Materials management

The Irwin Series in Management
and
The Behavioral Sciences

L. L. Cummings and E. Kirby Warren *Consulting Editors*
John F. Mee *Advisory Editor*

Materials management

DEAN S. AMMER, Ph.D.

Research Professor and Director
Bureau of Business and Economic Research
Northeastern University

1974   Third Edition

RICHARD D. IRWIN, INC.   Homewood, Illinois 60430
IRWIN-DORSEY INTERNATIONAL   London, England WC2H 9NJ
IRWIN-DORSEY LIMITED   Georgetown, Ontario L7G 4B3

Third Edition
First Printing, March 1974

ISBN 0-256-01556-2
Library of Congress Catalog Card No. 73–89114
Printed in the United States of America

Preface

MATERIALS MANAGEMENT problems are common to every organization. They are most apparent and were first to be recognized among profit-making manufacturing companies. Later the concept of materials management began to be recognized among service companies and, most recently, its greatest growth has been in the non-profit sector among government agencies, hospitals, universities, and like institutions.

Materials management problems often are not identified by that name. Instead, managements tend to relate them as specialized materials management subfunctions: purchasing, inventory control, production control, traffic, warehousing, receiving, shipping, materials handling, and related activities. The basic reason for this is that the formal materials management organization is much younger than any of its components. In fact, the concept of materials management as an integrated activity was relatively novel as recently as 1958 when I first wrote the series of articles on the subject which, in turn, led to publication of the first edition of this book in 1962.

Since that time, materials management has won many converts and it is now conventional practice to group together organizationally activities that are concerned with the purchase, movement, and storage of materials. As a result, there are increasing opportunities for persons trained to think as materials managers rather than as specialists in some materials management subfunction.

The basic purpose of this book is to describe the nontechnical, management-oriented skills needed for successful materials management. Specialized technical knowledge is also essential for successful materials management in almost any environment. For example, materials management for an auto company presupposes at least minimum knowledge of the workings of a car and its components as well as some knowledge of manufacturing processes. Similarly, while the materials manager of a hospital need not be personally qualified to remove infected tonsils, he must be able to discuss specialized medical-surgical supply problems with the physicians and surgeons who actually do the job. In addition, considerable technical expertise may be needed in parts of the materials management department—especially in those activities concerned with the design and operation of complicated equipment that may be used in the handling and movement of material. But it is not necessary to be a materials handling engineer to become a materials manager.

However, there is a body of knowledge that is common to all types of materials management and this is what I try to cover in this book. It is a combination of the broader skills required of the materials manager himself along with specialized managerial knowledge associated primarily with the major subfunctions of purchasing, production and inventory control, and traffic.

Chapters in this book are organized in terms of related skills. In some cases, these pertain to a single activity. For example, the chapter on traffic and physical distribution deals exclusively with traffic and its role in the physical distribution process. Most chapters, however, are concerned with skills applicable to at least two materials management activities. For example, the chapters on inventory control principles are applicable obviously not only to the purchased materials inventories that concern the purchasing manager and production control manager but also to the finished goods inventories that are the responsibility of the physical distribution manager. Similarly, chapters dealing with price determination, negotiation, and other buying skills should be of interest not only to the purchasing manager but also to the traffic manager, who is a purchaser of transportation services. And, the dispatching rules discussed in Chapter 8 represent a materials management skill with wide application among various materials management organizational units.

This book is written for the student and the business executive and is pragmatic in tone. Most of the material in it is derived from current and past practice but it also suggests ventures into uncharted areas. Scattered through the book are some ideas that have not yet gained wide practitioner acceptance: application of Bayesian decision theory to materials management, the materials management profit center, use of price indexes to measure performance, and others.

The basic text is written not only to describe materials management as it actually is but what it should be, in the author's view. The cases focus entirely on past or current practice. Along with the text material, they reflect three periods in my career: actual experience in both materials management and manufacturing; my visits to at least 200 companies in the course of my duties as executive editor of *Purchasing Magazine;* and, finally, my current role as writer, consultant, and lecturer in the field.

The cases are written primarily for use by instructors who wish to use this book as a text. But they should not be skipped over by the practitioner who is simply trying to broaden his knowledge of the field. Each case is related to the text material that precedes it and is designed to illustrate how a real-life organization copes with its materials management problems.

Finally, this preface would not be complete without grateful acknowledgement to the hundreds of executives who contributed directly and indirectly to this book through personal conversation and correspondence. I would also like especially to acknowledge the assistance of Professor Harold Fearon of Arizona State University and Professor Jack H. Holland of San Jose State University for their expert comments and criticism of the manuscript, my wife who spent many hours editing it, and my secretary, Patricia Hinds.

Boston, Massachusetts   DEAN S. AMMER
February 1974

Contents

List of cases

1

Introduction to materials management

MATERIALS MANAGEMENT is a basic part of any organization that produces a product or service of economic value. Thus it is essential not only to manufacturing but also to service industries, and it exists not only in profit-making enterprises but also in the public and private not-for-profit sectors of the economy. Neither is materials management uniquely American; it is carried on in every country of the world. In many cases, this activity is not separately identified, and, when it is, it is not necessarily called materials management. For example, in France it is *d'approvisionment* (which might be translated as "the supply process"), while the Swedish term translates into English as "materials administration."

Further, the term "materials management" is not used consistently in the United States. The identical activities are known variously as "materials administration," "supply," "material," "procurement," and by a variety of more exotic names. While materials management has always existed in every organization, it is only in the past 30 years that separate materials management departments have become commonplace. Roughly 40 percent[1] of American manufacturing companies now have separately identified materials management departments, although they are not always called by that name.

Apparently, materials management is even more popular abroad than

[1] These and subsequent statistics on materials management quoted in this chapter are based on my survey of 4,000 American manufacturing companies, financed by a grant from the American Production ond Inventory Control Society. Some of the results of the study were subsequently published in the *Guide to Purchasing*, of the National Association of Purchasing Management and in various commercial publications.

1

it is in the United States and Canada, an assumption supported (albeit unscientifically) by my own firsthand experiences on visits abroad. It is also suggested by the names of major professional societies concerned with materials management. The biggest of these in the United States is the National Association of Purchasing Management, which has roughly twice as many members as the American Production and Inventory Control Society, the second-ranking organization. While each of these groups is concerned with broad problems of materials management, it is significant that each focuses its major emphasis on a *segment* of the materials management process—purchasing in one case and production and inventory control in the other. The only professional group that purports to be dedicated to all phases of materials management is the International Materials Management Society. Despite its more ambitious name and program, it is considerably smaller and less influential than either NAPM or APICS. It is also more specialized than its title implies, giving heavy emphasis to the physical distribution aspects of materials management.

In contrast to the situation in the United States, materials management is firmly established in Japan, where the Materials Management Society is the major organization of its type. Similarly, the British equivalent of the National Association of Purchasing Management has been identified for some years as the Institute of Purchasing and Supply, in order to provide greater emphasis to materials management activities other than purchasing.

BASIC ECONOMICS

One possible explanation for the greater recognition accorded to materials management abroad is that manufacturing industries play a greater role in the economies of Western Europe and Japan than they do in the United States. More for historical reasons than because of economic logic, materials management is commonly associated with manufacturing more than with any other sector of the economy. Manufacturing was the most important sector of the American economy until well into the middle part of the 20th century, and manufacturing companies tended to pay more attention to their materials management activities than nonmanufacturers did. Now, in our post industrial economy, manufacturing is declining in importance, and services—both public and private—are accounting for an increasing share of the output.

Materials management is as essential to producers of services as it is to goods. In fact, the railroads were probably the first to identify materials management as a separate activity. More recently, however, nonprofit and public institutions have begun to recognize that they, too, are engaged in materials management, and they have established formal materials management organizations. Materials management is common to every organization simply because none is completely self-sufficient.

Value added by manufacture

The dependency on outside suppliers is most apparent in the manufacturing organization. Every manufacturer is a converter of materials purchased from some outside side. Even a huge, seemingly self-sufficient corporation like General Motors spends roughly 50 cents of each sales dollar on purchased parts, materials, and supplies. (See Figure 1–1.) This is almost twice as much as the company spends on payrolls.

FIGURE 1–1
How General Motors Corporation spends its sales dollar

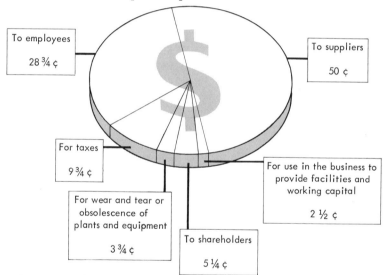

Source: **General Motors Corp.**, *Annual Report to Stockholders.*

General Motors, like every other manufacturer, is in the business of adding value to the products it purchases. In the case of General Motors, 50 cents worth of purchased material is transformed into $1 worth of finished product, primarily by adding value through manufacture. The value that is added represents the 29 cents General Motors spends on labor, plus an additional 21 cents for taxes, depreciation, and profit.

It is fairly easy to visualize the physical process of adding value by manufacture. With automotive products, it consists of hundreds of thousands of workers shaping metal into identifiable components and then, in various stages, fastening these components together, until they become a finished automotive product.

Value added by distribution

Distribution, the other value-adding process, is harder to visualize. This is the process by which the product reaches its ultimate user; value is added by distribution when a product is packaged, stored, shipped, and sold. The distribution process begins when the last manufacturing operation is completed and continues until the product reaches the ultimate consumer. When the manufacturing is extremely simple, almost all of the value added to the product is by distribution. For example, crushed stone may sell for $1 per ton at the quarry, but by the time it is delivered, the price is $3.50. The $2.50-per-ton trucking charge is a clear-cut case of value having been added by distribution. The stone is useless until it is trucked to someone who wants it.

Value is also added in less direct ways. In the course of the distribution process, material may be stored in a warehouse. Not only does the warehousing cost become value added by distribution, but so does the interest on the money that is tied up. Similarly, if merchandise is subject to spoilage or pilferage, then the loss becomes part of the value added by distribution to the products that finally do reach the user in satisfactory condition.

Value added by distribution may be roughly equal to value added by manufacture, even on complex products. For example, suppose General Motors adds $1,500 worth of value to a Chevrolet that it sells to one of its dealers for $3,000. The dealer, in turn, may sell the car to an ultimate user for $4,000. The marketing process from the end of the GM assembly line to the dealer then adds $1,000 worth of value by distribution—almost as much as that added by General Motors itself. And, as we will see later, much of the value that General Motors and other manufacturers add to their products comes from distribution, not from manufacture.

Of course, manufacturing and distribution are interrelated; one can not exist without the other. However, much of the value that is added by distribution is carried on by organizations that do no manufacturing. For example, a department-store chain purchases a refrigerator from the manufacturer for $200 and sells it for $300, adding $100 worth of value by distribution to the product. Or a gas company bills a home-heating customer $150 for natural gas it may have purchased from a pipeline company for $60, thus adding $90 worth of value by distribution.

Criteria for adding value

While most distribution is carried on by nonmanufacturing organizations, manufacturers also add value by distribution. In both manufacturing and distribution, value is added under these circumstances:

1. *Costs are incurred.* Things that are free, such as the air we breathe, have value, but no value is added in the economic sense until there is cost. Thus, if a foundry spends money on pollution control, it is thereby adding value by manufacture to the castings it produces, since restoration of the air to its former pure state is (or should be) a basic part of its process. Theoretically, all costs incurred by a manufacturing firm contribute either to value added by manufacture or to value added by distribution. If they do not, then company funds are being wasted, and management should be subject to either censure or dismissal.

2. *Capital is employed.* In a modern economy, it is not possible to produce anything without some minimum stock of capital (in the physical, not necessarily the financial sense). Investment in machinery, buildings, and in-process inventories is obviously essential if value is to be added by manufacture.

Capital requirements for distribution are less obvious, since the product is not transformed physically. Yet those who add value by distribution find it impossible to get along without a substantial investment in capital goods. A department store may require 50 to 75 cents worth of buildings, inventory, and other capital goods to support each $1 of sales. And, of course, the profit that is earned on sales represents the return that this capital must earn to be productive. Capital investment that does not "work" and contribute to profitability is sterile and should be eliminated. One of the major goals of materials management is to identify inventory that is not working to add value by distribution and get rid of it.

Hypothetical example

While the typical manufacturing company uses most of its capital to add value by manufacture, a substantial investment is needed to support distribution. Suppose, for example, that you are president of Appleton Corporation, a manufacturer of lighting fixtures. Your sales are $10,000,000 per year and profits after tax are $500,000. Your most recent balance sheet, shown in Figure 1–2, indicates that you require total assets of $4,000,000 (including $200,000 in cash) to carry on your business.

Evaluation of assets. Like every other businessman, you would be delighted to find a way to earn the same $500,000 profit with fewer

FIGURE 1–2
Appleton Corporation balance sheet

ASSETS

Cash		$ 200,000
Accounts receivable		1,000,000
Inventory		
Purchased materials	$400,000	
In-process stocks	200,000	
Finished goods	600,000	1,200,000
Net fixed assets (land, buildings, equipment)		1,600,000
Total assets		$4,000,000

LIABILITIES

Current liabilities	$ 500,000
Bank loan	1,000,000
Common stock and surplus	2,500,000
Total liabilities and net worth	$4,000,000

assets. However, if you try to get along with less plant and equipment, you simply will not have enough capacity to supply your customers. You would be more than happy if your customers would only pay their bills a little faster, since this would permit you to reduce your $1,000,000 investment in accounts receivable. But if you try to force customers to pay up faster, you know that sales volume will suffer, and the decline in profits will more than offset any saving you can make. You would also like to reduce your $600,000 investment in finished-goods inventory, but if you do, you know that you will not have stock on hand when customers require it. And again the loss of customer goodwill would more than offset any gain you could make by reducing finished-goods stocks.

Your $200,000 investment in in-process inventory represents unfinished products awaiting further manufacturing operations. They come about naturally as a part of your process, and, if you reduce them, your production capability would be severely curtailed. Similarly, you discover that you are unable to reduce your $400,000 purchased-materials inventories without adverse effects on your costs and profits. You need a stockpile of some materials to prevent your production lines from being shut down due to unexpected delays in future shipments by your suppliers. You also know that you have to buy substantial quantities of certain materials in order to purchase at the lowest price.

Thus, in your very well-run company, all assets are productive. If you try to make any reductions, you know that the benefit of lower capital investment will be more than offset by higher costs, lower sales, or both. In most cases, it is fairly easy to determine which of your assets are used to add value by manufacture and which are used to add value by distribution.

Manufacturing assets. You discover that your net investment in production equipment and machinery is $700,000 and that this investment is housed in buildings and land with a net value of $300,000. Thus, $1,000,000 of your $1,600,000 total net investment in land, buildings, and equipment is required in your manufacturing process. In addition, an investment of $200,000 is required for in-process inventory. So total assets employed in adding value by manufacture are $1,200,000 ($1,000,000 in net plant and equipment plus $200,000 for in-process inventories). Your total assets, exclusive of your cash balance of $200,000, amount to $3,800,000. Therefore, only 32 percent ($1,200,000 ÷ $3,800,000 × 100) of your "working" assets[2] are used in adding value by manufacture. The other assets, which amount to $2,600,000, are not needed in the direct manufacturing process.

Marketing assets. Let us now examine the role these nonmanufacturing assets play. If they perform no useful economic function, they should be eliminated. Your $600,000 investment in finished-goods inventory is obviously related to the distribution process; you must have it if your customers are to get your products when they need them. This finished-goods inventory is stored in a company-owned warehouse with a value of $300,000, and materials-handling equipment, sales offices, furniture, and so forth, account for investment of an additional $100,000. Thus, $400,000 worth of your buildings, plant, and equipment is directly associated with the marketing and distribution of your products; without these facilities, your products would never reach your customers. This is also true of your $1,000,000 investment in accounts receivable; financing of receivables is an essential part of the distribution process in all industries where sales are not made for cash. Thus, you need a total investment of $2,000,000 to market your product: $600,000 for finished-goods stocks, $400,000 for buildings and equipment, and $1,000,000 for accounts receivable. You therefore employ about 54 percent of your capital in the marketing process—substantially more than the 32 percent that is devoted to manufacturing.

Manufacturing companies recognize that they are usually engaged in two quite different businesses: making products and marketing them. It is not unusual for the marketing phase to be more important economically than the manufacturing aspect. Producers of packaged consumer goods, in particular, look upon themselves as being marketers much more than manufacturers. Outstanding examples of marketing-dominated manufacturers are companies such as Gillette and Revlon.

---

[2] For simplicity, I am assuming that cash is not a working asset. Of course, some minimum cash balance is essential to the operation of any business, to meet unexpected increases in costs and expenses or to compensate for unexpected delays in payments of outstanding receivables. The cash is obviously needed for both the manufacturing and distribution phases of the business. In most cases, it would probably be allocated proportionately to other assets used in distribution and manufacturing. If this were done, our allocation of 32 percent of Appleton's assets to manufacturing and 68 percent to distribution would be unaffected.

The organization structure of some companies even reflects the fact that adding value by distribution is quite different from adding value by manufacture—even though an identical product is sold. It would be easy, for example, for Appleton to reorganize itself into two separate companies: Appleton Manufacturing Company and Appleton Sales Corporation. One company would make the product, and the other would sell it. Each would employ capital and incur costs to carry on an economically useful activity.

Application to materials management

While managements have long been aware of the fact that manufacturing and marketing may be quite separate activities, they have typically been oblivious to a third basic economic activity that is carried on daily in their organizations: materials management. This activity meets the same basic value-adding criteria as marketing and manufacturing. In materials management, as in the two better known activities, *capital is employed and costs are incurred to produce something of economic value.*

Meeting value criteria.   The capital that is employed in materials management is primarily purchased-materials inventory, but it also includes the buildings and land needed to house this inventory, materials-handling equipment that may transport it, and office space and equipment used by materials management personnel. At Appleton (see Figure 1–2 above), the materials management investment might include not only the $400,000 purchased-materials inventory but also the $200,000 invested in land, buildings, and equipment.

Traditionally, capital employed in materials management has simply been lumped together with that used in manufacturing. While materials management existed, it was buried within the manufacturing organization. As a result, materials were often managed badly. It is fairly easy to submerge mediocre materials management activities within a rather efficient manufacturing management organization because the two functions are quite different economically. Materials management adds value by distribution. In materials management, as in marketing, products are not physically transformed but acquire additional value basically as a result of having been moved from their producer to their user. The materials management process adds value by getting material into the hands of manufacturing and other using departments; marketing takes material from manufacturing and gets it into the hands of a company customer.

Nothing for free.   While materials management is a perfectly obvious example of adding value by distribution, managements persist to this day in their belief that they get something for nothing in materials management. The belief is translated into practice by the conventional cost accounting system, which assumes that purchased material has a value at the stage where it is used that is equal to the original purchase price. For example, suppose that the Appleton Corporation purchases steel at a delivered price of 9 cents per pound. If the company has a conventional cost accounting system, it will be assumed, for example, that the cost of the steel is 9 cents per pound (if there is no waste) at the point where the steel begins to be shaped into a lighting fixture by the company's presses. This means implictly that no value has been added by distribution up to the stage of the process where value begins to be added by manufacture.

Test for added value. If no value is added by distribution prior to manufacture, why then is $600,000 invested by Appleton in inventories and various facilities related to materials management? It follows that this capital must be completely sterile. If it performs no economically useful function, it should be converted into cash and employed for something useful.

But, of course, no company can get along without a substantial investment in the assets that are essential to materials management, nor can it persuade its buyers, traffic coordinators, inventory controllers, and other materials management personnel to work without salary. Thus, value is inevitably added to purchased material in the materials management process. In a manufacturing organization, $1.00 worth of purchased material is usually worth at least $1.05 before it reaches its user; the value added by distribution in materials management then is 5 cents ($1.05 − $1.00). If the company spends 50 cents of each sales dollar on purchases, value added by materials management amounts to 5 percent of 50 cents and is therefore equal to 2½ cents of each sales dollar. Thus, in manufacturing companies, at least, materials management is never as important as marketing or manufacturing, the aggregate value added of which, in this example, would amount to 47½ cents of each sales dollar.[3]

In nonmanufacturing organizations, value added by the materials management process may be much greater. In hospitals or military organizations, there may be more than $1 of value added by materials management for each $1 of purchases. Thus, the true cost to the user of an item purchased from a supplier for $1 may become $2 or more after value is added by distribution in the materials management process.[4]

---

[3] Purchases account for 50 cents of each $1 of sales. This leaves 50 cents in total value added by the company's marketing, manufacturing, and materials management activities. Value added by materials management is about 5 percent of purchases, or 5 percent of 50 cents = 2½ cents. The remainder of 47½ cents (50 cents − 2½ cents) represents value added by manufacturing and marketing.

[4] A detailed explanation of how this comes about is part of the solution of Rhode Island Hospital (A), Case 1–2, at the end of this chapter.

Application of principle

As president of Appleton Corporation, you have access to all of the company's accounting records. With a little work, you can calculate value added in materials management, manufacturing, and marketing. You are, of course, already familiar with the conventional income statement in which a company lumps together all of its costs, subtracts this figure from sales, and arrives at a net profit.

Five basic costs. The special income statement shown in Figure 1–3 comes out with the same net profit of $500,000 as a conventional

FIGURE 1–3
Appleton Corporation adjusted income statement

Sales		$10,000,000
Less cost of purchases		5,000,000
Gross margin		$ 5,000,000
Less expenses		
Materials management expenses	$ 150,000	
Manufacturing payroll and expenses	2,000,000	
Marketing expenses	1,000,000	$ 3,150,000
Basic operating profit		$ 1,850,000
Less executive office and staff expenses		850,000
Net profit		$ 1,000,000
Income Tax		500,000
		$ 500,000

Allocated profit	Before Tax	After Tax
Materials management (14%)	$ 140,000	$ 70,000
Manufacturing (32%)	320,000	160,000
Marketing (54%)	540,000	270,000
	$1,000,000	$500,000

statement would report. The main difference is that all costs and expenses are grouped into five categories:

1. *Purchases.* This represents what you paid to outsiders for parts and materials used in your product and is the contribution or value added by your suppliers.

2. *Materials management.* In the course of getting purchased material from your suppliers to the point where the material was actually used, you incurred costs of $150,000. Payrolls, mostly salaries, are the single biggest expense, but also included would be depreciation on facilities and equipment employed in materials management, your best estimate of costs of utilities, and any other expenses incurred as part of the materials management process.

3. *Manufacturing.* You estimate that you spent $2,000,000 for wages paid to factory production workers and nonproduction employees such

as foremen, inspectors, and maintenance men who are directly concerned with your basic process. In addition, you would include depreciation, power, and all other costs directly associated with factory operation.

4. *Marketing.* Included among marketing expenditures of $1,000,000 would be salaries, advertising, depreciation on both office and warehouse facilities and equipment, and numerous other expenses.

5. *Executive office and staff.* Marketing, manufacturing, and materials management are the company's three "line" activities that directly add value to your product. But, of course, the company has other activiities—accounting, personnel, engineering—that you cannot get along without, even though their major role is to help the "value adders" rather than to add value themselves. Since you believe that managers of the three value-adding departments should be held responsible only for costs they control, you include in this miscellaneous $850,000 expense category the budgets of all activities, including those of the office of the president, which do not report to marketing, manufacturing, or materials management.[5]

Your total operating expenses would, of course, be identical with those shown on a conventional profit-and-loss statement. Both statements would show the same $500,000 after-tax profit. In the economic sense, this profit represents a reward to capital employed in adding value either by manufacture or by distribution. If we assume that Appleton's three basic value-adding activities were managed with equal proficiency, then each deserves a share of the $1,000,000 pretax profit in proportion to its investment.

Three basic returns. As we previously calculated, your company has 32 percent of its capital in manufacturing and 54 percent in marketing. The balance of 14 percent is invested in materials management. Therefore, as shown in Figure 1–3 above, profits earned by materials management, manufacturing, and marketing would be $140,000, $320,000, and $540,000 respectively. The value added by each line activity is equal to expenses of that activity plus its pretax profit. Since materials management expenses are $150,000 and profit is $140,000 at Appleton, the *minimum* value added by materials management is $290,000. The *minimum* value added by manufacturing is $2,320,000 ($2,000,000 + $320,000) and that by marketing is $1,540,000. To these minimum estimates, you would have to add the contributions made by the various staff activities. While these activities do not directly add

---

[5] If you wanted to be more precise, you would probably try to allocate the cost of these miscellaneous activities in proportion to the time spent with each of the line activities. For example, salaries of accounting clerks specializing in accounts payable would be allocated almost entirely to materials management, time of accounts receivable clerks would be charged to marketing, and the cost of operating the payroll department would be paid for primarily by manufacturing, which accounts for about three fourths of the company's employees.

to product value, they presumably all pull their own weight in helping the line departments add value.

Adding the "helpers." Note from the adjusted income statement for Appleton that the expenses of the non–value adders or "helpers" amount to $850,000, while the value adders have combined expenses of $3,150,000 and their invested capital earns a combined pretax profit of $1,000,000. Thus, total direct value added is equal to $4,150,000. Indirect contributions of $850,000 are 20.48 percent ($850,000 ÷ $4,150,000 × 100) of direct value added. If we assume that indirect contributions can be allocated in proportion to direct contribution, then we can increase each of the three *minimum* direct contributions by 20.48 percent to get an estimate of *total* value added by each activity, as follows:

Materials management:	120.48 percent × $290,000	= $ 350,000
Manufacturing:	120.48 percent × $2,320,000	= 2,795,000
Marketing:	120.48 percent × $1,540,000	= 1,855,000
Total value added	. . . .	$5,000,000

Dividing the sales dollar. Appleton's operations can then be looked upon as a series of three steps that adds value to purchased material as follows:

	Amount	Percent of sales	Cumulative total
Purchases	$ 5,000,000	50.0	$ 5,000,000
Materials management	350,000	3.5	5,350,000
Manufacturing.	2,795,000	28.0	8,145,000
Marketing	1,855,000	18.5	10,000,000
Total sales.	$10,000,000		

Thus the materials management process adds 3½ cents of value to each 50 cents' worth of purchased material. Manufacturing and marketing adds 28 cents and 18½ cents, respectively, giving a total of 50 cents in value added by all three activities to 50 cents worth of purchased material for each $1 of product that is sold. Also note that material increases in value by 7 percent in materials management, by 56 percent (of its original cost) in manufacturing, and by 37 percent in marketing.

As illustrated in Figure 1–4, a new type of "sales dollar" can be constructed from our estimates of value added. Instead of showing *payments*, which is essentially what is illustrated in the GM example in Figure 1–1, it shows *economic contribution*. The biggest single contribution in almost every manufacturing company is made by suppliers, and the smallest is always made by the company's own materials management process.

FIGURE 1–4
Typical manufacturer's sales dollar showing value added by four basic activities.

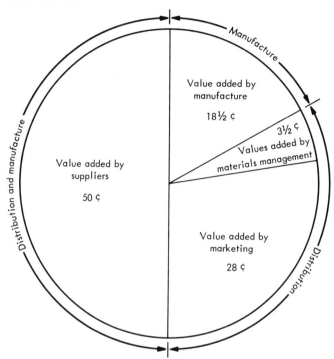

SCOPE OF MATERIALS MANAGEMENT

The contribution of the materials manager to his company's well-being is actually greater than Figure 1–4 suggests. In terms of basic value added to product, the materials manager is roughly but one fifth as important as the marketing manager ($3\frac{1}{2}$ cents of value compared with $18\frac{1}{2}$ cents) and only one eighth as important as the manufacturing manager ($3\frac{1}{2}$ cents compared with 28 cents).

Role of purchasing

The comparison above understates the contribution that a capable materials manager should be able to make.[6] The reason is that materials

---

[6] In most cases, it also understates the importance of the marketing manager relative to the manufacturing manager. While marketing may add somewhat less value to a manufacturing company's product than manufacturing, a marketing manager can usually exercise greater discretionary control over his environment than a manufacturing manager can. Marketing may, for example, persuade more customers to buy a company's product, but manufacturing can rarely persuade its employees to work significantly harder, and improvements which can reduce its cost usually require substantial increases in capital employed. Thus an outstanding marketing manager may have greater impact on a company than an outstanding manufacturing manager.

management exercises some discretion over the greatest product cost: purchases of parts and materials from outside suppliers.

Purchasing is the single most important materials management activity in most companies and institutions. If materials management adds value by distribution to purchased material, then obviously the process cannot take place unless someone buys the material. In fact, "the terms materials management" and "purchasing" are often used interchangeably. Executives whose responsibility is limited to purchasing sometimes have titles like materials manager and executives with titles like director of purchases are often given responsibilities that make them *de facto* materials managers.

The confusion is unfortunate, since many chief executives probably wind up believing that they are organized to do an effective job of materials management when they really are not. The fact is that purchasing is a specialized part of materials management, just as plant engineering is a specialized part of manufacturing and advertising is a part of marketing. Thus materials management is a basic function of the business that adds value directly to the product, and purchasing, like plant engineering and advertising, is a specialized staff activity that helps a value adder but does not really add any value to the product itself.[7]

Line and staff responsibilities

Line activities. To carry out its basic mission of adding value by distribution, materials management must embrace all activities that are concerned with getting purchased material from suppliers up to the stage where value begins to be added by manufacture. Included in this basic materials management activity would be not only the purchasing department but also all other activities concerned with handling, storage, or transportation of material prior to its incorporation into the manufacturing process.

When he deals with purchased material, the materials manager is a "line" executive responsible for a basic function of the business. His role is comparable to that of manufacturing manager or marketing manager. In many organizations, the materials manager also has a second "staff" role, comparable to that of the accountant. He is responsible for specialized services that logically fall under the control of either manufacturing or marketing. These services are delegated to materials

---

[7] In fact, one can say only half facetiously that purchasing is a "value subtractor." If the purchasing manager is doing his job, the 50 cents of the sales dollar that is spent on outside purchases will be whittled down to 49 cents or less. This *reduces* the value that is added to the product by the supplier! (But, as long as the buying company does not reduce the price of the end product, this reduction in value added by the supplier is offset by an increase in profit value added by the buyer's company.)

management simply because it has skills not ordinarily associated with manufacturing or marketing.

Marketing role. It is easy to differentiate materials management skills and marketing skills. In the profit-making manufacturing or nonmanufacturing company, the basic task of the marketing manager is to sell the product. Major marketing executives invariably concentrate their efforts on sales and advertising; in most cases, their previous experience has been in these two all-important marketing activities.

While it is only rarely that a marketing manager is a specialist in something other than the art and science of persuading customers to buy company products, the scope of the marketing activity is much broader than this. The total marketing process embraces all activities necessary to get the product from the last manufacturing operation to the customer. This normally involves a great deal more than simply persuading the customer to buy the product (although that activity is by far the most important marketing activity for most products). The product must be transported and stored, going through virtually the same process that is carried on when purchased material moves from the supplier to its point of use. This process of moving goods to the ultimate consumer is called *physical distribution.*

While the technical skills involved in physical distribution are virtually identical with those associated with materials management of purchased materials, responsibility for physical-distribution policy rests with the marketing manager rather than the materials manager. For example, it is a basic part of the company's marketing strategy to decide whether to stock a particular product in the company's warehouse or to require the customer to wait for delivery. Once this and thousands of similar decisions are made, however, the marketing manager may delegate responsibility for physical distribution to the materials manager, so marketing can concentrate its efforts almost entirely on sales. The materials manager then proceeds to apply virtually the same skills to finished goods that he is already applying to purchased materials. In the latter case, he makes his own rules (consistent with overall company strategy and policy); in the former, he tries to conform to guidelines given him by the marketing manager.

Manufacturing role. The relation of the materials manager to manufacturing is more varied and complex than it is to marketing, being strongly influenced by technology. In some cases, the relationship between materials management and production is quite well defined. In an electric utility, materials management delivers fuel to the generating station, and production uses the fuel in its boilers. Similarly, in a paper company, materials management delivers purchased logs, chemicals, and other materials, and manufacturing takes over from there.

In other manufacturing companies, the relationship between materials management and manufacturing is more complex. Many manufacturers purchase materials at various stages of fabrication; materials management may supply raw material, semifinished items, and parts, and may even bypass manufacturing entirely and purchase finished products. In other cases, a company may simultaneously purchase and make identical items. A complicated system of supply inevitably draws manufacturing and materials management closer together and makes it more difficult to determine where the responsibility of one ends and the other begins.

Nevertheless, it is always possible to separate the two activities after studying a company's unique situation. In general, materials management is responsible as a line function for anything that is purchased, up to the point where value begins to be added by manufacture. In addition, materials management may also serve manufacturing in a staff capacity, just as it does for marketing.

The manufacturing manager is more difficult to stereotype than the marketing manager, simply because there are so many different manufacturing processes. Yet all manufacturing managers seem to share these two basic assignments: to keep their processes functioning efficiently and to get maximum productivity from their labor forces. The manufacturing manager is an expert at getting as much work as possible from both people and machines. He almost always has some combination of these people-machine skills. When the process is highly automated, the technical skills may be dominant; when the process is simple, the leadership or people skill will be what counts.

Manufacturing management is concerned essentially with keeping equipment and manpower operating at top efficiency to produce products that marketing can sell. To carry out this basic mission, manufacturing often requires the same specialized skills as materials management. In manufacturing, as in materials management and marketing, material must be stored and moved physically from point to point. In fact, if the process is not completely automated, manufacturing is often engaged in adding value by distribution as well as adding value by manufacture. When a partially completed assembly is carried by a fork truck from one manufacturing location to another, value is being added not by manufacture but by distribution. Similarly, if a partially finished product is temporarily stored, a cost is incurred that represents value added by distribution.

While the manufacturing manager must ultimately be responsible for everything that happens during the entire manufacturing cycle, he may delegate specialized distribution tasks to the materials manager. With certain products, this delegation is all but essential if materials management is to function satisfactorily in carrying out its basic purchased-materials mission. In such cases, the manufacturing process may be subject to many unexpected changes, and materials management cannot hope to achieve continuity of supply of purchased materials if it is not directly involved in all of the internal supply problems in the entire manufacturing process.

Role varies widely. Thus, while the basic value-adding line function of materials management is universally applicable to all organizations, the staff types of activities vary widely. In organizations that produce a service, these staff activities are usually non-existent. Materials management does its job, and other parts of the organization produce and market the service, largely on their own. At the other extreme, the staff side of materials management may be more important than the basic activity in a company that produces a bulky finished product made from its own raw materials.

HISTORY OF MATERIALS MANAGEMENT

The scope of materials management in any particular industry is at least as much a product of historical development as it is of economic logic. Organizations in which materials management plays its optimum line and staff roles have rarely been created with a single stroke of the organization planner's pen. They have evolved gradually and, in most cases, have not yet matured.

Evolutionary process

The process of development in materials management is far from uniform but seems to follow this general pattern:

Stage 1. All materials management activities are carried on almost unconsciously, as sidelines, by executives who are primarily concerned with other activities.

Stage 2. Major materials management activities are recognized formally, but these activities report to a variety of executives and are not centralized organizationally. As a result, the only genuine materials manager in the organization is the president or general manager, who is usually preoccupied with seemingly more pressing problems.

Stage 3. Materials management activities concerned with purchased materials are grouped together under a single staff executive, who gradually begins to behave like a line manager.

Stage 4. Materials management becomes a genuine value-adding activity for purchased materials. It also provides maximum specialized staff assistance to manufacturing and to marketing in their physical distribution problems.

Slow progress. Three companies out of four have yet even to approach Stage 4 in the development of their materials management organizations. Most of those who claim to have reached this final stage in the evolution of materials management have yet to achieve the performance or play the role in general management they should ultimately be capable of.

The first stage of materials management predates the Industrial Revolution. All organized large-scale warfare, in fact, has been an exercise in materials management—or what present-day military planners would describe as "procurement" and "logistics management." In the past, wars that were seemingly lost on the battlefield were really failures in either procurement (buying the right material) or logistics management (getting the material to the point where it could be used). The Spanish Armada was months behind schedule largely because of botched materials management. If the job had been done properly, the Spaniards might have caught the British unprepared and defeated their smaller fleet. Similarly, Napoleon's ill-fated march to Moscow was largely a logistical failure. The French army was unbeatable until its supply system began to break down. In contrast, the Allied invasion of France in World War II was a masterpiece of logistical planning. Almost everything that was needed was in the right place at the right time.

The military, in its way, is now as adept at materials management as private industry is. But materials management as a separate body of knowledge is much more a product of the Industrial Revolution than it is of the campaigns of King Philip and Napoleon. Organized purchasing departments existed in the mining industry as early as 1832 and were quite common among railroads by 1887.[8]

The first factories

The concept of a separate and independent materials activity was still a novel one to most manufacturers even as late as 1900, when the United States and the leading Western European nations were already heavily industrialized. Nevertheless, since it is a basic function of the business, the materials management job was being performed. Each shop foreman or superintendent was pretty much his own materials manager. In most companies, he ran his department like a semiindependent feudal barony with remarkably loose ties (by today's standards) of allegiance to the company as a whole. The foreman scheduled his own production, bought his own supplies, and did his own hiring and firing—all with minimum interference from top management, provided he did the jobs with reasonable competence.

If someone had proposed a separate and independent materials department to the typical manager of about 1900, he probably would have been ridiculed. Why should a company incur extra overhead by hiring a purchasing agent or materials manager to do a job that could be

---

[8] Historical development of the purchasing function is discussed in detail in Harold E. Fearon and John H. Hoagland, *Purchasing Research in American Industry,* Research Study 58 (New York: American Management Association, 1963).

done as well or better by the shop superintendent or foreman? Besides, favors or kickbacks from suppliers were often a substantial part of a shop superintendent's income. If they were eliminated by transferring the buying power to someone else, the company would have to raise the salaries of its supervisors to prevent them from leaving to work for a competitor.

Specialists not needed. There is no basic need for a separate, independent materials activity if just one premise is accepted: skill in *managing* materials automatically accompanies skill in *specifying* and *using* materials. If one accepts this, one accepts the idea that a competent engineer or manufacturing manager is by definition a good materials manager, and materials automatically are managed as their specifications are developed and as they are used in operations. Thus there is no need for a materials manager.

This premise was widely accepted 50 years ago, and a few companies continue to do so today. But modern, progressive managements know it to be false. They believe there is a distinct difference between skill in specifying and using materials and skill in buying them. They know that a professonal buyer trained in business management and economics and familiar with the capabilities of hundreds of suppliers can do a much better job than an engineer or foreman whose training and orientation are less suitable for buying.

Other materials management activities probably did not even exist in the early factories. Inventory control meant simply having lots of material on hand when needed; production control may have consisted simply of asking the boss what should be worked on next. Traffic was handled by the teamster or railroad.

All of these materials management activities have evolved into specialities in the past 50 to 100 years. While they are now universally accepted functions, a majority of companies still do not delegate total materials management responsibility to a single integrated department. One basic reason for this backwardness is historical. It is the almost inevitable result of the evolution of the great corporation from the small family-owned business.

Development of functions

Materials management is just as essential to the firm with half a dozen employees as it is to the great corporation with half a million workers. The great corporation has full-time specialists in every phase of materials management (although they are not always grouped organizationally into a single unified materials department).

In the small business there is little functional specialization. The owner-manager handles all the administrative jobs. He is normally his own materials manager, chief engineer, controller, marketing manager, manufacturing manager, and personnel manager. He cannot afford the luxury of full-time staff specialists; about the only "experts" he does have are part-time attorneys and public accountants.

The two-manager stage. When the small business grows, the work load of the owner-manager gets heavier. Fortunately, profits grow with sales, and eventually he feels prosperous enough (or is sufficiently overworked) to hire someone to help him with his administrative chores. He either hires an "assistant" or someone to supervise fairly well-defined functional areas—an office manager or "someone to take charge of the shop."

Regardless of the title that is given this second manager, his addition is one of the most significant steps in the development of the business. It is at this point that an "organization" begins to develop. With it come problems in communication and division of work; responsibility no longer centers on just one person. As the organization continues to expand, it becomes far more complex. But the problems and changes are not nearly so far reaching as when work is divided in some fashion between two full-time administrators in a still minuscule organization.

In the one-manager organization, all materials management responsibility centers on the owner-manager. When a second manager is hired, the owner-manager usually delegates to him part—but not all—of the responsibility for materials management. For example, the second manager may have responsibility for determining materials requirements and buying supplies, while the owner-manager retains responsibility for buying major materials and controlling major inventories. Regardless of how responsibility is divided between the two managers, it is inevitably a permanant division; never again in the typical company are materials managed by a single executive. The job is eventually dispersed among a number of executives working at different organization levels, who report to executives interested in other functions—particularly manufacturing and finance. Most companies enjoy unified materials management only in their infancy; unfortunately, they are then still too small to enjoy the benefits a specialist in the field can give them.

The purchasing agent appears. As the company continues to grow and reaches the stage where it has a hundred or so employees, the two-manager type of organization becomes increasingly inadequate. More functional specialization is necessary; full-time managers of finance, production, sales, and engineering eventually appear. Finally, a separate purchasing department is formed. At first it may be run by someone who holds another job, too—that of office manager, controller, company secretary, personnel manager, or the like, but eventually a full-time purchasing agent is hired.

The purchasing agent is not a materials manager, by any means. In fact, he rarely even has complete responsibility for purchasing. He buys the less important items, formerly handled by the shop superintendent, various engineers, the controller, and others. He may also take over certain other activities, including operation of the storeroom for supplies, the receiving department, and so on. But the manufacturing manager continues to be responsible for inventory management, and top managers usually retain authority over all major contracts with out-side suppliers.

At this stage in its growth, the typical company establishes a separate purchasing department, mostly as a clerical convenience. The purchasing agent is definitely a second-string manager. He has yet to prove that he can make really significant contributions to the company's success. In fact, more often than not, top managers are still convinced (and in some cases, rightly so) that they can do a better job of buying than the professional buyers in their purchasing department. So they continue to dictate sources of supply for the half dozen or so major commodities that in most companies comprise as much as 75 percent ot total dollar volume of purchases. In some industries, the evolution of the materials function seems to have been arrested at this stage. For example, in big textile companies the purchasing department usually buys all needed supplies, while someone else, usually the company treasurer, handles the company's most important purchases—the cotton, wool, and synthetic fibers that are woven into cloth.

The purchasing agent, at this stage in the development of the com-pany, outranks shop foremen, but he is hardly the equal of the managers of finance, marketing, manufacturing, and engineering. However, if the purchasing agent is a good one, he may eventually convince his manage-ment that there is a lot more to purchasing than having lunch with suppliers and supervising a couple of clerks. Management eventually accepts the idea that there is a distinct difference between skills in buying materials and in using them, but this takes time. Almost every-one, from housewife to corporation president, not only thinks he knows how to buy things but also rather enjoys it. Even though they accept the theory that professional buyers buy better, many top managers are prone to make themselves exceptions to their own rules and inject their ideas into the company's buying operations.

Other activities emerge.   Other materials management specialties are developed in addition to purchasing, but these rarely arouse a similar do-it-yourself reaction among top managers. While buying can some-times be fun, such materials management activities as stock taking hold fewer charms for the nonpractitioner. In most companies, these other materials management functions evolve quietly, representing either work that had never been done before or the taking over of functions that had been handled by line supervisors. While such major functions as production and inventory control and traffic soon prove their worth, their managers rarely achieve top-management visibility comparable to purchasing department managers. There are no more than a handful of vice presidents in charge of production and inventory control and, outside the transportation industry, traffic managers are often hard pressed to achieve middle-management status.

Recognition of purchasing

Outstanding purchasing managers are beginning to be recognized as top-management material—in some companies, at least. They become "second-level" executives, reporting directly to a president or general manager, and not infrequently become not only vice presidents of their companies but also serve on the board of directors. In most cases, the change in title and organization status is a formal recognition of gradual changes that have taken place in the purchasing executive's job over a period of 20 years or more. The process is initiated as top management gradually grows more confident that the purchasing agent is the logical man to make the actual buying decisions on major purchased materials and gives him authority to do the job.

Contributions to profit. If he is a genuine professional buyer, the purchasing agent can almost always do a better job of buying than those who formerly did it. Since purchases comprise a major part of any manufacturing company's cost, the top purchasing executive must work closely with other key managers. As the company's biggest spender, his efforts must be coordinated with the controller's department, in order to control cash. Manufacturing depends on him for both the production materials and the supplies it requires. Close coordination between manufacturing and purchasing is essential for solving the inevitable problems in quality and delivery of purchased materials that arise. Since practically every company relies on suppliers of parts and materials for aid in engineering and product development, the purchasing and engineering departments must work closely together on new products, in order to enlist supplier assistance.

Purchasing also has gained recognition in the nonmanufacturing company. Transportation and utility companies have long realized that they could not operate effectively without a supply function, and gradually they began to be able to distinguish between effective and ineffective purchasing and to comprehend its relation to their business success. The purchasing function evolved much later in other nonmanufacturing organizations. For example, it was not until the current era of government-supported medical care that many hospitals began to approach purchasing and other materials management activities in an organized way. In the middle of the 20th century, some governmental agencies were still so ignorant of the principles of materials management that they assumed that inventory was "free" as long as there was money on hand to make a purchase.

Participation in decisions. Modern management recognizes that almost every decision made has some impact on purchasing and materials management. In addition, it is discovering that purchasing managers and materials managers can often make important contributions to problems that seemingly have nothing to do with their specialties.

Purchasing must be "in the know" regarding almost every activity in the company. It becomes almost essential that the top purchasing executive be a member of the company's key management group—its operating committee or executive committee. Because almost every major decision affects purchasing, he also often is a member of various other committees devoted to scheduling or production planning, make-or-buy decisions, cost reduction, standardization, and product planning, for example.

In companies with topflight purchasing departments, purchasing personnel make all major buying decisions. They also actively assist engineers by introducing them to suppliers or new products they can use, and sometimes even make specific recommendations for design changes. They assist in inventory control by buying in the most economic quantities, making special arrangements with suppliers to reduce the need for safety stocks, and so on. They assist the sales department with supplier relations programs and, in some cases, with actual sales leads.

EVOLUTION OF MATERIALS MANAGEMENT

To do its job effectively, purchasing must have a particularly close relationship with the traffic and production control departments. In most companies the three departments together control practically all materials management activities.

Production control was originally performed by the foremen, who scheduled their own production and sometimes kept records of inventories. Then parts of this job were performed by the superintendent's clerk, who kept necessary records while the superintendent continued to make the decisions. As more and more authority was stripped from line supervision and the scheduling process became more complex, the clerks eventually were superseded by a department of production control specialists.

Before the appearance of the traffic department, the traffic function usually was even more widely dispersed. Carriers were sometimes selected by suppliers, sometimes by the person responsible for the purchase, and occasionally by a top manager on the basis of personal friendship with a carrier representative. The other important functions of the traffic department were often performed casually by whoever selected the carrier, or they were not performed at all.

Managements in progressive companies realize that their purchasing, production control, and traffic departments have jobs so closely related that they can work together better to achieve common objectives if they are linked organizationally. With this integrated approach to materials management, all of the jobs encompassed by these activities would be under the overall direction of a materials manager.

Functions of materials management

There is no general agreement on what functions should be grouped organizationally for unified materials management. Most would agree, however, that in a typical manufacturing company they would embrace all activities concerned with materials *except* those directly concerned with designing or manufacturing the product or maintaining the facilities, equipment, and tooling. They would not, however, normally include receiving inspection. All large firms and many small ones routinely inspect every incoming shipment to make certain that the company is getting what it pays for. Production parts and materials are checked against blueprints and specifications. Nonproduction items are also reviewed, although most companies do not have specifications for them but simply compare the actual contents of the shipment with the description on the purchase order.

Receiving inspection. Some materials managers feel that receiving inspection should be under their jurisdiction, so that they have control over the complete materials cycle. It is wasteful, they argue, to separate receiving—where the shipment is identified and moved to an inspection area—from receiving inspection. When receiving and receiving inspection are separate activities, there is usually some duplication of work. In addition, there is a basic division of responsibility for the shipment. It is shared at this stage of the cycle by the supervisor of receiving and the supervisor of receiving inspection. One reports through channels to the materials manager; the other is responsible to the chief inspector or quality control manager. Each theoretically can pass the buck to the other should there be an error or a delay in handling the shipment.

However, most organization experts agree that quality control—including receiving inspection—should be a separate check and balance on the materials activity. It should be independent of materials management for the same reason that the accounts receivable section that actually pays for the material is independent. The group that is responsible for buying the material might be subject to too many temptations if it also paid for it and inspected it. In addition, receiving inspection is a specialized skill that is naturally related to quality control, not to materials management. If the quality control department is to monitor the quality of the entire production process, its job quite naturally begins the minute incoming purchased material hits the receiving dock (and even before this in companies where quality control works with the purchasing department to monitor the quality of the supplier's process).

With the exception of receiving inspection, materials management embraces all other functions concerned with ordering, storage, and movement of material. In the typical company, it would embrace the activities performed by the following major departments: purchasing, production control, stores, traffic, and physical distribution.

The specific duties of these departments vary considerably from company to company and industry to industry. In general, however, they include the following:

1. *Production and material control.* The production control manager helps set the overall production schedule and is responsible for making certain that manufacturing has the parts and materials it needs to meet it. He directs five basic activities:

a)   Computing detailed requirements for parts and materials—both purchased and manufactured—from up-to-date bills of material and specifications supplied by the product engineering department.

b)   Scheduling production or purchase of parts and materials needed to meet overall schedules for completed end products. This involves calculation of requirements for each item, taking into account such variables as inventory, lead time, on-order position, and so on.

c)   Issuing work orders to manufacturing departments and purchase requisitions to purchasing for parts and materials needed to meet overall production schedules. This includes following up to make certain schedules are met and revising schedules when necessary.

d)   Keeping detailed records of inventory, on-order status, and potential demand for each production part and material, and making periodic physical counts of stock to verify the accuracy of records.

e)   Maintaining physical inventories of all direct (i.e., production) materials[9] in various stages of fabrication, and administering controls necessary to maximize turnover and limit losses from spoilage, pilferage, or obsolescence.

2. *Nonproduction stores.* Techniques and procedures used to control nonproduction material (office supplies, perishable tools, and maintenance, repair, and operating supplies) resemble those used for production material, although they are usually less elaborate. Specifically, the stores department:

a)   Maintains physical stocks of nonproduction items to be drawn on as needed for operations or maintenance.

b)   Manages inventories of nonproduction materials and prepares pur-

---

[9] "Direct" or "production" parts and materials are incorporated directly into the end product. "Indirect" or "nonproduction" material is consumed in making the product but does not physically become a part of it. Screws used to fasten components of a product would be direct material. If the same screws were used for a minor repair in the plant, they would be a nonproduction maintenance supply. Solvent used to wash the product would be an indirect or nonproduction material. A standard package used to ship the product would probably be considered direct material by most cost accountants.

chase requisitions for needed material when stocks drop to the reorder point.

c) Keeps records and maintains controls to prevent duplication of inventories, minimize losses from pilferage and spoilage, and prevent stockouts.[10]

3. *Purchasing.* The purchasing department buys material in amounts authorized by requisitions it receives from the production control and stores departments. There are four basic purchasing activities:

a) Selecting suppliers, negotiating the most advantageous terms of purchase with them, and issuing necessary purchase orders.

b) Expediting delivery from suppliers when necessary to assure delivery in time to meet schedules, and negotiating any changes in purchase schedules dictated by circumstances.

c) Acting as liaison between suppliers and other company departments, including engineering, quality control, manufacturing, production control, and finance, on all problems involving purchased materials.

d) Looking for new products, materials, and suppliers that can contribute to company profit objectives, and acting as the company's "eyes and ears" to the outside world and reporting on changes in market conditions and other factors that can affect company operations.

4. *Traffic.* While purchasing buys parts and materials, the traffic department buys transportation service. It is always concerned with inbound shipments of purchased materials and is frequently concerned with outbound shipments of finished products to customers. There are four basic traffic activities:

a) Selecting common or charter carriers and routines for shipments as required.

b) Tracing inbound shipments of material in short supply as requested by production control or purchasing. Assisting customers in tracing outbound shipments when asked.

c) Auditing invoices from carriers and filing claims for refunds of excess charges or for damaged shipments when required.

d) Developing techniques to reduce transportation cost. This may involve negotiation with competing shippers, special studies on selecting the most advantageous plant location for new products, analysis of tariffs, and negotiation of any number of special arrangements for handling certain traffic.

5. *Physical distribution.* Finished goods must be moved from the production line to a company warehouse and, eventually, to a customer. This process is called physical distribution. The physical distribution

---

[10] Pilferage in particular can be a problem in stores management, since many of the items, like small tools, paintbrushes, and pencils, can be used in the home as well as in the plant.

manager may also be responsible for the physical movement of partially finished products within the plant and may receive and transport purchased materials to storage areas and to their point of use. The traffic function may also be included in the physical distribution department, but it is independent in many companies, particularly where shipment and storage of finished goods is not especially costly.

Place in the organization

In most manufacturing companies the five functions described above are separate, but not equal, organization units. Their relative status depends on their importance to the organization as well as on other factors, including custom, habit, and so on.

Purchasing usually has the highest organization status of the five basic materials functions. The purchasing manager usually reports directly to the president or general manager and is on the second highest level in the organization. In some cases, he may report to the manufacturing manager or finance manager and be on the third level. Very rarely is he on the fourth level.

The production control manager and the traffic manager usually report on the third level. The traffic manager would normally report to the sales manager, purchasing manager, or manufacturing manager; the production control manager almost always reports to the manufacturing manager or works manager. Occasionally, the traffic manager reports directly to the president, and, in a few cases, so does the production control manager. Both are found more often on the fourth level of the organization than they are on the second.

Physical distribution does not exist as a separate function in many companies. When it does exist (in companies with major problems in distribution of finished products), it is very important. Some companies have vice presidents in charge of physical distribution. In most, the physical distribution manager reports directly to the materials manager.

In addition to the major activities described above, materials managers are also responsible for a variety of minor activities, such as receiving and shipping. These secondary activities hardly ever report directly to the materials manager and sometimes not even directly to one of his immediate subordinates. While they are vital parts of the material management organization, they usually do not require much management attention and, once the rules are drawn up, can largely run themselves.

Nonmanufacturing applications

While materials management is far from standardized among manufacturing companies, variations in responsibility and in organization are even greater among nonmanufacturing organizations. Such organizations always purchase material, but there is no tangible finished product.

The purchasing, inventory control, and stores functions have essentially the same mission as their counterparts in manufacturing organizations. Usually there is no equivalent of production control.

Among transportation firms, as well as in military organizations, logistics management is a substitute for a physical distribution organization. The main difference is that logistics management deals with products that are going to be used, while physical distribution focuses on those that will be sold. Logistics management has much less of a marketing connotation than physical distribution has. Military problems of logistics management might include, for example, determination of the optimum number and location of specialized parts needed to repair or maintain warships or other military hardware. The peacetime version of logistics management would be an airline's distribution of key spare parts needed to service its fleet. A large airline might, for example, operate in and out of 50 different airports. Hundreds of parts can conceivably fail at any of these airports, and, obviously, the airline cannot afford to operate fully equipped maintenance bases at each of them. The basic problem in logistics management is to determine optimum investment and location of spare parts and maintenance equipment.

Hospitals also have an equivalent of a physical distribution or traffic function. Medical and surgical supplies must be transported from a central supply area to nursing stations or other points of use. Ideally, each nursing station should be stocked with exactly what is needed, but no more than that. Materials managers in hospitals and other service organizations also frequently get involved in peripheral activities—mostly because these activities have no other logical place in the organization. It is not unusual, for example, for hospital materials managers to run a laundry, to supervise the hospital's internal message service, and to operate a captive printing plant. Materials managers in industry can be involved in like activities—particularly captive printing (in companies not in the printing business) and the sale of scrap and surplus. These activities are out of the mainstream of materials management, however. In succeeding chapter, we will focus on the primary materials management functions that are common to every organization.

Cases

CASE 1–1. GAMELIN COSMETICS CORPORATION (A)*

Defining materials management activities

Gamelin Cosmetics Corporation started operations in 1936 when Rubette Gamelin began to market on a limited scale a line of cosmetics

---

she had originally developed almost as a hobby, while operating a highly successful beauty parlor in a large eastern city. The company gradually expanded and, by 1940, Miss Gamelin sold her beauty parlor in order to be able to devote all of her energies to the cosmetics business. By 1950, when the company became partly publicly owned, sales had grown to $2 million per year.

Sales more than tripled in the 1950s—almost entirely as a result of the company's original product line plus natural additions to it, such as a line of nail polish. Profits more than kept pace with sales. A few security analysts came to recognize Gamelin as a "growth stock" and began to acquire its shares. By 1961, the stock was selling for almost 30 times its record earnings that year.

The high stock price gave Gamelin a base from which it could easily step up its rate of growth by acquiring other companies through an exchange of its stock. Since the Gamelin stock had a higher price-earnings ratio than the stock of the acquired companies, each such acquisition tended to boost Gamelin's earnings per share. Unlike other companies that were following this same practice, Gamelin (*a*) stuck to companies in the cosmetics and related fine chemical fields and (*b*) did not attempt to grow by more than about 30 percent in any one year. Gamelin sales and profits leaped ahead despite this restraint. By 1970, the company's sales had topped $50 million. After-tax profits were $6 million and the company enjoyed a 38 percent after-tax return on net worth.

Despite this sparkling performance, the company was beginning to expand ahead of its cash flow by 1970. A combination administration-research building then under construction was expected to cost $5 million by the time it was finished in 1971. And although there were no definite plans for a new factory building, company executives knew their facilities were hopelessly out of date.

Almost all of the company's production—including that of the half dozen smaller firms that had been acquired in the last decade—were concentrated in a 60-year-old, rather ramshackle-looking factory building in an industrial suburb of a major eastern city. According to company President George Katz, "the existing facility is not only extremely expensive and costly to maintain but does not fit our image as a high-class manufacturer of cosmetics and fine chemicals."

Before starting plans for another major new building, Katz decided to have a consulting firm, the New Jersey Research Institute (NJRI) make a general study to review the company's prospects and to suggest how it should go about planning the new facility. Influenced by the NJRI study, the board authorized Katz to engage an architectural firm to design a new plant to be built on land adjacent to the company's almost-completed research and administrative facility. It was anticipated that construction would most likely be completed sometime in 1972.

By 1975, it was assumed that the company would have almost $25 million invested in the new plant and related facilities and equipment. This was more capacity than the company needed at present but it was assumed that internal growth alone—without any additional acquisitions—would cause sales to increase by 20 percent per year. The company's product mix provided exceptional cyclical stability (women apparently continued to buy the company's cosmetics even when their husbands were unemployed), and, in the past, the company's record to date made a 20 percent per year growth seem realistic.

As a by-product of its study, New Jersey Research suggested that inventory reduction might be a major source of capital to finance expansion. Company inventories of all types amounted to about $25 million at the time of the study. Most of this was invested either in finished-goods stocks or in raw materials. The company's processes and products were such that in-process stocks were negligible. However, there were substantial inventories of both raw materials and finished stocks. Certain raw materials were imported, and procurement lead times were sometimes long. In addition, a few critical items were refined from crops that were harvested just once a year. In such cases, the purchasing vice president had to commit for an entire year's supply, giving himself adequate reserve stocks both to ensure enough material on hand to meet demand and also to prevent being caught short should there be a partial crop failure the following year.

Finished-goods inventories were made higher than normal by the nature of the company's production processes. In order to maintain complete consistency of color and/or aroma on certain product lines, machinery had to be cleaned with exceptional care between batches. Sometimes the cleaning process tied up the machine for several days. In order to minimize cleanup, the production department tried to run large batches of major materials—particularly during periods when there was no clamor from marketing to run some other product which was badly needed. Fortunately, finished product shortages were relatively rare, since inventories were usually adequate to permit the company to maintain its overnight delivery policy to customers—even on products where demand was somewhat erratic.

New Jersey Research made a few preliminary calculations to support its contention that inventories were too high. First, it estimated that the company's cost of carrying inventory must be at least 25 percent per year. Then it made rough estimates of the setup or ordering cost of a few key items—taking into account, when necessary, the need for intensive cleaning of machinery and similar problems. In a few cases, setup cost was $1,000 or more for each batch because of the cleanup problem. In most, however, it was much less than this.

New Jersey Research then calculated economic lot sizes or order quantities, using the setup and carrying costs it had estimated in addition to usage data and unit costs culled from the company's record. The formula indicated that substantial reductions would be possible in lot sizes or purchase quantities of most items, even after taking into account special costs that tended to cause production runs to be lengthened.

However, according to New Jersey Research, most of the company's inventory "fat" lay in excess safety stock. This is apparent from the company's stocking policy. In general, the company purchases and manufactures on a quarterly basis. For example, if a sales forecast indicates that 10,000 pounds of product will be required in the second quarter of the year, then manufacturing will schedule 10,000 pounds during the first quarter and purchasing will buy the necessary raw material in the fourth quarter of the previous year. But, of course, sales forecasts are sometimes less than actual demand. Safety stock is needed in order to guarantee service to customers. At Gamelin this may amount to a six- to nine-month supply. For example, the average inventory of the material with the 10,000-pound demand per quarter may be 20,000 to 30,000 pounds.

While company President Katz agrees that inventories can probably be reduced, he does not want to do anything that will impair the company's service to customers. "Our reputation is based on quality and delivery to our customers," he points outs, "and it would be foolish to do anything to destroy this image." It occurs to Katz that one of the company's problems in inventory management may be organizational as much as it is procedural. He asks his planning vice president, Howard Roberts, to make a study of who actually makes inventory decisions.

Roberts and his staff trace back a variety of individual inventory decisions and also make a detailed study of the company's procedures in order to determine just who does get into inventory decisions. A few weeks later, Roberts makes his final report to Katz. In it he says:

> No one has probably ever consciously delegated inventory decisions to anyone at Gamelin. But, of course, they are made—seemingly by almost everyone. Since we do not have a formal corporate organization chart. I have attempted to construct an abbreviated version of such a chart (see Figure 1–5) in which I include everyone who seems to make these decisions. I have also included in the chart a "Materials Management Task Force," which I suggest you might consider creating to study the problem further. Obviously, if we are going to improve our procedures, we will need some sort of administrative body to recommend changes and, ideally, it should include representatives from all affected departments.
>
> As you can see, my supposedly abbreviated chart of materials management decision makers includes almost every manager in the company. The president and the vice president–planning are the only ones on the chart who get into the process only indirectly in the course of drawing up and approving forecasts, plans, and budgets. The role of everyone else is more direct.

FIGURE 1–5
Gamelin Cosmetics Corporation: Organizational relationships among activities involved in materials management.

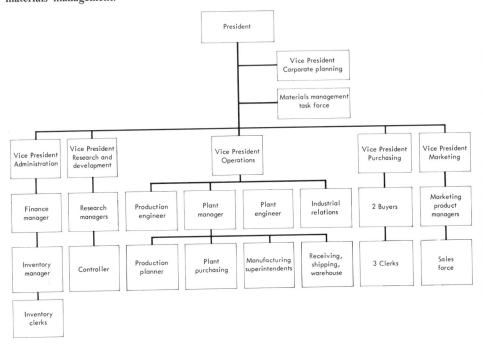

Administration. The vice president–administration and the finance manager play two major roles in materials management in their direction of the controller's office and that of the inventory manager. The controller is responsible for electronic data processing and, of course, we hope in the next few years to get our entire materials cycle on the computer. It will be the controller's responsibility to give other managers reports from the computer in a form that they need to make decisions.

The inventory manager is more directly involved. He will actually use statistics generated by the controller's EDP section. The position of inventory manager, as you know, is really new to us, even though we have had someone with that title for years. In the past, it was purely a clerical operation, concerned with gathering statistics and administering the annual physical inventory. It is only recently that this activity has shown promise of broadening itself beyond a mere record-keeping function. Obviously, this department will play a key role in any aggressive plan to reduce inventories—although its present role is still at least partly influenced by its more passive tradition.

Research and Development. As you know, the research and development department—particularly the managers concerned with flavors and fragrances—is very active in selection of suppliers. They will normally test samples submitted by each supplier and then work with the supplier in developing a product that fits our needs. In the process of development they must weigh the price quoted by the supplier against the aromatic and flavor characteristics of his samples. The vice president of research and development then reviews the information on sample tests and price and suggests not only the supplier but also the purchase quantity. In some cases, he may want to leave himself flexibility to change supplier should he feel that flavor or aromatic characteristics plays a direct role in determining inventory level of certain key purchased materials. The role of the purchasing department in such cases is a mere formality.

In theory, purchasing and almost everyone else in the organization knows that research and development has no business making purchase and inventory decisions. But no one is going to do anything about it as long as the present research vice president is there. He is a very strong figure and, apparently, he cannot be faulted on his decisions— even when they fall outside what some would regard as the limits of his jurisdiction.

Operations. The production engineer and the plant engineer have some influence on materials management in their own specialties. Each deals regularly with suppliers in his particular specialty and makes purchase decisions. Their role is quite limited, however, as is that of industrial relations, which is involved with inventory only as it affects stability of employment.

The plant manager plays a much more direct role. His production planner sets lot sizes in manufacturing and thereby directly influences the level of finished-goods inventory. He also works both formally and informally with the inventory manager and the purchasing vice president in ordering purchased material. Usually, this consists of estimating his materials requirements for the next quarter and then sending a requisition to purchasing. In other cases, he gives purchasing an estimate of his requirements and leaves it to them to determine how much to buy.

The plant purchasing agent's function should not be confused with that of the purchasing vice president. Plant purchasing is concerned only with supplies and other nonproduction items for the plant. In most cases, it acts upon requisitions that it gets from the operations staff functions (production engineering, plant engineering, and, occasionally, industrial relations) or from the line manufacturing organization.

The shipping and receiving department keeps a file of all open purchase orders for purchased materials and also maintains a conventional manually posted stock record for each major material and reminds the purchasing department to buy the material when stock reaches some predetermined order point. These records are maintained primarily for bulk materials which effectively are under the physical control of receiving and shipping. When inventory drops to the reorder point, shipping and receiving prepare a requisition and send it to purchasing. The bulk materials that are controlled in this way by the shipping and receiving supervisor are used in a number of products. Consequently, the production planner does not get involved in their ordering. He simply assumes they will always be on hand whenever they are needed, irrespective of what products are actually being scheduled. The inventory manager periodically compares his records (which are partially on EDP) with those of receiving and shipping. All records are revised periodically when physical inventories are taken.

Purchasing. The vice president of purchases is concerned almost entirely with production materials. He is responsible for selecting the production materials supplier in all cases except those in which research and development plays an active role. He is also sometimes influenced by reciprocal buying considerations and coordinates closely with marketing on purchases of certain chemicals, in particular. On a majority of major commodity purchases, the purchasing vice president exercises considerable discretion in determining how much to buy. He consults, of course, with marketing and with the production planner, but the ultimate inventory responsibility is his.

Marketing. Individual product managers work closely with the production planner, keeping him informed of expected changes in demand for company products. They also suggest when finished goods inventories should be increased to allow for anticipated sales gains. Marketing also works closely with research and development on new products and will, from time to time, deal directly with suppliers in development of these products. One of the marketing managers also coordinates with the purchasing department in order to make most effective use of the company's reciprocal buying power.

A few days after reading this report, Katz calls Roberts into his office and says:

> The report by your department pretty much confirms what you and I already knew, but I wanted you to check it out anyway. I agree with you on the task force but, frankly, I do not think it can do much more than make suggestions; committees never actually get any work done.
>
> One of the major jobs of the task force will be to explore ways in which we can reorganize our materials management organization in order to be able to focus our efforts more directly on inventory reduction. What I want from the task force is a consensus that reflects everyone's thinking. We do not want to get our organization all upset about a change. Our approach must be constructive. We don't want to fire anyone or, for that matter, even hurt anyone's feelings, if we can help it.
>
> I believe in making the organization structure fit the people rather than vice versa. We already have got one good man in Harold Singh, our new inventory manager. He is the first person in that job who has had actual training in EDP and some of those new control techniques. He is only 32 and has been with us but six months. But his department shows promise.
>
> We can probably also make changes simply because we are growing rapidly. Our sales should double in the next five years, and this is obviously going to increase both our need for and ability to support additional first-class people.
>
> We've also got two potential retirements to consider. Alfred Stein

is 64, so we will presumably be looking for a new production planner next year. This is probably just as well, since Stein is a little inflexible. Among the older men, Jim Jenkins is a lot more adaptable. Jim is 62, so he will be around as purchasing vice president for the next three years. He has never worked in any place but purchasing but he could probably take on extra duties if we liked, at least until we could begin to groom his successor. He certainly has not done a very good job on that score, and neither has Stein. Jenkins's subordinates are competent in their present jobs but not promotable, and Stein is a lone wolf. He has virtually created his own one-man department, so we should start thinking about what to do when he's gone.

The other members of the Executive Committee are as well informed as I am on the capabilities and limitations of individual members of our staff. You should keep these personality factors in mind on your task force but, probably, not discuss them openly. What we want from the task force is some sort of plan, and then we can worry about how to fit people into it, modifying the plan if necessary.

I am going to appoint you chairman of the task force. The other nominal members of the group will be the other five vice presidents. But, except for Jenkins, who I think should be active in the group, I think the others should appoint someone to represent them. I particularly want to get Singh and Stein involved on this committee. Maybe, if we get research and development committed to its success, they will play less of a prima donna role in selecting some of these suppliers.

I want the committee to meet as soon as possible and to give me a target date for a report recommending changes in the materials management organization. I then want a target date with specific plans for inventory reduction. I will give the committee all the support it needs from the Executive Committee.

CASE 1–2.   RHODE ISLAND HOSPITAL (A)*

Materials management in a health care setting

Rhode Island Hospital is one of the largest and best known hospitals in New England. It is a private, nonprofit institution offering a wide range of medical and surgical services. It is also committed to a variety of medical research projects and plays a major role in a number of medical education programs, including an affiliation with Brown University's School of Medicine. In 1972, the 700–bed hospital employed 3,842 persons and had a budget of $38,501,887.

Since 1968, the hospital has had an integrated Materials Management Department, reporting to Edward M. Boudreau. In 1970, Boudreau was

* Copyright © 1973 Bureau of Business and Economic Research, Northeastern University, Boston. Research for this case was supported by Grant Number HS 00844 from the National Center for Health Services Research and Development.

appointed an assistant director of the hospital and, in addition to his materials management responsibilities, is in charge of the buildings and grounds, office services, medical records, central transport, telephone services, and administration of the hospital capital expenditures budget.

Materials management at the hospital embraces four departments: Purchasing, General Stores and Inventory, Central Services, and Laundry. According to Boudreau:

> The Materials Management Department exists basically for the balancing and coordination of independent materials functions into a single work force. . . . The focal point of the department is transportation and processing efficiency through integration of functions and by implementing scientific application of machines for optimum utilization of personnel.
>
> Department emphasis is on creating awareness of total cost for items supplied to patients including purchase, receiving, storage processing, and final disposal. It is concerned with common materials-handling denominators in hospital operations and combined efforts to achieve economies.
>
> It is hoped that through cooperation and change, department goals of high-quality service at lowest possible cost will be achieved.

Purchasing

The hospital's purchasing expenditures total about $8,474,000 per year, or roughly 22 percent of total hospital operating costs. About $1,500,000 of these purchases are made through two purchasing cooperatives of which the hospital is a member: the Hospital Association of Rhode Island and the Hospital Bureau.

Eight persons are employed in the department, including the purchasing manager, two buyers, and five clerical employees. The department's 1972 operating budget was $75,233 per year.

In its annual report, purchasing typically reports savings of up to $200,000, roughly half of which come from advance buying to ward off price increases. The department issues about 25–30,000 purchase orders per year. Clerical costs, as well as errors, are reduced through the use of an IBM 870 machine and related equipment to type purchase orders automatically from data generated within the purchasing Department as well as that which is a product of the hospital's computerized inventory control system.

General stores and inventory

The hospital's inventories are divided into 15 categories, and the hospital's stores manager reported the following position as of September 30, 1972:

	Turnover 71-72	No. of items 71-72	Value 71-72	Value 70-71
Buildings and grounds	1.54	3,595	$ 42,554	$ 46,229
Blood bank	2.39	13	72,266	71,174
Dietary.	18.04	646	42,548	25,214
Dietary stores	2.45	76	12,561	25,311
Gift shop.	.25	27	1,700	1,837
Housekeeping	9.27	244	25,805	25,683
Laboratory	7.41	139	13,880	11,491
Linen and bedding	2.47	82	29,871	61,187
Medical and surgical	15.04	855	103,395	92,556
Medical and surgical O.R.	.02	1,022	100,691	86,653
Pharmacy	3.04	1,901	211,307	229,000
Data-processing forms	4.10	131	40,983	33,521
General forms	3.02	473	49,884	51,504
Office supplies	5.20	316	23,997	29,716
X-Ray film and supplies	2.44	16	13,619	16,532
Totals	77.04	9,536	$745,061	$807,678
Average turnover rate	5.13			
A net change of	$62,617, down			

The General Stores and Inventory Department employs 16 persons and has an annual operating budget of more than $100,000. Its activities embrace not only receiving and storekeeping functions but also delivery of material to nursing stations and other points of use throughout the hospital.

Some items distributed by the Stores Department are for single use. The Buildings and Grounds Department (also under Boudreau) is then responsible for their disposition. Other items are reusable, and responsibility for their recycling normally rests with the Central Services Department.

"Hospital materials management," Boudreau explains, "begins with the purchase of material, includes not only storage but also conversion processes needed to make it useful, and doesn't end until the material is used and finally discarded."

The Stores Department is responsible for operations of storerooms which accommodate approximately 65 percent of the hospital's total inventory investment of $745,061. The exceptions are the stores areas in the Dietary Food and Pharmacy departments. These departments operate their own storerooms primarily for convenience. For example, the dietary department naturally must have an inventory of food in close proximity to the kitchen.

When it does not control physical stocks of material, materials management is responsible for development and implementation of inventory control techniques, working with the appropriate department heads. The major exception to this is the pharmacy. The chief pharmacist both purchases the hospital's drugs and is also solely responsible for drug inventories.

In most cases, it is possible to get overnight delivery of drugs from vendor warehouses in Providence or Boston. While the hospital must be assured of a supply of any drug that is stocked, an overwhelming majority of the inventory investment is represented by relatively common drugs such as tetracycline, insulin, penicillin in various forms, barbiturates, tranquilizers, etc.

The hospital first began using its computer for inventory control in 1966. By 1973, all inventory centers were controlled by computer with the exception of the pharmacy, whose control techniques remained essentially manual. The hospital's chief pharmacist has been reluctant to make the changeover because he believes that drug requirements change so rapidly that he doubts if it would be possible to make sufficient reductions (without impairing quality of service) in drug stocks to be worth the effort of changing over to a computerized system.

The Materials Management Department agrees that it is no easy job to change over from a manual to a computerized inventory control system but believes it has now had enough experience with the process so that it can be carried off quite smoothly. Materials management [see Rhode Island Hospital (B), Case 10–1] believes that substantial improvement in inventory carrying costs can be attributed to computerization and other improvements that have been made in recent years. For example, inventories of medical-surgical supplies were cut from about $187,000 to roughly $100,000 almost immediately after the control system was computerized. With the old manual system, the materials manager never really knew what his inventory position was except just after the annual physical inventory was taken. With the computerized system, every materials transaction is keypunched and fed into the computer daily. Weekly printouts keep management up to date on the total inventory position. The reduction of about $87,000, or 47 percent, in medical-surgical inventory is essentially due to superior information provided by the computerized system.

This net reduction was made despite some increase in "official" stocks. In the past, head nurses simply requisitioned medical-surgical supplies, and each nursing station had its own inventory that was used up in accordance with patient needs. However, the hospital accounting system automatically charged the inventory to operating expense when the requisition was filled and, therefore, the inventory at the nursing stations did not officially exist.

The hospital's PAR delivery system virutally eliminates all such "unofficial" stocks. First, materials management specialists work with head nurses to determine usage of each item. For example, they might discover that a particular nursing station uses 100 disposable clinical thermometers per week. They might then establish a stock level of 150 thermometers. Each week they would check the inventory of thermometers at the nursing station, calculate the actual usage by subtracting from 150, and replenish the stock to bring it back up to 150. With this system, the nurses rarely need worry about having material on hand when needed and can concentrate strictly on nursing problems. In addition, the hospital enjoys the benefit of optimum inventories, and administrators also get a monthly printout of usage of each item by department for analysis.

Such printouts sometimes detect unusual patterns of usage. For example, the animal laboratory appeared on the inventory printout as a major user of incontinent pads. Since these pads are designed for use by human patients in medical-surgical units, materials management investigated and discovered that the pads were serving the same function that newspaper provides for the individual owner of a pet that is not housebroken. Used newspapers are free, while incontinent pads cost 14 cents each.

The Animal Laboratory Department manager was unwilling to use newspapers because he believed that there was no convenient way in which he could get an adequate supply. The final compromise resulted in the dogs using a cheaper incontinent pad that cost 5 cents instead of 14 cents. Since hundreds of these pads are used each month, the saving was substantial.

While the Materials Management Department expected the computer to help it police inventories, it assumed that relatively little further reductions in inventory investment could be made once the changeover to the computer was successfully completed. So far, however, the department has been able to continue to improve its inventory performance. For the last five years, investment in medical-surgical inventories has remained steady at roughly $100,000, in the face of steadily increasing usage of material and a rate of price inflation that has averaged at least 5 percent per year. Boudreau estimates that inventory turnover in physical terms has steadily improved at a rate of roughly 10 percent per year in response to a variety of techniques applied by materials management.

Much of this improvement is probably simply a result of paying more attention to inventories. "The using departments are concerned with doing their basic jobs," explains Boudreau, "and don't have time to worry about inventory levels. When we can suggest ways in which to improve performance, they are more than cooperative, but the initiative must come from a group whose primary concern is materials management performance." For example, the Buildings and Grounds Department is primarily concerned with keeping the hospital operating under all conditions and must have materials on hand should critical operating components, such as valves, fail on a week-end or holiday when it is impossible to get deliveries from suppliers.

When the Buildings and Grounds Department was responsible for its own inventory control, the department's focus was exclusively on having material on hand when needed. Consequently, there was a built-in tendency for stocks to accumulate simply because the department manager was fully occupied with keeping the hospital operating and did not really look upon minimizing inventory as one of his areas of responsibility or expertise.

Naturally, the Buildings and Grounds Department became more materials management conscious when Boudreau was appointed an assistant director and buildings and grounds and materials management were linked together by a common boss. The goal of always having critical materials on hand for emergencies was not abandoned, but it proved possible to make substantial cuts in inventory without imperiling hospital operation. For example, it is conceivable that the hospital might require one or two valves of a particular type should a failure occur on a week-end. But there was no chance whatever of 12 failures on that same week-end, so it is possible to reduce the inventory of that valve from 12 units to 2 units.

Central services

The central services, or central supply, function is unique to hospital materials management. In effect, hospital inventories can be divided into two categories: sterile and nonsterile. Most of the latter are handled by the General Stores Department, whose operation is little different from its counterpart in a factory or nonmedical service industry.

The Central Services Department also performs a materials management service when it maintains an inventory of sterile supplies, used primarily in the hospital's operating rooms. But, in the economic sense, it also adds value by manufacture when it sterilizes dressings and other materials, making up "kits" for the operating rooms and nursing units to use for various types of surgery and special care. For example, burn patients and some postsurgical cases require sterile kits provided by central services.

The Central Services Department at Rhode Island Hospital is responsible not only for dressings and other sterile fabrics but also for all other sterile supplies, including surgical gloves (about 60,000 pairs per year), syringes, intravenous solutions, and a variety of miscellaneous items that must be sterile. The department employs 27 persons, has an annual budget of approximately $350,000, and requires an inventory of about $24,000.

The economic role of central services at every hospital, including

Rhode Island, has been changed markedly by the introduction of disposables. In the past, almost everything handled by operating room personnel or by patients had to be processed through central services' sterilizers. Now most materials are received in sterile form from suppliers and discarded after being used just once. For example, the Rhode Island Hospital purchases and uses approximately 350,000 disposable syringes each year. Central services is concerned only with the supply of these syringes and need not sterilize them. In the past, the hospital had an inventory of nondisposable syringes which were sterilized in central services after each use.

Today, many hospitals even use disposable paper or nonwoven fabric in the operating room "packs" of sterile material that is used to drape patients and staff during surgery. However, Rhode Island Hospital continues to use conventional packs of woven cloth that is laundered and sterilized after each use. The decision to change over from nondisposables to disposables is basically economic. In every American hospital, it is apparently cheaper to purchase disposable syringes and surgical gloves than it is to sterilize and reuse nondisposables.[11] At Rhode Island Hospital, low laundry costs are a major reason it does not pay to use disposable surgical packs.

Boudreau is also concerned about the increased trash problems that disposables create. The hospital is already getting rid of 10 tons of trash each day at a cost of roughly 0.8 cents per pound and would prefer to avoid any increases. Boudreau believes that analysis of the cost of any material should include not only the conventional materials management costs but also the ecological and cash cost of getting rid of used-up material.

Laundry

While a large hospital laundry uses large quantities of trisodium phosphate, this is ecologically minor compared with getting rid of an equivalent quantity of disposables. Also, manufacturers of disposables have not yet been able to match conventional linens in both quality and cost. For this reason, even hospitals that have gone in heavily for disposables still incur enormous laundry costs. Increasingly, however, this is being done by outside suppliers which can handle laundry for a number of hospitals at low cost. Thus, laundering is increasingly becoming a purchased service for hospitals. Organizationally, this is the major rationale for including the laundry—which is really a manufacturing operation and not a supply function—in the Materials Management Department.

[11] Quality differences may also be important. A new, disposable hypodermic needle is sharper than a reusable one that has passed through the sterilizer a few times. In addition, proponents of disposables claim that they offer greater assurance of sterility since there is less danger of confusing sterile with nonsterile material when disposables are used.

Several years ago, Rhode Island Hospital was considering closing its own laundry and purchasing the service. At that time, its laundry operating cost was 12 cents per pound of laundry. In contrast, the Greater Boston Hospital Council offered its cooperative laundry service to member hospitals for just 9 cents per pound. This service was available to Rhode Island Hospital, since Providence is only about 35 miles from Boston.

Shortly after being appointed materials manager, Boudreau made a detailed study of the hospital's laundry operation and proposed that $87,000 be spent for three modern washing machines, two dryers, and a materials-handling system based on conveyors and chutes to minimize handling of both dirty and clean laundry. The new equipment permitted a sharp reduction in labor hours and, by 1970, the cost of laundry had been reduced to about $8\frac{1}{4}$ cents per pound. In addition to processing almost 4,000,000 pounds of laundry for its own needs, the improved facility is able to handle another 1,000,000 pounds per year for a neighboring hospital.

The laundry continues to be jammed into the same building it has occupied for many years, and this creates inefficiencies which simply cannot be eliminated. Nevertheless, the hospital's own costs have been cut by a third, and no cheaper alternative exists.

Coordination between the laundry and central services has also helped eliminate duplication of work that is common to many hospitals. The laundry is responsible for washing reusable packs used in the operating rooms, and the Central Services Department is responsible for sterilizing the material after it is laundered.

Naturally, the laundry folded each piece after it was washed. The material was then moved to central services, where it was stored until someone unfolded each item, inspected for holes, and then refolded it to be fitted in with other items in the surgical pack. If holes were found, as was often the case, the linen item was returned to the laundry for mending.

The unfolding and folding operation was eliminated by transferring seven women from central services to the laundry. This group takes material unfolded as it comes directly from the laundering operation and makes up surgical packs in a single operation. As a result, a buffer stock of unfolded laundry was eliminated, in addition to a net reduction of three employees. Boudreau estimates the saving to be at least $10,000 to $12,000 per year.

The saving would probably have been greater—or at least realized more rapidly—had there not been morale problems associated with the change. Central services is a higher status department than the laundry. Work in the former can be rationalized as "professional," even by less skilled employees, while the laundry worker suffers from no such illusions. While the actual work performed by the women who were transferred from the job did not really change, Boudreau believed that their perceptions of their jobs might well change. Consequently, he took great pains to make the group's new working area as comfortable and attractive as possible—including such a "frill" (for a laundry) as air conditioning. Air conditioning also permitted keeping the windows closed, so that flies, insects, dust and other foreign matter were kept away from the linen.

Cooperation between the laundry and central services has also helped reduce linen waste. Sheets and towels used on burn patients immediately become hopelessly stained from the silver nitrate that is used for treatment. Such linens can be reused for a while, at least, on other burn patients, but finally they become unusable for patients. They still have value within the hospital as rags (which would otherwise have to be purchased), but Boudreau discovered that hospital maintenance personnel refused to do this, preferring to use only discarded linen that was not badly stained. Apparently no one likes a bloody towel, even if he is using it as a wiping rag. The solution was to dye the stained linen a dark color. The cost of the dyeing process is only a fraction of the cost of purchased rags, and the dye makes the stained linen usable by squeamish maintenance employees.

The laundry has 62 employees, including the seven women transferred from central services. In addition to its basic laundering function, it is also responsible for delivering and picking up linen throughout the hospital. The direct operating cost of the basic laundry unit is about $235,000 per year; linen distribution costs about $188,000. In addition, the laundry manager is responsible for a sewing room and uniform room where uniforms for hospital personnel are stored and repaired as needed. This service is budgeted at about $57,000 per year.

Questions

1. Some hospitals as large as Rhode Island Hospital operate without a formally organized materials mangement department. Each department head is responsible for his own purchasing and inventory management. What benefits, if any, does Rhode Island Hospital gain from its materials management organization? What are the drawbacks?

2. What materials management problem(s) does Rhode Island Hospital presently have and what, if anything, can be done to solve them?

3. Which of the departments reporting to Boudreau are "legitimate" materials management activities, in your opinion? Which do you feel are not "legitimate," and how can they be justified as part of Boudreau's operation?

2

The materials cycle

MATERIALS MANAGEMENT is concerned with the flow of materials to and from the manufacturing departments. The materials manager regulates this flow in relation to changes in demand for finished products, actual or predicted prices of materials, supplier performance on quality and delivery, availability of materials, and other variables. He bases his decisions on information from other departments within his company, suppliers, and other sources, including news in business periodicals.

In its simplest form, most of materials management consists of learning how much to get, when, and from whom. Simple as this sounds, the job can be quite complex, both because of the fantastic amount of detail work involved and, as seen in Chapter 1, because of the tremendous impact of materials management decisions on a company's success or failure.

THE VACUUM CLEANER CASE

Suppose you were a materials manager for a small company making a relatively simple product like vacuum cleaners. What would your job encompass? What would be some of the problems you would be likely to encounter?

The job would be more difficult than you might casually suppose. Even though a vacuum cleaner is not very complex, the products of almost every industry would be needed to operate a plant. The cleaner itself would probably have components made of zinc die castings; molded plastics; brushes made of wood, hog bristle, and glue; steel screws made by cold heading; sheet steel stampings; and so on.

In addition, thousands of other nonproduction items would have to be purchased before the first vacuum cleaner could be shipped to a customer. Machinery, equipment, and a stock of spare parts to keep them in good repair would be needed, as would all the tools and supplies required to operate and maintain the factory and the office. These would include such diverse items as stationery, fuel for the plant's boilers, packaging supplies for the product, and countless others.

Materials management in even a small business often involves control of 8,000 to 10,000 different items, when all supplies are considered. However, the major materials management effort is directed toward the items that are "direct" material, that is, those that are incorporated directly into the product as parts, particularly the more expensive items. Usually 75 to 90 percent of the materials expenditures in a manufacturing company are for direct material, and often a few key items account for a large share of direct-material expense. Needless to say, materials managers try to spend more time on these major items than on minor ones, and most of them devote 75 to 90 percent of their time to direct material[1] and concentrate a big part of it on problems involving a few key materials.

Good materials managers try to "manage by exception." They try to organize their departments so that major problems requiring decisions are promptly called to their attention, while minor problems are automatically shunted to subordinates for solution. However, some managers delegate a minimum of authority early in the materials cycle, when the product is being designed. At this stage decisions are made that have an important effect upon every succeeding stage. Sometimes they may limit the materials department's flexibility in choosing supply sources for years to come, and bad design decisions can create innumerable problems at every stage of the cycle.

THE DESIGN STAGE

Prime responsibility for design rests with the engineering department, but the materials department plays a vital role. No company is so big that it can afford to have on its payroll scientists and engineers who are experts in the design, application, and processing of every part and material it uses. Suppliers make enormous contributions to every company's design efforts, to a much greater extent than most people realize. For example, in a familiar product like an automobile, spring-steel bumpers, chrome-plated wheel covers, power steering, automatic transmissions, overdrives, and numerous other components were originally developed by suppliers, not by the auto manufacturers themselves.

---

[1] Naturally this is not the case in educational institutions, in governments, or in companies that sell services.

The materials department is the company's prime contact with supply sources. It can act as a catalyst in bringing supplier know-how to bear on the company's technical problems. Veteran materials specialists often develop an expertise of their own, both from their educational backgrounds and from their association with suppliers. In some cases, they can assist with design problems that concern their specialities. For example, in a vacuum cleaner company, the materials specialist who handles zinc die castings could be the best-informed man in the company on die-casting technology. Engineers would be primarily interested in more critical parts of the cleaners, such as the brush action, and, especially if the company does no die casting in its own plant, their knowledge of this specialized field could be fairly limited.

Coordination of styling. Usually, the first step in creating a product whose appearance is important—such as a vacuum cleaner—is to make sketches of various styles. The final style selected would presumably offer maximum sales appeal for the lowest possible cost. Sales appeal can be determined by previous marketing experience, market research surveys, opinions of top marketing executives, and so on. Cost can be evaluated by comparison of proposed designs.

It is not easy to evaluate relative costs simply by looking at an artist's sketch of a product. At this stage, specifications for materials, dimensions, and processes have yet to be determined. The engineering approach to cost estimating, where material weights are calculated from blueprints and the like, just will not work. The cost estimate at this stage, in effect, is a well-educated guess. The company's future profits can depend on how accurate the guess is. Once a decision is made and tools are constructed to make a given design, it becomes expensive to make changes. Experienced materials personnel can estimate relative costs with almost uncanny accuracy because they are (or should be) comparing relative values of materials as a routine part of their day-to-day jobs.

Suppose that stylists propose several different designs for the outer cover of the cleaner. Each design can be executed in a variety of ways: they could conceivably be stamped from sheet steel; die cast from zinc or aluminum; or molded from polyethylene or some other plastic. The part might be perfectly satisfactorily made by any of the processes, so the final decision would be essentially economic and not engineering. When competent materials experts are permitted to review stylists' sketches, they can make rough approximations of relative costs and, possibly, also suggest ways in which costs could be reduced through minor changes in the shape of the item. Preliminary reviews of this sort not only make it possible to eliminate costly features that contribute relatively little to sales appeal or utility, but also help guide engineering to the type of process (such as molded plastic) that is most economic for this particular part.

Once the style is agreed upon, engineers proceed to translate the stylists' sketches into detailed specifications to guide the manufacture of each component. Materials specialists also should work closely with the engineers at this stage. They can assist by proposing standard components, bringing in suppliers to aid in development work, guiding design decisions, and acquainting engineers with new materials and techniques.

Standard components.   If a standard component can be used in a product, it usually costs less. In addition, there may be some saving in engineering and development cost, since the standard item is already available. Sometimes the standard item costs less than a special one, even though it may have features that are inherently more costly. For example, if the engineer's calculations in designing the vacuum cleaner indicate that a .45 hp. motor is required, what size motor should be specified? The answer is a ½ hp. motor. The slightly bigger motor is theoretically more costly, but its price would probably be lower because it is a standard size that motor manufacturers are already equipped to produce. Also, the price for the ½ hp. design may be based on relatively large production volume if other manufacturers buy a motor with the same specifications.

Supplier development.   If the cleaner is a new model, the key components will probably require some engineering development before they can be produced. Because suppliers have the specialized product know-how, it is usually desirable to have them do this for the components in which they specialize. For example, the vacuum cleaner motor might be an adaptation of some supplier's standard design.

In such cases, the company may effectively commit itself to buy from a certain supplier as soon as it asks for assistance on development. The supplier will incorporate his own specifications into the adaptation, and it will not be possible to get competitive bids from other suppliers. For this reason, the materials department should play a strong role in choosing the suppliers needed as engineering works on new-product development.

Guiding design decisions.   Engineers may have difficulty choosing from a number of acceptable designs and specifications. For example, it might be possible to make satisfactory wheels for a cleaner from wood, molded hard rubber, molded plastics, steel stampings, machined gray-iron castings, or die castings.[2]

The engineer can determine which materials and processes will do the job, but he can hardly hope to be an authority on the relative cost and availability of each. Nor can he always be guided by previous design decisions. Markets change; while it may have been economic

---

[2] In practice, there are rarely more than two or three acceptable choices among materials or fabrication methods. However, there are remarkably few products that do not have at least one alternative.

to make a component out of one material a year ago, an alternate material may be more desirable now. Relative prices and availability can change fast.

Introducing new materials. Good engineers try to keep up to date on all new products and processes that might help them. But even with a comparatively simple product like a vacuum cleaner, there can be just too many bases for the engineer to cover. Many different industries are involved, and no single engineering department can keep up with all of them.

The materials specialist can help engineers by introducing them to suppliers who are promoting new ideas. For example, for the vacuum cleaner, the materials specialist might suggest to his engineers that they test such new materials as molded Fiberglas for the exterior of the sweeper. Or he might propose molded nylon or sintered metal for the wheels—or anodized aluminum (instead of stainless steel) for the decorative molding.

Minor changes. Different suppliers may use slightly different equipment and processes to make identical items. Minor changes in specifications often are necessary to adapt a design to their equipment and processes. The materials specialist (or buyer) must coordinate such changes with his company's engineering department. Sometimes he also becomes involved in changes to permit quality standards to be met; in this case, he must bring together the supplier with both quality control and product engineers.

THE SOURCING STAGE

When the design is complete, the next basic stage of the materials cycle is sourcing.[3] Since very few manufacturers start with raw materials that they mine or grow themselves, this is largely a matter of determining the stage of fabrication at which a component or material will be purchased. At one extreme, a company may buy basic raw materials and perform all manufacturing and assembly operations in its own factories. At the other extreme, it may concentrate its efforts on engineering and merchandising its products, relying on outside suppliers to produce them complete.

Most companies follow a middle course between these extremes. They fabricate some items from raw material and rely upon outside suppliers for others. For example, the typical vacuum cleaner company might buy fasteners, moldings, and die castings as finished components. It

---

[3] This is an oversimplification. In practice, design and sourcing are almost simultaneous operations for a product. Suppliers often are assured of business when the design is in its preliminary stage, although orders usually are not formally placed until the design is complete. Also, individual components may be ordered months before the final design of the assembled product is completed.

might also buy semifinished items, like castings, forgings, copper wire, and sheet steel, which would be fabricated into parts to be assembled into finished cleaners. Since the typical company spends about twice as much on purchased parts and materials as it spends on its payroll, it can find it more advantageous to rely upon outside suppliers for many finished components and assemblies.

Make or buy. The decisions that determine which parts to make in the shop and which to buy from suppliers are by no means made exclusively by the materials manager. Since they can shape the company's future for years to come, they are nearly always reviewed by all of its top managers. Among the variables that influence make-or-buy decisions are estimated manufacturing costs, purchase costs, technical skills, availability of material, and capital resources.

The materials manager plays a vital role in make-or-buy decisions. Estimates of the variables of the marketplace (present and future price and availability of materials and components) depend almost entirely upon his judgment. If he is wrong, the company may make a decision that will hurt its profits for years to come.

For example, suppose the vacuum cleaner manufacturer must make a choice between investing in facilities and equipment to make his own sheet-steel stampings or molded plastic parts. The materials manager would estimate current purchase prices of both types of part and try to project future price trends. These estimates would be compared with estimates of the company's own manufacturing costs for these items. The difference between the purchase price and the company's own manufacturing cost would be the company's return on investment, should it decide to make the parts. If the purchase price declines in the future because of more competitive market conditions, the company's return on investment would also decline. On the other hand, if outside market prices rise, the return will rise. With a bad make-or-buy decision, the company's funds will be invested in equipment that yields small profits or, at worst, is an actual drain on the company's earning power.

Facilities procurement. Once decisions have been made as to which products and components will be manufactured and which will be purchased, definite commitments can be made for needed facilities and equipment. Occasionally, buildings will have to be purchased. The materials manager would be partly responsible (along with other top executives) for selecting the site of the new building and letting the contract for its design. He also would handle all dealings with contractors and subcontractors for construction.

Contracts for necessary machinery and equipment would, in most companies, be the joint responsibility of the materials manager and the chief plant or process engineer. The latter would determine the technical specifications for the equipment; the former would handle necessary negotiation with suppliers and administration of purchase contracts.

PLANNING PRODUCTION

Once a company has a product and knows what its manufacturing facilities will be, it is ready to plan production. The planning process starts with a sales forecast, which may be based on market research studies, actual orders from customers, and the judgment of the company's senior marketing executives.

The master schedule.   The materials manager rarely is directly concerned with the sales forecast, but he is part of the group that translates this forecast into a master production schedule. Sometimes the schedule is identical with the market research forecast; usually it is different. The schedule must take account not only of basic market demand but of other factors. A good schedule has a minimum of fluctuations to facilitate economic operation, and it must also take into account availability of labor and materials and basic capacity.

The master production schedule influences the operation of every department in the company. For this reason, its final preparation and approval are usually a committee effort. Represented on the committee are the materials manager, marketing manager, finance manager, manufacturing manager, and other key officials.

Calculating requirements.   Each product has a bill of material that indicates the name, part number, and usage of each component, and, usually, the subassembly in which it is used. Material control clerks "explode" the bill of material by taking the schedule and multiplying the number of units in each product by the scheduled output of that product. They post this information as "demand" on a record card that is kept for each individual component. Records are normally kept on a monthly basis. In posting, the clerk allows a predetermined lead time that is shown on the card.

Suppose, for example, that the company plans on building 10,000 vacuum cleaners in the month of August. Five units of a certain fastener are used in a subassembly of the cleaner. When the clerk explodes the bill of material, he knows that 50,000 fasteners will be needed for August production. But since these fasteners are not used in the final assembly operation, they must be available before August. In this case, the clerk's records might indicate that he should allow 30 days for subassembly operations ahead of final assembly; he then knows he needs 50,000 fasteners during July.

After the clerk posts all future requirements on the master record card for each component, he compares future demand with current inventories and commitments outstanding on purchase orders or work orders. The card should at all times reflect the latest information on demand, supply, and inventory of the part. All changes in production schedules are posted to it, as are all receipts or withdrawals of material from stores and any physical counts taken of material by stock checkers.

Changing schedules. Although they can be (and are) changed, schedules introduce inflexibility into the materials cycle. Individual components and the raw materials to make them must be ordered weeks or even months before the end product is assembled. During this period, there is danger that schedules will be disrupted. The demand for end products may change. Production problems with any one component can cause scheduling and assembly problems for countless other components and end products.

Clerks are quite capable of calculating what requirements will be when everything goes according to plan; materials managers must cope with the unforeseen. When one is controlling thousands of individual components, some problems are almost inevitable. There will be strikes at supplier plants, quality control problems, shortages of raw material, tooling difficulties, and so on. Materials management problems also arise when business is unusually good. If demand suddenly spurts, the flow of material must be accelerated. In such cases, materials managers look for the bottleneck items that will be most likely to prevent greater output and give them their personal attention, using techniques that will be discussed in future chapters.

THE ORDERING PROCESS

After a schedule has been determined for each item and requirements have been calculated, the ordering process begins. Requisitions and work orders are made up for each item. Typically these list unit requirements, either for a given customer's order or for total production for several months.

Purchase requisitions (Figure 2–1) provide the authority to issue purchase orders (Figure 2–2) to outside suppliers; work orders authorize the manufacture of components made in the shop. Work orders and requisitions are interrelated. If a work order is to be carried out on schedule, the purchase requisition for the raw materials must be executed on schedule.

For example, a work order for a motor assembly for the vacuum cleaner may automatically generate a purchase requisition for the bearings used in the motor. It may also generate a second work order, for the motor's commutator assembly, which in turn might create need for a third work order for the individual components of the commutator, which in turn would generate a purchase requisition for the silicon steel needed. Needless to say, a single failure in supply can raise havoc with the entire operation.

To prevent supply failure, materials managers must exercise considerable care in selecting vendors. Before contracts are awarded, suppliers' facilities and reputations are carefully investigated. Materials managers also review their companies' own records of how suppliers have handled

FIGURE 2–1
Purchase requisition form

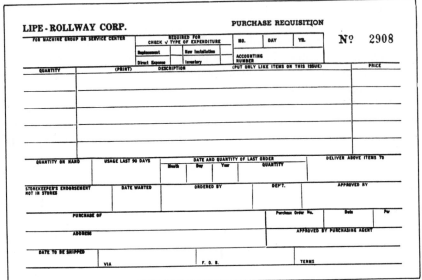

Courtesy Lipe-Rollway Corp.

The purchase requisition is the authority to buy material from an outside supplier.

previous orders; they naturally favor vendors who have done a good job for them in the past. But they also like to reduce prices they pay for materials, so they are prone to experiment with new suppliers who are willing to cut prices.

Placing the order. Buyers send quotation request forms (see Figure 2–3) to three or more competing suppliers when they believe they can reduce prices by competitive bidding. Often there are substantial differences between the quotes of the high and low bidders. If the high bidder has an excellent record on quality, delivery, and service, while the low bidder's record is more dubious, the materials manager has a problem. To whom should he award the business?

To find the answer, he must compare the saving made by buying from the low bidder with his estimate of the cost and greater probability of supply failure that might result from awarding the business to the low bidder. Since risks of this sort cannot be estimated precisely, such decisions are not easy to make. They depend to a great degree on the judgment and experience of the materials manager. They also depend on the materials manager's personality and the attitude of his superiors. Some materials managers are more willing to gamble on unknown suppliers than others. Most will back their bet on a new supplier either by protecting themselves with a larger than normal inventory or with

FIGURE 2–2
Purchase order form

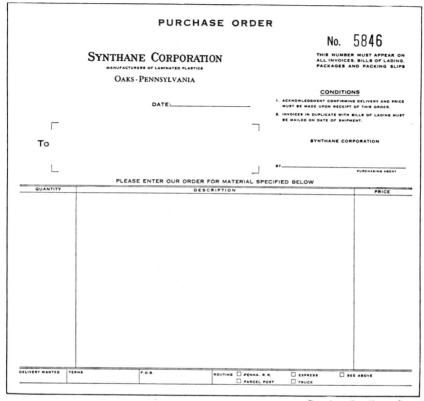

Courtesy Synthane Corp.

The purchase order authorizes the supplier to ship and invoice for material in accordance with its terms and provisions.

a second source of supply. When neither of these alternatives is practical, some managers refuse to gamble on a new source, regardless of the benefit. In big business and big government, the penalties for supply failure are quite real, while there may be little or no reward for brilliant success when the gamble pays off. A smart management encourages intelligent risk taking.

The purchase order formally confirms the choice of supplier. It becomes, when accepted by the supplier, a contract between buyer and seller. Before the contract is finally accepted by both parties, there may be legal problems to be ironed out. Special contract conditions may be negotiated, clauses may be added to the order, and so on. The materials manager must know enough about contract law to negotiate and write simple clauses. He must also recognize his own limitations and

FIGURE 2–3
Quotation request form

FORD DIVISION
Ford Motor Company

REQUEST FOR QUOTATION
BIDDER MUST FILL IN COMPLETE NAME AND ADDRESS

Gentlemen:

Please submit your price (less trade discounts) and terms of payment on materials listed below.

Omit Sales and Use Tax from your price, but include all other applicable taxes. Sales and Use Tax status will be indicated on the Purchase Order or Release. If you are legally required to pay this tax, we shall reimburse you for it in addition to the quoted price.

If unable to supply amount specified, please show hereon the quantity you can supply and your guaranteed deliveries.

Please insert unit price opposite each item and mail copy, properly signed, to this Company, retaining bidders' copy for your reference.

Quotation must remain open for acceptance for thirty days after receipt.

COMPLETE THE FOLLOWING INFORMATION

F.O.B.	TRANSPORTATION TERMS	PAYMENT TERMS
☐ CARRIER, SELLER'S PLANT	☐ COLLECT	☐ NET 20TH PROX.
☐	☐	☐

MINIMUM RUN (IN PIECES)	MIN.SHP.QUAN. (IN PIECES)	BEST DELIVERY DATE

PACKAGING AND/OR SHIPPING SPECIFICATIONS TO BE IN ACCORDANCE

WEIGHT	TO BE SHIPPED VIA	SHIPPING POINT

WITH ATTACHED FORM FD-1882-A, DATED_____

ADDRESS REPLY TO:

Purchasing Office, Ford Division FORD MOTOR COMPANY
P.O. Box 628, DEARBORN, MICHIGAN

ATTENTION _____ROOM _____ DATED _____

PARTS AND ACCESSORIES PART NUMBER	ENGINEERING PART NUMBER	PART NAME

FURNISH QUOTATIONS AS SHOWN BELOW

QUANTITY	PIECE PRICE	PACKAGING PRICE	TOTAL PRICE
IN PIECES	$	$	$
IN PIECES	$	$	$
IN PIECES	$	$	$

PPR. NO.

				BLUEPRINT DATE
☐ BLANKET ORDER	$	$	$	
INITIAL REQM'TS (PIECES)	AVG. MO. REQM'TS (PIECES)	DELIVERY REQ'D BY	DELIVERY REQUIRED AT	BID REQUIRED BY

IN ADDITION TO OUR STANDARD TERMS AND CONDITIONS, THE FOLLOWING WILL APPLY

ANY SUGGESTIONS RELATING TO PROPOSED CHANGES IN THE SUPPLIES COVERED BY THE REQUEST FOR QUOTATION WHICH YOU BELIEVE WILL RESULT IN IMPROVEMENTS IN THE SUPPLIER OR THEIR USE WILL BE WELCOMED. FORD MOTOR COMPANY ACQUIRES NO RIGHTS UNDER YOUR PATENTS BUT YOU ACKNOWLEDGE THAT SUCH SUGGESTIONS ARE NOT SUBMITTED ON A CONFIDENTIAL BASIS AND THAT ALL RIGHTS, CLAIMS AND REMEDIES IN RESPECT OF THEM (OTHER THAN THOSE ARISING FROM SUCH PATENTS) ARE WAIVED. PLEASE ADVISE US OF YOUR LOWEST QUOTATION FOR SUPPLIES CONFORMING TO BOTH THE BLUEPRINT DESIGN AND ANY SUGGESTED CHANGED DESIGN.

FIRM SUBMITTING QUOTATION

SIGNED BY AUTHORIZED REPRESENTATIVE	DATE

Courtesy Ford Motor Co.

Quotation request forms are filled out by potential suppliers for any purchases in which there is price competition among producers.

know when to call on an expert attorney for help with the more complex clauses that occasionally are necessary.

Follow-up.   The buying job does not end with the placement of the order. Not infrequently the supplier has difficulties with specifications, tooling, and so on. Even if there are no problems, a buyer cannot just issue a purchase order for an important item and then forget about it. He often follows the supplier's progress on the order in great detail, to make sure that nothing happens to prevent delivery on schedule. If the item is in particularly short supply, the buyer may even go so far as to stay in the supplier's plant and watch work on the order progress to assure that delivery will be made when promised. If the supplier has trouble getting raw material, the buyer may exert his pressure along with that of the supplier's buyer on the raw-material producer. Buyers occasionally use spectacular and rather flamboyant methods to assure delivery. Use of chartered planes is not unheard of when material is in short supply. One of the most imaginative buying feats was performed by a GM buyer during the Korean War, when nickel was in short supply. He managed to buy substantial quantities of Chinese coins, which were then melted down, and the nickel in them presumably wound up being plated onto Chevrolet or Buick bumpers and other parts.

Shortages can also develop as a result of failures within the materials manager's own plant. Thus, real-life materials management involves continuous follow-up not only of suppliers but also of internal operations. If the manufacturing manager is immediately alerted to a problem in one of his operations, he may be able to solve it before the entire schedule is thrown awry.

Materials management sometimes may be forced to reschedule inbound shipments from suppliers as a result of manufacturing problems. For example, if some problem developed in the manufacture of one model of vacuum cleaner, materials management would try simultaneously to increase output of some other model that was not affected by the problem and to cut off the flow of material for the model whose output was curtailed.

Packaging and transportation.   The materials manager is concerned with the flow of purchased material into the plant and the flow of finished products out of it. This involves him not only in the selection of carriers (trains, trucks, and sometimes planes) but also in packaging. Before the supplier can deliver, he must be given instructions as to how to package and ship. In some cases there is no problem, since the delivery may be in the supplier's truck and the product may require no packaging. In others, packaging specifications and transportation routing may be quite complex. Because transportation and packaging are so costly, many companies make elaborate studies of them and sometimes discover ingenious ways to reduce expenses.

Despite the most intensive cost-reduction efforts, transportation and packaging are still expensive,[4] and if their costs are reduced too much other problems result. Service is slower, and damage in shipment is greater. As with the selection of suppliers, the materials manager must compare the savings from lower cost packaging and shipping with the greater risk of loss he assumes. Even if transportation and packaging are specified without regard to cost, there are problems. Shipments go astray or are damaged in transit, claims must be made against the carrier for damages, and bills must be audited for errors.

THE RECEIVING PROCESS

When material is shipped, the supplier encloses a packing slip. The common carrier (if one is used) encloses a bill of lading and an invoice for freight. All of these documents identify the material when it arrives at the buyer's plant. The receiving clerk checks them against his file of open purchase orders. He then physically checks the shipment to make certain that it actually contains the material indicated on the supplier's packing slip and the buyer's purchase order. This check involves weighing or counting the shipment, along with a general identification; it does not involve investigation of the material's quality to assure that specifications have been met.

The receiving report. The receiving clerk customarily fills out a separate receiving report (see Figure 2–4) for each shipment. In it, he describes the material received, the number of the purchase order that authorized the shipment, and the name of the supplier. If there is a discrepancy between the quantity on the purchase order or supplier's packing slip and the quantity actually received, it is noted on the receiving report. Copies of the report accompany the material and also are sent separately to the purchasing department, the user of the material, and the accounting department.

Inspecting the material. The next step in the receiving process is inspection. In many companies, the quality control inspector works in the same area as the receiving clerk. He compares the characteristics of incoming material with specifications and blueprints, using gauges, laboratory tests, visual inspection, and other techniques. He reports his findings on an inspection report, which may be a separate form (see Figure 2–5) or part of the receiving report.

Copies of the inspection report usually go to both the buyer and the supplier (although sometimes the supplier does not get a copy if all material meets specifications), as well as to other departments in the buyer's company. If the material is rejected, the buyer will ask

---

[4] Probably 10 to 15 percent of the cost of the average product is transportation and packaging. In some cases, of course, transportation or packaging is the major cost. Sand and gravel cost more to ship than they do to quarry, and a toothpaste tube is worth more than the toothpaste it holds.

FIGURE 2–4
Receiving report

CESSNA AIRCRAFT COMPANY						
RECEIVING REPORT						
RECEIVED FROM					DATE	$
ADDRESS					P. O. NUMBER	
ORDERED FROM						
WEIGHT	TRANS. EXP.	NO. OF PACKAGES	VIA		P. S. NUMBER	
QUAN. RECD.	UNIT	PART NUMBER	DESCRIPTION			CODE
UNPACKED AND COUNTED BY	WRITTEN BY	DELIVERED TO	REQ.	CONTRACT NUMBER		
NO. F 50080				ACCOUNTING DEPT.		

Courtesy Cessna Corp.

The receiving report is used by the receiving department to notify interested departments of delivery of purchased material.

the supplier how it should be disposed of. The supplier may wish to have the material returned to him for either reworking or scrapping. If shipping costs are high, he will probably prefer to have the buyer either scrap the material or rework it himself at the supplier's expense. Buyer and supplier often have standing agreements on how material with certain types of defects should be handled, in order to reduce the volume of letters and phone calls.

If purchased material is returned to a supplier, the buyer must prepare a shipping notice that is, in effect, a purchase order in reverse, since it calls for the supplier to buy back the material he has sold. If the buyer reworks or scraps the material, he must negotiate an agreement with the supplier on the charges or credit for scrap.

Quality problems. If an item fails to meet the buyer's specifications, the major problem usually is not administrative. Rather, the materials manager may, as a result of the rejection, have a shortage that can disrupt production. Suppose, for example, that a supplier of vacuum cleaner motors needs five weeks' lead time to complete each order he gets

FIGURE 2–5
Inspection report form

FORM F-1003–REV.		DATE INSPECTED	INSPECTED BY	FOR REWORK, USE THIS NO. ON TIME CARDS
INSPECTION REPORT	CAN REWORK ☐ CAN SALVAGE ☐ MUST SCRAP ☐			**IR 14750**

PART OR MATERIAL DESCRIPTION		PART NO.	MATERIAL
REASON FOR REJECTION: SPECIFICATIONS SHOULD BE–	SPECIFICATIONS ARE–	JOB NO.	P.O. NO.
		LAST OPERATION NO.	RECEIVING REPORT NO.
		VENDOR	

WHO IS RESPONSIBLE?			CLOCK NO.	MACHINE NO.	QUANTITY INSPECTED		
					TOTAL	GOOD	REJECTED

REVIEW						NATURE OF REJECTS		
DATE	INSPECTION	ENGINEERING	PRODUCTION	SHOP	VENDOR	REWORK	OUR SCRAP	VENDOR SCRAP

OPER NO.	MACH NO.	REWORK INSTRUCTIONS	TOOLING	EST. TIME	DISPOSITION
					1–RETURN TO VENDOR: ☐ FOR CREDIT ONLY ☐ FOR CREDIT AND REPLACEMENT ☐ FREIGHT COLL. ☐ FREIGHT PPD.
					2–REWORK IN OUR PLANT: ☐ VENDOR'S EXP. ☐ OUR EXPENSE
					3–SCRAP ☐ CHARGE TO VENDOR ☐ OUR EXPENSE

INSPECTED DATE			1–DISPATCH	PURCHASING O. K.

The inspection report indicates whether or not purchased materials conform to specifications.

for motors. A shipment of motors arrives for the current month's production and is found defective. How does the materials manager prevent a shutdown of the cleaner assembly line, because of lack of motors? Sometimes he cannot prevent such a shutdown, of course, but he can usually get good motors from an alternate supply source, from inventory, by reworking the defective motors, by having suppliers work overtime at their plants (which raises the question of who pays for the premium paid to workers for overtime—the buyer or the supplier), and other measures.

Needless to say, vendors aren't happy when their shipments are rejected. If the defects are their rseponsibility, the loss to them can be substantial, particularly if the parts cannot be reworked and are a total loss. Occasionally, vendors will challenge the buyer's quality control procedures and maintain that specifications actually were met on the shipment. Or they will maintain that the defects were not their responsibility—either that they were not told certain specifications had to be met or that the parts were damaged after they left the supplier's plant.

The buyer must investigate all such complaints to make certain that the supplier has been treated fairly. He should always try to preserve amicable relations with suppliers, even if this sometimes means going more than halfway in reaching a compromise. He should also make certain that the supplier is familiar with his company's specifications and quality control procedures and will make an honest effort to correct quality discrepancies on future shipments.

INVENTORY CONTROL

If a shipment passes inspection, the receiving clerk usually prepares a "move" ticket that indicates to what area of the plant the material should go next. This ticket is physically attached to the shipment, along with the receiving report and the inspection report. The material is then transported either directly to the user or to a storage area. If the material goes into stores, which is true of almost all routine purchases, it becomes part of the company's inventory. It is carried on the company's balance sheet as an asset until it is incorporated into an end product that is sold to a customer.

Safety margin. Without inventories, the typical materials manager's job would be hopeless. Every minor delay in every minor component would cause a serious shortage. Production rates of components and subassemblies would have to be perfectly synchronized.

Inventories provide a safety margin for defects in scheduling and errors in forecasting the demand for and supply of materials. If its stocks are big enough, a company can operate for months without buying any raw materials at all.

For example, midwestern steel companies normally have at least six months' stock of iron ore each fall in order to avoid costly rail shipments during the winter months, when the Great Lakes freeze over and water shipments from Lake Superior ports and the St. Lawrence Seaway are cut off. Similarly, steel users always stock millions of tons of steel shortly before the contract between the steel industry and its union expires. Thus they usually are prepared to operate on inventories for two to three months if there is a strike.

In-process inventories provide a cushion between manufacturing operations. Without them, the entire plant might be shut down if a single machine tool failed to operate. In-process stocks also facilitate synchronization of production. If one machine produces 200 units per hour while another produces 400 units, production can be balanced only by building up stock from the faster machine and then shutting it down to permit the slower operation to catch up.

Cost of inventories. Although inventories solve many materials management problems, there are strong incentives for maintaining minimum stocks. Companies have a limited amount of cash to invest in inventories. Also, it costs as much as 20 to 30 percent per year to store materials.

The materials manager must have material available when needed, but he cannot afford to carry extra-large stocks just to make his job easier. He must balance the cost of carrying stock against the cost of possible shortages. His objective is the lowest overall average production cost. To achieve this, materials must flow smoothly through the plant. The proper quantities—no more, no less—of each of thousands of different items must be available at all times. Raw-material stocks should be larger than the minimum only if there is some special advantage to be gained. In-process stocks should be the minimum necessary to prevent serious production problems; the tighter the scheduling and material, the smaller the protective stocks needed.

Companies with poor materials management have both big inventories and frequent shortages. Their inventories do not prevent shortages because they are not balanced. There may be enough stock of some items to last for months or even years, and no stock of one or two critical items.

THE FINAL STAGES

When material is delivered on schedule to the manufacturing organization, the materials manager has done his most important job. When manufacturing completes processing and assembles the final product, the materials cycle is almost complete. All that remain are the packaging, storage, and shipment of the end product. These final stages rarely create as many problems for the materials manager as the earlier stages.

Packaging must usually be synchronized with the production process. In such cases, the workers who do the actual packaging may be under the supervision of a foreman or superintendent reporting to the manufacturing manager. The materials manager, however, retains responsibility for package procurement and may also be responsible for package design. The major effort on the part of the materials manager is directed toward improving packaging materials and equipment.

The storage of finished products is similar administratively to storage of raw materials. The materials manager, or his physical distribution manager, normally supervises the finished-goods warehouse. As the company's experts on inventory management and warehousing, the materials manager and the physical distribution manager also regulate inventory fluctuations. They try to minimize warehouse operating costs and inventory investment levels consistent with broad company goals. The materials manager is not the company's ultimate authority on finished goods inventories, however. Both the company's marketing success and its manufacturing efficiency are directly related to finished-goods inventory investment. Such stocks exist to protect customers and give them better service, and to permit more efficient operation of manufacturing plants. They also result when demand for end products is lower than anticipated

---

[5] Sometimes, for example, demand for finished products is seasonal, so the only way to operate the plant economically on a year-round basis is to build up stocks of finished goods during the slack season.

when schedules were made up. Decisions concerning finished-goods inventories are normally made by a top-management committee, of which the materials manager is a member.

The materials cycle for direct material ends with shipment of finished products to a customer. The materials department is always responsible for loading the finished goods into the carrier and preparing necessary shipping documents. If the customer does not have a traffic department, it may also be responsible for routing the goods to their destination.

MANAGING INDIRECT MATERIAL

The problems of managing indirect materials are similar to, but rarely as complicated as, the problems of managing direct material. The cycle for indirect material starts with the initiation of the need for the material in any department of the company—manufacturing, personnel, marketing, engineering, finance, or the materials department itself.

Nonrepetitive items. Each department needs certain materials and supplies in order to operate. It gets them by filling out a purchase requisition form if the item is not carried in stock. A buyer reviews this requisition against his purchase records, gets quotations, and issues an order to a supplier.

To this point, the materials cycle is quite similar to that for direct materials. There is one basic difference, however. Direct materials are almost always purchased in accordance with definite engineering specifications. This is not always the case with indirect materials; many are bought the way the housewife buys—by brand name. For example, if a buyer gets a requisition for a desk calculator, he does not send a set of blueprints to each calculator manufacturer. Instead, he and the user of the material evaluate various brands of calculators and compare their performance, features, and prices.

The purchase order will be for a specific brand of calculator. The materials cycle ends when the machine is delivered to the requisitioner who ordered it, and it operates satisfactorily.

Repetitive items. The conventional procedure for buying nonrepetitive items like desk calculators is wasteful if there is a continuing demand for the item. For example, it would be ridiculous to issue a separate purchase requisition and purchase order each time a light bulb burns out. Commonly used nonproduction items are bought in fairly large quantities and stocked in a storeroom. Users withdraw them from stores by presenting a stores requisition (see Figure 2–6) to the stores clerk.

The clerk posts withdrawals from stock to his stores record (see Figure 2–7). When his stock drops to a certain reorder point, he issues a purchase requisition to authorize another buy. The purchasing procedure is similar to that for other items.

FIGURE 2–6
Stores requisition form

	STORES REQUISITION				
NO. **89994**					DATE_____
SHIP TO—		ACCOUNT NO.			EQUIP. NO.
INTERNATIONAL MINERALS AND CHEMICALS CORP.	STOCK NO.	QUAN.	UNIT	DESCRIPTION	
	ORIGINATOR		AUTHORIZATION		

Courtesy International Minerals & Chemicals Corp.

This form authorizes material to be drawn from stores and is later posted to the stores record.

FIGURE 2–7
Inventory record card

INVENTORY RECORD									
Min. Point	Min. Quantity		Order Point	Order Quantity					
DATE	RECEIVED	DISBURSED	DISBURSED TO DATE	INVENTORY BALANCE	DATE	RECEIVED	DISBURSED	DISBURSED TO DATE	BALANCE INVENTORY
CODE NUMBER		ITEM							

Receipts and withdrawals from stores for each item are posted to perpetual inventory record cards.

Some nonproduction items are used in sufficiently high volume to justify a lot of time and effort in their buying. Some companies even go to the trouble of making elaborate specifications for key nonproduction items. Rather than buying by brand name, they invite a number of qualified suppliers to quote in accordance with their own specifications. This usually cuts costs, as well as eliminating the problem of brand preference by users. If the materials department is forced to buy a specific brand, its efforts to get competitive bids are inhibited. In addition, inventories may be higher. If supervisor X insists on brand A, and supervisor Y insists on brand B of the same item, then the item is duplicated in inventory.

Duplication is always a problem in nonproduction stores. It is almost impossible to draw up exact specifications for every item, and suppliers' descriptions and code numbers can be misleading. Stores personnel try to cope with these problems by using classification systems, periodic reviews of stock, standardization programs, and so on. But no system or program is foolproof. The only solution is constant vigilance by alert and intelligent materials personnel.

Cases

CASE 2–1. ZERO CORPORATION (A)

Establishing an independent materials department

Zero Corporation was founded in 1951 by George Frost, a former superintendent of a company that manufactured auto parts. The company commenced operations in a rented garage with a total of five employees. Because of its low overhead and Frost's manufacturing know-how, it was able to underbid larger competitors for contracts let by the Big Three auto manufacturers for small components used in their lower volume truck lines.

Zero grew steadily. By 1964 its annual sales were $600,000, and there were about 60 persons on the payroll. Because the company got its business by being low bidder in a very price-conscious industry with excess capacity, profits did not increase nearly so fast as sales. They were only $32,000 in 1963, the company's best year.

For all his work during this period, Frost had succeeded in paying himself only a moderate salary ($15,000 per year) and meeting obligations to his creditors. By 1964, he concluded that he was in the wrong business and began to look for a product where there was less price competition. He became acquainted with Robert Blank, a salesman for a firm making household refrigerators. Blank proposed to Frost that he manufacture refrigerated frozen-food display cabinets for grocery supermarkets. Although several other companies were already in the field, Blank was convinced that it was growing fast enough to support a newcomer.

Blank proposed that Frost hire him as sales manager, with a special salary and bonus arrangement. He also suggested that Frost hire Harold Brown, a young engineer who worked for the same large company as Blank, to head the design department. Frost talked to Brown, liked him, and suggested that he prepare a preliminary design proposal on a consulting basis in his spare time.

Frost then studied Brown's preliminary designs. He decided that he was equipped to produce some of the sheet-metal components of the cabinets and that he could assemble them with a minimum of additional investment—no more than $600,000 for plant, equipment, and inventory.

Meanwhile, Blank had not been idle. He discovered that a major grocery chain was contemplating a complete renovation of a number of its stores and would be in the market for as many as 10,000 cabinets. The chain planned to buy them piecemeal from a number of manufacturers. Frost suggested that Blank approach the chain's fixtures buyer and propose a contract arrangement for the entire 10,000 cabinets. The stores would not only get a lower price but would also get a design that was uniquely tailored to their needs.

The buyer was impressed with Blank's presentation and suggested that Zero Corporation present a formal proposal. Frost, Blank, and Brown went to work immediately. Working from Brown's preliminary specifications, Frost got quotations from major suppliers for such key components as compressors, electrical accessories, and steel. He then estimated his fabrication and assembly costs and added a moderate profit.

The store's buyer and director of purchases reviewed Frost's proposal and asked for additional price concessions. Frost complained that his estimated profit was already very modest and showed the buyers his unit cost estimate. A summary of the cost estimate indicated the following:

Purchased parts and materials	$405.30
Direct labor	72.60
Manufacturing overhead	90.75
Manufacturing cost	$568.65
Sales, engineering, and administrative expense	33.45
Profit	66.90
Unit selling price	$669.00

Frost pointed out that practically all of the $66.90 profit would be needed to amortize the special tooling that Zero would have to invest in for the new contract. He observed that the company would have to make an investment of $600,000 in facilities, tools, and equipment, so it would do little more than pay off this investment on the first order for 10,000 cabinets.

The prospective buyers considered this to be Frost's risk in doing business. They pointed out that about two thirds of Zero's sales dollar would go to outside suppliers. They felt that it was not enough just to solicit bids from a few leading companies when making a cost estimate. In their opinion, Zero should be able to get its material at least 10 percent cheaper by shopping around, and unit material cost should actually be no more than $360. They also suggested that since Zero had no previous experience in the field, the chain store was entitled to an extra-close price for risking its business with a new supplier. The buyers finally succeeded in persuading Frost to accept the contract at a unit price of $600, which would provide Zero with no profit at all unless actual costs were less than the estimate.

Frost accepted the order because without it he would find it almost impossible to raise the money to go into the refrigeration business. With the chain-store order in hand, Frost went to an investment banker and asked for help in raising the $600,000 he needed. The banker arranged a $300,000 loan and, late in 1964, another $300,000 was raised with a stock issue. Zero was in the refrigeration business.

Blank and Brown immediately became full-time employees of the company; the sales and engineering functions were well taken care of. Frost himself intended to devote his time to general management, with special interest in the finance and manufacturing areas. He already had a capable accountant and shop superintendent to assist him.

While the company was in the auto parts business, the job of materials management had been pretty much divided between Frost and the shop superintendent, Richard Howard. The job was not too complex, since the company's only product was steel stampings made to auto company specifications.

When the company quoted on a job, Frost studied the blueprint. From experience, he could readily estimate the blank size and cost of the steel sheets that were the company's major purchased material. He then determined the manufacturing operations that would be required and noted the equipment he would use if he got the order. He sent his estimated operation sheet and the blueprint to a friend of his who ran a tool shop for an estimate of the cost of the special dies that would be needed.

If he got the order, Frost ordered sufficient steel to handle the contract from a nearby mill. The superintendent scheduled production in accordance with requirements on customer orders. His system was simple. He kept a separate record for each piece of equipment and then "reserved" time on it for each job. For example, if a customer wanted 2,000 parts delivered during the month of August, the superintendent might schedule a press for the first operation on the fourth and fifth of the month, the second operation on the sixth, the third on the seventh, and so on.

Both the superintendent and the accountant purchased materials and supplies that they needed to do their work. They got Frost's approval for any unusual purchases but bought everyday items as the need arose. The accountant had a cabinet in which he stored office supplies; employees got supplies by coming to him. The superintendent had a storeskeeper who doled out material to the workers and the two job foremen as required. Materials that were bulky and not subject to pilferage were stored in open plant areas.

Frost now realizes that materials management will become more important because the company is entering the refrigeration business. It will be necessary to buy equipment and tooling to fabricate the stampings and assemble the completed units. The volume of purchases will increase and will also become more diverse. For the first time, the company will be buying components ranging from compressor assemblies consisting of several hundred components and costing about $60 to fasteners with a unit cost of a few mils.

The company will have to deal with at least 100 suppliers for production parts and materials, with plants located in many different areas. Formerly, it purchased its basic production material—steel—from two mills. Because of the wider diversity of operations, Frost believes that a greater variety of nonproduction materials will have to be purchased. Inventories of both production and nonproduction materials will increase, both because of the expected increase in volume of business and because of the greater complexity of the product.

Frost wonders if the materials management system that has worked quite well in the past will continue to work under these new conditions. He explains his doubts to his informal operating committee, consisting of the sales manager, the chief engineer, and the shop superintendent.

Both the superintendent and the chief engineer believe that the old system will continue to work best because, under it, administrative overhead will be minimized. The superintendent believes that he can schedule production and buy necessary tools and supplies just as he has done in the past. He thinks he may need a clerk to help him. The chief engineer points out that he will have to work with suppliers in developing final engineering details of the refrigeration equipment and that it will take but little effort on his part to follow through and actually place the orders for components. The sales manager disagrees with this view. He believes that materials management is a separate function of the business and should be handled by a materials manager.

Questions

1. Bearing in mind that the company wishes to keep administrative overhead at a minimum, what are some of the arguments that Blank, the sales

manager, should advance for the establishment of a separate materials organization at Zero?

2. What functions should the materials department at Zero embrace? What should be the materials department's relationship with the production and engineering departments?

CASE 2–2. NORGE DIVISION, BORG-WARNER CORPORATION*

Physical distribution and materials management

Though in the domain of physical distribution every company must wrestle with its own special problems and no two solutions can be identical, the experience of a representative company can offer some pointers to others. Norge Division of Borg-Warner Corp., for example, found that the revamping of its distribution system enabled it to increase profitability while reducing inventories.

Until 1964, the price of Norge's home appliances virtually doubled in moving from the end of the production line to the consumer. At least six departments at Norge, besides others at distributor and retailer levels, contributed to this rise in cost, but had no common direction or common policy.

"Each one, of course, was concerned with the costs it incurred," says A. B. Kight, president of Norge; but none cared whether incurring a higher cost in one department might lower total costs. Forecasts of overall sales levels made by the business forecasting department were revised by the sales department, then further revised by the plant scheduling department to suit plant convenience.

"Plant convenience, you know," says Kight, "means running a fixed model at a fixed rate forever."

The traffic department shipped "the best available way," which according to Kight means "shipping was purely a matter of expedience of the moment." Sometimes warehouses were underutilized, sometimes temporary outside space was needed. An excess of one product sometimes forced Norge into what the industry calls "a loading program"— pushing surplus product off on a dealer, with special concessions that boost accounts receivable, cut profits.

Complaints from Norge's parent company and from customers came with monotonous regularity.

At length, Norge called in a management consultant firm. The firm interviewed customers, distributors, field and plant people, sales people. It looked at what other consumer goods industries were doing, talked to transportation companies.

When its recommendations were in and management had fixed on a course of action, the real problems began. "Tradition and so-called standard operating procedures," says Kight, "can be very deep-rooted and, as you know, resistance to change increases in direct proportion to mental aging. So, there had to be a period of pain, early retirements, resignations, reorganizations."

Norge does not feel it has finished its program by any means, but it has made a beginning. Now, all functions starting with forecasting and production scheduling and going on to warehousing, order processing, and shipping have been consolidated under one department headed by a director of physical distribution. Much duplication has been eliminated, and the total process speeded.

"We have ceased loading distributors," Kight sums up. "We have substantially reduced our plant inventories, our distributors' inventories, and our accounts receivable. As a result, we have reduced our overall investment and at the same time have increased our profitability."

One specific step was to establish a regional warehouse in Utah for Norge's West Coast distributors. Norge plants around the U.S. ship to it the complete line of appliances—mostly in carload lots, at a freight saving. Norge can now make deliveries to Coast dealers in 4 or 5 days instead of 20, and has achieved a 50 percent reduction in dealer inventories and accounts receivable. The experiment will probably be duplicated elsewhere.

Norge, like other companies embarking on the physical distribution experiment, does not confine its thinking to finished products, but looks at the total flow. It worries about refrigerator motors coming from another manufacturer, even about where the copper that goes in these motors will come from. With a production lead time of 90 days or better, Norge cannot stop the line abruptly without having material keep on arriving for weeks afterward, or else incurring huge cancellation charges.

"An effective system of physical distribution," says Kight, "cannot begin at the end of the production line. It must also apply at the very beginning of the production process—at the planning, scheduling, and forecasting stages. It follows from this that the man who heads this activity must be a member of the top management team.

"He must not merely be aware," Kight adds, "of every plan and strategy, but must actively participate in the development of these plans and strategies, for physical distribution in a consumer products manufacturing company goes to the very structure of the enterprise."

Questions

1. Is Norge's director of physical distribution really a materials manager?

2. What is the essential difference between the physical distribution concept of organization, as practiced by Norge, and the materials management type propounded in this text? List advantages and disadvantages of each.

3

The objectives of materials management

THE MANAGER'S most basic job is to focus the efforts of his subordinates on the objectives of the enterprise. In materials management, this boils down to supplying material at lowest possible total cost. To achieve this fundamental objective, the materials manager must take into account both the long- and the short-term effects of his actions. He must also consider the impact of his operation on the costs of other activities within the organization.

The function of the materials manager is basically economic, even in nonprofit organizations. The most fundamental objective is survival. Managers come and go, but institutions live forever. If the materials manager is successful in his economic role, he will contribute to the survival of the organization. Among private companies, at least, profits are essential to survival; in the nonprofit sector, costs cannot exceed income for any prolonged period. Every enterprise also has objectives that are seemingly noneconomic. In the long run, they are ultimately economic, however, since if they are not achieved the enterprise will fail to prosper—and may not even survive. Among these noneconomic objectives are favorable community relations, maximum service to customers, pleasant working conditions and opportunities for advancement for employees, technological leadership, and others.

Each function of the business should work to achieve those objectives. The materials function is no exception. It contributes to survival and profits by providing materials at the lowest total cost. There are many ways it can achieve this overall objective; the most obvious is to pay minimum prices for materials. But the materials function also helps achieve this objective when it boosts inventory turnover or gets material of superior quality. In both cases, the true cost of material is reduced, in one because of less investment and in the other because of fewer rejections due to failure to meet specifications.

GOALS OF MATERIALS MANAGEMENT

We will next examine in detail some typical objectives of materials management. Each, in some way, contributes to the achievement of some overall company objective. If the contribution is made directly by the materials function, we call it a "primary" objective. If it is indirect, and results from the materials department's assistance to another department in achieving its objectives, we call it a "secondary" objective.

Primary materials objectives

Almost every materials department has at least nine primary objectives. These are low prices, high inventory turnover, low cost of acquisition and possession, continuity of supply, consistency of quality, low payroll costs, favorable relations with suppliers, development of personnel, and good records.

Low prices. Obtaining the lowest possible price for purchased materials is the most obvious materials objective and certainly one of the most important. If the materials department reduces the prices of the items it buys, operating costs are reduced and profits are enhanced. This objective is important for all purchases of materials and services, including transportation.

High inventory turnover. When inventories are low in relation to sales (inventory turnover = sales ÷ average inventories), less capital is tied up in inventories. This in turn increases the efficiency with which the company's capital is utilized, so that return on investment is higher. Also, storage and carrying costs of inventories are lower when turnover is high.

Low-cost acquisition and possession. If materials are handled and stored efficiently, their real cost is lower. Acquisition and possession costs are low when the receiving and stores departments operate efficiently. They also are reduced when shipments are received in relatively large quantities (thereby reducing the unit cost of handling), but they are increased if average inventories are boosted with the large shipments.

Continuity of supply. When there are disruptions in the continuity of supply, excess costs are inevitable. Production costs go up, excess expediting and transportation costs are likely, and so on. Continuity of supply is particularly important for highly automated processes, where costs are rigid and must be incurred even when production stops because of lack of material.

Consistency of quality. The materials department is responsible for the quality only of the materials and services furnished by outside suppliers. The manufacturing department is responsible for quality control of manufacturing processes. When materials purchased are homogeneous and in a primitive state (e.g., sand and gravel), quality is rarely a big problem for materials personnel. But when the product is in a highly advanced stage of manufacture and specifications are a tremendous challenge for suppliers to meet consistently (e.g., components of interplanetary rockets), quality may become the single most important objective of materials management.

Low payroll costs. The objective of low payroll costs is common to every department in the company. The lower the payroll, the higher the profits—all other factors being equal. But because no department can do its job without a payroll, the objective of low payroll must be viewed in proper perspective. It pays to spend $1.00 on additional payroll if earnings can thereby be boosted $1.01 through achieving other objectives.

Favorable supplier relations. As was pointed out in Chapter 1, manufacturing companies rely on outside suppliers to a far greater degree than is generally recognized. This makes favorable relations with suppliers extremely important. A company's standing in the business community is to a considerable degree determined by the manner in which it deals with its suppliers. A company with a good reputation in supplier relations is more likely to attract customers than one with a bad name.

Suppliers also can make a direct contribution to a company's success. Their product development and research efforts can be of tremendous assistance to their customers. Although such efforts naturally help the supplier too, it is important to remember that suppliers are human beings who respond to fair treatment. If a company has good relations with its suppliers, it will be far more successful in its efforts to stimulate superior performance from supplier personnel—extra service, cooperation on cost-reduction projects, a willingness to share new processes and ideas, and so on.

One of the major problems of materials management is sudden shifts in the demand for materials, requiring either rapid cancellation of existing commitments or extra output to prevent shortages. Cooperative suppliers can do much to help the materials manager with such problems.

Development of personnel. Every department in the company should be interested in developing the skills of its personnel. And each department head should devote special effort to locating in junior posts men and women who have the leadership potential the company needs for continued success and growth. They should try to develop these high-potential men and women as the company's future executives; the company's future profits will depend on the talents of its managers.

Good records. Good records are considered a primary objective of materials management, although paper work is a means to an end, not an end in itself. They contribute to the role of the materials department in the company's survival and profits only indirectly. They are necessary and useful; they help materials personnel do a better job. While this can also be said of office equipment, the maintenance of the materials department's stock of typewriters, adding machines, and the like would hardly be considered a primary objective. Good records, however, are considered a primary objective in the purchasing and traffic phases of materials management for the same reason that they are a primary objective in the accounting department.

Buyers spend company money and can be subject to tremendous temptation. Suppliers may wine and dine them and give them gifts for Christmas and other holidays. Although perhaps 99 percent of all buyers are above corruption, the opportunity does exist. Good records, along with well-planned administrative controls and periodic audits, can discourage corruption. They also partly remove the onus of suspicion from a completely honest individual working at a job that is popularly associated with graft and corruption.[1]

Secondary objectives

The secondary objectives of materials management are not nearly so limited in scope and variety as the primary objectives. Since they represent the materials department's contribution to the achievement of the primary objective of some other department, they can vary widely from industry to industry.

There are literally hundreds of possible secondary objectives in materials management. Among the more common ones are reciprocity, new materials and products, economic make-or-buy decisions, promotion of standardization, product improvement, good interdepartmental relations, accurate economic forecasts, and alertness to possible acquisitions.

Favorable reciprocal relations. When a company deliberately buys from its own customers as much as possible, it is practicing reciprocity. Sound reciprocity involves a balancing of the advantages and disadvantages of using one's buying power as an instrument for getting sales. Similarly, suppliers will use their own buying power as a sales tool.

In the consumer-goods industries, reciprocity is rarely a problem; sales are spread among many users. In producer-goods industries, however, reciprocity is a way of business life, particularly among industries where there is little product differentiation and prices are uniform. The

---

[1] This is particularly true in government procurement, but all buyers probably suffer some loss of social prestige because their jobs are unjustly associated with graft in the public mind. Groups like the National Association of Purchasing Management and the National Institute of Governmental Purchasing have done much to boost the prestige of the buyer by establishing ethical standards and promoting a high level of performance.

materials department in such industries often coordinates its purchases with the sales department to make certain that company customers get favored treatment.

New materials and products. Engineering and manufacturing managers are always interested in new products and materials that will help them operate more efficiently and thereby achieve one of their primary objectives. The materials department can help, because its personnel deal regularly with the suppliers responsible for the new developments. When they learn of anything of interest, they can call it to the attention of the interested parties in manufacturing, engineering, or other departments.

Economic make or buy. Make-or-buy decisions are often sparked by materials personnel since they are the group most intimately concerned with the selection of supply sources. By no means are they solely responsible for these decisions, however. As pointed out in the previous chapter, make-or-buy decisions should be a committee effort, representing the points of view of all departments in the company. The materials department, in its regular reviews of cost and availability of materials, often will spot the need for new make-or-buy decisions and should refer them to the committee for action.

Standardization. The fewer the items that need be controlled, the simpler and more efficient the materials management process. Thus it is to the interest of materials personnel to promote standardization and simplification of specifications. The engineering groups are primarily responsible for standards and specifications, but materials personnel can make a substantial contribution. They can periodically review stock to weed out nonstandard items; they can promote the incorporation of standard components into product designs to reduce cost; and they can promote standardization with suppliers.

Product improvement. This is perhaps the single most important objective of the engineering department. Materials personnel can assist, however. Their economic knowledge can supplement the technical skills of the engineers on programs to boost profits through product change. The engineering of practically any product is basically a compromise between design and economic objectives. Materials personnel can help engineers achieve their design objectives more economically by suggesting materials or components that will do a better or equivalent job at lower cost.

Interdepartmental harmony. The materials department deals daily with every other activity in the business. It not only can contribute to the success of every other department, but its own success depends on how successful it is in gaining the cooperation of personnel in other departments. In practice, most materials managers are fully aware of the importance of good interdepartmental relations. To prevent disputes, they are careful to define departmental responsibilities clearly (this will be discussed later in this chapter) and also try to familiarize others with materials objectives, policies, and organization.

Forecasts. To manage materials well, some conception of the future outlook for prices, costs, and general business activity is necessary. In large companies, professional economists make forecasts that are used for both sales and purchase planning. Materials personnel translate these general forecasts into specific forecasts for purchased materials. They may also provide the economists with data for forecasts because, more than any other group in the company, they are intimately familiar with the market and general business conditions through their daily contacts with suppliers.

In the smaller company that cannot afford a staff of professionals, the materials manager may double as company economist. In such a case, good forecasts become a primary, not a secondary, objective of materials management.

Acquisitions. Most company managements are interested in growing, not only by internal expansion but also by acquiring other businesses. It is no easy job to identify a possible candidate for acquisition and then to make the necessary overtures for eventual merger. The materials manager can often play an important role in acquisitions, since he normally has, through dealing with his many suppliers, more contacts with the outside business world than other executives in the company.

ACHIEVING OBJECTIVES

The primary and secondary objectives of materials management discussed above would be applicable to most manufacturing companies. However, these objectives vary in relative importance from industry to industry and even among companies within an industry. One company may devote considerable effort to one objective while another may concentrate most of its efforts on a different one. Four examples which can illustrate this point are given below.

Holding down prices. In the tanning and woolen textile industries, the raw material is always available—at a price. But price fluctuations can be violent. Wool and hides (and other commodities, like crude rubber, zinc, and copper) have been known to double or triple in price within six months or decline by a proportionate amount.

For users of the materials, the key objective is to pay minimum prices for them. It overshadows all others in importance. A shrewd materials manager can save 10—or even 100—times as much by intelligent timing of purchases as he can hope to save through achievement of other materials objectives.

Assuring reliability. In the aerospace industry, consistency of quality (i.e., reliability) is all-important. Almost any minor component can cause a $1,000,000 missile to malfunction. The odds favor failure. Because of the very complexity of the product, even a 99.9 percent quality standard may be inadequate. With this standard one part in 1,000 will be unsatisfactory. Since each missile contains more than 1,000 parts, it is then likely that each would contain a component that will fail.

Regulating inventory. In companies making a wide range of complicated products (instruments, machine tools, and similar items), the key problem usually is inventory turnover. Not only must the company have thousands of items available for product, but often it stocks tens of thousands of repair parts for customer service. If demand is erratic, there is always the danger that inventories will become unbalanced. The materials manager strives to prevent stockouts without tying up too much of the company's capital in inventory.

Cutting operating costs. If purchase prices are stable and inventory fluctuations are minimal, then the most important contribution the materials manager can make is to do his job at minimum cost. His focus will be almost entirely on how to maintain the same level of basic performance at lower operating cost. In hospital materials management, for example, this may be the single most important economic objective.

Effects of business changes

Objectives also can vary within the same company. When sales are expanding, the materials manager may concentrate on continuity of supply and consistency of quality. He is less interested in inventory turnover or low prices, since the economic expansion should bring both higher sales and high prices and these objectives may be achieved automatically.

But when business slumps, the story is different. Sales drop faster than output, so the materials manager is hard pressed just to keep turnover from dropping, and he must be nimble to avoid being greatly overstocked when the business cycle nears the bottom. During this period, he is also under considerable pressure to reduce purchase prices because his company may be forced to cut the prices of its end products despite slipping profit margins and lower sales volume.

During a war or some other period of extreme scarcity, the simple act of locating sources of supply may become the single most important materials objective. This is also true when a key supplier is shut down because of labor trouble. Even under reasonably normal conditions, there can be an unpredicted upsurge in the demand for a finished product that can put considerable pressure on the materials manager to locate additional sources of supply fast enough to satisfy the demand.

In a young company that is growing rapidly, cash is perpetually short. All earnings and all borrowings are plowed back into plant and equipment. Some must be invested in inventory, of course. But the materials manager is under considerable pressure to get along with as little stock as possible in order to make cash available for other purposes. To boost inventory turnover, he may buy in small quantities, even if this means he must forego quantity discounts and raise his cost of acquisition because of the greater number of receivals necessary to operate on a hand-to-mouth basis. He also may buy from suppliers with slightly higher prices, provided they will deliver with little advance notice.

Balancing of objectives

The examples above provide clues to one of the most basic parts of the materials manager's job: balancing of objectives. Objectives vary in importance. During certain periods, the materials manager may concentrate on one objective, and at other times he may concentrate on another.

Achievements bring sacrifices. Efforts to achieve one primary objective almost necessarily involve relaxation of efforts to achieve some other objective. The materials manager who concentrates on inventory turnover pays higher prices and has higher costs of acquisition because he must buy more frequently in smaller quantities. On the other hand, if he goes all out to get lower prices, he will buy in larger quantities to get quantity discounts. This will reduce inventory turnover. The higher average inventories will inevitably raise costs of possession, although unit costs of acquisition will probably decline because of the greater average size of each shipment. Continuity of supply and consistency of quality also may be affected. The materials manager will be tempted to go to "cheap" suppliers who cut prices and also cut corners on quality and fail to live up to their delivery promises. The objective of favorable supplier relations will suffer because of the shifting of business to the "cheap" suppliers and because of the steady pressure for price reductions.

Basic principle. All materials objectives are interrelated. As illustrated in Table 3–1, a gain in one objective means sacrifice on other objectives. In materials management you never "get something for nothing." You may, however, be getting something you do not really want or need. If an organization does not identify its material management objectives and develop a program to achieve them, it may be giving undue attention to some objectives and neglecting others.

In the organization where materials management objectives are not consciously identified, one objective—low operating cost—tends to be concentrated on to the exclusion of all others. In fact, top management often is not really aware that any other objectives exist (although it may be conscious also of the continuity-of-supply objective). In such organizations, $1 may be saved in operating cost at the cost of a $5 saving in purchase prices or inventory carrying cost. The objective in all too many organizations is to manage materials as *cheaply* as possible instead of as *profitably* as possible.

TABLE 3–1
Interdependence and potential areas of conflict in primary objectives of materials management

Primary objective	Other objectives adversely affected
Low prices for purchased items	High inventory turnover, low cost of acquisition and possession, continuity of supply, consistency of quality, favorable relations with suppliers.
High inventory turnover	Low cost of acquisition and possession, low prices for materials purchased, low payroll costs, continuity of supply.
Low cost of acquisition and possession	Low prices for purchased materials, high inventory turnover, good records.
Continuity of supply	Low prices for purchased materials, consistency of quality, favorable relations with suppliers, high inventory turnover.
Consistency of quality	Low prices for purchased materials, continuity of supply, favorable relations with suppliers, low cost of acquisition and possession, high inventory turnover.
Low payroll costs	Concentration on this objective can readily restrict achievement of all other objectives.
Favorable relations with suppliers	Low prices for purchased materials, high inventory turnover, continuity of supply, consistency of quality.
Development of personnel	Low payroll costs.
Good records	Low cost of acquisition and possession, low payroll costs.

Organization limits. In many cases, organization structure inhibits achievement of a proper balance of objectives. When materials management functions are scattered throughout the organization, each materials subfunction tends to develop objectives of its own which may not be consistent with company objectives. For example, if a purchasing manager is made subordinate to a marketing manager, he begins to take on marketing objectives rather than those of materials management. Every subordinate tries to please his boss. And, in this case, the boss-pleasing effort might cause him to pay undue attention to secondary objectives like reciprocity and relatively little to more fundamental materials management objectives.

The wrong objectives get undue emphasis even in cases where the boss does not interfere. For example, a purchasing agent may give undue emphasis to the price objective and all but ignore the equally important objectives of continuity of supply, inventory, and quality. Similarly, a production control manager may be so conscious of the need for continuity of supply that he all but ignores the inventory objective. Materials objectives are most likely to be balanced in a rational fashion when responsibility for achievement is clearly delegated—preferably to a materials manager who has authority to do the job. Even then objectives are not static. The materials manager must always reevaluate them when business conditions change or when they are affected by top-management decisions.

POLICIES AND PROCEDURES

After the materials manager determines the relative importance of his objectives, he devises a program to achieve them. In directing the program, the materials manager wants to manage by exception if possible. That is, he wants to delegate the achievement of the program completely to his subordinates. If everything goes according to plan, the materials manager does not interfere. But if something goes wrong because of a basic defect in the plan, the materials manager wants to learn of it. He may have to reevaluate the objectives and devise a new plan or take other remedial steps.

Written policies and procedures permit management by exception. They guide routine performance. With them, management decisions are needed only when an exceptional problem arises.

Definitions.   Policies are broad, overall guides to performance. Procedures are the specific administrative actions needed to carry out policies. Policies define in general terms the basic jobs of each department and its relation to other departments; they are derived from the general goals and objectives of the department itself and the company as a whole. Procedures are derived from policies. They describe routine operations in great detail.

Examples.   One big aircraft and auto parts manufacturing company includes low prices and favorable vendor relations among its materials objectives. To achieve these objectives, it has a written policy that "negotiations with vendors regarding price, terms, quality, etc. should be initiated, conducted, and concluded by the purchasing department."

This policy might be carried out with a number of procedures, such as a buying procedure whereby no purchase commitment is valid unless it is approved by a member of the purchasing department, or a procedure that prohibits anyone in departments other than purchasing from interviewing supplier salesmen without written approval of the purchasing agent.

A company with a policy of stimulating maximum competition among suppliers (in order to achieve an objective of low prices) might have a procedure calling for a minimum of three bids on each purchase.

Advantages of materials departments' manuals

Progressive materials departments codify literally hundreds of policies and procedures in manuals that may include several hundred pages. They invest in hundreds of hours of high-priced specialists' time for preparing the manual. Moreover, such manuals are no good unless they are kept up to date, so frequent revisions are necessary.

After all this work, what usually happens? Nine policy and procedure manuals out of ten may not be referred to for months or even years. They just gather dust on supervisors' bookcases. Very few persons in a well-managed company ever have much need to refer to a manual. Each knows his job, and if he has any questions he simply asks his supervisor. New employees don't have much use for manuals, either. They normally learn their jobs by observing their fellow workers and through verbal instructions from their supervisors.

Yet the best-managed companies have manuals for materials policies and procedures. They have them because manuals promote good inter-departmental relations (a secondary materials objective), make supervision easier, encourage standard practices, improve procedures, and aid in training.

Clarify interdepartmental relations. Even the best organization structure represents, to some extent, a rather artificial division of work. Departmental responsibilities overlap. Each department must work with the others if the overall job is to be done. Written policies and procedures define interdepartmental relationships. Thus they prevent many unnecessary jurisdictional disputes and also can prevent duplication of effort.

Written materials policies are particularly important because the materials department must work with other departments on problems where it is sometimes hard to determine jurisdiction. For example, although the materials department is responsible for selecting suppliers, using departments certainly have a right to receive the materials they need and to solicit suppliers for advice. Without written policies, jurisdictional disputes are almost inevitable when two departments are independently working with the same vendor on the same problem.

Make supervision easier. With written policies and procedures, a supervisor need not develop original solutions to routine problems. Nor need he even explain routine procedures to his subordinates (although he may wish to do so to make certain they understand them). The answers are in the manual. In most cases, the manual need not be referred to because employees already know what is in it. But were there no manual as a basic record, employees would gradually forget certain details of little-used procedures, and the load on supervisors would be correspondingly greater.

Develop standard practices. Without written policies and procedures, each supervisor would devise his own procedures to fit his superior's not-always-consistent instructions. As a result, eventually the same job would be performed in many different ways. Operations would be less efficient, communication slower, and supervision poorer. With written policies and procedures (called "standard practices," because that is what they are designed to promote), supervisors still deviate from routine when necessary, but they have basic guides to make them aware that they are deviating. These in themselves tend to prevent unnecessary changes in routine.

Improve procedures. When a manual is prepared, procedures are subjected to closer scrutiny than they may have received before. Improvements are almost inevitable. Unnecessary paper work can be eliminated, and tighter controls can be instituted if necessary. Periodic review and revision of the manual can prevent sloppy practices from creeping back into the system.

Aid in training. Although new employees are often lazy readers and prefer to get their training by watching and talking with fellow employees, the manual is helpful for reference. It is also useful to employees in other departments.

The job of preparing or revising a manual can be a training vehicle in itself. There is no better way to give a new high-potential employee a good grasp of the overall workings of the department and to permit him to apply his imagination and resourcefulness to improvements in procedures.

Preparing the manual

The materials department probably has more need for a policy and procedures manual than any other department in the company, mainly because of its contact with outside suppliers. Almost everyone in every department likes to buy and feels particularly competent to buy the items he uses. Controllers like to buy their own accounting machines, maintenance superintendents prefer to select brands of cleaning compounds, and product engineers feel they should select suppliers of parts and materials. This results in difficulties, which make preparation of a materials manual an especially long and tedious job. Since most of the important policies and procedures affect other departments, the person writing the manual must submit a draft of the proposed policy to each affected department head for approval. In many cases, hours are spent discussing precisely how a given policy should be worded so that each department's prerogatives are protected.

The usual procedure in preparing a manual is to determine what is being done and then to describe each operation in writing. After existing procedures are analyzed critically, the materials manager and his staff try to put down in writing what they would like to have done, as regards both policies and procedures. Existing procedures are then modified to fit these goals and drafts are submitted to all interested department heads for approval. The whole process always takes a few months and occasionally more than a year.

The effort is worthwhile, however. Written objectives, policies, and procedures provide the framework within which the materials organization does its job. But they are useless, of course, if the materials department does not also have the organization it needs to achieve the objectives. The principles of building a materials organization will be discussed in the next chapter.

Cases

CASE 3–1. GENERAL ELECTRIC COMPANY

Determination of materials objectives

The General Electric Company is one of the largest manufacturing corporations in the world. It employs about 350,000 persons, and its sales exceed $10 billion. Volume of purchases is more than $5 billion, and about $2 billion is invested in inventories. The company makes thousands of different products in hundreds of plants, including numerous consumer products, heavy capital goods, components and materials for industrial customers, and various defense products.

Organizationally, the company is broken up into more than 100 different operating departments. Each department specializes in a certain product line; for example, the company's Home Laundry Department in Louisville, Kentucky, makes washers and driers for the home. Each department is operated, to the greatest extent possible, as an independent business. Department managers have considerable latitude in choosing their staffs, negotiating for materials with suppliers, developing their own products and marketing strategies, and so on. The company's headquarters group, centered in New York City, exercises a minimum of authority over the departments. However, it does lay down overall policies that the department managers are supposed to follow. For example, the company has a mandatory policy requiring each of its department managers to comply fully with all government regulations and laws, including the antitrust laws.

In general, however, the headquarters staff tries to give the department managers maximum freedom to operate within the framework of company policy. The performance of managers is measured as much as possible in terms of the overall objectives of the company. These objectives are:

1. To carry on a diversified, growing, and profitable worldwide manufacturing business in electrical apparatus, appliances, and supplies, and in related materials, products, systems, and services for industry, commerce, agriculture, government, the community, and the home.
2. To lead in research in all fields of science and in all areas of work relating to the business, including managing as a distinct

and a professional kind of work, so as to assure a constant flow of new knowledge and of resultant useful and valuable new products, processes, services, methods, and organizational patterns and relationships; and to make real the Company theme that "Progress Is Our Most Important Product."

3. To operate each business venture to achieve its own favorable customer acceptance and profitable results; especially by planning the product line or services through decentralized operating management, on the basis of continuing research as to markets, customers, distribution channels, and competition, and as to product or service features, styling, price range, and performance for the end user, taking appropriate business risks to meet changing customer needs and to offer customers timely choice in product and service availability and desirability.

4. To design, make, and market all Company products and services with good quality and with inherent customer value, at fair prices for such quality and value.

5. To build public confidence and continuing friendly feeling for products and services bearing the Company's name and brands through sound, competitive advertising, promotion, selling, service, and personal contacts.

6. To provide good jobs, wages, working conditions, work satisfactions, and opportunities for advancement conducive of most productive performance and also the stablest possible employment, all in exchange for loyalty, initiative, skill, care, effort, attendance, and teamwork on the part of employees—the contributions of individual employees that result in "Value to the Company" and for which the employee is being paid.

7. To manage the enterprise for continuity and flow of progress, growth, profit, and public service through systematic selection and development of competent managerial personnel for effective leadership through persuasive managerial planning, organizing, integrating, and measuring for best utilization of both the human and material resources of the business; using a clear and soundly designed organization structure, and clearly expressed objectives and policies, as a vehicle for freeing the abilities, capacities, resourcefulness, and initiative of all managers, other professional workers and all employees for dynamic individual efforts and teamwork, encouraged by incentives proportionate to responsibilities, risks, and results.

8. To attract and retain investor capital in amounts adequate to finance the enterprise successfully through attractive returns as a continuing incentive for wide investor participation and support; securing such returns through sound business and economic research, forecasting, planning, cost management, and effectively scheduled turnover of all assets of the enterprise.

9. To cooperate both with suppliers and also with distributors, contractors, and others facilitating distribution, installation, and servicing of Company products, so that Company efforts are construc-

tively integrated with theirs for mutually effective public service and competitive, profitable progress.

10. To adapt Company policies, products, services, facilities, plans, and schedules to meet continuously, progressively, foresightedly, imaginatively, and voluntarily the social, civic, and economic responsibilities commensurate with the opportunities afforded by the size, success, and nature of the business and of public confidence in it as a corporate enterprise.[2]

Department managers at General Electric have considerable latitude in developing their organizations. There is no "standard" way to organize a GE department. However, most GE departments have materials managers who supervise the purchasing, production control, traffic, shipping, and receiving activities. These materials managers are expected to help their departments achieve their overall objectives.

Question

What specific objectives might GE materials managers develop to help their departments achieve their general objectives?

CASE 3–2. LAWTON PRODUCTS COMPANY

Determining materials management objectives

The Lawton Products Company was formerly known as the Lawton Camera Corporation. The new name was adopted in 1946 to reflect the company's broadened product line. Lawton was founded in 1915 by Howard F. Lawton, Sr., to manufacture and market a relatively expensive line of cameras designed especially for the amateur photographer. The company grew at first by widening its line of photographic equipment. Home-movie cameras, movie and slide projectors, and a best-selling line of 35 mm. "candid" cameras were introduced between 1920 and 1935.

The company prospered in the camera business not only because its products were of high quality and well merchandised but also because the company successfully avoided the problem of foreign competition with its products. Until World War II, the market for high-quality cameras was dominated by German manufacturers who had gained worldwide acceptance for quality and dependability. Although they were protected by an extremely high tariff, American manufacturers were hard put to compete even in their own market. Their products usually were

---

[2] As cited by General Electric's president, Ralph J. Cordiner, *New Frontiers for Professional Managers* (New York: McGraw-Hill Book Co., Inc., 1956), pp. 119–21.

not so widely accepted as the leading German brands. In addition, their costs were much higher; American camera workers were no more productive then German workers; but their wages were more than twice as high.

Lawton's solution to the problem of German competition was to buy major components from Japanese manufacturers, who could undersell both American and German firms. Lawton confined its efforts to design, assembly, and marketing.

The company was extremely successful, and by 1938 it had sales of $10 million, with profits of nearly $600,000 after taxes. In 1938, however, Howard Lawton became increasingly fearful of the threat to the company's survival if war should cut off his supplies of Japanese components, and so he decided to diversify. At that time, the company was doing almost no manufacturing. While Lawton desperately wanted to acquire manufacturing know-how on camera equipment, he had no desire to cut off his Japanese suppliers if he didn't have to. His solution was to buy the Abramson Company, a small manufacturer of optical instruments. In Abramson, Lawton got a profitable company with experience in optical equipment which could easily be converted to manufacture of camera components if necessary. The Abramson plant was located just a few miles from the Lawton plant, so there was no difficulty in integrating Abramson into the Lawton organization.

Pearl Harbor not only cut off Lawton's source of components, but it also cut off all manufacture of cameras for amateur photographers. The Lawton Corporation expanded its instrument line to serve the war effort. It also became one of the U.S. Navy's major contractors for optical fire-control equipment and gained considerable experience with the elaborate electric and electronic controls used in this equipment.

After the war, Lawton was able to use much of its expanded manufacturing capacity to broaden its line of photographic equipment. It also was able to apply its wartime skills in optics and electronics to a greatly expanded instrument line. In 1950 the company developed a closed-circuit television unit for industrial process control and added another line of process-control instruments to use with its TV systems. In 1951, the company reactivated its fire-control business when it got several major Navy contracts, and by 1969 the company had become a major supplier of fire-control and missile-guidance equipment for both the Navy and the Air Force.

The company's 1969 sales were $165 million, or more than 16 times as great as in 1938. Profits did not keep pace, however; they grew less than 500 percent in this period. The company's after-tax margin has deteriorated steadily since 1955, and in 1969 the company earned only 2 percent on sales and just over 5 percent on net worth. This was substantially below average after-tax returns of all durable good manufacturers (about 4 percent on sales and 8 percent on net worth).

In an effort to get to the bottom of the problem of declining profit margins, Howard Lawton, the company's president, hired the management consulting firm of Smith, Martin, and Conrad to make a broad survey of the company's organization, policies, and procedures.

The company's organization has grown a great deal since the 1930s, but its structure has changed very little. Reporting directly to Lawton are vice presidents in charge of sales, engineering, manufacturing, and finance. Reporting to the vice president of sales are an administrative assistant, advertising manager, public relations manager, sales personnel manager, general sales manager, and four product managers. The general sales manager supervises regional sales managers reponsible for sales of all of the company's products except cameras.

The product managers for instruments, defense products, and electronics each supervise a small staff. They are responsible for:

1. Coordinating complaints from customers with manufacturing and engineering.
2. Liaison with engineering on new products and design changes.
3. Production and materials planning, including the breaking down of orders from customers, preparation of purchase requisitions and factory work orders for parts, and preparation of overall schedules.
4. Preparation of quotations on new business from data secured from the cost department and interested activities.

Sales of camera equipment are handled somewhat differently. Since cameras are marketed through consumer channels, an entirely separate sales force is needed. It is under the direct supervision of the camera product manager, who is also responsible for market research on cameras, styling, coordination with engineering on new-product development, and purchase of all imported purchased components and complete products.

The company's purchasing manager, who reports to the vice president in charge of manufacturing, is responsible for buying all raw materials used in the company's products, as well as all nonproduction materials. Reporting to him are two buyers (one for direct material and the other for indirect), supervisors of the storerooms for both production and nonproduction materials, and the company's general foreman in charge of receiving inspection. In addition, the purchasing manager supervises a small data processing group that keeps records of all the company's inventories, including finished goods and in-process stocks. He also is functionally responsible for the purchasing specialists in the engineering department and provides them with forms, clerical services, and so on.

Also reporting to the vice president of manufacturing are the superintendents of the company's two plants, the production planning and control manager, the traffic manager, the factory personnel manager, the master mechanic, the cost estimating manager, the work standards manager, and the quality control manager.

The planning department prepares schedules, requisitions, and work orders for cameras from sales forecasts it receives from the camera product manager. It also participates in, but is not directly responsible for, production planning for other products.

The foremen of the shipping and receiving departments report to the traffic manager. Their activities require only a small amount of the traffic manager's time, most of which is spent on traffic problems on outgoing shipments of camera products and occasionally on assisting customers for other products when they do not specify any routing. The company has always relied on its suppliers to handle all inbound shipments. Even foreign suppliers take all responsibility for getting their shipments to Lawton and handle all details of shipping, customs, and so on.

The engineering department is organized almost entirely by product; there are chief product engineers for each of the company's lines. Reporting to each chief product engineer are various engineers who specialize in certain details of the product. Each chief engineer also has one or more buyers working for him who handle most routine contacts with suppliers. Individual engineers also work closely with the company's suppliers. On new products, they often rely on the supplier for substantial assistance in development. Suppliers do not charge for this service. They are rewarded indirectly, however, since the final specifications for the item usually are tailor-made to their processes, and, in some cases, they even indicate that the component should be purchased from the supplier who assisted in its development.

The engineering department is responsible for about 40 percent of the company's $110 million purchase volume. About 25 percent is spent by the camera department product manager on imported products and components, 30 percent directly by the purchasing manager, and the balance by the office manager for office supplies and by the master mechanic for machine tools and equipment.

The office manager reports to the general accounting manager, who in turn reports to the vice president in charge of finance. Also reporting to the general accounting manager are the supervisors in charge of office personnel, accounts payable, and accounts receivable. Invoices from suppliers go directly to accounts payable, where they are logged into a register and then sent for approval to the department responsible for the purchase. The department that made the purchase compares the invoice with the receiving report and the receiving inspection report and approves it if everything is in order. The approved invoice is then returned to accounts payable for payment. During an average month, accounts payable processes invoices for more than $9 million and manages to take discounts for prompt payment on all but about $500,000. Terms vary, but most suppliers offer a 1 to 2 percent discount if bills are paid within ten days.

Questions

1.   Should Smith, Martin, and Conrad recommend any changes in Lawton's approach to materials management?

2.   What are Lawton Products Company's probable materials management objectives?

3.   How can it better achieve these objectives?

4

Organizing for materials management

SOMEONE in every organization must make materials management decisions. Since, as noted in Chapter 3, materials objectives are interrelated, it is desirable to give one person authority over all activities concerned with materials management. Otherwise, no one—other than the president of the company—can be held responsible for materials decisions.

Suppose, for example, that materials authority is dispersed among a number of departments in a company (see Figure 4–1). A purchasing manager reporting to a finance manager is in charge of buying parts and materials. A traffic manager reporting to the sales manager buys

FIGURE 4–1
Divided responsibility for materials management

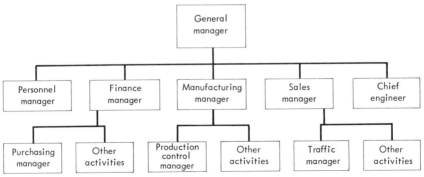

In this organization, the general manager is the only person responsible for all phases of materials management, including purchasing, production control, and traffic. Since he is involved with many other problems, materials are not managed as well as they should be.

transportation services. A production control manager reporting to the manufacturing manager schedules materials and controls inventories.

Problem of divided responsibility. Now suppose that one of the company's immediate objectives is to reduce materials cost by 5 percent. If the objective is actually achieved, the production control manager, purchasing agent, and traffic manager—and their respective bosses—all can share the credit. But who is responsible if the objective is not achieved? Each has a legitimate alibi. The production control manager is not responsible for negotiating prices of materials and services. The purchasing manager buys in amounts determined by the material control department, and his prices and bargaining power are determined by the quantities he buys. The traffic manager can't cut freight costs if purchasing insists on buying from suppliers in distant cities.

Duplication of effort. The divided materials organization not only makes it easy to pass the buck but it is wasteful. There is inevitably overlap of responsibility among materials functions—especially between production control and purchasing—and consequent duplication of effort. In the worst cases, production control and purchasing spend almost as much time jealously guarding their prerogatives against inroads of the rival activity as they do on the more constructive aspects of their jobs.

Sometimes the rivalry becomes genuinely destructive. In a large auto company in which I was once employed, both purchasing and production control quite correctly assumed that they were responsible for having purchased parts on hand to meet production requirements. So when a supplier failed to deliver, each activity rushed an expediter to the scene to straighten things out. There was just one difficulty. The competing expediters did not necessarily give the same instructions to the supplier. The purchasing expediter had a different set of priorities than the production control expediter did!

The difference reflected organizational level. Purchasing was centralized, and its priorities reflected what was theoretically a corporate view. The production expediter represented one of the company's major divisions, and its priorities on delivery of a wide variety of components were not the same as those of the corporate purchasing staff. The supplier presumably muddled through, trying to keep everyone happy but in reality performing less efficiently than if everyone had simply left him alone. It took the company 20 years to solve this organization problem. Today purchasing and production control are combined in a single materials management activity, so presumably the competition between the groups has been eliminated.

Lack of representation. Interfunctional rivalry can, however, be constructive, under certain conditions. Contrary to popular opinion, there is plenty of dissidence in a well-managed organization. Strong-willed executives often disagree. Each presents a point of view that reflects his specialty, and the decisions that result from this approach are likely to represent, on balance, the best that the organization can make at that time. For example, if engineering did not have a voice in top management, a manufacturing company might be prone to neglect research and development in order to boost short-term profit performance. On the other hand, an organization that is dominated by engineering might produce an excellent product, but it would cost too much to make and might not be marketable.

Materials management is conspicuous by its absence in the organization represented in Figure 4–1 above. If decisions reflect exclusively the viewpoints of personnel, finance, manufacturing, sales, and engineering, the best that can happen is that materials management is ignored. In the worst circumstances, however, it can be adversely affected. In one health-care organization where materials management was not represented at a high level, an expensive new facility was constructed in which almost no space was allowed for purchased materials inventory. Expensive alterations were later needed to make the facility workable.

The company's loss may be more subtle than this. It can safely be assumed that purchased materials inventory will not be under tight control unless there is a strong materials manager. The reason for this is that both sales and manufacturing performance tend to be improved if there is a large purchased-material inventory. The purchasing department's job is also easier. This leaves the finance manager as the only key executive with a vested interest in low inventory. He is not only outnumbered but also frequently unable to attack the problem, since his concern is entirely with dollar investment and change from some prior period. If inventory has always been high (as it often is in the company with weak materials management), then it cannot easily be cut back. A reduction is almost certain to cause severe disruption in manufacturing or in purchasing. In fact, when inventory investment is at its optimum level, production control and purchasing personnel, in particular, may feel that they are working in a state of near chaos. They are always on the verge of running out of material—and sometimes they actually do run out. This state of affairs is rarely welcomed by the salaried employees who must cope with it. In effect, the benefits of higher return on capital go to the company's stockholders and possibly to its top management. The ulcers are awarded to those who must actually cope with the problems of tight inventory.

WHO IS MATERIALS MANAGER?

Under the conditions described above, tough inventory management must be imposed from the top, with a key executive who understands the inventory process exerting continuous pressure to keep stocks down. A materials manager is needed.

Purchasing agent as materials manager

Sometimes the purchasing agent or purchasing manager becomes materials manager in fact, if not in title. He gets the job through a process of evolution, gradually assuming responsibility for all phases of materials management. When the purchasing agent is given responsibility for both traffic and inventory control, he is more materials manager than purchasing agent. At this stage, responsibility for almost all of the company's materials objectives centers on a single executive, and the company's organization structure is no longer a barrier to effective materials management.

Dozens of companies do an excellent job of materials management even though they employ no materials managers. Typically, the materials organization is headed by a vice president of purchases and traffic, who is also responsible for inventory control. This vice president is, in effect, materials management's representative in top management. His materials organization can be quite efficient. Three of the most important materials functions—purchasing, traffic, and inventory control—are linked together organizationally, and the company's efforts are consistently focused on a common set of materials objectives.

Criteria for effectiveness. The purchasing manager is most likely to make a satisfactory substitute for a materials manager in nonmanufacturing organizations—especially those with minimal inventory problems. The best example of this is a construction company. Purchased material is delivered directly to the site, and there is relatively little inventory. In this extreme case, of course, the materials manager is almost exclusively concerned with purchasing.

In most other cases, purchasing is not the only skill that is required, even though the materials management process effectively ends with delivery of purchased material to the ultimate user. For example, the purchasing agent of an educational institution is really a materials manager, even if he does not have that title, because he is almost always in charge of purchased inventories. Purchasing agents of manufacturing companies also frequently function as materials managers, particularly if there are no major materials management problems with in-process or finished-goods stocks. In the aerospace industry, for example, a purchasing manager in one company may have the same responsibilities as a materials or materiel manager in another company. In both cases, they may be responsible not only for buying but also for inbound traffic and control of purchased-materials inventory. In neither case do they have much to do with in-process stocks. Since the product is extremely expensive and made to customer order, there are no conventional physical distribution problems to interest the materials manager.

Limitations. In a majority of organizations, however, the purchasing manager makes an effective materials manager only if he has both skills and authority not ordinarily associated with his specialty. Two major problems prevent the typical purchasing manager from functioning informally as materials manager.

1. *Production control and inventory control cannot be readily separated from manufacturing.* The inventory control function is pivotal. Purchasing has a legitimate interest in this function because inventory level is determined by the quantity of material purchased. (This is explained in detail in Chapter 8.) Production control is also legitimately interested, since manufacturing schedules are intimately related to in-process and raw-materials inventories.

2. *Materials functions that remain in manufacturing do not have adequate "visibility."* Receiving, shipping, warehousing, and materials handling all tend to be neglected orphans in the typical manufacturing organization. Their activities are peripheral to manufacturing's main job—making the product—and their managers typically have the feeling that manufacturing has no interest whatever in their activities. Morale and performance are often improved when these activities are transferred to materials management, an activity in which movement and handling of material are primary concerns.

Fifty years ago, it was assumed that activities such as shipping and materials handling would more or less manage themselves. In recent years, however, management has become increasingly aware that a major part of its "manufacturing" cost has nothing to do with the manufacturing process itself but is concerned with the moving and storing of materials in various stages of fabrication. New management techniques have been developed to control these moving and storing costs. These can be applied most successfully if responsibility is given to a materials manager rather than remaining in manufacturing, where management is primarily interested in the manufacturing process itself.

Dual materials management

Problems in the purchasing–materials management relationship can be solved if purchasing is not considered part of materials management. In this case, materials management consists of all of the usual activities *except* purchasing. The materials manager takes over *after* the material is bought, and purchasing functions independently of materials management. As many as one tenth of the executives with the title of materials manager or its equivalent do not include purchasing in their departments. In some cases, the reason for this is entirely political. An ambitious executive is able to gather together all functions but purchasing, and the director of purchases is strong enough to keep his independence. Occasionally, these half-finished materials management departments will follow a more conventional pattern as soon as management finds it convenient to make further changes—often after a very senior purchasing executive retires and is replaced by a junior who is more amenable to becoming subordinate to the materials manager.

Occasionally, the existence of materials management and purchasing departments that are independent of one another may even be justified on a logical basis. A huge, multidivision company may prefer to do almost all of its buying at the corporate level so it has a large, corporate purchasing office. Other materials management activities are completely decentralized at the division level, however, with divisional materials managers responsible for everything except purchasing.

This setup automatically breeds the conflict of objectives discussed earlier. It would be workable in practice only if there were very little that the corporate purchasing office could do to thwart what might be quite different objectives of the divisional materials management departments. It is hard to believe that a better way cannot be found to organize for materials management.

Materials management subordinate to manufacturing

One alternative arrangement that is quite common is simply to group together all related materials management activities under a materials manger who, in turn, reports to manufacturing. In a smaller company, a similar version of this approach is to have managers of the major materials management activities all report directly to the manufacturing manager. In this case, the manufacturing manager really has two jobs: the one implied by his title and that of materials manager.

About half of the manufacturing companies with materials managers have an integrated department reporting to manufacturing. Materials managers would undoubtedly prefer to report to top management directly rather than to be subordinate to manufacturing, and it can safely be assumed they are given no choice. Legitimate arguments can be advanced for the role of materials management as a junior partner to manufacturing, however, including expediency, indivisibility, and span of control.

Expediency. In many cases, the only way a company can get an integrated materials management activity is by making it subordinate to manufacturing. Most or even all of the key materials management functions may have been under manufacturing to start with. The main change in this case is the act of grouping them together under a materials manager. Such a change is likely to be supported by the manufacturing manager only if he continues to retain overall responsibility for materials management. In other cases there might not be a separate materials manager, and the manufacturing manager would continue to function as an effective materials manager himself.

Indivisibility. In certain types of manufacturing processes, it is extremely difficult to determine where materials management ends and manufacturing begins. In general, the materials manager is responsible for the flow of materials through the shop (adding value by distribution), while manufacturing is responsible for the workers and machines that actually make the product (adding value by manufacture). In practice, however, the production and inventory control departments may be deeply involved not only in materials management problems but also in making decisions that are definitely manufacturing's responsibility. For example, a shortage of material may force production not only to reschedule equipment but also to shift workers from one production job to another. Materials management and production management decisions must then be made almost simultaneously and, since they are interrelated, should be made by the same department. Thus, in some industries, both materials management and manufacturing management can quite legitimately claim that production control belongs in their bailiwick. This ceases to be a problem if materials management is part of manufacturing to start with.

Span of control. The general manager may be so busy he wants to limit the number of executives who report directly to him. He feels he is too busy to be involved with materials management directly. As long as materials management cannot have much impact on the company's success, this view is correct. Materials management is not always so vital to the enterprise that its chief should be on the company's second level of organization, responsible directly to top management. This is generally true of companies that do not use substantial amounts of production parts and materials. For example, materials management can quite legitimately be made subordinate to manufacturing in a mining firm where the materials management job is primarily concerned with procurement of spare parts and similar items needed to keep the mine operating.

The case for independence

Unfortunately, the materials function is still subordinate to manufacturing in many companies where it could make a greater contribution to profits if it were independent. Increasingly, however, top managements are separating materials management from manufacturing. Automation is forcing the manufacturing manager to concentrate more of his energies on technological problems. He has less time for peripheral activities, including materials management.

EDP sharpens distinction. In addition, electronic data processing helps sharpen the distinction between manufacturing management and materials management. The typical EDP program automatically draws all related activities of materials management together. It is only natural that the company organization chart should reflect the way in which technology has regrouped activities. One activity, headed by a materials manager, is concerned with the data on inventory, orders, shortages, and lead time that is to be fed into the computer. Another group, under a manufacturing manager, dedicates its efforts to making machines and men meet schedules at lowest possible cost. Thus, as is explained in greater detail in Chapter 21, automation in the factory and data processing are forcing many companies to integrate their materials management activities and make a single executive responsible for all materials management decisions.

The only way. In the overwhelming majority of independent materials management organizations, the relatively small costs are offset many times over by the results. Materials should be managed by an executive whose success or failure depends entirely on how well this job is done. If materials management is a peripheral assignment for an executive with other responsibilities, it will get peripheral treatment. If the materials organization is a subordinate function, it will inevitably take on some of the objectives of the function to which it is junior. The best results and the highest morale are achieved when the materials management department must "sink or swim" in its specialty. This environment can best be created in an organization structure resembling that in Figure 4–2, where the division of work is by function. This and other types of organizational structure are discussed in the following section.

FIGURE 4–2
Division of work by function

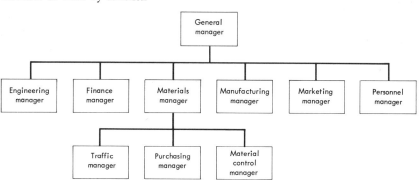

The overall job of management is delegated by its major functions. Division of work at the third level is also usually functional. For example, the materials management job is divided functionally into its traffic, purchasing, and material control elements.

BUILDING THE ORGANIZATION

Almost every materials manager requires a staff to help him achieve his objectives. Materials management is a big job. In a fairly small concern it may require 20 or 30 persons; in a big corporation, hundreds or even thousands will be needed. The overall materials job must be divided into many different jobs under some sort of organization structure. In the ideal organization, objectives are consistently attained at low cost and with a minimum of confusion. This ideal is hard to achieve, for organization is hardly an exact science. Two different managers will build entirely different organization structures, even though there are relatively few ways in which work can be divided in creating an organization. Among those that are feasible for a materials organization are division of work by: (1) function; (2) location; (3) product or project; and (4) stage of manufacture or process.

Organization by function

The most widely used organization technique is division of work by function (see Figure 4–2). The principle behind it is a sound one: jobs should be organized so as to promote maximum specialization of skills. With functional specialization, jobs are broken up so that they are as narrow as possible in scope. Each man is an expert in some highly specialized area.

There is considerable functional specialization in every materials organization. Breaking up the overall materials job into its components (purchasing, traffic, material control, and so on) is a form of functional specialization. Within these groups, there is even more specialization. For example, purchasing may be broken up so that one person receives purchase requisitions and prepares the records for a buyer. Another person, the buyer, contacts suppliers and actually places orders. Another specialist may do nothing but type purchase orders, and another files the necessary records. Still another specialist may follow up to make certain that the suppliers deliver on schedule. In a large purchasing organization, the buying job itself can involve as many as half a dozen different specialists, including assistant buyers, expediters, purchase analysts, and others.

Advantages. It is possible, in creating a materials organization, to divide work entirely by function. This would work fairly well in a small organization, although there might be problems in a larger one. Division of work by function is popular with good reason. It has many advantages, including the following.

1. *Economic use of high-salaried help.* With functional specialization, jobs can more readily be broken up into highly skilled and less skilled elements. A buyer does not type his own purchase orders (he probably wouldn't have this skill anyway); he relies on a typist whose salary is substantially lower. This permits the buyer to use his special skills more effectively. Functional specialization also makes it economic

to hire specialists whom the organization could not otherwise afford. For example, in the typical company, buyers in the purchasing department and various marketing executives all can make profitable use of periodic forecasts by a professional economist. By setting up a separate economics department to serve the entire company, each executive can get the benefit of an expert's advice. An additional function, economic forecasting, is created to serve a number of departments. Each executive served by the economist in effect delegates part of the forecasting element of his job to the economist, so that there actually has been a division of work by function.

2. *More efficient operation.* With functional specialization, it is possible to become extremely adept at one particular job. A clerk who runs a calculator all day in production control is bound to be more accurate and efficient in her work than one who uses the same machine only occasionally.

3. *More flexible organization.* An organization with a maximum of functional specialization can adjust more readily to changes in business volume. The reason is that it makes the most effective use of a few highly skilled persons who are always needed. When volume is low, they handle both skilled and unskilled jobs. When it expands, less skilled persons can be hired to take over elements of their jobs. There is no need to hire additional highly skilled people, who might not even be available in a period of business expansion.

4. *Concentration of buying power.* In the conventional materials organization, buying assignments are normally made on the basis of commodity specialization. One buyer handles stampings, another handles office supplies, and so on. With this approach, not only does the buyer become an expert in his field, but the plant's entire buying power is concentrated for each commodity instead of being dispersed among a number of "materials specialists" or "divisional materials managers." This can make for better procurement and lower costs.

Disadvantages. Unfortunately, excessive application of the principle of functional specialization can cause serious weaknesses in the organization. Among them are the following.

1. *Employee dissatisfaction.* People get bored when their jobs become too specialized; they like variety. Also, with specialization, the general objectives of the business can become too remote from the jobs of those who are supposed to achieve them. People may become so engrossed in their specialties that they begin to regard them as ends in themselves and not as means of reaching some broader company objective.

2. *Bureaucratization.* If jobs become too specialized, everyone is liable to "pass the buck" and disclaim responsibility for solving a nonroutine problem or for committing an error. Also, an organization with

a great deal of functional specialization is often "deep"—with many layers of supervision. This makes for a long chain of command and causes the decision-making process to be slow and complex.

Organization by location

In a large organization with many plants, the need for some application of the principle of organization by location is self-evident (see Figure 4–3). Each plant requires a materials organization, and at least

FIGURE 4–3
Division of work by location

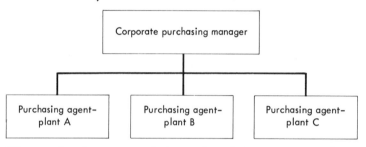

When similar functions are being performed in areas remote from one another, division of work by location is desirable at some level in the organization.

part of that organization must be physically located at the plant. Therefore division of responsibility by location is essential.

Organization by location is also practical in companies that operate only one plant. Many plants have more than one receiving, shipping, or stores department. In such cases, division of responsibility usually is by location, with each unit serving a given part of the plant.

When the materials organization is by plant, materials personnel can work more closely with the other departments in that plant. They become more intimately familiar with the plant's problems. The major disadvantage of organization by plant is that it tends to disperse the materials organization. Some of the advantages of specialization are lost, and buying power is often diluted.

Organization by plant is naturally essential for some elements of the materials job, notably shipping and receiving. Organization by area served is similar. In the materials department, it is particularly applicable to field expediters and traffic clerks. Field expediters can deal with suppliers in given areas. For example, one California aerospace company has field expediters in Cleveland, Ohio, and Hartford, Connecticut, to expedite needed shipments from eastern and midwestern suppliers. If a traffic clerk specializes in shipments from a given area, he will rapidly all but memorize tariffs of carriers serving that area and so will be able to do his job more efficiently.

For other parts of the materials department, organization by location is rarer. The disadvantages of this form of organization in purchasing, for example, usually outweigh the advantages.

Organization by product or project

Since the materials organization exists to help make some product or service more profitably, breaking up materials activities by product, process, or project is logical (see Figure 4–4). Each materials group

FIGURE 4–4
Organization by product

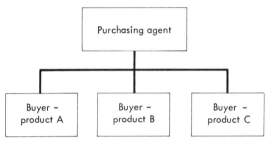

There is no better way to make a person conscious of profit margins than to give him responsibility for performing a vital function in the manufacture and marketing of that product.

is assigned to some product or group of products. For example, the purchasing departments of the General Motors Corporation are set up on a product basis. There is a separate purchasing department for each product division: Chevrolet, Pontiac, Frigidaire, and so on.

A project organization is a product organization with a finite life. Project organizations are temporarily set up to carry out a particular mission. When the job is done, they are either disbanded or melded into some new permanent organization. For example, a company that is contemplating manufacture of some new product would set up a project organization for that product headed by a project manager. Appropriate specialists from manufacturing, materials management, engineering, and other activities would then be assigned temporarily to that project. In many cases, they would simply return to their regular jobs when the project was completed. In others, they might form the cadre of a new permanent organization when the project organization evolved into a product organization with a permanent mission.

Within the materials department, division of work by product or commodity is quite common. Purchasing departments often are organized so that each buyer specializes in a few commodities. (This is a combination of functional specialization and product specialization.) One buyer may specialize in castings and forgings, another in sheet steel, and so on. The production control organization frequently follows the same pattern. In a cruder fashion, so do stores. Raw materials often go to one stores department, finished parts to another, and so on.

The big advantage of organization by product is that it permits personnel to become really familiar with the problems of a single group of products. As a result, they should be able to do their work more effectively. When the overall materials organization is broken up into a number of product groups, as it is at General Motors, each member's job is more closely related to the profit objectives in a particular product line.

The main disadvantage of organization by product is that it tends to disperse the overall materials effort. In a company as large as General Motors, this dispersal probably is no handicap. But it would be highly uneconomic, by contrast, to have the materials organization broken up into product groups in a company employing 1,000 persons and making 100 fairly similar products.

Organization by stage of manufacture

"Serial" organization, by stage of manufacture, is consistent with the basic concept of materials management as the administration of the flow of materials to and from production equipment. Some might regard the functional division of materials responsibility into purchasing, traffic, production control, and other components as also being a "serial" division, by stage of manufacture. Responsibility passes from department to department as the material or component moves from the idea stage to fabrication in the vendor's plant through the buyer's receiving and stores to the point where it is utilized in his manufacturing process.

Figure 4–5 shows how a materials department might be organized by stage of manufacture. Divisional materials managers reporting to the plant materials manager are responsible for all phases of materials management in certain areas of the plant. For example, one materials manager might serve the company' foundry, another the press shop, a third the assembly line, and so on. A divisional materials manager for nonproduction items would serve the entire plant and would also supervise the operation of the nonproduction storeroom.

Each materials manager would be responsible for determining his own requirements, managing his own inventories (but not managing the actual storeroom in most cases), placing his own orders, and doing his own expediting. The supervisor of traffic and materials handling could assist each division materials manager with traffic, materials-handling,

FIGURE 4–5
Organization by stage of manufacture

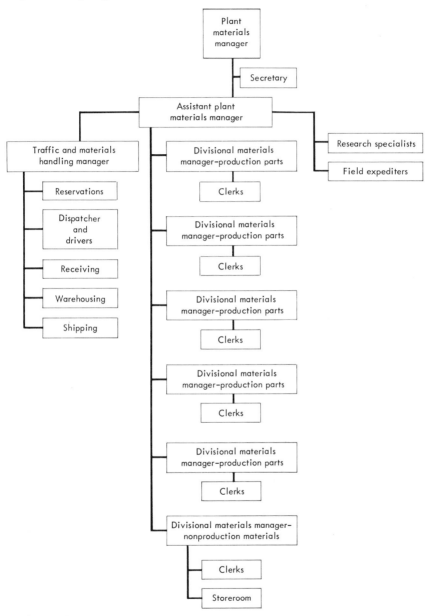

In the smaller materials organization that is dedicated either to a single product line or to many products made on a job-lot basis, organization by product is not practical. Organization by stage of manufacture is a good substitute in many cases.

and packaging problems, but the division materials manager would have basic responsibility for results. The traffic supervisor would also supervise plantwide services such as receiving, warehousing, reservations, dispatching, and so on.

One or more research specialists reporting to the plant materials manager could assist the division materials managers with value analysis or economic analysis. Such specialists might also develop performance measurements so that the contribution of each materials manager to the achievement of overall objectives can be evaluated and reported.

SPAN OF CONTROL

The four major ways in which to divide materials management work—organization by function, location, product, and stage of manufacture—have been discussed above. Another fundamental principle of organizing for materials management is the concept of *span of control* which is concerned with how many divisions should be made.

In a materials organization with 100 persons, should there be one general materials manager and 99 assistant materials managers? In this case, we are assuming that the general materials manager has a span of control of 99, that is, he can effectively supervise 99 persons. Most managers would not want to have that many persons reporting directly to them. In fact, they usually prefer to have fewer than ten persons reporting directly.

For this reason, most materials organizations with a staff of 100 would more likely have half a dozen or so "assistants" reporting directly to the general materials manager. Each of the assistants, in turn, might have half a dozen persons reporting to him, and these third-level people would in turn have subordinates. So the 100 people in the materials organization might be at four distinct organization levels.

This does not mean it is desirable to have an organization with many levels. On the contrary, such an organization has many disadvantages, and there are many reasons why an organization should be kept as "flat" (i.e., with a broad span of control and relatively few levels) as possible.

The flat organization. Morale tends to be higher in the flat organization (Figure 4–6) than in the deep one. Most people are much closer to the top echelon than they would otherwise be. They are more likely to have a better grasp of the problems of the business as a whole, and they are less likely to become so immersed in their own specialities that they lose sight of overall objectives. The flat organization is relatively democratic. To a great degree, everyone is his own boss and is forced to make his own decisions.

Since people are on their own to a much greater degree, individual skills must be greater in the flat organization. And, of course, the flat

FIGURE 4–6
Flat organization: Purchasing agent with broad span of control.

organization is a much better training ground for future top executives, since they get a chance to make decisions at a much earlier stage in their careers.

The deep organization. The deep organization (see Figure 4–7) also has advantages. In practice, most companies have fairly deep organizations, and they have them because they work. Proponents point out that there is a place for everyone in the deep organization. Highly routine, unskilled jobs can easily be found for the inexperienced and relatively inept at the bottom of the pyrimid, and the skills of the highly specialized and extra talented can be utilized to a much greater degree in some position near the top. Fewer experts are needed in the deep organization. Since there is a greater breakdown of work by skill, the services of everyone in the organization are used in the most economic manner.

FIGURE 4–7
Deep purchasing organization with narrow span of control

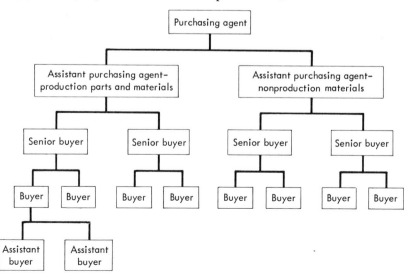

The deep organization has faults, too. It tends to be bureaucratic; decisions are passed upward from echelon to echelon. It can be inefficient; it requires more supervision than the flat organization does and, if carried to an extreme, this can reach the point where there are literally more chiefs than Indians. The deep organization also tends to discourage individual initiative; it is inherently more autocratic than the flatter organization. Promotions may be slow; in extreme cases, it can take exceptionally able persons years to reach jobs with sufficient responsibility for their skills to be recognized.

On the other hand, in a deep organization, supervisors are more likely to have time to train and counsel each of their subordinates on an individual basis. It is also possible to have tighter control over everyone's actions.

Wide or narrow span? In practice, every organization structure represents a series of compromises. This is the case with span of control. Some factors tend to widen span of control; others tend to narrow it.

It is possible to have a flat organization with broad span of control when:

1. Job objectives are clearly spelled out. A man who knows exactly what is expected of him obviously requires less supervision than one who knows what he is supposed to do only by frequent contact with his boss.

2. Job performance can be measured. When there are objective measures of performance, the supervisor's job is easier. It is no problem to determine the contribution of each subordinate to the business.

3. Jobs supervised are similar and repetitious. The less complex the job, the fewer the supervisor's problems. And, of course, the supervisor's job is much simpler when he supervises persons doing almost identical jobs, all relatively unskilled, than when he supervises persons who are highly skilled, each of whom is doing a different job.

4. Supervisors and supervised both are above average in job skill and administrative skill. Exceptional supervisors can effectively handle more subordinates, and exceptional subordinates can get along with less supervision.

5. Errors are not serious. If a man's mistakes do not have too much effect on the companys profit and survival, there is a greater inclination to put him in a spot where he can learn by making his own mistakes. If errors are too costly, supervision must be more intense.

Because errors *are* serious in a purchasing department, supervisors often have an extremely limited span of control. Each individual buyer may be spending hundreds of thousands or millions of dollars. Obviously, the company cannot afford too many mistakes, so his work is checked and rechecked by various supervisors. On the other hand, work in a receiving department is less vital to the profits of the business. An error made on a receiving report will undoubtedly cause confusion and could be expensive, but it is unlikely to be as critical as an error in buying. Therefore it is possible to have a broader span of control in receiving.

Span of control in the ideal organization is neither too broad nor too narrow. In such an organization, the manager tries to get some of the initiative that the flat organization encourages while retaining the ease of supervision of the deep structure.

In the typical materials organization, the span of control varies from 4 or 5 to 15 or 20. The top materials manager usually has fewer persons reporting to him than any other supervisor in the department. Receiving and shipping foremen may supervise as many as 15 or 20 men.

LEVEL OF ORGANIZATION

It is possible to build an effective organization simply by applying the principles of division of work to each major job within the limits of span of control. Managers whose activities embrace a big part of the organization would then report to major officials, while their subordinates would include managers with narrower responsibilities.

While every manager would prefer to report to the president of the company, because of the limits of span of control this is seldom possible. Only those in charge of the primary functions of the business—marketing, materials management, engineering, finance, manufacturing, and personnel—customarily report to the chief executive. Similarly, only the managers of the key functions of purchasing, material control, and traffic would report directly to the materials manager.

But there are exceptions. The materials manager may have lower ranking employees reporting to him as matter of convenience. These might include a secretary or administrative assistant, for example, or the manager of some activity that provides a service to the entire materials department—perhaps a clerical group that handles filing or provides stenographic services.

The materials manager may want to have a certain executive reporting directly to him because he wishes to give particular attention to a certain area. For example, suppose a company spends a large percentage of its purchase volume on a key raw material—crude rubber in a tire company, cloth in a clothing company, crude petroleum in an oil refining company. The materials manager may want to have the buyer of the key material report directly to him, along with the purchasing agent, traffic manager, and others. Theoretically, the buyer of the critical material should report to the purchasing agent along with the rest of the company's buyers. But the material is so important that it is worth extra attention and also may be worth the skills of an extra-talented buyer who, in salary and responsibility if not in title or nominal authority, is every bit the equal of the purchasing agent.

APPLYING ORGANIZATION PRINCIPLES

The materials organizations of the Lycoming Division of the Avco Manufacturing Company and the Jet Engine Division of the General Electric Company provide excellent examples for applying the basic principles of organization. They are similar in many ways. Both make aircraft engines. Each has a materials manager responsible for most phases of materials management. Each is too big to be typical, having several hundred persons in its materials department (although the organization structure of either could be satisfactorily adapted to a company with only a few hundred employees).

Despite these similarities, their materials organization structures are quite different. In the Avco organization, division of work by function is emphasized. In the GE organization, it is mostly by product.

The Avco-Lycoming Organization

The director of materials reports to the general manager of the Lycoming Division of Avco Manufacturing Co. (see Figure 4–8). Division of responsibility at this level is by function; the materials director is responsible for all materials management functions in the plant.

Managers of the four major materials activities at Lycoming—purchasing, expediting, traffic and transportation, and material control—report to the director of materials. Thus, division of responsibility is on a functional basis also at this level. The organization of the departments headed by these four managers is discussed below.

Purchasing. Reporting to the purchasing manager is a purchasing agent for production materials and another for nonproduction materials. One purchasing agent is responsible for all the parts and materials directly incorporated into the plant's products, the other for all the materials and services used in manufacturing and administration. Thus division of responsibility is essentially by product.

This is also true at the buyer level in the organization. The principle of commodity specialization is followed as much as possible. Each buyer handles a group of commodities (not shown on the chart in Figure 4–8). For example, one buyer may handle castings, another machined parts, and so on. With this type of organization, which is almost universally used in purchasing departments, buyers can become more familiar with suppliers, costs, manufacturing processes, and so on of the commodities in which they specialize. They can keep informed on all new technological and economic developments in their specialties.

FIGURE 4–8

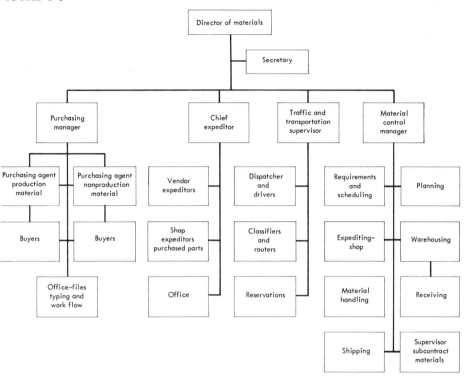

Division of work in the materials department of the Lycoming Division, Avco Manufacturing Co., is almost entirely by function. Managers of the four subdepartments divide work by function; division of work at lower levels is also predominantly by function.

A third person reporting directly to the purchasing manager (in addition to the two purchasing agents) is the office manager. His department handles all filing, typing, and miscellaneous clerical chores for the purchasing department. It frees the buying groups as much as possible from clerical duties, so they can concentrate their efforts on the buying process itself. Thus there is a functional division of the buying job, since much of the clerical phase is handled by a separate group. Lycoming feels this boosts efficiency. Routine clerical jobs can be more closely controlled if they are supervised by someone who is not distracted by other duties. In addition, certain records, such as copies of the purchase orders issued, must be kept centrally for the entire department, so the work must be organized on a department-wide basis.

Expediting. Many materials organizations do not have expediting departments. They consider expediting a basic part of the buyer's job and believe that his responsibility does not end until acceptable material is actually delivered from the supplier. Buyers retain basic responsibility for on-time delivery of purchased material at Lycoming, but a separate expediting department helps them with the clerical chores of expediting—another case of division of work by function. The expediting group is divided into three sections: vendor expediting, shop expediting on purchased parts, and office.

The division of work between vendor expediting and shop expediting is essentially by stage of manufacture. The vendor-expediting group deals with the supplier before the purchased part is manufactured or delivered. Shop expediting takes over when the part is delivered to the Avco receiving desk. If a part is on the critical shortage list, the shop expediter speeds its movement through inspection to the area in the plant where it is needed.

The office group in the expediting department is like its counterpart in purchasing. It handles typing, filing, and so on, as a functional subdivision of the overall expediting job.

Traffic and transportation. The traffic and transportation department is divided by function into its three basic sections: dispatching and drivers of company-owned cars and trucks, classifying and routing of inbound shipments from suppliers, and reservations. The first group operates the company's trucks. The second handles the conventional traffic department jobs: selecting common carriers and routes for inbound shipments and tracing shipments when necessary. The third group makes plane and hotel reservations for company executives when they travel.

Material control. The eight groups within the material control department at Avco-Lycoming reflect a combination of the stage-of-manufacture and the functional approaches to organization.

The requirements-and-schedules group translates customer orders into requirements for parts and materials. The planning group translates these requirements into purchase requisitions, taking account of quantities currently in inventory and on order. The receiving department unloads purchased material when it is delivered and issues a receiving report. The warehousing group stores material until it is needed. The shop-expediting group coordinates shortages that develop within manufacturing (i.e., when one manufacturing operation gets behind schedule and holds up the succeeding operation). The materials-handling group is responsible for moving materials in manufacturing from operation to operation. The subcontract-materials group is responsible for seeing that major subcontracted assemblies are available on schedule for final asssembly, and the shipping group is responsible for packaging and shipping the finished product.

Thus there is a separate group for each stage in the materials process. However, the organization is also functional, since each group performs a basic function in the overall materials job.

Although it is not shown on the chart, there is further functional division of responsibility within the material control department. For example, as with purchasing and expediting, separate little groups in planning and other sections within the material control department handle various specialized activities, such as typing and filing.

The General Electric approach

In most of its operating departments, General Electric Company has materials organizations that resemble Avco-Lycoming's with managers of purchasing, production control, traffic, and value analysis reporting to the plant material manager. However, General Electric uses a slightly different approach to materials management in its Evendale, Ohio, jet engine plant. Reporting to the plant's materials manager are materials supervisors who are in charge of materials management for each of the plant's major products. Also reporting to him are a purchasing agent, a supervisor of shipping, receiving, and stores, and two staff supervisors (see Figure 4–9). The purchasing agent is in charge of buying all items

FIGURE 4–9

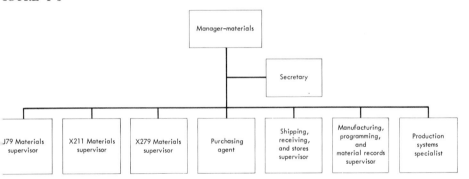

The materials department of the Jet Engine Division of General Electric is organized by product as much as possible. Materials supervisors handled all phases of materials management for each product. Division of work at the lower levels is also by product or type of material.

used throughout the plant (maintenance supplies, stationery, etc.). The staff assistants handle systems and procedures, manufacturing programming, records, and so on.

Product groups. The unique feature of this organization is the product groups. Each group is responsible for all phases of materials management for a particular product. It must:

1. Get basic requirements and design data from engineering.
2. Locate supply sources.
3. Determine required delivery dates and purchase quantities necessary

to meet the requirements of the overall program.
4. Place orders.
5. Expedite and follow up with suppliers to make sure that delivery promises are kept.
6. Maintain necessary property and inventory control records.
7. Schedule assembly buildups in the plant and handle necessary liaison on engine-test programs.

Thus each group is responsible for virtually all phases of materials management except shipping, receiving, and stores, and nonproduction buying. These remain centralized and continue to serve the entire plant.

Within the product groups, the same organization approach is used. "Materials specialists," who report to the supervisor of the product group, are responsible for various groups of commodities. Each has overall materials management responsibility and is assisted by clerical help.

The major difference between this organization and the more conventional materials organization represented by Avco is in the emphasis on functional specialization. At Avco, materials management is regarded as a series of related, but functionally distinct, activities. In the GE Jet Engine Division, materials management is regarded as a separate and almost indivisible function. Each materials specialist is a small-scale materials manager. Clerical and nonclerical phases on his job are separated when he delegates work to his clerks, but no effort is made to distinguish the functions of materials management—buying, expediting, material control, and so on.

Applications to Service Industries

An Airline. While materials management is primarily associated with manufacturing organizations such as General Electric and Avco, a surprising amount of materials management is also needed in large service organizations. For example, while United Air Lines's end product is a service, maintenance of its equipment takes on much of the character of a manufacturing operation. At its San Francisco maintenance base, United maintains an inventory of more than 100,000 different items used for both routine repairs and general overhauls of its equipment.

The materials organization (see Figure 4–10) at the San Francisco base follows roughly the same pattern as that of a manufacturing organization. The director of supply acts as materials manager. His purchasing manager heads a 127-man department that is primarily concerned with buying various types of spare parts. Buying responsibility is broken down into four product groups with separate managers for power plant parts, air frames, accessories, and equipment. The assistant to the purchasing manager is also responsible for traffic. A 291-man stores organization is responsible for receiving, storage, and shipping

FIGURE 4–10

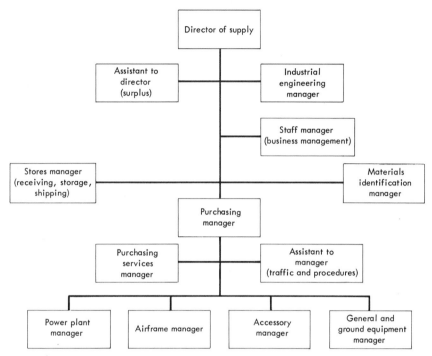

Materials management at San Francisco maintenance base of United Air Lines is organized much like a manufacturing organization, even though United's end product is transportation service.

and a 63-man materials identification group is concerned with other problems of material control. The United materials organization is "unconventional" in just two major respects: (1) there is no production control department because the base does no manufacturing, and (2) the industrial engineering manager reports to the director of supply, whereas in a manufacturing firm he would report to the manufacturing manager.

A large hospital. The materials management organization of a hospital is also quite different from that of a typical manufacturer. Like his industrial counterpart, the hospital materials manager is responsible for conventional purchasing and stores operations, but he also adds value by manufacture to purchased material when this is necessary to put it into usable form. For example, the organization chart in Figure 4–11 indicates that the materials manager is responsible not only for purchasing and stores but also for central supply, the laundry, and the print shop. Each of these departments is a manufacturing operation in the economic sense. Central supply sterilizes dressings and other supplies that must be free from bacterial contamination. The laundry and print shop represent "make" decisions for goods and services that

FIGURE 4–11

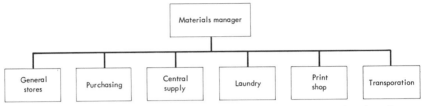

Materials management in a large hospital might embrace not only the obvious supply functions but also the hospital's "manufacturing" operations. In this example, these are the print shop and the laundry.

would otherwise be purchased and are linked to materials management organization both because of this complementary relationship to purchasing and because there is no other organizational niche in the hospital that is more compatible than materials management.

Materials management control of transportation is also partly a matter of organizational convenience. Transportation obviously does not belong in such hospital departments as nursing, dietary, and accounting. It fits in with materials management more closely than any other major activity in the hospital, and, in fact, there is a direct relationship between the hospital transportation function and the stores activities. The stores department is normally responsible for delivering materials from the storeroom to nursing stations throughout the hospital. In some hospitals, the stores facilities may be located some distance from the hospital premises—either because the hospital is already overcrowded or because warehouse space can be rented off the hospital site at much lower cost than buildings can be constructed on the site. The materials manager with an off-premises storeroom cannot possibly operate without at least one delivery truck, and typically he finds himself in charge of all of the hospital's automotive and materials-handling equipment. In this way, the materials manager can become responsible for all hospital activities relating to transportation, including such things as the hospital's internal message and mail service.

Other activities even more peripheral to transportation and materials management may eventually be included. For example, the materials manager of at least one hospital is in charge of the male orderlies who work on the nursing floors. Normally, the orderlies would report to various head nurses, but this tends to make the orderly's job a dead end for a responsible person interested in a career. The male orderly who helps the nurses cannot become a nurse himself without going through a professional training program and, in addition, an overwhelming majority of nurses are women. In contrast, an orderly who is attached to materials management need not have a dead-end job. As he gains experience he can be promoted to a clerical position in central supply or another materials management activity.

THE DECENTRALIZED ORGANIZATION

As the above examples illustrate, the materials management organization is flexible and can be adapted to suit the specialized needs of any profit or nonprofit institution. Any of the organizational forms discussed can also be expanded almost indefinitely to fit very large as well as smaller institutions.

The expansion process is quite simple. Each supervisor adds subordinates until the limits of his span of control are reached. Then another layer of supervision is added. When these new supervisors reach the limits of their span of control, still another layer of supervision is added.

For example, the purchasing department at Avco's Lycoming Division (see Figue 4–8 above) can be doubled by increasing the purchasing manager's span of supervision from two purchasing agents to four. It could be redoubled by adding a new level of supervision. Each purchasing agent would hire two assistant purchasing agents, each of whom would supervise a department identical to that formerly supervised directly by the purchasing agent.

Many small firms have grown to giant corporations by following this process. Eventually they may wind up with an organization 12 or 13 levels deep. The organization becomes cumbersome and bureaucratic. It responds slowly to change, and there is ample red tape in even the simplest transactions.

Managements of giant corporations lick the problem of size with decentralization. They break up the corporation into a number of smaller divisional units, each of which operates as a semiindependent business. Decentralization has many advantages. It brings managers closer to the objectives of the business, permits tigher control of costs, and provides a better environment for training future managers. It also helps stimulate improvements in products and methods.

Diluted buying power. Decentralization, however, creates a major materials management pi·oblem: diluted buying power. One of the advantages of a big corporation over a smaller one is its greater buying power. Big buyers can purchase in carload lots; in some cases they can buy a major proportion of or even the total output of supplier factories. With this buying power, they can get big price concessions. In addition, vendors often provide superior quality, delivery, and service to their very biggest customers.

With decentralization, management faces a dilemma. Should it go only part way and continue to have a headquarters buying staff responsible for all major purchases? Or should it completely decentralize the materials activities along with the rest of the organization? With the former approach, it preserves its buying power. With the latter, it gives the managers of the decentralized "little businesses" authority over all phases of their operations, including materials management. This is consistent with the management principle that you cannot hold a manager responisble for profits unless he has authority over all phases of his operation.

Only a few giant corporations operate with a single, highly centralized buying department. A few others are highly decentralized, with a number of buying departments completely independent of one another. Usually corporations that use similar or identical parts or materials at a number of plants tend to have a centralized buying organization to exploit their buying power. For example, most chemical, steel, and petroleum companies have a centralized buying organization, both to permit corporationwide buying of key raw materials and to facilitate handling of reciprocity problems. On the other hand, those that make a number of products with little resemblance to one another tend to have a decentralized buying organization. Good examples are the Borg-Warner Corporation and American Machine & Foundry. Both companies have buying departments in each of their divisions that operate independently. It is significant that both make a wide variety of products, most of which are unrelated to one another in terms of technology and markets.

Staff-and-line approach

Most major companies compromise: they try to get the advantages of both centralization and decentralization. They do this with the so-called "staff-and-line" approach (see Figure 4–12). At the top of the materials management organization is a corporate staff, often headed by a corporate director of purchases or materials manager. At this level, division of responsibility is by function. The materials manager, who often is a vice president, reports to the president or executive vice president. Usually strictly a staff executive, he is responsible for overall materials policies and plans but has no responsibility for the basic line activities of materials management.

Directly responsible for line activities are materials managers in each plant or division. These managers usually do not report to the corporate materials executive, although they do rely on him for advice on corporate-wide buying policies and procedures and for assistance on special problems. They report directly to the general managers of their respective plants or divisions, which is consistent with the principle of making the general managers responsible for every phase of their job.

With the staff-and-line organization, most of the advantages of centralized buying are preserved. The corporate purchasing staff is able to consolidate purchases of all items used by a number of plants in order to get the lowest possible prices. Usually it makes overall contracts directly; occasionally it restricts itself only to making available information on savings that might be made if the plants choose to pool their buying power.

FIGURE 4–12
Staff-and-line organizations

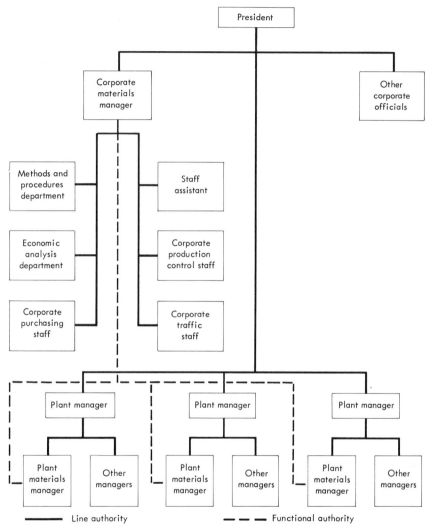

The staff-and-line approach to organization is widely used in very large corporations. A corporate materials manager coordinates policy and functionally supervises plant materials managers, who report directly to their respective plant managers.

Materials staffs' activities

Although the corporate materials manager in a big corporation does not supervise the plant materials managers directly, he usually has a small staff under his direct supervision. The staff provides specialized services to both the plant materials managers and top management.

Among its major services are value analysis, administrative planning, economic analysis, and electronic data processing.

Value analysis.   Value analysis refers to a series of techniques that are designed to reduce costs. The value analyst is a specialist with substantial training in engineering, cost estimating, and manufacturing methods. He assists buyers and others in the materials organization with cost-reduction projects.

Administrative planning.   The overall materials cycle is complex. Procedures, policies, and organization structures must be planned carefully. Records must be kept of the performance of every materials executive in every plant. Training programs must be administered. Budgetary controls are necessary. All these jobs and many others can be handled by a competent administrative assistant to the materials manager.

Economic analysis.   When and how much should a company buy? How much inventory should it carry? The answers to these questions depend on more than just the company's internal costs. They depend also on the external economic environment and on the trend of both overall and individual prices and costs. Economic analysis is essential in modern materials management, and a staff economist or statistician can provide invaluable assistance to the materials manager. (Specific applications of economic analysis to materials management are discussed in more detail in Chapter 6.)

Electronic data processing.   It is a rare materials organization that has its own computer or even does it own programming. These responsibilities are usually delegated for the entire organization to a specialized department on the controller's staff. Nevertheless, an increasing number of materials managers have at least one computer specialist on their staff who combines knowledge of computers with materials management. This specialist can work out computer problems and also suggest new EDP applications for materials management.

Other specialists.   These four types of staff specialist are the most common in industrial materials organizations. However, there are many others. A staff specialist on "trade relations" (i.e., reciprocity) is quite common in industrial purchasing departments. He works closely with the company's sales department and helps determine policies governing how far the company will extend itself in making purchases from suppliers who are also customers.

A number of big companies with thousands of suppliers have staff specialists handling vendor-relations problems. These specialists investigate complaints from suppliers who feel they have not been treated fairly by company buyers and also do everything they can to bolster supplier goodwill.

Many large companies find it convenient to have field expediters in key cities where there are a number of suppliers. These specialists expedite items in short supply for any buyer requesting their services. They investigate new suppliers, and they also help to get information about quality problems. Because they serve the entire materials department, they must report directly to the director of materials management or to one of his immediate assistants.

Results of staff-and-line organization

Breaking a department into line and staff activities provides additional functional specialization. Skilled specialists can be hired to serve the entire materials department. In addition, staff work provides excellent training for high-potential junior executives. They can be exposed to top-level decision making without the company's having to suffer the consequences of their mistakes.

The staff executive almost always has problems. To get anything done, he must work through line personnel and persuade them to cooperate. With strong staff men, dual subordination frequently results, that is, the line supervisor winds up reporting to both a staff executive and a line executive. Some writers on management charge that since staff has no real responsibility to contribute directly to the objectives of the business, it is inherently wasteful.

THE ORGANIZATION OF THE FUTURE

Staff specialists are useful, and there will always be a need for them, especially in large materials organizations. But I believe there will be a smaller staff in future materials organizations. In fact, as is discussed in greater detail in Chapter 21, the centralized materials management department in the large corporation seems to be fading away. Materials management is increasingly becoming a divisional-level activity in large organizations. The divisional materials manager reports either directly to the division's general manager or to some other manager who, in turn, reports to the general manager. Among manufacturing companies, about half of the divisional materials managers report (not through any choice of their own) to the manufacturing manager, while most of the others report to the general manager. Their organization structures resemble those illustrated in this chapter, with variations that primarily reflect differences in industry.

Cases

CASE 4–1. ALABAMA AIRCRAFT CORPORATION

Organizing for a new product line

Alabama Aircraft Corporation was founded in 1928. It has always specialized in fighter planes for the U.S. Air Force, and its products served the country well in both World War II and the Korean War. By 1959, the company employed 8,000 workers and its sales were almost $200 million. The company now faces one of the major turning points in its history. New orders for military aircraft are off sharply because of the growing use of missiles instead of fighter planes. Although the company may continue to produce airplanes indefinitely, management doubts that its airplane business will ever be as good as it once was. Missile orders will take up part of the slack, but the company will still be left with a tremendous unused investment in facilities and equipment to fabricate aluminum and steel.

Fortunately, the company's engineers had some advance warning of this problem and have been working for several years on a host of new products designed to fill the gap left by a slowdown of the aircraft business. Among these products are prefabricated aluminum highway bridges, house trailers, and a line of aluminum boats.

Alabama's marketing department expects that these new products will account for 25 percent of the company's sales volume almost immediately and will ultimately account for as much as 50 percent. The company already has substantial contracts with distributors and mail-order houses for some of these products, and it is convinced that the others will gain rapid acceptance. It anticipates few problems in selling products as long as its prices are competitive, but costs are a major problem. The company is used to producing aircraft-quality components where it would willingly pay as much as $1 for a simple bolt manufactured to aircraft standards. Now it must manufacture to entirely different standards and cannot afford to spend more than 5 cents for a bolt that would superficially look not much different from an aircraft bolt even if it were made from lower cost materials to looser tolerances.

Harry Spooner, the company's materials manager, anticipates that an entirely different approach to materials management may be necessary if the company is to keep its costs in line. He believes that an entirely different group of suppliers may be needed for the company's new civilian products. Aircraft suppliers are used to such high-quality standards that they may not be able to cut prices enough to compete for civilian business.

Spooner is also apprehensive about quality problems on the new line. He fears that Alabama's quality-control department is so indoctrinated with aircraft quality standards that it will reject components from his new suppliers. He knows that although instruments can be used to measure quality objectively on certain dimensions, quality is at least partly a matter of the inspector's judgment. If inspectors apply their aircraft background to civilian parts, they may set such high standards that Spooner will be forced to pay higher prices. Since purchases will comprise about 60 cents out of every sales dollar on the civilian line (about the same ratio as the military line), obviously the company cannot afford to pay higher prices for components than its competitiors do. On the other hand, if the company's inspectors set realistic quality standards for the new products, they may get too lax for the company's military line.

Spooner is responsible to management for meeting cost objectives on the new product line. However, he is virtually at the mercy of the quality control department in achieving them, since with a high reject rate he will have to insist that vendors institute more rigid controls over their manufacturing processes and inspect outgoing shipments more carefully. Inevitably, he will have to pay for this extra work.

Spooner believes that the best solution to the problem is to set up a separate receiving inspection department under his control that is staffed with inspectors who will work exclusively on the new product line. Currently, Spooner has a conventional materials organization. Reporting to him are managers of traffic, production control, and purchasing. The traffic department, the smallest of the three, has six transportation specialists working on routing, tracing shipments, and so on. In addition, the traffic manager supervises a foreman, who in turn supervises the company's trucks and drivers. The production control manager has seven supervisors reporting directly to him. One supervises shipping, receiving, and nonproduction storerooms; others supervise production raw materials, purchased parts, and a "bond room" in which parts are stored after they have passed inspection; and there is a supervisor in charge of in-process materials in each of the plant's main manufacturing areas. The purchasing agent supervises five senior buyers, each of whom specializes in a given group of commodities. Working for each senior buyer are three to six buyers, each of whom supervises an expediter and a secretary.

While Spooner is convinced that receiving inspection for the new line should be under his jurisdiction rather than that of the company's quality control manager, he is less certain about how he should reorganize his department to handle the new product line. Moreover, he believes that changes will be necessary, particularly in the purchasing department, where he would like buyers to be more price-conscious on the new line.

Questions

1. Should management accept Spooner's recommendation that a new receiving inspection department be established for the new line and be put under the materials manager's jurisdiction? What are the pros and cons? What are the alternatives?

2. How should the materials department be reorganized to cope with the new product? Support your recommendation with a new organization chart.

CASE 4–2. ALBERT ELECTRONICS CORPORATION

Centralized versus decentralized materials management

Albert Electronics is a New England firm that has gradually grown until it presently operates more than 20 plants from coast to coast. Last year's sales were more than $200 million, up 10 percent from the previous year. The company has hit a new sales record in nine of the last ten years, but profits have not kept pace. The company earned nearly $8 million after taxes six year ago, when its sales were only $100 million. Last year it earned only $10 million. A 100 percent increase in sales has brought a mere 20 percent increase in profits during a period when the company has also almost doubled its investment in plant and equipment.

This year the outlook is even bleaker. Dan Watson, vice president in charge of finance, predicts that profits will actually drop off a little even though sales are scheduled to rise to about $220 million. In addition, the company going to need more money to finance the extra inventories required by expanded sales. Current inventories total about $24 million. Watson estimates that they will give rise to $27 million, and the company's cash position will tighten so much that it will have to draw on its line of credit at several large banks.

The company has grown so rapidly that it has been forced to rely on outside suppliers for an abnormally large part—68 percent—of its sales dollar. It has a small top-management staff consisting of a president, two executive vice presidents, vice presidents in charge of sales, engineering, manufacturing, personnel, and finance, and a small group to assist these top officials. The two executive vice presidents each supervise 10 of the company' 20 plant managers. The other vice presidents have no direct responsibility for operations but serve primarily in an advisory and policy-making capacity in their specialities.

Each of the company's plants is responsible for making its own purchases. Organizations within the plants vary, since Karl Albert, the founder of the company, believes in giving his plant managers maximum autonomy so long as they achieve their profit objectives. In most cases the plant materials management job is divided among a purchasing department, a traffic department, and a production control department. Typically the purchasing agent reports directly to the plant manager, while the production control manager and the traffic manager report to the plant's manufacturing manager. However, in the largest plant (the Cleveland Works), which has a purchase volume of nearly $50 million, there is a materials manager who reports to the plant manager. This materials manager supervises separate production control, purchasing, and traffic departments.

No formal efforts are made to coordinate companywide purchases.

However, the Cleveland Works materials manager has made some informal efforts. Because his volume is so much greater than that of any other plant, he can sometimes get special concessions from suppliers on various mill supplies and other nonproduction materials. When he gets an especially good deal, he sends a memo to the purchasing agents of the other plants so they can call the supplier and demand the same terms on the basis of being part of the same corporation as the Cleveland Works. No one knows how many plant purchasing agents have taken advantage of these occasional opportunities.

Albert is becoming concerned because, while the company is successful in expanding its sales, its profit margin has gotten progressively narrower and now even total profits are threatening to drop off. He has engaged Merrill, Johnson & Connors, management engineers, to study the problem. In its preliminary report, Merrill, Johnson & Connors has suggested that a detailed study be made of the company's purchasing operations. Since the company spends nearly $140 million on purchases, it pointed out that relatively small improvements in this area can have a considerable effect on the company's overall profits. It believes that substantial savings could be made by consolidating purchases of certain materials.

Questions

1. Suppose you were a consultant working for Merrill, Johnson & Connors. What changes would you recommend in Albert Electronics's approach to purchasing?

2. Draw a new organization chart in which you show your suggested changes in the purchasing organization.

3. Compare the relative merits of the present completely decentralized purchasing organization at Albert Electronics with those of a completely centralized organization.

CASE 4–3. GENERAL ELECTRIC LARGE JET ENGINE DEPARTMENT

Reorganization resulting from work distribution analysis

Like other organizations, that of the materials department of the Large Jet Engine Division of the General Electric Company in Evendale, Ohio, has been changed periodically to reflect changes in work load, product mix, and other factors. By 1964, the organization shown in Figure 4–9 on page 109 had been modified somewhat, as indicated below in Figure 4–13. The organization continued to be basically by product, with each purchasing manager responsible for all materials functions on a group of commodities. The purchasing managers served two main "cus-

FIGURE 4-13

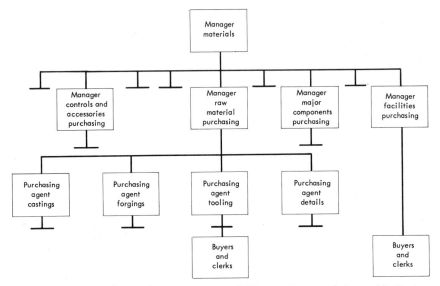

Organization of purchasing function at General Electric Company's Large Jet Engine Department in 1964, before work distribution analysis, was designed to serve two main "customers"—the assembly and the spare parts groups.

tomers"—the assembly and the spare parts groups. Each of the "customers" initiated its own requests for supplies and had its own follow-up and reporting procedure. Both ordered many of the same parts, which were processsed through the same purchasing routine at different times.

As one of GE–Evendale's managers recalls, "It had been obvious for some time that the purchasing operation had a problem. Everyone was very busy, but there just didn't seem to be enough time to get all the work done. Some of the buyers and purchasing agents were putting in a great deal of casual overtime. Most of this was spent catching up on paper work they couldn't get done during the normal working day when they were tied up with too many unscheduled dealings with people—at their desks, on the telephone, or in the receiving inspection areas."

The materials manager was aware of the problem and was planning improvements, but nothing could be done without first measuring the magnitude of the problem. So, the industrial engineering department was requested to make a classified work distribution analysis[1] of purchasing agents and buyers.

Before making the analysis, the industrial engineering department studied the department and classified its work into four basic categories:

---

[1] This is basically an application of the work-sampling techniques described in Chapter 20.

functions, activities, subjects and "who." Fortunately, one of the industrial engineers had once worked in purchasing and was able to define the operation accurately. Detailed breakdown of the department's work is shown in Fig. 4–14. Tasks, the smallest division of a work element,

FIGURE 4–14
Work classification used in GE purchasing study

TASKS	SUBJECTS	FUNCTIONS
Writing	Costs	Developing new
Paper	Delivery	sources
Forms	Quality	Quotes and order
Records	Quantity	Placement
Other	Labor	Negotiation
Walking	Design	Purchase order
Sorting or filing	Material	fulfillment
Getting out or	Facilities	Revision
putting away	Manpower	Shipping, receiving,
Other manual	General	inspection, storing
Reading		Closing the order
Forms		Keeping the supervisor
Correspondence		informed
Records		Measurement
EDP reports		Estimates and forecasts
Literature		Cost reductions
Drawings	ACTIVITIES	Policies
Specifications	Analyzing	Presentation and
Other visual tasks	Planning	communication
Discussion	Follow-up	Maintaining relationships
	Expediting	Job administration
NONPRODUCTIVE	Auditing	
TIME	Getting information	
Out of area	Guiding	
Delay	Interviewing	
Physically inactive	Documenting	

are also included in Fig. 4–14. Tasks are defined as purely physical operations while activities are methods used to perform the job—i.e., they are the "what" portion of the work element.

The materials manager then called a meeting of his staff to explain why the study was being done. He pointed out that observations would be made at random intervals, emphasizing that measurement of individual performance was not being undertaken for disciplinary reasons. This meeting helped keep resistance to the study to a minimum, and the actual work sampling of the participants presented no great problem.

Everyone was provided with a list of job definitions. In addition, there was a three-day trial run before the study began, to educate both observers and participants. This was done because experience showed that there were always situations in the work-sampling data collection period that required some clarification. For example, should waiting for a long-distance phone call be recorded as "discussion—phone," "delay," or "physically inactive"? Different observers might not make an identical interpretation. It was necessary, of course, to agree on a consistent classification of these and other operations.

The purchasing operation was subdivided into three areas, each of which contained roughly equal numbers of personnel who were grouped logically according to organizational lines. Three industrial engineers made 16 trips per day through the department, at predetermined random times. They recorded their observations of the sampled tasks. Buyers and purchasing agents were also interviewed to get data for the functions, activities, and "who" categories. When they were not in the area, the observer left a form behind on their desks to be filled out and picked up on the next round. The study continued for three weeks during regular working hours, with data being tabulated manually by observers between trips.

In processing the data, observations were converted to percentages for each item in each category. Tabulations were broken down by buyer, purchasing-agent group, subunit and unit, as well as for the entire purchasing group. Data for each category were compared. The objective was to detect imbalance, overemphasis, insufficient attention, or questionable totals in the work distribution.

Comparisons that proved significant were incorporated into the final report, which also included questions designed to guide supervisors in making their own analyses of the data. The industrial engineers had already analyzed the data, but they believed that their conclusions would carry more weight if the supervisor arrived at them as a result of his own analysis.

The basic analysis procedure was to challenge each comparison in each work element category by asking "what" and "why." Personnel comparisons were analyzed similarly by asking "where," "when," and "who." Finally, overall comparisons of classifications led to "how" questions. This process raised such questions as:

1. What is a reasonable amount of time compared to its importance in the results obtained?
2. Why are buyers keeping so many personal records on order status?
3. Who is the proper person to do this? All of it or special situations only?

The next step in the study was development of a standard of comparison for the work-sampling data. This was done by having purchasing agents rank the relative importance of each activity observed. These opinions were then compared with actual data. The device used to get the purchasing agent's opinion was called a "tale-tell" work element ranking chart. Each work element is listed on the chart and compared with some other element. The subject chooses one element from each pair and records the number on the chart. The element recorded most often gets the highest rating.

Findings from the tale-tell survey showed little correlation between the activities purchasing agents believed to be most important and those on which they spent most of their time. The survey showed that the most important activities were analyzing, expediting, planning, and follow-up. Most of the time, however, was actually spent on guiding and interviewing, analyzing, and expediting. Overall correlation was about 12 percent. On actual versus estimated time consumption there was better correlation—45 percent.

The industrial engineering department prepared charts showing the average work day of a buyer and of a purchasing agent and also made lists showing which units spent the most or least time on various work elements. It was stressed that "most" did not necessarily indicate best or worst; it merely pointed up the need to ask "why." Time distribution data was converted to dollars of salary in order to emphasize the cost of the various operations. These charts made a substantial impact when they were presented. For example, they revealed that it cost the purchasing department $21,200 worth of salaries for time spent giving "guidance and counsel on incoming phone calls" and $30,000 per year for "delivery work out of the area." One of the most expensive operations was "discussion with another person." This cost $113,000 per year.

The industrial engineering department then prepared a flip-chart presentation showing highlights of the study. This was given first to the materials manager and the purchasing managers and then presented again to each purchasing manager and his staff of purchasing agents. The industrial engineers pointed out that purchasing is a "delivery-oriented organization." The department studied had an extremely heavy communications work load, taking information from customer and vendor, swirling it round and round within itself, sometimes changing its form in the process, and then spieling it out again, mainly to customer and vendor. Most of this communication was concerned with delivery or lack of it.

The presentation also emphasized that interruptions were part of the daily work routine in the purchasing department. It was rarely possible for a buyer to complete one job without being interrupted either by the telephone, his supervisor, a clerk, or a supplier representative. As a result of all these interruptions, the preparation stages of the purchasing cycle seemed to be getting shortchanged. Very little time was being spent in the functions of developing new sources, negotiations and quotes, and order placement. The bulk was being spent instead on administrative functions such as purchase order fulfillment.

The study also compared the purchasing agents' official position description with their actual job performance. The formal descriptions indicated that the purchasing agents were supposed to be actively engaged in the buying process, assisting buyers and clerks in making buying decisions. In practice, however, the purchasing agent was spending almost all of his time on direct supervision and doing very little buying as such. What they did consisted mostly of fighting fires when buyers and clerks needed help.

Accordingly, it was recommended that one way to solve the problem might be to redefine the purchasing agent's job so that he was responsible for supervision only—with buyers actually being held responsible for getting the job done. Another possibility was that the purchasing agent be given specific responsibilities different from those of the buyer for whom they would still provide guidance. For example, the purchasing agents could conceivably be assigned responsibility for buying a few key items themselves and, in addition, would continue to supervise and assist their buyers on other items.

If the purchasing agents were relieved completely of functional responsibilities, their span of control could conceivably be widened, that is, they could supervise more buyers. On the other hand, if the purchasing agents undertook to buy a number of important items, their span of control would be reduced; it is even possible that their span of control would be eliminated entirely by doing away with their level of organization. Buyers—including some of the former purchasing agents—would then report directly to various managers of purchasing.

Questions

1. To what extent might GE Large Jet Engine's problems be a product of its organization structure—as distinct from its procedures or personnel?

2. What changes if any would you recommend in GE Large Jet Engine's materials organization as a result of the work distribution study?

5

Legal aspects of materials management

THE LAW OF AGENCY permits a materials manager, purchasing agent, or buyer to act as his company's agent in making contracts; his word or signature can be a binding contract for the company. Although he may make thousands of contracts, he is not a lawyer. *Specific legal problems on purchase contracts should always be reviewed by company attorneys.* Every nonroutine agreement should have the approval of the buyer's legal staff. In addition, lawyers, not materials managers, should draft all of the clauses used for routine purchases. Fortunately, there is no need to have a lawyer sitting in on every negotiating session. The subsequent written agreement that results from the conversation can be reviewed by the lawyer, if necessary. The written purchase contract will always take precedence over the oral one, even if it is substantially different.

BASICS OF CONTRACTS

Each purchase order that the materials manager approves is a contract. The materials manager can readily get advice from the company's legal staff on any special problems that arise. But since he does approve more than 99 percent of the contracts into which his company enters, he should be familiar with the general principles of contract law.

The basic steps in making a purchase contract are quite simple:

1. Each verbal or written quotation by a supplier is an offer to sell, which is usually subject to acceptance at the time the buyer issues the purchase order.
2. Each purchase order either is an acceptance of the seller's offer

or, if its terms and conditions differ somewhat from the supplier's quotation, is in effect a counteroffer.

3. Each acknowledgment of a purchase order by the seller confirms the contract and makes it binding, provided that the seller accepts all of the terms and conditions of the order. If the seller takes exception to any of them, he is in effect making a counteroffer, which must be accepted by the buyer before the contract is binding. If the seller does not acknowledge the order formally, he does so informally when he complies with its terms and ships the goods or services the order calls for.

4. Every purchase order change subsequently agreed to by buyer and seller becomes a part of the purchase contract.

Possible disputes

Many firms follow the procedure outlined above almost unwittingly year after year. About 40 percent of all manufacturing companies do not even bother to include any terms and conditions in their purchase orders.[1] They don't worry about legal "fine points," and they never have any problems. Any misunderstandings that arise are worked out in friendly negotiation with suppliers. While lawsuits involving buyers and sellers are common in commercial transactions, they are surprisingly rare in industrial purchasing. In most cases, industrial purchasing agents and their suppliers can amicably resolve their disputes.

Arbitration. If agreement fails, they may call on an impartial arbitrator for help, selecting him from detailed listings supplied by the American Arbitration Association. The arbitrator is sometimes an attorney but, in many cases, is simply an unbiased expert who has had substantial experience with problems similar to the issue in dispute. An arbitration hearing resembles a lawsuit in that both parties present arguments, and they are often represented by attorneys.[2] However, arbitration is both cheaper and faster than a lawsuit. The hearings are not public, so trade secrets can be protected. In addition, complicated commercial problems can often be settled more equitably if they are reviewed by a technically qualified arbitrator than would be possible in a lawsuit where neither judge nor jury would have the technical qualifications needed for an objective evaluation of the case.

Under common law, however, the ruling of an arbitrator is not binding, and either party may still sue if he is not satisfied with the arbitrator's ruling. However, common law has been superseded by arbitration statutes in almost all of the major industrial states. The statutes make the arbitrator's ruling legally binding on both parties once they agree to

---

[1] "How Legal Should Purchase Orders Be?" *Purchasing*, May 11, 1959, p. 11.

[2] A more detailed explanation of arbitration procedures is incorporated in Case 5–3.

submit their cases to an arbitrator who is mutually acceptable. Agreement to arbitrate may be reached on a case-by-case basis, but many firms include an arbitration clause in their purchase contracts. The following standard arbitration clause is recommended by the American Arbitration Association:

> Any controversy or claim arising out of or relating to this contract, or the breach thereof, shall be settled by arbitration in accordance with the Rules of the American Arbitration Association, and judgment upon the award rendered by the Arbitrator(s) may be entered in any Court having jurisdiction thereof.

Disputes with government. Contract disputes involving the federal government may also be arbitrated if both parties agree. In fact, the federal government's approach to procurement is necessarily much more legalistic than that of private firms. Procurement officials are governed by thousands of regulations (the Armed Services Procurement Regulations alone consist of more than 3,000 pages), and their every action must be within the precise letter of the law. Contractors sometimes find to their dismay that government agencies refuse to relax even the most insignificant regulations. For example, if a government invitation to bid has a deadline of noon June 21, then the firm that delivers its bid at 12:01 P.M. may find itself out of luck even if it is the low bidder.

Law of agency

A private firm need not be so inflexible. Some purchasing agents and materials managers in private companies, however, may be too lax about the legal aspects of their jobs. It is important that every company define the terms and conditions of each purchase contract as precisely as possible, not only to prevent misunderstanding but also to protect the company from potential liabilities.

Delegated authority. Basic authority for the acts of the purchasing agent and materials manager is derived from the law of agency, which, as noted above, gives the purchasing agent and the sales manager authority to act for the corporation, a legally separate entity. For example, if a purchasing agent agrees to purchase a ton of sheet steel from a supplier, the purchasing agent's employer—not the purchasing agent himself—is legally obliged to buy the steel. In fact, the company may be liable for a purchasing agent's actions even though they were not carried out with the approval of the company's top management. For example, if a purchasing agent committed his company for a ton of steel it neither needed nor wanted, the company could still be held to the contract as long as the supplier acted in good faith. If the company refused to perform in accordance with the contract, the supplier would have legal recourse against the company but not against the purchasing agent, to whom the company delegated its power to enter into contracts in accordance with the law of agency.

Big companies usually establish internal procedures so that the power to act as buying agent is not delegated too freely among the members of a large purchasing department. Typically, the procedure places dollar limits on the buying power of various organizational levels within the purchasing department. For example, one big company permits its assistant purchasing agent to commit the company for as much as $25,000. Orders in the $25,000 to $50,000 range must be signed by the purchasing agent; those in the $50,000 to $100,000 category by the vice president of purchases; and those over $100,000 must carry the signature of the company's chief executive officer.

A company may wish to protect itself against commitments by lower echelon purchasing personnel by notifying suppliers that only certain persons have been delegated the power of agency. In practice, this is not often necessary. Lower level purchasing personnel obey the rules anyway, and suppliers are usually well informed on the real sources of buying authority.

Salesman not agent. In dealing with their suppliers, purchasing personnel must exercise a degree of care. They cannot assume that the members of the supplier's sales organization with whom they deal are legitimate agents who can act in the supplier's name. In fact, salesmen who actually call on customers do not usually have this power. If a salesman tells a buyer that "we will deliver on June 15 and our price will be $19.22," he probably is not committing the supplier to these conditions. The buyer should assume that he actually has a binding contract only when the deal he has negotiated with the salesman is confirmed by the supplier's sales manager or some higher official.

Offer and acceptance

Under common law, a verbal agreement is perfectly binding on both the buying and selling corporations if agreement is reached between lawfully authorized agents. However, the common law which has evolved through precedent is often modified by legislation. Usually this legislation is at state level. As a result, companies that buy and sell on a national basis must be familiar with the laws of all 50 states. The Uniform Sales Act was drafted many years ago in order to prevent commerce from being unduly inhibited by conflicting statutes among the various states. It was followed by the Uniform Commercial Code in 1951. Most provisions of the code have now been adopted by almost every state, so laws regulating basic business transactions are now reasonably uniform throughout the nation.

When contract begins. The code and the act make major changes in the conditions under which a contract offer and acceptance are legally binding. Under common law, all verbal agreements between authorized parties are perfectly binding. The Uniform Commercial Code states that a contract of $500 or more must be in writing to be enforceable.

Under common law, a contract does not exist until seller makes an offer and buyer accepts it. Offer and acceptance must agree in every particular. For example, suppose a supplier offers a particular item for delivery within three weeks of receipt of order for price in effect at time of delivery. Buyer issues a purchase order on June 1 calling for delivery by July 1 at a price of $3. At this stage, there is no contract under common law, since buyer's acceptance does not correspond with seller's offer. As long as the seller did not agree with what in effect was a counteroffer, neither buyer nor seller is bound by the purchase order.

Under the Uniform Commercial Code, a contract would exist as long as both buyer and seller behaved as if there were a contract. For example, suppose that the seller went ahead when he received the purchase order and then the buyer changed his mind and canceled the order. Under common law, the buyer might not be liable for any work that was done under the order, since no contract existed. Under the Uniform Commerical Code, a contract would exist since both parties behaved that way—the buyer when he issued the order and the seller when he started to work on it.

Period of offer. The code also defines the period in which an offer may remain open. Under common law, there is no problem if seller places a specific time limit on his offer. For example, his quotation might indicate: "This offer not binding on seller unless accepted by seller within 30 days of date of offer." In this case, seller need not honor buyer's acceptance on July 2 of an offer made on June 1.

The case gets murkier if seller's offer has no particular expiration date. For example, suppose you get an offer dated July 1 that has no expiration date. If you accept this offer within a few days, it is reasonable to assume that you have a binding contract, but, obviously, you cannot hold the supplier's offer and accept it five years later. Problems arise from offers that have been open an unreasonable period of time in seller's opinion but a reasonable time in the opinion of the buyer. The Uniform Commercial Code helps provide a definition of what is "reasonable." If seller specifies no time limit, the code says that the offer can be assumed firm for a "reasonable" period of time, not to exceed three months.

Offer and acceptance never pose any legal problems as long as buyer and seller agree explicitly on all terms and conditions. Buyer should examine seller's proposal carefully and object in writing to terms he finds unsatisfactory. He may also include a clause on his purchase order which states that acceptance of seller's offer is conditional and limited by terms and conditions of buyer's purchase order.

Cancellation. For example, suppose that seller's proposal includes a clause permitting seller to cancel an order without penalty due to "causes beyond his control." The buyer would be out of luck if he simply issued a purchase order and then the supplier failed to deliver because of a strike. Under the Uniform Commercial Code, a court would hold that the buyer tacitly accepted the supplier's delivery clause as long as he did not object to it specifically in writing. A general clause on the back of the purchase order that binds seller to deliver on the required date and makes delivery an essential part of the contract would probably shift the burden of proof from buyer to seller. That is, the seller would have to prove why he shouldn't be liable for damages suffered by the buyer because of inability to deliver on schedule.

Sometimes, purchase order offer and acceptance become a battle of forms that is never really resolved until the merchandise is shipped and accepted by the buyer's quality control department. For example, I once worked in a defense plant where all purchase orders had to be approved by an Air Force contracting officer. At the contracting officer's insistence, a purchase order for steel was issued on a fixed-price basis: if the supplier quoted $6 per cwt. for the steel this was all he could charge. There would have been no problem if this had been acceptable to the supplier, but supplier's offers always indicated that adjustment could be made to "price in effect at time at delivery."[3] In addition, the supplier always took specific exception to the fixed-price provision in the purchase order. The buyer tried to persuade the supplier to accept a fixed price, but he refused. The contracting officer also was adamant and refused to accept the seller's terms. So there was really no binding contract, although in practice the supplier went ahead and shipped the order anyway. Fortunately, the price did not change, so there was no problem. Had there been a price increase, the buyer would have been forced to issue a new order at the higher price if he wanted the material.

---

[3] When a company quotes "price in effect at time of delivery," it charges the prevailing market price at the time of shipment. Producers of raw materials almost always sell on this basis, and the practice is logical for commodities whose price is determined by impersonal supply and demand forces. However, many purchasing officers feel that steel and aluminum should not be priced on this basis, since prices for these products are set by conscious acts of producers, not by an impersonal market. However, steel and aluminum producers defend the practice. They point out that with any other system of pricing, they would temporarily be selling the same commodity at different prices. For example, suppose that the price of a particular type of steel was increased from $6.00 per cwt. to $6.20, effective April 1. With price in effect at time of delivery, all shipments made after March 31 would be invoiced at the higher price. This would not be true if a steel company accepted fixed-price orders. The higher price would be effective only on new orders, and there would be an interim period in which the company was simultaneously shipping orders at the new price and those placed prior to April 1 at the old price. For example, on July 2, the steel company might ship one order placed on March 31 at the old price and another placed on April 1 at the new price.

PRICING

Price hardly ever poses any legal problems on goods that are available for immediate delivery. The transaction is simple and straightforward. Buyer indicates quantity desired and price[4] on the order. Vendor ships and bills. Sometimes the contract is completed before it is even formalized in writing. Buyer telephones supplier, giving him essential details and advising that he will issue a formal purchase order. Vendor ships and then bills after he has received the purchase order.

Changing prices. Legal problems in pricing are likely to arise when delivery is not "off the shelf" but must be made some time after the order has been placed. Prices of labor and raw material can change during this period, as can general economic conditions. In addition, if the item is made to order, the supplier's actual costs of production may be either substantially higher or lower than his estimate, so either buyer or seller may wish to change the price on the order. Neither can do so in the absence of mutual agreement or some advance provision that permits change. *A purchase order that has been unqualifiedly accepted by the seller normally legally binds both parties to the prices and quantities shown on the order, unless the order's terms and conditions specifically provide for changes.*

Many companies issue or accept purchase orders for delivery of material over a long period of time, with no provision whatever for change in prices. Occasionally they will negotiate price changes on these orders. In such cases, the provision for change is, in effect, made informally, as a result of a long-established friendly relationship.

Some private companies and all government bodies are more cautious. All orders they issue or accept have provisions for price changes incorporated in them if they anticipate the need for change. Most governments and government prime contractors employ standard provisions determined by regulation, while private firms are more flexible. The terms and conditions they use are limited only by their imagination and their acceptability to suppliers. However, these terms and conditions fall into five general categories: open-end pricing, cost plus, time and material, escalation, and price redetermination.

Open-end pricing. When there is an established free market for a material, it is possible that neither buyer nor seller will want to commit himself to a specific price for a long period of time. The purpose of

---

[4] Many purchasing departments follow the practice of issuing unpriced purchase orders for inexpensive, minor items. The supplier's invoice goes directly to the buyer who placed the order. If the price is consistent with previous prices paid for the material, the buyer approves the invoice. If it is not, he either negotiates with the vendor, or, on rare occasions, returns the material for credit. Although many departments have followed this practice for years without difficulty, this is not good purchasing. For reasons brought out in this chapter, it is always good practice to define every purchase order term and condition as clearly as possible for every purchase.

the contract is to assure a supply of material for some time in the future at the prevailing market price. In such cases, the purchase order need not be priced (although it may be convenient to list the current price for reference purposes). Its terms indicate that the supplier is to charge the "price in effect at time of delivery."

Open-end pricing is used for basic raw materials whose prices are determined on commodity markets by impersonal supply-demand forces. It also is frequently used for other purchases simply because the producers refuse to sell unless there is open-end pricing. Producers of steel, aluminum, and other materials whose prices are not determined on commodity markets insist on open-end pricing. So do most suppliers of patented items.

Buyers avoid open-end pricing whenever possible because it limits their flexibility. With open-end pricing, the supplier gets, in effect, a blank check. In most cases, it is easy to avoid even when buying commodities where price cannot be predicted in advance. In some cases, the price can be tied to some impartial price-reporting service. For example, a copper producer in the Philippines or Indonesia might sell to its American and Japanese customers on the basis of the current spot price for copper quoted on the London Metal Exchange. In other cases, uncertainties affecting price can be resolved by using one of the more specialized contracts discussed in the following paragraphs.

Cost-plus contracts. Sometimes a purchase contract is made for something that is so novel that neither buyer nor seller knows what the cost should be. In such cases, some sort of cost-plus contract may be the only solution. The seller agrees to do the job either at some fixed price per hour of work performed or at his cost plus some extra fee as profit. Such contracts should be avoided whenever possible. Under them, suppliers have little incentive to keep down costs. In fact, waste can even become profitable for the supplier, especially if he can successfully pad his "costs" to include some profit.

When cost-plus contracts are necessary, they should be controlled and circumscribed as closely as possible. Provision should be made for a detailed audit of the supplier's cost. It also is preferable to fix the supplier's profit on such contracts, so that there is no incentive for him to waste time. With a cost plus fixed-fee contract, for example, the supplier would recoup his exact cost plus some predetermined fee. With a straight cost-plus contract, he would recoup his costs plus some percentage profit on cost; the more the supplier spends, the more he makes.

Time and material. Costs can be somewhat more tightly controlled on a time-and-material contract. Typically, the buyer agrees to pay the supplier's material costs plus labor at some predetermined rate per hour. Time-and-material contracts are often used on research and development contracts where neither buyer nor seller knows how long it will take to develop some particular product. Buyer agrees to pay the supplier his actual audited cost of materials plus (in some cases) a modest mark-up for "handling." Seller's profit and overhead are recouped from the hourly rate charged for labor. Typically, the seller will take a markup of about 100 percent on actual labor costs. Thus, an engineering firm that pays its junior engineers $5 per hour will charge $10 per hour in order to recoup overhead and earn a profit.

Needless to say, time-and-material contracts give the seller an incentive to make the job last. In addition, consulting firms (who frequently work on a time-and-material basis) have sometimes been accused of using much of the time paid for by clients in working up proposals to get more business from the client. At least one very big management consulting firm gives its engineers special incentive pay if they can persuade clients to extend the contract.

Time-and-material contracts are probably in the buyer's best interest on jobs where costs are so uncertain that the only alternative would be a fixed-price contract that is heavily padded by seller with allowances for uncertainties. They may also be quite satisfactory for certain professional services where the basic commodity being sold is hours of service. In general, however, time-and-material contracts should be avoided because they do not effectively limit the buyer's costs. They may not be desirable even when some costs are uncertain. For example, most buyers of construction services prefer fixed-price contracts, even though the seller will inevitably give himself sort of contingency allowance when bidding on a particularly tough construction job. The fixed price gives the contractor incentive to overcome his difficulties without delay. A time-and-material contract might make these same obstacles seem almost insurmountable.

Escalation. Almost any long-term contract should have some provision for price change. Escalation clauses in contracts permit adjustment for unforeseen changes in basic costs but otherwise require the seller to stick to his original quotation. A wise buyer (or seller) tries to define the areas of price escalation; otherwise, he is likely to lose all the benefits he hoped to gain from entering into the long-range contract. For example, buyer or seller may invest millions of dollars in plant and equipment on the strength of some long-range contract.[5] Unrestricted escalation can make such investments unprofitable.

Escalation clauses permit a change in price if a key element of cost

---

[5] A classic case is a contract between the Tennessee Valley Authority and the Peabody Coal Co. TVA invested $100,000,000 in a steam-electric generating plant on the strength of a contract with Peabody to supply 65,000,000 tons of coal worth $191,750,000 over a period of 17 years from a nearby mine. TVA's basic reason for locating its plant next to the Peabody mine was the favorable price it had negotiated for the coal. The cost at the beginning was only $2.95 a ton, one fourth less than TVA paid on the average for coal for its other steam plants. Obviously, the contract must have some provision for price escalation because of its long duration. But escalation clauses must also be restrictive; uncontrolled price increases could conceivably raise TVA's costs to the point where its $100,000,000 investment became uneconomic.

changes. Usually this is labor or material cost, or both. Construction contracts often permit escalation if wages paid to the various building-trade workers change. Contracts issued by automobile manufacturers for electric storage batteries, on the other hand, may permit escalation if the prices of the key raw materials (lead and antimony) change. Sometimes escalation is linked to changes in some well-known price index issued by the Bureau of Labor Statistics or some other agency.

To prevent disputes, the formula for escalation should be completely clear. It should be based, whenever possible, on widely available economic information and not upon the seller's internal costs. For example, if there is an escalation clause to cover supplier wage increases, it is best to agree on a price adjustment for each cent-per-hour change in the Bureau of Labor Statistics average wage for the supplier's industry. This not only prevents arguments about the effect of a wage change on a supplier's cost but also gives the supplier an incentive to resist wage increases in collective bargaining that will make his prices higher on future bids.

When it is not feasible to base the escalation on some widely available cost data information and the supplier's individual cost data must be used, then the method whereby costs are determined should be agreed upon in advance. Also, it is usually desirable to have some top limit to escalation incorporated in the contract; 10 to 15 percent of the original price is typical.

Price redetermination. As the term implies, price redetermination clauses permit periodic renegotiation of contract prices. They are broader than escalation clauses, since the change in price is not necessarily tied to a change in wage rates or raw-material costs. The redetermination clause typically permits the price of an item to be changed about once a year, to reflect both changes in basic costs and the supplier's experience in making the item. They are useful for contracts that extend over a long period or for items with which neither buyer nor seller have had much experience.

Price redetermination clauses are most frequently used in military purchasing, but they also have civilian applications. They are particularly useful when a company subcontracts an entire product. For example, a department-store chain may issue a contract for its own brand of lawn mower to a manufacturer. If the supplier has never made lawn mowers before, he may not know precisely what his costs will be. He may also expect to reduce costs after he has more experience with lawn mowers, and costs will be especially low if the lawn mowers sell well. In this case, a price-redetermination contract might be ideal. Sometimes it will include an agreement permitting the buyer to audit the supplier's cost and to recoup any profits in excess of some predetermined percentage of sales. For example, Sears, Roebuck and Company has allowed certain suppliers an 8 percent profit on sales.

Ultimately, every contract is subject to redetermination even if there is no clause that permits it. No buyer who wants an assured source of supply can impose conditions so harsh that the supplier simply cannot meet them and stay in business. For example, the Japanese firm Mitsubishi Shoji had a fixed-price plus escalation contract with Kaiser Resources calling for delivery of millions of tons of coal from a Canadian mine over a period of years. Kaiser then discovered that the price it had agreed to was impossible to meet. In effect, bankruptcy was cheaper. So Mitsubishi had no choice but to renegotiate its seemingly fixed-price contract. Thus the terms of any contract must always be at least more favorable than the legal penalties for nonperformance. Otherwise, they may not be met at all.

OTHER ECONOMIC CONDITIONS

Payment terms

The cost of materials contracted for is not determined solely by the unit price of the material and quantity. Someone, usually the buyer, must pay for transporting the material to the buyer's plant. In addition, suppliers usually offer customers a trade discount of 1 to 2 percent if they pay for the material within 10 days of its receipt instead of within the customary 30 days. The buyer should always be certain that the trade discount is included in his contract. Sometimes this discount is negotiated between buyer and seller; usually it is a standard discount that the supplier offers to all of his customers.

Payment terms can become quite complicated on construction contracts and equipment purchases. Usually suppliers insist on progress payments, to be made at specified stages. For example, on a contract to design and build a machine tool, the order might call for payments to the supplier when the design is complete, when the machine is ready to be tried out, and final payment when the machine is operating in accordance with performance specifications.

F.o.b. point

Purchase orders should always indicate f.o.b. (meaning "free on board") point. This not only indicates who should pay freight and handling charges but also when title is passed on the goods. The following are some of the more commonly used f.o.b. terms and their legal implications to buyer and seller.

F.o.b. our plant. Responsibility for transport of the material should always be clearly assigned in the contract. Contracts for low-value materials purchased from local suppliers are customarily made "f.o.b. buyer's plant."[6] In such cases, the buyer takes title to the goods only when they are delivered to the loading dock at his plant; the supplier must pay any transportation charges. In addition, if the goods are damaged in transit, the supplier—not the buyer—is responsible for making a claim and negotiating a settlement with the carrier.

F.o.b. shipping point. When the contract is big and transportation charges are substantial, the terms are usually "f.o.b. shipping point." The buyer takes title when the seller loads the goods onto a common carrier. The buyer pays transportation charges directly to the carrier and also negotiates all freight damage claims and the like with the carrier. Most companies prefer to buy major materials "f.o.b. shipping point" because then their traffic departments can completely control inbound shipments. As a result, they often can cut freight charges substantially.

In some cases, a designation of f.o.b. shipping point may be too general. Suppose, for example, that a supplier does not have a railroad siding and must truck his product to a siding. Is the shipping point then the supplier's dock or is it the rail siding? Confusion can be prevented with more specific terms. If the purchase order reads "f.o.b. Detroit, Michigan, via New York Central Railroad," for example, then there is no doubt whatever that the supplier is responsible for getting the shipment to the rail siding and loading it. Conversely, if the terms are "f.o.b. supplier plant, via New York Central Railroad," then the buyer takes title to the shipment at the supplier's plant and can be charged separately for getting the material to the railroad siding.

Freight equalization. Producers of uniformly price commodities[7] such as aluminum, steel, and cement will often equalize freight charges with competitors whose plants are located closer to customers. For example, if the freight rate is 50 cents per cwt. from the plant of supplier A of a given commodity and only 25 cents per cwt. from the nearest supplier, supplier A will offer a 25 cents per cwt. "freight equalization" adjustment to the buyer. The buyer's purchase order to supplier A would then read "f.o.b. shipping point; 25 cents per cwt. freight equalization adjustment allowed." The buyer would pay the common carrier the full

[6] If the buyer is purchasing for more than one plant or there is some reason why such brief terms would create confusion, then more explicit terms should be incorporated.

[7] Usually, because of oligopolistic pricing, such commodities carry identical prices f.o.b. shipping point. With such a pricing structure, the lowest delivered price is naturally always obtained from the nearest producer. For example, a metalworking firm in South Bend, Indiana, would always get lowest delivered prices on steel from mills in the Chicago-Gary area. A Pittsburgh mill can get business in South Bend only by offering the South Bend firm the same delivered prices as Chicago mills, but it does not want to reduce its f.o.b. shipping-point price because it does not wish to cut prices to nearby customers. Therefore, the only solution is to reduce the freight charge to South Bend artificially by allowing the South Bend customer an allowance equal to the difference between the Pittsburgh–South Bend freight rate and the Chicago–South Bend rate.

50 cents per cwt. freight charge but would deduct the 25 cents per cwt. adjustment when he paid his invoice to supplier A. If the buyer does not happen to know the amount of the freight equalization adjustment, his purchase order can read "freight charges to be equalized with [name of city and state]," and supplier must take this into account when he invoices the buyer.

Free alongside ship (f.a.s.). This term is used for export shipments and reference is made to the port of export—, for example, "f.a.s. Hamburg." Buyer designates port, berth, and vessel. Vendor is responsible for getting it there and must provide a receipt indicating that goods were delivered to the ship's loading tackle in good order.

Cost-insurance-freight (c.i.f.). This term is used in export shipment when vendor is to be responsible for getting the shipment to a dock in a port designated by the buyer. For example, if an American buys something that is shipped to him from Le Havre on a "c.i.f. New York" basis, the vendor is fully responsible up to the point that the vessel docks in New York. It is then the buyer's responsibility to see that the merchandise is unloaded from the ship and delivered to its final destination in the United States. The term *c. & f.* (cost and freight) is similar, except that seller does not assume any risk if merchandise is lost at sea.

REJECTION OF DEFECTIVE GOODS

If goods are not satisfactory or do not meet specifications, buyers normally return them for credit. Sellers almost never object if returns are made promptly. In many states, the Uniform Sales Act governs warranties; in these states, almost all goods may be returned, provided the seller is promptly notified of rejection.

Warranty. The buyer has the right to conduct reasonable tests upon merchandise. If the merchandise is unsatisfactory, he should promptly notify seller of breach of warranty. His statement should identify the transaction (by purchase order number and shipment), describe the defect to the seller, and indicate that the buyer is asserting his legal right to reject the shipment.[8] If the buyer delays inspection and rejection of material for an "unreasonable" period of time, or if he notifies the wrong person in the supplier organization, his warranty may not be valid. Frequently goods that are rejected can be put in good order by the buyer. In such cases, the seller should agree in advance to any repair charges made by the buyer; normally he can request return of goods if he feels the charges are unreasonable.

While no seller planned it that way, the buyer of equipment may

---

[8] The supplier is normally notified of a rejected shipment with an inspection report form (see Figure 2–5 in Chapter 2), which may be sent to him separately or may accompany the rejected goods if they are returned for credit.

be at least partly protected against damages to persons or property that result from failure of that equipment—as long as there is reasonable evidence that the failure represented negligence on the part of the seller of the equipment rather than its purchaser. For example, if a car you purchase is involved in an accident because of a defective component, the courts may hold the manufacturer liable for damages, even if you have no formal warranty.

Samples. In many cases, a sample is the basis of the sale. This gives the buyer an implied warranty that the goods actually shipped must conform to the sample that was originally submitted by the seller. The Uniform Commercial Code makes this explicit when it says that "any sample or model which is made part of the basis of the bargain creates an express warranty that the whole of the goods shall conform to the sample or model."

Specifications. There is rarely a legal problem because of poor quality on purchases of standard, off-the-shelf items. In such cases the company's right to reject the merchandise is recognized. A company's relations with its suppliers for such materials are like a housewife's relations with a department store. If the merchandise is not satisfactory, it is returned for credit. The supplier then either sells the merchandise to another customer or returns it to his supplier.

Quality problems are not so simple when a company makes a product to the buyer's specifications. In such cases, the buyer may be the only user of the product. If he rejects a shipment, the supplier may suffer a substantial loss. Because of this, the buyer should incorporate specifications for the item in the purchase order. If the item is made to a blueprint, the purchase order should indicate that material is to be made in accordance with a particular blueprint number or specification accompanying the order. In such cases, the buyer need only accept the material if it meets the requested specifications.

Performance. With some purchases it is not possible to describe the product with detailed specifications. In buying machinery, for example, the buyer is interested not in the supplier's design of the equipment but in the performance of the equipment. So he uses a performance specification. Typical is this performance clause incorporated into a contract issued for a machine developed for Chesebrough-Pond, Inc. by one of its suppliers:

> The machine is to be guaranteed to produce at a minimum linear speed of 240 inches per minute, using a specific material, sample rolls of which were tested by the supplier. The seals produced by the machine are to withstand a minimum of 20 inches of vacuum at 70°F. Furthermore, the machine is to be test-run, prior to shipment, with representatives of our company present. In addition, agreement is to be reached for a specific delivery date, stemming from the date of final confirmation of all details.

If this machine did not actually produce at a speed of 240 inches per minute and meet all other performance specifications, then Chesebrough Pond would not be obliged to accept it.

Other provisions. Buyer or seller may also wish to include other explicit provisions with respect to warranty. The seller naturally likes to limit his warranty to the actual cost of the product he sells. For example, buyers of gray-iron castings sometimes do not discover that a casting is defective until some rather advanced machining operation reveals a porous section. In extreme cases, the buyer may have invested several hundred dollars of machining time into a casting that is worth no more than a few dollars. In such cases, buyer's legitimate damages are many times the cost of the casting. By trade custom, however, foundries limit their warranty to the actual cost of the casting and normally refuse to honor claims for machining time wasted on the defective casting.

Of course, buyer and seller can best prevent misunderstandings by explicitly defining the limits of the warranty. Inspection procedures may also be spelled out in detail. For example, an auto manufacturer may agree to accept nickel-plated parts only if a random sample of such parts can withstand 100 hours in a salt-spray bath without showing any signs of corrosion.

FAILURE TO DELIVER

The date that delivery is required should be clearly indicated on the buyer's order. If the seller accepts the order, he binds himself to deliver by that date. What happens if he fails to deliver? The Uniform Sales Act says that if "seller wrongfully neglects or refuses to deliver the goods, the buyer may maintain an action against the seller for damages for nondelivery."

If the goods that a seller fails to deliver are readily available, the buyer may collect general damages. Such damages are limited to the difference between the contract price and the price the buyer must pay on the open market. Suppose, for example, that a supplier accepts an order for material at 30 cents per lb. and then fails to deliver. If the buyer must pay 40 cents per lb. for the material, he may collect 10 cents per lb. damages from the supplier who failed to deliver.

If the goods are not readily available, the buyer may recover special damages. To do so he must prove that the damages he suffers from nondelivery could reasonably be anticipated by both buyer and seller. He must also be able to justify the amount of the damages.

Late delivery can often cause as much damage to buyer as no delivery. But if the buyer does not indicate a specific delivery date on his purchase order, the seller is bound by the Uniform Sales Act to delivery only within a "reasonable" time. Courts differ in the interpretation of the word "reasonable." Many buyers protect themselves against late deliveries by inserting a clause in their purchase orders to the effect that "if shipment is not made at the time specified, buyer reserves the right to cancel the order, or any part of it, without obligation." Public purchasing agencies sometimes require suppliers to post performance bonds. If the contract is not completed on schedule, the contractor may forfeit all or part of this bond. More frequently, both private and public purchasing agencies include penalty clauses for later delivery—particularly on construction contracts. Seller's price is automatically reduced by some predetermined rate for each week he is behind schedule.

OTHER LEGAL PROBLEMS

When a buyer issues a purchase contract, he may be innocently violating some law, infringing upon someone else's rights, or otherwise subjecting his company to possible lawsuits. Among the possible legal pitfalls for the buyer are patent infringement, the Fair Labor Standards Act, and the Robinson-Patman Act.

Patent infringement. A patent gives the inventor a legal monopoly for 17 years. If anyone manufactures, sells, or uses a patented device during this period without permission, the patent owner may sue and collect damages for infringement. Purchasers may innocently buy an item made by a supplier who is infringing upon the inventor's patent and still be liable for damages because they used the patented device.

Many buyers try to protect themselves against unwitting patent infringement by inserting in their orders clauses such as basic clause 2 in Figure 5–1. Such clauses do not enable the purchaser to transfer liability for infringement to the seller, but they can give him a basis for a claim against the seller in the event he is forced to pay damages to the inventor.

Fair Labor Standards Act. The hot-goods" clause (Section 15) of the Fair Labor Standards Act says that it is unlawful to buy and resell goods made in violation of the act. (The Fair Labor Standards Act regulates child labor and wages and hours.) Another section of the act permits a buyer to protect himself against innocent violation of the act by getting certification from seller that the act has been complied with. Such certification can consist of a clause in the purchase order (similar to basic clause 3 in Figure 5–1), indicating that the seller must comply with the act in producing the goods specified in the order. In addition, the buyer should insist that the supplier certify on each of his invoices that he has complied with the act.

Robinson-Patman Act. This law is designed to prevent a seller from unfairly discriminating among customers. It makes it unlawful, under most circumstances, for a seller to offer identical merchandise in similar quantities to different customers at different prices. One section of the

FIGURE 5–1
Useful purchase order terms

BASIC CLAUSES

(1) Time is of the essence on this order. Purchaser reserves the right to cancel this order, or any part thereof, without obligation, if delivery is not made at the time(s) specified.

(2) Seller warrants that there has been no violation of copyrights or patent rights in manufacturing, producing, or selling the goods shipped or ordered, and seller agrees to hold the purchaser harmless from any and all liability, loss, or expense occasioned by any such violation.

(3) All goods shipped against this order must have been produced in compliance with the requirements of the Fair Labor Standards Act of 1938, as amended, including Sections 6, 7, and 12, and regulations and orders issued under Section 14 thereof. Seller must certify this compliance on each invoice submitted in connection with this order.

OPTIONAL CLAUSES

In addition to the three basic clauses above, there is an almost infinite number of special clauses that purchasing agents may want to add to their orders. Among the more common are the following:

(1) The terms and conditions of sale as stated in this order govern in event of conflict with any terms of seller's proposal, and are not subject to change by reason of any written or verbal statements by seller, or by any terms stated in seller's acknowledgment, unless accepted in writing by us.

(2) We reserve the right to inspect all shipments after delivery to us and to reject any material that may be defective or not in accordance with specifications as to quality or performance.

(3) If price is omitted on order, except where order is given in acceptance of quoted prices, it is agreed that seller's price will be the lowest prevailing market price and in no event is this order to be filled at higher prices than last previously quoted or charged without purchaser's written consent.

(4) In the event any article sold and delivered hereunder shall be defective in any respect whatsoever, seller will indemnify and save harmless purchaser from all loss or expense by reason of all accidents, injuries, or damages to persons or property resulting from the use or sale of such article or which are contributed to by said defective condition.

(5) If seller performs services, or constructs, erects, inspects or delivers on buyer's premises, seller will indemnify and save harmless buyer from all loss or expense by reason of any accident, injury or damage to persons or property occurring in connection therewith.

(6) Purchaser may at any time insist upon strict compliance with these terms and conditions, notwithstanding any previous custom, practice, or course of dealing to the contrary.

These terms were suggested by the late Lyle Treadway, a purchasing agent for the Federal Glass Co. Mr. Treadway, a graduate lawyer, was a vice president of the National Association of Purchasing Management.

act also makes it unlawful for buyers to accept such discrimination. The act is not designed to prevent buyers from seeking lower prices, under most circumstances. In general, a buyer does not violate the act if he accepts a lower price, in good faith, in order to (1) permit a seller to meet a competitor's bid that was also made in good faith, (2) secure the benefit of purchases in bigger quantities or of some other arrangement that reduces seller's costs.

In practice, the Robinson-Patman Act has not been troublesome for buyers. Most cases brought against them have been dismissed by the courts. On the other hand, the act has helped curb monopolistic practices of certain sellers.

Damages in supplier plants. Suppose a company sends equipment or material to a supplier and it is damaged or destroyed while in the possession of the supplier. Naturally the company feels the supplier is responsible. Some companies like to clarify this situation in advance with a clause in the purchase order. For example, the B. F. Goodrich Company has a clause in its purchase orders that states: "Whenever Seller shall, by virtue hereof, have in its possession any property belonging to Buyer and/or Buyer's customer, Seller shall be deemed an insurer thereof and shall be responsible for its safe return to Buyer."

Workmen's compensation and liability insurance. When a company has a contractor working on its premises, it may be liable for any injuries inflicted on others by the contractor's workers or vehicles in accidents. Therefore, it should insist in its purchase terms that contractors be covered by liability insurance. Some companies go further; they demand to see copies of the insurance policies before they will let the contractor start work. A company can also be responsible for injuries suffered by a contractor's employees. It protects itself by making certain that the contractor has workmen's compensation insurance.

Tax exemption. Certain goods are subject to federal excise tax if they are used by the purchaser. But if they are purchased for further manufacture—as is the case with all production parts and materials that are incorporated into some end product—they are exempt from tax. To avoid the tax, the buyer must add an exemption certificate to his purchase order. Figure 5–2 illustrates the certificate used by the B. F. Goodrich Company.

A company also may purchase materials for direct resale without using them in manufacture. In this case, it is also exempt from the federal excise tax and should add an exemption clause to its purchase order. A special exemption clause would also be added if the material is to be exported.

Many states also have sales or use taxes. If a material is purchased for resale, incorporation into another product, or export, it will normally be exempt from the tax, but special clauses must be added in each case in accordance with the laws of the state in which the buyer does business.

Liens. When a company has work done by a general contractor, it is potentially liable for payment of subcontractors or their employees. If the general contractor does not meet his obligations, subcontractors and employees may secure a lien against the project on which they worked. Buyers are usually careful to get waivers of lien from all subcontractors before making final payments on contracts. They are far more likely to be negligent in the purchase of major used equipment, which also may be subject to lien. The creditors of the seller of the

FIGURE 5-2

EXEMPTION CERTIFICATE

PURCHASES FOR FURTHER MANUFACTURE
UNDER SECTION 4220 OF I.R.C.

Date: _____ 196 __

The undersigned hereby certifies that he is a manufacturer or producer of articles taxable under Chapter 32, sub-chapter A, of the Internal Revenue Code, as amended, and holds certificate of registry number 20 issued by the Director of Internal Revenue at Cleveland, Ohio, and that the article or articles specified in the accompanying order will be used by him as material in the manufacture or production of, or as a component part of, an article or articles enumerated in sub-chapter A to be manufactured or produced by him.

It is understood that, for all the purposes of such sub-chapter A, the undersigned will be considered the manufacturer or producer of the articles purchased hereunder and (except as specifically provided by law) must pay tax on resale or use, otherwise than as specified above of the articles purchased hereunder. It is further understood that the fraudulent use of this certificate to secure exemption will subject the undersigned and all guilty parties to revocation of the privilege of purchasing tax-free and to a fine of not more than $10,000 or to imprisonment for not more than five (5) years or both, together with costs of prosecution.

This certificate covers Purchase Order No. _____ dated _____ .

This certificate covers purchases from _____ to _____ .

THE B. F. GOODRICH COMPANY
By: _____
Title: _____

Many states have sales or use taxes, and the federal government has excise taxes on various products. Production parts and materials purchased for resale are exempt from these taxes, provided the buyer either includes the appropriate exemption certificate with his order or files it with the appropriate taxing authority. Above is an exemption certificate used by the B. F. Goodrich Company for purchases subject to federal excise tax.

equipment can sometimes collect from the buyer of the equipment if the seller is not able to meet his obligations. The buyer is completely assured of a clear title to equipment only if he has a lawyer investigate the supplier's financial condition.

CONTRACT CANCELLATION

Every materials manager issues purchase orders that he later must cancel because the goods are no longer needed. Purchase contract cancellations are particularly frequent in technologically dynamic industries. Materials and components rapidly become obsolete on account of product changes. In the materials departments of the big aircraft companies, as many as 50 persons may be employed full time on cancellations. When a buyer cancels an order before its completion, it is called "anticipatory breach." If the merchandise for which he has contracted is salable but only at a lower price, the Uniform Sales Act says that buyer is liable to seller for the difference between this lower price and the contract price.

If buyer cancels an order for materials made to his specification, he is liable for all of the costs incurred by the seller—including the seller's liability to his suppliers—of materials and services used in carrying out the contract. In addition, the buyer is liable for the normal profit the seller would have made on the contract.

Buyers should terminate contracts without delay once they determine that the material on order is no longer needed. They are liable only for costs incurred (less salvage value) by the supplier prior to termination. Once supplier has acknowledged termination, the buyer cannot change his mind and demand reinstatement of the contract unless the supplier concurs.

All major contracts should include a termination clause. Terms of payment for all potential liabilities should be defined as clearly as possible. Procedures used to determine costs of inventories, depreciated value of special tools, and so on, should be agreed upon in advance. It is usually wise to make provision for an audit of termination costs. Both buyer and seller are protected on termination of big contracts if there is agreement when the original contract is made. And there is no danger of unpleasant misunderstandings arising between them that will mar relations on future contracts.

It is particularly important that provision for cancellation be incorporated into purchase orders of defense contractors. Rapid changes in defense technology keep defense purchasing departments in a constant state of flux. In some firms, no more than one purchase order in two for parts and materials is ever completed. Continuous design changes make it necessary to cancel an enormous number of purchase orders before they are completely filled. Military needs also sometimes change rapidly As a result, purchasing departments in big aerospace firms sometimes are flooded with cancellations when a major contract change requires them to cancel hundreds of outstanding orders.

LETTERS OF INTENT

The letter of intent is a device that can reduce the risk of cancellation charges and misunderstandings between buyer and supplier. It is particularly useful when a buyer finds it advantageous to define purchase terms and conditions before he can formally commit himself to buy anything.

Typical application

Figure 5–3 shows a sample letter of intent used by the Airesearch Division of Garrett Corporation. This letter defines price and other conditions of purchase for two parts, No. 259771 and No. 256963, for a

FIGURE 5–3
Letter of intent to purchase

AIRESEARCH MANUFACTURING COMPANY

A DIVISION OF THE GARRETT CORPORATION

SKY HARBOR AIRPORT · 402 SOUTH 36TH STREET · PHOENIX, ARIZONA 85034

TELEPHONE 273-3011

A.B.C. Company
1234 Rightway Street
Los Angeles, California 90007

Attention Mr. John Doe

Gentlemen:

This letter of intent, in response to negotiations mutually agreed upon
between AiResearch Manufacturing Company and A.B.C. Company, is to
confirm the pricing and conditions for manufacture of barriers, parts
259771 and 256963.

The following conditions are noted as part of this agreement:

(A) The anticipated yearly quantities of 3000 to 3500 (part 259771)
and 1800 to 2300 (part 256963) are estimates only, and are not
to be considered binding quantities.

(B) To allow for payment of delivered units during the period of
this letter of intent, the individual purchase orders shall
reflect a price of $15.50 each for part 259771, and $5.50 each
for part 256963.

(C) At the end of the year's period, the buyer and seller shall
adjust the final price of each purchase order issued during the
year in accordance with the negotiated price established for the
year's accumulative total for each part per paragraph (D) below.

(D) Firm fixed prices, based upon the accumulative quantity manufactured during the one year period of the letter are as follows:

Quantity	Unit Price	Quantity	Unit Price
500	$21.30	3501 - 4000	$13.20
1000	17.60	4001 - 4500	13.10
1500	15.50	4501 - 5000	13.05
1501 - 3000	13.50	5001 - over	13.00
3001 - 3500	13.30		

Revision of individual orders at the end of the year to the
prices shown in the above aggregate quantities is based upon
subsequent orders being released in a manner that will allow

(H) The minimum quantity of any order placed per this letter shall
be 500 pieces.

(I) The period of this letter of intent shall be one (1) year from
the date of acknowledgement.

Very truly yours,

R. D. Lutz

Max O. Mitchell
Purchasing Department

RDL:sb

Acknowledged: _____
A.B.C. Company

Sample letter of intent shows how Airesearch defines conditions of purchase for two
parts it intends to buy, provided it gets a contract for the parts' end product.

period of one year. If the hypothetical supplier, the A.B.C. Company, acknowledges this letter of intent without qualification, then Airesearch is assured that it can buy these parts from A.B.C. in accordance with the terms of the letter of intent.

Price assured. Airesearch probably used a letter of intent for these particular parts because, at the time the letter was written, it did not have a contract for a finished product requiring them and it wanted to be assured of firm prices for purchased materials before it went ahead and quoted on a final assembly. Once Airesearch gets an order, it can then go ahead immediately with a purchase order that is consistent with the terms of the letter of intent. Even though this particular letter will not necessarily lead to the purchase of anything from A.B.C., it serves useful purposes for both A.B.C. and Airesearch. Letters of intent from customers permit A.B.C. to do a better job of planning. Although A.B.C. knows that not every letter of intent will actually lead to purchase orders, there is a high probability that some percentage of them will result in firm orders. As a result, A.B.C. can forecast more precisely its equipment and facilities so that it will be ready when the letters actually do become orders. In fact, if A.B.C. needs financing, the letters can be shown to banks as evidence supporting the need for loans which will be self-liquidating from future business.

Shorter lead time. Use of the letter of intent permits Airesearch to do a much better buying job than would be possible if it were to start from scratch on subcontracts when it receives a firm prime contract. Chances are that Airesearch will get the order for the end product only if it offers to deliver promptly. This usually means that orders for purchased parts and materials must be issued almost immediately after Airesearch gets a firm order from its customer. Then there might not be sufficient time to do the best possible job of buying each component, and costs of purchased components would not be firmly pinned down. Airesearch might find itself in the unhappy position where costs of purchased materials were so high that it was impossible to make a profit on the order. Or, if purchase costs turned out to be lower than anticipated, Airesearch might never get an order for the end product because its bid was inflated by an excess allowance for cost of purchased parts and materials. Letters of intent define quite precisely what purchased costs will be and provide assurance that there will be an adequate margin between purchased materials costs and selling price. They also permit the buyer to group similar items together with the same supplier in order to get the lowest possible price.

De facto orders

While the letter of intent shown in Figure 5–3 does not commit the buyer to make any purchase, other letters of intent may become de facto purchase orders. Suppose, for example, that in the course of negotiating the terms of purchase for parts 259771 and 256963, the buyer discovers that it is impossible to get delivery until at least three months after the supplier has received a firm purchase order. He checks with production control and discovers that Airesearch will need the parts within two months after it is able to give a formal go-ahead to the supplier.

Obviously, something must give. Either Airesearch must get the parts delivered in two months instead of three months, or it must accept the risk of being late in delivering its end product. In some cases, the best solution is to authorize the supplier to do some preliminary work in the letter of intent. For example, if the two parts are fabricated from steel, the buyer might authorize the supplier in the letter of intent to go ahead and purchase the steel but not to fabricate it. This automatically shortens the supplier's lead time and no one loses anything as long as the deal goes through. However, if the end product is not produced, the supplier will be stuck with steel he neither wants nor needs. Inevitably, the buyer would be required to compensate the supplier for any loss suffered. In this case, of course, the letter of intent becomes a partial purchase order for raw materials.

GOVERNMENT PROCUREMENT

Letters of intent and all other procedures followed by defense contractors must be consistent with Armed Services Procurement Regulations (ASPR). In addition, nondefense government agencies spend directly about one fifth of total national income for a wide variety of materials and services.

The basic principles of materials management are as applicable to government procurement as they are to private industry. In every case, materials management should be oriented toward the objectives of the organization it serves. The fundamental objective of the materials manager in government is not significantly different from that of his counterpart in industry. The materials manager in the private firm strives to maximize his company's profits over the long term; the public purchasing official attempts to get maximum value for the taxpayer's dollar.

Reasons for regulation

Differences between government and private industry procurement come not in basic principles but in legal environment. The private purchasing official has tremendous flexibility; the public official is regulated by a myriad of laws. Tight regulation makes public procurement inflexible and not always efficient, but it is politically essential for the two basic reasons discussed below.

To protect the taxpayer against corruption. In the past, public purchasing was the means by which those in power rewarded themselves. At best, public purchases could be (and sometimes still are) diverted to businessmen who support the party in power. At worst, public funds are simply misappropriated.

Contemporary public purchasing officials are at least as honest as their counterparts in private industry, but they remain circumscribed by literally hundreds of regulations designed to prevent malpractice. In some cases, these regulations protect the professional public purchaser from political pressures; in others, they simply make it difficult for him to do a competent job.

To promote noneconomic objectives. Legislative bodies have always assumed that public purchasing should take social as well as economic factors into account. Municipal and state purchasing officials may be forced to buy locally even when better values can be obtained from a supplier in another city or state. Similarly, the federal government is subject to regulations that discriminate in favor of American suppliers, particularly "small business" as defined by the Small Business Administration.

In addition, high-ranking officials at all levels of government often make no bones about interfering with the procurement process—particularly on major projects—in order to favor quite deliberately one group or region over another. At the local level, the town's major contractors often serve as elected or appointed officials. At state level, the party in power gets much of its financial support from those businessmen who do business with the state. And, at the federal level, decisions on where to locate major government facilities are at least as much political as they are economic.

Advertised bidding

Government procurement officials operate in a fishbowl; every act is a matter of public record. Local, state, and federal governments are required to advertise for bids whenever possible. Exceptions to this basic rule are possible only when the purchase is too small to be worth the time and expense of advertised bidding or when the nature of the product or service makes advertising impractical.

Mechanics of bidding. Advertised bidding requires highly detailed specifications. It is particularly useful for commodities where standards have already been set (such as foods) or for construction where detailed specifications must be drawn up anyway. Once the specifications are available, the advertised bidding process becomes highly mechanical, going through the following steps.

1. The government agency that is to do the buying gets a budget authorization and specifications from the agency that is to use the mate-

rial. The buying agency must be certain that the specifications are not restrictive and lend themselves to advertising. For example, specifications for canned fruit based on the standards of the U.S. Department of Agriculture would be appropriate for advertised bidding since dozens and perhaps hundreds of canning firms are able to meet these specs. On the other hand, advertised bidding would not be appropriate for a patented item, since only the patent owner or his licensee could supply it.

2.   Invitations to bid are prepared which set forth a specific place, date, and hour for opening of bids. These are sent to all qualified bidders on the procuring agency's list. In addition, the procurement may be advertised by posting it in public places or announcing it in newspapers. Federal government purchases in excess of $10,000 are also publicized in the Department of Commerce publication, *Synopsis of U.S. Government Procurement, Sales and Contract Awards.*

3.   At the specified hour, bids are opened. Names of bidders and their bids are recorded on an abstract of bids which is available for public inspection. Under normal conditions, no bidder may withdraw a bid once it has been submitted. In some cases, he is forced to post a performance bond which he forfeits if he refuses to accept a contract on which he is low bidder.

4.   The contracting officer evaluates the bids and makes an award. Bids that do not conform in every detail to the invitation and to specifications are rejected. The contracting officer also rejects any bids that are not "responsible"—that is, those that do not come from bidders who are regular dealers or manufacturers of the item being purchased. After culling out all bids that do not qualify, the contracting officer makes the award to the low bidder.

5.   The bidder is required to perform precisely in accordance with the terms of the contract. If he fails to perform, the contracting officer may be required by regulation to take legal steps needed to assure performance. For example, if the bidder fails to deliver, the contracting officer may choose to buy the item from another supplier at a higher price. He then forces the original bidder to make up the difference so that the government spends no more than what it would have under the original contract award. The contracting officer might also sue the original bidder for any losses occasioned because of late delivery.

Pros and cons.   Advertised bidding guarantees reasonable impartiality in public purchasing. A recognized supplier who is willing to bid low enough can almost always get an order from a public purchasing official. In contrast, the supplier who is not "in" with many big private firms may not be able to get an order regardless of what he quotes. Almost all information on bids and so forth is held in strictest confidence in private firms. This may inhibit the competition. With advertised bidding, every bidder can look at the recap and know exactly where he stands.

Despite this basic advantage, advertised bidding has rather serious weaknesses even for certain types of public purchasing. These include:

1. The contract is automatically awarded to the lowest bidder who possesses the minimum qualifications to do the job. This may not be the best firm in the business. In contrast, a purchasing official in a private firm might not issue his order to the low bidder but prefer to do business with a supplier he regards as more reliable or superior in some other respect.

2. The public purchasing official using advertised bids tries to get bids from a maximum number of firms. In some cases, it may be necessary to evaluate several hundred bids. In contrast, the private firm rarely solicits bids from more than a half dozen suppliers, and many qualified suppliers may not be solicited at all simply because the purchasing official feels that he already has adequate competition.

3. Advertised bidding is costly and time-consuming compared with the private method of buying. It may cost several thousand dollars to prepare bids and make an award.

4. Advertised bidding does not necessarily guarantee a competitor the lowest possible price, even when a large number of bids are solicited. In many cases, one firm enjoys such an enormous advantage over its rivals that it can quote a very high price and still be low bidder. This is particularly true of engineered items where one contractor has had substantial experience.

5. Highly detailed specifications are needed. There is no margin of error with advertised bidding. If the government forgets one important specification, then the bidder is perfectly free to ignore it and cut costs in any way he can as long as he adheres to specifications. The seller cannot afford to give the government anything more than the minimum he requests; otherwise, his bid may be too high. In contrast, the atmosphere in most private procurement is considerably less formal. If a private firm buys an automobile, it can reasonably expect to get a spare tire even if it does not ask for it. Conversely, it probably will not sue a seller who fails to deliver.

Despite these serious limitations, advertised bidding is a highly effective public purchasing technique when (1) specifications are detailed, (2) there are many qualified bidders, and (3) the purchase is important enough to be worth advertising. Thus, there is good reason why most government procurement agencies will advertise except on purchases where it is clearly not workable.

Negotiated procurement

Advertised bidding in federal procurement dates back to 1809, with exceptions allowed during wartime for procurement of munitions. Negotiated procurement did not really come into its own in the federal government, however, until 1947, with the enactment of the Armed Services Procurement Act. This act authorized "negotiated" procurement for purchases where advertising is not practical or would not lead to best value for the government. At present, about 80 percent of all military procurement is "negotiated." Advertised bidding is used more frequently for nonmilitary procurement not only by the federal government but also by state and municipal governments. Almost every government purchasing office has authority to buy certain items—particularly services and small purchases of any kind—by negotiation, however.

Meaning of negotiation. The term "negotiation" may be misleading. In federal government jargon any purchase that is not made through advertised bids is by definition negotiated. And, in fact, there is usually some discussion or negotiation with purchases that are legally negotiated. In contrast, no discussion or negotiation is necessary with advertised bidding. The seller submits his bid in writing and then is advised in writing when he gets the award.

There may be "negotiation" on even the most trivial negotiated purchase. For example, if a corner gas station repairs a flat tire on a government-owned car, payment may be made with what is legally a negotiated purchase order. The "negotiation" may consist simply asking the mechanic what he charges for fixing a flat and then paying the bill if the charge seems reasonable.

Discussions get much more involved on major negotiated purchases. In fact, competition may be keener than it is with advertised bidding because the contracting officer is less likely to accept the lowest bid that he gets. He may negotiate with one or more bidders in order to obtain even more favorable purchase terms. For example, a contracting officer may get bids of $10 million, $11 million, and $12 million for a Navy warship from three competing shipyards. Conceivably, the contracting officer could simply award the contract to the shipyard that bids $10 million. However, he may ask each of the competing shipyards to revise its bid and attempt to buy the warship for $9,500,000.

Truth in negotiation. Buyers for the military services are helped a great deal in negotiation by the "Truth in Negotiation" law, which requires government contractors to reveal their cost estimates and certify their accuracy, completeness, and currency. In theory, at least, the military buyer is then at least as well informed as his suppliers and enjoys an enormous advantage over his civillian counterpart, who is not able to demand reliable supplier cost estimates. The system is by no means foolproof, however. In many cases, neither the supplier nor the buyer really knows what the item is supposed to cost, and the actual cost may turn out to be greatly in excess of the original estimate.

Favoritism of sharp practices? In recent years, some defense contractors have had their prices hammered down in negotiation with the Pentagon and then have been stuck with contracts that, at best, yielded only nominal profits and sometimes caused major losses. Not surprisingly, both defense contractors and the congressmen who represent them have sometimes complained bitterly about this sort of negotiation, calling it "sharp practice." However, there is no doubt that government purchasers have saved taxpayers many millions of dollars through such negotiation.

The procurement officer who trades one supplier off against another is rarely accused of favoritism. There is considerably greater opportunity for favoritism—justified or unjustified—when the contracting officer must make a negotiated procurement from a single supplier. When the purchase is sufficiently small it simply isn't worth the effort to solicit bids from a number of suppliers.

However, congressmen don't complain about favoritism among corner garages fixing flat tires. The pressures come when big defense contracts are being passed out. A single contract may amount to hundreds of millions of dollars and create thousands of jobs in a congressman's district. Such procurement inherently tends to favor one supplier at the expense of another, and there is not much that can be done about it. One cannot, for example, advertise for bids for a new missile or bomber that has not yet been developed. The detailed specifications obviously do not exist, and competing aerospace firms might well propose substantially different designs to meet the same performance objective. Consequently, even if it is possible to develop detailed quotations, bids will not be comparable between competing producers, since they are not based on identical products. As a result, the contracting officer must consider qualitative factors such as design capability as well as prices and costs when he makes the award.

Rightly or wrongly, the award may also be influenced by factors that are completely noneconomic. This is often true of major military procurement. Competing firms will submit quite different design proposals. Not only must someone evaluate these designs, but political reality requires that the impact of the contract on a region's economy be taken into account. Congressmen from areas with substantial unemployment will fight hard to force the Department of Defense to favor contractors in their districts. In some cases, election results may be influenced by whether or not voters feel a candidate can get more federal money for businesses in his district.

Favoritism without corruption. Major procurement decisions may be difficult and controversial even when there are no overt political pressures. In many cases, the government is trying to buy something that has never been made before. Competing contractors must quote a price for something that does not exist. In addition, their technical approaches are often different. If the Department of Defense wants to buy a supersonic fighter plane with certain performance characteristics, one contractor may propose a delta-wing design, another may propose wings that change position as the aircraft increases its speed, and so on. In awarding the contract, the Department must take into account not only the cost of the proposed design but its practicability.

Major mistakes are inevitable when criteria for bidding are not well defined. Technical problems frequently cause costs to soar above original estimates. The competitive environment also encourages underestimating of costs. Every contractor is strongly tempted to underbid, since if his original estimate is higher than those of competitors, he probably will not get the contract. As long as the design has not been firmly established, it is usually possible to boost prices and recoup losses from underbidding. Also, if precedent is any guide to the future, the federal government will not permit a major defense contractor to go bankrupt simply because of unprofitable defense contracts.

With negotiated procurement of complex products, it is not only difficult to achieve workable competition prior to production but the government is also stuck with a single supplier even after the product has been in production for some time. For example, the F–5 fighter plane was produced for many years by the Northrup Corporation, and the Air Force has long had available highly detailed specifications for this aircraft. Theoretically, the Air Force or the Navy could send copies of these specifications to every aircraft company in the nation and solicit competitive bids on the next procurement. In practice, however, this would hardly be worthwhile. Northrup has already acquired so much experience in making this plane that its costs would be well below that of any other possible competitor. For example, if $2 million is a fair price for the plane from an experienced producer like Northrup, the lowest competitive bid might be $3 million from some other supplier who had had no experience whatever. Consequently, if the procurement were made strictly on the basis of competitive bidding, Northrup could conceivably charge $2,900,000 and still get the contract even though it made an enormous profit. Obviously, competitive bidding process just does not work when the product is very complex and a single contractor has had a great deal of experience with it.[9]

Contract clauses

Obviously, the Department of Defense in particular must use a wide variety of contract clauses if it is to get optimum value for the taxpayer's dollar. Some defense contracts are in effect "one of a kind," developed for some particular need. However, most negotiated procurement makes

---

[9] Naturally, buyers want to benefit from reductions in cost that result from experience. They do this by applying the learning curve, an analytical procurement technique that is discussed in detail in Chapter 16.

use of a wide number of variations of three basic contract clauses: fixed price; cost reimbursement; and special incentive.

Fixed-price clauses. No contract clause is needed for a firm fixed-price contract. The price on the purchase order becomes part of the contract, and the contractor is obliged to charge that price. Roughly one third of all Department of Defense purchases are for a firm, fixed price.

Escalation and redetermination. Other fixed-price contracts are not quite so fixed. The Department of Defense also uses escalation clauses on fixed-price contracts which typically permit a price to be increased as much as 10 percent for changes in wages, raw-material costs, or taxes.

The Department also uses price-redetermination clauses not unlike those described earlier in this chapter. A redetermination clause is ideal when the price quoted by the contractor is higher than what the government is willing to pay. The item may be so new that the contractor is often unwilling to quote the desired price because he feels he must make some allowance for contingencies. In this case, the buyer and seller negotiate a price and include a redetermination clause which permits the price to be renegotiated within some limit after the contractor has had experience with the item.

Incentive contracts. Of course, a conventional price-redetermination clause may not give the contractor much incentive to control his own costs. The contractor knows the government will reimburse him for all of his costs, so he simply spends the money. The fixed-price incentive contract may be more desirable in such cases. This contract requires the negotiation of a target cost, a target profit, a ceiling price, and a final profit formula which allows the contractor to participate in any savings that result. For example, suppose that the buyer and seller agree that a contract should have a target price of $1 million, with costs of $920,000 and $80,000 expected profit. On the other hand, buyer and seller recognize that unforeseen contingencies may cause costs to be higher than target, and so a ceiling price of $1,250,000 is negotiated. If actual costs are less than expected costs, 20 percent of the saving goes to the contractor and 80 percent to the government. For example, suppose that the contractor's actual costs are $900,000 instead of $920,000 as indicated in the target cost. Of this $20,000 saving, the contractor gets 20 percent, bringing his total profit on the contract up to $84,000. Thus, the contractor enjoys a 20 percent profit on any savings he can make below the target cost.

Conversely, the contractor's profit is reduced by a like amount when his costs go above target. Suppose, for example, that costs of $1,100,000 are incurred on the contract. The government is then willing to pay the contractor $1,080,000—the target price plus 80 percent of the excess. The contractor's loss is $20,000 because of his 20 percent share of the cost overrun. The ceiling price of $1,250,000 cannot be exceeded in any event, regardless of the contractor's costs.

This type of contract gives the contractor incentive to keep his costs down and also avoids giving him a blank check. Such contracts must be negotiated quite carefully, since obviously the contractor has considerable incentive to inflate his original estimate as high as possible and then to come under it in order to make excess profits.

Cost-reimbursement clauses. The government tries to make minimum use of cost-reimbursement contracts because of the obvious danger involved. However, sometimes it has no choice and roughly 5 percent of all Department of Defense procurement actions are of this type. In some cases, the contractor has a simple "cost" contract, with some allowance for direct costs and overhead but not for profit. These are most often entered into with educational and other nonprofit institutions.

Occasionally the contractor accepts a cost-sharing contract. Since the contractors stand to profit from the product that is being developed under the contract, he receives no fee and is reimbursed only for a portion of his cost. The government also issues cost plus fixed-fee contracts in which the contractor receives costs incurred along with some fee. Another variation of this is an arrangement whereby the cost plus incentive fee is increased if costs are kept under some predetermined maximum.

Special-Incentive clauses. Occasionally, the government issues a special-incentive contract which gives the contractor an extra profit if some performance objective is exceeded. For example, suppose that the Navy issues a contract for a nuclear submarine and the specification calls for a maximum speed of at least 40 knots. Since speed is vital in nuclear submarines, the contract may carry some added provision giving the contractor extra profit if he can make the submarine go even faster (without adversely affecting other performance characteristics).

Similarly, the Bureau of Ships, in particular, has had great success with adding value engineering[10] incentives. These contracts call for a value engineering appraisal to be made during the contract with savings to be shared between the contractor and the government. The Bureau of Ships has reportedly saved $12 for every $1 worth of value engineering that was authorized under such contracts.

Value engineering clauses and other types of incentive contracts give Department of Defense buyers considerably more flexibility than they had as recently as 20 years ago. But once the contract is signed, the defense buyer still has considerably less latitude than his counterpart in private industry. These and other clauses are the product of negotiation at the time the contract is placed. Negotiating techniques appli-

---

[10] This is the military version of value analysis, which is discussed in Chapter 18.

cable to both defense and nondefense buying are discussed in Chapter 7.

Defense materials system

The defense buyer in government, as well as in business, does enjoy one major advantage over all other buyers, however. Only he has the legal power to demand that a seller give priority to certain of his orders. Defense suppliers are required by the Defense Production Act of 1950 to give priority to orders that are certified as essential to national defense. DMS (Defense Materials System) priorities can be applied both directly by government agencies concerned with the defense effort and by their subcontractors. Priorities can extend back through the chain of supply all the way from the defense agency to the producer of basic raw materials.

Cases

CASE 5–1. SOUTHERN ELECTRONICS CORPORATION

Purchase order acknowledgments

Southern Electronics Corporation is an important prime contractor for the U.S. Air Force for missile guidance systems. All major purchases must be approved by the Air Force contracting officer, and periodic audits are made by the government's General Accounting Office to check conformance with procedures.

Most of the orders issued by Southern Electronics have contained no provision for price escalation. In almost every case, bidders have quoted fixed prices, and the business has been awarded to the low bidder. Because government regulations are quite strict, the company is careful about maintaining good records. Clerks even keep track of each purchase order acknowledgment. If the acknowledgment copy of the order is not returned within two weeks after the order is placed, the supplier gets a form letter requesting that he return it.

Once this procedure was set up, Errol Walters, the materials manager, and Clark Bedell, the purchasing agent, ceased to worry about acknowledgments. However, two incidents involving acknowledgments have recently been called to their attention:

1. An audit of the acknowledgment copy file shows that several suppliers have taken exception to the terms and conditions of the company's purchase orders when they have acknowledged them. Most notably, Apex Metals Corporation, one of the biggest companies in the world, insists on acknowledging Southern's orders with its own sales acknowl-

edgment forms, which have terms and conditions quite different from those on Southern's purchase orders. The contracting officer flatly refuses to accept Apex's terms. He particularly objects to Apex's clause: "Price subject to change without notice." He correctly points out that this condition, if accepted, would give Apex the right to charge almost any price it pleased when it actually delivered the order. Apex points out that it is against its policy to accept any restrictions on its pricing, or any terms but its own. It also points out that it has always been extremely conservative in pricing, and under no circumstances has it ever consciously sold its products at prices higher than those of its competitors. It says flatly that it must ask Southern Electronics to cancel its orders if it will not accept Apex's terms.

Unfortunately, Apex is the only supplier that can meet Southern's quality and delivery requirements. In addition, Apex's price is competitive, and no other producers in Apex's rather oligopolistic industry will offer better terms. Nevertheless, the contracting officer insists that Southern should not give Apex a blank check.

2.   Another Southern supplier, Moon Screw Products Company, accepted Southern's fixed-price order without qualifications. Now Moon finds that its costs on the order are much higher than anticipated. The order calls for it to receive only $10,000, and Moon claims that its total costs are $60,000 and the small company is now having trouble meeting its payroll. The specifications on the order have been much more difficult to meet than Moon anticipated. Bedell checks Moon's story by getting bids from other suppliers with experience on items similar to those made by Moon and finds that he would be lucky to get the parts for $60,000 from an experienced supplier. Now Moon is threatened with bankruptcy if Southern tries to force delivery at the contract price. In addition, Southern won't get delivery of the parts when it needs them if Moon doesn't have money to meet its payroll.

Questions

1.   What contract changes, if any, should Walters and Bedell recommend to the Air Force contracting officer on the Apex and Moon orders?

2. What, if anything, should Walters and Bedell have done before they placed their first orders with Apex and Moon?

CASE 5–2.   ZERO CORPORATION (B)

The use of escalation clauses

Zero Corporation (see Case 2–1 for additional history and information about the company) has redesigned the fan it uses to cool its compressors. The fan was formerly an assembly consisting of several steel stampings screwed to a gray-iron casting. The new design is a one-piece aluminum die casting that costs substantially less.

The supplier, Broderick Zinc and Aluminum Corporation, suggested the new design and is willing to sell at a guaranteed unit price of 70 cents. However, Mr. Allen, the Broderick sales representative, suggests that this may not be the best possible deal for Zero. When it guarantees a price, Broderick must include some allowance to protect itself against fluctuations in raw-materials prices. Currently, secondary aluminum alloy (No. 108) sells for 26 cents a pound. However, price changes of as much as 5 cents a pound during the course of a year are not at all uncommon. Since the casting weighs 0.9 pounds and Broderick must allow an additional 5 percent in calculating the weight of material used because of dross losses, the firm must obviously include some "fat" in any fixed-price quotation, to protect itself.

Allen says that his firm is willing to cut its price to 67 cents provided that Zero is willing to accept risks from price fluctuations in secondary aluminum. The 67-cent price is based on 26-cent 108 alloy, and Allen proposes that provision be made to adjust the price either upward or downward when the price of 108 alloy, as reported in the *American Metal Market*, changes. He suggests that the price be adjusted in exact multiples of 1 cent and that no adjustment be made unless the cost of aluminum used in the casting changes by at least that amount.

In addition, Broderick is willing to amortize the costs of molds used in making the die casting in the piece price. In other words, the $2,000 cost of the molds can be spread over the first order of 20,000 units with a 10-cent price increase. This arrangement permits Zero to pay for the tools as it makes savings from the use of the new lower cost design, and it need not make a big cash investment in tools. Both Zero and Broderick agree that since tools are being amortized, there should be a special cancellation clause in the contract that permits Zero to cancel only if it: (1) accepts responsibility for any parts that it authorized to be fabricated against the order, and (2) compensates the supplier for the balance of tool cost not yet amortized in the piece price at the time of cancellation.

Questions

1. Should Zero buy the die casting on the basis of a 70-cent fixed price or a 67-cent price subject to escalation due to changes in secondary aluminum prices? Justify your answer in terms of the price trend that has prevailed for 108 secondary aluminum alloy during the last year.

2. Suppose you are the Zero buyer negotiating this contract and you conclude that it is advantageous to accept the 67-cent price with escalation and also wish to amortize tooling the piece price. Draft the escalation and cancellation clauses that you would submit to your company's legal department for approval.

CASE 5–3. SOUTHEASTERN MILLS VERSUS TAMPA MANUFACTURING*

The case of the cancelled order

Cast of Characters

Tribunal Clerk	E. Robert Cregar
Southeastern Mills, Inc.	Edward C. Wallace, Attorney
	Peter T. Derringer, Sales Manager
Tampa Manufacturing Co.	Edwin L. Gasperini, Attorney
	Albert W. Carr, Purchasing Agent
Arbitrator	Edward M. Fuller

NARRATOR: Every year, industrial purchasing agents contract for billions of dollars' worth of goods and services. Most of these transactions are completed without any problem. Many differences that do occur are resolved by negotiation. But every once in a while, a buyer and a seller are unable to overcome their differences. They then face a choice of litigating their dispute in the public courts, or arbitrating in a private hearing room. You are about to see what takes place in a typical buyer-seller dispute when, as happens thousands of times every year, the parties choose the arbitration route.

There are many reasons for choosing arbitration. One is privacy. A company's reputation for fair dealing, and the good name of its product, represent large sums of money spent in advertising. These may be jeopardized if the public learns of a dispute. Another reason is speed. Crowded court calendars often make a prompt decision impossible, and a victory may be of little avail if business opportunities are lost and funds are tied up pending the outcome of trials and appeals.

A third reason is that in arbitration, as the late Judge Learned Hand observed, the parties can select as arbitrators men who are experts. As the Judge put it: men "who are familiar with the practices and customs of the calling, and with just such matters as current prices, merchantable quality, the terms of sale, and the like." Many other reasons may be cited: economy; ease of enforcement; convenience; the friendly atmosphere which encourages continued business relationships; and so on.

When the American Arbitration Association was notified of the dispute, the AAA's regional manager mailed to the parties identical lists of attorneys, accountants, and qualified trade experts. These names were taken from the Association's National Panel of Arbitrators, which now numbers some 16,000 experts throughout the country. When the parties made their selections from the lists, the regional manager appointed one arbitrator who represented a mutual choice.

Shortly after the arbitrator was chosen, a date and place were set for the hearing. The place turned out to be an AAA hearing room in one of the 18 cities where the association maintains its offices.

---

* This case is based on a filmstrip developed by the American Arbitration Association and the National Association of Purchasing Management. The film may be rented from the National Association of Purchasing Management, 11 Park Place, New York, N.Y. 10007 or the American Arbitration Association.

The arbitration is about to begin in this hearing room. There is nothing elaborate here. It is simply a convenient and comfortable place for the parties to meet and present their cases. The first participants to enter are from the Tampa Manufacturing Company. ALBERT W. CARR is the purchasing agent, and EDWIN L. GASPERINI is the attorney for Tampa. From the opposite side come PETER T. DERRINGER, sales manager for Southeastern Mills, Inc., and EDWARD C. WALLACE, attorney for Southeastern. Now the arbitrator, who is acceptable to both sides by prior agreement, EDWARD M. FULLER, enters, followed by the tribunal clerk, E. ROBERT CREGAR.

CREGAR: Mr. Fuller, on August 4, the American Arbitration Association received the following demand for arbitration from Edward C. Wallace, attorney for Southeastern Mills.

Tampa Manufacturing Company has refused to pay for 30,000 yards of nylon fabric. Tampa has also refused to pay $145 which Southeastern Mills paid to Hollywood Rubber Company for rubber-coating samples of the nylon fabric.

The demand for arbitration asks for $22,645. $22,500 is for the nylon, at 75 cents per yard, and $145 to cover the cost of rubber-coating the samples.

The demand for arbitration quotes an arbitration clause naming AAA as the administrator of arbitration. The clause, printed on a purchase order dated March 21, reads:

Except as otherwise provided in this order, any dispute, controversy or claim arising out of or relating to this contract or the breach thereof, which is not disposed of by agreement, shall be settled by arbitration in accordance with the rules of the American Arbitration Association. The award rendered by the arbitrator(s) shall be final and judgment may be entered thereon in any court having jurisdiction thereof. Pending final decision of a dispute, controversy or claim hereunder, the vendor shall proceed with the performance of this order.

In an answering statement dated August 26, Tampa Manufacturing denied that any sum was due Southeastern Mills. The answering statement was signed by Edwin L. Gasperini. Here are the papers in the case.

(CREGAR *hands demand for arbitration and answering statement to the* ARBITRATOR.)

ARBITRATOR: Thank you. Would either of you gentlemen like to examine these letters before they are accepted?

WALLACE: No. Those are the letters.

GASPERINI: That's all right.

ARBITRATOR: All right then. As Southeastern is the complainant, suppose we hear from Mr. Wallace first. Would you care to start with a brief opening statement, telling us what it's all about?

WALLACE: Gentlemen, early this year, my client received from Tampa Manufacturing Company an invitation to bid on the production of some 100,000 square yards of nylon fabric of a certain type which Tampa intended to make up into life rafts on a contract for the Navy. It appeared also that the fabric would have to be rubber-coated before delivery to Tampa. After certain conversations and correspondence which I will establish through my witness, an agreement was reached and a price of 75 cents per running yard was established. This was not to include rubber-coating. That was an extra charge by Hollywood Rubber Company, which is not really a part of this case, as you will see. After the purchase order which Mr. Cregar mentioned was signed, my client proceeded with production. He manufactured eight sample pieces and had them rubber-coated before going ahead with the rest of the order. Tampa approved the samples, and Southeastern thereupon proceeded with production. After some 30,000 yards were produced, Tampa notified us that the Navy had decided not to place that order for life rafts. Southeastern stopped production and expected Tampa to accept delivery and pay for what had already been done. Tampa refused to do so, which left Southeastern with no alternative but to institute the proceedings that brought us together here today.

Now, I would like to establish all the facts through a sworn witness.

ARBITRATOR: Yes, you may. But first, let's see whether Mr. Gasperini would like to make an equally brief statement now.

GASPERINI: Thank you, I will be brief. Much of what Mr. Wallace said is true, but he omitted to tell you that the entire purchase order was conditioned upon Tampa Manufacturing Company actually getting the order from the Navy that was promised. Pentagon officials had given us assurances that we were getting the order. But Southeastern knew that no work was to be done until everything was set. If, for their own reason, they chose to jump the gun, they were taking a calculated risk. Having taken that risk and lost, they are now trying to get my client to absorb the loss. There is no contractual basis for Southeastern's demands. I have more to say about this, but I would like to postpone the rest of my introductory remarks until I present my case.

ARBITRATOR: All right, then. Mr. Wallace, you may proceed with your first witness.

WALLACE: I call Peter T. Derringer.

CREGAR: Do you solemnly swear that the evidence you are about to give will be the truth, the whole truth, and nothing but the truth, so help you God?

DERRINGER: I do.

CREGAR: Please be seated. Will you state your position with Southeastern Mills?

DERRINGER: I am sales manager.

WALLACE: In your own words, Mr. Derringer, tell the arbitrator about your transaction with Tampa Manufacturing Company.

DERRINGER: Well, last January, Tampa Manufacturing Company got in touch with Southeastern Mills and asked us to bid on the manufacture of some 100,000 running yards of fabric of a certain quality that the Navy wanted made into life rafts. We estimated at 75 cents per running yard, and the estimate was apparently satisfactory, because Mr. Carr, an officer of Tampa Manufacturing, asked me to see him about further arrangements. He told me . . .

(The scene shifts to Mr. Carr's office. Mr. Carr is at his desk. Facing him, with his back to the camera, is Mr. Derringer.)

CARR: When this order comes through from the Navy we're going to need 100,000 yards of nylon cloth in about six weeks. Your price is all right, but do you have the plant capacity to produce in that time?

DERRINGER: You don't have to worry about that. We'll deliver. But just to make sure we aren't held up after we get the green light, I'd like to get all the samples approved in advance, including the rubber-coating. Where do you want that done, or did you want us to find the subcontractor?

CARR: That's all lined up. Hollywood Rubber will do it. Send your samples over to them and add their bill to your own.

DERRINGER: When do you want us to start production, assuming the samples are OK?

CARR: We'll send you a purchase order, and I'll be in touch with you. As soon as I get definite word from Washington, I'll pass it on to you.

(*The scene shifts back to the hearing room. Derringer is still testifying.*)

WALLACE: And what followed?

DERRINGER: Well, Hollywood rubber-coated eight pieces of nylon and they came back all right. We sent four of them over to Tampa. They still have them, and we have the other four. They were apparently satisfactory, because we got Tampa's purchase order and we sent them our confirmation-of-order form.

WALLACE: Let's put that into evidence. I hand you this paper. Will you tell the arbitrator what it is?

DERRINGER (*examining it briefly*): Yes, this is our copy of the purchase order for 100,000 yards of three-ounce nylon as per the sample, at 75 cents per yard, plus Hollywood's charge for rubber-coating.

WALLACE: (*to the arbitrator*): I would like this document accepted in evidence, and call your attention to the statement on the purchase order which reads: "Delivery is to be completed within six weeks after Tampa Manufacturing notifies Southeastern Mills that the order from the United States Navy has become final."

ARBITRATOR: Mr. Gasperini, would you like to examine this document and comment on its acceptibility as evidence in this case?

GASPERINI (*examining the purchase order brief*): Yes, this is the document the witness described. I was planning to introduce our copy of the same paper. If Mr. Derringer doesn't object, it might be received as a joint exhibit.

WALLACE: That's perfectly all right.

GASPERINI: But I would like to point out that the purchase order identifies the nylon fabric by its military number, MIL-C-5539, which shows the understanding of both sides that the transaction was dependent upon our order from the Navy.

ARBITRATOR: Mr. Cregar, you may mark the purchase order as Joint Exhibit No. 1. Please continue, Mr. Wallace.

WALLACE (*to the witness*): Now, then, we have established the point that the terms of the purchase were agreed upon. What happened next?

DERRINGER: What happened next was that I kept in touch with Tampa, as Mr. Carr had suggested I do. Finally, about April 15, Mr. Carr told me that it was a certainty that the order was coming through, and we started production. About two weeks later he called to tell me the deal with the Navy fell through. We stopped production, but by that time we had already made up about 30,000 yards.

WALLACE: Mr. Derringer, how did it happen that you started production before the Navy's order was final.

DERRINGER: Tampa Manufacturing kept assuring us that the deal was a sure thing and that delivery in no later than six weeks was absolutely necessary. We would not have started ahead of time if Mr. Carr hadn't told us that he had word from Washington that only some red tape stood in the way of official notice to start work.

WALLACE: When did this take place?

DERRINGER: That was on April 15. I had been calling every few days. On this occasion . . .

(*The scene shifts to Mr. Derringer's office. Mr. Derringer is on the telephone. Mr. Carr's voice is heard at the other end.*)

DERRINGER: Look, Al, what's the deal with the Navy? Did you get that order yet? We're holding off with some other customers for your work and we'd like to get going.

CARR: I told you before, Pete. Stop worrying. It's in the bag. There's some paper work snafu that's holding things up. But we're getting the order. That's definite. But while we're at it, I want to be sure you can give us delivery on time. That's critical.

DERRINGER: Our agreement is for 100,000 yards in six weeks. We can do it, but it will help if we don't delay unnecessarily.

CARR: I'm telling you, it's an order. You can depend on it.

(*The scene shifts back to the hearing room. Derringer is continuing his testimony.*)

DERRINGER: . . . So, with the definite assurance that the deal was on, and with all that pressure for speedy deliveries, we started production.

WALLACE: And it was for the convenience of the Tampa Manufacturing Company, not for yours, that you started production when you did?

DERRINGER: Definitely.

GASPERINI: Now just a minute. I object to Mr. Wallace leading the witness. You can argue when you summarize.

ARBITRATOR: The objection is well taken. Mr. Wallace, no doubt you want me to reach that conclusion, but it's still too early in the proceedings for that.

WALLACE: Just one more point. You spoke of 30,000 yards of nylon twill produced before the stop-work order came through, and you also spoke of eight pieces of canvas that were used for samples. Are those eight pieces included in the 30,000 yards?

DERRINGER: Yes, those eight pieces came to a total of 400 running yards. They were rubber-coated and we paid Hollywood Rubber Company $145 for their work. The other 29,600 yards never left our premises.

WALLACE: That's all. (*Turning to Mr. Gasperini.*) Your witness.

GASPERINI: Now, Mr. Derringer, you testified that Mr. Carr said to you that the order was "in the bag." Were those the very words he used?

DERRINGER: Well, more or less, that's what he said.

GASPERINI: What do you mean, more or less? We're not interested in whether he said more or less. We want to known exactly what he did say. Did Mr. Carr use the phrase "in the bag"?

DERRINGER: He said that, or "it's a sure thing," or words to that effect. I can't swear to every word.

GASPERINI: In other words, you're improvising. You're not giving us an accurate account of that phone conversation.

DERRINGER: I'm giving you the gist of it to the best of my recollection.

GASPERINI: Speaking of recollections, do you recall how many times you called Mr. Carr before that occasion you testified to?

DERRINGER: What do you mean, how many times did I telephone him?

GASPERINI: Yes, how many times did you call to ask whether it was OK to start manufacturing the fabric?

DERRINGER: Oh, I don't remember exactly. Three or four times, I suppose. He wanted speed, and we wanted the work. Is there anything wrong in that?

GASPERINI: Leave the questions to me. You just answer the questions. Those calls took place after the purchase order and confirmation-of-order forms were exchanged, didn't they?

DERRINGER: Yes.

GASPERINI: And by those calls, you showed that it was your understanding that until you got the word "Go" you were not to start work.

DERRINGER: Well, we expected to start the minute we were authorized to, and the phone call I told you about was the word we were waiting for.

GASPERINI: It has been brought out that delivery was expected in six weeks' time. As a matter of fact, didn't you have some doubt as to whether your plant was capable of producing 100,000 yards in six weeks?

DERRINGER: No doubt at all.

GASPERINI: Isn't 15,000 yards a week just about your maximum capacity?

DERRINGER: It might be if we worked regular hours only. But we can work overtime, too. And we can always increase production by putting off other customers for a while, if we have to.

GASPERINI: I submit to you that you ran ahead with production not for the convenience of Tampa but for your own convenience. You just speculated and lost.

WALLACE: Hold on a minute. That's not a proper question. That's argument. You can argue during the summation.

ARBITRATOR: That objection is well taken. I suggest you rephrase the question, if you want to ask one.

GASPERINI: Mr. Derringer, as a matter of fact, didn't you know that the whole purpose of your transaction with Tampa Manufacturing was dependent upon Tampa's getting that order from the Navy?

DERRINGER: Sure, I knew the fabric was for filling that order.

GASPERINI: And that if the order didn't come through Tampa had no need for the cloth?

DERRINGER: Naturally, but I had assurances . . .

GASPERINI: That's all.

(*Derringer begins to leave the witness stand. He is stopped by the Arbitrator.*)

ARBITRATOR: Just a minute, Mr. Derringer. This three-ounce nylon fabric you were talking about —is that a standard fabric, with an established market and price?

DERRINGER: Oh, no. That was made to Navy specifications, and no one else uses it. We quoted a price for the manufacture of the goods according to specifications, and there is no quotable price on the open market.

ARBITRATOR (*to Gasperini*): Do you agree with that?

GASPERINI: On the contrary, that nylon has many uses and can be bought and sold anywhere. I would like to offer evidence on that point, if you think if necessary.

ARBITRATOR: Of course, you may do so if you wish. You will have an opportunity when you present your case. (*To Mr. Wallace.*) Do you have other witnesses, Mr. Wallace?

WALLACE: No.

ARBITRATOR: All right. Mr. Gasperini, you said earlier that you wanted to finish your opening statement before presenting your first witness. Do you want to do so now?

GASPERINI: As a matter of fact, I don't think it is necessary. The claim has been shown to be so lacking in merit that if this were a court of law, I would move for a verdict in our favor without putting a witness on the stand at all. But I will call Mr. Carr.

(*Mr. Carr takes the stand and is sworn.*)

CREGAR: Do you solemnly swear that the evidence you are about to give will be the truth, the whole truth, and nothing but the truth, so help you God?

CARR: I do.

CREGAR: Please be seated. Will you state your position with Tampa Manufacturing Company?

CARR: I am purchasing agent.

GASPERINI: Now, Mr. Carr, it has already been established that the samples were found acceptable and that a purchase order and a confirmation-of-order form were exchanged. What happened next?

CARR: What happened next was that after promising us that we were getting the order all along, the Pentagon suddenly decided not to go through with this contract. I don't know why, and I don't know whether the project will be revived in the future. But as of right now, they don't want those life rafts. Naturally, as soon as I learned of this, I called Southeastern and gave them the bad news that the deal was off.

GASPERINI: And that was the end of it, as far as you were concerned?

CARR: Yes, and that was the first time I learned that Southeastern had jumped the gun without authorization and had actually started production.

GASPERINI: You had not authorized them to start production until the order from the Navy was received?

CARR: I specifically warned them not to start until I gave the signal. I did authorize the manufacture of samples, but that's all.

GASPERINI: Thank you, Mr. Carr. No further questions.

ARBITRATOR: Mr. Wallace, would you care to cross-examine?

WALLACE: Indeed I would. Mr. Carr, do you recall a telephone conversation with Mr. Derringer of Southeastern about two weeks before you notified him that the Navy was no longer interested in the life rafts?

CARR: Well, I recall many phone conversations. We were on the phone almost every day.

WALLACE: I refer particularly to a conversation on April 15 in which you told Mr. Derringer that the order was a sure thing and that he didn't have to worry about anything.

CARR: I don't recall that language exactly. Mr. Derringer was nervous about not getting official word to start production and he seemed to be anxious for this order to go through, so he called me every so often to ask what was happening. I told him the truth as I understood it at the time. We expected the green light from the Pentagon and I said so. I didn't tell him to start production.

WALLACE: You knew the purpose of Mr. Carr's call was to get authorization to start work so he could deliver on schedule, didn't you? Did you tell him to hold off until you got the final word?

CARR: I sure did. I testified to that. He came to my office when we discussed the deal and I said . . .

WALLACE: I am not asking about his visit to your office. I'm asking about that phone conversation when Mr. Derringer said he was anxious to start work. Did you tell him not to?

CARR: Not specifically, but he . . .

WALLACE: Never mind the buts. Your answer is that you did not specifically tell him not to begin production.

GASPERINI: Just a minute. I object to Mr. Wallace's interruption of the witness. Please let Mr. Carr answer the last question in full.

WALLACE: The witness answered. We're not interested in argumentation. You will have a chance to argue when the proper time comes.

ARBITRATOR: Now hold on a minute. The last question, as I recall it, was whether, in the phone conversation of April 15, Mr. Carr had told Mr. Derringer not to start production, and the answer was "not specifically." Is that your full answer to the question?

CARR: I was just going to say that it was understood Southeastern was not supposed to run ahead.

WALLACE: When you told Mr. Derringer that only some red tape stood in the way of a final order from the Navy, you intended him to understand that as instructions to start production, didn't you?

CARR: No.

WALLACE: And you were not, in fact, speculating on his starting work so that your company might have the advantage of quicker deliveries?

CARR: No.

WALLACE: I have no further questions.

ARBITRATOR: Mr. Carr, you heard Mr. Derringer testify that the nylon produced by Southeastern has no open market. Do you agree with that?

CARR: I do not agree. That's a regular three-ounce nylon, and as long as it hasn't been dyed or finished, it can be easily sold.

ARBITRATOR: All right, you may step down, Mr. Carr. Mr. Gasperini, have you any other witnesses?

GASPERINI: No. That's our case. But I would like to summarize, of course.

ARBITRATOR: Of course. But I think it would be best to proceed in the same order we followed in starting. I suggest we hear first from Mr. Wallace.

WALLACE: Mr. Fuller, we are dealing here with a simple matter of contract law. But somehow, a very subtle, but important, inaccuracy has been put into the record here. Tampa Manufacturing has been trying to give the impression than an order from the Navy was the circumstance that was to mark the beginning of production by Southeastern Mills. That is not correct. As the purchase order form makes clear, the condition precedent to production was *notification by Tampa to Southeastern that the order was final.* The distinction is important, for only Tampa was privy to the details of negotiations with the Navy, and only Tampa could signal the start of production. If Tampa gave the go-ahead signal in advance of the order—and this is what happened—my client is entitled to be paid for the work he did. You will notice that the purchase order does not say *how* notification is to be accomplished. It does not speak of notification by registered letter, or by writing of any kind. It speaks only of notice. Period. Notification to start production can occur by word of mouth, by a wink, or a nod. And in this case, as the evidence clearly shows, notification was accomplished by language that was deliberately contrived to mislead my client. Mr. Derringer kept calling Mr. Carr every few days to find out if the order was in. Finally, on April 15, it became apparent that unless Southeastern was told to start production, there might be delays. And so, without saying it in so many words, Mr. Carr gave Mr. Derringer reason to believe it was safe to start production, and Southeastern did just that. I submit, in conclusion, that my client had the notice required by the purchase order, and he is entitled to the remedy asked for in our demand for arbitration, notwithstanding the fact that the Navy did not after all, come through with the order.

ARBITRATOR: Thank you, Counsellor. And now, may we hear from you, Mr. Gasperini?

GASPERINI: Mr. Fuller, we have here a situation in which both parties knew that everything depended upon an order from the Navy, and without that order, that all these negotiations were so much wasted motion. The Navy order was almost within their grasp, but Southeastern knew that some uncertainty had to exist as long as the order was not official. Yet, knowing this, Southeastern Mills went into production prematurely. Why did they do that? Not because of any contrived signals from Tampa. That's nonsense. Mr. Derringer is a prudent, experienced businessman and he knows that in matters as important as this, one gets a clear yes or no answer before taking action. At all times, he got an honest answer, and if it seemed ambiguous, it was because the Navy order seemed certain, but was not yet completely so. I contend that Southeastern ran ahead with the work for its own convenience. It was because Southeastern had not been perfectly candid with Tampa. They didn't have the mill capacity for quick production that they said they had, and they were afraid they might have to default on the six-weeks delivery schedule, once the green light was given. They speculated; if the Navy contract had come through, no harm would have been done. And if, as events transpired, the contract fell through, they figured that they could still unload the goods on Tampa, through arbitration, if necessary. This is the kind of practice that should not be tolerated. In short, the condition precedent for work—that is, the Navy contract—did not exist when Southeastern started production, and Southeastern knew it. Without that contract, none of the commitments of the purchase order were binding. That is why I ask you to deny Southeastern's claim and rule for the respondents.

ARBITRATOR: All right, gentlemen. I want to congratulate both of you on a very able and helpful presentation of your case. Before I declare this hearing closed, will you affirm that all your evidence is in and that you have had an equal opportunity to be heard?

WALLACE: Yes.

GASPERINI: Our case is in.

NARRATOR: Under AAA rules the arbitrator has 30 days in which to make his decision. While he is studying the evidence and exhibits, perhaps *you* would like to discuss the case and come to your own decision. *You* be the arbitrator!

Question

As arbitrator, prepare an award form like the following sample. Explain in detail the reasons for your decision.

AWARD

_____Claim of Southeastern for $22,645 is allowed in full.
_____Claim of Southeastern is denied, except for payment of $145, the cost of rubber-coating the samples.
_____Southeastern is allowed $_____ to reimburse it for the loss incurred in selling material on the open market.
_____Claim of Southeastern is denied in full.
_____Other (explain). _____

6

Forecasting for materials management

IF THE MATERIALS MANAGER could forecast the future perfectly, most of his problems would disappear overnight. Unfortunately, regardless of whether or not he has any talent for it, the materials manager must behave as if he were an almost-perfect forecaster. To some extent he can hedge his forecasts with inventory, but he often must pay heavily for this privilege.

The materials manager is confronted with problems of uncertainty both in the supply of purchased materials and in the demand for finished goods and services for which these materials are purchased. Both the supply of purchased materials and the demand for finished goods are determined by factors over which the materials manager has no control and of which he can have only imperfect knowledge.

DEMAND FOR MATERIALS

Market responsibility

The demand for purchased materials is derived from the company's end-product demand. In most companies, the marketing manager is responsible for forecasting final demand for company products, but in some this forecasting responsibility is delegated by top management to the materials manager. The reasoning behind this is that the materials manager must have material on hand if manufacturing is to be able to fill every order that comes to it from marketing. Thus, whether the company succeeds or fails in its objective of having just needed material on hand—and no more—is the responsibility of materials management.

171

Therefore, materials management should be responsible for forecasting demand for finished goods. In such companies, marketing is responsible essentially for getting more orders, not for filling these orders. Marketing works closely with customers and is in the best position to predict what they will buy. The forecast of end-product demand that is made by marketing then becomes the basis of the materials manager's forecast of demand for purchased materials. For example, if the marketing department of an automobile manufacturing company predicts sales of 1,000,000 cars, the materials manager of the company will be prepared to buy that year 1,000,000 sets of headlights, 1,000,000 batteries, and corresponding amounts of other parts and materials.

As long as marketing's forecast is perfect, the materials manager has no demand forecasting problems. Unfortunately, forecasting is an inexact process. The auto company that hoped to sell 1,000,000 cars will often discover that actual demand is significantly different from its prediction. If demand exceeds the forecast, the materials manager may be hard pressed to have on hand sufficient amounts of material to permit the higher demand to be satisfied. On the other hand, if demand lags, he may have too much material.

In either case, for reasons we will later explore in considerable detail, the company's profits are lower than they would have been were forecasting a precise science. In such cases, the real-life materials manager would feel tempted to point his finger at marketing and say, in effect, "I can't help it if your forecasts are no good." This temptation would promptly be suppressed by the successful materials manager, however. The simple fact is that he is responsible for having exactly the right amount of material on hand (no more and no less), regardless of whose forecasts he uses. The materials manager, like the other key line managers of the organizations, is paid to make the right decision even when that decision is based on faulty information. His role is quite different from that of the economist who makes the forecasts that may go astray. Staff executives such as economists are responsible only for turning out high-quality professional work. As long as they are not negligent, it is the executive who uses their forecast who takes the responsibility for the final results.

Independent action

Because they must take the responsibility, materials managers in many companies do not feel literally bound to forecasts they receive from marketing. They may buy more material than what seems to be called for in the forecast, or they may buy less. If top management is to hold materials management responsible for results, it has to give the materials manager authority to make his own forecasting decisions.

In a few companies, top management goes one step further and gives complete authority for prediction of end-product demand to materials management rather than to marketing. These companies operate on the principle that it is up to marketing to sell as much as possible, while manufacturing and materials management stand ready to supply whatever can be sold. And, of course, materials management can determine how much material to buy only if it can forecast what can be sold. In these companies, the job of sales forecasting can be done as easily in materials management as in marketing because the product is one in which the marketing department is not in direct contact with users of the product. For example, neither the materials manager nor the marketing manager has any direct contact with the millions of men who use Gillette razor blades, so materials management is responsible for forecasting demand because it must have materials on hand to meet that demand. Marketing simply works as hard as possible to equal or to exceed some previous forecast.

Materials management would never play this strong a role in forecasting demand for a product that required considerable personal selling effort. For example, Boeing has fewer than 1,000 potential customers for its airliners. Company salesmen work closely with each customer, and, because of their contacts, they are in excellent position to predict demand, even before it materializes. In contrast, the Boeing materials department would have almost no contact with the company's airline customers, and its forecasts would err accordingly.

Minor product demand

While marketing in companies like Boeing is primarily responsible for forecasting demand of *major* end products, the forecasting of demand for the thousands of *minor* finished products these companies also sell is normally a materials management responsibility. Any company like Boeing, General Motors, Caterpillar, or IBM that makes a very complicated end product is also in .the business of marketing thousands of repair parts for the major product lines. In some cases, the total value of the repair parts over the life of the equipment is greater than the value of the original sale. Some of these parts are made by the original equipment manufacturer; others are purchased and resold. In either case, the materials manager may ultimately be responsible for forecasting demand for these spare parts. The forecasting technique is essentially statistical, based on the number of pieces of equipment in the field, the estimated failure rate in the field, and other variables.

Users of spare parts must also be able to forecast demand so that equipment is not shut down for long periods. The whole field of logistics management is primarily concerned with having the right spares on hand at the right place at the right time. In certain types of companies, this is the most important part of materials management. For example, the really critical materials management problem for an airline is to have spares readily available. This is normally far more important than the purchase price of the spares themselves. Every day a jet airliner sits on the ground waiting for parts represents a loss of more than $10,000. The cost of the part itself may be trivial in comparison to the loss from the idle equipment.

SUPPLY OF MATERIALS

The supply of purchased materials is subject to essentially the same vagaries as demand for these materials. Each supplier tends to be in much the same position as the materials manager's own company. It cannot control the demand for its end products, and it is also dependent on its own suppliers.

While the materials manager must use forecasts of demand for his company's end products, he normally need not worry about the ability of suppliers to satisfy his needs—provided he can afford to wait. His basic problem is usually how rapidly suppliers can respond to changing demand rather than their ultimate ability to respond. Almost all suppliers, for example, would be delighted to double shipments to their customers, but hardly any are able to increase their output substantially without weeks or even months of advance notice. Thus the materials manager's key problem is rarely his ability to get the material he needs; instead it is how to get it by some deadline. Nor need the materials manager really worry too much about the supply of material drying up (as long as some form of rationing is not imposed by government). His problem, instead, boils down to his company's willingness to pay the going price for materials that may be in short supply. In a free market, price works to ration supply and, since purchased materials account for 50 percent of the average manufacturer's sales dollar, the materials manager is very much concerned that the relationship between prices paid for purchased material and prices charged for the company's finished product remains favorable.

GENERAL BUSINESS FORECASTS

The materials manager is concerned with three basic types of forecast:

1. *Demand for purchased materials.* This is normally derived directly from demand for the company's end products.

2. *Supply of purchased materials.* In most cases, the primary concern is with lead time, the number of weeks or months that one must wait for delivery of particular materials after they have been ordered.

3. *Prices paid for purchased materials.* These have a direct relationship to the company' success. Very few organizations can afford to ignore fluctuations in prices of purchased materials.

Each of these three forecasts is shaped partly by unique forces. For example, if demand for a company's end products increases by 10 percent, it usually is pure coincidence if the demand for the company's suppliers' products also increases by 10 percent. On the other hand, it would be surprising if there were not relationship at all.

In general, all businesses are affected at least partly by broad economic forces. No materials manager is expected to be a professional economist, but he should be familiar with business statistics and know how they apply to his job.

Many big corporations have full-time professional economists on their staffs. In such cases, the materials manager should know how to apply the forecasts of the company's economists to materials management. In turn, he often can supply the economists with much useful information gleaned from his contacts with thousands of suppliers in many industries.

In the overwhelming majority of companies, however, the materials manager is strictly on his own as far as business forecasting is concerned. There are no staff economists to help him. He must read and interpret his own data and make his own decisions. In these smaller firms, particularly those with a limited number or type of customers, the materials manager is in the best possible position of anyone to act as company economist. He often is the only member of management with contacts outside the particular company's industry. Also, he is the manager most directly concerned with economic forecasts in the course of his day-to-day work.

Effect of business conditions

Why must management be familiar with the business outlook? Because in most industries, general business conditions play a vital role in determining the prices, availability, and demand of purchased materials.

Prices. When business booms, prices tend to rise; when it slumps, they tend to decline. If a materials manager is sure of the business outlook, he can make substantial profits for his company. If he believes prices are going to rise, he will increase inventories with forward buying. If he believes they are going to decline, he will hold off buying and operate with minimum inventories.

Availability. When business is booming, many industries are operating near capacity and materials take longer to get. In some cases, supplies become inadequate to satisfy the demand of all users. If the materials manager can successfully anticipate shortages, he can either stock up in advance or locate alternate sources of supply to protect his company against shortages.

Demand. Demand for a company's end products is at least partly determined by general business conditions. If the materials manager knows that general business will decline, he can cut back on purchase commitments, since less material will be needed. If he anticipates better business, he can increase commitments. Without good forecasting, it is easy to make serious errors in commitments for materials. Many items must be ordered months before they are needed, and if demand changes, the company either is stuck with excess stocks or loses sales because of lack of inventory.

It is no exaggeration to say that if the materials manager could forecast business conditions with absolute certainty, his job would become largely routine. So far no one has figured out a surefire forecasting technique. All the materials manager can do is to study certain key business barometers and make the best possible decisions.

Gross national product

The biggest, broadest business indicator in the United States is gross national product (GNP).[1] GNP, the estimated total spending for all goods and services, is prepared quarterly by the Office of Business Economics of the U.S. Department of Commerce. GNP components and their approximate relative importance as a percentage of total GNP are:

Personal consumption expenditures 63–66%
Net balance of foreign trade (difference between exports and
 imports) .... 1% or less
Government purchases of goods and services (federal, state, and
 local) 20–22%
Gross private domestic investment 14–16%

As the term implies, the personal consumption expenditures component of GNP is estimated total consumer spending for goods and services. Although it is the biggest component of GNP, it is one of the easiest to predict, because individuals spend a consistent percentage of their incomes. Big fluctuations in consumer spending come only on durable goods (automobiles, refrigerators, and so on) for which consumers can postpone spending without great hardship.

Foreign trade, the second GNP component listed above, rarely has much direct effect on the American economy. Exports normally exceed imports by a few billion dollars. However, when American costs get out of line with those of foreign producers, imports may exceed exports. In any case, the difference between exports and imports is a net addition to (or subtraction from) GNP.

Government spending, on the other hand, is a very important component. It now comprises almost 25 percent of our economy and shows

---

[1] The reader is reminded that this is a book on materials management, not economic theory. If explanations of economic phenomena seem either confusing or too superficial, it is suggested that he refer to one or more of the books listed in the Bibliography that deal in detail with economic theory and business cycles.

no sign of declining in importance. Government spending poses few problems for the forecaster, however. It is voted in advance by Congress and by state and local legislative bodies.

Investment spending

Thus, three out of four segments of GNP are reasonably predictable. Would-be forecasters fall flat on their faces only when they try to predict the fourth major component, gross private domestic investment. In a private-enterprise economy, business investment spending is a not-too-small tail that wags the overall GNP dog. Cutbacks in investment spending touch off recessions; increases spark booms.

The multiplier principle. The reason why the level of investment spending determines GNP and total economic activity is a commonsense one. To understand why this is so, compare the economic activities of a farmer raising pigs to those of a bricklayer.

When the farmer sells his pigs on the market, he increases the supply of nondurable consumer goods. When he spends his income from the pigs, he is increasing the demand for consumer goods by a like amount (assuming that he spends all of his income). The net result is that GNP rises by the exact amount of the revenue that the farmer gets from the pigs.

When the bricklayer cashes his paycheck, he also increases the demand for consumer goods. But the product of his labors, a new office building or factory (i.e., investment spending), has no immediate effect on the supply of consumer goods. So the bricklayer's economic activity produces an imbalance in the supply of and demand for consumer goods. His net increase in demand is a call for additional production and investment; the whole economy expands.

Thus, spending for pork increases GNP by the exact value of the pork. Spending for a bricklayer's services increases it by more than the value of his services because there is a net increase in the demand for consumer goods (since the bricklayer's production cannot be used for immediate consumption). This is what economists call the "multiplier principle" It is one of two basic reasons why investment spending is so important to the economy. The second reason is not hard to deduce: It is easy to postpone investment spending, but it is hard to postpone consumption spending. As a result, investment spending virtually determines total output of the entire economy.

Every long-range, overall economic forecast is really an attempt to determine the level of the three basic types of gross private domestic investment: new construction, producers' durable equipment, and changes in business inventories. The first two are discussed briefly below, and the third, and most important, is the subject of the next subsection.

New construction. The best barometer of new construction activity is the monthly report of contract awards by the F. W. Dodge Division of the McGraw-Hill Publishing Company. It is particularly useful since contract awards are indicators of future investment spending, but it must be interpreted carefully. Construction activity is highly seasonal (see Figure 6–1). It reaches a peak late in spring and is at a seasonal

FIGURE 6–1

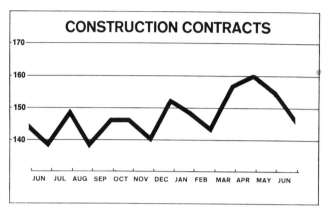

F. W. Dodge statistics on construction contract awards are useful to the business forecaster because they indicate future capital expenditures.

low in January and February. In analyzing contract awards, it is best always to compare current with year-ago figures; otherwise the analysis may well be distorted by normal seasonal fluctuations.

Producers' durable equipment. The U.S. Department of Commerce and the department of economics of the McGraw-Hill Publishing Company both run quarterly surveys on future plant and equipment spending. These surveys are widely reported and are extremely useful to the business forecaster. Materials managers in metalworking industries are keenly interested in the monthly report of the National Machine Tool Builders' Association on new orders for machine tools (see Figure 6–2). New-order statistics are especially interesting for forecasting purposes, since they are an excellent barometer of future investment in producers' durable equipment. The association's report is quoted widely in many publications. It should be read not only by materials managers interested in making a business forecast but by machine-tool buyers, who will find it a good indicator of the industry's ability to deliver promptly on new orders.

Inventory changes

Inventories are by far the most unstable component of investment spending. The reason is obvious. Businesses can change direction in

FIGURE 6-2

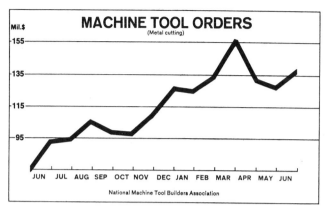

A drop in machine-tool orders can signal a general business downturn. When machine-tool orders rise, the economy is usually already booming.

inventory investment much more rapidly than in spending for construction or equipment. When business gets better, they can boost inventories in a period of weeks. But it can take months (or even years) to get new plant and equipment.

Relatively rapid changes in inventories by business are the single most important factor in the business cycle, and no one is closer to inventory policy than the materials manager. But even the materials manager can profitably supplement his unique know-how on inventory trends with data on changes in inventory in the entire economy.

The U.S. Department of Commerce issues monthly statistics on business inventories that are excellent leading indicators of future business conditions. Unfortunately, they come out six weeks late; for example, inventory figures for September are not available until about November 15. They also are subject to frequent revision.

Thus forecasters must try to guess approximately what inventories will be during the current month. A number of business barometers provide clues. Particularly useful are figures on new orders, freight carloadings, retail sales, and certain commodity prices.

1. *New and unfilled orders.* Statistics on new orders and unfilled orders are issued simultaneously with inventory figures by the Department of Commerce (see Figure 6–3). So they, too, are at least six weeks late, but they are still useful as barometers of future spending. Changes in order backlogs influence inventory planning. When new orders are rising, inventories eventually will rise as business stocks go up to meet anticipated new business. On the other hand, when new orders drop, business is likely to cut inventories in anticipation of lower business volume.

FIGURE 6–3

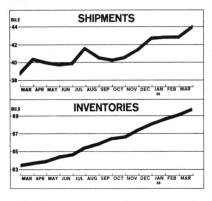

U.S. Department of Commerce estimates of shipments, inventories, new orders, and unfilled orders help confirm forecasts made from other statistics that are available sooner.

2. Freight carloadings. When business activity is high, carloadings are high. Statistics on total carloadings are sometimes misleading, since they include highly seasonal shipments of grain and other commodities that have little relation to industrial output. For this reason, for forecasting purposes economists have traditionally relied on "miscellaneous carloadings" data, which reflect movements of manufactured goods.

Carloadings are not a leading indicator. They are a rough barometer of shipments by manufacturers and are primarily useful in forecasting because they are available on a weekly basis. Properly interpreted, they can provide clues to inventory trends weeks before the Department of Commerce issues its monthly report on sales, inventories, and new orders.

3. Retail sales. Weekly Department of Commerce estimates of department-store sales also provide clues to inventory trends at the retail level. When retail sales are rising, department-store orders to suppliers will also rise, and this in turn will affect industrial sales, orders, and inventories.

Both retail sales and carloadings are subject to wide seasonal fluctuations, and the forecaster must be careful in making week-to-week comparisons. For example, retail sales always plunge during the last week of the year. This doesn't mean the beginning of a recession; it is only the end of the Christmas shopping season.

4. Commodity prices. Industrial materials traded on commodity exchanges generally fluctuate widely in price. Slight changes in supply or demand are almost immediately reflected. By watching these prices, the economist can deduce what changes in inventory policies are going on. If commodity prices rise, inventories are probably rising. When they are dropping, users of the commodity may be buying less than they are consuming.

Unfortunately, inventory changes are not the only factors that influence commodity prices, so it is easy to be misled by price changes in individual commodities. For this reason, forecasters rarely take commodity price changes too seriously in making overall forecasts, unless other barometers confirm the trend of prices. It is especially hazardous to rely on any one commodity as a barometer of the general business trend Speculation can cause the price of a commodity to move counter to the general trend. For this reason, indexes such as the Dow-Jones commodity index are useful barometers, for they reflect the prices of a group of various commodities.

Consumer durables. If personal consumption expenditures are determined primarily by investment spending, why should it be necessary to analyze spending for durable consumer goods in making a business forecast? The answer is that consumer durables are an exception to the general rule for an important reason. Consumers have a hard time postponing expenditures for the nondurables and services (food, clothing, electricity, telephone, etc.) that comprise about 85 percent of total personal consumption expenditures, but they can and do postpone spending for consumer durables. For example, if Detroit's car models are real hits with the public, the entire economy can boom as a result. On the other hand, if the public decides to make the "old buggy" last another year, overall production and national income will be adversely affected.

Weekly figures for automobile production and for steel output provide good clues as to spending on consumer durables. These are issued by *Ward's Reports*, an auto industry publication, and by the American Iron and Steel Institute, respectively.

Another good barometer of spending on consumer durables is the Federal Reserve Board's report on installment credit. Remarkably few major consumer durables are bought for cash; practically everyone gets an installment credit loan. When repayments of old loans exceed new borrowing, net installment credit declines; this indicates subnormal spending on consumer durables. When credit is rising rapidly, spending for consumer durables may well be the driving force behind an expansion of the entire economy. For example, installment credit increased almost as fast as national income between 1961 and 1965. Consumers not only spent their higher personal incomes, but general prosperity encouraged them to borrow at an accelerated rate.

LEADING INDICATORS

The materials manager should watch the trends of all the economic barometers discussed so far in this chapter. In addition, he must watch all production and price statistics dealing with his own industry or with those industries with which he deals for major purchased materials. Unfortunately, despite all this study, changes in the business cycle will still often catch him napping. The reason is that many of the barometers discussed so far either: (1) move with the general business cycle or lead it by only a short time, (2) are difficult to interpret, or (3) have statistics that take so long to prepare that the lead they provide on general business is lost while they are being prepared.

NBER indicators

The National Bureau of Economic Research has made detailed studies of every business cycle in the nation's history. These studies indicate that certain indicators usually—though not always—lead changes in general business conditions by several months to a year or more. Other indicators move pretty much with the cycle, and some lag behind it. Reports on the status of these leading, coincident, and lagging business barometers are published monthly by the U.S. Department of Commerce in *Business Conditions Digest.*

Short list. Of particular interest to the forecaster is the "short list" of twelve leading barometers:

1. Average workweek, production workers, manufacturing.
2. Average weekly initial claims, unemployment insurance.
3. Net new business formation index.
4. New orders, durable goods industries.
5. Contracts and orders, plant and equipment.
6. New building permits, private housing.
7. Change in book value, manufacturing and trade inventories.
8. Industrial raw-materials prices.
9. Prices, 500 common stocks.
10. Corporate profits, after tax.
11. Ratio, unit price to labor cost, manufacturing.
12. Change in consumer installment debt.

Individual barometers in the short list are combined into the composite index shown in Figure 6–4. This series is a broad measure designed to predict what will happen to the overall economy. As can be seen in the figure, it is a pretty good forecaster of recessions. The series started heading downward at least a few months in advance of each of our postwar recessions. Unfortunately, it also gave two major false signals—in 1966–67 and in 1951–52. The decline in the leading indicators in each of these periods was as steep as that for a real recession, but no recession materialized. On the upside, the leading indicators are quite reliable. Unfortunately, as indicated in Figure 6–4, they do not really lead the business cycle up, but they more or less move with it.

FIGURE 6–4
Composite leading indicators of the National Bureau of Economic Research

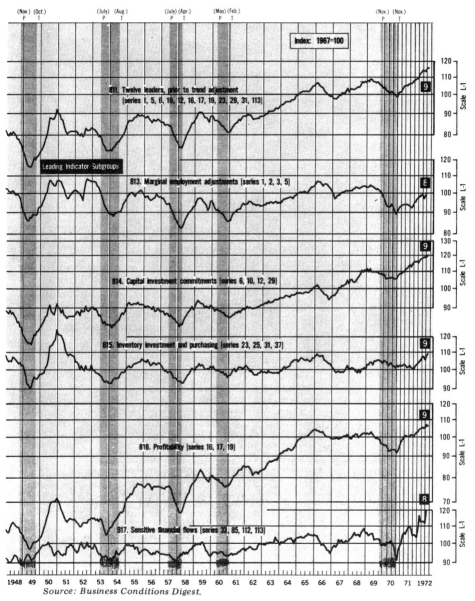

Source: Business Conditions Digest.

This may not pose too great a handicap for materials managers. Figure 6–4 also shows five subgroups of composite leading indicators of employment, capital investment, inventory investment and purchasing, profitability, and sensitive financial flows. In recent years, the purchasing and inventory subgroup has lagged behind the business cycle by many months on the upside. This implies that materials managers need not respond immediately to a business upturn by increasing inventories and bidding up industrial materials prices. There seems to be plenty of time for the materials manager to act when business is recovering. He is most likely to get in trouble when he fails to anticipate a major recession.

Purchasing barometers. The materials manager will also follow with interest three leading indicators that are developed by the National Bureau of Economic Research from data furnished by the National Association of Purchasing Management and the Purchasing Management Association of Chicago. As illustrated in Figure 6–5, these are the pur-

FIGURE 6–5
Three leading barometers of purchasing policy

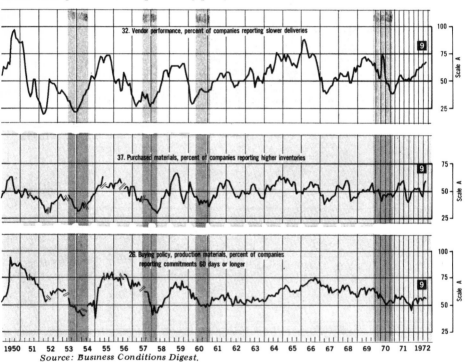

Source: *Business Conditions Digest.*

chased-materials index, vendor performance index, and buying policy index.

The purchased-materials index measures the percentage of firms reporting higher inventories. It tends to reach a peak some months in advance of the business cycle, when 65 to 70 percent of the respondents to the survey will be boosting their inventories. The index seems to bottom out just as a general recession is about to end; at this stage of the cycle only 30 to 40 percent of the participating firms are boosting their inventories.

The buying policy index represents the percentage of industrial purchasing agents reporting commitments 60 days or longer. This index typically reaches a peak some months ahead of the general business cycle when purchasing agents are committing their companies months into the future in order to assure an adequate supply of parts and materials. At this stage, as many as 70 percent of the respondents (who represent a broad cross section of industrial purchasing agents) may be committing themselves ahead by 60 days or more. At the bottom of the business cycle (when this index behaves more like a coincident barometer than a leading barometer), less than 50 percent of the respondents are making commitments 60 days ahead.

The vendor performance index represents the percentage of purchasing agents reporting slower supplier deliveries. This index reaches a peak six months to a year or more ahead of general business and touches bottom a few months ahead of the general business cycle. At the peak, 70 percent or more of the respondents may be reporting slower deliveries, while at the bottom 25 percent or fewer report them.

Purchasing opinion survey

The buying policy and purchased-material indexes described above are derived from the monthly reports of the Business Survey Committee of the National Association of Purchasing Management. Each month approximately 200 members of this committee, who all are top purchasing and materials management executives in representative manufacturing companies, are asked to fill out the form illustrated in Figure 6–6. Their report on their companies' production volume, new orders, commodity prices, purchased-materials inventories, employment, and buying is tabulated almost overnight. The results are promptly published in the *Bulletin* of the National Association of Purchasing Management, the *Wall Street Journal,* the *Journal of Commerce,* and on the business pages of most regular major newspapers.

Reasons for importance. The NAPM survey is perhaps the single most important forecasting tool for the materials manager, for the following reasons.

1. *Results of the survey are directly related to the forecasting problems of materials management.*

2. *Publication comes several weeks to more than a month ahead of comparable government statistics.* While the NAPM survey does not provide absolute data (such as total investment in inventory), it does provide relative data which may be just as useful in forecasting.

3. *There is no substitute for some of the NAPM data.* The government publishes statistics on production, inventory, new orders, employ-

FIGURE 6–6

FROM: REPORT FOR:

REPORT FOR N. A. P. M. NATIONAL COMMITTEE ON BUSINESS SURVEY

TO: E. F. ANDREWS
Vice President — Purchases
Allegheny Ludlum Industries, Inc.,
Pittsburgh, Pennsylvania 15222

NOTE: Please mail this report so that it will arrive close to but not later than the date specified above.
The information on this form is for the exclusive use of the chairman of the Business Survey Committee and will be held strictly confidential.

NOTE: Check marks and comments should reflect conditions in your own business. But, whenever possible, please include additional remarks on prevailing local conditions. Refer to explanation sheet for further details.

1. GENERAL BUSINESS CONDITIONS:

PRODUCTION
(Check)   Remarks (Explain fully.):
☐ BETTER THAN MONTH AGO
☐ SAME AS MONTH AGO
☐ WORSE THAN MONTH AGO

NEW ORDERS
(Check)
☐ BETTER THAN MONTH AGO
☐ SAME AS MONTH AGO
☐ WORSE THAN MONTH AGO

2. COMMODITY PRICES: SPECIFIC COMMODITY PRICE CHANGES
(Check)   UP
☐ HIGHER THAN MONTH AGO
☐ SAME AS MONTH AGO   DOWN
☐ LOWER THAN MONTH AGO

3. PURCHASED MATERI-   Remarks: (Explain reason for change from previous month):
ALS INVENTORIES:
(Check)
☐ HIGHER THAN MONTH AGO
☐ SAME AS MONTH AGO
☐ LOWER THAN MONTH AGO

4. EMPLOYMENT: Remarks: (Explain reason for change from previous month):
(Check)
☐ GREATER THAN MONTH AGO
☐ SAME AS MONTH AGO
☐ LESS THAN MONTH AGO

5. BUYING POLICY (Check)   Remarks: (Explain reason for change from previous month):

HAND TO MOUTH	30 DAYS	60 DAYS	90 DAYS	6 MONTHS	1 YEAR		
						PRODUCTION MATERIALS	
						MRO SUPPLIES	
						CAPITAL EXPENDITURES	

6. ITEMS IN SHORT SUPPLY   (Explain reason for shortage.)

7. GENERAL REMARKS (Give frank opinion on general business conditions and any condition, local or national, which affect purchasing policies.)

Use reverse side or attach separate sheet if additional space is necessary.   (OVER)

ment, and prices. But only the NAPM can report buying policy and shortages. Also, the NAPM price survey reflects "buyers' prices" as distinct from the "sellers' prices" reported by the Bureau of Labor Statistics. Theoretically, there should be no difference between the two series. Obviously, there must be a buyer for every seller. But at critical junctures in the business cycle, there can be discrepancies. In times of shortage, buyers purchase from marginal suppliers whose prices may be higher than those reported by conventional producers to the Bureau of Labor Statistics. Conversely, during periods of oversupply, sellers are forced by competition to "shade" their prices on an individual basis to their customers, but they may continue to report officially the higher prices they would really prefer to charge were it not for keen competition. For example, the official price of aluminum ingot was pegged at 29 cents a pound for two years, but the actual "buying price" during this period fluctuated between 25 and 20 cents a pound.

4. *The NAPM survey is sometimes more accurate than government statistics at critical turning points in the economy.* The U.S. Department of Commerce series on new orders and inventory is especially vulnerable. The first figures published by the Department can never be taken as the "last word." Sometimes, they will be followed over a period of several years by three or four revisions and, at turning points in the business cycle, the first figure may have been downright misleading. In contrast, the NAPM figures have been almost completely consistent at these critical turning points in the business cycle.[2]

Interpreting the results. The NAPM survey is published as a simple tabulation of results. It is not adjusted for seasonal fluctuations, and results are sometimes influenced markedly by major strikes and other disruptions. In addition, the basic format may be misleading to the unsophisticated analyst. Respondents to the survey typically check "better," "same," or "worse" for each business condition as it applies to their own company. Then the results are tabulated, giving equal weight to each respondent. For example, during a particular month, the chairman of Business Survey Committee may report that 42 percent of the responding companies reported more new orders received by their company than in the previous month, 22 percent reported the same, and 36 percent reported a lower level of orders.

Since 42 percent of the committee reports more orders, while only 36 percent reports fewer orders, we can probably assume that there was a moderate increase in total manufacturers' new orders during that month. And, in an overwhelming majority of cases, this conclusion will be consistent with the Department of Commerce data that are subsequently published.

This does not mean, however, that business is getting better—even if the survey results for production, prices, inventories, and employment are consistent with those for new orders. What counts is not so much the absolute results of the survey but the rate and direction of change. For example, suppose that last month 52 percent of the respondents

---

[2] A detailed explanation of this phenomenon, along with an explanation of how to make more effective use of the survey, appears in Dean S. Ammer, *The Effectiveness of Opinion Surveys.* Copies of the study can be purchased from the National Association of Purchasing Management, 11 Park Place, New York, N.Y. 10007.

reported an increase in new orders and 63 percent reported an increase the previous month. Even though new orders are apparently still increasing in an absolute sense, there is a relative decline. The rate of change in new orders is obviously negative. This may indicate a major change in the business cycle if it cannot be explained by seasonal fluctuation.

Correctly interpreted, the NAPM survey gives very few false signals. On several occasions, it has signaled a recession months ahead of other business barometers. With practice, the various chairmen of the Business Survey Committee have become increasingly adept at interpreting survey results. The chairman's complete analysis is published, along with the basic survey, each month in the NAPM *Bulletin.*

Market sentiment

Monthly changes in the NAPM business survey are an excellent barometer of market sentiment. Purchasing managers, like all intelligent businessmen, follow the trend of business. They carefully read comments on the business outlook by professional economists. Many of them analyze the business statistics discussed above. Yet in general, businessmen are wrong on business forecasting as often as they are right. One reason they are wrong is that forecasting is far from an exact science, and it is extremely easy to make serious mistakes. A second reason is even more basic. Forecasts can be self-defeating if they gain wide acceptance.

Suppose every economist and businessman agreed that we will be in for the biggest boom in history next year. What would happen? Each businessman would prepare for it by expanding plant, equipment, and inventories. The surge in demand would push up prices and employment. The boom would no longer be a year away; it would already have arrived. In fact, in a year the expected boom might prove to be a mirage, for there would be a slump as soon as business was completely prepared for the coming boom and tapered off its investment spending.

Investment decisions are based not on current activity but on businessmen's estimates of future activity. Business forecasting is the art of anticipating future business decisions. Analyzing current statistics is not enough; the forecaster must predict how businessmen will react to these statistics and the forecasts on which they are based. If he has a knack for it, the materials manager is in a much better position to do this than the professional economist is. Economists can be expected to catch swings in business sentiment only when they show up in news releases and business statistics. The materials manager, on the other hand, is in daily contact with leaders of the business community—his suppliers. If he is an intelligent listener, he can sense changes that will not be reflected in GNP statistics for months to come.

PRICE FORECASTS

From statistics, his evaluation of the market sentiment, and the forecasts of professional economists, the materials manager reaches his own conclusions as to the future course of the economy. He then tries to translate this general forecast into specific forecasts for various key commodities.

Most materials are always available at a price. Materials that are bought and sold in commodity markets are always available; the price automatically equilibrates supply and demand. Even scarce materials whose prices are "administered"[3] are available if the materials manager is willing to pay enough. For example, although steel was scarce when ordered through regular supply channels at published prices right after World War II, it was almost always available from "gray market" dealers at prices 50 to 100 percent higher than those charged by the major producers.

But what materials manager wants to pay premium prices for materials? His job is to get the required materials at minimum prices. And, to the greatest extent possible, he wants to be able to predict what prices will be in the future so he can plan his purchases accordingly.

The materials manager can influence the prices of most of the items he buys. All parts and a few raw materials have "administered" prices; in most cases, they are established by negotiation between buyer and supplier. While the materials manager will make use of economic forecasts when buying such items, he is not at the mercy of an impersonal market, and in practice he can predict such prices with considerable accuracy.

In some cases, he participates intimately in the price-setting process, using purchase price analysis techniques and subsequent negotiation of prices as described in Chapters 16 and 17. In other cases, the materials manager simply does not have enough bargaining power to influence prices directly. For example, not even the biggest purchaser of electric motors can normally sit down and negotiate the price for a 25 hp. motor with General Electric, Westinghouse, and other producers.

Forecasting administered prices

In some cases, the producer has sufficient power to set a price almost independently of any market. In most cases, however, the producer must take into account the reactions of both competitors and customers. The materials manager who is trying to predict such prices will consider both cost of production and the supply-demand situation that exists in particular industries.

---

[3] That is, set by a few big producers whose pricing decisions are based on demand, competition, cost of production, and other factors.

Suppose, for example, the materials manager is trying to estimate the future price of gray-iron castings. He should consider the following six factors.

1. *Effect of general business conditions.* The predicted GNP will have a varied effect on the industries that use gray iron castings. If GNP rises 3 percent, demand for gray-iron castings may not rise at all, or it may rise substantially more than 3 percent. The materials manager often can guess quite accurately what the overall effect of a change in GNP on demand for castings will be by studying what happened in previous years.

2. *Predicted changes in major sectors of the economy.* The U.S. Department of Commerce periodically makes input-output studies of the U.S. economy.[4] These show the interrelationship that exists among various primary industry groups. For example, input-output data might indicate that each $1 worth of output in the transportation equipment industry requires 12 cents of output in the primary metals industries, whose output would include gray-iron castings. With input-output data, it is possible to derive forecasts of demand for one industry's products from basic forecasts of demand for the products of other industries. The technique is still in its infancy but has tremendous promise if more highly refined statistics become available.

3. *Estimated changes in supply.* By using general business statistics and also drawing on his knowledge of the expansion plans of key suppliers in the industry, the materials manager can deduce how much additional capacity is planned.

4. *Cost trends in the industry.* If contracts between foundries and the unions representing their workers are being renewed, the materials manager should estimate the cost of the settlement and its probable effect on the foundries' cost of production. He also should be familiar with the probable trend of the prices of key raw materials in gray-iron castings: pig iron, scrap iron, coke, and so on. And further, he should try to estimate what effect new equipment and various laborsaving devices will have on suppliers' costs when they are introduced.

5. *"Temper" of the market.* The materials manager and his buyers should be in regular contact with all important suppliers. In this way they are always apprised of the state of the market. If producers are extremely confident, the near-term outlook is probably for firm prices. Sophisticated buyers know how to evaluate their suppliers' comments on the market. They are sharp enough to spot market weakness when the optimists sound a little less optimistic and the pessimists moan a little louder than usual.

---

[4] Input-output data are published occasionally in the *Survey of Current Business* published by the U.S. Department of Commerce. Use of the technique is lucidly described in William H. Miernyk, *The Elements of Input-Output Analysis* (Random House, Inc., 1965), pp. vii, 156.

6. *Prices on new contracts.* If the materials manager has been successful in making new purchases at lower than expected prices, the market is obviously weakening. Similarly, if prices are rising slightly, the market is firmer. When current prices are changing, the materials manager can safely predict a change in total prices in the same direction, and rarely will he be wrong. Price trends take time to reverse themselves. In addition, not all prices paid reflect the effects of new prices at the same time; prices usually are adjusted only when a new purchase is made and deliveries are made. For these reasons, purchase price indexes can be extremely useful tools for predicting short-term trends in prices.

Subjective evaluation. The materials manager's evaluation of the six factors that influence the price of gray-iron castings is partly subjective—although it should be based on objective data as much as possible. The materials manager may wish to assign a percentage weighting of the importance of each factor in making his final estimate of the probable price change in castings. This may give the estimate an appearance of objectivity, but the final decision remains highly subjective and depends almost entirely on the materials manager's skill and experience.

In a large company, the materials manager may want to back his judgment up with that of a "Delphi" panel of experts—particularly if an accurate forecast is critical to the company's success. The basic idea is to give each member of the panel all information pertinent to the forecast. Each panel member then makes his individual forecast and adds any new ideas that occur to him after he has read the composite contribution of the panel. It is possible to have several Delphi "rounds" in the hope that the panel will continue to gain insight from the collective contributions of other members of the panel to the forecast.[5]

Free market commodities

The Delphi approach can also be applied to materials whose prices are determined almost entirely by supply and demand. Unlike producers of administered-price items, commodity producers have almost no control over price. The producer of a gray-iron casting or an electric appliance sets a price for his product. This price reflects what competitors would charge for an equivalent product, but it is possible to have slight and sometimes even substantial differences. The producer does not have this option when price is set entirely by supply and demand. Theoretically, the producer of a free market commodity can produce and sell as much as he likes at the market price, but he can sell nothing should he try to charge slightly more than market.

---

[5] The Delphi technique is applied to economic forecasting in Dean S. Ammer, "What Businessmen Expect from the 1970's," *Harvard Business Review,* January–February 1971, pp. 41–52.

Many free market commodities are agricultural in origin—wheat, crude rubber, corn, corn oil, soybeans, cotton, wool, and hides. Others are either the products of primary producers of various types or of scrap—scrap metals of all types, plywood, lead, tin, zinc, and various chemical and petroleum products.

Many of these products are traded on commodity exchanges, and the price on the exchange determines the price paid by every producer. In other cases, the material is not formally traded on an exchange but the price is widely publicized, moving up and down in response to changes in supply and demand. The general business outlook and cost of production ultimately affect demand and supply, but over a short term prices are determined entirely by sellers and buyers whose bids and asks determine prices on commodity exchanges.

Demand and supply.　Demand for these commodities fluctuates considerably. When the business outlook is basically bullish, businessmen buy not only for current production but also to add to inventories. When businessmen are pessimistic about the future, they will use up their inventories and buy practically nothing, even for current production. Demand depends more on business sentiment and expectations than on actual business conditions.

While demand is subject to extremely wide swings, supply changes quite slowly. It takes time to bring additional facilities into production in response to high prices. And businessmen are reluctant to shut down marginal facilities until prices fall to ruinously low levels. The result of this supply-demand situation is highly unstable prices.

Materials managers who buy these volatile commodities can make or lose large sums of money for their companies. For example, an automobile manufacturer might use 2 million pounds of copper in its radiators per month. Suppose copper goes up 4 cents a pound. Costs rise $80,000 per month—but not for a while, at least, if the materials manager has anticipated the increase and has increased inventories. On the other hand, if copper drops 4 cents, the materials manager can get maximum benefit from the decrease only if he had cut his stocks "to the bone" before the price dropped.

Available statistics.　Industry statistics provide clues to future price changes. They are published in abbreviated form in the *Survey of Current Business* and in great detail in specialized journals. For most commodities, it is possible to get reasonably up-to-date figures on stocks-on-hand, current production, and sales. In theory, at least, a buildup of inventory tends to bring prices down, and reduction of inventory may be a harbinger of higher prices. In practice, most commodity prices have a habit of turning around before statistics become available. Thus, the buyer may learn only after the price change has occurred.

While commodity buyers carefully study all available statistics in order to make rational decisions, they can never be completely certain that a particular price trend will continue. The general rule is that a current trend will prevail: If prices have been rising, they will probably continue to rise, and if they have been falling, they will continue to decline. But, of course, there is always a turning point—and this is what is most difficult to predict.

Slight changes in supply and demand often have a magnified effect on price. Demand and supply for most commodities is relatively inelastic over the short term. This means that, regardless of the price, buyers will keep buying and sellers will keep selling—over the short term, at least. When supply or demand get out of balance, the imbalance continues simply because neither buyer nor seller is inhibited very much by the price. In fact, for a time at least, price change may induce behavior that continues the trend. For example, if copper rises by 2 cents per pound after a period of stable prices, buyers may well be tempted to build stocks in anticipation of further price increases. This extra demand pushes up prices even more, and the rising trend continues until eventually supply begins to get a little ahead of demand—either because production is increased or because every buyer has built up his own inventory as much as he wishes.

Timing of purchases

Price fluctuations introduce an element of risk into materials management that cannot be avoided. Realistic materials managers know that they may be wrong almost as often as they are right in forecasting. Nevertheless, they try to time their purchases to reflect predictions of future price and availability and use inventories as a hedge against uncertainty. Materials managers have always tried to make the timing process as precise as possible—using forecasts and all other information they can lay their hands on. But, as one materials manager pointed out, "There is no formula that will tell me when and how much to buy. The best I can do is to review all available information, try to interpret it as best I can, make my decision, and then hope I'm right." He adds, "Regardless of how long you've been in the business, you're often wrong."

It is almost impossible for any materials manager to be consistently "smarter" than the market. All buyers are constantly analyzing general business conditions and supply-demand relationships in particular commodities. So are thousands of speculators. As a result, changes in sentiment are almost immediately reflected in prices. Buyers tend to reach the same opinion regarding future prices at almost the same time. Consequently, their total buying—or lack of buying—tends to cause prices to readjust to the new conditions. Therefore, buying tends to be heavy when prices are high and light when prices are low. Obviously only a minority of buyers are in the market when they should be, i.e., when prices are low.

There is good reason for this situation. The materials manager's prime mission is to provide needed raw materials for operations. Unfortunately, he usually needs materials least when prices are low. Prices generally slump with overall business, and most materials managers must cut back purchases because of a drop in their company's sales. When prices ar high, on the other hand, the materials manager often must buy regardless of whether or not he thinks the material can be bought more cheaply at a later date. His factory is running full blast and needs a steady flow of parts and materials. There is no single right formula applicable to timing of purchases in all situations. However, most successful materials managers follow the general procedures outlined below.

1. *Estimate materials needs.* The usual approach is to try to make a rather firm estimate of materials consumption for at least several quarters, and possibly a year ahead. In addition, the materials manager tries to get a more tentative estimate of materials needs for a five-year or even a ten-year period. Both the long- and short-term estimates are revised at periodic intervals to bring them in line with the latest sales projections supplied by the company's market research department.

At all times, the materials manager's estimates should be based on the best available forecasts. During the period of the estimate, the materials manager knows he will have to buy at least enough material to satisfy estimated use (less any reduction in inventories that might be desired). So purchases must always be timed to meet use requirements. In other words, the materials manager can buy "ahead" of materials requirements. But he cannot afford to buy "behind" actual requirements; he must always have material available when it is scheduled to be used.

2. *Develop tentative plan of purchases.* At this stage in his planning, the materials manager ignores the effect of future price changes and the like on his purchase timing. He breaks up his requirements into economic lots and programs their delivery, allowing sufficient lead time to prevent stockouts if suppliers fail to adhere to delivery schedules. This process is described in detail in Chapter 7.

3. *Watch for buying opportunities.* Whenever prices look unusually favorable, the materials manager should consider buying in excess of requirements. He should work closely with his company's financial officials on forward buying. Most companies have limited funds available for forward buying, and the amount available can vary from month to month.

When a buying opportunity does appear, the materials manager is still faced with a timing problem. Should he buy ahead now, should he spend all the money available for forward buying, or should he hold off? The Bayesian decision rule can sometimes be helpful. The procedure is identical with that described in Chapter 7 except that the price change becomes a prior (or first) probability rather than a conditional (or secondary) probability, as it does in the example where a possible steel strike is followed by a possible price increase.

4. *Consider formulas.* Materials managers also frequently get good results with various timing formulas. One such plan might work in the following way: The materials manager expects the price of a material to average 30 cents a pound during the year. He makes up a buying plan based on this assumption. If the price is 30 cents or more, he will buy only the absolute minimum of material needed for production. But for every 1-cent drop in price below 30 cents, he will use 10 percent of his forward-buying fund to accumulate inventory. He does this cumulatively. For example, if the price drops 1 cent he spends 10 percent of the fund; if it drops an additional cent (to 2 cents below the estimated average of 30 cents), he uses another 20 percent of the fund; and so on.

The advantage of this formula is that it encourages stock accumulation when prices are low and discourages it when they are high. However, the buyer is not protected against severe price drops, since he will use up his fund before the bottom is reached. Nor will he be buying most advantageously should prices inch up progressively throughout the year. Formulas, when they are used, must be developed on a tailor-made basis to suit the needs of the materials manager applying them. They can never be used as substitutes for the judgment of a skilled and experienced materials manager.

REDUCING MARKET RISK

Unfortunately, it is almost impossible to be on the "right" side of the market at all times. The general rule is that the economic expectations of all users of and speculators in a particular commodity change at about the same time. As a result, everyone tends to accumulate or liquidate inventory at about the same time. Thus prices change quite rapidly after periods of stability, which makes it even more difficult to manage inventories profitably. The key to successful forward buying in commodities was described by one buyer as "knowing in advance what other buyers think will happen in the future; that is, it's knowing the future of the future." That is no easy task.

Many buyers try to neutralize the effects on profits of fluctuations in commodity prices. They do this in four ways: averaging their purchases; budgeted buying; hedging in futures markets; and last-in, first-out inventory accounting.

Averaging purchases

Averaging purchases is the simplest (but not always the most effective) method of coping with the price risks of volatile commodities.

It involves keeping inventories as low as possible at all times and then buying on a hand-to-mouth basis for current production. With this approach, the average cost of the commodity used in production will be about the same as the average price for that commodity during the year.

The average-purchase technique permits a company to concentrate its efforts on making and selling a finished product without giving a thought to commodity market fluctuations. It works well only when: (1) the commodity is not too important in relation to overall product cost, (2) increases in the cost of the commodity can be passed on immediately to customers buying the end product, (3) the commodity is not subject to particularly violent fluctuations; or (4) the commodity is not produced abroad or under other circumstances where supply lines are long and complex and likely to be disrupted by political upheavals,[6] labor trouble, and the like.

Budgeted buying

If prices regularly fluctuate around some mean, it is possible to beat the market with budgeted buying. The materials manager budgets regular amounts to be spent for the material, regardless of its selling price. As a result, the company automatically buys more when prices are low and less when they are high.

Table 6–1 illustrates a budgeted policy for a commodity whose usage is 120,000 pounds per month. The materials manager assumes that the price will fluctuate around a mean of 10 cents per pound, so he calculates that, on the average, he can get required quantities by spending $12,000 a month on the material. When the price is higher than 10 cents, he buys less than 120,000 pounds and draws on inventories for production requirements. When the price is lower than 10 cents, he spends $12,000 anyway and buys more than 120,000 pounds.

Table 6–1 covers a commodity over a six-month period in which its price averaged 10 cents per pound and varied from a high of 12 cents to a low of 8 cents. When purchases are averaged, requirements of 120,000 pounds were purchased each month at the market price. During the six-month period, they totaled 720,000 pounds and the cost was $72,000. With budgeted purchases, $12,000 was spent each month for material at the market price, and total purchases were 732,423 pounds, or 12,423 pounds in excess of use. This addition to inventory, worth

---

[6] It is for this reason that users of crude rubber, tin, and other materials produced in politically unstable countries thousands of miles away traditionally carry extremely heavy inventories, often amounting to enough for production needs of a year or more.

TABLE 6–1
Averaging purchases versus budgeted buying

Month	Market price	Quantity required (in lbs.)	Averaging purchases		Budgeted buying	
			Quantity purchased (in lbs.)	Cost	Quantity purchased (in lbs.)	Cost
January.	10¢	120,000	120,000	$12,000	120,000	$12,000
February.	9	120,000	120,000	10,800	133,333	12,000
March	8	120,000	120,000	9,600	150,000	12,000
April	10	120,000	120,000	12,000	120,000	12,000
May	11	120,000	120,000	13,200	109,090	12,000
June	12	120,000	120,000	14,400	100,000	12,000
Total			720,000	$72,000	732,423	$72,000

$1,490.76 at the June market price, is the "profit" earned through budgeted purchasing in this period as compared with averaging purchases. In both cases total expenditures were $72,000, but with budgeted purchasing it was possible to buy 12,423 pounds of additional material.

Limitations. Unfortunately, a budgeted buying program is successful only when the materials manager can predict the average price that will prevail with reasonable accuracy. For example, suppose prices declined steadily for a long period of time. The materials manager simply could not afford to continue to buy in excess of current requirements indefinitely, and he would be stuck with a large inventory worth, at market prices, less than he had paid for it. Similarly, if prices went up steadily for a long period, a budgeted-buying program would not work. Month after month the materials manager would be buying less than the amount being consumed and eventually he would run out of inventory, which he would then have to replenish at peak prices.

Despite its shortcomings, budgeted buying is a useful technique for certain commodities—especially when the materials manager is reasonably certain what the overall price trend will be.

Hedging in futures markets

If a company must carry large inventories of a commodity for various reasons, it is always in danger of suffering substantial losses when the commodity drops in price. This is strictly a "paper loss" as long as the company is not forced to reduce the selling prices of its products when the commodity drops in price. In such cases, the "loss" is the additional profit that would have been made if the company had postponed its purchase and got the commodity at lower prices, thereby making its profit margin bigger.

The loss becomes more painful if the company must cut its prices when the commodity drops in price.[7] If the company has a big stock of material, its costs will be much too high at the new market selling price for its finished products. With some commodities, the buyer can avoid this risk by hedging in the futures market. He can sell a contract for future delivery of an amount equal to the quantity in his inventory. Then, for the period of the contract, he will neither lose nor make money on his inventory.

A typical transaction. Suppose, for example, a company has a contract to make tires for a mail-order house. As is not untypical of contracts requiring substantial investments in raw materials that are subject to wide price fluctuations, buyer and seller agree on an escalator clause. (See Chapter 5.) This requires the final selling price to be adjusted to reflect the market price of crude rubber at time of delivery.

The company needs 1,000,000 pounds of crude rubber for the order and buys it at the current price of 30 cents a pound. If crude rubber continues to sell at 30 cents a pound, the company estimates that it will make a $200,000 profit on the order. However, final selling prices for the tires must be adjusted to reflect changes in crude rubber prices in accordance with the escalator clause. If rubber prices jump by 10 cents a pound to 40 cents, the company can boost prices by 10 cents × 1,000,000 pounds, or $100,000. This will, of course, be extra profit, since the rubber actually used in making the tires was purchased at the time the contract was signed for 30 cents a pound, not at the 40-cent price that prevails when the order is completed.

On the other hand, suppose rubber declines by 10 cents a pound between the time the rubber is purchased and the tire order is completed. The company is then forced to reduce its selling prices to reflect the rubber market prevailing at time of shipment, reducing its profit by $100,000.

Some companies will risk an inventory loss in order to have a chance of making a gain. Others would prefer to make their profits strictly from manufacturing and let others assume the risks of price change. They can do this with a hedging transaction—selling a futures contract at the same time they make a purchase.

Suppose, for example, that the company gets the original order in October and it calls for delivery of tires in June. The company then purchases 1,000,000 pounds of rubber in the "spot" market for immediate delivery at the prevailing price of 30 cents a pound. Simultaneously it

---

[7] This would be the case with a brass mill, for example. Brass prices move up and down in unison with copper prices. Contrarily, if a steel mill takes an inventory loss when steel scrap drops in price, this is merely lost profit, since steel prices do not fluctuate with scrap prices.

sells short for 30 cents a pound a futures contract calling for delivery in June.[8] This short sale requires the company to deliver the equivalent of 1,000,000 pounds of crude rubber to the purchaser of the contract the following June.

If rubber prices do not change at all, the company can simply buy back the futures contract at 30 cents and it will lose nothing but broker's commissions on the two transactions. Suppose, however, that rubber prices decline by 10 cents a pound when the tires are shipped. The company is forced to cut prices, and it makes just $100,000 profit on the order instead of the expected $200,000. However, it will be able to buy crude rubber in the open market for just 20 cents a pound to deliver against the short sale. Thus, the company's trading in the futures market yields a profit of approximately $100,000—$300,000 received from the short sale when the price was 30 cents, less $200,000 paid out to purchase the rubber at 20 cents to close out the short sale.

Now suppose that rubber prices increase by 10 cents a pound during this same period. The company can boost its prices by $100,000 in accordance with the escalator clause and make a $300,000 profit on its contract. Unfortunately, it loses $100,000 on its futures contract. The short sale yields $300,000 at the 30-cent price but the company must buy at the 40-cent price, with total cost of $400,000, in order to close out the trade.

Thus, hedging not only eliminates risk of loss but also prevents a company from making profits on its inventory. The transaction is easy to follow once you grasp the concept that it is possible to sell a contract for future delivery. This makes it possible to sell something you do not have and then buy it to fulfill your obligation at some future date when the market price may be quite different.

But, of course, there must be a buyer for every seller. It is understandable why a tire company might want to sell a contract in April that calls for delivery of 1,000,000 pounds the following June. But who would want to buy such a contract? One possibility is the mail-order house that is going to buy the tires.[9] If it buys a futures contract at 30 cents, its profit on the contract will offset the higher prices it must pay for tires if crude rubber goes to 40 cents the following June.

---

[8] A "short sale" is a transaction in which the seller does not own the commodity that he sells (i.e., he is "short" of it) but simply agrees to deliver the commodity he has sold at some future date. A producer of a commodity may sell short in order to take advantage of current prices and then deliver the commodity physically at some future date. A speculator will simply close out his short sale by making a purchase at some later date.

[9] This is purely a hypothetical example. In practice, it would be extremely foolish for both buyer and seller to hedge in a commodity market. It would be far wiser for them to make a contract wherein all market risks would be taken by one party, which could then do the hedging for both of them. Hedging is not free; brokerage commissions and other costs are incurred. With intelligent management, these can be minimized.

Futures contracts are frequently purchased by users of material who want to be assured that material will be available for future delivery at current prices. They may be sold by raw-material producers who prefer to guarantee their profit by selling material they have not yet produced rather than risk being forced to sell later at a loss. Most trading, however, is done by speculators who close out their contracts just before delivery is due and either pocket their profits or take their losses.

Disadvantages of futures hedging.   Most materials managers make little or no use of futures contracts. Although brokerage commissions are nominal on individual transactions (less than 1 percent of the value of the contract), they become significant if a company does a lot of trading. In addition, capital may be tied up that can profitably be invested elsewhere were it not for the hedging transaction. A company that hedges against its inventory must not only have cash invested in inventory but must also have cash tied up in a broker's account (although sometimes it can simply pledge a physical stock of material if it sells short).

Even more important, the transaction often does not work out quite as neatly as it did in our example, where we assumed that spot and futures prices of rubber were precisely the same—30 cents a pound. In actual practice, the spot and futures prices are rarely identical, and often there is a significant spread between them. Each price is determined by somewhat different supply and demand forces. A majority of the time, the futures price is slightly lower than the spot price. This difference reflects the risk that a buyer takes when he commits himself for future delivery when there is no obvious advantage to doing so. If the spot price of rubber is 30 cents a pound, then the futures prices might be only 28 or 29 cents. This automatically increases the cost of a hedging transaction.

Spot prices and futures prices are different because each represents a different value. A contract to buy crude rubber for immediate delivery is quite different from a contract calling for delivery six or eight months in the future. The spot price reflects the interaction of current supply and demand; the futures price reflects present estimates of what future supply and demand will be. Thus a summer drought may have little effect on the spot price of corn in July, but it will probably drive up futures, prices as speculators take into account the probability that the crop will be poor.

Because of the disadvantages of hedging, most managers simply prefer to let their inventories swing up and down with the business cycle. With last-in, first-out accounting (LIFO), companies that can vary their selling prices with raw-material costs need not worry too much about the effect of inventory losses on the profit-and-loss statement anyway.

Last-in, first-out accounting

Conventional accounting procedures are based on a first-in, first-out (FIFO) treatment of inventory, in which the items that are received earliest are regarded as being used first. In some businesses, this handling of inventory literally fits the accounting practice. In a grocery store, for example, every effort is made to turn over stock physically on a first-in, first-out basis. That way there is no spoilage, provided not every housewife tries to beat the system by reaching for the fresher merchandise at the back of the shelf.

In a manufacturing business, the first-in, first-out concept is not so logical. A stock of raw material is really a permanent investment, something that is as essential to operation as plant and equipment. This material may not be perishable. For example, in a die-casting plant, zinc slabs received a couple of years ago are just as useful as those received yesterday. This basic stock is regarded almost as a permanent investment in the business and is carried on the books at original cost. Purchases are regarded almost as immediate operating expenses; cost of production is charged the most recent purchase cost. This is called last-in, first-out, or LIFO inventory accounting.

Effect on profits. When material costs vary a great deal, reported profits can be affected substantially by the inventory accounting method used. For example, suppose a company making zinc die castings has 1,000,000 pounds of zinc in its inventory. Assume that 500,000 pounds were bought when the price of zinc was 15 cents a pound, and at a later date an additional 500,000 pounds were purchased at a price of only 10 cents a pound.

Now suppose the company gets an order for finished die castings in which 100,000 pounds of metal will be used. The order price is based on the current market price for zinc, 11 cents a pound. So, the total cost of metal will be as follows:

At market price: 100,000 lbs. at 11¢/lb. = $11,000.
Cost on FIFO basis: 100,000 lbs. at 15¢/lb. = $15,000.
Cost on LIFO basis: 100,000 lbs. at 10¢/lb. = $10,000.

Naturally the company's prices must be based on the current market for materials; otherwise it is liable to lose out to competitors who can offer finished castings made of metal bought at the prevailing low price. But what happens if it keeps its books on a FIFO basis? Then its cost of production will be based on the prices paid for the "oldest" metal in the inventory, that bought at 15 cents a pound. Thus costs will be $5,000 higher than anticipated.

If accounts are kept on a LIFO basis, this will not happen. If the materials manager decides not to increase inventories because of this order, production cost will be based on the "last" zinc received, which will be "used" in that order.[10] As a result, costs will be 1 cent a pound lower than anticipated, and the company will show an added "profit" of $1,000 ($.01 × 100,000 lbs.) on the order. Finally, if the company decides to increase inventories because of the order and buys more zinc at 11 cents, it will make the anticipated profit if its records are kept on a LIFO basis.

With last-in, first-out accounting, changing prices for raw materials have considerably less effect on stated profits. This takes some of the pressure off the materials manager to time purchases properly. However, even with LIFO, profits over a long term will be affected just as much by timing of purchases as with any other accepted accounting system. LIFO can only keep the full impact of an unfavorable swing in inventory prices from being reflected immediately in the profit-and-loss statement. It also, of course, prevents a big rise in raw-materials prices and consequent "paper" gains in inventory values from being immediately translated into higher profits.

Cases

CASE 6–1: OHIO BATTERY COMPANY

Forecasting lead prices

Ohio Battery Company makes automobile batteries for the replacement market. As with all battery manufacturers, its single most important cost is the lead that is cast into plates in the battery. For example, the company has the following costs for one of its cheaper, more popular batteries.

Lead (22 lbs. @ 14¢/lb.)	$3.08
Other materials	1.97
Direct labor	0.36
Overhead	0.72
Manufacturing cost	$6.13
Sales and distribution cost	1.35
Total cost	$7.48
Profit	0.32
Selling price to dealers	$7.80

[10] Students should note that there is usually no connection between accounting practice and actual physical usage of the material. In fact, the workman who actually moves the zinc slabs out of inventory usually does not have the vaguest idea whether the inventory accountant assumes that the "oldest" metal (FIFO) is being used first or the "newest" (LIFO). Regardless of the inventory accounting practice, the production organization would probably tend to use the "older" metal first—unless its storage system made the "new" metal more convenient to use.

Prices to dealers are revised periodically to reflect changes in cost. Ohio Battery never tries to be the price leader. Instead, it waits for its larger competitors to adjust prices and follows with an identical price change a few days latear. Major swings in the lead market always bring price adjustments on batteries. Producers cannot afford to absorb a substantial increase in lead prices, and competition forces them to pass on major reductions in lead costs to their customers.

Changes in the lead market provide Ohio Battery with unusual opportunities for both profit and loss, since the company does not have to adjust its prices until its competitors' adjust theirs. For example, if the company has a large inventory of lead acquired at low prices and competitors raise prices to reflect higher costs, Ohio Battery can also raise prices and enjoy high profits while it uses up its low-cost inventory. On the other hand, if the company has a high-cost lead inventory and competitors cut prices because of a declining lead market, the effect on the company's profits can be almost disastrous. For example, the price breakdown above is based on lead at 14 cents a pound. If the lead market declined to $12\frac{1}{2}$ cents and competitors cut prices by 33 cents (22 lbs. $\times$ $1\frac{1}{2}$/lb.), the company's profits would be wiped out completely until it managed to use up its inventory of 14-cent lead.

The company tries to protect itself against such violent fluctuations in stated profits with a last-in, first-out inventory control system. As a result, gains and losses in the lead market are not immediately reflected in the company's income statement. Lead inventories, with the oldest inventory listed first, are currently valued as follows:

10,000 lbs. @ 10¢	$ 1,000
90,000 lbs. @ 9¢	8,100
11,000 lbs. @ 12¢	1,320
6,000 lbs. @ 14¢	840
Total	$11,260

Demand for the company's products is seasonal. The peak is in fall, when dealers stock up for the wave of battery failures that come with the first cold weather, after four months of summer doldrums. The company anticipates the following pattern of lead usage:

January	100,000 lbs.
February	100,000
March	100,000
April	70,000
May	60,000
June	60,000
July	60,000
August	60,000
September	100,000
October	120,000
November	120,000
December	100,000
Total	1,050,000 lbs.

Questions

1. Prepare a one-year price forecast for lead based on *current* spot and futures prices, refiners' stocks, production, consumption, general economic outlook, and analysis of price trends in lead and other commodities.

2. Prepare a plan of purchase based on your price forecast. Assume that the company president is willing to carry as much as three months' inventory, provided you can convince him that it will be worthwhile.

3. On the basis of your forecast and plan of purchase, calculate the difference between the company's stated profits with its last-in, first-out system and a first-in, first-out system of inventory control.

CASE 6–2. NEW ENGLAND SHIPBUILDING CORPORATION

Forecasting purchase prices

New England Shipbuilding Corporation is one of the largest shipyards in the United States. It builds not only various types of warships and supporting craft for the U.S. Navy but also cargo ships for private ship lines. Like other American shipyards, the company would not exist were it not for Navy orders and heavy subsidies on merchant marine orders. While New England Shipbuilding and other major American shipbuilders believe they are at least as efficient as their foreign competitors—particularly the Japanese—their methods are not so superior that they can compete in world markets with foreign yards that pay wages at one half the level prevailing in American yards. Consequently, despite government subsidies, the company is in an almost perpetual profit squeeze.

Its problems are compounded by the basic economics of shipbuilding. Individual ships require as much as three years to construct, and a shipbuilding firm may, at any given time, have no more than three or four ships under construction. Naturally, it does not know how much profit it realizes on any particular order until after the ship is completed. Any interim calculations represent no more than an educated guess. While the company does receive subsidies on its work, competition among American shipyards for available business is so keen that profit margins are extremely narrow both on Navy work and on merchant ship construction. In addition, shipbuilders have relatively little control over many of their costs. A shipbuilder is basically an assembler of steel and other components made by specialized suppliers and, in the case of New England Shipbuilding, purchased parts and materials account for more than 60 percent of the sales dollar.

Naturally, when a project stretches out over a period of two or three years, costs of purchased parts and materials can run way ahead of original estimates. In the past, the company has been able to protect itself against unanticipated fluctuations in material costs by incorporating price-redetermination or escalation clauses into its contracts. These clauses generally permit reasonable increases in both labor and material to be passed on to the customer. In recent years, however, customers have demanded more protection against unanticipated price changes, and competition has been so vigorous that the major shipyards have been forced to accede to their customers' requests.

The company is now bidding on a $30 million order. It hopes to get an edge on competitiors if it can offer the customer a completely fixed price. The company estimates that work on the order will extend over a three-year period and that purchases of parts and materials for the order will amount to almost $20 million. Naturally, a wide range of purchased materials and parts will be required, although most of them will fall into three general categories: metals and metal products, electrical machinery, and nonelectrical machinery and equipment.

Walter Rogers, the materials manager, estimates that, roughly, $8 million will be spent for electrical machinery and equipment of various types, $6 million for nonelectrical machinery, and the balance for various types of metal parts and products. He assumes that prices he pays for the products will advance roughly in line with the Bureau of Labor Statistics wholesale price indexes of metals and metal products, and machinery. He also notes that in the past prices of machinery have tended to advance about half as rapidly as general wage rates. That is, if general wages advance by 5 percent during any particular year, the price of machinery would go up by roughly 2½ percent. This is only an overall average, however. In practice, machinery is more likely to advance almost as much as wages when demand is strong, while in periods of weak demand machinery manufacturers and suppliers of other materials and parts usually absorb any contract increases they incur in wage rates.

A decrease in prices paid for purchased parts or materials seems highly unlikely. Rogers is certain that, at best, he will be able to hold the line with existing costs and prices over the three-year period in which deliveries of the parts and materials will be made. At worst, he suspects that a full 15 percent escalation (which the company has gotten on contracts in the past) would be required.

He has been ordered, however, not to pad his estimate of material costs by the maximum amount of escalation. That is, if it seems certain that prices will not increase by more than 15 percent in the next three years, Rogers cannot protect himself by increasing his estimate of purchased parts and materials from $20 million at present prices to $23 million at the price level that will prevail three years later. The company needs the new order badly and cannot afford to lose out to competitors. On the other hand, Rogers has also been warned not to underestimate material costs. In fact, George Warren, the president of the firm, told him, "I want you to estimate the lowest possible material cost on this job and then stick to your cost. We can't afford to pad our estimate on this job. We need it too badly. On the other hand, the profit margin will be so narrow that we can't afford to spend $20,500,000 for materials if our bid is based on material cost of $20 million. We're not in business for our health, either."

Rogers believes that delivery of materials will be spaced fairly evenly over a three-year period. This, of course, would blunt the effect of any continuing inflation of prices and cost, since the maximum inflation would be incurred only on material that is delivered toward the end of the contract, while no inflation over original prices is incurred on material that is purchased immediately. However, Rogers cannot afford to commit the company to buy and take delivery of the material before it is actually needed. The company does not have the cash to invest and will not have it until it gets progress payments from the customer. In addition, it is subject to cancellation clauses that would prevent the company from being reimbursed for materials that are purchased too far ahead of actual needs.

Question

Assume that New England Shipbuilding's costs of purchased parts and materials follow the pattern of the BLS wholesale price indexes for metals and metal products, nonelectrical machinery, and electrical machinery. Based on *present* economic conditions, what should New England Shipbuilding include in its estimate of material costs?

7

Materials management planning

PLANNING is a major part of every executive's job. In general, the higher the executive's rank, the greater the futurity of his planning. The chief executive officer should be almost exclusively occupied with long-term planning. Especially in a large organization, there is relatively little he can do to influence the performance of his organization within the near future. The chief executive is normally concerned with such decisions as selection of key operating executives, construction of new facilities, introduction of new product lines, major financing, and so on. The impact of these decisions is not usually felt for at least a year.

The day-to-day success of the company is in the hands of a chief operating executive. In large corporations, the chairman of the board may be the chief executive officer, while the president is the chief operating officer. Regardless of the titles of the executives, however, every organization has two distinctly different types of management problem: long-range, concerned with the basic direction in which the organization is headed; and short-range, which focuses on day-to-day operating problems.

In most organizations, the materials manager can make significant contributions to the long-range planning process. Trends in purchase prices, for example, may be the single most important factor influencing a company's decision either to make something it is now buying, or vice versa. Like all other executives, the materials manager is also responsible for the professional development of his subordinates. While this effort may have almost no impact on current operations, it is vital to the achievement of broad, long-range plans.

Although he can almost always make important contributions to long-range planning, the materials manager is far more concerned with short-term planning. As a major operating executive, he helps develop the organization's basic operating plan. In most cases, the time period covered by this operating plan is one year, broken down into quarters or months. This plan is designed to permit the company to use its resources most effectively during the coming year to achieve its perceived operating objectives. In every organization, the operating plan consists of two basic documents.

1. *A forecast of revenues.* In a profit-making organization, this would be a conventional sales forecast. In a nonprofit organization, the equivalent would be a forecast of such revenue-producing activities as tax collections, tuitions, or hospital patient days.

2. *A budget.* This is a breakdown of expenses that are expected for some particular level of revenue. There is almost always a direct correlation between the revenue forecast and the budget, but it is rarely a one-to-one relationship. In most cases, a $1 change in income produces less than $1 of change in expenses.

At the same time that he is participating in the preparation of the company's overall operating plan, the materials manager prepares plans for his own activities. The materials management plan is interrelated with the organization's overall operating plan. It indicates what materials management must do if overall objectives are to be achieved, as well as contributions it can make to company success that are more or less unique. In making up his year-ahead plan, the materials manager not only must take into account the company's short-term goals but also indicate what, if anything, he hopes to contribute to longer term goals.

Typically, a materials manager might start to work on his plan three to six months before he submits it to top management for approval. In the course of the next three months, he may have to make several revisions in his plan to bring it in line with the plans of other activities of the business and to reflect changes in basic assumptions. After the plan is approved, there may be further changes. If the assumptions on which the plan is based change during the year, the materials manager would again revise his plan. Also, during the course of the year he would report progress in achieving objectives of the plan.

ACHIEVEMENT OF OBJECTIVES

The materials-planning process always should be in terms of objectives. In his plan, the materials manager should indicate how he proposes to achieve each of his basic objectives. For example, suppose that his objectives are identical with those listed in Chapter 3. (Remember, however, that objectives vary from company to company and industry to industry; each materials manager must determine his own.) Some typical ways in which a materials manager might plan to achieve these objectives are discussed below.

Low prices. Individual purchasing decisions obviously reflect price objectives. But the materials manager also should have an overall objective. Based on his economic forecast, knowledge of competitive conditions, and so on, he may wish to set an overall target for cost reduction—for example, 2 percent of total purchase volume, or $300,000 total savings.

High inventory turnover. To achieve this objective, the materials manager might institute programs to reduce the number of items carried in stock. He could also persuade vendors to carry special stocks available for immediate delivery, work to tighten lead times, and use similar techniques that will be discussed in later chapters of this book.

Low-cost of acquisition and possession. This objective can be achieved with various programs to reduce the cost of inbound freight, using techniques that will be discussed in the chapter on traffic management. It also can be achieved through improvements in the handling and storage of materials—materials-handling equipment, better controls, and so on.

Continuity of supply. To a considerable extent, this objective is largely dependent on selection of suppliers and inventory policies, but it also can be achieved in part by improved liaison with other departments in the company that use materials. In this way changes in their needs can be rapidly communicated to suppliers.

Consistency of quality. If quality is a problem, this becomes one of the most important objectives. The materials manager may propose joint programs with the quality control department to educate suppliers concerning the company's quality standards. He may propose a program of statistical quality control and vendor certification. If the quality problem becomes serious enough, he may plan on introducing new suppliers who can meet specifications or propose a joint program with engineering to develop alternate designs whose specifications suppliers can meet better.

If quality is not a problem and vendors are likely to continue meeting specifications, the quality objective may require almost no planning by the materials manager. In fact, it is possible that he may go even further and propose that suppliers with lower quality standards be introduced if he feels the company is paying for quality it does not need.

Low payroll costs. The materials manager should plan on introducing laborsaving devices, such as electronic data-processing equipment, in order to keep his clerical costs as low as possible. He also should review his organization at least once a year to determine changes in its structure that will permit jobs to be done by fewer personnel. He certainly should also try to prevent overtime expense by planning work ahead to even out work loads, hiring additional personnel if necessary and improving organization and methods.

Favorable supplier relations. A program to improve supplier relations may include "supplier days" on which vendors are invited to tour company facilities, hear speeches, and so on. It also may include efforts to prevent favoritism in buying and to stimulate supplier interest in developing new products for the company. Improvements may even be made in parking, lobby facilities, and the like to make salesmen's calls more pleasant.

Development of personnel. On-the-job training programs and night courses for high-potential personnel can help achieve this objective. So can plans for a more informal development of personnel. Ideally, the materials manager should include in his report evaluations of all key personnel and steps planned to improve their job skills. He also should include plans to prepare for job openings that may come with expansion, retirements, and so on.

Good records. Each record and procedure should be subjected to "regular trials for life," and those that are unnecessary should be eliminated. Periodic studies also may indicate a need for new records or better record keeping.

Other objectives. The objectives that have been discussed so far are all basic ones. Most materials managers will have other objectives as well. These might include favorable reciprocal relations, better relations with other departments, improved liaison with engineering on new products and design changes, promotion of standardization, and better make-or-buy decisions. In each case, the materials manager should present the objective and indicate how he plans to achieve it. If other departments in the company are involved, this should be made clear in the plan. Naturally, these departments must concur with such a plan before it is put into action.

Ideally, the materials-planning process should start at the bottom and work its way up. That is, the overall materials plan should represent a composite of the plans of the various individual departments that report to the materials manager. The planning process might begin with a meeting of the materials manager and his subordinates. At this stage, the group would agree on some very broad plan that seems to be consistent with top-management objectives. After agreeing on these very broad goals, each key subordinate would then make up his individual plan showing how he proposes to meet materials department objectives within his own group. This plan would then be reviewed by the materials manager and other key subordinates. If it seems consistent with the overall plan, it would then be consolidated into a combined statement of objectives for the materials department which the materials manager would submit to top management for approval.

FUTURE PRICE AND AVAILABILITY

The materials manager must supplement his broad plan to achieve objectives with highly detailed plans directly related to his basic jobs of buying, storing, and moving materials. The materials-planning process starts with an economic forecast. Using the forecasts of professional economists and applying the principles discussed in the previous chapter, the materials manager tries to predict the general trend of prices, wages, and costs for at least a year ahead. He must also make certain assumptions about his company's sales and production prospects for the coming year and even further in the future, if possible.

Price Forecasts

From broad forecasts and plans, the materials manager tries to develop specific predictions. He is careful not to misuse his forecasts. For example, if his forecasts indicate that overall wholesale prices will rise 2 percent, can he then conclude that the average prices he will pay for materials and components will rise 2 percent? Of course not. Some of the prices he pays will rise; others will decline. The change in his average prices may be greater or less than an overall average. To make an intelligent forecast, the materials manager should divide his commodities into groups. Such a division for an office-equipment manufacturer is shown in Table 7–1.

TABLE 7–1
Major purchased commodities for a manufacturer of business machines and equipment

I. Production parts and materials
    A. Semifinished and raw materials
        1. Plastic molding compounds
        2. Zinc
        3. Sheet steel
        4. Gray iron and castings
        5. Steel forgings
        6. Miscellaneous materials
    B. Component parts and assemblies
        1. Sheet steel stampings
        2. Ball and roller bearings
        3. Fractional horsepower electric motors
        4. Plated zinc die castings
        5. Miscellaneous components and assemblies
II. Nonproduction materials
    A. Machine tools and equipment
    B. Maintenance, repair, and operating supplies
        1. Perishable tools
        2. Lubricants and cutting oils
        3. Other supplies
    C. Construction
III. Transportation costs

Administered prices. The materials manager should develop forecasts for each major commodity. No materials manager can hope to forecast price or availability perfectly. With a material whose price is administered, such as steel, availability is likely to be more difficult to forecast than price. Prices of such materials respond quite slowly to changes in supply and demand, since producers exercise considerable discretion in price administration. On the other hand, availability can be a problem either when overall demand exceeds supply or when producers are shut down because of labor trouble or other reasons.

Competitive prices.   The situation is just the opposite with materials whose prices are determined almost entirely by impersonal supply-demand forces. As we saw in Chapter 6, these materials are almost always available at a price. When supply is reduced or demand is heavy, prices can rise precipitiously. Demand will then drop not because buyers are unable to get the material but because they are unwilling to pay the going price. Unfortunately, it is no easy job to forecast prices of such materials. Nevertheless, the materials manager who uses them is forced to make some sort of forecast whether he wants to or not. This is true even of materials managers who deny that they attempt to predict what the market will be. A materials manager's buying and stocking pattern is intrinsically based on market assumptions, whether he wants to admit it or not.

Of course, a materials manager can say, "I don't know what the market is going to do" and use various buying and accounting techniques designed to reduce risk. These include averaging of purchases, budgeted buying techniques, last-in, first-out accounting, and hedging. All these techniques prevent bad timing of purchases and poor forecasting from being immediately reflected in the profit-and-loss statement. But few materials managers would deny that they can boost profits substantially through shrewd timing of purchases—particularly when dealing with commodities that fluctuate a great deal in price.

Availability

Happily for the materials manager, most materials are readily available to the buyer who is willing to pay the going price. The major concern usually is not basic availability but the speed with which suppliers can respond to changes in demand. This responsiveness varies widely by commodity. In some cases, the position of the materials manager is no worse than that of the housewife who wants to buy an extra sack of potatoes. If he wants more, all he need do is ask for it, and the additional material is available immediately. At the other extreme, it may not be possible to satisfy an increase in demand for months or even years.

Unexpected changes.   Naturally, the materials manager tries to predict his needs as precisely as possible so he will not be forced to ask his suppliers to respond rapidly to an unexpected change in demand.

However, every organization occasionally makes major errors in forecasts. If the materials manager is totally unprepared for a sharp *increase* in demand, he may scramble uncertainly trying to respond and then ultimately fail to get the additional material when it is needed. A sudden *decrease* in demand may be equally unfavorable; the materials manager then finds himself deluged with a supply of material he cannot cut off fast enough. Excess costs of storage and handling as well as scrap are inevitable.

The rational manager has a formal or informal contingency plan to guide him in responding to a major shift in demand for each major commodity. Conceptually, it is sometimes useful to think of the demand estimate (which is usually derived from a sales forecast for the end product) as the mean of some distribution of estimates. For example, the materials manager whose major commodities are listed in Table 7–1 above may estimate that demand for his company's office equipment will require 10,000 tons of cold-rolled sheet steel to be used in the company's manufacturing operation. While this is the best estimate he has, he knows full well the company probably won't need *exactly* 10,000 tons. Instead, this is the *mean* of the distribution of a number of possibilities. Under normal circumstances, however, the materials manager believes that demand will be for at least 9,000 tons and will not ordinarily exceed 11,000 tons.

Response. The materials manager then figures out how he will adjust to expected variations around his mean estimate. In most cases, this is easy; inventory provides the buffer. When usage runs somewhat ahead of normal, the company draws on inventory; when usage drops below expected levels it lets inventory build up until it has a chance to cut back on orders to suppliers.

Major shifts in usage pose a greater problem. In some cases, every solution is very expensive. Costs are held down, however, if the materials manager considers every possible alternative so he has time to make the best possible decision. Suppose, for example, that demand for the company's office equipment jumps unexpectedly by 25 percent. The materials manager who had been buying about 800 tons of steel per month now must have 1,000 tons per month. He first considers the normal lead time for the material—with steel, at least three months. Thus it would ordinarily take the supplier three months to respond to the demand. During this three-month period, the materials manager could satisfy demand only if he had an extra 600 tons on hand for this contingency. The cost of this additional inventory would have to be weighed against other possible strategies, such as those suggested below.

1. *Do nothing.* The odds are against it, but the most profitable decision might be simply to let the company run out of steel and make customers for finished products wait their turn.

2. *Buy premium-priced steel.* Steel service centers carry large inven-

tories of most of the popular types of steel for immediate delivery. Naturally, their prices are higher than those charged by the steel mills.

3. *Expedite delivery.* The materials manager may be able to persuade his regular supplier to respond more rapidly to an increase in demand. This is quite likely during a period of depressed general business conditions and all but impossible during a boom.

4. *Make special arrangements.* In some cases, the contingency plan may be based on some special arrangement. The supplier may agree to "guarantee" some extra reserve capacity to be available on short notice, or possibly the problem can be solved by carrying a stock of semifinished material that can be rushed into production if it is needed.

Delivery failures. Under ordinary circumstances, a contingency plan is needed only if there is an unexpected change in demand. Otherwise, normal inventories can serve as a buffer to even out expected fluctuations in supply or in usage. However, normal buffer stocks are never adequate to cope with a strike or a catastrophe such as a major fire. Natural disasters are usually all but impossible to allow for in contingency plans, but materials managers can and do protect their companies against the effects of strikes at supplier plants or strikes by common carriers. When making their plan, they take into account scheduled labor negotiations. If they feel that operations might be affected by a supplier strike, they try to prevent supply failures with some sort of contingency plan. Similarly, if a strike is expected at one of the company's own plants, the materials manager's plan might call for finished-goods stocks to be built up in advance of the strike.

BAYESIAN ANALYSIS

Traditionally, materials planning has been carried out on an "all or nothing" basis. For example, suppose that a materials manager is concerned about coming union contract negotiations in the steel industry. Obviously, his plan of purchase should take into account a possible strike and, conceivably, a steel price increase following settlement of the strike. The traditional way to do this is to look at all the facts and then attempt to forecast precisely what will happen. For example, a materials manager might conclude that, as a result of contract negotiations, the steel industry will have a two- to three-week strike, followed by a 3 percent general increase in steel prices. He would then go ahead and plan his purchases accordingly—most likely building up a substantial inventory in advance of the strike deadline.

Decision under uncertainty

Of course, such a decision is not made with 100 percent probability. A well-informed materials manager can do a better job of predicting what will happen than the man on the street, but he can easily be way off base. There may not be a steel strike at all, and prices may not increase. As a result, he may make a bad decision, spending thousands of dollars to build an inventory of steel that will not be needed. Bayesian analysis is a technique that permits a more realistic approach to decisions made under conditions of uncertainty. With the Bayesian approach, the materials manager does not have to suck in his breath and decide whether or not there is not going to be a strike or there is going to be a strike—a situation that simply is not realistic. Instead he makes his decision reflect relative probabilities. That is, he admits he doesn't know what will happen but, after careful consideration of the facts, estimates the probability of various events occurring.

This approach also permits the relative value of each alternate decision to be taken into account. For example, the cost of running out of steel may be ten times greater than the cost of stockpiling it. Consequently, the materials manager might want to stockpile steel even if the odds are heavily against a strike. Theoretically, the materials manager might intuitively take this into account when making a decision. The Bayesian approach gives him a quantitative basis for weighing the relative values of alternate decisions, along with the probability of their occurrence.

Determination of probability. The Bayesian approach requires that a probability be assigned to each possible outcome. The sum of these probabilities is, of course, equal to 100 percent. In planning ahead for a possible steel strike and steel price increase, the materials manager might want to take a number of probabilities into account in making his decision.

To keep the arithmetic simple, assume, however, that there are just two basic probabilities: no strike or a 90-day strike. Looking six months or more ahead to a union contract expiration date, no one can predict with certainty whether or not there will be a strike. So the best that can be done is what a bookie does on a horse race: make an expert study of the available facts and then estimate the odds.

The materials manager should take all factors into account. These would include the following.

1. *Past labor relations in the steel industry.* If the steel industry almost always has had a strike every time the contract comes up for renewal, it becomes reasonable to expect a strike during the succeeding period.

2. *Attitudes of present union and company officials.* Personalities sometimes play a major role in labor relations. A strike becomes much more likely if the union elects new officers who need to "prove" how effective they are in winning gains for the rank-and-file workers.

3. *General economic conditions.* In general, the likelihood of a strike increases greatly during periods of booming business and declines drasti-

cally during periods when there is substantial unemployment. For example, in the past, steel strikes have always come off when the industry has had very little slack capacity and is hard pressed to meet orders. There has rarely been a strike during periods when there is plenty of slack capacity and the steel workers are suffering from underemployment.

Because he is objective, the materials manager who is on top of his job should be able to estimate the odds more reliably than many industry insiders who may become emotionally involved in the various issues. Suppose that the materials manager, after considering all of these factors, decides that the odds are 70 to 30 against a steel strike $[P(S) = .30$ and $P(NS) = .70]$. Theoretically, this means that if he took a random sample of all steel negotiations made under similar conditions, there would be no strike 70 times out of 100 and a 90-day strike the other 30 times.

Cost of protection. If the cost of protecting against a strike were exactly equal to the losses suffered as a result of not having prepared for it, the decision should be obvious: do nothing. But, of course, the losses are most likely much greater than the cost of protection, so the issue is in doubt until the materials manager takes both probability and relative cost into account.

Suppose that protection against a 90-day strike requires an extra investment of $1 million in inventory to be on hand when the union contract expires. The inventory buildup might begin 90 days before the contract expiration date. If there were a strike, it would be worked off during the 90-day period after the strike begins. Average additional investment in inventory would be $500,000 during this six-month period.[1]

If the carrying cost of the inventory is 30 percent per year[2] or 15 percent for the six-month period that the company will be holding the inventory, extra carrying cost is 15 percent of $500,000, or $75,000. This must be compared with the losses that the company would incur if it were forced to shut down for 90 days because of the steel strike. Such losses are not easy to estimate. Some customers would undoubtedly wait until the company was able to resume deliveries of finished products, while other sales might be lost forever. In addition, the shutdown would undoubtedly hurt the company's market prospects—particularly if the company's competitors had stocked up on steel and were able to keep on delivering to customers without interruption.

Suppose that, after taking all of these factors into account, manage-

---

[1] The average investment is equal to half of the original investment. This is explained in Chapter 8 in detail; Figure 8–2 is of particular interest.

[2] Carrying cost would include rental of storage space, transportation of the inventory to and from the storage space, interest on money tied up in the inventory, and allowance for possible spoilage. The concept of carrying cost, or cost of possession, is explained in more detail in Chapter 10.

ment estimates that a 90-day shutdown for lack of materials would cost $1 million. Then the Bayesian decision rule would be applied, taking both estimated probabilities and relative cost into account. The "expected value" of a shutdown is 30 percent of the $1 million cost of the shutdown, or a $300,000 loss. Similarly, the expected cost of protection against a strike that does not come off is equal to the $75,000 cost of carrying additional inventory, multiplied by the 70 percent probability that there will be no strike—or a $52,500 loss.

Thus the company stands to lose less if it is protected against a strike that does not happen. Therefore, it would protect itself against a strike even though the odds are 70 to 30 in favor of a peaceful settlement.

Conditional probability. In the example above, the Bayesian rule was applied to alternative possibilities of a single event. But, of course, in real life events are interrelated. One event may lead to others with alternative possibilities. In Bayesian jargon, these secondary events are "conditional probabilities."

For example, the expiration of a union contract in the steel industry first gives rise to the probability of some increase in steel prices following either a peaceful settlement or a strike. Assume that there are just three possibilities: no price increase, a 2 percent price increase, or a 4 percent increase. Each of these probabilities exists, regardless of whether there is a strike. However, they take different values with different strike outcomes. If there is no strike, assume that there is a 50 percent probability that there will be no price increase $[P(0)|NS = .50]$, a 30 percent probability of a 2 percent increase $[P(.02)|NS = .30]$, and a 20 percent probability of a 4 percent price increase $[P(.04)|NS = .20]$[3].

On the other hand, if there is a strike, the steel industry will almost certainly be stuck with a much higher wage settlement, and the climate will be more favorable to a price increase. So the probability pattern shifts upward. With a strike, assume there is but a 20 percent probability of no price increase $[P(0)|S = .20]$, a 50 percent probability of a 2 percent price increase $[P(.02)|S = .50]$, and a 30 percent probability of a 4 percent increase $[P(.04)|S = .30]$.

The Decision Tree

There now are eight different probabilities to be considered. To prevent confusion, the materials manager may want to lay them out in a "decision tree" like that in Figure 7–1. The tree begins with the first

---

[3] To the statistician, these are conditional probabilities, and the notation | can be translated as "after." For example, $[P(0)|NS]$ can be read as the probability (P) of no price increase (0) after $(|)$ an agreement has been reached and there is to be no strike (NS).

FIGURE 7–1
Decision tree on steel

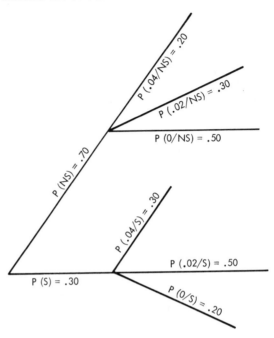

set of probabilities, and each new set of conditional probabilities creates new sets of "branches."

The decision tree makes it easy to calculate the probability of various individual events. Conditional probabilities can be calculated by multiplying the probabilities indicated on each of the branches of the tree, beginning at the base in each case. For example, the probability that there will be a strike and a 2 percent price increase $[P(.02|S)]$ on the decision tree is equal to the basic probability $[P(S) = 0.30]$ that there will be a strike multiplied by the conditional probability $[P(.02)|S]$ = .50 that there will be a 2 percent price increase following the strike. This probability is, therefore, 0.30 multiplied by 0.50, or 0.15.

Thus, there is a 15 percent probability that there will be both a strike and a 2 percent price increase. We will also want to calculate the probability that there will be a 2 percent price increase, strike or no strike. This is equal to the probability that there will be a 2 percent price increase and a strike *plus* the probability that there will be a 2 percent price increase and no strike. The decision tree indicates that the latter probability is equal to $P(NS)$ multiplied by $P(.02|NS) =$ .70 × .30, or .21. Thus there is a 21 percent probability that there will be a 2 percent increase, and no strike. Therefore, the probability that there will be a 2 percent price increase, strike or no strike, is equal to 0.21 + 0.15, or 36 percent. Following this same approach, the probability that there will be no price increase, strike or no strike, is 41 percent (6 percent if there is a strike plus 35 percent if there is no strike). And there is a 23 percent probability that there will be a 4 percent price increase, strike or no strike (9 percent with a strike plus 14 percent without a strike).

Calculating expected value

It is now possible to estimate probable steel costs during the coming year, which amounts to $4 million per year at current prices. With a 2 percent price increase, these costs would rise to $4,080,000 (calculated by multiplying 1.02 by $4,000,000). With a 4 percent increase they would be $4,160,000. These costs are then weighed by their probabilities, as follows:

$$
\begin{array}{ll}
\$4,000,000 \times 41\% = & \$1,640,000 \\
\$4,080,000 \times 36\% = & \$1,468,800 \\
\$4,160,000 \times 23\% = & \underline{956,800} \\
\text{Expected value} & \$4,065,600
\end{array}
$$

Thus, there is an expected value that steel costs will increase by $65,600 per year or about 1.5 percent as the result of the coming labor negotiations in the industry. Note, however, that costs will *not* increase by precisely $65,600. There will still either be no increase in price at all, a 2 percent price increase that will cost $80,000 per year, or a 4 percent price increase that will cost $160,000. The $65,600 expected value merely indicates what average cost would be if a company were confronted with the same problem many, many times and outcomes occurred at random.

While the company will not be hit with an actual $65,600 increase in steel costs, regardless of what happens, this is the most realistic esti-mate to use in planning, since it takes all probabilities into account. If Bayesian analysis is applied to all other forecasts of purchase costs, total purchase costs would work out pretty much as planned because, of course, deviations from the expected values would occur at random and cancel each other out. If Bayesian analysis is not used, it would be necessary to forecast precisely what the steel price increase would be. Inevitably, major errors would be made simply because not even the best-informed materials manager can do more than guess under such circumstances. There is tremendous uncertainty, and all a well-informed manager can hope to do is to suggest a range of probabilities.[4]

---

[4] The weatherman has finally caught on to this concept, too. He no longer says dogmatically it will rain today or it will be sunny. Such a forecast implies, of course, that meteorology is a much more advanced science than it actually is. The best the meterologist can do is to predict that there is a strong probability

Limitations

Not even the most well-informed person really knows what the probabilities are. While this is an obvious limitation to Bayesian analysis, it does not prevent it from being a useful technique. The fact is that all business decisions—including most of those made by materials managers—are made under conditions of uncertainty. If the materials manager knew exactly what was going to happen, he could presumably delegate his decision making to a computer and, in this case, there would not be much need for a materials manager.

The qualified materials manager should of course, be better able than anyone else in his company to come up with an estimate of the probability of a steel strike and the conditional probability of a price increase. In making his estimate, he would not only rely on his gut "feel" for the situation but also get the opinions of his subordinates as well as suppliers and outside economists. However, the ultimate responsibility for decisions made to cope with uncertainty belongs to the materials manager alone (or to top management, if it makes the final decision).

PREPRODUCTION PLANNING

Purchase prices and availability are by no means the only uncertain elements in the planning process. Every project involves a series of steps, and the success and timing of each are often in doubt. Along with other key executives, materials managers are periodically involved in planning for some new activity. In a nonmanufacturing enterprise, this is usually the introduction of some new service or the construction and breaking in of some new facility. Typical nonmanufacturing projects which would involve the materials manager in planning are the opening of a new maintenance base for an airline, the construction of a new wing to a hospital, or the construction and initial operation of a new power-generating facility.

Basic process

In a manufacturing company, comparable activities would be the planning stages prior to production of some new product. If the new product is to be introduced on schedule, a long series of events also must take place on schedule. Naturally, some of these events involve the materials department.

---

of a certain type of weather. Now the weatherman officially admits this and, rather than forecasting rain tomorrow, he may say that there is a "60 percent probability of rain" (or if a nice day is in store, he may say there is a "10 percent probability of rain").

Holding to schedule. Typically, the first event involving the new product occurs in the engineering department. Engineering makes up an elaborate schedule for completion of the design of the product and normally plans to release a steady flow of blueprints and other specifications to other departments in the company.

Each major activity in the company is responsible for holding to its own schedule. If one department slips behind schedule, it will almost inevitably put additional pressure on other departments to make up lost time. For example, if engineering is not able to complete the design of a particular component on schedule, then either purchasing or manufacturing will be under pressure to complete its share of the job. If the next department is not able to make up lost time, the whole program may fall behind schedule, and the company will ultimately suffer losses.

If the product is complex, the planning process can become extremely involved. To see how the process might work, however, consider a fairly simple product with just two components, subassembly A and subassembly B. These components are joined together to make a particular end product.

Before top management gives a final go-ahead on the product, each department reviews its role in detail and estimates the time required to complete each phase of its job. Usually, information from various activities concerned with the project is consolidated into a single master schedule. Each existing department is normally responsible for its phase of the schedule. However, the company may wish to create a special organization to handle the new project rather than delegate it on a functional basis to the various departments.

Organization by project. The company might create a "project team" that functions as a special division until a new product gets into production. Following the principles outlined in Chapter 4, this team would be responsible for all work up to the point where the product enters production and thereby becomes a regular activity of the company. Typically the project team includes representatives from all major departments concerned with the product. The team decisions are passed back to the appropriate departments, and the team members expedite within their own departments to make certain that schedules are adhered to.

For example, once purchase specifications are avilable, the materials representative on the product team might agree that he could get suppliers to deliver subassembly A in adequate quantities within 30 weeks and subassembly B within 20 weeks. These estimates, in turn, would be broken down for internal control into time estimates for each basic step in the materials cycle, starting with the process of getting quotations from the suppliers and ending when the supplier finally begins to deliver in production quantities. For purchased items, the materials cycle might consist of the following steps:

1. Get competitive bids.
2. Evaluate quotations and place orders.
3. Follow up on progress made by the supplier in tooling for production. If the supplier must purchase special tooling, this might also involve review of progress of the supplier's supplier.
4. Follow up to make certain that samples made from production tools are inspected and approved on schedule by the buyer's quality control department.
5. Make certain that production begins on schedule.

The materials department attempts to estimate realistic times for each of these steps. In some cases, the time allowance is more than adequate. Certain parts can be obtained almost overnight and could not possibly cause any problems. In such cases, however, the materials department does not make its own job too easy. It would not want to buy an item six months before it was needed just to make certain it was on hand, because this would tie up funds in inventory unnecessarily. It would hold off buying the item until just before it was actually needed, giving itself an adequate lead time.

In many cases, delivery of purchased parts and materials has to be closely coordinated with tooling programs in manufacturing. The materials management department is concerned not only with delivery of purchased parts but also with follow-up of progress in purchasing any equipment that might be needed and in trying out and installing this equipment. Its preproduction control job is finished only after the initial pilot run of the new product has been completed.

Certain items would almost certainly be critical to the overall program. These are the ones for which the procurement or production cycle is longest. A delay in any of these critical items could cause the whole program to fall behind schedule. From experience, the project team knows which items might cause trouble, and progress on these items is followed up periodically to make certain that they are on schedule.

The Gantt chart

Procedures used in the follow-up process vary widely. Many of them, however, make use of one version or another of the Gantt chart (named for its inventor). The chart shown in Figure 7–2 is typical. Like other Gantt charts, this one makes it easy to compare actual and scheduled progress on a particular project.

Scheduling basic jobs. The first step in developing the Gantt chart for a particular project is making up a schedule of the basic jobs required. For example, the chart in Figure 7–2 indicates that engineering drawings should be completed on subassembly A sometime in the 7th

FIGURE 7-2
Gantt chart for new-products program

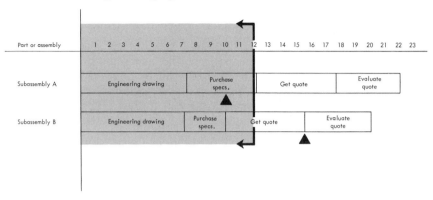

week, purchase specs should be ready in the 12th week, quotations should be received in the 17th week, and these quotations should be evaluated some time in the 22nd week.

The Gantt chart has a movable arrow or some other marking device to mark off the weeks as they roll by. In Figure 7-2, the shaded area indicates that the project is now in its 12th week. Actual progress on the project is also recorded on the chart, as indicated by the two small solid triangles underneath the schedule for each subassembly. One triangle indicates that, as of the 12th week, purchase specs on subassembly A are still being worked on in the engineering department and, in fact, they are only a little more than half complete. The arrow is therefore placed under the tenth week. This indicates that the work on subassembly A is now about two weeks behind schedule, and engineering is at the stage it should have reached by the 10th week.

In contrast, work on subassembly B is ahead of schedule. As of the 12th week, the purchasing department should have sent the specs out to suppliers for quotations but would not expect to get them back for another four weeks. However, the arrow indicates that all of the quotations are in, so this subassembly is four weeks ahead of schedule.

Unfortunately, the wrong item is ahead of schedule. The materials manager can glance at the chart and conclude that he can afford to be a little behind schedule on subassembly B, since the entire job on this item up to placement of the order only takes 20 weeks, while that for subassembly A should take 22 weeks. Consequently, the fact that subassembly B is ahead of schedule does him no good whatever. It just means there will be additional slack time that is not needed. However, subassembly A is critical. If it is two weeks behind schedule, the product that is assembled from A and B will be two weeks behind schedule. Consequently, the materials manager can tell at a glance that work must be speeded up on subassembly A, and he would undoubtedly request the engineering department to try to speed up its development of purchase specifications, by working overtime or by some other means.

Basis for follow-up. A Gantt chart like that shown in Figure 7–2 can also be used by a project group for follow-up, since it includes all activities necessary for the project. The materials group would be likely to keep a detailed Gantt chart only for its phase of the operation, which in this case begins with the securing of quotations. Some follow-up might still be carried on to make certain that the engineering department is on schedule in delivering specs on subassembly B in the 10th week, as scheduled, and on subassembly A in the 12th week. But the materials department would not, of course, be responsible for following up on each detailed phase of the engineering job.

In the past, many companies kept Gantt charts on almost every component of a new-product program. Only a few of the individual components were troublemakers, but it was difficult to determine in advance what they would be—and, in fact, hardly anyone tried. Sometimes, however, for various reasons, a component like subassembly B—which seemingly had plenty of slack time—would be held up and would become a bottleneck in the program.

The PERT technique

In the past 20 years, new techniques have been developed to spot potential bottlenecks in a program and to permit management to ignore the parts of a project that will not give any trouble. This relatively new technique is known as PERT,[5] or the critical path method. In every project, there are a number of activities going on simultaneously. In a really complicated project, such as development of a space vehicle, there may be literally tens of thousands of such activities. Most of these are not critical; that is, if they are delayed, the overall program will not be held up. However, in every project there is at least one bottleneck or "critical path" that will hold up the entire project if it gets behind schedule. This is the chain of events that requires the longest time to complete.

Simple network. Figure 7–3 shows a PERT network that could be constructed for subassembly A and subassembly B. The time indicated for the procurement cycle is identical with those in the Gantt chart in Figure 7–2, except that the PERT network assumes that no decision

---

[5] The initials stand for program evaluation review technique. PERT was originally developed by the Navy to control the Polaris missile program but is now widely used by all of the armed services, the National Aeronautics and Space Administration, and various defense and other areospace firms. When the same technique is used in non-defense-related industries, such as construction, it is often called critical path method (CPM).

FIGURE 7–3
Typical PERT network

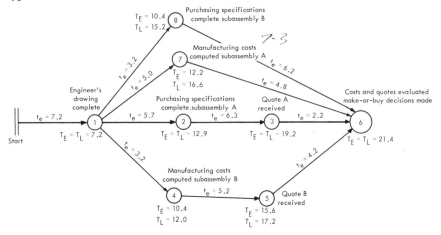

Computations for PERT Network

Preceding event	Event	a (optimistic)	m (realistic)	b (pessimistic)	t_e	T_E	T_L	$T_L - T_E$
Start	1	1	4	26	7.2	7.2	7.2	0
1	2	2	5	12	5.7	12.9	12.9	0
1	4	1	3	6	3.2	10.4	12.0	1.6
1	7	2	4	12	5.0	12.2	16.6	4.4
1	8	1	3	6	3.2	10.4	15.2	4.8
2	3	4	6	10	6.3	19.2	19.2	0
3	6	1	2	4	2.2	21.4	21.4	0
4	5	3	5	8	5.2	15.6	17.2	1.6
5	6	1	4	8	4.2	19.8	21.4	1.6
7	6	1	5	8	4.8	17.0	21.4	4.4
8	6	4	6	9	6.2	16.6	21.4	4.8

The PERT network consists of a number of events (circles) joined by activities (arrows). Event times, T_E and T_L, are earliest and latest times event can be reached without upsetting overall schedule. Activity times, t_e are averages of three estimates of the time needed to complete each activity. Network in example is a simple one; complete networks can be built from networks similar to this.

has yet been made as to whether this item should be purchased or made by an outside supplier. For this reason, there are four "paths" in the network. Two paths are for purchase of subassembly A and subassembly B and two cover manufacture of A and B. All four paths come together when manufactured costs and purchase quotations are evaluated for a make-or-buy decision. The network would, of course, extend on from this point, joining with other paths until the product or program is completed.

In constructing construct a PERT network such as that in Figure 7–3, you first write down each activity needed and note what other activity must be completed before this one can be started.[6] You then make estimates of the time (in days or weeks) needed to do each job: an "optimistic" time, a, a "realistic" time m, and a "pessimistic" time b. You then calculate the expected time of the event, t_e, with the formula $t_e = \dfrac{a + 4m + b}{6}$.

This formula is an easy-to-calculate substitute for a normal distribution. Every estimate of time required to do a job can be looked upon as the mean of some distribution. The maximum and minimum times that are also estimated provide an approximation of three standard deviations variance around that mean. In theory, the mean estimate represents the best estimate of the time to do the job, and the actual time should fall between the minimum and maximum at least 99 percent of the time. The formula gives an approximation of the time that would be estimated were all possible times in the normal distribution "added up" by means of integral calculus.

After calculating expected times for each operation, you proceed to construct a PERT network similar to that in Figure 7–3. The critical path—the path that requires the longest time—includes events 1, 2, 3, and 6, and the total expected time, T_L, is equal to the sum of the expected times of each of these events, or 21.4 weeks. If events in this critical path get behind schedule, the entire project will be held up.

Noncritical to critical. There is slack in the other paths. Events on noncritical paths can fall behind schedule without affecting the over-all project. Slack time for each noncritical path shows how far these noncritical paths can get behind schedule before they become critical.

For example, look at event 4 in the table in Figure 7–3. The expected time, t_e, of this event is 3.2 weeks, and the cumulative expected time, T_E, for the path up to event 4 is equal to the sum of the expected times of events 1 and 4, or 10.4 weeks. The path is not complete, however, until events 5 and 6 are completed. The expected times on this path for these remaining events are equal to 9.4 weeks (5.2 weeks to get from event 4 to event 5, and 4.2 weeks to get from 5 to 6). Since the total expected critical path time is 21.4 weeks, the project probably will not be held up as long as you can get up to event 4 in 12.0 weeks (21.4 weeks minus the 9.4 weeks expected time to get from 4 to 6). This becomes T_L, the latest that you can reach a point on a path without holding up the project. And, of course, T_L minus T_E is the slack, which is 1.6 weeks for the path up to event 4. If we are more than 1.6 weeks behind schedule, this path may then become critical.

Management normally limits its attention either to paths that are

---

[6] This in itself would make the PERT network worthwhile, even if it did nothing else. Before PERT, many companies embarked on new-product programs almost blindly, with little or no advance planning of the exact steps in the process. They could, of course, have used Gantt charts, but in practice they often did not.

already critical or to those about to become critical. Typically, an entire PERT network is programmed into a computer. All transactions concerned with the network are then keypunched and entered into the computer. The computer then will calculate and recalculate critical paths, focusing management's efforts on events that are likely to delay the entire program.

PERT is particularly useful for extremely complex products, while a simple Gantt chart is usually adequate when there are no more than a dozen possible paths. Thus it is not surprising that PERT is used almost entirely in defense-related industries or construction, where the end product is made in relatively small quantities and is extremely complicated. Producers of conventional civilian products usually use a version of a Gantt chart, although they often rely on a computer to do the basic work of the chart.

PRODUCTION PLANNING

Job lots

Variations of the Gantt chart are often used for production control of existing products as well as new ones, especially for products made in batches or "job lots." With job-lot production, the organization behaves almost as if each order were a separate project, unrelated to other orders. In the production of a weekly magazine, for example, the production department would have a separate plan for each issue of the magazine, which calls for completion on the date a particular issue is due to be mailed to subscribers.

Manufacturing applications. In a factory, job-lot planning is used when each order fills some special customer need. In some cases, such as companies making specialized machine tools, the job lot is identified with a particular customer's order. In others, customer orders for like material are grouped together. For example, a drug company might periodically manufacture batches of a compound that is sold to a number of customers.

In every case, the production-planning process is a joint effort between materials management and manufacturing. Materials management is responsible for having the material on hand when it is needed, and manufacturing must have manpower and equipment available on schedule. With most processes, these two tasks are hopelessly interrelated. It is wasteful to have material on hand when manpower and equipment are not available to use it. Conversely, no company can afford to have machines and workers idle because there is no material to work with.

In the ideal situation, manpower, machinery, and materials for a particular job lot all come together at exactly the right time. This is easiest to accomplish when a single executive is responsible for getting them there. In most manufacturing companies, this executive has a title like production and inventory control manager. As indicated in Chapter 1, in a growing number of manufacturing companies he reports to the materials manager—although his job is partly materials management and partly manufacturing management.

Three resources. At any time, the ability of a company to deliver its products to customers on schedule is limited by at least one of three basic resources: manpower, equipment, or materials. The supply problem is largely one of having the material there when the equipment and manpower are available to work on it. There is seldom a simultaneous shortage of both equipment and manpower.

At times when equipment is in short supply relative to manpower, production control is primarily concerned with planning the most effective utilization of the bottleneck equipment, making certain that adequate amounts of material and labor are always available. In other cases, manpower is the effective bottleneck. The company occasionally is not able to hire needed skills. More commonly, however, it wants to maintain a stable labor force with high productivity. This objective can only be achieved if there is always another job waiting for the worker who completes an assigned task ahead of schedule. The material must be on hand already, along with the appropriate equipment.

Equipment planning

The trouble with equipment is that it is not homogeneous. Even a homeowner's workshop may have a half dozen pieces of equipment, each of which performs a specialized function. Thus it is useless to own a band saw if you need to drill holes. Factories have the same problem on a much bigger scale. They almost always have many pieces of equipment that are being used only on a part-time basis. When general business conditions are favorable, they also usually are confronted with a shortage of certain types of equipment. Unfortunately, it is rare that the surplus equipment can be adapted to substitute for that in short supply. Band saws just cannot be made to drill holes.

Forecast of demand. In most companies, equipment planning must be based on a forecast of demand for equipment. This would normally be derived from long-term forecasts of product demand, following the principles outlined in Chapter 6. It would also reflect the company's immediate past experience. For example, a manufacturer who had a severe shortage of screw machine capacity last year will probably also suffer from one this year—provided there is no major adverse change in product mix or aggregate demand.

In job shops, the production control department typically bases its equipment-planning decisions on records it keeps of the demand for each type of equipment. When a company has hundreds or thousands of pieces of equipment these records are normally maintained by a computer. The basic principle is the same when there are just two pieces of equipment.

Imagine that you operate a small printing business equipped with four presses and a machine that collates and binds printed sheets of paper into booklets. Some of your customers want you to produce various pamphlets and booklets for them, and therefore they require both your printing and binding services. Others require just printing or send you material for binding that they have had printed elsewhere.

You normally operate just one shift, 40 hours per week. Therefore, you have just 40 hours per week of binding capacity and 160 hours of press capacity from your four presses. Every time you get an order, you add the estimated press time and binding time to your backlog. When an order is completed, this time is subtracted from the backlog.

For example, suppose you accept an order requiring 30 hours of press time and 5 hours of bindery time. You already have orders calling for 770 hours of press time and 35 hours of bindery time. Adding in the new order gives you a revised backlog of 800 hours and 40 hours, respectively. Since your four presses each can operate a normal 40-hour week and therefore provide 160 hours per week of press time, your backlog of press time is now exactly five weeks ($800 \div 160$). But your bindery backlog is just one week, or 40 hours' work.

Imbalance. Thus it appears that you have an imbalance between press and bindery capacity. Unless you get more orders, your bindery will soon be idle and losing money. But customers who want both printing and binding will be dissatisfied because your big backlog for printing makes your service poor. There are two obvious short-term solutions to your problem.

The first solution is to solicit orders from other printers for binding. Since your bindery is about to be shut down anyway because of a lack of orders, you will be quite willing to quote low prices in order to get more binding.

The second is to farm out some of your printing to other printers, so you will be able to accept more orders calling for both printing and binding. This solution presupposes that your ability to accept new business is limited by your printing capacity because your customers insist on delivery sooner than is possible with your five-week backlog.

If yours were a large organization, the production control manager would probably call this imbalance in capacity to the attention of either the sales manager, who would solicit additional orders, or the purchasing manager, who would arrange for subcontracting.

Subcontracting might also be a preferred solution over the longer term. In a large organization, the materials manager and the manufacturing manager would jointly review capacity and estimate approximately how much work should be farmed out and how much should be done in house. The alternative would be extra capacity—through either over-time operation or purchase of additional equipment. Manufacturing would decide how it was going to achieve the additional capacity and material management would buy whatever equipment was needed.

Surplus disposal.   Not infrequently, review of equipment needs indicates a surplus. In some cases, equipment can be disposed of without any adverse effect on production. For example, a company that owns 12 turret lathes may discover it can operate just as well with 11. Its depreciation, taxes, and other operating costs will be reduced if it sells the unneeded lathe. And, of course, the proceeds from the sale can be used profitably in other parts of the business.

Profits may also be increased by getting rid of equipment that is used only part time. For example, in your printing business, you may discover that it is virtually impossible to keep your bindery busy enough to be profitable. In that case, as is explained in detail in Chapter 11, you may wish to dispose of this equipment and rely on subcontractors for your binding.

Manpower planning

Any change in the equipment inventory of your printing plant would also affect your labor force. In fact, manpower planning is probably a greater problem for the very small business than the big one. In a small business, the unexpected resignation of a single highly skilled employee can have an adverse effect on profits. In a big business, employee resignations usually can be predicted statistically and be taken in stride.

Sales fluctuations.   However, utilization of manpower is a major problem for both large and small organizations. It is particularly acute when there is considerable fluctuation in demand for the company's end product.

In such cases, a company really has only three choices:

1. *Employment level can be varied with demand.*   For example, a construction contractor will hire skilled workers on a day-by-day or week-by-week basis. The workers float from contractor to contractor and have no permanent employer. However, this continuous process of hiring and laying off is much too expensive in all but a few industries. Most companies avoid like the plague situations where employment levels zoom up and down with the ebb and flow of sales on a weekly or monthly basis. A company that lays off an employee in May only to discover that it needs the same skills in June may incur two losses: (1) unemployment benefits paid to the laid-off employee, and (2) the training costs associated with his eventual replacement.

2. *Inventory can serve as a buffer between varying demand and stable employment.*   Stocks of unsold goods will accumulate during periods when demand lags behind production and can be sold off when demand

exceeds production. This policy works well over the short term as long as the company is able to produce something for which there is certain to be a future demand. Over the longer term, the policy becomes too costly. For example, no company can afford a situation where it produces in excess of demand for a period of several years, and a majority of manufacturing companies will cut back production immediately after an unexpected slump in sales.

3. *The backlog can serve as a buffer between demand and capacity.* If a company always has a few more orders than it can handle immediately, its employees never run out of work, and a backlog of unfilled orders builds up. This backlog is reduced during periods when demand lags behind expectations and builds up again when demand leaps ahead of production. As long as customers are willing to wait (and they often are not), a backlog is an ideal solution to any organization's manpower-planning problem.

Line production

Backlogs are most likely to be acceptable to customers when the product is made on a job-order basis, especially when it is made to the customer's unique specifications. For example, producers of capital goods almost always work from backlogs and do not usually carry any finished-goods inventory. In contrast, manufacturers of consumer goods normally produce ahead of demand, feeding their production into finished-goods inventories.

In most cases, goods are produced in a continuous flow rather than in batches. For example, an automobile plant assembles a variety of models that move down the same assembly line in a continuous flow. In contrast, if autos were produced by a batch process, the workers would first complete one lot of blue, super deluxe four-door sedans, then they might switch to pink station wagons, then to black two-door sedans, and so on.

Optimum plan. The ideal production plan has the following characteristics:

1. Demand is satisfied. No sales are lost because products were not available when customers wanted them.
2. Minimum labor costs are incurred. Employment remains stable, and there are no interruptions in production.
3. There is minimum investment in purchased, in-process, and finished-goods inventories.
4. Equipment is fully utilized.

Unfortunately, no production plan can be ideal. Achievement of any one of these objectives brings sacrifices in the others. For example, the company that hopes to achieve full utilization of equipment (1) may not be equipped to cope with unexpected surges in demand, (2) will probably incur excess labor costs in the form of standby employees or overtime premiums, and (3) will likely accumulate extra inventory during periods of lagging demand.

Every production plan is a compromise which reflects the best possible balance of marketing, manufacturing, and materials management objectives. An overall production plan must be a joint effort by the managers of these three basic functions. However, the actual preparation of the detailed plan may well be a materials management responsibility. Planning is often a trial-and-error process. Past experience is usually the most important guide to the future, although computer simulations and other operations research techniques can help reduce the probability of planning errors.

Example of plan. Table 7–2 shows a line production plan for a hypothetical manufacturer of air-conditioning units. Total annual demand is forecast at 80,000 units, with a selling price of $100 per unit. For obvious reasons, this demand is highly seasonal. Customers do not begin to buy at retail until spring, and by late summer, the season is over and retailers are cutting prices to avoid having to carry over stock until the following year. Shipments from manufacturer to distributor and from distributor to dealer must lead retail sales by at least a month or two. The manufacturer anticipates that shipments to distributors will begin in December and continue through June, with monthly sales (in dollars) shown in Column 6 of Table 7–2.

In order to stabilize employment and use manufacturing facilities more efficiently, the company chooses to operate for almost 12 months of each year, even though it expects to make almost no sales to distributors between June 30 and October 31. During this slack period, all production is stored in a warehouse. As indicated in Column 8, it is assumed that this extra investment in finished-goods inventory will cost 6 percent per year, or .05 percent per month, in interest charges, under the company's credit agreement with its bank. If all goes according to plan, the company's total interest charges for its extra investment in inventory will be $81,320.

Extra storage and insurance costs also will be incurred under this plan. These are shown in Column 9, along with overtime premiums the company anticipates paying to its workers during the peak production months of January and February. Premium costs, exclusive of interest, are expected to total $52,264. Added to interest charges of $81,320, the total extra inventory carrying cost is estimated at $133,584.

For these extra costs, the company gains a reasonably stable production rate, steady employment, and some flexibility. The basic production rate is 32 units per day. Column 2 of Table 7–2 indicates the number of working days expected in each month at normal operation, after allowing for paid holidays. In July there are only 10 working days be-

TABLE 7-2
Production plan for 80,000 air conditioners

(1) Month	(2) Number of work days	(3) Production in units	(4) Beginning inventory	(5) Additions	(6) Shipments	(7) Ending inventory	(8) Interest @ 0.5% per month	(9) Other excess costs	(10) Total extra costs
July	10*	3,200	—	$320,000	—	$ 320,000	$ 1,600	$ 320†	$ 1,920
August	22	7,040	$ 320,000	704,000	—	1,024,000	5,120	1,024	6,144
September	20	6,400	1,024,000	640,000	—	1,664,000	8,320	1,664	9,984
October	21	6,720	1,664,000	672,000	—	2,336,000	11,680	2,336	14,016
November	21	6,720	2,336,000	672,000	—	3,008,000	15,040	3,008	18,048
December	22	7,040	3,008,000	704,000	$ 500,000	3,212,000	16,060	3,212	19,272
January	20	9,600	3,212,000	960,000	1,500,000	2,672,000	13,360	20,672‡	34,032
February	20	9,600	2,672,000	960,000	2,000,000	1,632,000	8,160	19,632§	27,792
March	23	7,360	1,632,000	736,000	2,000,000	368,000	1,840	368	2,208
April	20‖	6,400	368,000	640,000	1,000,000	8,000	40	8	48
May	16#	5,120	8,000	512,000	500,000	20,000	100	20	120
June	15**	4,800	20,000	480,000	500,000	—	—	—	—
Totals	230	80,000			$8,000,000		$81,320	$52,264	$133,584

* Two-week vacation shutdown.
† Consisting of taxes and insurance of 10 cents per unit on inventory stored in plant's own warehouse.
‡ Equal to $18,000 overtime premium plus $2,672 storage cost.
§ Equal to $18,000 overtime premium plus $1,632 storage cost.
‖ Start on four-day week last two weeks of April.
Four-day week.
** Four-day week with three-day layoff at end of month.

cause of the company's vacation shutdown, and beginning in mid-April, the company plans to cut back to a four-day week, which will continue to the end of the fiscal year on June 30. If demand does not exceed the present forecast, the company also expects to lay off its entire work force about three days before the annual vacation begins in June.

Need for flexibility. There is some flexibility built into the plan. If demand seems to be lagging behind expectations, the company can quite easily eliminate the overtime it is planning during the January-February period of peak demand. If demand continues to lag behind sales, the vacation shutdown can be advanced accordingly. On the other hand, overtime operations may continue into March—and conceivably even into April—if demand exceeds forecasts. In addition, if there is a late surge in demand from dealers and distributors, the company can keep its plant operating five days per week during the final 10 weeks of the fiscal year, instead of the four-day week called for in this plan.

This plan, like any other the company might make, is a compromise. It is not ideal. Theoretically, for example, the company might wind up with slightly lower costs if it hired more employees and produced perhaps 340 units per day instead of 320. This higher basic production rate would eliminate much of the overtime premium that is now expected in January and February. It would also permit more production if the sales estimate turns out to have been too low. Unfortunately, these benefits do not come without cost. A higher production rate would also increase inventory carrying cost early in the year, when stocks would be accumulating at the rate of 340 units per day instead of 320. In addition, if the company's sales estimate proved too optimistic, extra employees would have to be laid off.

In the present era of computer simulation, it would be possible for the company to experiment with literally hundreds of different possible plans. Bayesian decision theory could also be applied to the planning process, since almost all of the key variables of the plan are really probability distributions rather than simply "point estimates," as is implied in Table 7–2.

PLAN OF PURCHASE

One of the major factors determining the final production plan is the ability of manufacturing to respond to change in demand. The quicker the response, the lower the potential premium costs of overtime, layoffs, or inventory. This is also true of plans of purchase derived from the production plan. The materials manager must get his purchased materials delivered before they are actually needed in production. The earlier he brings them in, the greater the inventory carrying cost. But this cost is at least partly offset by the benefit of having material on hand to meet unexpected increases in demand or potential future delays in supply. Procurement lead time is also determined by the stage of the manufacturing process at which the particular purchased item is used. The carton for an air conditioner that is completed on June 30 can be delivered from the carton supplier on June 29, if necessary. But a casting which must be machined before it is incorporated into a major component that is assembled into the finished product might have to be on hand sometime in May if there is to be no delay in the process.

Example of plan. Table 7–3 shows how a plan of purchase is developed for a gray-iron casting used in the air conditioner whose production plan is shown in Table7–2. The production planner first checks the specifications to determine how many castings are used in each air conditioner. In this case, just one casting is actually used, but the company expects that about 5 percent of the castings purchased will be lost as scrap in the machining process or will simply disappear. Therefore, the company plans on buying 84,000 castings instead of just 80,000 during the coming year. If losses seem to be running less than the 5 percent allowance, purchases can be cut back slightly toward the end of the year.

The plan of purchase, like the production plan, assumes that this particular model of air conditioner will not be produced after the fiscal year ends. If the company decides to continue the model, next year's plans can simply be joined on to this year's without difficulty.

The purchasing department predicts that the price of this casting will increase by 10 percent, from $1.00 to $1.10, about January 1. Therefore, as indicated in Column 3 of Table 7–3, all castings purchased after December 31 are priced at $1.10 each rather than $1.00 each.

The purchasing department also believes there is some small chance of a strike at the foundry that supplies this casting. The foundry's labor agreement expires on December 31, and the purchasing department believes the foundry will reach an agreement with its union calling, of course, for higher wages. Since the market for gray-iron castings is already strong, this wage agreement will give the foundry the excuse it needs to boost prices. The purchase manager proposes that the company try to purchase its total requirements of 84,000 before January 1, with the supplier following a shipping schedule similar to that suggested in Column 5 of Table 7–3. This schedule would offer advantages over the plan indicated in Column 1, which is simply designed to have material on hand when its is needed. These advantages are:

1. The revised plan calls for shipment in full truckload quantities. The traffic department estimates that 8,000 of these castings would fit into the company's truck, which will be used to pick up the castings at the supplier's. The supplier can also conveniently manufacture in lots of 8,000, and his $1.00 price is based on shipments of at least 8,000. If the unadjusted plan indicated in Column 2 were followed, the com-

TABLE 7–3
Plan of purchase for a gray-iron casting

	Actual production requirement			Suggested purchases			
(1) Month	*(2)* Quantity	*(3)* Cost	*(4)* Inventory	*(5)* Quantity	*(6)* Cost	*(7)* Inventory	*(8)* Change in inventory
May.	6,720	$ 6,720	$ 6,720	8,000	$ 8,000	$ 8,000	$+ 1,280
June	7,392	7,392	14,112	16,000	16,000	24,000	+ 9,888
July.	3,360	3,360	14,112	None	—	20,640	+ 6,528
August.	7,056	7,056	13,776	8,000	8,000	21,248	+ 7,472
September	7,056	7,056	14,112	8,000	8,000	22,528	+ 8,416
October	7,392	7,392	14,448	16,000	16,000	31,472	+17,024
November	10,080	10,080	17,472	16,000	16,000	40,416	+22,944
December	10,080	10,080	20,160	12,000	12,000	45,024	+24,864
January	7,728	8,501*	18,581	—	—	34,944	+16,363
February	6,720	7,392	15,893	—	—	24,864	+ 8,971
March	5,376	5,914	13,306	—	—	17,136	+ 3,630
April	5,040	5,544	11,458	—	—	10,416	− 1,042
May.	—	—	5,544	—	—	5,040	− 504
June	—	—	—	—	—	—	—
Total.	84,000	$86,487		84,000	$84,000		

*10 percent Price increase expected.

pany truck would have to make several additional trips to the supplier's foundry during the year. In addition, the supplier might demand a price increase because he would be shipping in lots of fewer than 8,000 most of the time.

2. If the company purchases its full years' requirement of 84,000 castings before January, its purchase cost will be only $84,000 (as indicated in the total for Column 6). If it buys according to the plan in Column 1, costs for the year will be $86,487 because it will probably be necessary to purchase 24,864 castings at the higher price expected to go into effect on January 1. Thus the expected cash saving from the revised plan is $2,486 (24,864 castings × $.10/casting).

3. If the revised plan is followed, there is considerably less risk of delivery failure resulting from a strike. The materials manager might want to use Bayesian decision theory to estimate the expected value of the loss from a strike occurring sometime between January 1 and April 30, if the plan suggested in Column 1 is followed. Suppose, for example, he estimates the loss at $300,000. Even if the probability of a strike long enough to cripple the foundry's production schedules is only 5 percent, the expected loss would still be $15,000 (.05 × $300,000).

4. Upward revisions in production are easier with the purchase plan in Column 5. The company may discover later in the year that its sales estimate has been too conservative. If it has the bare minimum of castings on hand at the time it decides to boost its production schedule, it may have to wait several months before there are sufficient finished castings to permit an increase in the final assembly schedule. The supplier will not be able to respond immediately to the request for more production; chances are he will need at least a month's advance notice. In addition, there is roughly a two-month lead time with the company's own operations. Thus a total of three months may elapse before the decision to boost output can be reflected in increased shipments.

Suppose, for example, the company decides in July it would like to assemble an additional 2,000 air conditioners per month. In August (with good luck) the supplier may be able to ship 2,000 extra castings, and by October (with even more good luck) an extra 2,000 air conditioners will roll off the line.

In contrast, increased output would pose no problem for castings, at least, if the plan indicated in Column 5 is followed. The castings would already be on hand. In addition, if the company wanted to increase its assembly schedule at the end of the year, there is a 95 percent chance (assuming no strike) that the castings could be ordered any time in January or February.

Unfortunately, every plan also has its costs. If the company followed its original plan, it could fairly easily cut back on purchases of castings any time up until March (assuming the vendor needs 30 days' notice of a cutback). With the revised plan, the company is firmly committed to purchase 84,000 castings by some time in November—months before it would probably come to realize that its sales forecast had been too optimistic.

In most real-life companies, the castings not needed could be stored and used in the following year. But inventory cannot be stored for free. Even if the company's sales forecast is perfect, inventory carrying cost will be higher if the schedule in Column 5 is followed. Column 8 compares the inventory balance indicated by the plan in Column 1 with that in Column 5. For example, during the month of May, the first plan calls for an ending inventory of $6,720. This balance reflects planned receivals of 6,720 castings with no withdrawals from stock, since shipments are not scheduled to begin until July. In contrast, the plan in Column 5 calls for purchase of 8,000 castings in May with no withdrawals. The difference of $+$1,280 ($8,000 − $6,720) represents the extra inventory investment that is the major price paid for obtaining the advantages of the revised plan.

During the year, this revised plan increases purchased-materials inventory by an average of $10,486.[7] Interest on this additional investment at 6 percent per year would amount to about $630. Total cost of carrying this inventory might amount to $2,500 or more, for reasons to be discussed in Chapter 10. However, the cash savings from the revised purchase plan are so much greater that there is little doubt that this is the better plan. Taking into account only the cash saving of $24,864 from buying the entire year's supply at the $1 price, the company should earn a return of about 237 percent ($24,864 ÷ $10,486 × 100) on its extra average investment of $10,486 in inventory. This return would be reduced by any additional cash storage costs that might be incurred, but these would be insignificant compared to the saving.[8]

Cost reduction. Each commodity purchase plan should also allow for the buyer's cost-reduction efforts. In a footnote to this plan, for example, the buyer should indicate what, if anything, he proposes to do to avoid paying the 10-cent price increase on the casting next year. His efforts to reduce costs would then become part of next year's plan. He might search for new gray-iron casting suppliers or, conceivably, he might propose that a die casting or sheet-metal stamping be substituted for the casting.

Cost reduction should be considered not only when making plans for individual commodity groups but also on a consolidated basis, with recommendations as to how to achieve definite goals by the application of specific cost-reduction techniques (discussed in later chapters).

However, lower costs are not the only objective of materials manage-

---

[7] $\dfrac{\$1,280 + 9,888 + 6,528 + 7,472 + 8,416 + 17,024 + 22,944 + 24,864 + 16,363 + 8,971 + 3,630 - 1,042 - 504}{12 \text{ months}} = \$10,486$

[8] The principles behind these calculations are explained in Chapters 9 and 10.

ment. As we saw in Chapter 3, there are a number of primary and secondary objectives. These objectives are interrelated; success in achieving one may impair performancse in achieving one or more of the others. The art of materials management is successful balancing of objectives into a coordinated plan and then achieving the goals of the plan.

Conflict of objectives is illustrated in the plan of purchase for gray-iron castings in Table 7–3. In this case, the objective of high inventory turnover is deliberately made secondary to achievement of the objectives of low prices and good delivery performance. Stocks are built up in anticipation of higher prices and possible shortages. In making his purchase plan for each major commodity group, the materials manager is really balancing achievement of various objectives. When making the plan, he should consciously consider its effect on prices, inventory turnover, continuity of supply, relations with suppliers, quality, and low cost of acquisition and possession.

KEY-PARTS CONTROL

The plan of purchase indicates exactly the inventory the materials manager plans to carry of each commodity. If the materials manager made a plan of purchase for every individual item, he could readily anticipate exactly what his inventory position would be during the period of the plan. All he would have to do is add up each plan of purchase to get a total. In practice, this is never done. It is not practical to make detailed plans of purchase for each item, and materials managers usually make plans only for major items; less important materials are ordered and stocked in accordance with the principles discussed in Chapters 9 and 10.

The plan of purchase may also be too general to be really useful in forecasting product costs. For example, a plan of purchase might be made (as it was in Table 7–3) for gray-iron castings used in all of a company's products. This plan would be extremely useful for inventory planning and allocating purchases of castings among suppliers, but it would not necessarily be useful for forecasting product cost, since the castings might be used in dozens of different products.

An obvious solution to this problem would be for the materials manager to make overall plans of purchase for his major commodity groups and then break these plans down in detail into plans and forecasts for each product. In a typical materials department, however, this is an almost impossible job. It would be necessary to keep extremely accurate records and make rather elaborate calculations for literally thousands of different items. The cost would be high and errors frequent.

In practice, the "purchase plan" consists essentially of an overall estimate of requirements that is adjusted to take into account scrap, shipping quantities, and other factors. Normally these calculations are made by computer and do not take into account such "soft" factors as expected price changes or strikes.

80 percent buys 15 percent. Price performance is more readily planned by keeping special price records of a sample of key items in each commodity group. Usually, 80 to 90 percent of the money is spent on only 10 to 15 percent of the items. If careful records are kept of these "big money" items, overall changes can be accurately estimated with a minimum of paper work. This is the key-parts approach to cost control and forecasting.

Suppose a company finds that its key-parts sample (which may be 15 percent of all items) represents exactly 90 percent of total expenditures. If prices of the items in the sample increased exactly 1 percent, the value of *all* items increases 0.9 percent, even though there have been no changes at all in the prices of the nonsample items. In practice, of course, the nonsample items change in proportion to the sample items. A carefully selected sample not only includes expensive items but is also reasonably representative of the overall sample as to type of material, industry, method of fabrication, and so on.

The mechanics of preparing a key-parts index are not hard to understand. However, the job can be done easily only if the company already has the basic data on punched cards and can program its computer to do all the hack work. Otherwise the clerical effort is a major barrier in setting up such an index. It is necessary to compile a complete list of every item purchased and compute the value of the usage of each by multiplying unit price by usage. The high dollar-volume items are then culled from each commodity or product group so that the sample represents approximately 80 to 90 percent of the dollar volume.

Controlling product XYZ. Key-parts control is normally by product for production parts and materials because management needs product information for pricing and cost control purposes. Table 7–4 shows key-parts control for hypothetical product XYZ. It is a summary of groups of key parts for each commodity group. The sample's value on January 1 is $100. The materials manager classifies the changes affecting price and projects them for the coming year.

The total price reduction of $2.70 for "negotiation" for the year is his estimate of savings that can be made. The total is based on individual forecasts of economic and competitive conditions for major commodity groups and on estimates of the probable success buyers will have in applying the cost-reduction techniques discussed in later chapters.

The predicted $0.38 cost increase due to "product change" is based on the materials manager's estimate of the cost of planned design changes. The $3.10 change classified as "other" arises from a make-or-buy decision. Both of these changes affect product mix. Since they are not economic, they will not be used to measure the success of the materials department in achieving its cost-reduction objectives.

TABLE 7–4

Budgeted materials cost changes, product XYZ, 1974

Month	Beginning cost	Negotiation	Product change	Materials cost	Supplier change	Other	Total change
January.	$100.00	$(0.42)	$(0.22)	$0.14	$(0.05)		$(0.55)
February	99.45	(.28)	.60	.75	(.35)		.72
March	100.17	(.40)			(.10)		(.50)
April	99.67	(.40)			(.10)		(.50)
May.	99.17	(.40)			(.10)		(.50)
June	98.67	(.40)			(.10)		(.50)
July.	98.17	(.40)		1.05	(.10)		.55
August	98.72				(.10)		(.10)
September	98.62				(.10)	3.10*	3.00
October	101.62				(.10)		(.10)
November	101.52				(.10)		(.10)
December	101.42				(.10)		(.10)
Total at end of year	$101.32	($2.70)	$ 0.38	$1.94	($1.40)	$3.10	$ 1.32

*Addition of new parts to sample formerly made in the shop and purchased from outside suppliers, effective September 1, 1974.

An increase of $1.94 per unit is anticipated because of higher materials costs. This could include both increases in the cost of purchased raw materials and increases in prices of components as suppliers pass along higher raw-material costs. In calculating the effect of increases in materials costs, the materials manager would estimate the amount of the increase per unit of raw material (using techniques that have already been discussed) and multiply by the amount of raw material in the product. For example, suppose that a 2 cents per pound increase in the price of copper were anticipated in January. If 7 pounds of copper were used in the product—either in shop-made or purchased components—the unit product costs would rise by 14 cents,[9] as indicated in Table 7–4.

The final major price change column in the materials plan is one that allows for "supplier change." It is an estimate of savings that will be made by bringing in new suppliers who charge lower prices than existing suppliers. It is based on both an evaluation of competitive conditions and an estimate of how successful buyers will be in performing one of the basic parts of their job.

[9] In practice, this would rarely be literally correct. In many cases there is a lag of at least a month between the time a raw material increases in price and the time suppliers of parts fabricated from the material request a price adjustment. To allow for this, the materials manager would allow for two adjustments because of a change in materials costs: one for the material purchased directly, and a second, later adjustment for parts made of the material.

COMMODITY PRICE INDEXES

Key parts systems work well in companies that produce a limited number of products in large volume. They are used, for example, by several leading automobile manufacturers.

They will not work well in companies that produce many products on a job-order basis. In such cases, individual products are manufactured intermittently and it is seldom worthwhile to maintain key-parts control over every product. Management is interested primarily in the overall trend of costs; it needs information that will help it do a better job of estimating costs on new jobs that come in.

A commodity price index is best suited for this purpose. It is similar to key-parts control except for two basic differences: index numbers are used instead of actual dollar costs, and cost data are classified entirely by commodity instead of by product.

To see how such an index might be set up, consider the example of a hypothetical manufacturer of highly specialized, custom-made business machines that require the commodities listed in Table 7–1 above. Such a company might buy as many as 20,000 different items and make 100 different products, even though it employs no more than 1,000 persons. Almost every customer would require a product that was engineered specifically for his needs.

Selecting the sample. The mechanics of compiling the index are much like those used in developing key-parts control. Average monthly expenditures for each commodity are calculated from purchase records, and the more expensive items are selected for the sample. However, in developing the index, it is necessary to take particular pains to select a sample that is a truly representative cross section of the commodities purchased. Because the company makes so many different products in relatively small quantities, it is not true that 10 to 15 percent of the most expensive items account for 80 to 90 percent of the dollar volume of purchases. It may be necessary to work with a sample that comprises only 30 to 40 percent of total dollar volume.

The procedure used in calculating the base cost of the index sample is different from that used in key parts. Usage is not taken into account. Base cost is calculated simply by adding the unit prices of each item in the sample. This makes it vital to take relative usages into account when choosing the items represented in the sample.

For example, suppose the business-machine manufacturer compiles an index of castings costs. If he uses an average of two small castings as miscellaneous components for every larger casting used for the machine base, then the sample should be divided 67 to 33 between the large and small castings.

Making the index. After the sample is selected, price changes are tabulated. The technique is similar to that used in Table 7–4. Imagine, in fact, that Product XYZ in Table 7–4 is an index of castings costs for the hypothetical business-machine manufacturer. The beginning cost in January is $100. The unit price changes during January on the castings in the sample reduce total cost of the sample by $.55—as in Table 7–4—to $99.45. But since this is an index, the index number of 99.45 is used instead of the dollar amount. This is because the total value of the sample has no significance; unlike a product index, it is merely the sum of current prices for a selected group of materials. It is easier to judge the effect of price changes with index numbers that automatically indicate the number of percentage points in change from the base period. Actual dollar figures rarely come to the convenient $100 figure of the example.

With a commodity index, it is simple to estimate the effect of price changes on overall costs. For example, if a company were spending an average of $10,000 a month for castings, a drop in the castings price index from 100.00 to 99.45 would indicate a saving of $55 per month.

Commodity indexes can be used for both production and nonproduction items. However, when they are used to measure changes in cost of a nonproduction group such as maintenance, repair, and operating supplies, the sample must be constructed with extra care, because a wide variety of items with erratic usage patterns falls into this category.

Composite indexes. Commodity indexes also can be used to build product indexes of composite products. If a company makes a wide variety of products on a job-order basis, it cannot afford to keep cost indexes for each product. It can, however, construct an index of a composite product; the company's various products are sufficiently similar so that cost changes of each follow similar patterns.

A composite index is made up of indexes for major commodities; it is weighted by the relative importance of each commodity in the typical end product. Table 7–5 shows the construction of such an index for a hypothetical machine-tool manufacturer. Studies might show that

TABLE 7–5
Composite index of materials costs—machine tools

Component group	Percent weight	January		February		March	
		Index	Exten-sion	Index	Exten-sion	Index	Exten-sion
Electrical.	35	100.00	35.00	102.00	35.70	101.00	35.35
Castings	20	100.00	20.00	90.00	18.00	90.00	18.00
Bearings	5	100.00	5.00	100.00	5.00	99.00	4.95
Hydraulic	15	100.00	15.00	96.00	14.40	97.00	14.55
Miscellaneous	25	100.00	25.00	100.00	25.00	94.00	23.50
Composite index			100.00		98.10		96.35

the average purchased-material cost for each machine tool is divided as indicated in the second column of the table: 35 percent for electrical, 20 percent for castings, and so forth. The monthly price index for each commodity group is then multiplied by its percentage weight (e.g., multiplying the electrical component index of 100.00 by its 35 percent weight gives an extension of 35.00), and the products are added to get the composite index.

Table 7–5 shows that material for a composite machine tool in January cost its precise base price of 100.00. In February and March, prices of components declined until the index reached 96.35, indicating an average 3.65 percent reduction in materials cost of machine tools.

USES OF INDEXES

Indexes and key-parts cost controls are expensive. They can take hundreds or even thousands of man-hours of work to set up, and even a relatively simple system can take 500 man-hours of work a year to maintain. Cost is undoubtedly one of the main reasons that indexes are not used more widely in materials management. Companies that do use them rarely abandon them; they are convinced that they are worth their cost. Indexes and key-parts controls permit more accurate forecasting of costs, stimulate superior materials performance, and help make the materials management job easier.

Provide accurate forecasts. An index or summary of key-parts cost is based on prices currently being paid for materials. But because of supplier and manufacturing lead times and inventories, there is always a considerable lag between the average order date for material and the date when the material is actually incorporated into an end product. In some industries, today's purchases appear in products six months hence; in few industries is this lead time less than two months. Indexes or key-parts systems permit material costs to be forecast with 99.99 percent accuracy during the lead time. When they are combined with the materials manager's price projections, it is possible to predict materials costs with considerable accuracy a year or more in advance.

The company controller can use projections of key-parts prices to plan his cash flow, to develop a projected profit-and-loss statement based on the sales estimate, and to develop data for pricing. Composite price indexes cannot be used so directly, but they are useful in forecasting cost trends. For example, if a composite index drops 3.65 percent (as in Table 7–5) and materials cost constitutes 50 percent of the sales dollar, management knows it can reduce average prices by 1.825 percent (i.e., 50 percent of 3.65 percent) in bidding for new business without narrowing its profit margin. It also can plan on spending 3.65 percent less for materials for the same physical output and can budget its cash accordingly.

Stimulate performance. Index and key-parts information provides a convenient yardstick for performance measurement. Comparison of actual key-parts prices with projected prices or with general price indexes indicates how well materials personnel have done their work and also stimulates improvement.

Simplify management.   Materials management involves thousands or even millions of individual transactions each year. Materials managers can do their job effectively only if they avoid the distraction of numerous unimportant details and concentrate on significant problems. Price indexes help them function more effetively because they summarize the exact effect of thousands of materials transactions on cost and profits. They also make it easy to evaluate accurately the effect of future changes in materials prices on operating costs.

For example, suppose management becomes concerned about a possible price rise for a key raw material. With key parts or index data, it is an easy matter to calculate what product costs will be at various price levels for the raw material. It also is possible to calculate precisely when it pays to change to a substitute material or to initiate a program to redesign the product so that it no longer requires the material.

Indexes can also simplify inventory management. It is often practical to make a plan of purchase for each index item. When the materials manager adds up the projections in these plans, he knows exactly what 80 to 90 percent of his inventory investment will be months in advance. If he must change his plans because of faulty sales or price forecasts, he knows almost exactly how rapidly he can change with a minimum of detail work. For example, suppose a materials manager's current inventory of index items is equal to two months' production and he is already committed to a buildup to three months' stock. Because of a shortage of cash, management decides to cut back to one month's stock. The materials manager can do the job quickly and efficiently by concentrating his attention on the index items that comprise the biggest part of his costs.

Cases

CASE 7-1. DONALDSON CHEMICALS, INC.

Poor forecasting eliminates profits

Donaldson Chemicals, Inc. is a middleman in chemical manufacturing. It buys basic chemical raw materials and converts them into more complex chemicals, which it sells to manufacturers of chemical end products. For example, it buys a basic material like naphthalene and converts it into a product such as pthalic anhydride, which it sells to other companies for making paints and for other uses.

Donaldson has grown rapidly in its specialized business. In 1960, its sales were $99 million—up 67.4 percent since 1956. The story on profits has not been quite so impressive. In 1960, Donaldson's management forecast a $5 million profit, but actual profits were only $3 million—less than they were in 1956. The drop in profits could be traced to a single cause: the high cost of naphthalene.

Naphthalene is one of Donaldson's single most important raw materials. Steel companies are the biggest source of supply. They generate naphthalene as a by-product when they convert coal into coke in their coke ovens. Naturally, the steel companies try to get the best possible price for their naphthalene, but they have little or no direct control over the amount of naphthalene they produce. If naphthalene prices are high, the steel mills will not make more coke just to get naphthalene. Their sales and profits come primarily from steel. When demand for steel is strong, the mills produce more coke and, consequently, more naphthalene. When demand for steel is weak, the steel mills cannot afford to stockpile coke, so their naphthalene production falls off, even though naphthalene prices may be relatively high.

In 1960, demand for steel was weak. In January, the steel industry was operating at about 90 percent of capacity. By June it was operating at less than 60 percent of capacity, and operations continued below 60 percent capacity until April, 1961. Although the demand for steel had fallen, the demand for chemicals made from naphthalene was stronger than ever. As a result, the price of naphthalene soared from about 6 cents per pound late in 1959 to 17 cents by December 1960.

Donaldson uses about 100 million pounds of naphthalene per year. An increase of 10 cents per pound in naphthalene prices can thus raise costs by $10 million per year. To some extent, Donaldson can pass on higher materials costs to its customers, but it must always meet competitors' prices. If competitors do a better job of buying naphthalene, the effect on Donaldson's profits can be almost disastrous.

Donaldson experienced just such a disaster in the first quarter of 1961. In late 1960, Donaldson's management was desperate for naphthalene to keep its plant operating. It had held- off buying naphthalene in more than hand-to-mouth quantities for months. It had hoped that steel production would rise (and naphthalene prices fall), so it had gradually used up its inventories. Steel operations were at less than 50 percent of capacity in December 1960, and naphthalene cost 17 cents per pound. Unfortunately, Donaldson had to have naphthalene or go out of business. So it purchased 25 million pounds—enough for its first quarter's needs—at 17 cents.

Because it was using high-priced naphthalene, Donaldson's operating costs were abnormally high throughout the first quarter of 1961. Unfortunately, selling prices could not be raised without losing business to competitors. As a result, Donaldson had one of the worst quarters in its history. It lost $200,000 on sales of $24 million.

Ironically, while Donaldson was eating up its profits with its 17-cent naphthalene, the market price of naphthalene was declining. By May, when Donaldson used the last of the 17-cent material, the price had dropped to 7 cents. And by July, it reached 6 cents, as the steel industry's operating rate reached more normal levels.

The 1960–61 gyrations in the price of naphthalene are reasonably normal. The steel industry is highly cyclical, and this automatically makes for wide fluctuations in naphthalene production and prices. To some extent, of course, naphthalene output does respond to demand. Usually demand for naphthalene is greater when the business cycle is at its peak and steel mills are running full tilt. And it is weakest when the cycle is nearing bottom and steel production is in a slump. However, naphthalene demand does not fluctuate as much as steel demand. As a result, it is relatively cheap and plentiful at the peak of the business cycle and scarce and expensive at the bottom of the cycle.

Naphthalene need not be a by-product of the steel industry, of course. It can be made from almost any hydrocarbon. If the price of naphthalene is sufficiently attractive, oil companies, for example, are perfectly willing to make it from crude oil. In August 1961, partly as a result of its unhappy experience in the previous year, Donaldson signed a contract for naphthalene with the Wabash Oil and Refining Company. The contract calls for delivery of 20 million pounds of naphthalene per year at a price of 11 cents per pound. The price is subject to escalation should crude oil prices rise or decline, but escalation is limited to 15 percent in either direction for the five-year term of the contract. One of Donaldson's competitors has signed a similar contract with another oil company. Another competitor continues to buy all of its naphthalene in the open market.

Question

Based on today's market conditions, what plan of purchase would you propose for Donaldson Chemical, Inc.?

CASE 7–2. OWEN ELECTRIC COMPANY (A)

Developing a plan of purchase for copper

Owen Electric Company is a small manufacturer of fractional horsepower electric motors. In the fall of 1958, despite depressed business conditions, it is about to complete a record business year with sales of $5 million. The company's marketing department predicts that business in 1959 will be even better, with sales reaching $6 million.

The general business outlook is equally bullish. The economy is showing strong signs of recovery from the recession that prevailed early in the year. The Federal Reserve Board's index of industrial production has advanced to 138 (1947–49 = 100) from its April low of 126. Copper prices have advanced 5 cents per pound in the same period, and other sensitive commodities have moved up by similar amounts. Inventory liquidation has virtually ceased; the most recent figures show inventories of durable goods manufacturers to have been almost unchanged for three months at about $28 billion.

Richard Owen, Jr., Owen Electric's purchasing manager, is particularly concerned about the outlook for copper, the company's single most important purchase. The company's sales increased faster during the year than Owen had anticipated, and it was necessary to draw on inventories. Currently, the company is operating on almost a hand-to-mouth basis.

The production forecast indicates that 10,000 pounds per month of copper magnet wire will be required through June 30. During the summer months, requirements will drop to 7,000 pounds per month, and, if sales are as high as current plans indicate, they will rise again to 13,000 pounds per month during October, November, and December.

Since inventories currently are barely adequate to maintain production, Owen already has allowed for some buildup early in the year and has ordered 22,000 pounds of copper for delivery during January and February. Owen Electric uses several different types of copper magnet wire. At present, their weighted average cost is 45 cents per pound. Richard Owen estimates that this will probably increase by 1.2 cents for every 1-cent increase in the price of ingot copper, as copper fabricators attempt to pass on the cost of wage increases. On the other hand, he believes that fabricators will be forced to pass on to their customers the full benefit of any drop in ingot prices.

Copper producers freely predict higher prices. Deliveries of refined copper in the United States totaled 120,793 tons in October 1958—a sharp increase over the 86,982 tons in August and the 101,064 tons in September. This is the best October that copper refiners have had since 1955, when the demand for ingot was so heavy that prices were pushed to more than 40 cents per pound. Copper consumption frequently reaches a seasonal peak in spring because of heavy usage in the auto industry and other areas. Owen anticipates no difficulty in buying copper wire in any reasonable quantity with two months' lead time at the price in effect at time of delivery.

There is no storage problem for copper, but the company's cash position is not ideal. The controller advises Owen that no funds are available for inventory accumulation beyond present commitments. However, the controller anticipates no difficulty in getting additional short-term loans at about 6½ percent interest should the company's board of directors approve an inventory buildup.

Questions

1. Develop a plan of purchases for Owen Electric's requirements of copper wire for the year 1959. Use the data provided; state any additional assumptions

that must be made. Prepare a defense of your plan for the company's board of directors. Indicate the cost of your plan to the company, based on:

a) Your own assumptions of price and availability of copper wire.

b) No change in the price or availability of copper.

c) Higher copper prices: a 6-cent advance during the year, spaced as a 1-cent increase every two months starting in January.

d) Lower copper prices: a 2-cent increase in price in January followed by three 2-cent decreases in April, July, and October.

2. Evaluate your plan of purchase with a Bayesian analysis, using the following probabilities:

a) No change in price—20 percent.

b) Higher prices with, most likely, a 6¢ advance during the year, spaced as a 1¢ increase every two months starting in January—30 percent.

c) Lower prices, with a 2¢ increase in January followed by three 2¢ decreases in April, July, or October—50 percent.

CASE 7–3. OWEN ELECTRIC COMPANY (B)

Developing a plan of purchase for steel

"As if I didn't have enough trouble with copper," Richard Owen, Jr., Owen Electric's purchasing manager, complained as he read *The Wall Street Journal,* "I've also got to worry about the steel situation. David McDonald, president of the steel workers' union, has had things his own way just about every time steel negotiations come up. There was a strike in 1952, then another one in 1956, and I'll just bet there will be a strike in 1959."

Steel is Owen Electric's second most important commodity after copper and, in late 1958, the company's steel inventory situation is far from favorable. In fact, sales have bounced back so fast from the 1957–58 recession that the company is operating almost on a hand-to-mouth basis with steel as well as with copper. Looking ahead, the company anticipates that it will require 50 tons per month of steel through June 30; 35 tons per month until September 30; and 65 tons per month for the balance of the year 1959. Owen has already ordered 170 tons of steel for first-quarter rolling since, even if the company does not decide to build inventory in anticipation of a strike, he would like to get a little bit of cushion in its inventory. If all goes according to plan, first-quarter purchases will exceed usage by 20 tons, giving the company a little safety stock—which it does not have in the fall of 1958. Adequate steel inventories are particularly important because the company estimates that it stands to lose irrevocably about $2,000 for every day that operations are shut down for lack of material.

Owen, like most other purchasing agents he knows, believes that there will almost certainly be a strike when the steel contract expires July 1, 1959. Steel company salesmen have been urging their customers to buy ahead in anticipation of a strike, and lead times for steel have already been lengthened. Owen doubts if he can even get on any of his steel suppliers' first-quarter 1959 rolling schedule for any tonnage over and above what he already has on order. However, he can probably increase his purchases by as much as 100 percent during the second quarter and get delivery before the union contract expires on July 1.

The company does not have space available to store any extra steel inventories over and above the 20-ton safety stock it hopes to accumulate during the first quarter. However, adequate storage space could be rented for an average cost of $1.50 per ton per month, plus $2.00 per ton to move the steel from the warehouse to the Owen Electric plant. In addition, the company anticipates other modest losses as a result of damage from extra handling, rust, and so forth, which might amount to 1 percent of the value of the steel stored. Purchases could be financed with a 6½ percent bank loan.

The last steel industry strike, in 1956, lasted about three weeks. Unlike the Truman administration, which intervened in the 1952 steel strike, the Eisenhower administration in power in 1956 and still in power in 1959 believed in minimum interference in labor-management disputes. The steel strike in 1956 lasted about three weeks and resulted in what both steel producers and users regarded as an inflationary wage settlement. This wage settlement helped trigger an 8 percent increase in the BLS index for composite steel prices during the year 1956. Steel companies not only passed on their higher wage costs but also took advantage of an opportunity to pass on miscellaneous increases in various other costs and to attempt to restore what had been shrinking profit margins.

In late 1958, the steel companies are not only faced with higher wage costs but are also feeling the effects of much higher scrap prices. The Pittsburgh price of No. 1 heavy melting steel scrap has advanced about $10 per ton from its low of $35 earlier in the year. Steel companies are using a charge of as much as 50 percent scrap steel in their open-hearth furnaces. [10] During periods of peak demand, as much as half of this scrap must be purchased on the open market. The balance is generated within the mill as part of the steel-making process.

Owen Electric's weighted average price for various types and grades of steel used in 1958 is $148 per ton. Richard Owen estimates that even if there is no strike in 1959, there is a 50 percent probability that steel prices will increase by about 5 percent and a 40 percent probability that the increase will be limited to about 3 percent. He guesses that there is only a 10 percent probability of no price increase at all—even with no strike.

However, if there were a strike, Owen believes there is zero probability of no price increase and a 30 percent probability of an increase

---

[10] Present-day technology requires much less scrap.

of as much as 7 percent. He guesses that the probability of a 5 percent increase would be about 40 percent and that there is a 30 percent probability of a 3 percent increase if there were a strike.

Owen believes that the odds strongly favor a strike, although, of course, he is not certain how long it would last. He sees four broad possibilities, however: a probability of 20 percent for no strike, a probability of about 40 percent for a three-week strike, a probability of 30 percent for a strike lasting three to six weeks, and only a 10 percent probability of one that would last six to eight weeks. Owen does not believe that a strike could possibly last more than eight weeks before either a settlement is reached voluntarily or President Eisenhower invokes the Taft-Hartley Act. Under the Taft-Hartley law, the President can order the strikers back to work for a period of 90 days if he feels that the strike is adversely affecting the economy. Owen guesses that if President Eisenhower invokes the act, there would be no second strike, and labor and management would almost certainly reach an agreement.

Questions

1. Recommend a plan of purchase and evaluate it with a Bayesian probability analysis.

2. With the benefit of hindsight, we now know that steel production was crippled for more than 100 days in the summer of 1959 until President Eisenhower finally invoked the Taft-Hartley Act, forcing the steel company employees to go back to work. However, the composite index of steel prices remained at $.0698 per pound from November 1958 through 1960. Partly because of indirect government pressure but mostly because of falling demand and growing inroads from cheaper foreign steel, American steel producers were not able to raise their prices above the 1959 level for more than five years thereafter.

  a) How would your plan of purchase have worked during the 1959 strike?

  b) Could Owen have protected himself against a steel stockout, given the assumptions on which he based his decision?

8

Production and inventory control basics

Production control is the process of monitoring the performance of a group of workers or equipment and comparing the results of their efforts with a predetermined plan. The production controller's function is to see that the objectives of the plan are being met and that human and physical resources are being used as efficiently as possible.

SCOPE OF PRODUCTION CONTROL

If a factory is supposed to make 10 widgets on a particular day, it is the production controller's job not only to compare actual results with the objective but to measure the resources used in the process. If the 10 widgets were not made, he would describe the problems that caused the failure and, ideally, anticipate causes of future failures.

Nonmanufacturing applications

The production control function is not limited to manufacturing. It is universal to all economic activity, although it cannot always be easily identified. The traffic department of an airline or railroad is engaged in production control[1] when it decides to have equipment on hand in a particular city. The registrar of a university is engaged in production control when he determines that a particular classroom will be used for a particular course in materials management at a particular hour. The manager of a retail store is engaged in production control when

---

[1] And *not* in traffic, as we define it in this book (see Chapter 15).

he determines that eight salesclerks will be needed on Saturdays but only six on weekdays.

Production control is concerned with all of the resources needed to get a job done. Thus its scope extends beyond materials management as narrowly defined in Chapter 1. The production control manager is concerned with having not only the materials on hand to do the job but also the labor and equipment. The latter resources are often more important than the material and, of course, they are the direct responsibility of the operations manager responsible for getting the job done.

Materials management function

How, then, can one justify production control as a part of materials management rather than the operating management activity itself? There are basically four reasons.

1. *Of the three resources used in production, material is the only one that is external to the organization.* Over the short term, the labor and equipment are already there. Production control is, in large part, a matter of making sure that enough material is on hand so that workers and machines can be productively employed and customers will be satisfied.

2. *The skills required for materials management can readily be applied to production control problems involving labor and equipment.*

3. *Production control problems involving material, labor, and equipment are inevitably interrelated.* The basic production control problem is to bring all three resources together at the right time in the proper quantities. This is a single interrelated function; responsibility for it must be centralized in one group. To divide it between materials management and operations management is to invite chaos.

4. *The materials management organization is often considered part of operations management.* The author does not regard this as good practice in most cases, but it does have the advantage of resolving the problem of whether production control is part of materials management or operations management. When operations management embraces materials management, production control easily can be part of both, with no real conflict. In contrast, when production control is part of a materials management department that is independent of manufacturing or operations management organization, its decisions involving the scheduling of labor and equipment must nevertheless be consistent with manufacturing's objectives, just as the physical distribution part of materials management serves marketing's objectives. Otherwise there will be conflict.

The production control process is both easy and difficult to visualize. In small organizations it is carried on so inconspicuously that it does not seem to exist. In large organizations its existence is all too apparent, and the process becomes so complex that it is difficult to comprehend.

In the small organization, for example, production control consists primarily of a worker asking the boss which job he should start on next and, from time to time, the boss checking up and asking the worker how he is coming along. This is more or less what happens in a very large organization, but here there may be tens of thousands of workers and thousands of bosses assisted by thousands of other production controllers. In large organizations oral instructions are no longer adequate; in fact, there are so many activities going on simultaneously that it is difficult for any single person to grasp what is happening. The total report of whether or not everything is going according to plan can be found among tens or hundreds of millions of "bits" of information stored in computer memory, magnetic tape, punched card, or written records. Thus, in a large organization, production control is a maze of records and numbers that can be extremely confusing even to an outsider who claims expertise in the field.[2]

A MODEL PRODUCTION SYSTEM

The best way to grasp how production control works is to create a situation that is so easy to comprehend that no formal system is needed. Imagine that you are a small manufacturer with this equipment: two automatic lathes, one milling machine, and one drill press. Your finished products are custom made to customers' specifications. In some cases they require assembly operations incorporating purchased parts and parts machined on your screw machines.

Application of manpower and equipment plans

Following the principles outlined in Chapters 6 and 7, you do the best job you can of planning and forecasting. Your equipment plan consists of making do with what you have. Your manpower plan calls for 40 hours work per week by each of your four employees. Two of your employees are machinists who are able to operate with equal proficiency any of your machine tools. The other two are assemblers. In a pinch, the machinists could help the assemblers, but the assemblers have no training as machinists. The best an assembler could do would be to operate the drill press after one of the machinists set it up for him.

---

[2] Despite 25 years' experience in the field, I still find initial review of any large company's production control system to be an exercise in confusion and frustration. Even though the principles behind the system are completely clear, it takes many hours of intense study to determine whether the system really works, or even whether the numbers it generates have any meaning.

Calculate backlog. A simple production system can be based on calculation of backlogs of manpower and equipment (see Table 8–1).

TABLE 8–1
Calculation of total and active backlogs

Department	Weekly capacity (hours)	Orders on hand		Active backlog	
		Hours	Weeks	Hours	Weeks
Facilities and material					
Automatic lathes	80	800	10.0	32	0.40
Milling machine	40	220	5.5	8	0.20
Drill press	40	100	2.5	2	0.05
Assembly	80	1200	15.0	200	2.5
Manpower					
Machinists	80	720	9.0	26	0.33
Assemblers	80	1200	15.0	200	2.5

As orders flow in from customers, you estimate the time they will require in each department and then add these hours to the backlog. When an order is completed in a particular department, you deduct from your backlog. In your business, you keep separate backlogs concerned with the utilization of equipment the utilization of manpower. Your goal is always to have enough of a backlog to keep your employees busy and also to utilize your equipment economically—especially your two automatic lathes, which are much costlier than your milling machine and drill lathe.

Adding an order to a backlog is a clerical operation. Table 8–1 indicates that you have in your files orders from customers calling for a total of 800 hours of lathe time, 220 hours of milling machine time, and so on. This does not mean that you are presently in a position to start all this work. Material must be on hand before work can begin. Therefore you must also keep track of an "active" backlog for each department.

Active backlog. In the lathe department, for example, you are presently ready to start jobs calling for 32 hours of machine time. Since your capacity in this department is 80 hours per week (two machines each working 40 hours), this 32-hour active backlog represents 32 ÷ 80, or 0.40 weeks (two days) of work for the automatic lathes. If you are the boss, this means that your employees can probably work on their own for the next two days without having to come to you for further instructions.

Most of your orders are started on one of the automatic lathes. The active backlog on subsequent operations depends at least partly on performance of equipment used in performing preceding operations. Thus, the active backlog for milling and drilling depends primarily on whether or not the parts currently being produced in the lathe department require subsequent milling and drilling. At present, there is only a 0.20 week (one-day) backlog for the milling machine and a 0.05 week (two-hour) backlog for the drill press. If one of the jobs presently on the screw machines does not require milling or drilling, it is likely that not only the drill press but also the milling machine will soon run out of work. While these machines have theoretical backlogs of 100 hours and 220 hours, respectively, the only orders that are at a stage where milling or drilling can actually be done amount to only one day's work for the milling machine and two hours' work for the drill press.

Goals. Your production plan assumes that your milling machine and drill press will not be fully utilized. You plan to employ just two machinists. If you anticipated continuous operation of the drill press and the milling machine, you would need three machinists. Under your present plan, you normally expect to employ one machinist virtually full time to operate the two automatic lathes. The second machinist would operate either the milling machine or the drill press. However, if there is a substantial active backlog for both milling and drilling, you may temporarily shut down the automatic lathes and assign one machinist to the drill press and the other to the milling machine.

Your major goal is to prevent active backlogs from temporarily shrinking to the point where one of your employees temporarily runs out of work and, in effect, gets paid for doing nothing. Your calculation of total and active manpower backlogs shows you how much work you presently have for your employees. For example, your two machinists have a weekly "capacity" without overtime of 80 hours per week. Since one machinist operates two automatic lathes, an 80-hour backlog of lathe time is equivalent to a 40-hour backlog of the lathe operator's time. Thus the total 800-hour backlog of time on the two lathes is equivalent to a 400-hour backlog for the machinists.

The drill press and milling machine each require one operator, so their 100-hour and 220-hour order backlogs represent an identical backlog of machinists' time. This, therefore, amounts to 220 hours + 100 hours = 320 hours. Adding the 320 hours to the 400 man-hour backlog on the lathes gives a total machinists' backlog of 720 hours. This is equal to exactly nine weeks when the two machinists each work a 40-hour week. However, the present active backlog for the machinists amounts to only 26 hours or .33 weeks—equal to 2 hours on the drill press, 8 hours on the milling machine, and one half of the 32-hour active backlog on the two automatic lathes.

Preventing idle time. You would be quite concerned about an active backlog of only .33 weeks (or less than two days) for your machinists if the machinists were used only to operate production machines. You could temporarily prevent one of your machinists from running out of drilling or milling by quickly scheduling on the automatic lathes a job that requires a great deal of subsequent work on the drill press and milling machine. But your overall order position clearly implies that you have an imbalance between demand for automatic lathe work and for the subsequent machining operations. The lathe backlog represents 10 weeks' work for a machinist, while the combined milling machine and drill press backlog represents just eight (5.5 + 2.5) weeks' work. Assuming no change in your order mix, the day will come when your drill press and milling machine sit idle while the automatic lathes continue to operate.

Your solution to this problem is simply to transfer a machinist to assembly work. Fortunately, your active backlog in the assembly area is now two and one half weeks. You will probably transfer a machinist to assembly in the next day or so. This will cause the active backlog in assembly to shrink more rapidly. With three workers in the assembly area, your weekly capacity temporarily becomes 120 hours instead of 80 hours. You would immediately check to make certain that additional material was delivered to the assembly area so that its active backlog would continue to be adequate. This material would probably consist of in-process inventory coming from one of the three machining departments, as well as purchased parts you are not equipped to make.

Releases to purchasing and manufacturing

Proper timing of both purchases and manufacturing operations is vital to successful production control. As noted above, the production control process begins when an order from a customer is analyzed and requirements for both purchases and manufacturing operations are estimated. In the case of your small business, this boils down to estimates of machining and assembly times as well as calculations of specific purchase requirements. When an order is received, the estimated hours needed to fill it are added on to the backlogs of the various departments shown in Table 8–1.

Starting date. At this stage, no specific starting date has necessarily been determined for the order—even though the customer probably indicated when he wanted delivery and your salesman made a specific delivery promise. For example, suppose it is June 1 and your salesman accepted an order calling for 100 hours of automatic lathe work and 20 subsequent hours on the drill press, to be delivered by August 15. Backlog on the automatic lathe would automatically increase to 900 hours or 11½ weeks, after the 100 hours of new demand was added to the existing 800-hour backlog shown in Table 8–1. Similarly, the backlog on the drill press would increase to 120 hours, or three weeks.

At this time you would probably want to estimate when you will "release" this job for production. Under ordinary circumstances, your very latest release date would allow enough time for the order to be completed before August 15. Since you would probably run this order for 100 consecutive hours on just one lathe, this operation alone would take two and one half weeks. The 20-hour drilling operation will require another half week. The total cycle would therefore be at least three weeks if there were no delays. Thus you must release the job no later than July 25 if you are to meet the customer's requested delivery date.

Ordering material. Raw material for this order must also be on hand before July 25. You would undoubtedly get the raw material delivered at least a few weeks before the July 25 deadline. This would give you some safety margin should your supplier be late in delivering and would also permit you to start production well ahead of the required date if you found it convenient to do so. In this particular case, you would probably order the raw material on June 1 and get delivery on it in the next few weeks, if you did not already have it in stock. However, if the order were not to be released for many months, you would most likely hold up ordering raw material until a couple of months before you are ready to start production. There would be no point in committing yourself to material too long before you actually need it, and your customer would not allow you to buy too far ahead if he were held responsible for the material.

Your requisition to purchase material would be sent immediately to the purchasing department, which would then follow the procedures outlined in Chapters 12–14. This order and dozens of others would then figuratively—and perhaps literally—sit in a file cabinet pending further action. You might, in fact, have two separate files of orders—one covering orders for which materials are on hand and the other for orders where material is not on hand. In the latter file would be included some orders where material should have been delivered but has not been, for various reasons. From this you might well make up a "shortage" list indicating what materials were needed, checking at regular intervals with buyers in the purchasing department to see how suppliers were progressing in filling orders for materials not yet delivered.

Dispatching

When the raw material is on hand for an order, you can "release" that order for production and "dispatch" it from department to department until it is completed. The minute an order is "dispatched" it becomes part of the active backlog of some department in manufacturing, until the order is finally completed. The process in your company is such that work on orders normally starts in the automatic lathe department. Table 8–1 above shows an active backlog in this department of just 0.40 weeks (two days), even though total backlog is 10.0 weeks.

Minimize inventory. This does not mean that there is sufficient purchased material on hand for just two days of production. Instead, it almost certainly reflects a deliberate policy of rationing the flow of new work to the shop. The production controller tries to release just enough new jobs to keep all departments operating according to plan. Nothing can be gained by releasing any more than this minimum, and in fact, manufacturing costs will probably be increased. In general, the greater the active backlog, the greater the investment in inventory. Also, efficiency usually declines when there is a large active backlog. This is partly psychological[3] and partly physical, since extra handling operations are often required when a shop is jammed with excess in-process inventory.

First come, first served.   Orders may be dispatched on a first-in, first-out basis. In this case, the order's initial release date can be estimated from the order backlog. For example, Table 8–1 shows a 10-week order backlog on the automatic lathes. If the first-in, first-out rule is followed in dispatching, the next order added to this backlog would not be released for 10 weeks. Thus, if Table 8–1 reflects your backlog as of June, an order received on June 2 would not be started through the automatic lathe department until about August 15. While the order received on June 2 might be started later than all orders received on earlier dates, it would not necessarily be the last one finished. Each work station would have its own first-come, first-served queue. An early order requiring many operations might therefore take much longer to complete than a late order that passed through just one or two work stations.

The first-in, first-out rule of dispatching is easy to comprehend. It also prevents orders that would otherwise warrant a low priority from sitting around for weeks or months, with possible deterioration of material. Otherwise the first-in, first-out system has no advantages and, in practice, is almost always superseded by other dispatching rules designed either to keep customers satisfied or simply to maximize the producer's profits.

Customer-oriented priorities.   Pleasing customers is a legitimate materials management objective that can be reflected in dispatching procedures. A company may decide that it is "fair" to its customers if it releases orders in a sequence determined by the dates on which customers desire delivery. If all orders from all customers require essentially the same operations, customer-oriented priorities are easy to set: an order calling for delivery on August 15 is released before one calling for delivery on the 16th, and so on.

Under this dispatch rule, all orders will be ready for delivery ahead of schedule as long as the company's volume of orders is less than its capacity. On the other hand, if the company is trying to deliver more than it is capable of producing during any period, its performance will get progressively worse. The first order completed during the period may be on time, the second may be a day or two late, the third will be almost a week late, and so on.

---

[3] This is explained in detail in the discussion of short-interval scheduling later in this chapter.

Calculation of customer-oriented priorities requires more than a simple sorting of orders by customer's desired delivery date if different orders require different manufacturing processes. In this more typical case, an order requiring a lengthy process must be started before an order calling for just one or two operations. For example, an order requiring eight weeks of processing would get a tentative starting date of February 1 if the customer wanted delivery during the last week of March. On the other hand, an order with a delivery date of February 28 might get a tentative starting date of February 8 if three weeks' process time were estimated. Thus the latter order would be started after the former, even though it would be delivered sooner. It should be noted, however, that neither order would necessarily be started on these dates. If the shop had more business than it could handle, all orders would start late. If business were slack, the orders would be ahead of schedule.

Producer-oriented priorities. All other factors being equal, most manufacturers try to please their customers. Unfortunately for the customers, all factors frequently are not equal—especially during periods of high demand. Other dispatching rules often take priority over those that are exclusively concerned with pleasing the customer. These rules, which can become quite complex, are concerned with minimizing costs and maximizing profits.

In the situation outlined in Table 8–1, your primary concern would probably be maintenance of a work load that will keep all four of your employees busy. Priority in dispatching might be given to jobs that require time on the milling machine and the drill press, so there will be work for both machinists. If jobs requiring milling and drilling simply dry up, you will probably try to give priority to jobs with lots of assembly work. With the milling machine and the drill press shut down, you need just one machinist on the automatic lathes. The second machinist would be transferred to the assembly department, increasing your manpower in that department by 50 percent. Your present active backlog of two and one half weeks' work for two assemblers would immediately become a 1.7-week active backlog with three assemblers. You would almost certainly run out of work for the assemblers if you did not immediately begin to release jobs for production that require a substantial amount of assembly time.

Chances are you would alternately follow just two dispatching rules with the model shown in Table 8–1. You would be concerned first with releasing types of work that make it possible to keep all four of your employees busy. Then you would probably follow a customer-oriented priority.

There are a variety of other dispatching priorities that you could conceivably follow. Among these are:

1. *Shortest cycle or least work.* The goal here is to rush through

all jobs that require relatively little work. These jobs require a minimum investment in in-process inventories and also can be delivered and invoiced quite rapidly.

2. *Longest cycle work.* Usually the most lucrative jobs in terms of total profit are those that require the most time. It also takes fewer of these jobs to load the shop with work, so they can mean less congestion, longer production runs, and greater profit.

3. *Fewest remaining operations.* If an order has been processed through most operations and is held up owing to some bottleneck operation, it might be given priority at this point simply to get rid of it (and to collect from the customer).

4. *Maximum delay rule.* If a job has been held up for some maximum period, it might be given priority both to please the customer and to prevent a particular job from floating around in the system for an indefinite period because no other priority can be applied.

Problems of rescheduling

In a very small shop, the production controller might apply various dispatching rules without really being conscious of them. He simply evaluates each order on its merits and determines its priority, taking all relevant factors into account. In a larger organization, specific rules are needed to guide the dispatcher. In the situation described in Table 8–1, the specific rules might be quite simple: dispatch orders in a sequence designed to meet completion dates desired by customers as long as this sequence permits all four employees to be employed productively. In a large shop, the dispatching rules would be much more complex. And in every shop, small or large, circumstances would frequently require that exceptions be made in the dispatching rules. Either a customer's needs change, or the company finds it is unable to follow its existing schedule. Here are some typical problems.

Change in customer demand. You might have an order that you did not plan to release for another month. But, unexpectedly, your customer asks you if you can deliver as soon as possible. If the customer is a good one, you will try to accommodate him if you can.

If purchased material needed for this customer's order is not already on hand, you will have to contact your supplier and ask him to speed up delivery. Then you will investigate to see what effect an earlier than expected release of this order will have on your own operations and on service to other customers. If business conditions are fairly slack, you may not have any problem. If other customers are also clamoring for early delivery of their orders, you may be able to please everyone only by working overtime—and you may pass this extra cost on to your customers.

Customer cutbacks may cause as many changes in your schedule as customer requests for speedy delivery. A cancellation of an order can be particularly inconvenient if it comes just as you are getting ready to release that order. You may not have purchased material on hand to permit you to start some succeeding order, and the cancellation may cause some of your equipment to be unexpectedly idled. In any case, the cancellation will force production control to scramble to revise the production plan.

Quality failure. Quality problems can occur at any stage of the process. When purchased material fails to meet specifications, production control attempts to find out when satisfactory material can be delivered and meanwhile must adjust schedules so that other orders can be filled using material that is already on hand. If quality failure occurs within the plant, the material that is ruined must be replaced. In addition, schedules might have to be readjusted to prevent a particular failure from affecting succeeding operations.

For example, suppose your shop is working on a particular order that requires an automatic lathe operation, milling, and subsequent assembly. Quality problems are encountered on the milling operation. This failure may touch off a whole chain of events in which production control must:

1. Determine when the problem will be solved by consulting with appropriate executives in the quality control, engineering, and manufacturing organizations.
2. Order additional raw material to replace products that were scrapped because of the quality failure.
3. Advise the company's marketing department of the effect of the quality failure on the schedule for completion of this order and any side effects it may have on other orders.
4. Revise dispatching sequences to reflect customer priorities indicated by the marketing department. This particular order can be completed in reasonable time only if it is now given priority over other orders. The quality failure will almost certainly cause at least one order to be late, and marketing would advise which customers it prefers to favor.

In addition, production control may have to change dispatching sequence in order to prevent internal operations from being dislocated. The order that is delayed at the milling machine was destined to move on to assembly. Unless another order is quickly dispatched, the assembly area may temporarily shut down, and excess costs will be incurred.

No material. A supplier may be late in delivering purchased parts and material. If the company itself is responsible for previous operations, excessive absenteeism or labor disputes may cause internal operations to get behind schedule. Equipment failures also can reduce effective capacity. Regardless of the cause, material that is not available will delay an order either at the start of the manufacturing cycle or at some work station in the plant. Production control must therefore go through a process similar to that required for a quality failure.

Short-interval scheduling

Shifts in demand, quality failures, or materials shortages can create such hopeless snarls in dispatching that routine procedures will not work, and the manager must step in to follow progress on an hour-by-hour basis. The technique he uses is called short-interval scheduling (SIS). The term is misleading because it implies that something is different about the scheduling. In reality, SIS is a method of *dispatching;* the schedule or sequence in which work is performed may not change at all.

Close supervision. With conventional dispatching, the worker moves from job to job, much on his own, following a system of priorities that has been presented to him by management. With SIS, the priorities may not change but the manager personally dispatches each job, one at a time. He is then on the spot to inquire why a particular job is taking longer than anticipated and to correct immediately any conditions that inhibit optimum performance.

Workers will respond to SIS essentially because the boss is monitoring their performance almost hour by hour, and he is also ready to help them with problems. SIS may also help workers overcome psychological handicaps. A huge backlog of work may be so frightening to basically conscientious employees that it causes them to slow down rather than to work faster. In extreme cases, the backlog may be so terrifying that the employee becomes almost completely unproductive, and no work whatever is done. When the manager applies SIS, productivity is restored because the worker emotionally must concern himself only with one job at a time, the one handed to him from the backlog by the supervisor. In many cases, SIS permits far more complex dispatching rules to be followed simply because the manager has the best grasp of the impact of any particular dispatching on all phases of the business. Thus, the manager can do something the employee cannot possibly do; he can vary the dispatching priority from job to job in order to fulfill current demands best.

Costly technique. The major disadvantage of SIS is the extra-close supervision entailed. There may also be more record keeping. Despite these disadvantages, SIS has broad applications not only in working off large backlogs in manufacturing operations but also in clerical operations. For example, the productivity of a typist may decline sharply if she is presented with a backlog that represents six months' work. In some cases, she may become so discouraged that output declines as a result of a subconscious decision. In other cases, the decision to make 6 months' work last for 12 months may be made quite consciously, since it is difficult for management to measure output over such a prolonged period in the absence of well-defined work standards. In either case, SIS may be the best answer. The work is passed out in small increments, and it is quite easy to monitor performance on each increment.

Expediting

When short-interval scheduling is used, there is no need for extensive expediting. The technique automatically limits the number of jobs in process, and it is relatively easy to locate each job and to measure its progress. However, with conventional dispatching, changes in production plans may be made so frequently that it is anyone's guess when a particular order will be completed. In fact, until computers became commonplace, it was not always an easy job even to *find* an order in process. Companies often employed expediters who were employed full time to physical track down in-process orders so they could report on progress to the company's sales department and to customers.

Basic problem. With conventional dispatching, an order is physically released to its first operation. The release "package" might include not only the raw material needed for the order but also specifications and operations sheets, which describe precisely what machines and tooling are to be used in completing the order. Each operation is then checked off as it is completed, and the partially fabricated material is moved to the next department, where it waits for a subsequent operation. Even in a medium-sized plant, each operating department might have dozens or even hundreds of different orders piled up in a not particularly orderly fashion. The foreman in charge of the department eventually processes each order, following whatever dispatching rules he has been given.

Neither the foreman nor anyone else in such a situation can accurately predict when a particular order will be completed. This would be difficult even with simple dispatching rules. For example, if the dispatch rule were simply "first come, first served," without exception, it would be easy to determine the relative priority of each order, but it would still be difficult to predict when the order would actually reach the head of the line. Process times on prior orders can vary substantially. In addition, a foreman can never predict what his effective labor force or equipment inventory will be. The labor fluctuates each day because of absenteeism and turnover. Equipment also is subject to breakdowns. To make matters worse, probably no company has a single dispatching rule. With a complex dispatch rule, it is difficult to determine the relative priority of a particular order. In addition, company expediters may effectively be changing the dispatch rule on a daily or even hourly basis.

Role of the expediter.   An expediter may track down a particular order by literally walking from department to department until he locates it physically. If it appears that the order will be delayed if it is simply left to the prevailing priorities, the expediter may ask the foreman to give it special attention. This represents, of course, a new dispatching rule. What often happens is that the expedited order displaces some other order which then becomes the object of future expediting, and so on. Orders that receive no expediting keep being put aside in favor of expedited orders, and the expedited orders themselves may leapfrog ahead of one another as one expedited order yields priority to another expedited order, which, in turn, causes the first order to drop behind schedule and to be expedited again.

The computer has done much to eliminate overexpediting. Typically, a card is keypunched every time an operation is completed on an order. The computer can then print out summaries that show exactly where each order actually is at any particular time. The computer can also dispatch orders, following extremely complicated dispatching rules with ease. The computer's calculations can always be overridden, of course, Ideally, however, this is done only after taking into account not only a particular order that management wishes to speed up but also the effect that expediting will have on other orders in the system.

Key weakness

With the production control system discussed so far, the key weakness is that the manager never really knows when a particular order is going to be completed. He can predict when a particular order will be released relative to other orders, but the absolute release date depends on how much work is already in the system and how rapidly it is being completed.

Once the order enters the system, its completion date is determined by the dispatch rules that are applied as it moves from operation to operation. In the absence of expediting, the order either may be completed well ahead of the customer's desired date or it may be late. In many cases no one can predict when the order will emerge from the system.

For a company handling many small orders, this seemingly casual approach may be the most efficient system it can afford. Otherwise the cost of administering the order may be greater than the total value of the order. This may also be true of a company with a few very large orders—especially if the product is not complicated. In this case it is fairly easy to keep track of what is going on without a formal system. Organizations that fall between these extremes usually try to schedule output fairly precisely. They not only estimate in advance how much time each order will require at each work station but also try to predict precisely when this work will be done.

Use of Gantt chart

The Gantt chart[4] in Figure 8–1 shows progress on a series of orders passing through your small company's lathe, milling machine, drilling, and assembly departments. It is now the second day of week 3, as

FIGURE 8–1
Use of Gantt chart for production planning and control

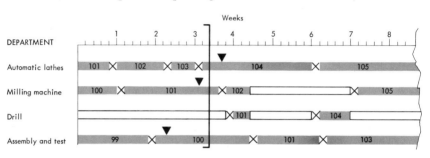

indicated by the marker passing through the chart. The schedule calls for the automatic lathes to have been working on order No. 104 for about a day. However, the ▼ shows that work on this job is more than one day ahead of schedule. Unfortunately, the milling machine is more than one day behind schedule on order No. 101, the assembly department is more than a week behind on order No. 100, and the drill press is shut down due to lack of work.

Spotting problems. The Gantt chart shows exactly how much progress has been made on each order, and the manager can quickly estimate how far ahead or behind schedule each order is. The chart also shows potential conflicts. Suppose that the manpower plan associated with Figure 8-1 is identical with that associated with Table 8–1—namely, two machinists and two assemblers. There was clearly a problem when the Gantt chart in Figure 8–1 was laid out. If everything goes according to plan, the drill press would be working on order No. 101 during the first two days of week 4, at a time when the milling machine would still be working on order No. 102 and the automatic lathe would be working on order No. 104. Thus there would temporarily be enough work for three machinists in a shop that employed just two machinists.

If the planner schedules the drilling on order No. 101 to begin after milling for order No. 102 is completed, then order No. 101 would not be ready for assembly on the third day of Week 4, as called for in the schedule. The alternative is to schedule the drilling of job No. 101 ahead of the milling on job No. 102. This is possible, but it causes order No. 102 to be held up for an additional three days. No assembly work

---

[4] Gantt charts are explained in Chapter 7.

is required for this order, and it would be desirable to perform the milling operation as soon as possible so as to complete the order.

The planner could easily see that no harm would be done by postponing a decision when he laid out the chart. In week 3 he can make a better decision, because it is now obvious that order No. 101 will not be needed in the assembly area until the early part of week 5. This makes it possible to perform the milling operation on order No. 102 immediately after the milling on order No. 101 has been completed. Order No. 102 will then be complete, and the operator will still have time for drilling on order No. 101 before that order is needed in the assembly area. The production controller may not be too concerned about the delay in the assembly area. Order No. 100 will probably be late, but chances for getting back on schedule look good. Once jobs 101 and 102 are machined, there will be plenty of slack time on the drill press and the lathes so that one of the machinists will be able to help the assemblers.

Major weakness. Versions of the Gantt chart are at least as widely used in production control as the simpler system of calculating total and active backlogs, as shown in Table 8–1. Their major weakness is that they are a nuisance to change if production control makes last-minute changes in dispatching. For example, Figure 8–1 shows jobs starting on the automatic lathe in numerical sequence: 101, 102, 103, and so forth. The chart would have to be completely rearranged if the actual dispatching order turned out to be 105, 101, 104, 102, 103. This major disadvantage can be overcome by use of a computer, which can print out the equivalent of a new Gantt chart every time it is given a different set of planning assumptions.

THE INVENTORY OBJECTIVE

The models illustrated in Table 8–1 and Figure 8–1 imply that production control is concerned with making certain that customers get finished products on schedule, as well as with keeping manufacturing departments supplied with sufficient material so that labor and equipment are never idle. Under ordinary circumstances, these manufacturing and marketing objectives can be achieved as long as the company is willing to invest a good deal of money in purchased materials and in-process and finished-goods inventories. The bigger the inventory, the easier it is for both marketing and manufacturing to do their jobs. If manufacturing has ample supplies of purchased materials and in-process stocks, its efficiency is limited only by the reliability of its equipment and the perseverance of its labor force. If there is a huge investment in finished-goods stocks, marketing need not be concerned about its ability to satisfy customer demand or about the flexibility of manufacturing's response to changing markets.

The materials manager, in contrast, is very much concerned with inventory investment. Every company could spectacularly increase its profitability if it could hire a super materials manager who could magically whisk material from suppliers through manufacturing to customers so rapidly that the company could collect from its customers before it was forced to pay its employees and suppliers.

Need for inventory

Since organizations hire ordinary mortals as materials managers, they often find themselves saddled with a substantial permanent investment in inventories that is automatically generated by the materials management process. Even the extremely simple production control system outlined in Table 8–1 generates as much as five different piles of inventory for each order. There is an investment in purchased-material inventory before conversion to in-process inventory by the automatic lathe. Three different types of in-process inventory pile up ahead of the milling machine, drill press, and assembly area. Finally, there is an investment in finished-goods stock up to the time the company's customer accepts delivery and pays his bill.

Successful production control is largely the art (with some science) of keeping these investments as low as possible, with minimum adverse effects on manufacturing and marketing. When companies have too little inventory and run out of stock, manufacturing efficiency and customer relations are bound to be hurt. Stockouts of essential materials mean some interruption of production, which raises costs. They may also delay delivery of finished products to a customer. After a few such delays, even the most patient customer will start looking for a supplier who will give him better service.

Cost. The situation is almost as bad for the company that carries too much inventory. It may have material available when it is needed, but its costs will be so high that it will not make any profit on the business it gets by having material available. Inventories tie up a company's capital; they generate storage costs; and they deteriorate or become obsolete in storage. In all, as will be discussed in greater detail in Chapter 10, inventories may cost as much as 25 percent per annum to carry; it can cost a company as much as $250,000 per year (and sometimes even more) to carry a $1,000,000 inventory. Obviously, if through intelligent materials management the same company can get along with just $500,000 invested in inventory, the savings will be substantial.

Since a company with a $1,000,000 inventory may have sales of no more than $8,000,000 and profits of only $800,000, it does not take too much imagination to grasp how efficient inventory management can make a tremendous contribution to company profit objectives. Similarly, it is easy to guess what will happen to company profits if costs are raised 5 or 10 percent because of frequent delays in manufacturing due to lack of inventory, or what happens to both sales and profits if customers find they can get prompter service from a competitor who is able to have material on hand when it is needed.

Conflict. Thus, as in all the other phases of materials management, there is a conflict of objectives in inventory management. The objective of high inventory turnover conflicts with the objective of continuity of supply and other objectives (discussed in Chapter 3). Of all business assets, inventories are the least stable and most difficult to control. Unfortunately, both for their profits and for the economy as a whole, American corporations do a rather bad job of inventory management. Their inventories tend to be high when they should be low, and vice versa. Bad inventory planning has been one of the major causes of almost every business recession.

In the typical business cycle, inventory accumulation helps push business activities to a new high. Business then tapers off, but inventories continue to rise. Stocks become excessive. Businesses not only stop buying in excess of needs, but they buy substantially less than current consumption. This underbuying causes production to drop even more and so helps accelerate the downturn. Finally, equilibrium is reached at the bottom of the business cycle, and recovery begins. Usually the recovery catches business unprepared. Sales temporarily exceed production, and inventories drop further. When production catches up with and eventually exceeds sales, inventories start increasing, and the cycle begins all over again.

Nature of the problem

All businesses have difficulty managing their inventories. The major reason is inability to forecast accurately. When a materials manager adds to inventory, he is anticipating a need for the material. In many cases, the need comes later than anticipated, and sometimes it never materializes at all. The result is excessive inventory. Or, if demand comes sooner or is stronger than anticipated, the inventory is inadequate.

Slow movement. The materials cycle is remarkably sluggish. Typically, more than a year may pass before a quantity of raw materials is transformed into a finished product. Theoretically, it would take less than a week to perform every operation necessary to transform various raw materials into a product like a television set. Chances are, however, that the iron ore, copper ore, bauxite, and other minerals used in making the TV set completed today were mined nearly a year before. The materials spent months either in various stockpiles or in transit between operations or plants. It may take only a few seconds to drill a hole in a small component on the TV set, but the material can lie on a factory floor for two days waiting to be scheduled on a machine that will perform this operation. Even completely automated processes have "pipelines" full of inventory awaiting processing.

Inventory functions

No business can operate without inventories. It needs them as a protection against uncertainty, for efficient processing of material, and to permit transit and handling.

Protection against uncertainty. Because the materials cycle is long and complex, the materials manager must anticipate his needs at each stage. Inventories protect him against unforeseen failures in supply or increases in demand. Without inventories, a large plant would cease operations each time a motor on a machine tool failed. Even a flat tire on a supplier's delivery truck could interrupt production if it delayed a shipment of needed material. Inventories protect production against unanticipated delays.

Similarly, inventories also protect against sudden upsurges in demand. Even with the most advanced market research techniques, few manufacturers can estimate demand accurately—particularly for various individual models of their products. The room air-conditioner industry is an extreme example of this. Sales are greatly affected by both season and weather. During a hot, humid summer, sales may be 50 percent higher than during a cool summer. Air-conditioner manufacturers must not only guess how many appliances the public will want but which models it will prefer. And these decisions must be made in the fall and winter, months before the public is in a buying mood. If a company wants to sell as many air conditioners as the market will absorb, its only protection against a really hot summer—and soaring demands—is an extra-heavy inventory.

Efficient processing of material. Unit costs normally are lowest when material is purchased, handled, and processed in large quantities, which in turn generates larger inventories. In addition, inventories act as a "cushion" between operations or processes. Production at various stages of a manufacturing cycle can never be synchronized perfectly; inventories take up the slack when one stage operates at a rate different from that of the preceding or succeeding stage.

The components of any product are manufactured at widely varying rates of production. For example, it may be possible to make the fasteners used in a television set at the rate of 20,000 pieces per hour. TV assembly lines might operate at the rate of about 200 sets per hour. It would be completely impractical to synchronize fastener production with TV set assembly. In practice, fasteners are assembled onto the TV sets from an inventory strategically located near their point of use on the assembly line.

Transit and handling. Materials may be transported thousands of miles before they are incorporated into an end product. Jamaican bauxite may travel by ship to British Columbia to be made into aluminum ingot. From there it may be shipped to New Jersey to be rolled into aluminum sheet, which moves by rail to Detroit to be fabricated into a component for an automobile, which moves by truck to rail to an auto assembly plant, whence it is finally trucked to a dealer as part of a finished auto that eventually is sold to its ultimate user. All the time it is in transit, which may be a period of several months, this material is part of someone's inventory.

For the reasons given above, every manufacturer must carry a certain minimum inventory. In practice, almost every manufacturer carries an inventory that is substantially greater than the minimum. He does so because:

1. His sales and manufacturing departments find it convenient to have stocks that are more than ample.
2. He expects prices of materials to rise and therefore stocks up at lower prices.
3. Scheduling, production control, and inventory management are more difficult and costlier when stocks are kept at optimum level. The manufacturer may lack the skills necessary for such control or be unwilling to incur the control costs, so he carries extra inventory in order to prevent stockouts.

Determining inventory levels

The amount of inventory a company carries is determined by three basic variables: order quantity, lead time, and safety stocks.

Order quantity. The greater the order quantity, the greater the average inventory. For a company using 100 units of an item per week and ordering in lots of 200 units whenever it runs out of stock, maximum inventory would be 200 units right after a new shipment is received and minimum inventory would be 0 units when the stock is used up. Since usage is steady, its average inventory would be 100 pieces—exactly halfway between the maximum and the minimum. If inventory were plotted against time, the result would look like the sawtooth pattern illustrated by the upper part of the drawing in Figure 8–2.

If the company should double its order quantity while usage remains unchanged, its maximum inventory would double; there would be 400 pieces in stock immediately after a shipment is received. It takes twice as long—four weeks instead of two weeks—to use up the inventory. As a result, the average inventory also is twice as great. It consists of two weeks' stock, or 200 units, instead of just one week's stock.

Lead time. There is always some interval between the time the need for material is determined and the time the material is actually

FIGURE 8–2

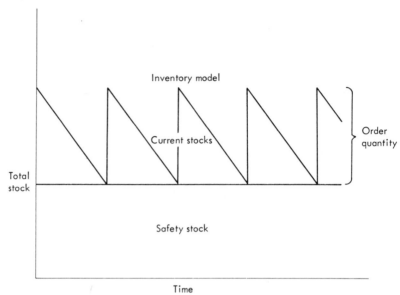

Inventories normally do not drop below the safety stock level. They reach their peak when a new shipment is received, when they usually equal the order quantity plus the safety stock. When usage during the lead time is greater than planned or when deliveries are late, the safety stock protects against a stockout.

manufactured and delivered. This period is the lead time. For example, if an office manager requisitions an electronic calculator on February 1, a buyer issues a purchase order on February 3, and the calculator is delivered on February 11, the total lead time for the purchase is ten days. The total lead time has two components, administrative lead time and supplier lead time. In the case of the calculator, these are two days and eight days, respectively.

The shortest lead-time items are those a local supplier has in stock for immediate delivery. Even in such a case, a company will usually allow a week's lead time between the day the purchase requisition is prepared and the actual delivery of the purchase, to permit both buyer and supplier to process the order efficiently and economically. When there is an immediate need for an off-the-shelf item, however, the lead time usually can be shortened to less than one day.

Much longer lead times are necessary for items made to order by out-of-town suppliers and for more complex items. Steel mills normally will accept orders with a lead time of 60 to 90 days. Auto companies often allow their parts suppliers—who fabricate steel and other raw materials into finished components—as much as five months' lead time. And the lead time for a complex piece of custom-made equipment may be two to three years.

Lead times also vary for identical items. One supplier may require a greater lead time for a given item than another supplier will, and the same supplier may have different lead times for a given item at various stages of the business cycle. When business is depressed and the supplier is operating well below capacity, with almost no new orders coming in, lead time will be short. When the supplier is working at capacity and has a huge order backlog, the lead time will be long. Variations in lead time can be quite substantial. For example, machine tool manufacturers may require only two months' lead time when business is depressed, but at the peak of a boom it may stretch to a year or more.

Changing lead time is one of the most difficult problems of materials management. Suppose, for example, the normal lead time for an item is four weeks. If a buyer orders material on February 1, he can expect delivery on February 28. What happens if the lead time changes and the buyer is not aware of the change? If the lead time increases, the order that the buyer places on February 1 will not be delivered when it is needed on February 28. At best this will be an inconvenience; at worst it can cause an entire factory to shut down temporarily.

If lead time suddenly decreases, the effect is not quite so bad. Suppose the lead time shortens by 50 percent and the item that is due February 28 is actually delivered on February 14. In that case, the buyer's plant will be carrying substantially more inventory than is needed, for when lead time shortens, the need for inventory also is reduced.

In order to prevent a stockout, a company must have an inventory that is at least adequate for usage during the lead time. If lead time is four weeks for an item with a usage of 100 units per week, there must be at least 400 units in inventory when the order is placed in order to prevent a stockout. This means that the lowest theoretical average inventory is 200 units (with an order quantity of 400 units). On the other hand, if lead time drops to two weeks, there need be only 200 units in inventory before it is necessary to place an order to replenish stocks. In this case, the lowest theoretical average inventory is 100 units, which happens when 200 units are ordered every two weeks.

Often the lead time changes unexpectedly. For example, a company may have originally ordered an item during a period of slack business when the lead time was two weeks. Business is booming the next time the item is ordered, but the stock clerk (or the computer) uses the same old lead time. The item actually arrives four weeks after the order is placed—two weeks after it was actually needed.

A stockout is a forceful reminder that lead time has lengthened. In contrast, a shorter lead time that causes excessive inventory investment may never be detected. If an item is first ordered during a period of general shortage, the lead time will be long. Then each time the item is reordered, the lead time allowance will be excessive, causing the company to carry inventory it does not really need. For example, 400 units of lead time usage might have been necessary when the item was first ordered, but only 200 units are needed now. While excess stocks that arise from unduly long lead times are difficult to detect with manual control methods, computers can readily be programmed to expose them.

Safety stocks. If usages and lead times could be predicted exactly it would be possible to limit maximum inventory of an item to the order quantity, with the usage pattern described above. A new shipment would arrive just as the last unit of the existing stock was used. Maximum inventory would equal the order quantity; average inventory would equal one half the order quantity; and minimum inventory would be zero. In practice this cannot be done. Suppliers fail to keep delivery promises, and usage forecasts are inaccurate. Extra inventory is needed to protect against unreliable forecasts. This extra inventory is called "safety stock." A company should carry just enough safety stock of any item to give it the protection against stockouts it is willing to pay for. Excess safety stocks boost inventory investments; inadequate safety stocks fail to give the desired protection. Most companies set their safety stocks on a trial-and-error basis, but, as will be seen in Chapter 10, more scientific techniques are available.

When forecasts of lead time and usage are accurate, the maximum inventory is equal to the order quantity plus the safety stock, and the minimum inventory is equal to the safety stock (see Figure 8–2 above). If usage is steady, the average inventory equals half the order quantity plus the safety stock. For example, if order quantity is 400 units and safety stock is 50 units, then average inventory is 250 units.

JOB-LOT ORDERING

Companies that manufacture on a job-lot basis have the easiest job of inventory control. Each customer order is treated, in effect as a brand-new product. The materials department reviews the bill of material for the customer's order and buys what is needed to do the job. If its timing is perfect on lead times, the company's raw-material inventories are negligible. For example, if you used the production control system illustrated in Table 8–1 and Figure 8–1, purchased-material inventory would be converted by the automatic lathes into in-process stock almost immediately after it was delivered. If your scheduling were reasonably tight, in-process inventory would be moderate, and finished-goods stocks would be disposed of by immediate shipment to customers.

The purest examples of job-lot ordering are found in the construction industry. When a construction firm wins a contract, its materials personnel must go to work immediately to get the material needed for the contract. There usually are no inventories to draw on, since construction firms almost always have suppliers deliver raw materials directly to the site. It would not be economic for a construction firm to carry an inventory of bricks, for example, since there would be too much handling expense in storing the inventory between jobs. It is much cheaper to buy the bricks needed for each contract and have the supplier deliver them to the site as needed.

Manufacturers of products that are largely made to customer specifications—machine tools, various types of equipment, special instruments, and so on—have problems similar to those of construction firms. Although they do all their work at the same location, each order is substantially different from its prececessors, and it is almost impossible to anticipate materials needs. Many firms do not even try; they simply calculate what material is needed for each order and then buy it.

Problems of control

With a system of job-lot ordering, each order must be scheduled separately. Different materials and components for the job are needed at different stages of construction or manufacture. The long lead-time items needed at earlier stages naturally get top priority. Materials personnel usually deliberately hold off buying short lead-time items until they have to. For example, they may know in January that an item with a lead time of three weeks will be needed in June, but they will make no commitment for the item until, perhaps, the last week in April, and even then they may request that the vendor hold up delivery until early June, although he actually might be able to deliver a few weeks ahead of schedule.

Purchased material on hand will not be released to start through the production process until in-process inventories of material are as low as possible. With perfect dispatching, each work station is about to run out of material just as a new order is moved in from preceding station.

Minimized losses. With good material control, materials are purchased and released for production only when needed for another reason: to minimize losses. The goals are to keep liabilities to a minimum should an order be canceled, reduce the cost of last-minute changes in specifications, and tie up a minimum of storage space for materials not needed immediately.

Problems arise when the lead time turns out to be different from the plan. Frequently an entire order can be held up because a supplier fails to deliver on schedule. Materials personnel try to spot lead-time problems as far in advance as possible. They also try to use all possible expediting methods (discussed in Chapter 14) to bring the lead time back to normal. Should a shortage develop, they immediately inform the manufacturing and sales departments so the job can be rescheduled. A typical form used for this purpose is shown in Figure 8–3.

Order quantity also can be a problem in job-order systems. Theoreti-

FIGURE 8–3

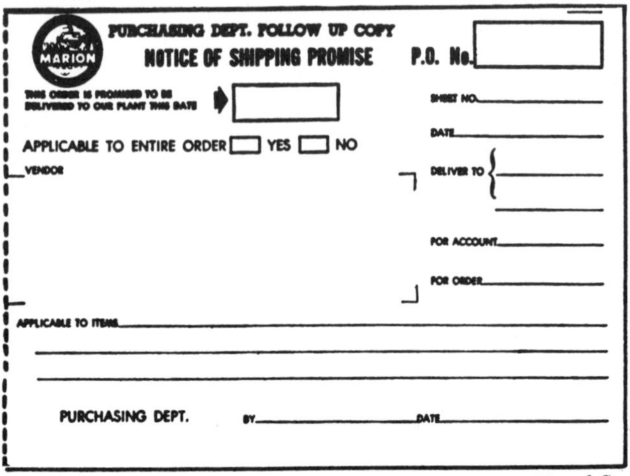
MARION

PURCHASING DEPT. FOLLOW UP COPY

NOTICE OF SHIPPING PROMISE

P.O. No.

THIS ORDER IS PROMISED TO BE DELIVERED TO OUR PLANT THIS DATE

SHEET NO.

DATE

APPLICABLE TO ENTIRE ORDER ☐ YES ☐ NO

VENDOR

DELIVER TO

FOR ACCOUNT

FOR ORDER

APPLICABLE TO ITEMS

PURCHASING DEPT. BY DATE

Courtesy Marion Power Shovel Co.

Lead times and delivery dates of purchased material are extremely important in a job-lot ordering system. The purchasing department of the Marion Power Shovel Co. uses this form to advise the production department of supplier shipping promises.

cally, the materials department simply can order the material specified in the bill of material for each job, and there are no problems. But what happens if usage is greater than anticipated because of miscalculations, spoilage in manufacturing, or shrinkage? Unless this is allowed for by ordering a little extra material, production may be plagued with work stoppages due to lack of material. It is no easy job to determine in advance how much extra material will be needed, and any material that is not used for the job may be wasted.

Solution by rules of thumb. Most companies try to solve problems of control with rules of thumb based on past experience. For example, they may not overorder at all on materials with a unit cost of more than $100, but materials in the $50–100 range may warrant a 2 percent overorder and greater cushions would be allowed on even cheaper materials. It is pointless to be stingy with low-cost materials and, in fact, may not even be possible to do so. Suppliers often insist on selling in certain minimum quantities and may prefer not to be bothered at all with orders that amount to $5 or less. As a result, a company which needs 100 cotter pins for a particular job, at a cost of no more than $1 per thousand, may be forced to order many times more cotter pins that it actually needs.

Application of Bayesian Rule

Occasionally the Bayesian decision rule (discussed in Chapter 7), can be helpful in determining the proper order quantity for a job lot. Suppose, for example, that a machine-tool manufacturer has an order to make a highly specialized piece of equipment for a customer. The equipment is designed for a very particular job, and there is little likelihood that there will ever be a repeat order for it. One of the components of the equipment is machined from a forging. In all, there are more than 150 machining operations on this particular component. Many of them are extremely precise. It is likely that at some stage of the long machining cycle someone will goof and cause the part to be scrapped. There may then be no choice but to start all over again with another forging.

Risk of scrap. The company actually needs only one good component for the equipment, but it intends to purchase several forgings and start them through the machining process simultaneously. Presumably most of the forgings will be scrapped at some stage of the machining process, but, if the company estimates its needs correctly, at least one forging will make it all the way through the process. The problem is to estimate how many forgings should be ordered and started through the process. If not enough forgings are ordered, the company may scrap one that is started and be forced to begin all over again. This would put the entire project months behind schedule. Conversely, it is wasteful to buy and machine more forgings than are actually needed; only one good one will ever be needed.

There is no quick and easy solution to a problem of this sort. Most companies would study the machining cycle carefully and then simply make the best possible estimate of their machining losses. They would then add some safety allowance, hold their breath, and go ahead, hoping that everything would work out. There is no way to avoid risk in making such decisions; this is what executives get paid for. The Bayesian decision rule, however, can help the materials manager and the manufacturing manager make a more rational decision, taking all risks into account.

Suppose the purchase price for the first forging made in the lot is $350, and each additional forging costs $200. Cash cost of machining the forgings is $500 each. To simplify calculations, assume that this cost is incurred even if the forging winds up being scrapped at some stage of the machining process.

The superintendent of the machine shop believes that the scrap rate is certain to be at least 50 percent and a minimum of two forgings must be started through the process. He believes there is a 60 percent probability that one of these castings will be good. He further guesses that there is a 90 percent probability of getting a single good part if 10 forgings are started through the machining process, and the probability of getting a single good part will increase to 99 percent if 30 forgings are started.

No one knows precisely how much will be lost if every forging is lost in the machining process. The general manager, however, believes that at least $25,000 will be lost if the company is not able to produce this component on schedule.

These probabilities and costs are no more than rough estimates based on previous experience. Many executives might take them into account almost subconsciously and then simply make a decision. In this case, for example, the manufacturing manager and the materials manager might arbitrarily agree that 12 forgings should be purchased and started through the machine process. This will prove to be the best of all decisions, of course, only if exactly 11 forgings are scrapped in the process. It will be a wasteful decision if only one or two forgings are scrapped, and it will be almost disastrous if all forgings are scrapped.

Three possible decisions. Bayesian analysis will not eliminate the uncertainty from such a decision, but it forms an orderly basis for rational review of the relative risks. There are three possible solutions to the problem outlined above:

1. Buy and machine two forgings and accept a 40 percent risk that both forgings will be scrapped.

Purchase cost of two forgings	$ 550
Machining two forgings	1,000
40 percent probability of $25,000 loss.	10,000
Total cost plus expected value	$11,550

2. Buy and machine ten forgings and accept a 10 percent risk that all ten forgings will be scrapped.

Purchase cost of ten forgings	$2,150
Machining ten forgings	5,000
10 percent probability of $25,000 loss.	2,500
Total cost plus expected value	$9,650

3. Buy and machine 30 forgings and accept a 1 percent risk that all 30 forgings will be scrapped.

Purchase cost of 30 forgings.	$ 6,150
Machining cost of 30 forgings	15,000
1 percent probability of $25,000 loss	250
Total cost plus expected value	$21,400

Since the cost of the risk is lowest with the second alternative, the company should buy a lot of ten forgings and accept a 10 percent risk that this will not be enough. This example is perhaps unrealistic in that only three probabilities are considered, in order to prevent calculations from becoming unduly cumbersome. But it is realistic in showing that it usually does not pay to take actions that virtually guarantee that there will be no stockout. Purchasing a lot of ten forgings represents a hedge that is within the usual range of fluctuations that can reasonably be expected in this case. Purchasing a lot of 30, on the other hand, would protect against a most unusual situation. Under most circumstances, a company cannot afford to protect itself against something it expects to happen only very rarely. In every situation, of course, it is desirable to make every effort to consolidate requirements of different orders so that common items are ordered simultaneously.

Modified job-lot control

While construction contractors order almost everything on a contract-by-contract basis, manufacturers almost always draw on inventories for commonly used materials and job order only those that are unique to a particular order. This reduces the cost of job-lot ordering and eliminates some of its basic defects. Each customer order is regarded as a demand on a portion of a common pool of materials and components. While no materials and components are stocked until an order comes in to generate a demand, customer orders are not handled so independently that it is impossible to pool requirements and so reduce cost.

Figure 8–4 illustrates the production and inventory control record used by a manufacturer of a widely diversified line of office equipment. The company manufactures more than 500 different products, and material control involves more than 15,000 different items.

FIGURE 8–4

	4 TRAY NO.	PRODUCTION *•₀ INVENTORY CONTROL RECORD DIEBOLD, INC.		INVENTORY			UNIT		PART NO.
CODE SEGREGATION				ACCOUNT 804	CLASS	MEASURE EA	WEIGHT		01-39424

Courtesy Diebold, Inc.

inventory control card for the modified job-lot ordering system used by Diebold, Inc. Sales orders are posted as demand for material; purchase order or manufacturing work orders supply this demand.

The company cannot afford to manufacture so many different products to stock, nor is it economic to stock all the materials and components it uses. Thus job-lot material control is essential. Some of its disadvantages are eliminated by using as many common parts as possible in each product. Requirements for each individual item are combined by listing each item on a separate card so that purchases reflect the demand of each product in which the item is used.

As the company receives orders for its machines, a "demand" is generated that is posted to the record. For example, suppose the company received an order requiring 100 pieces of part No. 01-39424 (see Figure 8–4). On February 1, the record is posted to indicate that 100 pieces are reserved for sales order A 11190, with delivery required March 20.

The reservation is posted by an accounting machine that compares the requirement with existing inventories and previous reservations. Since this is the first entry, the machine shows a negative balance of 100 pieces available after it takes account of the new reservation. This generates a demand for the material. Since the lead time is 30 days[5] and the material is needed on March 20, the order must be placed by February 20. However, the material planner decides to place it immediately because the sprocket is supposed to carry an extra reservation of 150 pieces for unusual usage. So on February 6, purchase order J 8091 is issued for 1,000 pieces—the predetermined economic order quantity. The machine operator takes account of this order by posting the "on order" amount of 1,000 pieces and allocating 100 pieces of this amount to cover the reservation and 900 "available" for future reservations.

When the order is delivered on March 3, the records are posted to eliminate the 1,000 pieces on order and add 1,000 to the "balance in stores" column. On March 17, 100 pieces are drawn out of stores to be used for sales order A 11190, and the reservation that was made for this order on February 1 is canceled.

Electronic data processing can also be used (see Chapter 19 for details) to do essentially the same job. Orders for finished products and their scheduled delivery dates are keypunched and transferred to the computer. Parts lists for each product are also either on magnetic tape or in the computer's "memory." The computer would then automatically issue purchase orders and perform other operations in response to various other transactions that are keypunched as they occur and then fed into the computer.

ORDERING FOR INVENTORY

Even a modified job-order system has weaknesses. Material is not purchased until there is a definite need for it, so it often is not on hand for emergencies. There is no way to plan ahead and anticipate requirements so that large quantities of materials may be purchased

---

[5] Shown in the upper right-hand corner of Figure 8–4.

at lower prices. Also, manufacturing costs are high, and customer service is slow. Because of these disadvantages, companies use job-order systems only when they are forced to do so because it is impossible to predict materials requirements for each order. Even companies that make thousands of semi-custom-made products avoid job-order material control whenever possible. All material that is common to a number of products is carried in stocks that are drawn on as needed.

Two-bin system

The oldest and simplest system of inventory control is the "two-bin system." One bin holds a reserve supply of material equal to the amount that will normally be consumed during the lead time, plus an extra amount for safety stock. The other holds the balance of the inventory. When stock in the second bin is used up, the order point is reached. A clerk requisitions a new supply of material and then draws on the reserve supply for his needs. When the order is delivered, the reserve supply is brought up to its former level, and the balance of the order is put into the other bin to be drawn on for immediate needs.

The two-bin system is simple to operate because there is no need for records. And, in most cases, there is no need even for two bins. The only requisite for successful operation of the system is that the order point of reserve stock be physically separated from the balance of the stock. This often can be done quite simply.

For example, suppose the item being controlled is pencils, for which usage averages four boxes a week and maximum lead time is one week. The reserve supply in a two-bin system might then be five boxes, including one box as safety stock for unexpected changes in usage or lead time. This supply need not be kept in a separate bin. It can be identified simply by putting a rubber band around it and then using up the other boxes in the inventory first. When the stock drops down to the point where it is necessary to use the boxes held by the rubber band, the order point has been reached.

The two-bin system is best suited for items of low value, fairly consistent usage, and short lead time. It is most commonly used for office supplies, and in smaller plants it also is used for maintenance, repair, and operating supplies. It rarely is suitable for production materials because it does not provide any record of stock on hand and is not sensitive to changes in demand or lead time.

Perpetual inventory

The two-bin system actually is a primitive version of a conventional perpetual inventory control system.[6] The main difference is that in the

---

[6] Also called a "max-min" system because inventories fluctuate between a maximum equal to the order quantity plus the safety stock and a minimum equal to the safety stock.

regular perpetual system there is no need to segregate stock. Control is maintained with record cards (see Figure 8–5) for each item.[7] All materials transactions are posted on these cards.

FIGURE 8–5

Material description											Location		Commodity number	
NONPRODUCTION MATERIAL RECORD														
Used for or by												Order Quan.	Unit of Meas
MONTHLY USAGE														
Jan.	Feb.	March	April	May	June	July	Aug.	Sept.	Oct.	Nov.	Dec.	Min. Bal.	Order Time	
Date	Reference	Quan. on order	Quantity received	Quan. disb.	Bal. in stock	Date	Reference		Quan. on order	Quan. received	Quan. disb.	Bal. in stock		

Typical nonproduction inventory control record card provides a perpetual inventory of the item. All receipts and additions to stock are posted; the balance is periodically verified with a physical count of stock on hand.

The stores clerk disburses material only when he gets a storage requisition. Data from requisitions is later posted to the record cards. Similarly, when an order point is reached, the clerk prepares a purchase requisition and posts the "on order" section of his record card. When material is received, the clerk posts the record card from his copy of the receiving report.

Each transaction can be substantiated by some document such as a receiving report, or requisition form. As a result, the clerk can be held responsible for any discrepancies between his records and actual inventories. Losses from pilferage or unauthorized use are minimized. In addition, the records always show the balance on hand and on order, so it is possible to calculate the value of the stock at any time. While the perpetual inventory system is much more expensive to operate than the two-bin system without records, its cost usually is more than justified for relatively valuable items subject to losses from pilferage.

---

[7] The form shown in Figure 8–4 also can be used in a perpetual inventory control system. The order point is indicated in the "Min. Available" box on the form. A new order is issued whenever the balance on hand and on order drops below this minimum.

Perpetual inventory systems are widely used not only by manufacturers but also by distributors and retailers. In most cases, the records are kept by a computer rather than a clerk, but the principle is the same. Some version of the perpetual inventory system can be adapted to almost any item that is used or disbursed regularly and whose stocks are periodically replenished.

While perpetual inventory systems are most commonly associated with items that are purchased, they are also used by many manufacturers to control finished-goods inventories. Instead of ordering from an outside supplier when inventory drops to the reorder point, a work order is processed by production control for manufacture. In most cases, a dispatching and releasing process similar to that outlined earlier in this chapter is followed.

Critical ratio

Close coordination between the physical distribution department and production control is essential if the company is to achieve manufacturing and marketing objectives without having excessive inventories. Integrated materials management, which embraces production control and physical distribution, has helped solve one problem that has traditionally plagued both marketing and manufacturing departments: fluctuating lead time.

Suppose, for example, that a company sells annually 1,000 units of product X, which it makes in its own plant. As other company products, X is made in batches or job lots which are stored in the company warehouse until they are sold. Product X is manufactured in lots of 250, and production control estimates that a lead time of one month is needed to manufacture a new batch; thus a new batch requested by the physical distribution manager on June 1 should be delivered to the warehouse on July 1. Thus there should be at least a one-month supply, or about 83 units, of X in the warehouse when a new order is sent to manufacturing.

Lead-time problems. Everything will work perfectly so long as (1) lead-time demand is the expected 83 units, and (2) the manufacturing lead time is exactly one month, as predicted. In this ideal situation, the company will not have excess inventory, nor will it be unable to fill customer orders promptly. Real life is almost never so idyllic. There will tend to be either too little or too much of product X because:

1. *Sales may surge ahead during the lead-time-period.* In this case, if manufacturing is not able to deliver a new lot of product X in *less* than one month, there will be a stockout.

2. *Sales of product X may lag behind expectations during the lead-time period.* In this case, the physical distribution manager will receive a new lot of product X before he needs it. As a result, he will temporarily

have more money tied up in inventory than he would like. He may also have trouble finding space for the additional material.

Worse yet, he may discover that although he has too much product X, he has run out of product Y. Demand has been greater than expected for Y, and the reorder point for Y was reached shortly after that for X. Consequently, the badly needed lot of Y will be delivered after the unneeded lot of X. If manufacturing had known that Y was the critical item, it could have given it priority over X, and the company would have enjoyed both higher sales and lower inventory.

3. *The factory may be ahead of schedule.* In the worst of all cases, the factory may have just laid off employees whom it now must recall because of an unexpected surge of demand for X and other products. Its costs would have been much lower if it could have anticipated this demand and maintained a steady rate of operation. On other occasions, the shorter lead time does not result from the factory's need for orders but, for example, from greater availability of raw materials. The physical distribution manager should then cut back on lead time; otherwise, inventories will be too high.

4. *The factory may be behind schedule.* When this is the case, the effective lead time will be more than one month. Delivery of product X will be on time only if the physical distribution manager sets an order point that is greater than the previously predicted 83-unit minimum. Note, however, that the factory's total output cannot be increased simply by ordering sooner. If the factory's capacity is temporarily lagging behind demand, the physical distribution manager may be able to prevent stockouts by selective ordering of those items where a stockout is almost certain. His flow of orders to the factory would be reduced to what the factory could handle, and orders would be postponed on items not immediately needed. Inventories would then fill the gap between supply and demand.

Maintaining balance. For many companies, keeping the factory's output in balance with demand is one of the most difficult tasks in materials management. In the past, the job was almost impossibly difficult because there was no quick way for production control to compare current demand and inventory with production. Records simply could not be brought up to date fast enough. As a result, the factory was often producing products that really were not needed for current sales, and it learned too late about items in high demand.

The computer solves at least part of this problem. It permits overnight tabulation of production, orders, and inventories for every product, so production can be adjusted to demand much more rapidly than before. The computer also can easily perform calculations that show the rates at which inventories are being used. The key calculation is the "critical ratio" that shows the relationship between stock currently available and the minimum stock needed during the order lead time. With product

X the critical ratio would reach 1.0 when the stock on hand (plus that already on order from the factory) dropped to the lead-time usage of 83 units.

The computer periodically recalculates critical ratios for every product. The new ratios reflect the latest orders from customers as well as new production. In a large company, literally hundreds of critical ratios may be calculated. Suppose there are just three products, with the following critical ratios:

Product	Ratio
X	1.0
Y	.9
Z	1.5

In this simple example, there will probably be a stockout of product Y unless it is given priority in dispatching. Therefore, as long as Y is not competing with dozens of other products that also had critical ratios of less than 1.0, it will move toward the "head of the line" at each work station through which it is to be processed. Chances are that this would shorten the effective lead time enough to prevent a stockout.

Product X would also be released for production immediately, but it might not require expediting. The critical ratio of 1.5 for product Z indicates that it need not be run immediately. However, production control might choose to release it for production anyway, if it appears that the factory will need the work.

Using the critical ratio. In theory, production control tries to match the operating rate of the plant with expected demand, in accordance with the basic production plan. Over the short term, however, demand and supply will often get out of balance.

There will be periods when supply is temporarily ahead of demand. In that case, production control will release for production products whose critical ratios are greater than 1.0. This policy automatically builds up finished-goods inventories. For example, production control may find it must release for production all products whose critical ratio is 1.1 if it is to avoid layoffs and idle equipment. Total inventory investment theoretically could then increase by as much as 20 percent[8] The higher inventory costs may be more than offset by the lower costs of stable

---

[8] For example, suppose there is no allowance for safety stock ordinarily and the order quantity is 100 units. The average inventory would then be 50 units, as stock levels vary between a peak of 100 and a minimum of 0. Setting an order point that is 10 percent or 10 units higher generates a built-in safety stock of 10 units. Average inventory would then be 60 units—10 units from the built-in safety stock and 50 units from the order quantity. This is further explained in Chapters 9 and 10.

production—or at least they should be if this policy is followed consistently.

There may also be periods when sales of finished goods exceed manufacturing capacity. Production control will then discover that it has more items with critical ratios of 1.0 or less than the plant can possibly handle. For example, it might discover that during a particular week it has on hand orders with critical ratios of 1.0 or less that call for 12,000 hours of labor and machine time. The plant, however, is capable of turning out only 10,000 hours of production. If the "pipeline" of in-process inventory is already at an optimum level, production control would be foolish to release more than 10,000 hours of work to the shop. The other 2,000 hours should be held over until the following week.

The critical ratio becomes the criterion that determines what work is to be released. All other factors being equal, work with the lowest critical ratio is released first. In a plant that is not able to keep up, the critical ratio of all work released for production will normally be less than 1.0. In a plant that is producing ahead of its sales, critical ratios will probably be greater than 1.0, but the items with lower relative critical ratios will still be released ahead of items with higher ratios.

The critical ratio of items entering the production process is a guide to future changes in basic capacity. If critical ratios are creeping up and the trend shows no sign of reversing, management must eventually cut its capacity by laying off employees and, ultimately, by getting rid of redundant equipment. If critical ratios are in a persistent declining trend, management will be forced to turn down sales (or to make customers wait) if it does not soon increase its effective capacity through overtime, hiring more employees, subcontracting, or other measures.

INVENTORY RECORDS

Critical ratios and other calculations in production and inventory control make it mandatory that a company identify parts of material with some sort of numerical system. Even small companies may carry thousands of different items in inventory. Obviously some system of classification is essential to prevent duplication of stock and to permit each item to be located readily. Almost every company assigns individual part numbers to its production parts and materials, and most companies also have some classification for nonproduction items.

Classification

The principles of classification are the same for all inventory items. In every case, the best approach is first to classify them into broad general categories and then progressively reclassify within each category. For example, one very broad category might be "tools"; a subcategory would be "machine-powered cutting tools," of which one type might be "milling machine cutters." The final classifications identify the specific classifications by size and type. For example, the specification number for a particular tool might be 18–26 444. The first digit might indicate that the item was a tool, the second that it was a machine-powered cutting tool, the next two that it was a milling machine cutter, and the last digits would identify the particular cutter.[9]

Classification systems permit similar items to be stored in close proximity to one another, both for convenience and to facilitate joint ordering of similar items. Assignment of classification numbers also helps prevent duplication of inventories. Master lists indicate specifications of each item and the brands that meet specifications.

Chrysler's System. For example, the Chrysler Corporation assigns its specification No. NPUV 204 to an iron valve gate with outside screw and yoke, capable of withstanding pressures of 125 W.S.P. and 200 W.O.G.[10] Chrysler does not have valves made to order; it uses standard types supplied by a number of manufacturers. Each supplier also has its own specification number. For example, the Chrysler NPUV 204 value is the equivalent of the 465½ valve supplied to Chrysler by Crane, the 1430 valve furnished by Lunkenheimer, the 651-A of Jenkins, and so on.

In the Chrysler storeroom, certain Jenkins, Lunkenheimer, or other valves may be located side by side under the same Chrysler specification number. If Chrysler did not use its own numbers, it could readily carry duplicate stores. For example, if a Lunkenheimer 1430 valve failed in service, the stores clerk might think it necessary to buy another 1430 valve; he might not know that the Crane 465½ valve would do the same job, unless there was some classification system to group together like products of competing manufacturers.

Duplication and obsolescence. Even the best inventory systems are not perfect. Constant vigilance by materials personnel is necessary to prevent duplication and obsolescence of inventories. From time to time, engineers will specify new parts and materials when the job can be done with items already stocked, or requisitioners will insist on slightly different brands and automatically increase the number of items in stock. These problems are discussed in detail in later chapters.

Disposition of surplus

Duplication of inventory almost always leads to surplus. For this and other reasons, almost every company has surplus inventory that should

---

[9] Some classification systems are so highly refined that the last digits also have very special meaning. For example, they may indicate the particular size of the tool, the parts or products on which it is used, and so on.

[10] Chrysler Corporation Standards, Valve & Cock Specification Index, January 1958, p. UV 3.

be weeded out and disposed of. Materials management is responsible not only for identifying the surplus but also for getting rid of it. Methods for doing so are described in Chapter 13.

How surplus develops. If a company buys only what it needs, one might wonder why surplus stock is such a common problem. One reason is that even if an item can clearly be identified as surplus, there is a natural tendency to save it. Suppose, for example, that a company stocks extra ball bearings for a particular machine tool. From time to time, bearings wear out in the machine tool, so it pays to keep them in stock in order to minimize production shutdowns while the machine is being repaired.

Imagine that a particular bearing is used on just one machine and, finally, the machine itself is replaced. Suppose that there are two bearings in inventory at the time the machine is sold and that each of these originally cost $6. Thus the company has $12 worth of inventory it no longer needs.

What will happen to these bearings? With many inventory control systems, the answer is nothing. The bearings may just lie on the shelf for years and years. Ordinarily the only way such inventory can be disposed of is for a company to make periodic checks to determine whether there has been any "activity" for each item carried in inventory. The materials manager then sets rules—usually quite arbitrary—that material that has not been "active" for a period of perhaps a year is automatically disposed of.

A policy like this is quite easy to carry out in companies that use electronic data processing for inventory control. The computer can be programmed to automatically print out a list of inventory items on which there has been no activity for some predetermined period of time. These items are then investigated, and anything that is obsolete is sold for the best price the company can get.

Obviously it makes sense to get rid of items that you are sure you will never need. However, even though people may be aware of this intellectually, even in well-managed companies they may be emotionally inclined to save some items that will never be needed. This simply is not economic, even if an enormous loss must be taken on the item when it is disposed of. A $6 bearing that is no longer needed is worth nothing to the company, and it should be eliminated from inventory even if no more than 6 cents is realized from it. The loss that is taken on obsolete inventory can, of course, be charged off against income, and the company reduces its taxes. Equally important, inventory carrying cost is also reduced. For example, if the company's cash inventory carrying cost is 15 percent per year, then each $6 bearing costs 90 cents per year to carry in inventory.

It is hard enough for an organization to weed out inventory that actually may never be needed, but it is even more difficult to educate an organization into throwing out stuff that will eventually be needed but whose rate of usage is so low that it will take many years to use it up.

Weeding-out process. Suppose, for example, that a company has a regular usage of 100 units per month of some item and that it is economic to order this item in lots of 1,000. Everything goes along routinely as long as usage stays at 100 units per month. A new order is placed when inventory drops to some reorder point. Then a new shipment of 1,000 units arrives and the company has about a ten-month supply of that particular item.

Now, suppose the company loses one of the contracts that require this particular item. Usage drops to five pieces per month. At the time this happens, the company has 1,000 units in inventory, so it now has a 200-month inventory, enough to last about 17 years at the new rate of usage. With many inventory control systems, no changes would be made to account for this much slower rate of usage. The item would just stay in stock and gradually be used up over a period of 17 years, if usage continued at about five units per month.

This is extremely wasteful, however. The company will spend far more to carry the item in inventory for 17 years than it would to throw away the same item now and purchase it again in 16 years. Suppose, for example, that the company's cash carrying cost of inventory is a mere 10 percent per year (which, of course, is lower than it is for most companies). If the purchase price of the part is $10, the annual cash carrying cost would be 10 percent of $10, or $1 per year on each item. Even if interest is not compounded, total carrying cost would be $17 for each item by the end of 17 years. And if the carrying cost is compounded at 10 percent per year, total carrying cost would be more than $40. The fact is that it is impractical to carry an item in inventory more than seven years with a 10 percent carrying cost—even if it is necessary to give it away in order to get rid of it. A $1 per year carrying cost, compounded at 10 percent per year, has a value of $9.48 after seven years. In eight years, it reaches $11.44, which is more than the original cost of the item.

In this example, it would pay to save only a seven-year supply, or about 420 pieces, at the present rate of usage of 5 pieces per month. The other 580 pieces should be scrapped. If the item has a salvage value, inventory should be reduced even further. Of course, companies do not really know what their future usage of an item will be. All they really know is present usage. As a general rule of thumb, it rarely pays to carry more than a five-year inventory of anything, even if the item has negligible scrap value. In other words, a company holding more than a 5-year supply at present rate of usage that knows of nothing that will increase this usage had best throw the stuff out. It pays to get rid of it. Many companies, in fact, apply even harsher rules, especially if they can convert the particular item into something that is useful or can obtain a substantial salvage value for it.

Unfortunately it often is not easy to detect this type of obsolescence. It can only be done by comparing present rates of usage with existing inventory. Without computerized inventory control, this can be an awkward, slow process. With a computer, it is possible to program so that current inventory can be compared with current rates of usage, and any excess stock can be weeded out.

Inventory accounting. All purchases and withdrawals from stock must be accounted for. In addition, company accounting departments issue periodic reports on inventories. The materials department uses these reports but usually is only indirectly concerned with their preparation. In most cases, the accounting department keeps separate records and gets copies of all documents concerned with materials transactions.

Accounting systems vary widely, and, since this is not a text on accounting, they will not be discussed here. However, essential to every system is some periodic review to make certain "theoretical" inventories indicated by stock records and the like correspond with actual inventories. This review usually is made by materials personnel (with assistance from other departments). Since it normally involves a physical count of all inventory items, it often is done during a vacation shutdown, to prevent disruption of operations. Discrepancies between actual inventories and theoretical balances shown on records are a reflection on the company's inventory control and the efficiency of its materials personnel. For this reason, many companies do not like to have physical inventories counted by the same person responsible for keeping the records of the stock. They prefer an independent check by an accountant.

Cases

CASE 8–1. QUEENSTOWN CHEMICAL COMPANY (A)

Developing an inventory reduction program

Queenstown Chemical Company is a leading producer of specialty chemicals. It makes thousands of different compounds for almost all of the major drug and fine chemical producers. George Mead, Queenstown's director of purchases, is responsible for both raw-material and finished-goods inventories, in addition to directing the company's purchasing activities. At present, his biggest single problem is managing finished-goods inventories, which in the last year have increased from $2 million to more than $10 million. Not only is the company running short of storage space, but its cash position is getting tight.

There is no easy solution to the problem. Queenstown's customers are aware that chemical shortages are a thing of the past, and they insist that the company stock their needs for immediate delivery. Where customers formerly carried 30 to 60 days' inventory to allow Queenstown plenty of lead time on new orders, they now insist on getting delivery in 10 days or less. If they do not get this rapid service, they can buy from Queenstown's competitors, who are willing to carry stock for their customers. Unfortunately, competition and overcapacity are facts of life in Queenstown's industry, and everyone believes it will be many years before producers can once again require customers to allow adequate lead time so they can schedule their production for each order and carry minimum finished-goods inventories.

It occurs to Mead that he might try the same approach on his suppliers and get them to carry inventories for Queenstown. At present the company has $1 million invested in nonproduction inventories and $6 million in raw materials. Usage of nonproduction items is about $100,000 per month, and usage of raw material is about $2 million per month. Queenstown uses a perpetual inventory system. All materials transactions are posted to inventory records for each item, and clerks set order points based on past usage, lead-time estimates they get from purchasing, and their own experience. Whenever there is a shortage, they increase the safety stock. In general they are criticized for shortages, but, except for occasional campaigns to reduce inventories, management has rarely expressed concern over excess stocks.

Mead believes that inventories can be reduced substantially by requiring suppliers to carry inventories. "If we carry inventories for our customers, there is no reason why our suppliers shouldn't be willing to carry them for us," he declares at a meeting of the corporation's executive committee. He proposes that Queenstown make contracts with each of its major suppliers that call for them to maintain certain minimum stocks of materials available for immediate delivery. Queenstown will not pay for the material until it is delivered, but it will guarantee the supplier a market for it eventually.

For example, in its processes Queenstown uses a "9280" type of valve that must be replaced periodically. Usage of this valve varies widely from month to month but averages about 400 valves per year. Currently, Queenstown reorders when its inventory drops to 20 valves, and delivery takes about two weeks. Mead believes that the division could get along with just two valves if it had a deal with the valve distributor guaranteeing that 30 valves would always be on hand for overnight delivery. Since these valves cost $150 each, Mead's plan would reduce inventory investment by $2,700 on this item alone.

Mead's assistant, Robert Stark, disagrees with his boss's plan. He points out that it costs the supplier just as much to carry inventory as it does Queenstown. In addition, Mead's plan would require more frequent ordering, which raises costs for both buyer and seller. The result would be that overall costs would be higher than they are at present. He grants that Queenstown would probably be able to persuade its suppliers to stock without having to pay a premium. However, he feels that in the long run the division has to pay for every service it gets from its suppliers. As an alternate solution, he suggests that Queenstown discuss the problem with its suppliers and try to persuade them to offer lower prices because Queenstown is not requiring them to carry inventories. He admits, however, that this approach may not work too well on items that are price fixed.

Stark also suggests that Queenstown might be able to reduce inventories by trying to schedule its needs for maintenance items in advance. For example, the life of the "9280" valves can be accurately predicted. If the maintenance department were to schedule replacement far enough in advance, there would be no need to carry inventory. Orders could be placed for each job, and it would not be necessary to carry more than two or three valves in stock.

Question

How do you evaluate Mead's and Stark's proposals? Develop an inventory reduction program for Queenstown.

CASE 8–2.   A.E.D. DIVISION*

Predicting process losses

In September 1950, National Motors Corporation received a contract to tool a large government-owned facility in the Chicago area in order to become a second supplier of Hornet engines for the U.S. Air Force. It proceeded immediately to establish a new Aircraft Engine Division (A.E.D.) to carry out the contract. The division was to tool for a capacity of 30 engines per day and received an initial production order for 1,000 engines. Price for the engines was to be negotiated. It was assumed that, after the plant became operative, the division's costs, because of automation, would be substantially below the then prevailing price for the Hornet engine of approximately $75,000. Before A.E.D. could commence production of acceptable engines, however, it had to produce two prototype engines which would be subject to extensive testing. These engines were to be assembled from parts made by A.E.D. and its suppliers. Until these engines were flight tested and approved, A.E.D. could not go into full-scale production.

In some cases it was acceptable to order semifinished components for the prototypes from existing suppliers of engine components. For example, A.E.D. intended eventually to develop a second supplier of crankshaft forgings. Naturally it would take some time before the new

* Copyright © 1968, Dean S. Ammer.

supplier could deliver acceptable material. Meanwhile, it was agreeable to the Air Force that A.E.D. buy crankshaft forgings from the existing supplier of forgings and run these forgings over its own machine tools in order to produce finished crankshafts for the two prototype engines that were needed to get approval to go into production.

The crankshaft was a particularly critical component. It required more than 70 machining operations, and many of these required considerable precision. Even the less critical operations could conceivably create problems, since all operations would be on brand-new machines staffed with new employees.

The production control department did not know how long it would take to pass a forging through a complete machining cycle, but its guess was several months. One major problem was engineering changes. Production control wondered if it dared schedule long production runs on crankshafts because there was a steady stream of design changes, and some of these changes could not be incorporated at the company's leisure but had to be put in immediately. Nevertheless, it seemed that it would be all but impossible to have a machining cycle of much less than three months. That is, a forging which was begun on June 1st probably would not be completed until about September 1st.

One problem that production control faced immediately was the ordering of the crankshafts needed for the two prototype engines. From that time on, it was assumed that crankshaft forgings would be coming from a new supplier which the purchasing department was in the process of developing. It was absolutely essential, however, that production control get enough crankshaft forgings on hand from the existing supplier so that there would be at least two completed crankshafts after all of the new machine tools were tried out. Production control was, of course, fully aware that some crankshaft forgings would be lost in the process, through either malfunctioning of the new equipment or—even more likely—errors made by inexperienced operators.

In the opinion of the production control manager, an allowance of about 5 percent for nonreworkable scrap on each operation would be adequate for the first production run. Since there were 70 operations, this implied to him that the scrap allowance should be 350 percent of the number of finished pieces actually desired. Since only two crankshafts were needed, his guess was that the company should start 12 forgings through the machining process. The production control manager knew full well that a big safety margin was necessary, since if the two forgings were not made on schedule, the program would be set back. For example, if all 12 forgings that he proposed to order were scrapped late in the machining cycle, the entire program might be set back at least six months before the division could get new forgings delivered from the supplier and start them through the machining cycle again.

On the other hand, it did not pay to buy too many forgings. First, the cost of each forging was $600 and, in addition, even the rough forgings were in danger of becoming obsolete because of engineering changes—especially if too many of them were carried in inventory. There was also a great advantage in having only a minimum number of forgings from the existing supplier, since the company wanted to get its new forging supplier approved and shipping forgings as soon as possible. Its price with the new supplier was based on the assumption that the supplier would get 100 percent of the business (although the other vendor, which would continue to supply the second prime contractor, was presumably available in the event of a strike). Thus, both A.E.D. and the other prime contractor would have the protection of two forging suppliers, while each of them paid only to tool a single supplier.

While the production control manager thought that an initial order for 12 forgings would be plenty, this was not a decision he made himself. He conferred with the division works manager and the general purchasing agent. These three executives, in turn, jointly recommended to the division general manager that 100 forgings be ordered at a price of $600 each.

When the senior buyer of forgings questioned the general purchasing agent about the large quantity of forgings being purchased for just two prototype engines, he was told the potential loss from failure to complete the two prototype engines was so great that A.E.D. could not afford to take any chances. "Bill Murray [the division general manager] told me that he would be willing to buy almost any number of forgings if this would guarantee him two good finished crankshafts on schedule," the general purchasing agent explained to his senior buyer.

The forgings were ordered in March 1951. Meanwhile, the company began receiving its initial shipments of machine tools and gradually began to lay out its crankshaft department. The first machining operations were performed on the 100 forgings in July 1951 and the company was confident that at least two forgings would be completed for installation for assembly by January 1952. Production of engines was scheduled to begin the following June, with output to be steadily increased up to 30 engines per day by late 1952. In the interim, the company had received several other production orders for variations of the same engine and was in the process of tooling for these variations and also making parts needed for prototype testing.

The crankshaft department was plagued with start-up problems throughout 1951. Deliveries of certain critical machines were behind schedule; tooling did not always function properly; and a steady stream of design changes helped create additional confusion. As a result, the lot of 100 forgings passed through the long machining cycle much more slowly than had been anticipated, and the scrap rate greatly exceeded the estimate of the production control manager. By March 1952, the division still had not completed a single crankshaft, and in May the last of the 100 forgings was scrapped. Additional forgings were purchased and the first acceptable crankshaft was completed in November 1952— roughly six months behind schedule.

Question

Given no advance knowledge that scrap rates would exceed even the most pessimistic estimates, could A.E.D. have done anything to prevent its crankshaft machining problems from apparently holding up the entire program by about six months?

9

Order-point and periodic control systems

THE INVENTORY CONTROL SYSTEMS discussed so far are all fixed reorder-point systems. That is, when stocks drop to a certain level (approximately the safety stock plus lead-time usage), a new order for a fixed quantity is prepared. With these systems, stocks fluctuate in a pattern like that illustrated in Figure 8–2 in the preceding chapter.

As has been pointed out, the average inventory balance is determined by order quantity, safety stock, and lead time. These three factors also influence the probability of a stockout. The greater the order quantity, the less frequent the exposure to risk of stockout. For example, when order quantities are so great that it is necessary to order only once a year, only one stockout per year is risked when inventories drop to the reorder point. The safety stock reduces the stockout risk as inventories drop to the reorder point. It also takes up the slack if there are unanticipated changes in demand during the lead-time period, when additional stock is on order but has not yet been delivered. This period, which is the only time during the inventory cycle when there is risk of a stockout, is equal, of course, to the total lead time. Stockout risk also is reduced by selecting suppliers that have short and consistent lead times and never fail to keep delivery promises.

A PROBLEM IN ORDER-POINT CONTROL

When demand can be predicted with reasonable accuracy and the value of the item is not too great, it is fairly easy to determine safety stock and order quantity. Commonsense rules can be applied.

Suppose, for example, that a company uses 20 typewriter ribbons per week and can get a 10 percent extra discount if it buys them in lots of one gross. Total lead time is only a week (or less, since the ribbons are available from a local office-supply distributor). What should be the order quantity, safety stock, and order point?

Determining order quantity. The order quantity is easy to determine: It should be 144 ribbons in order to get the discount. By buying just a little more than seven weeks' supply with each order, costs are reduced 10 percent. This means that at the maximum the company is carrying three and a half weeks' more inventory than it would if it operated on a hand-to-mouth basis on typewriter ribbons. The 10 percent saving earned in three and a half weeks is equal to an annual return of more than 100 percent on the money invested in this inventory. In addition, it is more convenient and administrative costs are lower when the company buys in larger quantities.

What if there were no quantity discount, if the price for the typewriter ribbons were the same regardless of the quantity purchased? Chances are that most companies would still choose to buy in lots of roughly 144 ribbons if their usage were about 20 ribbons per week. With this order quantity and usage, average inventories of ribbon would be roughly four weeks' supply, including safety stock. Most managers would feel that it would not be worth the trouble and clerical expense to order such a minor item more often than six or seven times a year, even if this policy did result in carrying somewhat larger stocks of ribbons than absolutely necessary.

However, this attitude would be quite different if the ribbons were an extremely expensive material that accounted for a large percentage of total inventory investment. In such cases, materials managers are quite willing to order weekly or even daily in order to minimize their inventory investment. Most materials managers, as we shall discuss in detail later in this chapter, classify inventory items by dollar value of usage and then establish rules for determining order quantity. For example, a materials manager might not permit an order quantity greater than two weeks' usage for an item whose dollar value of usage is $10,000 per month, while he would require a minimum order quantity equal to twelve weeks' usage for an item whose dollar value of usage is only $10 per month.

Determining safety stock. The safety stock is determined by analyzing the past pattern of usage. Suppose that weekly usage during the past year has been as shown in table at top of page 298.

If, with the pattern of usage above, the reorder point were set at 20 ribbons, there would be no safety stock at all, since 20 ribbons are used on the average during the one-week lead time. How many stockouts would there have been each year because of variations in demand?

The first answer that might come to mind is 14, since there were 14 weeks in which actual usage was greater than the average lead-time

Number of ribbons used	*Number of weeks with this usage*
15 or fewer	6
16	3
17	4
18	6
19	7
20	12
21	5
22 to 30	8
30 to 40	0
More than 40	1

usage of 20 ribbons. On second thought, you might come up with a different answer when you consider that the order quantity was 144 ribbons. This is equal to more than seven weeks' usage, so it is only necessary to order between seven and eight times per year. Thus, at the very most, a stockout is risked no more than eight times per year with the usage pattern above; at any other time stocks are more than ample.

In actual practice, there would be considerably fewer than eight stockouts for an item with this usage pattern, an order quantity of 144 units, and no safety stock. The week when the previous order was almost used up would have coincided with the week when usage was greater than 20 units. Chances are (the probability can be calculated with precision, of course) that this would not happen more than two or three times per year.

With this pattern of usage and an order quantity of 144, a typical inventory planner would probably set the safety stock at 10 ribbons. The order point thus would be reached when stock dropped to 30 ribbons. With a safety stock of 10, there would be an occasional stockout (perhaps once every seven years) during the rare week when usage was greater than 30 ribbons and the order point would have been reached even if usage had been normal.

A good case could be made for setting a safety stock even lower than 10 units, were the cost of the ribbons not so low that the saving from the reduced investment in safety stock probably would not offset the inconvenience of an occasional stockout. For example, a safety stock of five ribbons might bring one or two stockouts per year. This might cause slight inconvenience but certainly no serious problems, since typewriter ribbons are not that critical. They can be bought in a few hours on a rush basis. Chances are that the typists would not need fast service, anyway, since they often keep spare ribbons in their desks.

THE ABC SYSTEM

Materials managers rarely, if ever, worry much about stockouts of typewriter ribbons. This is not the case with many other items, particu-

larly production parts and materials. In many cases a stockout of even
a minor production part can be costly. For example, the bolts that hold
the engines to the wings are just as important to an airframe manufacturer as the engines themselves; production is held up if either item
is out of stock. But the engines may cost $100,000 each, while each
bolt may be no more than a few dollars. A safety stock of eight bolts
would cost only a few dollars a year to maintain, while a safety stock
of eight engines would cost thousands. Obviously the investment in
safety stock for the bolts is a much better value than investment for
the engines, since it provides the same protection at a fraction of the
cost.

Safety stocks almost always are a better value for low-cost items
than they are for expensive ones. Modern inventory control systems
take this into account by classifying items by value of usage. The high-
value items have lower safety stocks because the cost of protection is
so high. The low-value items carry much higher safety stocks.

10 percent of items, 70 percent of value. The basis of the "ABC"
approach to inventory control, which provides maximum overall protection against stockouts for a given investment in safety stocks, assumes
10 percent of items and 70 percent of value of inventories for the most
costly items. In every company, a big percentage of the investment
in inventory is concentrated on relatively few high-value items. The
first step in the ABC approach is to estimate average demand for each
item in inventory and multiply this figure by unit cost to determine
value of usage. For example, an item that costs $10 and has an annual
usage of 1,000 units would have a usage value of $10,000, while an
item that costs $100 with a usage of only 50 units per year would have
a usage value of $5,000. Values of usage for each item are then listed
in order of importance, with the greatest dollar-volume item topping
the list.

The items are separated into three groups. The 10 percent that are
most costly are A items; the next 20 percent are B items; and the balance
are C items. In every case the A items will account for a heavy percentage of total expenditures and the C group will account for a surprisingly small percentage. The following relationship is typical:

Category	Percent of items	Percent of value
A.	10	70
B.	20	20
C.	70	10

Although there are one seventh as many A items as C items, seven
times as much is spent on A items as on C items. Thus the average
expenditure of an A item is 49 times greater than the average expenditure for a C item. Investment in safety stock for the A item must be

49 times greater than for a C item in order to afford the same protection against stockouts (provided all other factors are equal).

Selective control. The ABC system permits selective inventory control. Safety stocks are kept low for the high-value items, which should be subject to extremely close control by materials personnel, anyway. The low-value items get less attention from materials personnel; stockouts are prevented by maintaining much higher safety stocks.

With ABC control, it is possible to risk fewer stockouts and reduce investment in inventories. This is proved by comparing ABC control with overall control. Inventories are divided into three classes: the expensive A items account for 10 percent of the total and roughly 70 percent of the value; the B items for 20 percent of the total and about 20 percent of the value; and the C items for 70 percent of the total and about 10 percent of the value.

Suppose, for example, that a company stocks 1,000 items in inventory and that its average investment is six weeks' usage, or $1 million, of which $200,000 is safety stock. Average order quantity is eight weeks' usage, and there is two weeks' safety stock. With this order quantity and safety stock, assume that the company experiences ten serious stockouts every year. These are distributed at random among the 1,000 items carried in inventory, and they are equally effective in disrupting production.

Now suppose that the company classifies its inventory by the ABC system. It breaks down as follows:

	Number of items	Average inventory investment	Investment in safety stock
A items	100	$ 700,000	$140,000
B items	200	200,000	40,000
C items	700	100,000	20,000
Total.	1,000	$1,000,000	$200,000

The ten stockouts expected each year are distributed at random among all the 1,000 items. Thus, the chances of a stockout on an A item are the same as those for any B or C item. However, since C items comprise 70 percent of the total number of items in inventories, it is reasonable to expect that 70 percent of the potential stockouts will occur on these items, with just 20 percent on B items and 10 percent on A items. Thus, under normal circumstances, the following pattern can be expected: one stockout on the 100 A items; two on the 200 B items; and seven on the 700 C items.

Note the enormous difference in the prices paid for protection against stockouts. $700,000 is tied up in inventory, including $140,000 in safety stock, to hold the stockout rate to 1 percent per annum on A items.

Seven times as many C items can be protected with a total safety stock investment only one seventh of that required on the A items. Thus the average investment in safety stock per A item is $1,400 ($140,000 ÷ 100 items) and only $28.57 ($20,000 ÷ 700) for each C item.

The same or better protection against stockouts can be provided at much lower cost by concentrating investment on the cheaper items, where protection can be bought more cheaply. For example, the company might decide to get along with no more than two weeks' average inventory of A items, of which only one half week is safety stock. The B items might not be changed at all, while safety stocks of C items would be doubled, leaving order quantities unchanged, as shown in the table below:

	Number of items	Average inventory investment	Investment in safety stock
A items.	100	$233,333	$ 56,667
B items.	200	200,000	40,000
C items.	700	120,000	40,000
Total.	1,000	$553,333	$136,667

Note that the company has succeeded in reducing inventory investment by $446,667—almost 50 percent. For reasons explored in detail in the next chapter, this could reduce operating costs by as much as $100,000 per year. Despite this spectacular cost reduction, protection against stockouts is actually increased. The stockout rate on C items was probably reduced by more than 50 percent when the safety stock was doubled, so no more than three stockouts of these items can be expected in the next five years, instead of seven. The rate on B items remains unchanged. The company is therefore ahead even if it triples its stockout rate on A items (three stockouts every five years, instead of just one), because of the sharp reductions in both order quantity and safety stock which cut average inventory by two thirds.

In practice, it probably is not necessary to suffer any increase in stockouts of A items. With the ABC approach the company has not only different inventory policies for the more expensive items but also different control procedures. Because there are so few A items, it may be economic to review their inventory status almost daily to spot deviations in demand and to maintain extremely close follow-up on suppliers to make certain they adhere to lead times. In other words, on costly items, tight control is substituted for the protection of inventory. This is economic, since it permits substantial reductions in inventory investment.

With the low-cost items, it is cheaper to carry inventory than to pay the salaries of the personnel needed for close control. It would take seven times as much effort to maintain tight control over the 700 C items as it would for the 100 A items, and it would be possible to reduce investment in C items by only one seventh as much as the reduction in the investment for A items. With the B items, a middle-of-the-road policy would probably be followed. There would be some control, but the company would also rely to a greater extent on inventories to protect against stockouts than it would with the A items.

DETERMINING LEVEL OF CONTROL

It should be concluded that inventories are always essential to prevent disruption of production. In some cases a company using an order-point control system can operate successfully with no inventory investment in many key parts and materials.

No finished goods.   Suppose, for example, that a manufacturer of upholstered furniture offered hundreds of different types of furniture, each available in dozens of different fabrics. The product line would be so diverse and the product so bulky that it would be impossible to carry a finished-goods inventory. Production of any particular piece of furniture would begin only after a firm order was received from a customer, but, of course, competitive pressures would force the company to ship as rapidly as possible after it got the order.

The problem is solved by carrying a diverse in-process inventory. While no upholstered furniture firm carries an inventory of finished furniture, all do carry stocks of finished components and fabrics that can rapidly be assembled into finished furniture. These stocks are drawn on as orders flow in. As long as the company's lead time for the finished product is greater than the lead time required for final assembly, the company can keep its delivery promises without an investment in a finished-goods inventory.

This introduces an additional dimension to inventory management: level of control. If a product is complex, the materials manager must analyze it and determine the stage of fabrication that is critical. Usually, his inventory control process is automatic as long as stocks are in control at the critical level.

In a furniture factory, for example, this critical level might be the stocks of parts and other materials that are assembled directly into finished pieces of furniture. The company can respond reasonably rapidly to orders by drawing on parts inventories, which are maintained on an order-point basis. Production control would release materials for final assembly in accordance with some dispatching rule. In a furniture factory, dispatching priority would be strongly influenced by the desirability of shipping full cars of furniture to a single destination whenever possible. This dispatch rule might, for example, cause a North Carolina factory to delay shipment of furniture to a retailer in St. Louis until there were enough orders from this area to make up a full boxcar.

Applying the principle

This principle is better understood with a more complex example. A company makes product A, whose sales lead time is six weeks. Product A is assembled from subassemblies B and F and purchased component T. Subassembly B consists of manufactured components C, D, and E, which in turn are made from purchased parts and materials Y and Z. Similarly, subassembly F consists of manufactured components G and H and purchased component V. G and H in turn are made from purchased materials X and W.

Time-cycle chart. Each material, component, and assembly requires some lead time. If the materials manager starts with the lead time for final assembly of the product and then adds the lead times of the components, he can construct a time-cycle chart like that shown in Figure 9–1. The chart shows that, starting from scratch with no inventories at all, about 22 weeks' lead time would be needed before a finished product could be produced. The bottleneck item is material X, which must be fabricated into G, which in turn is assembled into F, which becomes part of A.

Obviously, the company must have inventories if it is going to offer delivery to customers in six weeks. It could carry protective stocks at every stage of manufacture, but there is an easier way which involves less control and usually will also reduce inventories. Stocks are maintained for only a few critical items; the others are puchased or manufactured only when there is a definite demand for them.

The concept is best explained graphically. Note that there is a horizontal line in Figure 9–1 at the six-week mark; this represents the sales lead time. Only those items whose lead time intersects this six-week line need be started. These include components C, D, E, G, H, V, and T.

For example, suppose the materials manager decides from experience that a safety stock of 100 units each of C, D, E, G, H, V, and T will allow the company to take care of all foreseeable demand from customers. To simplify the arithmetic, assume that it is operating entirely on a job-lot basis; except for safety stock, it buys or fabricates exactly enough material to complete each order received from a customer.

Suppose a customer orders 20 units of product A. Components C, D, E, G, H, V, and T are drawn from stock. In order to deliver within six weeks, the chart shows that work must start on subassembly F within one week. If it suits convenience (and it may, since every factory manager likes to even out work loads in order to get more efficient operation), work on subassembly B can be held off for two weeks.

FIGURE 9–1
Time-cycle chart

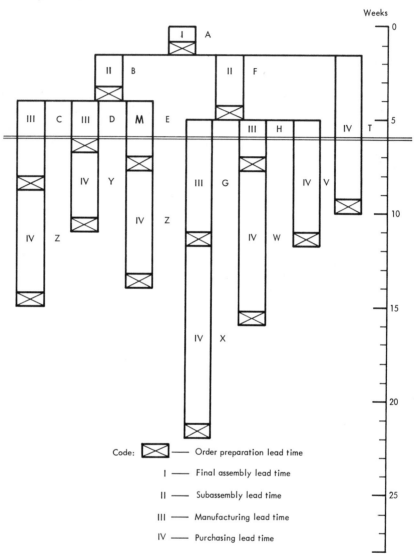

The time-cycle chart makes it easy to determine which inventories require safety stock protection. For example, if sales lead time is six weeks, the parts C, D, E, G, and H require protection at manufacturing in-process level while purchased parts stocks are required of V and T. No other safety stocks are needed.

Or, of course, work can be started immediately, to give the customer extra-prompt service.

Steps must also be taken to replenish safety stocks. Therefore materials and parts T, V, W, X, Y, and Z are ordered in sufficient quantities so that they ultimately can be manufactured into the key components for which safety stocks are carried.

Possible problems. The example above is greatly oversimplified. The assumption that identical safety stocks of the various key items could be carried is not correct. In actual practice, a much greater safety stock would be carried for part G, whose raw material X must be ordered 22 weeks ahead of final assembly, than for T, which requires a total lead time of only 10 weeks. If there were a 100-unit safety stock of T, a 220-unit safety stock of G would probably be needed to get the same protection against stockout, because of the difference in lead time.

In addition, it would not be possible to handle orders for much more than 100 units during any six-week period. Even if the later stages of the process could be accelerated, supply lines of purchased materials and semifabricated components would be emptied out.

Nor would the parts fabricating shop necessarily be operated strictly on a conventional "max-min" basis. Most likely would be a critical ratio approach, (described in Chapter 8), in which those parts where the critical ratio was lowest would be run. This would keep the fabricating shop operating on a fairly steady basis even if work at the later stages were intermittent and fluctuated with customer demand. Also, certain items would probably be purchased in excess of actual requirements, in order to reduce purchase costs.

It is not difficult to see how this selective control system can be applied to any of the inventory control systems described in this chapter and the previous chapter. It can also be used in conjunction with an ABC system. The components and materials controlled selectively could be classified according to their value. Inventory levels would then be adjusted to afford varying degrees of protection in accordance with ABC rules.

STATISTICAL ANALYSIS OF DEMAND

Limitations of max-min systems

All of the inventory control systems discussed so far have been order-point, or max-min, systems. Control can be improved and inventory investment reduced through application of ABC systems, selective control, and other techniques, but these systems still have one fundamental weakness: They work well only when the lead time and the demand for material during the lead time can be predicted with reasonable accuracy. Unfortunately, usage and lead times of many items vary enormously. Many companies increase their production by 50 percent in an exceptionally prosperous year, and demand for individual products can change even more. What happens when demand suddenly surges upward on an item under a max-min system of inventory control?

Effect of demand change.   Assume that an item normally has a usage of 1,000 units during its one-month lead-time period and that the previous year's usage pattern indicates a safety stock of 250 units to be more than adequate. If demand rises by 50 percent during the year and, as is often the case when business is increasing, lead times lengthen slightly, a whole series of stockouts is possible. The first stockout will come when usage during the lead time is 25 percent greater than normal. The inventory planner may consider usage abnormal and not increase safety stocks after this first stockout.

A second stockout will almost certainly touch off an analysis of the item's usage. Usually order point will be increased. Suppose that the item that used to have an average usage of 1,000 units a month has these usages for six months: 1,050, 1,100, 1,400, 1,250, 1,300, and 1,400. The planner notes that average usage during this six-month period was 1,250 units. He also notes that maximum usage was 1,400 units. He may increase the order point to 1,500 units, giving him a safety stock of about 250 units if lead-time usage continues to average 1,250 units.

If demand continues to rise, the inevitable result is another stockout. If the company is controlling thousands of different items with a simple max-min system, it will be plagued with stockouts. Eventually, however, order points and safety stocks are increased to the point where inventories are more than adequate to cope with peak demand. And, in fact, it is probable that they will be increased well beyond this point. In a period of rising demand, inventory planners are subject to almost daily harassment from production and sales executives because of shortages and stockouts. On the other hand, there will be few immediate complaints if they raise order points and safety stocks to the point where stockouts are highly unlikely, regardless of how much usage increases. Consequently planners not only boost order points to meet present demand but also allow for future growth of demand.

For example, an item that once had an order point of 1,250 units and a safety stock of 250 might wind up with an order point of 2,000 and a safety stock of 500, even though record consumption might not exceed 1,800 units. Eventually, planners would attempt to anticipate increased demand and build up stocks ahead of usage.

If this increase in demand were temporary, the results would be expensive. Suppose, for example, that on account of a businesss depression or some other cause the company's usage dropped well below its old norm of 1,000 units to 700 units a month. In such a case, its investment in inventories would initially be at least three times greater than necessary, and it would continue to be substantially excessive until max-min quantities were gradually adjusted back to the old levels.

Weaknesses of max-min. Few companies experience such a stable demand for materials that they can rely entirely on a max-min perpetual inventory control system such as that described above. Companies surveyed by the National Industrial Conference Board (NICB) in a study of inventory control indicated that they believed "maximum-minimum stock levels are no substitute for effective inventory management." According to the NICB study, max-min control has the following weaknesses:

1. Stock levels are actually set by clerks, since managers do not have the time to study inventory levels of individual items.
2. Reorder points and safety stocks often are not changed for years on end.
3. Delay in posting records makes them useless for control. Reorder of a critical item can be held up until the clerk gets around to posting the last withdrawal, indicating that the reorder point has been reached.

Impact of EDP. Widespread application of electronic data processing has done much to strengthen order-point, max-min inventory control systems. Records can routinely be brought up to date simply by keypunching each inventory transaction. This process is not entirely foolproof, but theoretically, at least, it is an easy matter for a company to run off an accurate report on its inventory position once or twice per week. The computer also makes it easier to manage inventory by exception. Decisions then need not be made by low-level clerks. Instead, the computer can be programmed to call to the attention of higher level management any situation in which order points appear inconsistent with present or projected demand.

Basic factors in forecasting

The computer also makes it practical to use numerous statistical techniques to forecast lead-time demand and to signal management that some change may have taken place. The easiest way to estimate lead time is simply to assume that what happened in the past will probably happen in the future. For example, suppose that an item was reordered when stock on hand was 100 units and that inventory had declined to 20 units by the time a new order was completed. Lead-time usage, therefore, is 80 units. This represents the most recent experience with the item; a computer can automatically reorder on the basis of previous lead time plus some safety stock allowance. Unfortunately, if this straightforward system is followed slavishly, the inventory system will automatically have all of the faults cited in the NICB survey. The computer will be doing exactly what the clerks were doing—and, if anything, the smartest computer is even dumber than the dumbest clerk.

Demand for inventory is determined by four independent variables.

It is probably pure luck if these variables cancel one another out and there has been no change in demand since the last time the item was ordered. The basic variables are secular, cyclical, seasonal, and random.

Secular change. Demand for every product is determined over the long term by one or more basic factors. For example, over the long term, the demand for housing is determined largely by new household formations—the number of single persons or couples who set up house-keeping for themselves each year. All other factors being equal (which they never are), builders would try to build enough new housing units each year to equal the number of new household formations and replace housing that is no longer usable.

Every item an organization may carry in its inventory is also subject to some secular influence, although, in many cases, it may be so insignificant that it can be ignored. In other cases it may be highly significant. For example, suppose that an auto parts distributor stocks mufflers that can be used only on 1974 Chevrolets. Demand will inevitably decline secularly from year to year as the number of 1974 Chevrolets on the road gradually declines. By the year 2000, the population of active 1974 Chevrolets would presumably be close to zero, and demand for this muffler would no longer exist.

Whenever secular change can be identified, a company would want to allow for it. For example, the auto parts distributor that estimates lead time usage for 1974 Chevrolet mufflers will be 1,000 mufflers on orders it places with suppliers in 1975 might reduce its estimate to 950 mufflers in 1977. And by 1985, the secular adjustment might amount to at least 500 mufflers, since by that time presumably about half of the 1974 Chevrolets will have been scrapped, and muffler demand will have been reduced accordingly.

The secular trend can usually be measured statistically. Actual data are plotted and the points are connected with a curve, using the least-squares method. This method is explained in detail in almost every basic statistics text. However, much cruder techniques will normally work just as well in materials management. The materials manager is always concerned with *future* secular trends. While the past is often a valid guide to the future, it normally makes little difference whether the materials manager calculates precisely that the past secular growth rate, for example, was 2.21 percent per year or relies on the sloppier estimate of roughly 2 percent.

In many cases the past trend will have to be adjusted anyway to take into account the cumulative effect of past production and other changes. For example, the aluminum industry formerly enjoyed a secular growth trend of about 7 percent per year—substantially greater than the growth of either manufacturing activity or population. This growth was possible because aluminum was being continuously substituted for other materials, such as steel, wood, copper, glass, and zinc.

Of course, no industry can gain indefinitely at another's expense. In the case of aluminum, most of the substitutions of aluminum for competing materials (such as aluminum for steel or glass in beverage containers) have probably already been made. As a result, aluminum's secular growth rate has declined, and it would be misleading to base a forecast on a simple linear extrapolation of the old growth rate. As this is written, the current secular growth rate for aluminum is estimated at 4.5 to 5 percent, or only a little higher than the expected growth rate of overall industrial production.

If an error is made in forecasting secular change, its greatest impact will be on facilities rather than inventories. Companies that are overly optimistic on long-term growth trends find themselves saddled with capacity they will not need for years to come. Conversely, underestimates of the secular trend lead to loss of market position and opportunities for profit.

Cyclical variation. Unexpected changes in secular trends are so gradual that they rarely have any effect on short term materials forecasting and planning. Errors in cyclical forecasting are far more likely to affect materials management. An unexpected shift in the business cycle works like a two-edged sword on materials management: it affects both the restocking lead time itself and also the lead-time usage. For example, suppose that under "normal" conditions an item has a lead time of one month and a lead-time usage of 100 units. The item is only ordered about once a year. Business begins to boom during a one-year period between orders, but order point continues to be based on the one-month lead time, with lead-time usage of 100 units. The item is reordered at the normal time but, owing to a huge backlog of orders, the lead time is now six weeks. In addition, the business boom begins to affect demand for the item itself. Demand is now 150 units per month instead of 100 per month. Thus, the anticipated lead-time usage of 100 is inadequate; 100 pieces are used up about three weeks after the new order is placed instead of one month. And, of course, the supplier is two weeks late, so the company is out of stock for a period of roughly three weeks.

During a recession, the two-edged sword works in reverse. Lead time usage is less than expected, and the lead time itself is shorter. For example, the order may be completed in three weeks instead of one month, as planned. In addition, usage is down to about 75 units per month. Thus, an extra 50 units are on hand when the new order is delivered. If this happens repeatedly, the company will find itself with far too much of its cash tied up in inventory.

Unfortunately, cyclical fluctuations in demand are far from uniform. They may lead, lag, or coincide with the general business cycle, as explained in Chapter 6. In addition, there may be an inverse relationship. For example, demand for new heavy trucks tends to fluctuate with the business cycle. Trucking companies add to their fleets when general business conditions are favorable. On the other hand, demand for spare parts for older trucks may have an inverse relationship with the business cycle; it flattens out and may even decline at the peak of a cycle. But parts demand may increase substantially when business is depressed as truck owners postpone purchases of new equipment and try to keep their older vehicles in operation through stepped-up spending on spare parts.

Seasonal demand. It is critical to distinguish cyclical changes in demand from seasonal ones. For example, suppose that a trucking company experiences a sharp drop in demand in the month of January. If this is a cyclical shift, the company should immediately cut back on plans for expansion. On the other hand, if extra-cold weather and heavy snowstorms are simply causing a greater than normal seasonal slump, the company should be ready for an upsurge in demand in the warmer months and may even want to lease additional equipment and hire extra employees.

Almost every product or service is subject to some seasonal variation. In most cases it is fairly easy to identify. For example, hospitals normally experience a drop in occupancy in the summer months and also during the period between Christmas and New Year's. Patients prefer to have elective surgery done during other periods, and so do their surgeons. Similarly, snow tires are almost never purchased in spring and early summer (in the Northern Hemisphere, at least), only bargain hunters buy Christmas tree ornaments in January, and so on.

In some cases, the seasonal variations are far more subtle. A government agency, for example, may discover that there is some seasonal variation in demand for office supplies, even though demand for that agency's services seems independent of seasonal variations. One reason for this is simply that the number of working days per week and per month is not consistent. Holidays may reduce a standard five-day week to three or four days; demand for supplies during that period will decline accordingly. Cold weather brings increased absenteeism and thereby reduces demand. Vacations have the same effect during July and August. If demand is measured monthly, there is automatically some seasonal variation simply because the months themselves do not have the same number of working days. February may have only 19 working days (assuming that Washington's Birthday is a holiday), while March may have as many as 23 working days in an organization that operates a regular five-day week.

Seasonal variations in demand can usually be predicted fairly precisely. However, continuous review is usually essential. Seasonal patterns gradually change. For example, there is now a sharp seasonal decline in overall industrial production in the month of July. This reflects the growing custom of shutting down factories for vacation. Fifty years ago, blue-collar workers did not get paid vacations, and the July seasonal slump was much more moderate.

The simplest (but not always most precise) way to estimate seasonal fluctuations is to assume that the pattern that prevailed in the past will prevail in the future. For most materials managers, this assumption may come sufficiently close to the truth so that more complex techniques of determining seasonality are not needed.

Suppose, for example, you want to measure seasonality of an item you have stocked for many years. You know of nothing that has happened (such as a tendency toward more vacation shutdowns in July) to change the seasonal pattern of demand, so you simply calculate the average monthly demand over a number of years. The results, which are shown in Column 1 of Table 9–1, indicate an overall average demand of 1,353 units per year or 112.75 units per month. Averages for each month show a clear seasonal pattern. Peak demand occurs in spring and fall, and there are two marked periods of seasonal slump—in July and August and in January and February.

Seasonal variations like those shown in Table 9–1 must be taken into account if you are to interpret current sales trends correctly. For example, suppose that demand this year increases from 94 units in February to 110 units in March, a 17 percent increase. If you were ignorant of seasonal trends, you might regard this as a reason for celebration and be tempted to hire more workers and increase production. A glance at Table 9–1 shows how wrong you would be. Actually, the increase to 110 units is a *less than seasonal* increase, and your sales performance is weak rather than strong.

Seasonal adjustment (or "deseasonalizing") permits you to observe nonseasonal influences more readily. You adjust for seasonal variation by dividing average monthly (or weekly) demand by average demand for that month. For example, Table 9–1 shows that average demand in January is 110, while average demand for all months of the year is 112.75 units. Dividing 110 by 112.75 gives a seasonal adjustment factor of .976. This means that owing to seasonal factors, demand during January is 97.6 percent of normal (Column 2 in Table 9–1) and, therefore, a +2.4 percent seasonal adjustment (100.00 − .976) should be added to January data to make it comparable on a seasonally adjusted basis with data for other months.

Changes in seasonally adjusted data are assumed to be due to causes that are not seasonal. The change in demand in the example above from 94 units in February to 110 units in March represents an actual increase in demand of 16 units. But Table 9–1 shows that seasonal factors alone should increase demand by 20 units during this period. For almost all products, the rate of secular change is so slow that it would barely be discernible during a one-month period. Cyclical variation is a possibility. If the product were an important one, you would want to investigate

TABLE 9–1
Calculation of seasonal variation in demand

	(1) Average demand	(2) Average demand for month	(3) Seasonal adjustment (percent)
January	110	0.976	+ 2.4
February.	95	0.843	+15.7
March	115	1.020	− 2.0
April	118	1.047	− 4.7
May	120	1.064	− 6.4
June	125	1.109	−10.9
July	90	0.798	+20.2
August	100	0.887	+11.3
September.	120	1.064	− 6.4
October	125	1.109	−10.9
November	120	1.064	− 6.4
December	115	1.020	− 2.0
	12 ⟌ 1353		
Average all months	112.75		

to see if the drop in demand is being influenced by the business cycle. If that were the case, you would probably cut back on your next order.

Random fluctuations.   It is quite possible, however, that the failure of demand to register a normal seasonal increase cannot be explained rationally. Such changes occur frequently at random. Some random fluctuations are related to seasonal factors, for example, sales of natural gas and fuel oil for heating, which reach a seasonal peak in January. But demand may be either lower or higher than expected, depending on the January weather in the northern part of the country. Similarly, a wet spring will flatten out the seasonal peak that is anticipated in fertilizer sales simply because mud prevents farmers from working their fields as early as they would like.

Weather is one of the few random fluctuations that can be identified and clearly related to a change in demand. Other random fluctuations are harder to identify. A major danger is that a change in demand will be looked upon as random—and therefore nonrecurring—when the cause is really secular, cyclical, or seasonal. For example, suppose an appliance manufacturer carefully identifies secular, cyclical, and seasonal factors and predicts a demand for 10,000 refrigerators during the month of March. He actually sells only 6,000 refrigerators. Is this deviation of 4,000 refrigerators from forecasted sales a random fluctuation, or can it be related to some cause? If it is random, then the company should simply ignore it and not cut back production.

With genuinely random variation (as in flipping a coin or throwing honest dice), periods when the company "loses" will be exactly offset by periods when it "'wins." Thus a random decline in demand for refrigerators will be followed by a random increase in demand, and the best policy is simply to go on producing at the planned rate, which takes into account secular, cyclical, and seasonal changes in demand.

In an organization where human beings must make decisions, it is all too easy to write off the unpleasant and unexpected as chance happening. This may also be a sure route to the poorhouse. Conceivably, the unexpected shortfall of 4,000 refrigerators represents a cyclical fluctuation the company has not been perceptive enough to identify. Or some other nonrandom cause may be the villain; for example, a competitor may be cutting prices. In any case, if the cause is nonrandom, the company should do something.

Applying probability

A company can use statistical theory to help determine whether or not change is random and can therefore be ignored. First, it would try to adjust for any seasonal factors that might be influencing sales. Conceivably the sale of 6,000 refrigerators instead of 10,000, for example, may indicate a slower than expected seasonal pickup in sales following the winter lull. This might happen, for example, if the weather were exceptionally bad. It is also possible that sales of refrigerators may be influenced by an unusually early or late Easter. If seasonal factors have apparently had a negligible effect, the company might then compare the unfavorable variation of 4,000 refrigerators with expected random variations.

Based on its past experience and analysis of the market, the company might try to estimate the maximum random variation it can expect from its forecast after all explainable variations have been taken into account. Statistically, this estimate represents an estimate of three standard deviations, or 99.72 percent of all occurrences. If the company has sufficient data it may even be able to calculate precisely the standard deviation of fluctuations due to random causes with the following formula:

$$S_X = \sqrt{\frac{\Sigma(x - \bar{x})^2}{n - 1}}.$$

The company may get exactly the same answer using both of these approaches: its maximum expected fluctuation is 3,000 refrigerators and its calculated standard deviation is 1,000 refrigerators. In both cases, the company then estimates the standard deviation to be 1,000 and three standard deviations to be $3 \times 1,000$, or 3,000.

If this estimate is correct, the company would expect random fluctuations in monthly demand to be 3,000 refrigerators or less, 99.72 percent of the time. The odds thus overwhelmingly imply that a shortfall in demand of 4,000 refrigerators is at least partly nonrandom in character. Therefore, some action should be taken.

In fact, the company may infer that fluctuations well within the range of three standard deviations may be nonrandom. Elementary statistics tells us that almost two thirds of all random fluctuations should fall within a range of one standard deviation. For the refrigerator company, this would be 1,000 refrigerators more or less than the basic forecast. In this case, the odds are heavily against purely random variations that *consistently* fall outside a range of one standard deviation. For example, if demand seemingly lags behind the forecast by 2,000 units for several months running, the odds are that this is not a random fluctuation, but some unidentified nonrandom factor is at work.

Averaging and smoothing techniques

If the product is a major one like a refrigerator, management would carefully study demand fluctuations on an individual basis. Variations due to nonrandom causes would be identified and appropriate decisions made. Random variations would be accommodated by allowing inventory levels to go up and down.

Minor items simply do not deserve that much management time. For better or worse, decisions must be made by clerks or computers. In some cases, it is easiest to assume that all fluctuations in lead-time usage are random and to protect against stockouts with adequate inventory. At the other extreme, it is possible to develop very complex statistical techniques where a computer takes into account secular, cyclical, and seasonal factors as well as random fluctuations in setting order points.

Most companies settle for a compromise between these two extremes. They periodically revise estimates of lead-time usage with techniques that partly, but not always entirely, take into account secular, cyclical, seasonal, and other variations.

The moving average. The simplest such technique employs moving averages. They permit usage figures to be brought up to date at regular intervals so order quantities will reflect the latest changes in demand. For example, a company might use a four-week moving average to measure demand. Each week a new average demand is calculated, as follows:

Week No.	Usage	4-week average
1	10	
2	11	
3	12	
4	11	11
5	14	12
6	14	12.75
7	16	13.75

With the moving average, demand gradually changes to reflect current usage. Each week's demand is weighted equally.

The weight given current usage depends on the span of the moving average. For example, a four-week moving average is more sensitive to current demand than an eight-week average. On the other hand, an eight-week average is more likely to smooth out short-term random fluctuations that are not significant.

Moving averages always lag behind current usage. In addition, they present programming problems when used with electronic data processing equipment. For these reasons, many companies have adopted exponential smoothing techniques to measure demand.

Exponential smoothing. With exponential smoothing, current usage is weighted more heavily than past usage in forecasting demand. Exponential smoothing is easy to apply. One merely updates the previous demand or usage average by a fractional constant A. This formula is:

New average = Old average + A (current demand − old average).

For example, suppose that a demand of 80 units is forecast for the week and actual usage is 90 units. If a value of 0.1 is used for the constant A, the new average equals $80 + 0.1 (90 - 80) = 81$. If demand drops the following week to 71 units, the new average equals $81 + 0.1 (71 - 81) = 80$ units.

Note that the value of the constant A determines the effect of current demand on the new average. For example, a constant of 0.1 gives results close to those obtained with a nineteen-period moving average, while a constant of 0.5 is the equivalent of a three-period moving average.

Change in trend. The exponential smoothing formula used above lags behind actual demand. To correct for lag due to trend, it is necessary first to measure the change in trend. Our formula is: Current trend = New average − old average. We can use exponential smoothing to measure the average trend just as we did for the demand itself:

New trend = A (current trend) + $(1 - A)$ old trend.

Then,

$$\text{Expected demand} = \text{New average} + \frac{(1 - A)}{A} \text{ new trend.}$$

To see how the formulas are applied, assume that averages have been increasing by two units per period. In the current period, they have increased by just one unit (from 80 units to 81 units). The new trend is calculated by substituting:

New trend = A (current trend) + $(1 - A)$ old trend
$$= 0.1 (1) + (1 - 0.1) 2 = 1.9 \text{ units.}$$
Expected demand = New average + $(1 - A)/A$ (new trend)
$$= 81 + 0.9/0.1 (1.9) = 98.1 \text{ units.}$$

To use this forecast of demand to set an order point, it is necessary to first project the demand through the lead time. For example, if lead time is four weeks and the expected demand is 98.1 units, then the demand during the lead time will be 4×98.1 units, or 392 units. To take trend into account in the lead-time forecast, the following formula is used:

Lead time expected demand

$$= \frac{\text{Lead time (lead time} + 1) \text{ (new trend)}}{2} + \text{expected demand}$$

$$= \frac{4 \times 5}{2} (1.9) + 98.1 = 117 \text{ units.}$$

The actual order point is equal to 117 units plus a safety stock that allows for uncertainties of demand (which may be calculated by applying the Poisson distribution discussed in Chapter 10).

Limitations. Exponential smoothing is not a perfect technique for forecasting demand. Like other statistical techniques, it is based on past demand and obviously cannot allow for new and unpredicted changes in demand. In addition, it may help increase inventories because, as was demonstrated in the example, small shifts in weekly demand can be magnified into substantial shifts in order points when trend is taken into account. Despite its weaknesses, however, exponential smoothing is an excellent technique, especially when used in conjunction with electronic data processing to control order points of thousands of low-value C items.

Lead-time change. Exponential smoothing is designed to adjust order points to changes in demand. But order points are affected also by supply. For example, suppose that usage of an item is 100 units per month. If vendor lead time is two months, then the order point must be set at 200 units plus safety stock. If vendor lead time increases to three months, the order point must be adjusted upward by 100 units.

Vendor lead times tend to fluctuate with the business cycle, usually leading it by a few months. Lack of planning becomes obvious when business is on the upswing. Materials managers are repeatedly plagued by stockouts as lead times lengthen. They react by increasing their order points. All too often, these order points are never cut back again when the lead times begin to shorten. At this stage of the cycle, there is no automatic mechanism that forces management to reset the order point.

A control for the order point can be built into an EDP system by having buyers check periodic printouts of vendor lead times. The materials manager can then easily set up controls to assure that order points are adjusted with the business cycle. Otherwise, inventory that creeps into the system because of shorter lead times may be difficult to weed out. There is no automatic forceful reminder of it, as there is when inventories are inadequate. Companies try to keep inventories from creeping up by insisting that suppliers adhere to delivery schedules. If the lead time allowed for an item is five weeks, they may insist that the supplier deliver during the fifth week even if he is quite capable of shipping within two weeks. This policy is not easy to police, however. For example, a company's receiving department cannot always be ordered to refuse all shipments that are more than one week early. The shipment is usually already delivered before the receiving clerk has a chance to check the "due date" on the purchase order. Also, many shipments arrive ahead of schedule at the request of the buyer, and it may be difficult for receiving clerks to distinguish between shipments that are supposed to be early and those that are not wanted.

PERIODIC ORDERING

If a company receives daily or weekly shipments of material, the controls used for order-point systems may break down completely. Inventories will be excessive and records may be misleading. The best solution to the problem may be periodic control or a hybrid sytem that combines periodic and order-point control.

Application

All the inventory systems discussed so far have been order-point systems, in which a certain quantity of material is ordered whenever stocks drop to the reorder point. Inventories are regulated by the period between orders; the order quantity is fixed. Periodic reordering is just the opposite: Inventories are regulated by the quantity ordered, and the period between orders is fixed. In other words, orders are placed at regular intervals for amounts needed to bring stocks up to the desired level.

Necessary conditions. Periodic reordering is commonly used when one or more of the following conditions prevails:

1. The item is ordered frequently and expenditures for it are sufficient to warrant tight control.
2. Inventory balances are determined only periodically, making an order-point system impractical.
3. Many items are ordered from the same supplier, and ordering jointly reduces prices, transportation, or paper work.
4. Usage is discreet or irregular. For example, an item may be withdrawn from stock just one day in a month.
5. The item is purchased in large quantities and requires a substantial percentage of a supplier's capacity.

6. Either price does not vary with quantity purchased or quantity discounts are available even though an order is scheduled for partial shipments.

Periodic reordering is used almost always by companies that make a limited product line in large quantities. For example, it is widely used to control production parts inventories in the automobile and appliance industries. In these industries, where identical products are finished on assembly lines day after day, inventory management is regarded as the regulation of a flow of parts and materials. It is not thought of as a series of additions to and withdrawals from stock, as it is in job-lot systems or perpetual-inventory systems used for nonproduction material.

An example. This flow concept is best illustrated by an example. Suppose an appliance manufacturer has scheduled 10,000 units of a particular model each month and requires a component that is unique to that model. The supplier quotes on the basis of 10,000 units per month but, usually, the purchase order itself does not authorize him to fabricate any parts or buy any raw material. This is authorized by releases from production control that amend the order. A system of releases with periodic ordering limits the buyer's liability for raw materials and finished stock should production be cut back. It also makes it easier to increase orders should requirements temporarily be greater than planned.

Table 9–2 shows the pattern of weekly usage, inventory, and releasing for the appliance manufacturer. In week no. 1, which is several months after the purchase order was placed, the supplier is authorized to ship 2,500 pieces. He had previously been authorized to fabricate two months' usage (20,000 pieces) and buy raw materials for five months' usage. In week no. 2, production control authorizes the supplier to make another shipment of 2,500 pieces, and the supplier has already given the buyer's traffic department the routing and car number for the first shipment, which is in transit.[1]

In week no. 3, the first shipment is received and a third shipment of 2,500 pieces is authorized. In week no. 4, production starts. A stock checker makes a count of stock on hand, and a usage of 3,000 pieces is indicated. Production control notes that usage has been greater than planned because of rescheduling. It warns the supplier but does not increase the weekly shipping authorization. In the following week usage jumps again, to 3,200 pieces, and the shipping release to the supplier is increased to 3,500 pieces in order to build up stocks that are now below normal.

---

[1] Companies that buy identical parts and materials for a number of plants sometimes reroute shipments in transit if shortages develop at a particular plant. Even companies with a single plant like to keep tabs on shipments in transit so they can ask the carrier to trace them if there are any delays.

TABLE 9–2
Material control with a periodic ordering system

	Weekly data					Cumulative data				
Week No.	On hand	In transit	Received	Apparent usage	Released	Fabrication authorized	Material authorized	Released	Received	Used
1	0	0	0	0	2,500	20,000	50,000	2,500	0	0
2	0	2,500	0	0	2,500	20,000	50,000	5,000	0	0
3	2,500	2,500	2,500	0	2,500	20,000	50,000	7,500	2,500	0
4	2,000	2,500	2,500	3,000	2,500	20,000	50,000	10,000	5,000	3,000
5	1,800	2,500	2,500	3,200	3,500	30,000	60,000	13,500	7,500	6,200
6	1,800	3,500	2,500	2,500	2,500	30,000	60,000	16,000	10,000	8,700
7	4,800	2,500	3,500	500	1,500	30,000	60,000	16,500	13,000	9,200

Note: With a periodic ordering system, stock levels are checked and orders placed at regular, predetermined intervals. In this example, suppliers fabricate approximately two months' usage of material and purchase raw material for an additional three months' usage. They then make weekly shipments of the exact amount of material needed.

Since it is the end of the month, the supplier's fabrication and material authorizations are reviewed. No changes in usage are predicted, so the supplier is authorized to buy material and fabricate an additional month's usage of 10,000 pieces. This increases cumulative fabrication authorizations to 30,000 pieces and material authorizations to 60,000, and the supplier continues to have a lead time of two months for fabrication and five months for materials.

During the sixth week, stocks remain unchanged and 2,500 units are received; thus usage is 2,500 units. The following week there is a wildcat strike at the plant, and the stock checker's report indicates that line stocks are up to 4,800 units and usage therefore is down to 500 units. Production control now cuts the supplier back to a shipment of 1,500 units.

Advantages and disadvantages

Note the similarity between the releasing procedure for periodic control and the dispatching system for job lots described in Chapter 8. In both cases, production control tries to keep material flowing to manufacturing at a rate that will keep every machine busy but will not cause excess stocks to be built up. The main difference is that with job-lot control, each order passing through the system calls for a different product; with periodic control, the product is identical.

Safety stocks. Despite the extremely close control it offers, periodic ordering does not eliminate the need for safety stocks. As with order-point systems, some protective stock is needed between the times material is ordered and delivered in order to allow for unanticipated delays in delivery or for extra usage. The process of determining safety stock is not unlike that for order-point systems. Investment in safety stocks can be reduced through application of ABC systems methods. The high-priced A items have the smallest safety stock. Protection against stock-outs is achieved by reducing the period between orders. For example, stocks of A items might be checked for reorder twice weekly, B items every other week, and C items once a month.

Using the ABC approach with periodic ordering, automobile assembly plants make daily checks of stocks of high-priced materials such as engines, transmissions, and major body components, but check stock weekly or even monthly for minor items such as upholstery tacks. The principles of selective control can also be applied to periodic ordering. Suppose, for example, that the time-cycle chart in Figure 9–1 illustrated the lead-time cycle of an assembly controlled with periodic ordering. If the entire manufacturing process were so interrelated (through conveyor lines, automated equipment, and so on) that in-process inventories were automatically regulated, then it would be pointless to control anything but purchased parts and materials. In this case, there would be periodic control of all purchasing lead-time items only. Inventories of other items would always be exactly equal to the space they occupy on conveyor lines and in-process equipment, less any scrap that was generated.

Close control, high cost. Applications of periodic ordering are limited almost entirely to mass production industries, where enormous quantities of a relatively limited number of items must be controlled. Periodic ordering permits such companies to operate with minimum inventories that often are only a fraction of what would be required with order-point control. Periodic ordering also has major disadvantages (which is why its applications are limited). It is expensive to operate, since it requires more clerical manpower than order-point systems do. Also, it usually is not practical unless usage is high or the item is extremely expensive. Otherwise it costs too much, because more frequent ordering can raise both unit shipping costs and prices of materials.

TOP-MANAGEMENT CONTROL

Regardless of the system used, periodic ordering or order point, top managers cannot hope to control the thousands of items in inventory on an individual basis. This is a job for clerks or computers. Management can only hope to control inventories on an overall basis. One of the best ways to do this is through standards used in conjunction with an overall materials plan.

For example, suppose the plan assumes that production and sales will be $1 million per month for the first three months of the year and then will increase steadily to a peak of $1.5 million in June. Obviously some inventory buildup is necessary to accommodate the sales increase. However, it is not necessary to increase inventories in proportion to the increase in output. Plants can operate with higher stock turnover ratios as production increases to near-capacity levels. What happens, in effect, is that materials move through the plant more rapidly when production increases. Thus, the need for in-process inventory may not increase as rapidly as output. Raw-materials inventories may not change at all. The extra demand causes stocks to drop more rapidly to their reorder points. Outstanding purchase commitments would grow, but, if everything goes according to plan, actual stocks of purchased materials would not necessarily increase. In practice, however, they would probably tend to creep up, since stockouts would otherwise become more frequent simply because order points are reached more often.

With a 50 percent increase in sales, it might be possible to get along with as little as a 20 percent increase in inventories of purchased parts and raw materials. Inventories might increase, for example, from $500,000 in January to $600,000 by May 1. Then a drop in inventories to $400,000 might be projected through July. In other words, during the peak production period, management might anticipate cutting inventories if sales are expected to drop sharply when the peak is passed.

Once the plan is agreed upon, managers can maintain control by comparing the standards set in the plan with reports of actual performance. Since it normally takes a rather elaborate study to calculate precisely what inventories are, managers usually maintain control with weekly or daily reports of purchases, receivals, and output, which can provide approximate inventory balances. When these reports indicate deviation from standard, the materials manager investigates and takes necessary corrective action.

Should actual output vary substantially from the plan or should the sales forecast change, the materials manager must be ready to set new standards quickly. If he does not move fast, either there may be shortages or inventories will build up rapidly because of accumulated commitments. Suppose, for example, that sales and production in June are actually $1 million instead of $1.5 million. This automatically means an inventory buildup if there has been no advance warning, since it is impossible to cut back commitments too much within the procurement lead time. The materials manager must then devise a plan to get stocks back in balance. If sales are greater than expected in succeeding months, his problem is solved almost automatically. But if they are less than expected, new purchases may have to be cut back sharply for a number of months before a new equilibrium is reached.

When there are no unexpected changes in either demand or supplier lead times, the inventory management process can be made largely automatic. In many cases, optimum inventory levels can be calculated with a high degree of precision through the use of various analytical techniques. These techniques are discussed in detail in the next chapter.

Cases

CASE 9–1

A problem in order-point control

Suppose you work for a company that controls its inventories on a max-min basis, using perpetual inventory cards. Your company is introducing a new line of products that will result in greatly increased usage of a particular component. You analyze the sales forecast for this new product line and calculate that it will cause demand for the component to rise by about 800 units per month. Naturally, you decide to analyze the history of the component to determine what lead time and order quantities should be. You note the following data on the perpetual inventory card:

Date	Purchase requisition issued	Receipts	Disburse-ments	Balance on hand
1/2				922*
1/7			400	522
1/12	500			
1/29			400	122
2/10		500		622
2/15	500			
3/13		500		1,122
3/16			400	722
5/1	1,000		722	0
5/18		1,000		1,000
5/19			278	722
7/12	500		400	322
8/10		500		822
10/26.			600	222
10/27.	500			
11/18.		500		722
12/12.			200	522

*Balance carried forward.

It is expected that demand for the component will be more regular from the new product than it will be from other products, which will continue to vary erratically as it has in the past. The unit price f.o.b. buyer's plant is $1 in lots of 100 to 499 pieces, 95 cents in lots of 500 to 999 pieces, 92 cents in lots of 1,000 to 4,999 pieces, and 90 cents in lots of more than 5,000 pieces. Normal lead time is four weeks, but in emergencies you can get delivery in two to three weeks by doing a great deal of expediting.

Question

Calculate purchase quantities, safety stock, and order-point quantity, based on the data above.

CASE 9–2. GAMELIN COSMETICS CORPORATION (B)*

Developing a program for inventory reduction

In accordance with its mandate (see Gamelin Cosmetics Corporation (A), Case 1–1) from company president George Katz, the newly formed Materials Task Force first considered the problem of the company's materials management organization. After submitting its report on organization, it then went on to develop plans for inventory reduction. Since Katz had requested that an inventory reduction program be instituted immediately, and, if need be, in advance of any changes in organization that might be made, Harold Roberts, vice president–planning and chairman of the materials management committee, assigned Alfred Hayes, his young administrative assistant, the task of investigating the company's inventory procedures so that the committee could develop specific recommendations for Mr. Katz.

Hayes proceeded to meet with various members of the committee and others in the company on an individual basis to discover exactly how inventories were generated at Gamelin. The process seemed to begin in marketing, where each product manager prepared a quarterly estimate of sales. The forecast at the beginning of one quarter covered sales for the succeeding quarter. For example, each product manager was supposed to have a detailed sales forecast for the third quarter of the year ready for approval before April 1. Occasionally, in the past, top management had raised the product manager's forecast when it felt that marketing was not setting a tough enough target for itself. Usually, however, the product manager's forecast became the basis for production planning without any modification whatever. In addition, Hayes noted that when management had raised the forecast, the new target was not always met; in fact, the product manager seemed to have a better grasp of what sales would actually be than top management, which seemed interested mostly in what sales goals it would like to achieve.

After approval by top management, detailed sales forecasts for the quarter were keypunched and matched with materials usage data stored on magnetic tape in the company's computer. This information was then "exploded" in the computer, which converted end-product sales for the coming quarter into estimated requirements of materials and compounds. For example, suppose each 100 units of product X required 5 pounds of compound Y and each pound of Y required 1.1 pounds of Z. If estimated final demand for X is 100,000 units, then the computer would calculate that 5,000 pounds of Y would be needed during the quarter and this, in turn, would require 5,500 pounds of Z. The usage figures programmed into the computer normally included a 20 percent allowance for "shrinkage" and process losses. For example, the computer would assume that 1.1 pounds of Z was required for each 1.0 pounds of Y even if a finished pound of compound Y actually contained only 0.9 pounds of Z.

The adjusted usage for the quarter was then multiplied by 3 to give a nine-month "reserve requirement." Thus, 15,000 pounds of compound Y and 16,500 pounds of Z would be required. Inventory on hand or already scheduled or committed was subtracted from this total. The difference represented what was to be scheduled for purchase or production during the coming quarter. Theoretically, this policy would result in a 4½ month average inventory of both raw materials and compounds. In practice, inventories are somewhat higher because the company's record system does not permit ready calculation of inventories of compounds on hand or in process at the time the calculations were made. For this reason, they were not subtracted from the nine-month require-ment in calculating the balance scheduled for production.

The computer then calculated a theoretical schedule for the quarter, assigning priority codes to each finished product. The program for setting priority took into account the relative urgency of demand, as indicated by the present inventory position as well as the need to group certain items for manufacturing convenience.

The priority served as a guide to individual production superin-tendents and was not arbitrary. The superintendents freely altered the plan, partly to reflect changes in demand as passed on to them by in-formal contact with the product managers and also because of problems with quality, reruns, and so forth which sometimes occurred. Production also adjusted, of course, to changing availability of material and labor. In practice, no one other than the individual superintendents knew what was being produced at any given time, although, of course, the superin-tendents did produce overall requirements during the quarter. These requirements sometimes changed, almost at the last minute, if large new orders came in. In this case, the superintendent, the production planner, and the appropriate marketing executives worked together on a new schedule.

Hayes noted that New Jersey Research Institute had suggested that inventory carrying cost must be at least 25 percent per year and was probably higher than this, considering Gamelin's extremely high oppor-tunity cost of capital. However, Hayes was able to get nothing more definitive from Gamelin executives than the NJRI rough estimate. Nor did anyone claim to know the true cost of a stockout—although there was universal agreement that the true cost, whatever it was, probably varied rather widely.

The production superintendent agreed that the NJRI estimate of a maximum of $1,900 for setup cost between batches was, if anything, gen-erous. And it appeared that the average changeover cost—exclusive of foregone profit and overhead absorption when the company was operating at capacity—was probably no more than $200. The Flav-Aire Division had developed estimates—which it admitted were very rough—that showed (see Table 9–3) setup or order cost varying between $10 and $300, depending on the type of commodities.

Hayes discovered that 5,000 out of 10,200 items carried in purchased or finished-goods inventories had had no turnover in the past 16 months. However, the dollar value of these inventories was just under $1,000,000, or only about 4 percent of the company's total inventory investment. He gathered from talking with the superintendents that most of this stock represented overruns. Since yield from most of the company's processes varied, it was necessary to schedule consistently a little more than what was actually needed in order to assure that requirements

TABLE 9–3. Flav-Aire Division inventory analysis, February 1969

Inventory group (Annual item usage value)	Items		Total usage		Inventory		Months supply	Order cost ($)	Lead time (months)
	Number	Percent	($000)	Percent	($000)	Percent			
Purchased goods									
Usage ≥ $100,000	28	1.8	8,858	59	2,292	48	3.1	20	1
10,000	150	9.7	4,977	33	1,695	35	4.1	20	1
1,000	294	19.0	1,057	7	612	13	7.0	10	1
100	283	18.3	111	.7	110	2	11.9	10	1
10	213	13.8	9.3	.06	34	.7	43.9	5	½
0	117	7.6	.4	<.01	15	.3	511	5	½
No usage	459	29.7	(-.1)	–	44	.9	–	–	
Total	1,544	100.0	15,007*	100.0	4,802	100.0	3.8		
Purchased goods modified									
Usage ≥ $10,000	4	10	161	75	44	88	2.8	20	1
1,000	12	29	51	24	4	8	.9	10	1
100	7	17	3	1.3	1.6	3.4	6.6	10	1
10	7	17	.2	.2	.3	.6	16.8	5	½
0	3	7	<.01	<.01	.02	.04	80.0	5	½
No usage	8	20	–	–	.03	.06	–		
Total	41	100	216	100.0	49.95	100.10	2.6		
Manufactured goods									
Usage ≥ $100,000	32	4	9,202	61	1,659	40	2.2	300	½
10,000	156	22	5,080	34	1,854	45	4.4	150	½
1,000	181	25	686	5	457	11	9.0	75	½
100	116	16	47	.3	72	2	18.3	35	¼
10	61	8	3	.02	23	.6	92	20	¼
0	40	6	0.1	<.01	2.1	.05	252	20	¼
No usage	141	19	–	–	39	1	–		
Total	727	100	15,018	100.0	4,105	100.0	3.3		
Compounds									
Usage ≥ $100,000	5	.1	1,471	27	358	42	2.9	75	.2
10,000	98	2.2	2,535	47	182	21	.9	50	.2
1,000	356	8	1,096	20	143	17	1.6	30	.1
100	716	16	265	5	66	8	3.0	20	.1
10	803	18	31	0.6	17	2	6.5	10	.1
0	524	12	2.1	.04	7	.8	39	10	.1
No usage	2,005	44	(-6.0)	(-.1)	79	9.3	–		
Total	4,507	100	5,394	100.0	852	100.0	1.9		

would actually be met. In some cases, the leftover material might not be used for many months. When storage space began to get tight, the superintendents would check over this inventory of material, and substantial amounts of these "leftovers" would be scrapped and written off the books.

Hayes discovered at first hand that the company's boast of top service was justified by actual performance. A study of orders—both "rush" and routine—disclosed that 85 percent were shipped on or before the date desired and 99 percent were no more than three days late. When orders did get behind schedule, the most frequent cause was manpower or scheduling problems (42 percent). In addition, 18 percent were purposely delayed for various reasons, and 20 percent of the delays were caused by administrative or equipment problems. Only 14 percent of the order delays were due to lack of inventory.

Total inventory turnover (sales ÷ inventory) had declined slowly in the past five years from a level of just over 2.0 to its current 1.58. Hayes was able to discover no explanation for this, since the company's stocking policies apparently had not changed at all during this period.

Most of the company's operating divisions had not given much thought to inventory. The sole exception was the Flav-Aire Division, which had attempted to group its stocks by value in order to help focus its efforts on possible cost reduction. This study, which also included estimates of setup or order cost, was now almost obsolete, having been made more than a year before, but Flav-Aire's relative inventory picture was believed to still be consistent with it. In addition, it was believed that studies of other divisions would yield roughly comparable data, since there was not that much difference among the divisions either in materials mix or inventory policy—and, for that matter, the divisions relied on common manufacturing facilities.

Question

Based on Hayes's findings, what specific recommendations for changes in inventory policy should the materials management committee make, and what timetable should it propose for inventory reduction?

CASE 9–3. BLUE MOTORS CORPORATION (A)

A problem in periodic ordering

Production and inventory control is not an easy job at Blue Motors, a large auto manufacturer. The company's investment in raw material and in-process inventories exceeds its investment in plant and equipment, and thus it is the company's biggest single asset. Control of production parts and materials inventories is particularly difficult at the company's automobile assembly plants, where the proper components to assemble hundreds of different trim and color combinations of the company's models must be on hand when needed. The company cannot afford to stop its assembly line because of a supply failure. On the other hand, storage space is limited. The company could not carry more than a few days' inventory of such bulky components as engines, radiators, and seat springs even if it were not the least bit concerned about tying up too much of its working capital in inventories.

The company tries to limit inventory investment with an ABC system. It carries less than a week's inventory of the bulky and expensive A items—engines, bodies, transmissions, and similar components. B items normally are limited to about two weeks' stock, and plants may carry as much as three months' stock of C items, although they try to hold it to 30 days' stock.

Blue Motors uses periodic ordering for all production parts and materials. Suppliers are authorized to purchase materials five months in advance and to fabricate two months in advance. Blue Motors stock checkers make periodic counts of material on hand. This information is compared with data on the number of parts that are on order and in transit. The total available supply is then compared with the demand indicated by the production schedule. Suppliers get new production releases each month that authorize them to fabricate and buy material for an additional month's requirements. The ordering and inventory control procedure used by Blue Motors is much like that shown in Table 9–2 on page 319.

The stock checkers use different review periods for different types of item. Any item that is in critical supply is reviewed daily, regardless of its value. Most A items are reviewed daily, B items usually are reviewed twice a week, and C items always are reviewed at least once a month.

Until recently, all of Blue Motors's basic products have been assembled in reasonably large quantities. The company's lowest volume item has been its convertible coupe, output of which has dropped to as low as two units per day at certain of the company's assembly plants. The company's newest product is what its advertising department calls a "customized" sports car. The new product is designed to compete with the sports cars turned out by various European manufacturers. Its price will be about $12,000. The company's marketing strategy is tailored to relatively few buyers who wish to own a high-quality automobile with unique design features. It already has widely advertised that production of the new car will be limited to 200 units per year in order to "protect the investment of its discriminating owners."

Current plans call for assembly of the car at the company's main plant in Detroit. Its production volume is so low that practically all of the components, few of which are interchangeable with the company's other cars, will be purchased. The company's own manufacturing plants prefer to concentrate on the more profitable, high volume components of the company's other products.

Suppliers of major components have been reluctant to accept orders unless they are authorized to fabricate an entire year's requirements in one production run. Since production is limited to only 15 units per day during the period of peak demand, in spring, and will probably drop to 5 units during the slack season, the company's normal ordering procedures for ABC items may not be applicable. For example, a supplier might object to shipping small screws in lots of 50 or 100. Similarly, it would be costly to use a supplier truck to deliver only ten units of an A item like a radiator. On the other hand, the company wants to tie up as little of its valuable factory floor space as possible on the new program. Also, if an item cannot be delivered directly to the assembly line, where there is a limited amount of space, it must be stored in some other area of the plant, and a second handling will be necessary. This would raise costs, particularly for high-volume components.

Question

Recommend an ordering system for Blue Motor's new sports car. In making your recommendations, assume that a radiator is a typical A item, a door handle a typical B item, and a fastener a typical C item.

10

Analytical inventory
control techniques

AVERAGE INVENTORY LEVELS are determined by both order quantities and
safety stocks. Order quantities are influenced by price and ordering
cost. Safety stocks are influenced by certainty of demand and lead time.
Businessmen have applied these principles for years to develop the inventory control systems described in Chapters 8 and 9. These systems
work reasonably well, but they can hardly be described as analytical.

It is only in recent years that the average company has made any
effort to determine quantitatively the safety stocks and order quantities
that yield maximum profits. Modern analytical techniques have taken
much—but by no means all—of the guesswork out of inventory management. No longer need stock levels be determined by habit, hunch, or
accident. Formulas are available to determine order quantities, and statistical probability theory can be applied to determine safety stocks.

Most of the quantitative techniques described in this chapter have
been available for 50 years or more, but it is only since the 1960s, when
computers began to be widely used in materials management, that they
have been applied on a widespread scale. As recently as 1966, a survey
by *Factory* magazine[1] reported that only about half of the participating
manufacturing companies used ABC control (discussed in Chapter 9)

---

[1] "Exclusive Survey Shows New Directions in Production and Inventory Control,"
Factory, October 1966, pp. 105–10. The survey was conducted among members
of the American Production and Inventory Control Society, who presumably would
be more likely to use quantitative inventory control techniques than nonmembers
of the society, since one of the society's basic objectives is to acquaint its members
with modern production and inventory control techniques. Thus a survey limited
to society members would probably imply that application of quantitative inventory
control techniques is more widespread than is actually the case.

and economic order quantity formulas. A mere 10 percent applied probability theory to safety stock determination, and even smaller percentages applied other quantitative techniques, such as those to be discussed in this chapter. In most cases, the reasons for not using them have not been valid ones: ignorance, resistance to change, and the like. Relatively few men and women have been trained in modern materials management techniques. Undoubtedly there will be wider adoption of these techniques when the supply of trained personnel comes anywhere near meeting the demand. However, there is no denying that some companies are thoroughly familiar with the techniques discussed in this chapter but refrain from using some of them because they feel that their advantages are more than offset by their cost, as well as by other disadvantages. Nonprofit organizations have been inhibited not only by indifference and ignorance but also by the fact that rational inventory management requires some assumption of a cost of capital. This is not too difficult for the profit-making organization but can be tortuous for the organization that professes no interest in profit.

DETERMINING ORDER QUANTITY

As we have noted, the bigger the order quantity, the bigger the average inventory investment. A policy of buying in large quantities also has its virtues. Unit prices usually are lower. In addition, the larger the order quantity, the fewer the number of orders that must be processed and the fewer the shipments that need be handled. This reduces costs.

Consequently the materials manager is torn between a desire to keep inventories low by ordering in small quantities and a desire to reduce costs by buying large quantities. The cost of carrying inventories is called "cost of possession," and the cost of purchasing and processing the order is called "cost of acquisition." One of the most important goals in materials management is to strike the most economic balance between cost of possession and cost of acquisition in determining order quantities.

Cost of possession

Many companies estimate that it costs as much as 20 to 25 percent per year to carry inventories; that is, each $1 million in inventory costs $200,000 to $250,000 per year to maintain. There are three major costs of possession: storage, obsolescence, and capital cost.

Storage cost. This is the most obvious inventory carrying cost. It includes rent for storage facilities, salaries of pesonnel and related storage expenses, taxes, and so on. Storage costs vary widely with the type of material stored, type of storage facilities used, and so on. Usually they are equal to at least 5 percent of the value of material stored per year.

Obsolescence. When there are no inventories, there can be no obsolescence. But when many items are stored, it is inevitable that some of them will not be used, will shrink or disappear, or will spoil. Needs cannot be estimated with perfect accuracy, even with the most rigid inventory control systems. Well-managed companies ruthlessly weed out surplus inventory and dispose of it. The general rule is never to hold inventories for which there is no foreseeable need. In fact, companies sometimes dispose of materials even when there is a definite future need for them. If stocks are held long enough, the accumulated carrying charges will exceed their value.

Suppose, for example, that a company has $100 invested in a certain material for which there will be no use for at least two years. Carrying costs are 20 percent a year, or $40 for two years. It pays the company to sell the material immediately if it can find a buyer willing to pay $60 for it. In practice, many companies would be willing to sell the material for less than $60 because they prefer to have capital in cash rather than in inventory, and also because there is always some uncertainty in predicting a need for material a year or more in advance.

Although some obsolescence is inevitable, it cannot be predicted (or it would be prevented simply by not investing in inventory). Therefore a part of the cost of possession is an allowance of "insurance premium" to cover losses from obsolescence. The charge naturally varies widely, but few companies can hold it to less than 1 percent of the value of the inventory per year.

Cost of capital. Inventories tie up a company's most versatile asset, cash. Every business has a limited amount of capital available to it from its owners and creditors. Each tries to use it as efficiently as possible to earn bigger profits. One barometer that shows how efficiently capital is being used is inventory turnover: the ratio of sales to inventory. A company can raise this ratio either by reducing inventories or by increasing sales without a corresponding increase in inventories. In either case, its earnings on investmest are boosted.

Suppose, for example, that a company's sales are $1 million with total assets of $200,000—including $100,000 in inventories. If its profit margin on sales is 5 percent, profits of $50,000 provide a 25 percent return on assets. Inventory is turned over ten times a year ($1,000,000 ÷ $100,000). If the turnover rate can be doubled, the company's sales will be $2 million with the same assets. Profits increase to $100,000 and return on investment is 50 percent.

Capital never is so readily available that it can be invested in inventory at no cost. Were it not in inventory, it could always earn a return at least equal to the interest on government bonds. In many cases, it could get a much higher return.

The "opportunity cost" approach[2] is one of the best ways to estimate the cost of the money tied up in inventory. It assumes that the capital costs whatever it would earn were it invested in the most advantageous alternatives. The minimum opportunity cost is the 4 to 6 percent return the capital would earn if it were invested in short-term securities or used to reduce the company's debt. The maximum can be much higher—even 50 percent or more, if the company is very pressed for cash and has many opportunities to employ capital profitably.

Opportunity cost varies widely not only from company to company but also from year to year (or even month to month) within a company. Because of this, a company's cost of possession can vary widely. In a company subject to wide swings in business, carrying costs can be extremely high at the peak of the business cycle, when there are many very profitable alternative investments available for the capital tied up in inventory. It also can be quite low in a business slump when few investment opportunities are available. When a company's business is seasonal, its carrying costs (with the opportunity cost approach) also will vary seasonally, being very high at the peak of the season and low off season. Inventory management, never an easy job, is almost impossible to perform perfectly when changes in the cost of possession are taken into account.

Cost of acquisition

Despite their desire to use capital efficiently and minimize storage cost and obsolescence, most companies deliberately carry inventories substantially bigger than they need be for protection against stockouts. They do this to reduce their cost of acquisition, since by ordering and buying large quantities they reduce both purchase cost and ordering cost.

Purchase cost. When a company buys in larger quantities, it usually pays lower unit prices. Suppliers will cut prices because their costs are lower when they get a single large order instead of several small ones. Not only are their administrative expenses reduced, but often they also can manufacture in larger lots and reduce unit costs. In addition, the buyer's bargaining power is increased by placing a large order, and it is easier to wangle concessions from suppliers. If the purchased material is fabricated in the company's own plant, costs may also be reduced if the shop gets jobs with long production runs.

Setup and ordering cost. Each lot that is manufactured may require a separate setup. Production equipment is shut down and a skilled mechanic makes necessary adjustments to ready the equipment for the

---

[2] The reader interested in a detailed explanation of opportunity cost and other approaches to capital budgeting should study Joel Dean, *Managerial Economics* (New York: Prentice-Hall, Inc., 1951). This is the classic in the field. There are now dozens of equally articulate competitors that cover essentially the same material.

next lot. There also are costs associated with each purchase—salaries and overhead in the purchasing department; expediting, receiving, and paying for the material; interplant and intraplant transportation; packaging, and so on.

Suppose, for example, a company decides to buy material in two separate lots rather than one big lot. It costs just as much to issue the purchase order for the smaller lot as for the bigger one. Therefore purchase order costs double, since two orders are required to buy two lots. There also is twice as much paper work in the accounting, receiving, and inspection operations. Physically it will usually take more time to handle two smaller shipments than a single large one.[3] And, in most cases, a single big shipment can be packaged more economically and shipped for a lower tariff than two smaller shipments. Thus, the bigger the amount purchased, the lower the unit ordering cost.

Ordering cost is insignificant only with purchases of very high value. The cost of purchasing many small items may be substantially greater than the value of these items. For example, one large corporation made a study that revealed it cost its purchasing department $14.60 for each order it issued and it cost $3.86 to receive and inspect each shipment. High ordering costs make it desirable to carry rather large stocks of low-value items.

Setup costs in manufacturing vary even more widely than ordering costs. In some cases they are almost insignificant. For example, a furniture factory may be able to change the width or length of lumber that is being cut in a minute or two. In contrast, in an automobile factory it may require hundreds of man-hours of skilled labor to install all of the dies needed to make roof panels.

EOQ formulas

Many formulas have been devised to weigh the variables of cost of acquisition, cost of possession, and usage in order to determine the most economic order quantity (EOQ). If usage does not vary much from week to week, the formulas are not too complex mathematically. When the usage pattern is complex, so are the formulas.

No quantity discount. The following formula can be used to determine EOQ when unit price is the same regardless of order quantity:

$$\text{EOQ} = \sqrt{\frac{2 \times (\text{annual usage in units}) \times (\text{order cost in \$/order})}{(\text{unit cost of material in \$/unit}) \times (\text{carrying cost in \%/Yr.})}}$$

Suppose, for example, annual usage of a material is 1,200 units and it costs $10 to handle an order for this material. The price is $1 per

---

[3] The difference varies with the bulk and weight of the shipments. It usually takes nearly twice as much time to handle two five-pound shipments as one ten-pound shipment. But it takes about twice as much time to unload a two-carload shipment as it does a one-carload shipment.

unit regardless of quantity purchased, and carrying cost of inventory is 24 percent per year. Then

$$EOQ = \sqrt{\frac{2 \times 1,200 \times \$10}{\$1 \times 0.24}} = 316 \text{ units.}$$

Quantity discount. If, as is frequently the case, the price does vary with the amount purchased, it is more difficult to calculate EOQ. A separate table for each carrying cost and order cost used is required. It consists of tabulations of total procurement cost (purchase cost plus ordering cost plus carrying cost) for a series of order quantities and annual usages.

Calculations to compile such a table are not difficult to make. For example, assume that a certain material has an annual usage of $1,200 and each purchase covers a three-month supply. With a $10 order cost and a 24 percent carrying cost, total annual procurement cost is $1,276 and consists of the following components.

Purchase cost	$1,200
Order cost (4 orders @ $10/order)	40
Carrying cost (24% of $150)[4]	36
Total annual procurement cost.	$1,276

When these calculations are made for various values of annual usage and order quantities, a table similar to that in Figure 10–1 can be constructed and used to determine minimum annual procurement cost when purchase price varies with quantity purchased. For example, to find the $1,276 total annual procurement cost calculated above, first look at the "value of annual use" column in Figure 10–1 and locate the row for $1,200. Then go across this row to the column for three months' order quantity, which indicates that the total procurement cost is $1,276 when annual use is $1,200 and purchase quantity is equal to three months' usage. This table is valid, of course, only when carrying cost is 24 percent and order cost is $10.

Using the Table. An example illustrates how the table would be used in a real-life purchasing problem. Suppose a supplier has the following price schedule:

Order quantity	Unit price
1–499	$1.00
500–999	0.95
1,000 or more	0.925

---

[4] Note that even though $300 worth of material is ordered every three months, average inventory is $150, not $300. When the order is received at the beginning of the period, inventories rise by $300. Halfway through the period (after one and one half months), half of the order, or $150 worth, has presumably been consumed. At the end of the period, the entire order has been used. Average stock carried during the period therefore is $150, if usage has been reasonably regular.

FIGURE 10–1

VALUE OF ANNUAL USE	1	2	3	4	5	6	7
				TOTAL ANNUAL COSTS (IN DOLLARS)			
				ORDER QUANTITY IN MONTHS' SUPPLY			
$ 100	221	162	143	134	129	126	124
102	223	164	145	136	131	128	126
104	225	166	147	138	133	130	128
106	227	168	149	140	135	132	131
108	229	170	151	142	137	134	133
1,050	1,181	1,131	1,122	1,122	1,127	1,133	1,141
1,060	1,191	1,141	1,132	1,132	1,137	1,144	1,151
1,070	1,201	1,151	1,142	1,143	1,148	1,154	1,162
1,080	1,211	1,162	1,152	1,153	1,158	1,165	1,173
1,090	1,221	1,172	1,163	1,164	1,169	1,175	1,183
1,100	1,231	1,182	1,173	1,174	1,179	1,186	1,194
1,110	1,241	1,192	1,183	1,184	1,190	1,197	1,205
1,120	1,251	1,202	1,194	1,195	1,200	1,207	1,216
1,130	1,261	1,213	1,204	1,205	1,211	1,218	1,226
1,140	1,271	1,223	1,214	1,216	1,221	1,228	1,237
1,150	1,282	1,233	1,225	1,226	1,232	1,239	1,248
1,160	1,292	1,243	1,235	1,236	1,242	1,250	1,258
1,170	1,302	1,253	1,245	1,247	1,253	1,260	1,269
1,180	1,312	1,264	1,255	1,257	1,263	1,271	1,280
1,190	1,322	1,274	1,266	1,268	1,274	1,281	1,290
1,200	1,332	1,284	1,276	1,278	1,284	1,292	1,301
1,210	1,342	1,294	1,286	1,288	1,295	1,303	1,312
1,220	1,352	1,304	1,297	1,299	1,305	1,313	1,323
1,230	1,362	1,315	1,307	1,309	1,316	1,324	1,333
1,240	1,372	1,325	1,317	1,320	1,326	1,334	1,344
19,750	20,068	20,205	20,383	20,570	20,762	20,955	21,150
19,800	20,118	20,256	20,434	20,622	20,814	21,008	21,203
19,850	20,169	20,307	20,486	20,674	20,867	21,061	21,257
19,900	20,219	20,358	20,537	20,726	20,919	21,114	21,310
19,950	20,270	20,409	20,589	20,778	20,972	21,167	21,364
20,000	20,320	20,460	20,640	20,830	21,024	21,220	21,417

Table shows total annual cost for various values of annual use and various order quantities when carrying cost is 24 percent and ordering cost is $10. Total annual cost equals the sum of the value of annual use, the order cost, and the carrying cost.

If usage is 1,200 units per year, the value of the usage is $1,200 at the price of $1.00, $1,140 at the $0.95 price (i.e., 1,200 × $0.95), and $1,110 at the $0.925 price. The table indicates that minimum total procurement cost for a usage value of $1,200 per year is $1,276. This minimum is achieved with a three-month order quantity (i.e., 300 units per order).

With a usage value of $1,140, a company must order at least five months' supply (500 units) to get the $0.95 price. The table shows that total procurement cost is $1,221 with five months' supply and higher still if the company has bigger orders. Similarly, to get the $0.925 price and $1,110 annual usage, it must order ten months' supply at the minimum. In this case, a total annual procurement cost of $1,233 can be calculated readily. Obviously it pays the company to buy in lots of 500 at a unit price of $0.95.

Making EOQ fit the budget

So far, we have dealt only with the applications of EOQ formulas to individual items. They also can be useful tools for top-management control of overall inventory levels.

Suppose that you are a materials manager, and at a meeting of your company's executive committee it is agreed that inventories should be reduced by 10 percent. Your company is short of cash or the committee feels that sales and earnings will drop off sharply in coming months. If you were an old-style materials manager, you might have your staff review every item in stock to see where stocks could be reduced by ordering more frequently, or you might even make rather arbitrary cuts in safety stocks and order quantities.

EOQ formulas permit a more analytical approach. What, in effect, has management decided when it makes a decision to cut inventories? In the economist's jargon, its liquidity preference has increased. It has raised the interest rate on which it bases its investment decisions. This means that the inventory carrying cost in the EOQ formulas should be increased to reflect this higher "cost" for the use of the company's capital.

Suppose inventory is $1,200,000, including a $200,000 safety stock, and that the economic order quantity had been computed with a 16 percent carrying cost. Management wants a 10 percent (or $120,000) reduction in inventory investment without any change in safety stock. This means that the average inventory due to order quantity must be reduced from $1,000,000 to $880,000. It is easy to determine the new carrying cost. From the formulas, we know that order quantity varies inversely with the square root of carrying cost (CC). We also know that average inventory exclusive of safety stock (AI) is determined by order quantity. Therefore,

$$\sqrt{\frac{CC_1}{CC_2}} = \frac{AI_2}{AI_1}.$$

Substituting,

$$\sqrt{\frac{16}{CC_2}} = \frac{880,000}{1,000,000},$$

and
$$CC_2 = 20.6\%.$$

The new inventory policy can be carried out by using a 20.6 percent carrying cost in calculating order quantities instead of a 16 percent cost. The new carrying cost should be used in calculating economic order quantity for all *new* stock items. There is no need to recalculate for items where EOQ was already figured with a carrying cost of 16 percent. As the calculations above demonstrate, the EOQ for the new carrying cost is 80 percent of that for the old. Companies that use electronic data processing systems to control inventories would simply program in the new 20.6 percent carrying cost, and the computer would automatically generate the appropriate order quantities.

EOQ for production parts

The economic order quantity for raw material is usually quite different from the economic lot size for fabrication of that material. Unless the purchasing and production control departments work very closely together, purchasing may buy in lot sizes that are not economic to manufacture. Suppose that the part with the EOQ that is calculated to be 316 units in the example used to explain the EOQ formula is a casting purchased for $1 that is then converted into a finished component, with an additional cash cost of $2. Cash cost of manufacture would include only direct labor and variable overhead. Other costs would not be included in the analysis, since they would be incurred independently of the lot size in which the part is manufactured.

Carrying cost is 24 percent per year, order cost $10 per order, and usage is 1,200 units per year. The purchasing department goes through the EOQ calculations illustrated and comes up with 316 units. Meanwhile, production control (which has its own computer) decides it will get scientific, too. Out-of-pocket machining cost of the part is $2, variable setup cost is $50, and, of course, annual usage and carrying cost are 1,200 units and 24 percent, respectively. Substituting into the economic lot size formula (which is the same as the EOQ formula except that machining cost is used instead of purchase cost and setup cost is substituted for order cost), production control discovers that:

$$\text{Economic lot size} = \sqrt{\frac{2 \times 1,200 \times \$50}{\$2 \times 0.24}} = 500 \text{ units}$$

An independent purchasing department would buy in lots of 316, while the shop would machine the purchased casting in lots of 500. Obviously, one or the other is wrong. What the company should do is consider the purchase and manufacture to be interrelated (which is exactly what the computer program would do). Order cost for the material and setup cost are considered as a single cost totalling $60. Purchasing and machining cost also are added together. Substituting in the formula arrives at:

$$\text{EOQ} = \sqrt{\frac{2 \times 1,200 \times \$60}{\$3 \times 0.24}} = 450 \text{ units}$$

Thus, purchasing should buy in lots of 450—a compromise between the EOQ of 316 units and economic lot size of 500. This seeming conflict is fairly easy to resolve, especially in an organization in which both purchasing and production control report to a materials manager, who can reconcile any conflict of interest. However, EOQ formulas have weaknesses that are not so easy to resolve. As a result, few companies depend entirely on these formulas to determine order quantities, and some very successful firms do not use them at all.

Weaknesses of EOQ formulas

1. *Erratic usages.*   The formulas we have used assume that usage of material is both predictable and evenly distributed. When this is not the case, the formulas are useless. Different, far more complex formulas can be developed for wide swings in usage, so long as those swings can be predicted. But if usage varies unpredictably, as it often does, no formula will work well.

2. *Faulty basic information.*   EOQ calculations are only as accurate as the order cost and carrying cost information on which they are based. It is no easy job to calculate order or setup cost. In practice, order cost varies from commodity to commodity. Carrying cost, as we have seen, can vary with the company's opportunity cost for capital.

Both carrying cost and order cost calculations include elements of fixed and nonvariable costs that would be incurred over the short term regardless of the procurement actions taken. For example, included in a $10 order cost might be an allowance of 40 cents for the share of the purchasing agent's salary that would be allocated to that order, Theoretically, if the company can eliminate an order its costs should be 40 cents lower. But in practice, the purchasing agent's salary would not vary with the number of orders issued; he would be needed even if the company were to reduce its orders (by buying larger quantities) by 50 to 75 percent. Therefore, at least 40 cents (plus all other fixed costs) of the $10 order cost is incurred regardless of whether the order is actually placed or not.

Similarly, the true cash cost of an expensive setup may be negligible. Suppose there is sufficient slack time so that a machine shut down for setup would not be needed anyway. In addition, it is possible that there would be no work for the setup man if he were not used for a particular job. However, the company would not dare lay him off because it needs him for other work on that same day. In this extreme case, the variable cost of a setup could be ignored.

Consideration of fixed and nonvariable costs can result in two different economic order quantities, one for short-term inventory management and another for long term. The former takes account only of cash out-of-pocket costs in calculating costs of possession and acquisition. The latter includes fixed and nonvariable costs. For example, a company's total cost of ordering may be $10 and total carrying cost may be 24 percent, but its cash out-of-pocket costs may be only $2 and 8 percent, respectively. Naturally, using out-of-pocket costs in the formulas gives answers that indicate economic order quantities different from those that result when total costs are used. Which answer is the right one? There is no general agreement on this. However, many cost accountants would say that total costs should be used when one is developing an overall, long-term inventory control program, while out-of-pocket costs give a more realistic EOQ when the formulas are being applied to individual purchases on a short-term or one-shot basis.

3. *Costly calculations.* It is no easy job to estimate cost of acquisition and cost of possession accurately. This requires hours of work by skilled cost accountants. Unfortunately, each major commodity group requires a different study, since the acquisition and possession costs of various commodities can vary widely. Actual calculation of EOQ can be time-consuming even when the simple formulas for steady usage (discussed earlier) are used. More elaborate formulas are even more expensive. In many cases, the cost of estimating cost of possession and acquisition and calculating EOQ exceeds the savings made by buying that quantity. Also, savings often are reduced because the company cannot buy the exact economic order quantity. If that quantity is 176 units, for example, it may have to buy the closest round lot—2 gross or 288 units, for example.

Applications of EOQ

Despite their weaknesses, economic order quantities can be applied to at least part of the purchases of almost every organization. They are particularly useful in companies equipped with electronic data processing equipment, which can eliminate much of the burden of calculation and also enables the use of more complex formulas.

EOQ formulas are particularly suitable for materials that have:

1. *Reasonably steady and predictable usage.* For example, a large insurance company with a stable work force and work load could profitably use EOQ formulas to buy supplies, but they would not be too useful in ordering materials for which demand is erratic.

2. *Relatively low cost.* A manufacturer might profitably use EOQ

for thousands of different supply and maintenance items, which, in the aggregate, account for 10 or 15 percent of his purchases. But he would almost never use it for one or two key raw materials that might account for 50 percent of purchase volume. The high-volume items would get individual attention daily, and order quantities would reflect not only objective information (existing inventories, balances on order), but also subjective opinions on market sentiment, price expectations, and the like. Also, if a material is purchased in large quantities, it often is best controlled if regarded as a flow of material rather than as a series of separate order transactions. It thus becomes suitable for a periodic ordering system. The EOQ approach does not apply, since with periodic ordering the order quantity varies, while the review period between orders is kept constant.

3. *Short lead time.* EOQ formulas are best applied when there is little uncertainty about delivery promises. When lead time is long and delivery is less certain, the order quantity should be adjusted to reflect the materials manager's evaluation of the situation. For example, a company might wish to use EOQ formulas in ordering steel from a local warehouse that offers overnight delivery, but few companies would them in ordering large quantities of steel directly from mills with a lead time of two to three months.

DETERMINING SAFETY STOCK

Average inventory levels are affected almost as much by safety stock as they are by order quantity. Safety stocks are necessary because it is not always possible to predict usages and lead times perfectly.

Figure 10–2 shows a year's usage for a typical item. Total usage for the year was 468 units, or an average of 9 units per week. Actual weekly

FIGURE 10–2

DEMAND BY WEEKS FOR A PURCHASED INVENTORY ITEM							
Week	Demand	Week	Demand	Week	Demand	Week	Demand
1	7	14	6	27	7	40	12
2	16	15	8	28	10	41	10
3	5	16	7	29	11	42	9
4	9	17	5	30	4	43	11
5	13	18	9	31	9	44	14
6	8	19	11	32	7	45	6
7	9	20	6	33	10	46	10
8	1	21	10	34	8	47	12
9	10	22	7	35	11	48	7
10	7	23	11	36	6	49	13
11	8	24	13	37	12	50	11
12	5	25	8	38	8	51	6
13	9	26	9	39	14	52	13

usage varied erratically from a low of 1 unit per week during the 8th week of the year to a peak of 14 units during the 44th week.

Lead time for this item is five weeks, so the order point would be 45 units (the average usage during the lead time) were there no safety stock. With a safety stock of 8 units, the order point would be 53 units. With this safety stock, as Figure 10–3 shows, there may have been one stockout during the year.

FIGURE 10–3

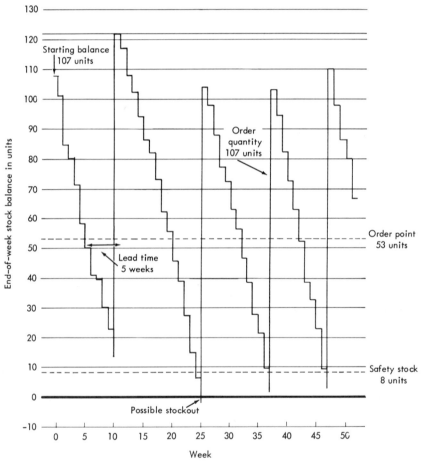

Inventory history of an item with the usage shown in Figure 10–2, a lead time of five weeks, an order point of 53 units, and a safety stock of 8 units.

Applying probability theory

Probability of future stockouts with given safety stocks can be determined by analyzing usage history. The first step is to convert the number of weeks' usage into percentages, that is, one week's usage is about 2 percent of a year's usage, two weeks' is about 4 percent, three weeks' is 6 percent, and so on. The next step is to make a chart in which one axis represents the demand in units and the other axis the percent of weeks in which there was this demand.

Figure 10–4 shows a chart for the data listed in Figure 10–3. Since

FIGURE 10–4

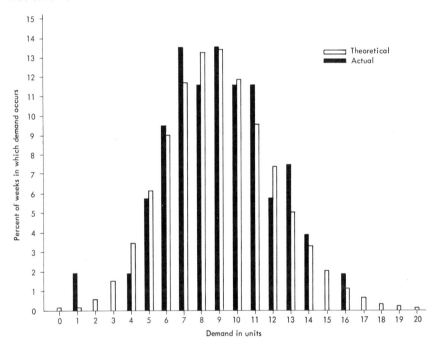

Comparison of actual distribution of demand for an item having the usage history illustrated in Figure 10–2, with theoretical distribution based on Poisson distribution.

one unit of usage occurred during a single week of the year, the chart shows, for example, that weekly demand was one unit for 2 percent of the year (i.e., about one week out of 52); four units per week for another 2 percent of the year; and so on. When actual data is plotted in this fashion, as it is in Figure 10–4, the result is a chart that closely resembles a Poisson distribution, which is also shown in Figure 10–4. This makes it possible to calculate the probability of a stockout with considerable precision, since the characteristics of the Poisson curve are known.

Simplifying assumptions. Real-life inventory managers make other simplifying assumption to make their jobs even easier; they use the normal curve to approximate the Poisson distribution.[5] This assumption makes it possible to apply all the principles learned in an elementary statistics course.[6] Standard deviation can be calculated for each distribution and used to measure the dispersion of the occurrences.

We know, for example, that the distribution in Figure 10–4 has a mean value of 9 units per week or 45 units during the five-week lead time. Suppose, for convenience, that the standard deviation of this distribution is five units. Two standard deviations, therefore, are 10 units. We know from memory[7] that when we move two standard deviations away from the mean of a normal curve we include approximately 95 percent of the area of the curve. That is, 95 percent of all occurrences will have values that fall within two standard deviations of the mean value. Therefore, if the mean is 45 and two standard deviations are equal to 10 units, 95 percent of all occurrences will have values that are at least 35 units and no more than 55 units. The other 5 percent of the values that fall outside the limits of two standard deviations are either less than 35 or more than 55. Since the normal curve is symmetrical, usage is greater than 55 units 2.5 percent of the time and less than 35 units the other 2.5 percent. But, of course, a company would only be interested in periods when it is in danger of running out of stock. This happens only when average lead-time usage is greater than 45 units. Thus, with a safety stock equal to two standard deviations or ten units, it would be protected against stockouts 97.5 percent of the time.

As long as the lead-time usage pattern is almost normally distributed, the company can easily calculate the level of protection it would get with various safety stocks. For example, 15 units of safety stock would give the equivalent of three standard deviations of protection, limiting stockouts to less than 1 percent of all occurrences. Conversely, one standard deviation of protection would embrace only about 68 percent of the normal curve, and roughly 32 percent of the occurrences would fall outside these limits. However, only half of these occurrences would represent usages greater than the mean, so it would expect stockouts on about 16 percent (half of a 32 percent) of its reorders.

Thus, it is easy to see that as long as demand is normally distributed, the amount of safety stock needed depends entirely on the standard deviation of average usage and the number of standard deviations of protection desire. This gives rise to the formula:

$$\text{Safety stock} = K\sigma_x,$$

---

[5] In practice, the two look almost alike. The Poisson distribution resembles a normal curve whose distribution is skewed slightly to the right. Students should note, however, that a Poisson distribution is *not* a normal curve, and one can be a working approximation of the other only in very special cases.

[6] If you haven't taken such a course, the discussion that follows is guaranteed to be confusing. But you can still use the safety stock formula introduced in this chapter without difficulty.

[7] And, if you can't remember, every statistics text has an appendix that includes a table of area under the normal curve from which you can get this information.

where K is the number of standard deviations and σ_x is the standard deviation. If K is equal to 2, for example, and the standard deviation is 5 units, then you would get 97.5 percent protection against stockouts with a safety stock equal to 10 units, as in the example.

This formula can be simplified even further by using the square root of the mean lead-time usage as a substitute for the standard deviation.[8] This eliminates the tedious calculation of the standard deviation with the formula

$$\sigma_x = \sqrt{\frac{\Sigma(X - \bar{X})^2}{N}}$$

Our revised working formula becomes simply:

$$\text{Safety stock} = K\sqrt{\text{Average demand during lead time}}$$

We then construct a table of K values like that in Figure 10–5. The combination of "acceptable average number of years between stockouts" and "order quantity in months' supply" gives us the value of K that

FIGURE 10–5

Acceptable average number of years between stockouts	Order quantity in months' supply											
	1	*2*	*3*	*4*	*5*	*6*	*7*	*8*	*9*	*10*	*11*	*12*
20	2.64	2.39	2.24	2.13	2.04	1.96	1.89	1.83	1.78	1.73	1.69	1.64
15	2.54	2.29	2.13	2.01	1.92	1.83	1.76	1.70	1.64	1.59	1.55	1.50
12	2.46	2.20	2.04	1.92	1.82	1.73	1.66	1.59	1.53	1.48	1.43	1.38
10	2.39	2.13	1.96	1.83	1.73	1.64	1.57	1.50	1.44	1.38	1.33	1.28
9	2.36	2.09	1.92	1.79	1.68	1.59	1.52	1.45	1.38	1.33	1.27	1.22
8	2.31	2.04	1.86	1.73	1.63	1.53	1.45	1.38	1.32	1.26	1.20	1.15
7	2.26	1.98	1.80	1.67	1.56	1.47	1.38	1.31	1.24	1.18	1.12	1.07
6	2.20	1.92	1.73	1.59	1.48	1.38	1.30	1.22	1.15	1.09	1.02	0.97
5	2.13	1.83	1.64	1.50	1.38	1.28	1.19	1.11	1.04	0.97	0.90	0.84
4	2.04	1.73	1.53	1.38	1.26	1.15	1.05	0.97	0.89	0.81	0.74	0.67
3	1.92	1.59	1.38	1.22	1.09	0.97	0.86	0.76	0.67	0.59	0.51	0.43
2	1.73	1.38	1.15	0.97	0.81	0.67	0.55	0.43	0.32	0.21	0.10	0
1	1.38	0.97	0.67	0.43	0.21	0	0	0	0	0	0	0

factors used to calculate the safety stock needed to provide various levels of protection against stockout for items whose usage pattern is similar to a Poisson distribution.

---

[8] This approximation and the others we have made are possible only because mathematical conclusions are only as reliable as their least reliable component. In the case of safety stock computations, this is most likely our underlying estimates of lead time and usage during that lead time. In making them, we assume that what has happened in the past will necessarily occur in the future. But, of course, lead times and usage are affected by many nonrandom factors that we may not be able to identify. Consequently, short-cut computation methods are a lesser error and we need not worry about assuming that something which roughly resembles a Poisson distribution is normal and that the square root of the mean is the standard deviation. As long as the empirical formula works better than anything else available, the mathematical niceties can be overlooked.

is appropriate to an ordering and stockout policy. For example, suppose that a company is willing to suffer one stockout every ten years and that order quantity is equal to a three-month supply. Thus, it orders four times per year or 40 times in ten years and is willing to risk one stockout. This is a stockout rate of 2.5 percent ($\frac{1}{40} \times 100$). The table indicates that the appropriate K value is 1.96. That is, if safety stock is equal to 1.96 standard deviations,[9] usage will exceed the mean value plus the safety stock only 2.5 percent of the time.

Using the Poisson distribution. We can now practice on a sample problem. Assume that a company is willing to run out of stock every two years (why it wants to take any risk at all is explained a little later). The item in the example (Figures 10–3, 10–4) has an order quantity of 107 units and an annual usage of 468 units. Thus orders are placed approximately four times per year, and during the two-year period in which it expects one stockout it risks a stockout eight times, when inventories drop below order point during the order lead-time period. So it expects that one inventory cycle in eight (12.5 percent, or .125) will result in a stockout.

With this probability, $K = 1.15$. We find this in Figure 10–5 by looking up the value for an order quantity of three months and an average of two years between stockouts. Since lead time is equal to 45 units of usage, we substitute in our formula

$$\text{Safety stock} = 1.15 \sqrt{45} = 8.$$

With a safety stock of 8 units, the order point becomes $45 + 8$, or 53 units.

Cost of a stockout. Whether or not eight units is really the correct safety stock depends on whether or not the company can afford to run out of stock once every two years. To find this out, we must determine the cost of the safety stock. If each unit is worth $100, then safety stock increases inventory by $800. If carrying cost is 24 percent, the safety stock costs 24 percent of $800, or $192 per year, to maintain. We could, by similar calculations, determine the protection against stockout and cost of other safety stocks. For example, we could reduce probability of stockouts to one in every 20 years with a safety stock of 15 units. This would cost $350 a year to maintain. Thus, for an extra cost of $158 per year, stockout frequency could be reduced from once every two years to once every 20 years.

Which is the right safety stock? The answer would be fairly easy if a company could calculate precisely the effect of a stockout. Suppose, for example, that a stockout cost $1,000. If there were a stockout once every two years, the annual stockout cost would then be $500; if frequency were cut to once every 20 years, it would be $50. In this case,

---

[9] Which we rounded off into two standard deviations in the previous example.

an extra $158 of inventory carrying cost would reduce average annual stockout cost by $450, and it would clearly pay to carry the extra safety stock.

Correct decision. In real life, the decision is not so easy to make. It depends on both intangible and tangible factors. Each company must study the variables and calculate its own costs. If a stockout costs only a few hours of expediting time to persuade a supplier to shorten lead time by a few days, it obviously pays to keep safety stocks low. If, on the other hand, it means loss of business on an important contract, it may pay to carry very high safety stocks. Materials managers also should consider the profitability of the item and its effect on overall production and customer goodwill when they estimate their willingness to risk a stockout.

In general, managements tend to overprotect themselves against stockouts. All too often they are unwilling to accept the idea that if they want tight inventory control they must be willing to risk an occasional stockout. It takes a courageous materials manager to risk running out of stock when he knows it pays to take the risk. When the stockout does occur, his boss is all too likely to think only of the immediate loss and forget the enormous gains that come from low safety stocks and close control.

Application to ABC control

Probability theory can be applied to ABC systems of control. Representative A, B, and C items are selected. Then cost of various levels of protection can be calculated, using the formula for safety stock, the table of K factors in Figure 10–5, the value of the item, and the carrying cost. Costs of each item can be averaged to get a representative cost of a certain level of protection for the inventory class. Each calculation is then plotted, and the final result is a chart resembling that in Figure 10–6, which is based on a carrying cost of 24 percent. Note that if management decides it is willing to risk a stockout once every five years on all items in inventory, it incurs the following costs:

	Investment in safety stocks	Carrying cost of safety stocks
A items.	$ 620,000	$148,800
B items.	450,000	108,000
C items.	320,000	76,800
Total.	$1,390,000	$333,600

With the ABC approach it is possible to get both greater overall protection against stockouts and lower carrying costs. For example, suppose that management is willing to accept the risk of a stockout once

FIGURE 10–6

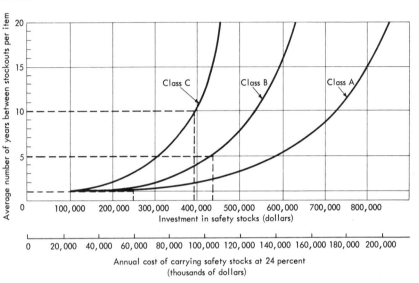

Protection
against
stockouts

a year on A items, once every five years on B items, and once every ten years on C items. Using Figure 10–6, we see that the following costs will be incurred:

	Probable interval between stockouts (years)	Investment in safety stock	Carrying cost of safety stock
A items.........	1	$ 250,000	$ 60,000
B items.........	5	450,000	108,000
C items.........	10	390,000	93,600
Total..............		$1,090,000	$261,600

In this case, the ABC approach permits inventories to be reduced by $300,000 (from $1,390,000 to $1,090,000) and carrying costs are cut by $72,000 per year. Risk of stockout also is reduced. Protection on C items, which comprise 70 percent of the number of items in inventory, is doubled. Protection on B items is unchanged. Only the A items, comprising 10 percent of the total, are more vulnerable to stockout. Since these items get close control anyway—because they represent 70 percent of the inventory investment—their low safety stocks need not pose insurmountable problems.

CONTROL OF PERIODIC ORDERING

Quantitative techniques for controlling periodic ordering systems are similar to those used in order-point systems. Both compare cost of acquisition with cost of possession. The major difference is that order-point systems are governed by order quantities, while periodic systems are governed by order review periods.

Comparison with order point

EOQ and safety stock.   Figure 10–7 shows monthly demand for a purchased inventory item over a two-year period. During this period,

FIGURE 10–7

Month	Demand	Month	Demand	Month	Demand
1	6	9	0	17	5
2	2	10	3	18	6
3	4	11	7	19	5
4	6	12	9	20	8
5	12	13	7	21	9
6	5	14	3	22	4
7	6	15	9	23	3
8	8	16	10	24	7

Monthly demand for a typical purchased item controlled with a periodic ordering system.

total demand was 144 units, and average monthly demand was 6 units. Assume that procurement lead time is one month, carrying cost is 24 percent per year, ordering cost is $10, and unit price is $20. With a conventional *order-point* system, the economic order quantity would be calculated as follows:

$$\text{EOQ} = \sqrt{\frac{2 \times 72 \text{ units per year} \times \$10 \text{ per order}}{\$20 \text{ per unit} \times .24 \text{ per year}}} = 17 \text{ units}$$

With an order quantity of 17 units and a usage of 72 items per year, a company would issue 42 orders over a ten-year period. Now assume that it is willing to risk a stockout once every 10 years. This is roughly one order in 40 or 2½ percent of all occurrences, representing a limit of two standard deviations, giving a K value of 1.96. We already know that average monthly usage is six units and lead time is one month. Therefore, we can use the formula,

$$\text{Safety stock} = K \sqrt{\text{Average lead-time demand.}}$$

Substituting:

$$\text{Safety stock} = 2.0 \sqrt{6} = 5 \text{ units.}$$

The order point would therefore be set at 11 units—the safety stock of 5 units plus the lead-time usage of 6 units. If the company orders in lots of 17, inventory would fluctuate between an average high of 22 units and an average low equal to the 5-unit safety stock.

Periodic system. What would happen if we applied periodic control to the same item? Lead time continues to be one month and, of course, carrying cost and ordering cost remain 24 percent and $10, respectively. With periodic control, order quantity will vary with usage. But we must determine the most economic review period and safety stock.

We will start with review period and temporarily ignore the safety stock problem. A company would need no safety stock, of course, if it knew in advance what lead-time usage would be. So we will temporarily assume perfect knowledge that demand will follow precisely the pattern indicated in Figure 10–7. We will also arbitrarily set the review period at two months.

The company would start a month prior to month no. 1 and order 8 units, which is exactly what is needed in months 1 and 2. In month 2, it would then order 10 units, satisfying demand for months 3 and 4. If we assume it will continue to follow this pattern of ordering every

FIGURE 10–8

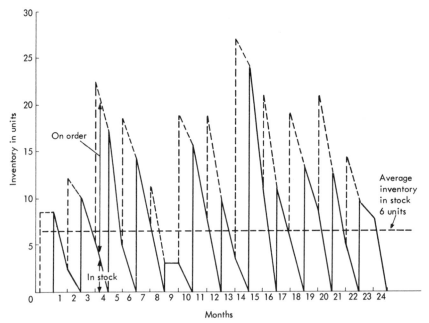

Inventory fluctuations of the item with the demand shown in Figure 10–7, lead time of one month, and review period of two months. Solid line indicates inventory that is actually on hand, while broken line indicates total inventory on hand and on order. For example, at beginning of month 2, there are 2 pieces actually on hand and 12 pieces on hand and on order.

other month and we plot the results, we get a chart like that in Figure 10–8. The dashed lines in the chart indicate the balance that is both on hand and on order at any given time, while the solid line shows the amount actually on hand. For example, the solid line indicates that at the beginning of month no. 2, there were two units in stock. The broken line indicates that an order for 10 units was placed, bringing the balance on hand and on order up to 12 units.

With the two-month review period, the company would naturally order six times per year. Since it costs $10 to issue each order, annual ordering cost would therefore be $60. If we were plotting annual cost for various review periods, this $60 cost for a two-month period would become point *A*, as in Figure 10–9.

Now we can calculate carrying cost. During the two-year period plotted in Figure 10–5, the company issues 12 orders for a total of 144 units. Therefore, average order quantity is 144 ÷ 12, or 12 units. Average inventory is equal to one half of the average order quantity and is therefore six units (which is precisely what it would be with a comparable order-point system). Since unit price is $20, the value of this average inventory is 6 × $20, or $120 Carrying cost is 24 percent of $120, or $28.80 per year. This is plotted as point *B* on Figure 10–9.

Optimum review period

Graphical analysis. Assume that we have gone through similar calculations for a number of other review periods and, in each case, plotted the appropriate annual ordering costs and carrying costs. We then wind up with two curves like the bottom two in Figure 10–9, which show ordering costs and inventory carrying costs for various review periods. The third curve in Figure 10–9 represents the sum of the other two curves. Thus, this curve represents total ordering costs and carrying cost for various review periods. It is plotted by simply adding together the appropriate ordering and carrying costs. For example, point *C* on the curve represents the sum of the $60 value of point *A* plus the $28.80 value of point *B*, giving a total annual cost of $88.80 with a review period of two months.

Review period formula. Inventory carrying costs steadily increase as the review period is stretched out. Conversely, ordering costs steadily decline because fewer orders are issued as the review period increases. Total costs of ordering and carrying inventory first decline and then increase. Obviously, the ideal review period is that which occurs at the point of inflection of the curve. Visually, we can determine from Figure 10–9 that this is equal to about 2.8 months.

Of course, Figure 10–9 is valid only when unit price is $20 ordering cost is $10, carrying cost is 24 percent, and annual usage is 72 units. Other curves must be drawn to determine the optimum policy under other

FIGURE 10–9

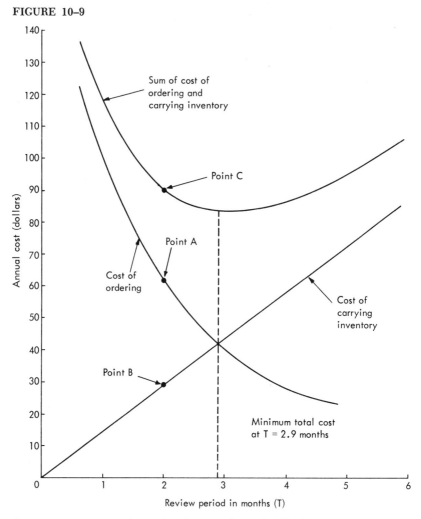

Optimum review period can be determined graphically by plotting total annual cost (purchase cost + ordering cost + carrying cost) for various review periods. It is just under three months for an item with annual usage of 72 units, unit price of $20, ordering cost of $10, and carrying cost of 24 percent.

conditions. Fortunately for those who do not like to draw charts, the same problem can be solved mathematically, using differential calculus. The end product is a simple formula that makes it possible to calculate optimum review period for any ordering cost, annual usage, unit price, and carrying cost. Its only limitation is that, like the EOQ formula for order-point systems, usage must follow a reasonably regular pattern. The formula is:

$$T = \sqrt{\frac{288\,S}{A\,CI}},$$

where:

T = Review period (in months).
S = Variable cost of ordering (in dollars).
A = Annual usage (in units).
C = Unit cost (in dollars).
I = Annual carrying cost (as a decimal).

Using the data in the example, $S = \$10$, $I = 0.24$, $A = 72$, and $C = \$20$. Therefore $T = \sqrt{(288 \times 10)/(72 \times 20 \times 0.24)} = 2.9$ months, which is consistent with our graphic solution.

The optimum review period for an item can change. When sales are high, order quantities will be raised and average inventories will increase. If there is enough change, it may be necessary to reduce the review period between orders so as to have optimum costs. Similarly, the optimum review period is increased when sales fall. The point at which it pays to change can easily be calculated. If a company has two review periods, T_1 and T_2, the point of change comes when carrying cost and ordering cost for the two review periods are equal. Using our equations, this can be done as follows:

$$12\,S/T_1 + T_1\,ACI/24 = 12\,S/T_2 + T_2\,ACI/24.$$

Solving for AC, with the data in our example, we get:

$$AC = 288\,S/T_1 T_2 I.$$

Since $S = \$10$ and $I = 0.24$, then $AC = 12000/T_1 T_2$. Again using the data in the example, $AC = \$6,000$ when $T_1 = 1$ and $T_2 = 2$; \$2,000 when $T_1 = 2$ and $T_2 = 3$; and so on. The result is the following table of optimum review periods for values of AC:

Value of annual use	Review period (months)
$6,001–up	1
2,001–6,000	2
1,001–2,000	3
601–1,000	4
401–600	5
Up to 400	6

Safety stocks

So far we have assumed that the company knows in advance what demand will be, so there has been no need for safety stocks. If demand is uncertain, however (as it almost always is in actual practice), it must protect against stockouts with safety stocks. In practice, most safety stocks used in periodic ordering systems are developed by trial and error. Fluctuations in lead-time usage are not genuinely random, and it may be incorrect to assume that usage follows a Poisson distribution, which, of course, is what we assumed when we developed the safety stock formula for order-point systems previously in this chapter. In many cases, however, these same basic assumptions can be made for a periodic-ordering system, and we can use a similar formula to determine safety stock. The major difference between the safety stock formula used for periodic systems is that the key variable is review period rather than order point or lead time. The formula for determining safety stock with a periodic ordering system is:

$$\text{Safety stock} = K \sqrt{\frac{\text{average usage during}}{\text{lead time} + \text{review period}}} \times \text{average size of demand.}$$

Returning to the example illustrated in Figures 10–7 and 10–8, demand averages six units per month and lead time is one month. If the company uses a review period of three months, average demand during lead time plus review period is 24 units. From Figure 10–5, we see that K is 1.96 if it wants to risk one stockout every 10 years. Then, if all the demands are each one unit, we can substitute in our formula:

$$\text{Safety stock} = 1.96 \sqrt{24} \times 1 = 10 \text{ units.}$$

Order quantity then is equal to the safety stock of ten units plus the average demand during the lead time plus the review period of ten units *less* whatever units are available in stock at the time each order is being placed. Figure 10–10 shows how this system would have

FIGURE 10–10

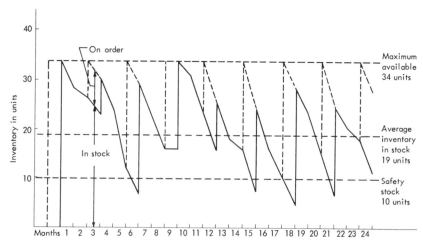

Inventory history of an item with usage history shown in Figure 10–7, review period of three months, and order quantities equal to 34 units less whatever stock is already on hand when the order is placed.

operated during the past two years, using a maximum of 34 (10 + 24) units.

Cases

CASE 10–1. RHODE ISLAND HOSPITAL (B)*

Inventory control in the nonprofit organization

Edward Boudreau, assistant director of the Rhode Island Hospital [see Rhode Island Hospital (A), Case 1–2] has a problem: despite considerable success in cutting inventories, his storage areas are so badly jammed that operating efficiency is being adversely affected. The situation is certain to get even worse before it gets better. The hospital is in the midst of a major expansion program and, inevitably, purchases and withdrawals of supplies from inventory will increase and new items will probably have to be added to stocks.

The hospital will soon be opening a new $22,000,000 day-care center that will draw its medical-surgical supplies from the same stores facilities that serve other buildings in the hospital complex. The main storeroom for medical-surgical supplies covers 4,620 square feet of floor space in the basement of one of the hospital's older buildings. The Materials Management Department has already made the aisles so narrow in this storage area that it is not only impossible to use modern materials-handling equipment, but there is barely room for two persons to pass abreast of one another. Shelves extend from floor to ceiling and are usually jammed with material. It is necessary to rearrange material periodically simply to find space to store new shipments.

The Materials Management Department also has available to it two other warehouse facilities which are not located on the hospital premises but are nearby. One of these facilities is rented for $354 per month and the other for $450. These facilities are used primarily for stationery and other supplies but are available for any overflow of medical-surgical supplies from the main storage area. However, not only is this extra storage space limited, but it is costly to transfer material from one storage area to another.

As indicated in Rhode Island Hospital (A), total inventory of medical-surgical supplies is approximately $100,000 and considerable progress has been made in increasing inventory turnover to its current level of almost 15 times per year. Boudreau is convinced that there is very little "fat" in this inventory. Physical counts are taken of each item every time it comes up for reorder and these are checked against the balances

* Copyright © 1973, Bureau of Business and Economic Research, Northeastern University, Boston. Research for this case was supported by Grant No. HS 00844 from the National Center for Health Services Research and Development.

indicated by the computer. Furthermore, the computer selects 15 items at random once a month for an additional physical check. These periodic comparisons of actual physical balances with theoretical balances generally indicate there is relatively little room for further improvement.

The computer also produces a quarterly inventory aging report which indicates which items are slow moving and which are nonmoving. The latter are often sold back to the original supplier; otherwise, they are disposed of for the best price the Purchasing Department can obtain. Nonmoving items are no longer really a problem. The most recent report showed a balance of but $200.

Slow-moving items are inevitable because of both changing technology and changes in preferences of requisitioners. However, Boudreau doubts if any additional major improvements can be made in detecting such items and readjusting order points much more promptly than is already being done.

Physical congestion in the storage area is also reduced to an absolute minimum as a by-product of the Materials Management Department's PAR delivery system. In order to reduce congestion in hospital corridors and elevators, supplies are delivered by materials management to the various nursing stations between 11 P.M. and 7 A.M. This not only speeds up the process, thereby cutting labor cost, but causes most withdrawals from stores to be made during periods of the day when stocks are not being replenished with new purchases from the hospital's suppliers.

While Boudreau would love to build a new facility with up-to-date materials-handling equipment, his plan is not without obstacles to be overcome in convincing the hospital administration and trustees that it absolutely must have one. Unlike most similar institutions, the Rhode Island Hospital is well financed from endowment funds and does not need to borrow funds for new construction. If it were to borrow, however, Boudreau guesses that 6 or 7 percent might be an appropriate interest rate. While no formal estimates have been made, it is reasonable to estimate that a 20,000 sq. ft. stores building would cost at least $500,000—and possibly much more if it had architectural features comparable to the other new buildings in the Rhode Island Hospital complex.

Land would be a problem even if the hospital were willing to construct a new stores building. The ideal facility would be interconnect with other buildings in the hospital complex, and there simply is no convenient space available. Nor can additional land be purchased easily. The hospital premises are surrounded by old, privately owned buildings on small plots of land. Since the hospital is a private institution, it cannot acquire surrounding property by eminent domain. This makes it difficult, if not impossible, to acquire major plots of adjacent land rapidly, even at inflated prices.

Other hospitals have "solved" the problem of inadequate stores areas by leasing a central warehouse at some distance from the hospital. The cost of this space might be $3 per square foot per year. In addition, the hospital would have to invest in at least one truck whose operating cost, including drivers, might run at high as $15,000 per year.

Boudreau is presently pondering whether or not he should recommend some new stores facility to the hospital's administration and trustees. He has discovered that repairs, maintenance, and operation of the building in which the present storeroom is located run about $124,000 per year. This building has 55,000 square feet of floor space, of which 4,600 square feet in the basement are used to stored medical-surgical supplies. No one really knows how much of the total expenses of $124,000 for the building should be allocated to materials management, although accountants tend to allocate such costs on the basis of square feet of space utilized. It should be noted, however, the basement space in a commercial building is always cheaper than space above ground.

The hospital calculates depreciation on its equipment to help determine which costs are reimbursable by Blue Cross–Blue Shield and other agencies but does not take depreciation into account on its older facilities. As a nonprofit organization, the hospital pays no taxes but does pay insurance premiums which, allocated to materials management, apparently amount to about $430 per year.

Obsolescence and shrinkage are reduced substantially as a result of the extremely close control that is maintained over inventories. No estimate has ever been made, but losses are probably less than 1 percent.

At present, both order points and purchase quantities are determined largely by judgment. The former is determined primarily by lead time and past usage and the latter by price breaks as well as by a desire to achieve maximum inventory turnover. Since the computer now makes it feasible to perform the needed calculations, Boudreau has been considering adoption of some sort of economic ordering procedure. He does not actually know the marginal costs of ordering and storing material, but the hospital's accounting system does provide average cost data. In addition to the overall costs of repairs and maintenance to the building in which it is located, the stores activity has an annual budget of $113,971, of which $105,551 is represented by salaries for 11 employees. The related receiving function, which occupies 1,675 square feet of loading dock and "break-out" area adjacent to the 4,600 sq. ft. main stores area, has a total budget of $38,000, of which $34,000 is represented by salaries for four employees. However, only about 15 percent of the 38,000 receivals that are made each year are for medical-surgical stores. The others are either noninventory or go to other storage areas in the hospital complex.

The Purchasing Department has total annual direct costs of $75,233, of which $66,275 is payroll and, as with receiving, approximately 15 percent of all purchase orders issued are applicable to medical-surgical stores. Similarly, accounts payable, with six employees, has total annual direct costs of $45,000 and, of course, 15 percent of the orders it processes are applicable to items carried in medical-surgical stores.

Questions

1. Does Boudreau have sufficient information on carrying cost and ordering cost to use EOQ formulas?
2. Suppose that Boudreau's rough estimate of $500,000 for a new stores building turns out to be correct and that land adjacent to the hospital's other buildings becomes available. How would Boudreau go about justifying a request to the hospital's administrator and trustees for funds to construct the building?

CASE 10–2.   OWEN ELECTRIC COMPANY (C)

Applying formulas to periodic ordering systems

Owen Electric Company (see Cases 7–2 and 7–3) controls inventories of hardware used on its assembly line with periodic ordering. Weekly reports from stock checkers are sent to appropriate buyers, who post them to their records and periodically issue orders to bring stocks up to the required balance.

For example, the company uses about 10,000 pieces of a small screw machine part each month. On the 15th of each month, the buyer looks at his latest stock report and issues an order for a quantity sufficient to bring the inventory balance up to about 15,000 pieces when the order is delivered. Thus, if the stock checker's report indicates an inventory of 12,000 pieces and estimated usage during the 30-day lead time is 10,000 pieces, the buyer will place an order for 13,000 pieces. Should the next month's inventory rise or the usage forecast drop, he would adjust the order quantity accordingly. For example, he would order only 9,000 pieces with a 30-day usage projection for 8,000 pieces and a current stock of 14,000 pieces.

The unit price of the part purchased in quantities of 5,000 to 10,000 is $.10. But the supplier is willing to cut the price to $.095 if he gets orders that average 20,000 pieces. Owen Electric's controller estimates that it costs $10 to make each purchase, and the carrying cost of inventory is 24 percent.

Questions

1. Should Owen Electric take advantage of the supplier's offer?
2. What is the company's most economic order period if the supplier's price does not vary with order quantity?

11

Sourcing: Make, buy, or lease

THEORETICALLY, a company has a choice of three basic decisions in sourcing a new product. It can:

1. Purchase the product complete from a contract manufacturer.
2. Purchase some components and materials and manufacture and assemble the balance in its own plant.
3. Manufacture the product completely, starting with the extraction of basic raw materials.

In practice, almost no companies can seriously consider the third alternative. Even relatively simple products require an amazing diversity of materials in various stages of fabrication. The largest, most highly integrated companies rely on outside suppliers for at least some components and materials.[1] And some companies choose the first alternative and obtain a new product completely from an outside supplier. They usually do this either because they are a merchandising or engineering organization with no manufacturing facilities or because the product is not suited to their facilities. Sears, Roebuck's purchases of its own brands of appliances are a good example of the former; a business-machine maker's purchase and resale to customers of special forms to use in its machines is an example of the latter.

---

[1] For example, the U.S. Steel Corporation spends about a third of its sales dollar for outside purchases, even though it has completely integrated steel-making facilities and also mines its iron ore, coal, and limestone. Ford Motor Company makes all major parts of its automobiles and much of the raw materials used in making them, including steel, glass, and so on. Yet Ford spends about half of its sales dollar on outside suppliers—more than twice as much as it spends on wages and salaries.

The general rule, however, is that an organization will make some things and buy others. This applies even to service organizations. Large hospitals, for example, often operate their own print shops and laundries but are purchasers of food, drugs, and numerous other items. Both service organizations and manufacturers sometimes generate their own electric power. They may even carry on service or manufacturing activities having nothing to do with their basic business, either because they happen to have the raw material or because the activity simply was not being performed by anyone else.

For manufacturers, make-or-buy decisions must constantly be made. No manufacturer makes all of his own raw materials, so it is largely a matter of deciding at which stage of fabrication a component should be purchased. The company may buy a component complete from an outside supplier, buy it semifinished, or buy the raw material.

MAKE-OR-BUY CRITERIA

Companies usually prefer to do their own fabricating. They buy only raw materials or semifinished parts in cases where the following is true of the finished component:

1. Can be made more cheaply by the company than by outside suppliers, or might require the company to rely on a limited number of vendors for its supply.
2. Is vital to the company's product and requires extremely close quality control.
3. Is readily manufactured with the company's existing facilities and is similar to other items with which the company has had considerable manufacturing experience.
4. Requires extensive investment in facilities that are not already available at supplier plants.
5. Has a demand that is both relatively large and stable.

Companies will usually buy a finished component from an outside supplier when:

1. They do not already have facilities to make it, and there are more profitable opportunities for investing company capital.
2. Existing facilities can be used more economically to make other components.
3. The skills of company personnel are not readily adapted to the making of the component.
4. Patents or other legal barriers prevent the company from making the component.
5. Demand for the component is either temporary or seasonal.
6. The supplier can utilize economically specialized equipment to make

the product by grouping orders from several customers, and demand is not so great that any individual customer could economically utilize this equipment.

Other factors. Some companies, by tradition, prefer to make almost every component of their products. Others prefer to buy as much as possible from outside suppliers. In general, an aggressive company in an industry that is expanding very rapidly with many technological changes (e.g., electronics) will prefer to buy many of its components from outside suppliers. In such industries, the company has many opportunities to employ its capital profitably through horizontal diversification—expanding its line of finished products.

A company in a stable or declining industry, on the other hand, has fewer attractive opportunities to invest its capital in expanding sales of its end products. It will be attracted, almost by default, to integration—making a bigger share of its sales dollar in its own manufacturing plants—in order to boost profits.

For example, the major auto companies have steadily increased the percentage of product that they make in their own plants. In most cases, they have been tempted to make the items that yield high profits to suppliers. Both Ford Motor Company and Chrysler Corporation have built plants to manufacture automobile glass, but it is no coincidence that neither has shown any signs of building textile mills to make upholstery cloth for cars. Efficient glass producers earn about a 20 percent return on their investment, while in the highly competitive textile industry even efficient producers consider themselves fortunate if they average a 10 percent return.

A company may be effectively prevented from making an item by its own labor relations policies. If it is extremely generous with wages and fringe benefits for its employees, there will be some industries where it simply is not competitive even if its methods are better than those of potential competitors. For this reason, if no other, a high-wage employer like IBM or Eastman Kodak could probably never earn even modest profits in the low-wage textile industry. And it is far cheaper for the highly unionized auto companies to buy certain items from nonunion suppliers than to attempt to make the same items themselves.

Cost comparison. When a company decides to make an item that it has been buying, it always eliminates the supplier's sales expenses and usually eliminates some freight costs. If its production costs are identical to those of the supplier,[2] the company also gains the supplier's profit and usually at least part of the fixed overhead expenses incurred by the supplier.

---

[2] Of course, few suppliers will give their customers detailed cost estimates, particularly if they think the buyer plans to use them for a make-or-buy study. However, it sometimes is possible for a buyer to estimate supplier cost quite accurately, using techniques discussed in Chapter 16.

Suppose a supplier had the following unit cost on a component:

Direct material	$.20	
Direct labor	.10	
Variable overhead.	.12	
Direct cost.		$.42
Fixed overhead	$.08	
Manufacturing cost.		.50
Sales expense	$.02	
Administrative expense.	.01	
Total cost		.53
Profit.	$.06	
Supplier's price		.59
Inbound freight	$.01	
Buyer's cost.		$.60

If a company were to make this item rather than buy it, it could conceivably reduce its costs from 60 cents per unit to 42 cents. This might be true if the company has idle equipment that could be used to make the part and if its only additional overhead expenses would be covered by the 12 cents allowance for variable overhead in the unit-cost estimate. Even if the company had to invest in additional facilities and incur normal fixed overhead, its cost would presumably be only 50 cents per unit if it could use the facilities as economically as the supplier.

Savings sometimes illusory. Companies often are confronted with opportunities to make rather than buy that yield theoretical savings comparable to these. In some cases they try to take advantage of them. But they often continue to buy the item even though they may be capable of making it. In most cases it is not to their advantage to make the item for a number of reasons, including:

1. The company's direct costs may be substantially higher than the direct costs of the supplier. The supplier presumably is one of the most efficient producers of the item and has achieved his existing costs only after management and labor have acquired considerable experience. And even if the buyer can produce as efficiently as the supplier, his saving will be reduced by start-up cost. No company can immediately produce a new item at peak efficiency; costs on initial production runs are always well above standard.

2. A company has less flexibility with "make" items. It can easily change suppliers if it wishes to redesign the item so that it makes use of different materials. This can be expensive if the company has invested in equipment to make the item. Similarly, the company can exploit changes in market conditions on "buy" items and take advantage of lower prices offered by suppliers eager for new business.

3. Savings in overhead often are illusory. Fixed overhead rarely

rises immediately after a company starts using idle facilities to make a part it has previously purchased, but eventually it creeps up. When business expands to capacity operations, fixed overhead increases and must be absorbed by each component that is produced. Similarly, if business slumps, fixed overhead is underabsorbed, and unit cost rises. For example, the eight-cent allowance for fixed overhead in the preceding cost breakdown is valid only for a given volume. If business dropped 50 percent, the allowance would have to be doubled, to 16 cents. If the part were purchased from an outside supplier, he also would have difficulty absorbing fixed overhead when volume declines.[3] But he would not dare try to recoup the added unit costs by increasing prices. In fact, competition might become so intense during a slump that he would be forced to cut prices.

4. There may be better profit opportunities in other areas. Each "make" part requires some investment in facilities, inventories, and top-management time. Even though this investment is profitable, the company may be able to earn even bigger profits by using its resources to expand the business it knows best—its end-product line.

Buy instead of make. Often companies decide to buy items that they have been making. In some cases they even dispose of plant and equipment used to make the item. Such decisions are almost always economic if the supplier's price is lower than the company's direct cash cost of making the part.[4] Sometimes they are worthwhile even if the company has been making substantial profits on the item, for it may be able to use its resources still more profitably on other items.

Similarly, when a company's facilities are temporarily taxed beyond capacity, it may decide to buy part of its needs from an outsider supplier. For example, a company with a captive foundry may temporarily buy part of its castings from outside suppliers when business is exceptionally good. Even if the prices of the purchased castings are higher than the company's own costs, the company may not wish to increase its investment in foundry facilities when the need for them may be temporary. When business drops off, the company can return to making all its own castings and need no longer rely on an outside supplier.

Companies that follow this practice may incur the resentment of suppliers who get orders from them when business is good and they need them least and then lose the orders when business is bad and they need them most. Suppliers may not cooperate when the company wants to

---

[3] If the supplier successfully diversifies his business, he might not be badly hurt if customers in a single industry have a bad year. For example, a manufacturer of fasteners may supply dozens of industries. If business from one industry dropped off but other industries suffered no setbacks, the effect on the fastener supplier might be insignificant.

[4] Provided that the supplier's price is not just a temporary bid to get the business and will not be increased at some later date.

subcontract again.[5] In addition, their ill will may have an adverse effect on the company's sales. Either the supplier may also be a customer, or he may "knock" the company and its products to his own suppliers and customers. Ethical materials managers never try to convince suppliers that business is permanent when they know it will move back into the shop as soon as capacity is available to handle it.

Split items. A company may simultaneously make and buy certain materials and components. For example, Ford Motor Company makes part of the steel for its cars in its own steel mills and buys the balance from independent steel producers such as National Steel Corporation. When a company does this, it enjoys most of the advantages of making without losing the advantages of buying. Its profits from making the item can be calculated precisely because there is an exact market price from the outside supplier. The company is protected, at least partly, against strikes at the supplier's plant or other supply failures. It enjoys the benefits of both its own and the supplier's improvements in technology. In addition, when a company has its own facilities to make an item, a supplier may hesitate to increase prices because his costs of production can be precisely estimated and the captive plant stands ready to take a bigger share of the business if it becomes profitable to do so.

A company often can reduce its average costs by buying part of its requirements and making the balance. The captive facility then can operate near capacity almost regardless of business conditions. When business is good, the supplier may make 50 percent and the captive plant 50 percent. When business is bad, the captive plant's production remains steady despite the decline in demand, and its share may increase to 80 percent or 90 percent, while the outside supplier feels the brunt of the business decline. His share drops to 10 or 20 percent of the business, and his actual output drops by an even greater amount. Needless to say, suppliers are not happy when they are asked to bear more than their share of a business slump, and sometimes they demand a contract providing that the percentage split be fixed regardless of general business conditions.

CONTROLLING CAPTIVE ITEMS

When a company makes and buys the same item, it knows precisely how competitive its manufacturing operations are. Ideally, every com-

---

[5] Apparently this is rarely true in practice. A survey by *Purchasing* "Does the Trend in Make or Buy Decisions Follow Market Conditions?" December 1954, p. 71) indicated that 81 percent of the purchasing agents responding did not believe that making items when business was bad and there was overcapacity had a sufficiently adverse effect on vendor relations to be a handicap when a company's capacity was overtaxed in the future and its purchasing agent tried to buy the same items once again in a tight "seller's" market.

pany would like the cost of each of its operations to be as low as those of the most efficient outside producer. The materials manager can render his company a real service by devoting a substantial amount of effort to locating shop items whose costs are higher than those of leading suppliers.

Stimulate improvement. When captive manufacturing operations are not subjected to outside competition with frequent make-or-buy decisions, they may become complacent and inefficient. Their methods may not be up to date; they may be lagging in productivity, and their costs may be much higher than those of efficient outside producers. When this happens, the company's overall competitive strength can dwindle.

Suppose, for example, that one company making finished electric refrigerators were to attempt to make all of its components from basic raw materials, while a competitor elected to manufacture parts only when it could do so at substantially lower cost than it could obtain from outside suppliers. If the captive manufacturing operations of the integrated company had costs that were higher than the market prices paid for parts by its competitor, then its total product costs would be correspondingly higher. Its profits would be less despite its greater investment in facilities that would be needed to make all components.

All well-managed companies try to keep their manufacturing facilities up to date. They also try to keep costs under control with budgets and the like. If the component itself is not sold directly to a customer but is incorporated into one of the company's products, however, it never faces the acid test of market competition. The materials manager can help manufacturing simulate such competition by periodically reviewing various items made in captive operations to make certain that their production costs do not exceed market prices.

Decentralize buying. Big companies go even further. They have decentralized organization structures in which one division may sell all of its output to one or more of the company's other divisions. For example, Ford Motor Company's Engine & Foundry Division sells its auto engines to the Ford Division, which is responsible for assembling cars and trucks.

In such a decentralized structure, the buying division (which is the unit responsible for the end product) treats the manufacturing division as much as possible as an outside supplier in order to simulate conditions in a competitive market. In some cases it can do this rather directly. For example, if the supplying division makes a product that the using division is also buying from an outside supplier, the market price is known. Similarly, if the manufacturing division makes something for which there is a published market price (steel or crude oil) it is not difficult to set a realistic market price.

Simulate competition. A problem arises when the captive operation makes a product that is unique and for which quotations are not readily available from outside suppliers. For example, the Fisher Body Division of General Motors makes body stampings that are shared by all GM cars. No outside supplier is equipped to make these bodies in the quantities required by General Motors, nor would it ever seriously consider buying any major part of its body stamping needs from an outside supplier, because of its enormous investment in Fisher Body's facilities. Under such circumstances, the best the materials manager can do is to simulate market conditions for the captive operation. He can vigorously negotiate with the captive plant to get it to price its output at a level he feels would be competitive if alternate suppliers were available. In negotiating, he uses all of the cost analysis techniques that will be discussed in succeeding chapters.

Some materials managers spend a great deal of time on intracompany purchases from manufacturing plants. Why do they go to the trouble? After all, if a buying division persuades a supply division of the same company to reduce its prices by $1, the two divisions are just trading dollars. The buying division's profits go up $1 because of the lower price; the supplying division's profits decline $1. The net effect on overall company profit is nil.

Realistic profits. One reason big companies go to such trouble is that they feel their manufacturing divisions will be more efficient in the long run if they are subject to as much competitive pressure as the materials manager can exert. Another equally important reason is that a company can calculate realistic profits for an operation only if its output is priced at market levels. If a plant whose prices are competitive does not earn adequate profits, either its management is at fault or it is in the wrong business. With realistic profit figures, a company can measure its managers' performance and also can direct new investments into areas that yield maximum profits.

Suppose, for example, that a television manufacturer makes his own cabinets. Each televison set costs $135 to make, and the company sells them to distributors for $150. Therefore the company makes $15 profit on each TV set, or 10 percent on sales.

If the company's cost of making each cabinet is $13.50, how much profit is the company earning by making its own cabinets? An amateur accountant might say that since the company is earning a 10 percent profit on each set it must automatically be earning 10 percent on each major component. But the fact is that it would be impossible to say whether the company's cabinets operation is profitable or not, since the company sells no cabinets. Possibly the company is producing a cabinet worth $30 for a cost of only $13.50. In that case, it should expand its cabinet line to supply outside companies and go out of the TV set business itself. Or, as is more likely, the cabinet that costs $13.50 may be available from a specialist producer for $14. In that case, the cabinets, with a return of less than 4 percent on sales, are eating into the company's profit margin. If the company can dispose of its cabinet plant and invest the proceeds in a more profitable part of the business, it can boost its overall profit margin.

Opportunity cost. The materials manager is the natural link between a company's own manufacturing operations and competitive operations of outside suppliers. Ideally, he should be constantly prodding manufacturing to make items he is currently buying, if these items are potentially profitable. At the same time he should be working to take items out of manufacturing that do not belong there.

The materials manager's basic yardstick for make-or-buy analysis is the company's own opportunity cost of capital. This, of course, represents the return that the company should be able to earn on new investments. For example, a company that consistently earns a 15 percent return on its net assets probably has an opportunity cost of capital of about 15 percent.

The higher the opportunity cost, the more limited the company's ability to make things instead of buying them. For example, a highly profitable company with an opportunity cost of 30 percent or more would find it profitable to buy almost every component of its end product. The reason, of course, is that it is impossible to earn this sort of return in most businesses, and the company's own suppliers would have to settle for lower returns. Conversely, a company in a declining industry with declining opportunity costs and huge cash flow might be a lot less fussy and settle for a lot less.

LEASING

Companies with very high opportunity costs of capital often prefer to lease many of their assets. For example, a company that earns 20 percent on its own capital might prefer to lease a fleet of cars for its salesmen rather than buy them. The leasing firm might be willing to settle for a 10 percent return on capital. Consequently, even if the company could buy, sell, and maintain cars as efficiently as the leasing firm, its opportunity cost of capital would be so much higher that it would perfer to delegate the job to the leasing firm.

Leasing has grown enormously in popularity in recent years. A survey[6] showed that 71 percent of the manufacturers participating leased capital equipment. Respondents also mentioned the types of equipment they leased. Office machines were most popular, with 31 percent of the mentions. Also mentioned were transportation equipment (23 percent), materials-handling equipment (18 percent), machine tools (17 percent), and other machines and equipment (11 percent).

---

[6] "Does Industry Lease Capital Equipment?" *Mill and Factory*, July 1960, pp. 73–74.

Advantages. Companies that lease do so both to avoid the responsibility of ownership and to make capital available for other purposes. They prefer to lease certain highly specialized types of equipment because they need not worry about its maintenance or possible obsolescence; all they need do is operate the equipment, with none of the responsibilities of owning it. In adddition, a company gets some tax advantage by leasing. Rent can always be charged entirely as an operating expense and thus is completely deductible from taxable income.[7] On the other hand, if a company owns equipment, it must capitalize its cost. Depreciation charges deductible as operating expense must be spaced over the life of the equipment.

In some cases the lessor may be willing to pay for the lessee's tax privileges. Capital-intensive industries like airlines frequently generate more investment tax credit and accelerated depreciation than they can profitably use in reducing their own tax liability. One solution is to sell new equipment to third-party lessors who can make better use of the investment tax credits. The airline then leases back the equipment and enjoys the advantage of a financing scheme that does not increase the amount of debt on its own balance sheet.

Except when there is an extraordinary tax break, the lessee must pay for these advantages. The rent he pays not only includes an adequate amount to cover probable maintenance, depreciation, taxes, and other expenses but also a healthy profit for the lessor. Typically, a lessor might allow for a 10 percent return on his investment in calculating his rent. The return would be higher yet on equipment on short-term lease that is subject to high obsolescence, and it would be lower on buildings with very long-term leases.

Why then do most insurance companies and banks prefer to lease electronic data processing equipment when they are eager to make an investment with a guaranteed return of 5 to 6 percent? Such institutions rarely want to own this equipment. Its maintenance is much too costly and too highly specialized for them. When equipment is leased, the supplier must fix it if it breaks down. In addition, EDP equipment is subject to rapid obsolescence. This need not worry the lessee; he does not have to get rid of the old equipment when new models are developed or his needs change.

Companies also lease solely to use capital for other purposes. In some cases, they may even sell and lease back assets to get what amounts to a loan that is not shown as a liability on the balance sheet. For example, a company might sell one of its buildings to an insurance company and then sign a long-term lease for its use. The building be-

---

[7] In the writer's opinion, many businessmen have been oversold on the tax benefits of leasing equipment. Taxes are lower because profits are lower, since leasing in most cases costs more than owning. It is rarely good business to reduce profits simply because the government gets its share through the corporate income tax.

comes the equivalent of collateral on a loan for the insurance company, and the lease includes a rent sufficient to cover depreciation of the property over its life as well as a return on investment. Sale and lease-back is desirable when the company either cannot raise money more cheaply with a direct loan or does not wish to impair its credit standing by having a loan show on its balance sheet, or it can make a larger profit on the proceeds from the sale of the asset than the return it gives the lessee in rent.

In the past, companies could also reduce financing costs substantially through sale and leaseback from municipalities in which their facilities were located. In order to encourage the company to build its plant and provide employment, a city would become legal owner of the plant, financing it with tax-free municipal bonds issued on the strength of the company's long-term lease of the facilities. This permitted the company to get financing for perhaps 4 or 5 percent instead of the much higher interest rate that would be charged if the financing were carried out through conventional channels. This tax loophole is currently available only for pollution-control projects.

Decisions to make, buy, or lease affect both manufacturing and materials activities. They should not be made without the approval of both the manufacturing manager and the materials manager. Other departments also help shape make-or-buy decisions, which are among the most basic decisions in the management of a business. Once the decision is made to buy, however, the materials manager and his buyers become the dominant factors in selecting the supplier. The next three chapters discuss the buying process in detail.

Cases

CASE 11–1. MIRACLE TOY CORPORATION

Make-or-buy decision on corrugated cartons

The Miracle Toy Corporation is one of the largest manufacturers in its field. It has been consistently profitable since it was founded by Hubert Mack in 1936. The Mack family still owns more than 60 percent of the company's stock. For this reason, dividend policy has been extremely conservative. A dividend payout averaging no more than 33 percent of earnings has been more than adequate for the family's needs. The company has been able to finance all of its growth internally, and it currently has the most up-to-date facilities in the industry.

Despite heavy expenditures for plant and equipment, the cash flow from earnings and depreciation has been so great that the company's financial position is very strong (see balance sheet in Table 11–1). In fact, Howard Carlson, the company's treasurer, is becoming concerned

TABLE 11-1
Summary of condensed financial statements of miracle toy corporation

ASSETS			LIABILITIES	
Cash	$3,922,000		Current liabilities . . .	$ 3,364,200
U.S. government			Common stock and	
bonds	3,265,000		surplus.	15,846,000
Accounts and notes			Total.	$19,210,200
receivable	1,910,000			
Inventories.	2,050,000			
Current assets. .		$11,147,000		
Plant and equipment .	$9,881,900			
Less: Depreciation	2,000,700			
		$ 7,881,200		
Land		182,000		
Total		$19,210,000		

Income Statement for Year Ended June 30

	1962	1963	1964	1965	1966
Sales	$18,902,000	$18,786,000	$21,942,000	$23,942,000	$24,020,000
Net profit be-					
fore tax . . .	2,020,000	1,682,000	2,689,000	2,532,000	2,910,000

lest the U.S. Internal Revenue Service charge that the company has been accumulating cash it does not really need by holding back on dividends to wealthy stockholders, who are subject to extremely high surtax rates on their personal income. Carlson feels that it is in the best interests of the company to have available a healthy reserve in cash or marketable securities to protect the company during a business downturn and also for any profitable investments the company might wish to make.

Robert Axelrod, manager of the company's manufacturing engineering department, thinks he may have a solution to the excess cash problem. He proposes that the company invest in a small plant to produce cartons.

The company currently spends about $800,000 per year for various types and sizes of cartons. At present, it buys them from three suppliers. Two of these suppliers are divisions of much larger corporations. One, however, is much smaller and depends on Miracle Toy for about 25 percent of its business. Prices for cartons fluctuate somewhat. When there is excess capacity, they drop; when capacity is tight, they inch upward. Current prices reflect a recovery from a previous price-cutting period.

Axelrod believes that the company can profitably invest in a plant capable of turning out all but $50,000 of its current annual carton needs. (The plant would not produce the small number of cartons that require special lithographing.) At the start, Miracle Toy would be able to take less than half of the plant's production for its own use in packaging toys; the balance (about $1 million worth of cartons) would be sold to outside customers. As Miracle Toy's business grew, it could rely on the carton plant for its increased needs and cut back on sales to outsiders.

Total investment in facilities would be approximately $1,100,000. This estimate does not include any allowance for land, which the company already owns and which probably is worth $50,000 to $75,000. Nor does it include any allowance for start-up costs—the unusually high operating costs that are almost always incurred when a plant starts producing. Axelrod estimates that these costs will be at least $50,000.

Axelrod estimates that the plant would earn a 10 percent profit on sales to outside customers and would also save the company about $90,000 in boxboard costs (see Table 11–2). He believes that sale of

TABLE 11–2
Miracle Toy Corporation, estimate of costs and revenues on proposed carton plant at standard volume

Sales to outside customers		$1,000,000
Reduction in purchases of cartons from outside suppliers		750,000
		$1,750,000
Cost of purchased paper board	$710,000	
Inks, plates, and other factory supplies.	165,000	
Wages and salaries.	495,000	
Depreciation, taxes, and other expenses	190,000	
		1,560,000
Profit from carton operations.		$ 190,000

the extra capacity would be no problem, since most of the company's suppliers purchase cartons. He points out that suppliers should be willing to buy Miracle Toy cartons provided that they were competitive in price and quality. In fact, Miracle Toy is already indirectly buying a substantial number of cartons in addition to those it buys directly to package its end products, since many of Miracle Toy's suppliers use cartons to package the company's purchases.

Question

Suppose you were the materials manager of the Miracle Toy Corporation. How would you react to Axelrod's proposal? State your position and make a detailed analysis of his proposal.

CASE 11–2. ILLINOIS CHEMICAL CORPORATION

Investment in new facilities

The Illinois Chemical Corporation is a major producer of a diversified line of industrial chemicals. One of its most important products is polystrand,[8] which it sells to plastics fabricators who mold it into a wide variety of industrial and consumer products. One of the major raw materials in polystrand is trimethylacetate. The company uses 10 million pounds of trimethylacetate per year. It buys from two suppliers, the Blue Chemical Corporation and Gamma Company. Blue Chemical's price is 61.6 cents per pound, and Gamma's price is 62 cents. The business is split evenly between the two sources. Currently Gamma and Blue Chemical are the only producers of the chemical. Their prices have been steady for more than two years, despite rising labor and raw-material costs.

TABLE 11–3
Manufacturing cost summary, supplier's operation (ten million pounds per year, trimethylacetate)

	Unit	Unit cost	Quantity	Annual $M	¢/lb.
Raw materials:					
Compound X	M lb.	$30.00	5,500	$ 165	1.7¢
Compound Y	M lb.	17.50	5,380	94	0.9
Others	M lb.	10.00	260	3	*
Total				$ 262	2.6¢
Wages and salaries:					
Wages	Man-year	$5,000	48	$ 240	2.4¢
Salaries	Man-year	$7,000	10	70	0.7
Security	10% of wages and salaries			31	0.3
Total				$ 341	3.4¢
Supplies	$1,000/operating employee			$ 48	0.5¢
Utilities:					
Steam	M lb.	$ 0.40	45,000	$ 18	0.2¢
Electricity	MKWH	10.00	6,000	60	0.6
Cooling water	M gal.	0.02	128,000	3	*
Others				15	0.2
Total				$ 96	1.0¢
Services:					
Technical	3¢/lb. product			$ 300	3.0¢
General	$1,500/employee			87	0.9
Total				$ 387	3.9¢
Occupancy:					
Maintenance	4% of investment			$ 400	4.0¢
Shops and stores	2% of investment			200	2.0
Insurance and taxes	1% of investment			100	1.0
Depreciation	6% of investment			600	6.0
Total				$1,300	13.0¢
Total manufacturing cost				$2,434	24.4¢

* Insignificant Amount

[8] Names of chemicals are fictitious to prevent identification of the manufacturer who cooperated in furnishing data for this case.

Illinois's materials manager, Jim Hartley, estimates that Gamma's capacity is 25 million pounds and Blue Chemical's is about 20 million pounds. Both companies are expanding their capacity, and in the next two years, Hartley estimates, their combined capacity will be 60 million pounds. He also understands that they are making improvements in their processes.

Demand for polystrand has mushroomed in recent years, and Illinois estimates that it may double its sales of the plastic in the next five years. Other chemical companies noting the heavy demand for the material, have been attracted not only to the end product (where competition is growing more intense) but also the major raw material (trimethylacetate). Three other producers have announced plans to enter the trimethylacetate business. If these producers carry out their plans, Hartley estimates that total industry capacity will be well over 100 million pounds per year in the next three years.

Because it expects continued growth in demand for polystrand, Illinois is now considering investment in facilities to product the key raw material, trimethylacetate. Heretofore, Illinois has preferred to invest its capital primarily in equipment to process end products and has relied on suppliers for raw materials. However, Edward Van de Venter, vice

TABLE 11–4

Sales price summary, Supplier's operation (ten million pounds per year, trimethylacetate)

	$M	$/lb.
Capital investment:		
Fixed investment:		
Battery limits	$10,000	$1.000
Allocated		
Utilities	600	0.060
Services	400	0.040
Shops	200	0.020
Total.	$11,200	$1.120
Working capital	$ 490	$0.049
Total capital investment	$11,690	$1.169
Return on total investment (after taxes), 15%		
Annual net profit	$ 1,753	$0.175
Annual income tax	1,753	0.175
Annual gross profit	$ 3,506	$0.350
Annual cost of sales		
Manufacturing cost	$ 2,434	$0.244
Corporate overhead @ 4%	247	0.024
Total	$ 2,681	$0.268
Annual sales revenue	$ 6,187	$0.618

Selling Price—¢/lb., 61.8¢/lb.

president in charge of manufacturing, has long been urging the company's executive committee to approve construction of facilities to make raw materials. Van de Venter's staff has prepared an analysis (see Tables 11–3 and 11–4) that indicates that the company can earn a 15 percent return on invested capital by investing in trimethylacetate manufacturing facilities. This is approximately what the company is currently earning on existing facilities. While the company's bonded indebtedness is already heavy, it could undoubtedly borrow the $11,690,000 it would need for the project—although it would then have to postpone any additional expansion for at least a year or two.

Hartley does not share Van de Venter's enthusiasm for the project. He has asked his administrative assistant, Henry Waterman, to prepare a study in which he considers both the pros and the cons of going into the trimethylacetate business.

Question

What factors should Waterman consider in his study?

12

Finding qualified suppliers

THE BUYING PROCESS is deceptively simple. Competing suppliers submit bids. If each offers acceptable delivery, quality, and service, a purchase order is issued to the lowest bidder. This is the clerical framework. Within it operates a buying process that requires both extensive knowledge and remarkably keen judgment.

Good buyers never ask a supplier to quote unless they have some knowledge of his qualifications. In fact, they would prefer to solicit quotations only from suppliers with perfect records for quality, service, and delivery. If they could do this all the time, their jobs would be much easier. All they would need to do is request quotations from three or four such suppliers and then award the business to the low bidder.

Unfortunately, real-life suppliers are not so perfect. Most buyers are not completely satisfied with the quality, service, and delivery of even their best and most reliable suppliers. In addition, they must spend a great deal of time looking for new suppliers capable of taking care of their changing needs. No company can stand still. It must continuously be developing new products and processes, which in turn require new suppliers. No supplier can afford to stand still, either. Each is looking for new customers, and each must be investigated carefully by the buyer before being trusted with an order.

BUYING ERRORS ARE COSTLY

The costs of mistakes in buying are always substantial; sometimes they are staggering. If buyers pay suppliers higher prices than are justified, a company's profits and competitive position may be undermined. As was pointed out in Chapter 1, in the average company a 2 percent change in total materials cost brings a 10 percent change in profits.

If a buyer buys materials of unsatisfactory quality or a vendor fails to deliver, the costs may be enormous. Imagine what would happen if an auto company purchased parts for a critical component like a steering gear or brakes that failed completely after a year's service in the field. Hundreds of thousands of cars would be defective. The company's reputation would certainly suffer. In addition, it would incur losses from lawsuits and from the enormous expense of replacing the defective part in thousands of cars.[1]

Quality failure can be a nightmare when it is not detected until long after the product is in use. It can even be costly when it is spotted immediately by sharp-eyed inspectors. A shipment of material that does not meet minimum quality specifications is the equivalent of no shipment at all. Worse yet, it may mean continued delivery failure until the supplier can correct the defect.

If a supplier fails to deliver an item and the buyer's inventories are exhausted, the costs of the production stoppage that results can be huge. Customers are dissatisfied; sales and profits are lost that can never be recouped. In addition, the direct cost is substantial. A plant employing about 300 persons has fixed costs of several thousand dollars per day, which are incurred whether the plant is operating or not.

If a buyer fails to achieve the fourth buying objective, service,[2] in his dealings with suppliers, the consequences are not nearly so spectacular as with a major quality or delivery failure. In some cases, however, they can be even more significant economically. Outstanding suppliers sometimes provide their customers with products and ideas that can have tremendous impact on sales and profits for years to come.

CHANNELS OF DISTRIBUTION

Industrial buyers commonly buy materials both directly from producers and through various local distributors. In general, they buy production materials used in fairly large quantities directly from the manufacturer, in order to get lowest possible prices. Nonproduction materials and supplies normally come from local mill supply houses or distributors, who buy from the manufacturers in large quantities and then resell to their customers in smaller quantities.

---

[1] Such failures have become commonplace in recent years. In most cases, they result from a problem not anticipated by the manufacturer's engineering department. In some, however, the failure results directly from sloppy worksmanship in a supplier plant that was not detected until after thousands of cars containing inferior components had been sold.

[2] The objective of service is comparable to the favorable supplier relations objective mentioned in the discussion of primary materials management objectives in Chapter 3.

As a general rule, industrial buyers prefer to deal directly with the manufacturer whenever possible. There are no middlemen making extra profits on each purchase, and communication is easier when the buyer has technical problems to discuss with the manufacturer. However, industrial distributors do have a legitimate economic role. When the buyer requires their services, the higher prices they charge are more than justified. In fact, when quantities are relatively small, they are usually the most economic form of distribution.

Buying direct

When a company uses reasonably large quantities of production parts and materials, it almost always pays to buy directly from the manufacturer. Suppliers of standard and semistandard items—steel, chemicals, ball bearings, paper, and so on—sometimes require a minimum factory order on direct purchases.[3] All large users, however, buy directly from the factory or mill. Suppliers of parts that are custom made to the buyer's blueprints and specifications almost always sell direct, even if quantities are small.

Full-time salesmen. Supplier salesmen are the liaison between their customers and the home office and factory. The salesmen of practically all large and many small companies are full-time employees. They usually are paid a straight salary plus some bonus based on performance and company profits. They may also receive a commission based on sales volume, which may or may not supplement a regular salary.

It is probably to the buyer's advantage to deal with salesmen who are paid a straight salary, since they might be more interested in providing outstanding service to their customers, even at the expense of immediate gains in sales volume. However, there is not much a buyer can do to control the way in which a supplier pays his salesmen. Nor, in most cases, can he even find out the method; most suppliers are extremely reluctant to discuss such an intimate detail of their business with customers.

Manufacturers' representatives. Many smaller firms sell through manufacturers' representatives. They pay a flat commission on sales volume, which ranges from 1 percent or less on extremely high-volume items to more than 10 percent on equipment and parts purchased in very small quantities. Typically, each manufacturers' representative serves several noncompeting firms in an area. In most cases, they sell products

---

[3] For example, mills demand a minimum order of 10,000 pounds for most types of sheet steel. Users who want smaller quantities must buy from a steel warehouse firm that specializes in buying mill quantities and then reselling in smaller quantities to users in its area. Warehouse prices usually are at least 25 percent higher than mill prices. Warehouses earn this premium by offering prompt delivery of small quantities and other services.

to the same customers, so the representative often can service several accounts on a single sales call.

While some buyers complain that the commissions earned by manufacturers' representatives are too high, this method of selling is probably the most economical one for the firms that use it. The company need not maintain sales offices in areas where they would not be economical. Its sales costs are not rigid but vary directly with sales volume.

On the other hand, a manufacturers' representative usually cannot give any one company all of his time, nor can he be expected to know as much about the company's products as a full-time sales representative. As a result, critics say that neither buyer nor seller gets the best service through a manufacturers' representative. When problems arise, the manufacturers' representative often is only an errand boy between the buyer and the supplier. He usually is not empowered to make more than minor decisions for his employer. On the other hand, some, but by no means all, full-time salesmen are thoroughly familiar with the details of their product and are able to make many decisions without consulting the home office.

Buying from distributors

A distributor is a dealer who handles a wide range of products for a number of manufacturers in an area. He may have an exclusive franchise for a manufacturer's products and not handle competing brands. In other cases, each distributor in an area would handle all major brands. Distributors usually buy materials in fairly large quantities, store them, and then resell in small quantities to customers in their area. About 23 percent of the typical distributor's sales are drop shipments,[4] in which the material is shipped directly from the factory to the user. In such cases, the distributor still takes title to the goods, even though he does not handle them physically. But in this case his function is really no different from that of a manufacturers' representative.

Even on drop shipments, however, the manufacturer invoices the distributor, who reinvoices the user of the material. The distributor's profit comes from the difference between the price at which he sells and the price at which he buys. Unlike the manufacturers' representative, the distributor receives no commission and, except where it is prohibited by so-called "fair trade" laws, is perfectly free to resell at any price he chooses.

Distributor markups vary with the quantity and type of material sold. One study showed that the average gross margin of the distributor was 21.19 percent of sales.[5] To earn this margin, the distributor anticipates

---

[4] Robert D. Buzzell, *Value Added by Industrial Distributors and Their Productivity* (Columbus: Ohio State University Press, 1959), p. 26.

[5] Ibid., p. 55.

the needs of his customers in his buying, stores the material until there is a demand for it (an average period of three months[6]), and then delivers it to the user.

Role of the salesman

The modern salesman is not necessarily a bubbling extrovert, but he almost always does have a reasonably pleasant personality. The fact is that many salesmen get business simply because customers enjoy doing business with them. If all other factors are equal, why shouldn't a buyer deal with someone he likes and trusts? Personality factors are just as important in buyer-seller relations as they are in other phases of business.

While every buyer is certainly influenced to some extent by the personalities of the salesmen who call on him, he also has more objective reasons for preferring some salesmen to others. A good salesman knows not only his company's products but also something about his customer's problems. He is around when the buyer needs him but does not make unnecessary calls that waste time for both of them. When the salesman is an able one, there are few problems regarding quality and delivery. The salesman will follow up on most of them himself and thus save the buyer considerable trouble.

Firms with able sales representatives always get more business. And they deserve it, for they offer superior service to their customers. Able salesmen naturally seek out prospective customers; many a company learns about a supplier only because one of his salesmen happened to call. The professional buyer doesn't always play such a passive role, however. He spends a substantial amount of time actively looking for new suppliers who can serve his needs better.

FINDING A SUPPLIER

Buyers most commonly find suppliers for an item either by drawing on their experience with comparable items or by inviting quotations from the same suppliers who made the item on a previous order. Every buyer must often locate new suppliers, however. He wants to stimulate competition on items he regularly buys, and he must also buy new items that present suppliers are not equipped to handle. Buyers usually locate new vendors by checking purchasing directories and catalog and vendor files or through personal contacts with supplier salesmen or other buyers.

Directories.   There are numerous directories that list potential suppliers both alphabetically and by type of product sold. Probably the most widely used directory is the buyer's local telephone book. In the yellow pages are listed all local suppliers for various merchandise.

---

[6] Ibid., p. 71.

Purchasing directories, like *Thomas' Register of American Manufac-turers, Conover-Mast Purchasing Directory,* and *MacRae's Blue Book,* are widely used by industrial buyers. Each is carefully edited to include only those products that are useful to the industrial buyer, and each lists upwards of a quarter of a million supply sources, both alphabetically and by product. A buyer can quickly locate almost every domestic sup-plier of an item simply by turning to the product classification in the directory in which he is interested.

Many states publish directories of all industries within their bound-aries. Every buyer should have the directory of his home state if there is one. It can be an extremely useful supplement to his general purchas-ing directory, which might not list all suppliers or commodities in which he might be interested. Trade associations also issue purchasing direc-tories for specialized commodities. The *Rubber Red Book* is typical of these; it specializes in very detailed listings and product classifications for rubber products manufacturers and so is an invaluable reference for a buyer of such products. Every buying department should be equipped with all available specialized commodity directories in its fields of interest.

Catalog files and vendor lists.   The typical purchasing department is bombarded with thousands of pieces of direct-mail sales literature every year. Although they discard at least 90 percent of this mail, most purchasing men carefully review and save any catalogs that might be of use in buying. A big purchasing department may have several thou-sand different supplier catalogs in its files.

Some purchasing departments try to boost the usefulness of their catalog files by carefully classifying their contents both by supplier name and by-product. For example, they may store the catalogs on shelves or in file cabinets alphabetically by supplier name and then keep a separate card file by type of commodity. Some companies have even developed numerical file cards on which they imitate the Dewey decimal system used in libraries, assigning a code number to each commodity group.

The purchasing department of a manufacturer of office staplers and similar items uses these basic groupings:

1000—Bearings and bushings
2000—Electrical equipment and supplies
3000—Factory equipment
4000—Gears
5000—Mill supplies
6000—Office supplies and equipment
7000—Steel, brass, aluminum, etc.
8000—Taps and drills
9000—Miscellaneous

The third digit in the identifying number indicates the type of material, and the fourth digit classifies it further. For example, in category 7000, 7010 identifies a general steel product, while 7011 is for steel wire, 7012 for steel bars, and so on. Specific catalogs are then identified in numerical sequence, with a decimal point after the commodity number. For example, the number 7011.01 might refer to a U.S. Steel catalog of steel wire, which is the first of several wire catalogs on file. 7011.02 might be Republic Steel's wire products catalog, and so on.

Buyers specializing in high-volume production parts and materials rarely rely on catalogs, since everything they buy is custom made to company specifications. But they would probably use some sort of vendor list. The simplest of these would be a file of 3 × 5 cards arranged alphabetically by supplier name. On each card would be the supplier's address, telephone number, names of officers and sales representatives, and an indication of the type of work the supplier is equipped to handle. The buyer then can review this list whenever he must buy a new item to see if anyone on it is interested in quoting.

Personal contacts. Buyers talk to salesmen of potential vendors even when they have no immediate need for the products they sell. When a need does arise, they can refer to the salesman's calling card or "leave behind" sales literature to see if his company should be considered.

Buyers often get tips on potential suppliers for offbeat items by asking other buyers for assistance. Many of them use their membership in the National Association of Purchasing Management or some other purchasing organization as a vehicle for becoming acquainted with purchasing personnel in other companies who can be useful sources of information. They also carefully read many trade publications regularly. When they see an ad by a company that might be a potential supplier, they tear it out and file it for future reference.

Similarly, buyers get information about potential new suppliers through regular attendance at trade shows where suppliers have booths and display their products. Some companies take even more direct measures to stimulate sales calls from promising new suppliers. They have displays of their products in their lobbies, so that suppliers will know precisely what they buy. Some companies have even set up (during a defense program, when they had to get many new suppliers in a hurry) exhibits of the items they buy in public halls and invited all potential suppliers to come and look at them.

INVESTIGATION OF SUPPLIERS

No buyer should place orders with a supplier about whom he knows nothing. At best, there is danger of substandard performance in price, quality, delivery, or service. At worst, there is danger of fraud. Almost every buyer occasionally is approached by a sharp operator trying to pass off shoddy merchandise at exorbitant prices, and sometimes the swindler is successful. In a survey of industrial purchasing agents, 15 percent of the respondents admitted that they had been victims of industrial racketeers.[7]

Caveat emptor. In one of the rackets mentioned in the survey, a pencil salesman calls and claims that his company has printed the name of the buyer's company on several thousand pencils[8] because of confusion with another customer who has a similar name. If the name of the buyer's company is Universal Screw Machine Corp., for example, the salesman might claim that his firm has accidentally printed this name on pencils ordered by the Universal Screw Products Corp. The salesman appears to be upset over the error and offers the buyer distress prices if he will take the pencils off his hands. The salesman is lying, of course. The company's name is printed on the pencils only after it orders them. And the buyer doesn't get a distress price at all; he pays a high price for the poorest quality of pencils available.

In another, similar racket the salesman claims to be representing a firm that is financially hard pressed. If the buyer will pay cash, he promises extra concessions. What happens is that the buyer winds up with low-quality merchandise worth about half of what he paid. Since it is not economic to sue and the transaction usually is perfectly legal anyway, the buyer is bilked.

Rackets such as these would disappear if every buyer carefully investigated each supplier before placing an order. But everyone likes to get something for nothing, and if the racketeers can convince the buyer that he must move fast, he might forego investigation in his eagerness to exploit what appears to be an opportunity for a bargain. The fact remains that every supplier should be investigated, even those whose morals and ethics are above reproach.

Unfortunately for the buyer, a completely honorable supplier can also cause losses to the buyer's company, for he may be incompetent, a poor manager, and unable to keep promises made in good faith. For this reason, many buyers avoid asking a supplier even to quote on business until they have learned something about his facilities, personnel, financial resources, and reputation.

Facilities

Suppliers often are remarkably eager to get orders they are not equipped to handle. From the supplier's point of view, the best way

---

[7] "Buyers Beware—The Racket Boys Are Back," *Purchasing*, July 18, 1960, p. 72. Since many people, particularly professional buyers, do not like to admit that they have been cheated, presumably more than 15 percent of the respondents were actually victimized.

[8] The racket obviously would work with any item that has the company's name printed on it, including advertising specialties like blotters, calendars, and so on.

to expand a business is to get the orders first and then worry about buying the needed equipment. The buyer has a somewhat different point of view. He almost always buys best when he deals with suppliers who already have the equipment and skills needed. Costs usually are lower and quality is higher when the supplier performs almost every operation on the product or service himself.

Equipment lists. The buyer should listen carefully to the salesman's description of the supplier's facilities. If he is buying parts made to his specifications directly from a small manufacturer, he should ask for a list of machine tools and equipment. He then can accurately determine if the supplier is actually equipped to do the job. The buyer also can get useful descriptions of a supplier's facilities from a Dun & Bradstreet report (see Figure 12–1) or from the current issue of *Moody's Industrials.*

If the supplier is located nearby, the buyer should always arrange to see his facilities. If the contract is sufficiently important, the buyer should visit the supplier's plant even if it is hundreds of miles away. And he may wish to bring along product, process, or quality control engineers from his own company to assist him in evaluating the supplier's facilities.

A buyer's tour of a distributor's facilities can be more superficial than one of a supplier's manufacturing plant. The distributor should certainly be adequately stocked. Equally important to the buyer are the distributor's employees. If their morale is high, if they seem alert and intelligent, the buyer has a reasonably good chance of getting prompt service with a minimum of errors. The distributor's housekeeping also may be significant. The buyer usually has good reason to expect sloppy service from sloppy-looking facilities.

Plant visits. A manufacturing plant usually is much more complex than a distribution facility and takes much more skill to evaluate. Every buyer who has ever been conducted through a supplier plant has heard the salesman boast of its modern facilities and equipment. If the buyer is an expert in the supplier's industry, it will not take him long to see if the salesman's praise is justified.

If the buyer is not thoroughly familiar with the industry, he can still get clues as to the quality of the facilities by seeking answers to these questions:

1. Is the equipment up to date? If the equipment looks new and modern (and doesn't just have a fresh coat of paint on it), the buyer usually can assume that it is reasonably efficient and in good condition. In some cases, he might bluntly ask the supplier when the equipment was purchased. If he notices a number of machines shut down for repairs, he may conclude that the equipment is older than it looks.
2. Is there effective material control? If the supplier has in-process

FIGURE 12–1

Dun & Bradstreet, Inc.

Please note whether name, business and street address correspond with your inquiry.

BUSINESS INFORMATION REPORT

BASE REPORT

SIC	D-U-N-S	© DUN & BRADSTREET, INC.		STARTED	RATING
34 69	04-426-3226	CD 13 APR 21 19--		1957	DD I
	ARNOLD METAL PRODUCTS CO	METAL STAMPINGS			

53 S MAIN ST
DAWSON MICH   49666
TEL 215 999-0000

SAMUEL B. ARNOLD)
GEORGE T. ARNOLD) PARTNERS

SUMMARY

PAYMENTS	DISC
SALES	$177,250
WORTH	$42,961
EMPLOYS	10
RECORD	CLEAR

CONDITION STRONG
TREND   UP

PAYMENTS

HC	OWE	P DUE	TERMS	APR 19--	SOLD
3000	1500	1	10 30	Disc	Over 3 yrs
2500	1000	1	10 30	Disc	Over 3 yrs
2000	500	2	20 30	Disc	Old Account

FINANCE

On Apr 21 19-- S. B. Arnold, Partner, submitted the following statement dated Dec 31 19--

Cash	$	4,870	Accts Pay	$	6,121
Accts Rec		15,472	Notes Pay (Curr)		2,400
Mdse		14,619	Accruals		3,583
		----------			----------
Current		34,961	Current		12,104
Fixt & Equip ($4,183)		22,840	Notes Pay (Def)		5,000
CSV of Life Ins		2,264	NET WORTH		42,961
		----------			----------
Total Assets		60,065	Total		60,065

Annual sales $177,250; gross profit $47,821; net income $8,204. Fire insurance mdse $15,000; fixt $20,000. Annual rent $3,000. Signed Apr 21 19-- ARNOLD METAL PRODUCTS CO by Samuel B. Arnold, Partner.
-----0-----
New equipment purchased last Sep was financed by bank loan. Monthly payments on loan are $200.
Arnold reported sales for the three months ended Mar 31 were up 10% compared to the same period last year. Increase was attributed by management to additional capacity provided by new equipment.
Profit is being made and retained resulting in an increase in net worth. Current debt is light in relation to worth. Inventory turnover is rapid.

BANKING

Balances average high four figures. Loans granted to low five figures, secured by equipment, now owing high four figures. Relations satisfactory.

HISTORY

Style registered Feb 1 1965 by partners. S. ARNOLD, born 1918, married. 1939 graduate of Lehigh University. 1939-50 employed by Industrial Machine Corporation, Detroit, and 1950-56 production manager with Aerial Motors Inc., Detroit. Started this business in 1957. G. ARNOLD, born 1940, single, son of Samuel. Graduated in 1963, Dawson Institute of Technology. Served U.S. Air Force 1963-1964. Admitted to partnership Feb 1965.

OPERATION

Manufactures perforated metal stampings for Industrial concerns. Sells on Net 30 day terms. Has twelve accounts. Territory greater Detroit area. Employs ten including partners. LOCATION: Rents 5,000 square feet in one story cinder block building in normal condition. Located in central business section of main street. Premises neat.
4-21 (803 77) PRA

Although they are most often used to check a customer's credit, Dun & Bradstreet reports are also good sources of information about potential suppliers' facilities and finances.

inventory piled haphazardly throughout the plant, his production scheduling may be defective, or equipment breakdowns may be creating production bottlenecks.

3. Are working conditions good? The buyer is more likely to get the quality and output he wants from a plant that is well lighted and

well ventilated and that has guards on machines to prevent accidents.
4. Are facilities well maintained? If a supplier skimps on maintenance in obvious areas, he may also skimp in the less obvious ones that cause shutdowns.
5. What are the supplier's fire-protection facilities? If the plant has its own water tower and sprinkler, fires will cause less damage and will be less likely to hold up work on the buyer's orders.
6. Is the work pace fast but unhurried? A well-operated plant doesn't have idle workers in one area and harried workers in another.
7. Does the supplier have the equipment to handle the buyer's order? The buyer should ask to see the equipment that is to be used on his orders. He should ask about the approximate capacity of each machine, to make certain that his needs can be accommodated. He may also wish to make note of each machine's model number and specifications so that he can review the supplier's facilities with experts at his own plant.
8. Does the supplier have efficient receiving and shipping facilities? The buyer should note particularly whether the supplier can ship his order by the most economical type of carrier. If the buyer's traffic manager would prefer shipment by rail, for example, the supplier cannot ship at low cost unless he has his own siding.
9. Is the supplier currently making products similar to those in which the buyer is interested? If the buyer's order will be different from the supplier's usual line, there might be problems. If it is similar, the buyer can get a good idea of how his order will be handled by watching work on similar orders.

Many companies require buyers to make out detailed reports each time they visit a supplier plant. These reports are filed and can be referred to by other buyers interested in doing business with that supplier. However, a company should not use one report as a guide indefinitely. Follow-up visits are essential to keep up to date on changes the supplier may have made. A series of reports can then be analyzed for trend. A company naturally is more willing to place business with a supplier that is progressively improving than with one that is standing still or even slipping behind.

Personnel

Although buyers should do their best to evaluate a supplier's facilities objectively, this is sometimes difficult and occasionally almost impossible. Some facilities simply do not lend themselves to the type of superficial appraisal a buyer can give on a plant tour. For example, both efficient and inefficient chemical plants look like a maze of pipes and storage tanks to the casual observer. Supplier managements may also superficially appear to be homogeneous, but they are not. It is the buyer's job to distinguish between really competent managements and the also-rans.

Regardless of their products and processes, all companies depend heavily on the caliber of their managers; a good supplier always has good managers. The buyer is particularly qualified to evaluate the supplier's materials manager. He should insist on meeting him, as well as other company executives. He may also, if the contract is an important one, arrange for these executives to meet their counterparts in his own company. If each of the supplier's department heads knows his job thoroughly, the buyer has less to worry about when he places the order.

If the contract is a major one, the buyer should not confine his study of the supplier's personnel to the top managers. He should meet lower level supervisors as well. The supplier's key men should be backed up by bright, alert subordinates who are being trained to take over in the future.

The supplier's labor relations also should interest the buyer. Do the workers appear contented and reasonably interested in their jobs? Or are they sullen and obviously doing work they hate simply because they must eat? In the latter case, the buyer should not be too surprised if he sometimes gets substandard workmanship on his orders. The buyers should bluntly ask the supplier to show him records on strikes and work stoppages. If they have been frequent, the buyer can expect both an environment leading to poor quality and frequent failures to meet delivery promises.

Financial resources

Why should a company be interested in the financial strength of its suppliers? It need not rely on their credit, nor is it making an investment in them. The answer is that the best suppliers are financially strong and are making healthy profits.

Advantages of strong suppliers. In general, it is sound to prefer an extremely profitable vendor to a less profitable one—all other factors being equal. The company with big profits is in a much better position to reduce prices (if it can be persuaded to do so). Its methods and management usually are superior. It also is more likely to be a better source of new products and techniques than its more marginal competitors.

Certainly no buyer wants to give important purchase orders to a weak supplier and then have him suddenly go bankrupt. Also, a supplier who is making adequate profits and is strong financially can take temporary losses if he underbids or has trouble with an order. The buyer need not worry about such a supplier's coming back after he has accepted an order and demanding extra payments to complete it, financial advances, and so on.

If the company is large and publicly owned, the buyers should ask its sales representatives for a copy of the latest annual report to stockholders. Such reports often contain interesting descriptions of company operations as well as basic financial data. If the company does not widely distribute its financial reports to stockholders, the buyer has other sources of financial information. He often can get balance sheet and income data and similar basic information from the latest edition of *Moody's Industrials*. Or, if the supplier is too small to be listed in *Moody's*, the buyer can get a Dun & Bradstreet report. The D & B report will usually include a financial statement. In addition, it will indicate the company's credit standing with its suppliers and the overall credit rating assigned it by Dun & Bradstreet.

Financial analysis. The buyer, or better yet, a financial analyst on the materials manager's staff, should periodically review the latest balance sheet and income statement of each major supplier. If the balance sheet shows that the supplier's business is deteriorating, the buyer should investigate; he may want to change suppliers before the company's financial condition becomes critical.

The buyer should also be particularly interested in the trend of the company's profits. If profit margins are widening, he may have a legitimate basis for asking the supplier to reduce prices. And certainly he should complain vigorously if such a supplier should increase prices. If the profit margin is narrowing, it may mean that the supplier is gradually becoming less efficient and less competitive. Or it could mean that his prices are too low and the buyer can expect pressure for price increases.

No buyer or materials manager is expected to be an expert financial analyst. However, he should be sufficiently familiar with balance sheets and income statements to make intelligent comparisons of competing suppliers and to spot individual strengths and weaknesses.

The financial statements of a hypothetical supplier are illustrated in Table 12–1. How would a financial analyst go about reviewing them? One of the best approaches is to calculate various financial ratios for the supplier and compare them with ratios for competing suppliers.[9] The following ratios are particularly significant:

1. *The current ratio.* This is the ratio of current assets to current liabilities. It indicates the ability of the company to pay its immediate obligations. In the ABC Company (Table 12–1), this ratio is 2.5 ($500,000/$200,000). Most analysts agree that it should be at least 2.5 and when it gets below 1.0 the company usually is on the brink of default on its obligations. The ratio of cash plus accounts receivable

---

[9] Each year, Dun & Bradstreet publishes 14 important financial ratios for 72 different industries. The title of the publication changes from year to year. Businessmen can get complimentary copies by writing to Dun & Bradstreet, 99 Church Street, New York, N.Y. 10008.

TABLE 12–1
Condensed financial statement, ABC Company

ASSETS			LIABILITIES		
Cash	$100,000		Accounts payable	$ 50,000	
Accounts receivable	200,000		Wages payable	50,000	
Inventories	200,000		Accrued taxes	100,000	
Current Assets		$ 500,000	Current Liabilities		$ 200,0
Land	$ 50,000		Long-term debt		100,0
Plant and			Common stock	$100,000	
equipment $500,000			Capital surplus	100,000	
Less: De-			Earned surplus	500,000	
preciation 100,000					700,0
	$400,000				
Fixed assets		$ 450,000			
Good will, etc.		50,000			
Total Current Assets		$1,000,000	Total Current Liabilities		$1,000,(

Income Statement

Net Sales		$2,000,000
Less:		
Purchases	$1,000,000	
Payrolls	500,000	
Other expenses	200,000	
Operating costs	$1,700,000	
Less: Sales and administrative expense	100,000	
Total costs		1,800,000
Operating profit		200,000
Less: Taxes		100,000
Net Profit		$ 100,000

to current liabilities ($100,000 + $200,000/$200,000 = 1.5 for ABC Company) is an even better measure of liquidity. Inventories cannot be quickly converted into cash, so they are excluded from current assets. If a manufacturing company is in good financial condition, this "quick" ratio or "acid test" should be at least 1.5.

2. *Profit ratios.* Profitability can be measured by earnings both as a percent of sales and as a percent of net worth. The ABC Company's after-tax earnings are 5 percent of sales and just over 14 percent ($100,000/$700,000) of net worth. Average earnings on sales and net worth vary from industry to industry and also from year to year. Large companies tend to be more profitable than small firms. ABC's relative profitability can best be measured by comparing it with sales and earnings statistics published by the Securities and Exchange Commission and the Federal Trade Commission in the *Quarterly Financial Report for Manufacturing Corporations.* The *Report* (which is available from the U.S. Government Printing Office on a subscription basis) would probably show ABC to be relatively more profitable than other firms of comparable size, and it might even be above the average of its industry.

3. *Debt ratios.* A company that is heavily in debt will have difficulty

raising money to invest in improvements. Two ratios measure the extent of a company's indebtedness. The ratio of funded debt to net working capital should rarely exceed 1.0. In the case of the ABC Company, it is 0.33 ($100,000/$300,000). The ratio of current debt to tangible net worth should normally be under 0.75, ABC's is about .28 ($200,000/$700,000).

4. *Inventory turnover.* Dividing net sales by inventories indicates how rapidly the company is turning over its inventories. This is a barometer of the company's materials management skill. ABC's ratio of 10.0 is probably above average, although the only good way to determine whether the ratio is high or low is to compare it with that of other companies in ABC's industry.

The ratios given above are danger signals. A buyer can successfully deal with a supplier who is financially marginal for years, but he should not do so blindly. Whenever any of the key financial ratios of a supplier are substandard, the buyer should investigate. He may directly ask the supplier to describe his problems, or he may request that his own company's controller make a more detailed analysis of the supplier's financial statements.

Financial limitations. Regardless of how strong a supplier is financially and how able he is in every other respect, few buyers care to concentrate too great a percentage of their purchase volume on a single supplier. Nor do they care to have the supplier become dependent on them for too great a share of his overall business. When they place too much business with a single supplier, buyers not only limit competition but they unnecessarily restrict their freedom of action in changing suppliers. No buyer need worry too much about taking a small order away from one supplier and giving it to a competitor. But only a cold-blooded ogre would cancel orders on short notice when they are almost the sole source of the supplier's income and hundreds of workers (sometimes entire communities) depend on the orders for their livelihood.

Suppliers who have staked too much on a single corporation have lived to regret it, too. For example, at one time the Murray Corporation of America depended on Ford Motor Company for as much as 30 to 40 percent of its sales. Then Ford decided to make almost all of its own auto body stampings. Murray was hit with a sharp drop in business from which it has never recovered fully. Chrysler Corporation had an even closer relationship with Briggs Manufacturing Company, which depended on it for practically all of its automobile business. When Chrysler decided to make its own automobile bodies, Briggs's only solution was to go out of the auto body business completely and sell its facilities to Chrysler.

There are no hard and fast rules as to how much business can be safely concentrated on a single supplier, but few companies want to use more than 10 percent of a supplier's capacity unless there is some special reason for doing so. When companies break this rule, there is usually some special angle. An obvious one is nepotism. A father who controls one corporation may set his son up in another firm as a supplier. This practice is usually frowned upon—although it does not necessarily work against the best interests of the purchaser.

Other companies may become wed to some particular supplier for even more legitimate reasons. A company may become interested in the work that a particular supplier is doing and then place a majority of its business with that supplier after it acquires a financial interest. This is often the cheapest way for a large corporation to acquire the technological know-how of some specialized supplier.

Reputation

If a potential supplier has a bad reputation, one should clearly avoid doing business with him. Credit reports often provide clues to a supplier's reputation. They describe the backgrounds of the principals and also mention any outstanding litigation. The buyer should also ask a new supplier for a list of his major customers and vendors. Chances are that he may be acquainted with at least a few of the executives of these firms who can give him an unprejudiced view of the potential supplier's reputation. If the buyer belongs to a group like the National Association of Purchasing Management, he may get tips on suppliers' reputations from his fellow members.

When he investigates a supplier's reputation, the buyer will be interested not only in conformance to ethical standards but also in experience others have had with the supplier in regard to meeting quality standards and keeping delivery promises.

DEVELOPING NEW SUPPLIERS

Ideally, a supplier should have the equipment, know-how, and financial capacity needed for each order he accepts. In real life this often is not the case. Buyers may deliberately give business to inexperienced suppliers. Sometimes they have no choice, but, usually they have good reason for deliberately gambling on a new supplier.

New products. If a buyer is looking for a supplier of something that has never been made before, he must obviously select an inexperienced supplier. Sometimes, of course, the buyer is taking little risk. The latest design of automobile bumper guard may look entirely different from last year's model, but last year's suppliers can probably handle it without great difficulty. The products that give the buyer problems are those that are completely different from anything that has been made before. For example, the first buyer who had to find a source for a space capsule nose cone really had a problem. The product was extremely difficult to make, and there was no producer with experience.

Competition.   Buyers go to great pains to develop new and untried suppliers even when there is nothing new or revolutionary about the product and there are several qualified producers. Their usual reason is to stimulate competition in the field. When there are few producers of an item, competition can be less than vigorous. At worst there may even be collusion among producers on bidding. This results in higher prices for the buyer and occasionally also sloppy service and poor quality.

Sometimes a buyer may wish to develop a new supplier even when his existing sources are doing an excellent job. He may feel there is not enough capacity in the industry to take care of his needs. Or he may wish to develop a supplier in a particular area that is not too convenient for the plants of existing producers.

The development process.   Regardless of the motive, most good buyers are always in the process of developing at least one or two new suppliers. They cannot always use conventional techniques to locate them, particularly if they are considering introducing a supplier to work that is not presently in his line. Sometimes they develop new sources by suggesting that certain dependable suppliers broaden their product lines. Often they play a more passive role; the supplier suggests to the buyer that he be considered for an order not presently in his line. The more aggressive buyers may even go out and actively solicit bids from potential suppliers with management and equipment that they believe could be adapted to a particular item.

The most important criterion by far in selecting suppliers that are to be developed on new products is management. If the supplier's management is good enough, some buyers are willing to ignore almost all other criteria. In fact, when they want the new supplier badly enough, they will go to great lengths to help him. They may lend him money, equipment, and skilled personnel and be extremely generous in pricing orders until the new supplier gains experience.

In most cases, of course, buyers are not quite so eager to develop a new supplier. But in order to induce a well-managed firm to enter a particular line, they may be willing to place long-term contracts to make it worthwhile for the supplier to invest in plant and equipment needed to enter the new field.

Buyers usually like to start a new supplier with a small part of their total needs. Then, if the supplier has difficulties, they can still fall back on more experienced suppliers for the majority of their requirements. They naturally prefer to negotiate prices from the new supplier that are lower than those charged by established producers. In many cases they are successful in this, particularly when the supplier is being introduced because the buyer considers prices charged by existing producers excessive. Buyers may be forced to discard accepted criteria in supplier selection when they are developing a new source, but they do this only when there is no other choice.

BUYING ABROAD

The ground rules may be quite different when the buyer brings in a foreign supplier. Buying abroad is a post–World War II phenomenon as far as the typical industrial purchasing agent is concerned. Of course, Americans purchased billions of dollars worth of imports prior to the 1950s, when foreign purchasing became commonplace among American industrial purchasing agents. But (to oversimplify a little), at that time American imports fell into two broad categories: raw materials and various other items that were not available in the United States, and specialized finished goods that foreign firms had developed. Nickel and crude rubber are examples of the former category; Scotch whiskey and French perfume are examples of the latter.

Why imports have grown

Prior to World War II, industrial purchasing agents were limited almost entirely to American suppliers for almost everything they bought (except the specialized raw materials not available in the United States). It is only since the late 1950s that many foreign firms have effectively penetrated U.S. industrial markets. This phenomenon was triggered by many developments. Most important of these were a general easing of trade restrictions in the United States, rapid economic development in Western Europe and Japan, development of the international corporation, and more rapid communication.

Trade barriers. The United States was a high-tariff nation from the 19th century until the 1940s. Tariffs were originally raised to permit infant industries to compete with more efficient firms in England and elsewhere in Europe. For example, when the iron and steel industry began in America, it was much less efficient than the British and German industries. High tariffs permitted American steel firms to charge higher prices, giving them the profits they needed to prosper and grow. By the late 19th century, this "infant industry" argument could no longer be used to justify high tariffs. The United States had become the world's greatest industrial power. Despite high wages, its manufactured products were among the lowest cost in the world.

But high tariffs continued to protect most of our industries. In fact, the overall tariff schedule reached an all-time high when the Smoot-Hawley Tariff was enacted in 1930. This raised the average duty to 52.8 percent of the average value of imports. In addition, of course, duties on many individual items were so high that there were no imports at all.

The Smoot-Hawley and other high tariffs were lobbied through Congress with the argument that they were needed to equalize American and foreign costs of production. How could an American firm, it was argued, compete with foreigners willing to work for one-tenth the American wage rate? Economists knew this argument was basically false and that American wages could be high only because American costs were basically low.[10] But legislators were impressed with the argument, and American tariffs generally stayed high.

U.S. tariff policy changed during the Roosevelt administration in the 1930s, and tariffs have been cut substantially since that time. As a result, by the 1960s tariffs offered only a modest barrier to imports of many products. Paper and products had a rate of but 1 percent; the rate for steel was 8 percent; inorganic chemicals, 6 percent; and electrical machinery, 13 percent. Consequently, there are countless products where an efficient foreign producer can hope to compete on reasonably even terms for American business. As a result, American purchasing agents are buying millions of tons of Japanese and West European steel and are also relying on overseas suppliers for countless other items, including ball bearings, office equipment, machine tools, electrical components, and so on.

Economic development overseas.   Contrary to public opinion, lowering of tariff barriers usually does not bring a flood of imports from "cheap labor" countries. In fact, nations with the lowest wages in the world generally could not compete in American markets even if there were no tariffs or shipping costs. Factories in low-income areas of Latin America, India, and the other desperately poor areas of the world are almost always so inefficient that their costs are high despite pitifully low wages.[11] To compete with American firms, the industrial purchasing agent looks almost entirely to the high-wage nations of Western Europe and Japan. These nations have all made enormous technological progress in the past 25 years. The richest (Sweden) has wages and standards of living that are comparable to those of the United States, while the poorest still have levels of living that are more than ten times as high as those of the really poor nations of the world.

Manufacturers in these nations compete primarily in the same way American firms compete, namely, by being more efficient than their rivals. The Japanese steel industry, for example, offsets its competitive disadvantage of being forced to import most raw materials by locating

---

[10] If this were not true, a nation could increase its wealth simply by enacting high tariffs and then raising its minimum wage. But, obviously, this would not work, or a nation like India could become as rich as the United States overnight through an act of its Parliament.

[11] This generalization is usually valid even if the factory in a poor nation is managed by Americans or West Europeans. For example, American auto manufacturers who assemble their cars in Latin America find costs are substantially higher even though the Latin wage level is but a fraction of that paid in Detroit.

its mills near harbors and making more intensive use of the efficient oxygen steel-making process than American firms do.

The purchasing agent who buys abroad is not an exploiter of coolie labor but is simply broadening his supply base. If there are ten qualified producers of a particular product in the United States, there may well be another ten producers in the rest of the world. Some of these foreign firms will be among the most efficient; others still will not measure up to the standards set by American firms. Sometimes there are differences within an industry. For example, Japanese steel firms can easily undersell American producers for most types of steel in world markets. But Volkswagenwerk and other European auto makers still prefer American-made auto body steel and import it at substantial cost.

The international corporation. Many big firms buy and sell to themselves across international borders. A subsidiary of a firm in one nation may specialize in products that it markets to subsidiaries in other nations. The economies of the United States and Western Eruope are becoming more and more dependent on the activities of giant international corporations whose plants are increasingly being built without regard to national borders and whose managements are multinational. Purchasing agents in these firms, more than any other, look upon the world as their potential source of supply.

Perhaps 90 percent of the international firms are American based. The United States still represents their biggest market, but usually overseas operations have more growth potential. Among the biggest American internationals are firms such as General Motors, Ford, Exxon (Esso), USM, International Telephone & Telegraph Corporation, John Deere, International Business Machines, and Singer. Among the foreign-based internationals are the Shell Oil Group (British and Dutch), Swedish Ball Bearing, Phillips Lamp (Dutch), Ciba Pharmaceuticals (Swiss), International Nickel (Canadian), and Unilever (Dutch and British).

Buyers within the international corporation almost automatically look beyond national borders when searching for new suppliers. A few of the internationals have purchasing representatives in almost every major capital. For example, Ford Motor Company not only buys in England and in Germany, where it operates huge plants, but also in Japan. And a Ford purchasing representative in Germany or England is not necessarily concerned only with purchases for use within these countries. He may be searching for a supplier for a Ford plant in some other country.

Jets and telephones. Industrial purchasing is basically a communication process. When he is in the office, the industrial purchasing agent is usually either in a meeting with suppliers or other executives in his own firm or he is talking on the telephone. He also may spend as much as 25 percent of his time outside the office visiting existing or potential suppliers. The jet plane now brings the New York City–based purchasing agent as close to London as he used to be to St. Louis in the prop-plane era. And purchasing agents in the big international firms routinely make overseas telephone calls. As a result, American purchasing agents can now keep in close touch with overseas suppliers and can, therefore, rely on them to do jobs that could have been delegated only to domestic firms a few decades ago. As a result, national boundaries become less significant each year.

Problems in buying abroad

Development of the Common Market and other free-trade areas has, of course, been a tremendous stimulus to the growth of international buying. There are no tariffs at all within the Common Market, so a buyer in Germany need not be the least inhibited about placing orders in Belgium or France, for example. Barriers between trading blocs are also crumbling, so international buying will undoubtedly continue to grow. But there is no denying that, all other factors being equal it is still easier to deal with the supplier who is just down the street.

Communication. Language is often the biggest barrier to successful foreign purchasing. Industrial purchasing is a highly technical process. It is essential that buyer and seller be genuinely fluent in the same language. Unfortunately, the American purchasing agent sometimes has difficulty communicating even with the British. The language is the same but the precise vocabulary is sometimes sufficiently different to pose problems in communication between firms that have never done business with each other. The problem is worse, of course, in dealing with firms on the Continent and, in dealing with the Japanese, the American can normally just speak English and hope he is understood. The communication problem is made more difficult by cultural differences among the various nations. As a result, there is always a danger of slight misunderstandings in international buying, even between firms that have been doing business with each other for years.

Legal and financial. Purchase law is different in each country. Consequently, buyer and seller must exercise much greater care in negotiating contracts, because each is working from a different legal framework. Trade terms must also be carefully defined. Most purchases from American suppliers are made either f.o.b. on some common carrier at the supplier's plant or the price includes delivery to the buyer's plant. Foreign buying usually involves water freight and greater variety of terms and conditions is naturally available.[12] The International Chamber of Commerce publishes a directory of trade terms which many buyers find helpful.

Financing of foreign purchases is more difficult—at the start, at least. Purchases may be made in either buyer's or seller's currency. In some

---

[12] Some of these are described in Chapter 5.

cases, it may not be possible simply to mail the supplier a purchase order and expect him to bill you when he makes shipment. Bills of exchange must be used where, in effect, the seller is guaranteed payment ex dock or on some other basis.

Fortunately, these initial difficulties can usually be worked out, and many American firms use precisely the same procedures in buying from foreigners as they use with domestic firms. The purchase order calls for payment in U.S. dollars, the supplier ships the material and invoices, and the invoice is paid by simply mailing the supplier a check.

However, basic commodities such as tin are often purchased with the seller's currency, while parts and materials made to the buyer's specification may be purchased with buyer's or seller's currency. When firms have not had much previous dealing with one another, more elaborate terms of payment must be used which assure the seller of payment on delivery of merchandise. The details can easily be worked out with banks that specialize in foreign trade—but the process is more time-consuming than domestic purchasing.

Quality standards. The industrial buyer likes to get precisely the quality that he needs. Poor-quality products will perform unsatisfactorily; premium-quality products will be wasteful if the extra quality is not needed. In dealing with American suppliers, the purchasing agent has thousands of standards to guide him. He can tell a supplier, for example, that he wants a "Class 3" fit on a particular item, and there are engineering standards to guide both buyer and seller as to precisely what a Class 3 fit is. The European version of a Class 3 fit may not be the same as the American. The problem is complicated by the fact that most other nations today use the metric system of measurement and, of course, all of their engineering standards are metric. The foreign manufacturer who wants American business must be prepared to meet American engineering standards, but his lack of familiarity with these standards may cause quality problems.

Sometimes American buyers compensate for this simply by setting slightly higher quality standards when buying from foreigners. Of course, this is wasteful if they get more quality than they really need. In fact, some American buyers have complained that European suppliers are inclined to be too fussy and wish they could speed things up a little and cut costs.

When American purchasing agents start buying abroad they also discover that they require quality characteristics that have never been spelled out in formal specifications. These rump specifications were developed over time as buyer and seller got to know each other's needs and abilities. The foreign supplier will not necessarily have this background, and there will be quality problems until buyer and seller get used to each other. Unfortunately, the physical distance that separates buyer and seller makes even simple quality problems difficult to work out. This difficulty is being resolved in part by increased use of the overseas telephone and travel, but there is no doubt that it is still a barrier to foreign purchasing.

Lead times and inventories. While many purchasing agents travel around the world by jet plane, the products they buy abroad usually move by slow boat. As a result, lead times are almost always much longer when buying abroad. If an item has a three-month lead time in the United States, it may be necessary to allow six months when buying it abroad. Greater protective stocks are needed to protect against unexpected fluctuations in supply and demand of the material being bought. Even if the foreign supplier is as reliable as his American competition, international shipping schedules are an added variable, particularly in winter months when gales often sweep the North Atlantic shipping lanes. The United States and the United Kingdom in particular are also vulnerable to periodic strikes by dockworkers and various other maritime unions. These can cut off supplies for months on end.

Thus, there may be a greater real cost in buying overseas which can only be offset if the price charged by the foreign firm is a little lower than that charged by his domestic competitor. In some cases, however, the buyer can have his cake and eat it too. The foreign supplier may offer both a lower price and speedier delivery. This happy situation is most likely to occur when the U.S. economy is at the peak of the boom, while foreign economies have at least a little slack capacity. In addition, some foreign suppliers—most notably the Japanese—are so eager to export that they will offer better deliveries for overseas customers than they offer in their own home market.

Purchasing agents experienced in foreign buying usually protect themselves with adequate inventories even when the foreigner quotes speedier delivery. The foreigner is at least as prone as his American counterpart to be overoptimistic on delivery. In addition, the buyer is not as well informed on foreign economic conditions as he is on the domestic situation. He is much more likely to be caught unprepared by unexpected developments. So he wisely protects himself with greater safety stock.

The foreigner—except perhaps the British supplier—has one built-in advantage over his American competitors: relative freedom from strikes. Factories in the other advanced nations of the world are at least as heavily unionized as those in the United States, but labor and management in foreign firms recognize that they will lose export markets if deliveries are held up because of strikes, so agreements are usually reached amicably. The Japanese workers often "strike" by working so hard that their supervisors are embarrassed and lose face. This type of "strike" is effective in the Japanese culture and, of course, it does not cause export orders to be held up. The northern European worker does not worry about embarrassing the boss by working too hard but arbitration almost always prevents labor-management disputes from erupting into work stoppages—except in Great Britain and Canada, where strikes occur about as frequently as in the United States.

What to buy

There is no doubt, however, that additional competition is beneficial to both the American suppliers and their foreign competitors. Unfortunately, in some cases, the domestic producer may enjoy a natural monopoly even if he is less efficient than the foreigner. It is rarely, if ever, economic to import bulky, relatively cheap commodities that are plentiful in the United States. For example, the United States may not be the world's lowest cost producer of cement, but it costs so much to ship that only a few areas of the United States could afford to use the imported cement even if the foreign producer all but gave it away.

Breaking domestic monopolies. In contrast, products with a very high value per unit of weight and volume are naturals for foreign buying. Sometimes this may be the only way to break what is effectively a domestic monopoly. For example, the United States is undoubtedly the world's lowest cost producer of heavy electrical equipment. Yet, in the 1950s, the Tennessee Valley Authority and various privately owned public utilities found that foreign producers provided the only real source of price competition. It later was proved that the domestic firms had illegally conspired to fix prices.

Foreign producers may also be the only real source of price competition, even when there is apparently no violation of the antitrust laws but the market is dominated by a limited number of producers who avoid price competition. There is little price competition among American steel producers, for example. Each firm knows that if it cuts prices, rival firms will meet its price. The end result is a price war in which all producers earn lower profits than before. Consequently, American steel prices have not tended to respond to changes in competitive market conditions. Foreign steel producers have been more flexible; they know they have to cut prices in order to make inroads into the American market. This upset the price equilibrium that prevailed among domestic producers, and there is now more price competition in the steel industry than at any other time in the 20th century.

Competition is sometimes even limited on an international basis. Competition may be limited to producers in a single nation while all other producers are dedicated to stable prices. The ball bearing industry is a good example. The Swedish firm SKF operates plants in the United States and in Western Europe. It has competitors, but ball bearing buyers in the United States have discovered that there is only modest price competition between SKF and major American firms such as the New Departure Division of General Motors Corporation. Much of the needed price competition has come in recent years from Japanese firms such as Toyo Bearing which are eager to establish themselves in the American market.

U.S. competitive strengths. Bearings are, of course, almost an ideal product to consider for foreign buying. They are high in value relative to their weight and bulk. Their material content is relatively low and their labor content relatively high. In general, raw-material costs in other industrialized nations are at least as high as they are in the United States. More often than not, they are higher. In fact, the United States is an exporter of many industrial raw materials, so American manufacturers enjoy costs as low as any in the world. An American steel mill, for example, might pay $20 per ton for metallurgical coal delivered from a mine in West Virginia. A German mill would pay $30 or more per ton for the same coal shipped across the Atlantic. Similarly, American steel mills would pay $40 to $50 per ton for steel scrap, while the delivered cost to a Japanese mill of that same American scrap might be over $60. Both American and foreign steel mills rely heavily on ores imported from various nonindustrial nations such as Brazil and India. Delivered costs of the ore are roughly comparable.

Costs of plant and equipment are also often roughly comparable in the United States and in other foreign nations. If it costs $10,000,000 to build an ammonia plant in the United States, it probably will cost roughly the same amount to build a similar facility in Germany or Great Britain. In some cases, the foreign construction cost may be higher—perticularly if the plant represents technology that is imported from the United States. The American producer also may enjoy lower investment per unit of output because of economies of scale. If it requires a $1,000,000 investment to produce 1,000 units per year of a particular product, an investment of only $1,800,000 may be needed to produce 2,000 units of the product. The American market is as big as that of all of the other free industrial nations of the world combined, so American producers are more likely to be able to afford huge plants that require minimum capital investment per unit of output.

Financing costs of the foreign plant are almost always higher. The American manufacturer can usually borrow at lower interest rates than his foreign competitors. He also can raise money fairly easily by selling stock. In contrast, financial markets in every European country except Great Britain are relatively undeveloped. In Germany, for example, almost all financing is done by a few big banks, and businessmen find it difficult to sell their securities direct to the public.

Lower capital costs and sometimes lower construction costs per unit of output give American producers an enormous competitive advantage in capital-intensive industries. American producers of such products as industrial chemicals, steel, cement, petroleum, synthetic fibers, paper, and other products requiring a high capital investment per worker usually enjoy the lowest production costs in the world. If their prices are higher than foreign producers, it is the result of inferior technology or competitive conditions.

Foreign strengths. The foreign firm can penetrate American markets only when it is smarter than its American competitors or when it can take full advantage of lower wage rates. The highest wage foreign firms must almost always be smarter to compete successfully in the American market. For example, the Swedish firms Atlas Copco, Saab, and A. G. Volvo enjoy substantial sales in the United States, not because their costs are particularly low (Swedish wage costs are only a little below American levels) but because of product acceptance. Similarly, Scotch whiskey enjoys a big market in the United States even though it can be produced no more cheaply than American whiskey.

However, when an American firm shops abroad for something it can easily get in the United States, it is most likely to be successful with products having a high labor requirement, relatively low material cost, and limited capital investment per unit of output. The foreign producer's only real advantage in such cases is a lower wage level. Typically, all of his other costs are at least as high as those of his American competitors. In addition, part of the foreigner's wage advantage is fictitious. One cannot assume that foreign labor costs are half as much as American costs just because the wage rate may be but one half as high. The real advantage is probably closer to 25 or 30 percent and may even be less than this. Foreign workers usually enjoy more holidays and other benefits than American workers. Also, the work pace in foreign shops is often slower than that in the United States.

In addition, the foreign producer does not always have a competitive advantage even on products with high labor input. Machine tools are a good example. Their labor requirement is very high; raw-material cost per unit of product is relatively low; and plant and equipment investment per dollar of product sales is moderate. Thus, machine tools would seem to be an ideal product for a foreign producer. In some cases they are. European and Japanese manufacturers make many excellent machine tools and equipment which they successfully export to the United States. But, on balance, the United States exports more machine tools than it imports. We are very low-cost producers of heavy specialized machine tools, large stamping presses, and various other capital goods. American and foreign producers both use unautomated methods to produce such products. Higher American wage rates are not, therefore, offset by a high degree of automation. The American advantage is derived from the enormous scale of the home market. Consequently, American producers can design and build their products in larger lots than foreigners. An American firm may be able to spread fixed costs of designing and building a particular machine over perhaps 100 units, while the market of the foreign firm may be limited to perhaps

10 or 20 units. This gives the American firm a tremendous competitive edge over its foreign competitors which the foreigner can overcome only if he is successful in developing a superior design. Some foreign firms have become dominant in their fields for this reason, even though their home market is extremely limited. For example, the Swiss firm of Brown Boveri is a world leader in electric melting furnaces even though the Swiss market probably takes only a small part of its output. Similarly, the Swedish firm, Atlas Copco, is a world leader in construction tools.

Relations with foreign vendors

Locating suppliers. The process of locating foreign suppliers is essentially the same as that for finding the domestic variety. In many cases, the buyer's role is quite passive. Salesmen representing the foreign firms will call on him and solicit his business. The buyer then proceeds to investigate the supplier in the usual way. If the contract warrants it, the buyer would insist on seeing the seller's plant abroad.

In fact, many companies now aggressively seek out foreign suppliers and send their buyers abroad to establish contact with potential suppliers. Leads on potential suppliers can come from foreign purchasing directories, word-of-mouth recommendations from fellow American purchasing agents, customs brokers, and the foreign nation's commercial attaché or chamber of commerce. Various major industrial shows also can provide leads. Among the best known are the Hanover Trade Fair in Germany and the Tool Show in Milan, Italy. Both shows are international in scope. Those who find it inconvenient to attend can request catalogs that list major exhibitors and the products they are displaying. The giant Japanese trading companies—Mitsui, Mitsubishi, Sumitomo, and Itoh—can also provide leads. They maintain offices in major American cities and can provide a variety of services.

Negotiation. The bigger foreign firms are used to doing business with Americans and can be expected to behave much as American firms. National personality does affect supplier relations, however. The Japanese, in particular, are famous for being indirect. American buyers, who are interested in getting right down to business, sometimes complain of what they have called the "snow job" they get when they visit Japanese firms. From the moment they land at Tokyo airport they are feted by their eager Japanese hosts. The food and entertainment are enjoyable but, for the American not used to this, the Japanese seem to take a long time to get down to business. Of course, the American buyer must adapt to foreign business customs. In Japan, in particular, business is mixed with a great deal of wining and dining—so the buyer might just as well be prepared to proceed with his actual business somewhat more slowly than he would in the United States.

Negotiations, particularly with the Japanese, must be quite indirect. Typically, a foreigner visiting a Japanese supplier would be invited to a room where tea is served and hot towels are offered for the hands and face. Several hours might be spent in courteous light conversation before the subject at hand is approached. The buyer's hosts are ultra hospitable. In fact, while American buyers usually grow to become genuinely fond of their Japanese suppliers, they often return from visits to Japan in a state of complete exhaustion from the continuous hospitality of their hosts.

Business relations with Communist countries also pose special problems. Dealings are with a government agency rather than a private firm, which tends to slow the process of negotiation. As long as political relations between the United States and a particular country are going along rather smoothly, the industrial purchasing manager will be welcomed. All of the Communist nations would like to increase their imports from the capitalist West but are limited by lack of foreign exchange. The purchasing agent may be able to do the exporting branch of his company a real service if he can find something to buy on a reciprocal basis from the Communist country. In some cases, out and out barter trade is essential.

Ethical problems.   Each culture develops its own code of ethics. Practices that may be perfectly acceptable in one culture are not in another. Business ethics among the economically advanced nations of the world are usually similar, but problems sometimes arise. When they do, the buyer must use his best judgment. In extreme cases, it may be wise to explain American practices to the foreigner. In others, it is best to go along with local practice. For example, it is not at all uncommon for businessmen to exchange gifts in Japan and Europe. The American buyer who visits Japan, in particular, should have a gift for each of his hosts which he can present at the time of his departure. The practice is also not uncommon in Europe.

While social customs may be substantially different in dealing with foreign suppliers, the analytical buying techniques discussed in future chapters are known and practiced in the other advanced nations of the world. So after they become acquainted with foreign suppliers, American buyers can treat them pretty much as they would their American competitors.

Cases

CASE 12–1. LAWRENCE PLASTICS COMPANY

Dealing with dishonest suppliers

The Lawrence Plastics Company is a medium-sized molder of both injection-molded and compression-molded plastics. It makes various toys for a department-store chain, knobs for several manufacturers of television sets, and miscellaneous parts for a number of other manufacturers. The company employs 250 persons and its stock is owned entirely by the Lawrence family and certain key executives. The company's founder, George H. Lawrence, serves as president and chairman of the board, and his son, Walter G. Lawrence, is vice president and general sales manager. Other members of the company's top-management group include a treasurer, a superintendent, a chief engineer, and a purchasing agent.

Albert Harrison, the purchasing agent, has complete responsibility not only for the company's buying but also for inventory control of both raw materials and supplies. To a limited extent, he is also the company's traffic specialist and handles most contacts with carriers. In addition, Harrison is responsible for receiving and shipping, and the foremen of these departments report to him.

While he has a secretary who assists him on routine purchases, Harrison himself conducts all interviews with suppliers. This takes about one third of his time, but Harrison is convinced that it is worth all of that— and more. The company has a firm rule that no commitments can be made for purchased materials and services by anyone outside the purchasing department. Operating personnel are permitted to talk to suppliers, but they are expected to make it completely clear that purchases can be authorized only by the purchasing department.

Harrison feels that this rule is workable only if he makes a genuine effort to investigate each supplier thoroughly to see if he has anything at all to offer that will help operating personnel do a better job. If the supplier has something to offer that might be worthwhile, Harrison then asks the appropriate operating executive for his opinion. For example, one supplier recently offered a new type of floor-cleaning compound that he claimed was superior. Harrison permitted the supplier to give his presentation to the maintenance foreman, who thought the new product warranted a trial. Harrison got a sample for the foreman to test. The foreman reported that he liked the new compound, so now Harrison buys it.

Two weeks ago, Harrison had a caller by whom he was not impressed. His name was Harold LaPorte, and his card indicated that he was president of the LaPorte Tool Company. LaPorte mentioned that he was a good friend of Howard Lawrence, the brother of the president of Lawrence Plastics. He said that Howard Lawrence (who operates a business in a city 500 miles away) had suggested that he call on Lawrence Plastics because he was certain they would be interested in LaPorte's service. LaPorte claimed he had developed a "metallic revitalization process" that could make old worn tools and dies as good as new. While he refused to discuss the details of his process (he had to keep it secret until he worked out the details of the patent application), he implied that it involved plating or coating the worn tool with some special hard alloy. He supported his presentation with testimonial letters from several satisfied customers in the city where Howard Lawrence's business is located. He said he hoped that Lawrence Plastics would become another satisfied customer so it would recommend LaPorte to other companies in the area.

In order to get Lawrence to try the service, LaPorte proposed that he be given a trial order for demonstration purposes. No fee was mentioned, but Harrison assumed that the first order would be at nominal cost. Nonetheless Harrison was cool to LaPorte's proposal. He had never heard of any of LaPorte's customers, was automatically biased against secret processes, and also reacted unfavorably to LaPorte's personality. He said he would think over LaPorte's proposal, discuss it with other Lawrence executives, and get in touch with him in a few weeks. As soon as LaPorte had left, Harrison requested a credit report on the La-Porte Tool Company.

A few days later, Harrison received the credit report. It was not favorable. Harold LaPorte had operated under two other names at various times in his career. He had been arrested and convicted in 1938 for nonsupport of a child. In 1943 he was arrested, but not convicted, on a charge of violating the regulations of the Office of Price Administration in dealings in scrap metals. In 1949 he was involved in a suit that charged him with selling used cars under misleading circumstances. The report indicated that LaPorte was in the "metal business" but credit investigators could find no record of any facilities or bank accounts and recommended that no credit be granted to LaPorte. The report thus confirmed Harrison's suspicions. He dropped LaPorte from consideration as a supplier under any circumstances and made a mental note to mention LaPorte at the next meeting of his local purchasing agents' association so that other companies in the area might not be hoodwinked by his sales pitch.

A week later, Harrison received an invoice calling for Lawrence Plastics to pay LaPorte $185 for reworking an extrusion mold. The controller had passed it on to Harrison because he had no record of any purchase order being issued for the mold to be reworked. Harrison investigated and discovered that LaPorte had managed to impress the foreman of the tool room with his presentation. The foreman had given the mold to LaPorte so that LaPorte's "engineers could study the mold to see how they could apply the LaPorte process to it."

Harrison now called LaPorte and asked him why he had sent Lawrence an invoice for $185 for just "studying" the mold. LaPorte replied that the bill covered engineering time in developing an application of the process. He said that the process could be applied should Harrison authorize it, and that there would be an additional charge of $185. Harrison replied that he had investigated LaPorte's record and did not want to have any dealings with him, and he asked him to return the mold (which it would cost Lawrence about $2,500 to replace). LaPorte refused to do so until his invoice for engineering time was honored.

Questions

1. What action should Harrison take?
2. What, if anything, could he have done to prevent this problem from arising in the first place?

CASE 12–2. MUSKEGON FURNITURE COMPANY

Investigating a new supplier

Muskegon Furniture is a medium-sized manufacturer of wooden office furniture. It buys its lumber and most of its hardware. Its manufacturing facilities are devoted primarily to finishing wooden parts and assembling finished products. One of its high-volume purchase parts is a metal drawer pull used in its most popular line. This part, along with all other metal hardware parts, is handled by George Schwartz one of the company's buyers. Schwartz has purchased the part from the Akron Stamping and Hardware Corporation for a number of years. Akron has never changed its price of 40 cents for the part despite several increases in labor and material costs. Apparently, increased volume (from about 50,000 units a year at the beginning to about 250,000 currently) and various improvements in manufacturing techniques have offset rising costs.

While Schwartz is completely satisfied with Akron's quality and service, he feels that it is about time he got competitive quotations on the drawer pull. So he solicits bids from several of Akron's regular competitors. In addition, he invites Americon Industries to quote. Until a few weeks ago, Schwartz had never heard of Americon. At that time, Americon's president, a Mr. Sloan, called on Schwartz and asked for the opportunity to bid on a job. He showed Schwartz a list of his equipment and also indicated that he was already making a number of small parts for several well-known customers.

Schwartz reviews Americon's sales literature and is impressed enough to mail Sloan blueprints of the drawer pull and to ask him to quote. However, he warns Sloan that he won't necessarily get the job even if he is low bidder, since price is not the only factor that determines Muskegon's buying decisions.

Americon's bid, based on tooling for 250,000 units per year, is 30 cents. It is the only bid Schwartz gets that is below Akron's price of 40 cents. Schwartz checks Americon's bid carefully. While it is obvious that Americon is figuring costs closely and will have to work hard to make a fair profit, Schwartz becomes convinced that the bid is a legitimate one that Americon can live up to. He checks with two of Americon's current customers, whose purchasing agents he knows through his membership in a local purchasing agents' association, and finds that they are thoroughly satisfied with Americon's quality and service.

Schwartz visits Americon's plant and discovers that, while it is a little smaller than he anticipated, it is equipped to make the drawer pull. However, the company has only one press capable of forming the part. As long as there is no breakdown, this press is quite capable of handling all of Muskegon's needs, although Americon might have some difficulty in meeting schedules if Muskegon's requirements increased substantially.

Schwartz then gets a copy of Americon's most recent financial statement. The balance sheet shows total assets of $330,000, including $12,000 in cash, $30,000 in accounts receivable, $125,000 in inventories, and the balance in plant and equipment. Current liabilities are $105,000, there is a mortgage of $95,000, and the balance represents the owners' equity. Last year's sales were $300,000, and profits after taxes were $19,000.

Question

Prepare a report analyzing the pros and cons of buying drawer pulls from Americon and recommend a buying decision.

CASE 12–3. GNU STEEL CORPORATION

A problem in reciprocity

The GNU Steel Corporation is an integrated steel producer with mills strategically located in several cities on the Great Lakes. Its products include low-carbon sheet steel, strip, plate, and bars, in addition to a broad line of alloy and stainless steels. Reciprocity has always been a problem for GNU because the company both buys from and sells to thousands of different companies.

The company's director of purchases, W. H. Arnold, tries to award business on a reciprocal basis as long as by doing so he suffers no penalty in price, quality, or delivery. His decisions are based on a master book that shows exactly how much GNU both bought from and sold to its suppliers and customers the previous year.

Arnold tries to split his business as equitably as possible among competing customers. For example, last year GNU sold $35 million worth of steel products to automobile manufacturers. The Blue Motors Corporation was the company's single biggest customer, taking $18 million worth of steel. Central Motors bought $8 million worth, and the Acme Automobile Company spent $9 million with GNU. Arnold allocated his purchases of automobiles accordingly. This year he purchased 65 new passenger cars and 135 trucks. Acme makes no trucks, so Arnold bought all of his passenger cars (except for three cars used by salesmen calling on Central and Blue Motors) from Acme. He then purchased 100 trucks from Blue Motors and 35 from Central Motors, which was roughly in proportion to their importance as customers. The auto companies know that GNU divides its auto business as fairly as possible on the basis of the proportion of steel business they give GNU, and they have never complained.

GNU also spends substantial amounts for chemicals and gases. It is a particularly large user of oxygen and divides its business 50–50 between the two largest domestic producers, the Midwest Chemical Corporation and Allied Air Products. Both these companies are part of very large chemical corporations, both of which are overall big steel users. They are approximately equal in importance as GNU customers, each taking about $2.5 million worth of steel per year. GNU in turn buys about $5 million worth of oxygen from each of them.

Arnold has recently been approached by the Zibitsu Chemical Corporation, Ltd., of Kyoto, Japan. Zibitsu has excess oxygen capacity and is offering it at a laid-down cost to GNU that is 25 percent less than the prices charged by Midwest and Allied. Zibitsu is not able to handle all of GNU's requirements but can guarantee delivery for 20 percent of its needs. Arnold investigates Zibitsu and finds it has an excellent reputation for living up to its agreements.

Knowing the reciprocity problem concerning oxygen, Arnold presents his proposal to Kevin Roberts, GNU's vice president in charge of sales. Roberts agrees that Zibitsu's offer is tempting but points out that both Midwest and Allied will be unhappy if Arnold accepts it. Arnold then presents the problem quite frankly to his two suppliers. Roberts's guess was correct: both companies threaten to cut back their steel purchases from GNU if Arnold accepts Zibitsu's bid. They admit, however, that Arnold must consider Zibitsu's price attractive and finally offer (Midwest makes the offer and Allied says it will adjust prices to remain competitive with Midwest) to cut prices 10 percent to keep Zibitsu from making inroads on the domestic market. They also point out that Zibitsu is trying to get rid of excess capacity and may, sometime in the future, raise its price when capacity gets tight again. They also observe that while their purchasing departments know that Belgian and German steel producers will sell pipe more cheaply than American producers such as GNU, they have continued to buy American steel because they feel that mills like GNU are more reliable. They suggest that they may be forced to change their minds if business gets tough enough and they lose a major customer like GNU.

Questions

1. Should GNU accept Zibitsu's offer?
2. What factors should be considered in making the decision?
3. What executives are involved, and who should make the final decision?

13

The buying process

THE BUYING PROCESS is directly concerned with four basic materials management objectives: low prices, continuity of supply, consistency of quality, and favorable supplier relations. The preceding chapter dealt with the selection of potential suppliers, or, more specifically, with the evaluation of a company's ability to supply. This chapter will discuss the process of selecting among a number of qualified potential suppliers. Essential to this process are an understanding of quality and an ability to evaluate prices quoted by competing suppliers for goods that sometimes vary in quality.

QUALITY IS PARAMOUNT

Of the four basic buying objectives, quality may well be the most important. If the buyer does not get the quality of material needed, he gets nothing of any worth. Price, delivery, and favorable supplier relations become unimportant.

Quality is also the least understood buying objective. The price, delivery, and service objectives are fairly obvious. The quality objective seems obvious—but it is not. For example, professional buyers are always interested in paying the lowest prices for material and getting the delivery and service they need, but they do not necessarily seek the highest possible quality. On the contrary, they usually are interested in getting the minimum quality necessary for the material to perform its function satisfactorily. For example, for most applications silver is a higher quality metal than copper. It is easier to draw and has superior electrical conductivity. Yet silver is almost never used to make electrical wire, despite the fact that it is the best metal for this purpose. The reason, of course, is price. Silver is 40 to 50 times more expensive than copper, which does an adequate job.

Quality and price. Quality is usually linked with price. A $6,000 Cadillac automobile is of better quality than a $3,000 Chevrolet. Which car is the better value depends on its function. If the car is to be used for company errands, the Chevrolet is undoubtedly the car to buy. It will serve the function somewhat better than the Cadillac because it is shorter and easier to maneuver. It will last almost as long, be cheaper to operate and maintain, and costs half as much. But if the car is to be used to impress company customers, the Cadillac will probably serve the function more than twice as well as the Chevrolet.

Note that quality is related to function. In one sense, the Chevrolet is actually a higher quality car than the Cadillac. Similarly, a $3 pair of blue jeans can be of higher quality than a $50 pair of fine woolen slacks, if they are to be used as work clothes.

Every salesman tries to convince his prospects that his products are superior in quality to those of competitors. In fact, if a buyer tells a salesman his price is too high, the standard rejoinder is that the quality is high, too. In such cases, the buyer and the salesman both may be right. Then it is up to the buyer to determine if the salesman's company is offering the quality he really needs.

Setting quality criteria. Quality determination is only partly the buyer's responsibility. Also vitally interested are the departments concerned with using and specifying the purchased material. Ideally, the users and specifiers should set objective quality standards for each purchased item. Then the buyer need not concern himself with quality so long as the supplier meets those standards. Unfortunately, for many items this cannot be done in practice. Often it is impossible or impractical to establish standards sufficiently detailed so that the buyer would be assured of satisfactory quality if the supplier met them. Sometimes, the users and specifiers do not really know what standards should be set. They want the "best available at a reasonable price." In some cases each supplier's product is different and performance is the user's only really dependable guide to quality.

Thus quality criteria vary from product to product. No company can use the same criteria to measure the quality of every item it buys. And, regardless of the criteria used, quality is always a problem. Specifications can rarely be so precise that an unscrupulous supplier cannot find a way to beat them. "It's amazing," one contracting officer for the U.S. Army once said, "how ingenious contractors are in spotting loopholes in specifications."[1] One supplier almost succeeded in selling back to the Army canned sweet potatoes that had been sold as surplus because

---

[1] Paul V. Farrell and Dean S. Ammer, "The Truth about Military Buying," *Purchasing,* October 1957, p. 119.

they were spoiled.[2] Other contractors have been successful in beating Army specifications.

What makes quality?

Ethical suppliers will not try to pass off obviously shoddy goods, but they can and do ship substandard merchandise. The quality of any material can never be better than the process by which it is made, but, unfortunately, it can always be a lot worse. The basic theory behind modern quality control practice is that every process tends to produce material with specifications that fall within a predictable range. If the process is "in control" specifications are within this range, and if it is "out of control" they fall outside it.

Role of engineering. Quality determination usually begins in the buyer's engineering department. The engineer specifies the range of qualities that is acceptable and will sometimes even directly specify the process by which the product should be made. For example, suppose a product has a half-inch hole in it that is needed for ventilation. Almost any old hole will do and the engineer does not care how it is made. So he might just mark "½″ D" on the blueprint to indicate the half-inch diameter. By engineering convention, this would mean that the hole could be made with a standard half-inch drill or punch, and the supplier need not worry about it. If the engineer were cost-conscious, he might go one step further. He would actively discourage close tolerances on this hole by marking the hole "for ventilation only" on the blueprint so that everyone would know that it could be made with the cheapest process that was available and that tolerances were not important.

Holes that the engineers really care about are marked either with tolerances or with the specific process. For example, an engineer might mark a half-inch hole on the blueprint as ".500″ ± .006′″" or he might mark it ".500″ REAM." With the former, the engineer does not care what process is used as long as the holes can be held within the desired tolerances; in the latter, he is requesting a specific operation—reaming. In the first case, the supplier can probably hold the hole to plus or minus 0.006 inch (or between 0.494 and 0.506 inch) with a single drilling or punching operation. In the second case, the requirement that the hole be reamed makes two operations necessary, since reaming is a finished operation that must be preceded by drilling or punching.

If the engineer does not indicate tolerances for the reamed hole, engineering convention would indicate that they should fall within the normal range of reamed holes but that, apparently, the dimensions will be no problem as long as the hole is reamed. On the other hand, if the engineer is really interested in the diameter of the reamed hole, he should indicate this with specific tolerances.

---

[2] Ibid.

Mean and dispersion. In no case can the engineer require that a hole be exactly one-half inch in diameter, or 0.500000000 inch. Every process, regardless of how good it is, produces a range of dimensions. The more precise the process, the narrower the dispersion. But the engineer must always be realistic; he should never specify tolerances that are tighter than the process is capable of producing when it is in control.[3]

If the process is in control, the mean characteristic is about equal to specification, and the actual range falls within that specified by the engineer. For example, a half-inch drilling operation might be in control if the mean diameter of the holes drilled was 0.500 inch and the range fell between 0.494 and 0.506 inch.

Quality can be statistically controlled if it is assumed that the process yields a normal distribution about its mean. In the example above, it would be assumed that the control limits of 0.494/0.506 inch were three standard deviations about the mean diameter of 0.500 inch. With a normal distribution, 99.72 percent of all occurrences would therefore fall between these control limits.

If a supplier is on the ball, he will be able to hold any process within its "natural" limits of three standard deviations.[4] In fact, the materials manager who says he buys quality is really insisting that the supplier adhere to two basic rules:

1. Make the product by the required process indicated (implicitly if not explicitly) in the buyer's specifications.
2. Hold the process within three standard deviations of its normal range of fluctuation so that acceptable characteristics are achieved 99.72 percent of the time.

Buyers' specifications

Suppliers usually will make an item by the required process. The buyer is normally concerned almost entirely with whether or not the

---

[3] The only exception to this would be a case where the best process just is not good enough. Then, what you must do is use that process and keep using it until by coincidence you get a product that meets your specifications precisely. This can be extremely costly, of course, and should be avoided if at all possible. One way to avoid it is by selective fitting with a mating part. For example, tolerances on ball bearings and the races in which they roll are normally held to only about 0.001 inch, but the equivalent of a tolerance about ±0.0001 inch can be achieved by selective assembly. A race that is 0.0001 inch oversize can be mated with a ball that is also 0.0001 inch oversize, and so on. This gives effective tolerances much tigher than the process is capable of producing.

[4] This discussion of statistical quality control is admittedly superficial and will undoubtedly be confusing to the reader who has never had a basic course in statistics. To go into the subject much further, however, would extend beyond the scope of this book. A more detailed explanation can be found in Dean S. Ammer, *Production Management and Control* (New York: Appleton-Century-Crofts, 1968) or in any production management or quality control text.

supplier is keeping the process in control. He measures the effectiveness of the supplier's process with specifications. The buyer's quality control program is only as good as the specifications by which quality is measured. There are three basic types of specification commonly used to measure quality: technical, performance, and brand name.

Technical specifications. Quality can sometimes be measured objectively and impartially with instruments and gauges. The specifications may either be industrywide standards or be determined by the buyer's engineers. Most raw materials are bought to some industry or professional specifications. For example, the Society of Automotive Engineers, the American Iron and Steel Institute, and other organizations have developed specifications for steel. If a buyer orders one-inch bar stock made of SAE 4320 steel, he can define quality standards with considerable precision by using recognized industry specifications. When the order is delivered, his inspectors can measure the diameter, concentricity, and finish of the bars to see if they conform to standards. The quality laboratory can make an analysis of the steel to see if it contains precisely the right alloys in the right amounts. It also can test the material to make certain that its hardness, yield strength, ductility, and so on all are within the specified tolerances.

Similarly, if a company buys parts, its blueprints can specify the type of material and also the exact dimensions and other characteristics that are desired. For example, if the part is to be machined from the one-inch bars described above, the blueprint would indicate each dimension with its permitted tolerance. One dimension might be 0.875 inch with a tolerance of plus or minus 0.020 inch. In some cases much closer tolerances might be needed, but the engineer should never specify a closer tolerance than is really needed if the extra quality contributes nothing to the usefulness of the product.

Performance specifications. When a company buys a finished product designed by the supplier, it is not particularly interested in a laboratory analysis of the materials or the dimensions of the product's components. Its primary interest is the performance of the product itself. Companies measure quality of such vendor-designed items as machine tools and maintenance, repair, and operating (MRO) supplies with performance specifications.

Performance specifications are sometimes combined with technical specifications. For example, one company requires that the aluminum paint used by its maintenance department dry tack-free in two hours and hard in six hours. It also specifies that the paint must not crack when a test panel is "rapidly bent 180° over a ⅜-inch diameter mandrel." Hiding and hardness qualities also are specified. All these are performance specifications. The company determines whether or not they are being met by applying the paint to a test panel and then measuring drying time and other characteristics.

The procedure for determining conformance to technical specifications is a little different. Tests are made on the product itself, not on its application. For example, one technical specification requires that the paint be 13.5 percent pigment and a minimum of 59 percent nonvolatiles. Conformance to it can be determined in a laboratory, by heating the paint to boil off volatiles and by other tests.

Approved brands. In some cases neither performance nor technical specifications can be developed satisfactorily. In addition, neither type of specification can be developed without incurring some costs. For this reason, most smaller organizations are forced to buy almost everything on a brand-name basis, and even very large organizations do some buying by brand name. For example, it would be difficult even for very large users to develop worthwhile specifications for products such as pickup trucks, copying machines, and electric typewriters. Each manufacturer's brand would be a little different, even though it might be designed to provide almost identical performance at the same prices charged for competing brands. Each manufacturer naturally would claim that his product was the best value. The only objective way the user could evaluate this claim would be to test several brands over a period of years to see if they performed satisfactorily. Careful records of breakdowns, repair bills, and user preference would eventually provide objective evidence of quality.

However, the buyer can still make errors with such records. Manufacturers sometimes change specifications and qualities, and a manufacturer whose products have a good history may currently be producing a product inferior to those of his competitors. For this reason, many purchasing departments try to keep abreast of quality changes by asking users of equipment to report regularly on the quality of all newly purchased items (see Figure 13–1).

Whenever possible, the buyer should be given the widest possible choice of competing brands that are equivalent in quality. Most companies test every major brand. Chrysler Corporation's quality standards for electric typewriters are a good example. All major brands—International Business Machines, Remington Rand, Royal-McBee, Underwood, and Smith-Corona—are approved. Individual characteristics of each brand are analyzed in Chrysler's specifications. The specification then provides that "selection of the models shall be determined by the requirements of the work to be performed." It further provides that "all factors being equal, the selection of the manufacturer, based upon competition, shall remain with Central Purchasing."

Restrictive specifications

To prevent misunderstandings, specifications should be as clear and explicit as possible. They should be written so as to encourage a maxi-

FIGURE 13–1

Nº 257	PURCHASING DEPARTMENT REQUEST FOR QUALITY REPORT	Part No.

Notification of: new part,   new vendor,   new material,   part change,   cost reduction.

Estimated annual savings:

Quantity............Location of sample:

Description of sample:

Description:

Date

PO No............Date decision requested:

Vendor

Product

To: Comments:

Purchasing Dept.

To: Comments:

Sometimes the user's opinion is the buyer's best guide to quality. One purchasing department sends this form to users of material whenever it makes changes in suppliers or specifications.

mum number of suppliers to bid. Preclusive specifications that restrict the number of bidders to a few are a problem in almost every company. They allow for a minimum of competition, and buyers find it impossible to do a first-rate job.

Materials personnel can never relent in their efforts to prevent specifications from becoming restrictive. Working against them are almost all of their regular suppliers and many specifiers and users of material in their own company. Every supplier dreams of customer specifications tailored to his products or processes. No longer would he have to fight for business against a number of competitors. Instead, he would automatically get an order whenever a need arose.

Brand name.   Supplier sales efforts are directed at both materials personnel and the engineers who specify the material. Salesmen try to convince engineers in particular that their product and processes are uniquely superior. In some cases, they may succeed in convincing engineers that theirs is the only product that will do the job. When this is the case, the engineer feels obliged to specify the supplier's product in his design or requisition. He may simply include the supplier's brand name in his specification, or he may describe the product with performance or technical specifications that can be met only by one supplier's brand.

User brand preference is a particularly acute problem in nonprofit organizations. The purchasing manager's argument that profits will be higher if lower cost brands are purchased simply does not carry any weight in an organization where profit is not an objective. It is no accident that companies that specialize in supplying the nonprofit sectors of the economy, such as educational and hospital supply firms, enjoy rates of return on capital greatly in excess of those earned by companies whose products are subject to intense price competition.

The buyer can sometimes sidestep the brand-name problem by persuading the user to add the phrase "or equal" to his specifications. This permits the buyer to purchase equivalent, competing brands from a number of suppliers. For example, a specification for electric typewriters might read "International Business Machines or equal." The buyer then would be perfectly free to buy from Remington Rand, Underwood, Royal-McBee, or Smith-Corona if he chose to do so, because they are standard, accepted competing brands.

There are more subtle ways in which to make specifications preclusive than convincing engineers that a certain brand is superior. A supplier can achieve the same objective by persuading engineers to incorporate specifications that are unique to his products or processes. Such specifications need not be completely preclusive; all they need do is give the supplier a slight advantage that permits him to underbid competitors without hardship. This is one of the major reasons that suppliers assiduously cultivate company engineers and other requisitioners of material.

Selling with service.   More sophisticated suppliers do not necessarily spend much time or effort trying to convince engineers of the intrinsic superiority of their product, particularly when they are so similar to those of competitors that such a claim would be an insult to the engineers' intelligence. They have a more positive approach: They assist the engineers in product development. As a result of their help, the specifications either become at least partly preclusive or the supplier gets such a headstart on his competitors that he gains the equivalent of restrictive specifications.

This is the best selling approach, since both seller and buyer may gain from it. The seller gets an edge on his competitors and so does not have to compete quite so vigorously on price. The buyer gets the benefit of the seller's technical know-how. The only problem, from the buyer's viewpoint, is that the loss of competition resulting from his giving an advantage to one supplier may more than offset the benefits of the supplier's assistance. Buyers try to overcome this drawback by retaining complete control over which suppliers are chosen to give technical assistance and by working to keep the specifications that are developed as nonrestrictive as possible.

The least restrictive specifications are those that impartially measure technical characteristics or performance. The system of approving certain brands is inherently more restrictive, since such tests can never be completely objective. No set of specifications is foolproof, however. Each inevitably freezes out at least some potential suppliers, but so long as an adequate number remain who are eager to bid, the buyer need not worry too much.

SECURING QUOTATIONS

When the buyer has reviewed specifications to make certain that they are as unrestrictive as possible, he is ready to solicit quotations from potential suppliers. With new items, buyers try to get at least three competitive quotations (provided the item is not proprietary). For major purchases, six to eight quotations are not uncommon, and, when the buyer has difficulty in finding a supplier, he may issue as many as 100 quotation requests.

While buyers should not hesitate to permit any qualified supplier to bid, they obviously cannot permit every possible supplier to quote for every projected purchase. They simply do not have the time or the clerical help to prepare that many quotation requests. Many buyers methodically rotate their lists of potential suppliers in requesting quotations. If a supplier is high bidder on several quotations, his name is temporarily dropped from the list. Suppliers who already have a substantial amount of the buying company's business may also be dropped temporarily if the buyer wants to avoid taking too great a percentage of their capacity.

Buyers often are too generous with quotation requests. It is pointless, for example, to go to the trouble of formally requesting a quotation from a supplier who consistently refuses to sell at prices different from those shown in his catalog or published price lists.[5] Nor should a buyer ever request a quotation from a supplier with whom he has no intention of doing business. Quotations are expensive to prepare, and it is unethical to ask suppliers to prepare them when they will not get an order regardless of what price they quote. In general, price should be the only unknown about the supplier at the time the quotation is requested. The buyer should already have investigated the supplier's potential quality, delivery, and service capabilities, although sometimes it is not worthwhile to make a really intensive investigation until the supplier has submitted a favorable quotation.

Exceptions to quotations

The quotation request should include complete specifications for the material, the quantities required, and a tentative delivery schedule. In addition, most purchasing departments indicate a deadline for submission of quotations; some, including almost all government buying offices, refuse to consider late bids. Some companies also print their purchase terms and conditions on their quotation requests.

If suppliers return quotations with all the information requested and

---

[5] The buyer should not automatically assume, however, that a supplier will not offer concessions on published prices if he is requested to do so by the buyer or is required to do so by competitive forces.

take no exception to any terms or conditions, the buyer is ready to analyze his quotes and select the supplier. However, this is frequently not the case. More often suppliers propose changes in specifications, delivery schedules, and purchase terms, and they also may make errors.

Exceptions to specifications. On production parts, suppliers frequently take exception to specifications. They usually suggest minor changes that will permit them to make the part more economically. Occasionally, they may even propose a complete redesign. Most companies try to encourage such suggestions, since they frequently reduce the cost of the item. Some companies even go so far as to include a statement in their quotation request that suggestions are welcomed. For example, Ford Motor Company quotation requests include this statement:

> We will welcome suggestions regarding design changes that you believe will facilitate the tooling or fabrication of the part or both. However, all such changes must have the approval of our Engineering Department and arrangements must be made to incorporate such changes on our blueprints because our purchase orders will specify delivery as per our blueprint.

As the Ford statement indicates, the purchasing department must submit all proposed changes to the engineering department for approval. Most large companies have routine procedures to handle such changes and use quotation request forms similar to that in Figure 2–3 in Chapter 2. The buyer can do nothing with the supplier's quotation until engineering approves or rejects the proposed change. If the change is approved, he usually will get new quotations from other bidders.

Changes in schedule. If a supplier cannot deliver material when it is needed, he is automatically disqualified. But sometimes suppliers propose delivery changes that are not so clear-cut. The delivery date requested by the buyer may be unrealistic, and the supplier simply must be given more time to fill the order. In this case, the buyer may have to propose a change in schedule to the various managers in his company who are concerned.

Occasionally a supplier may make what amounts to a counterproposal on delivery terms. For example, the buyer may have requested a quotation for 10,000 units of an item with delivery in ten monthly shipments. Suppose a supplier suggests either a single shipment of 10,000 pieces or two shipments of 5,000 pieces each. Obviously that supplier's bid is not comparable to bids that agree to the original plan.

The buyer should request the supplier to requote on the same delivery basis as originally requested. Then he should compare the two bids from the same supplier. If the supplier offers a lower price for different delivery terms, the buyer should analyze them to see if they are really advantageous. Suppose the supplier quotes a price of $1.00 per unit if he can ship in a lot of 10,000 pieces and a price of $1.10 if he must schedule his shipments over a period of ten months at the rate of 1,000 units per month. In effect, the supplier is offering to reduce the total cost of the purchase by $1,000 ($.10 × 10,000) if the buyer will accept the entire order in a single shipment. For this saving the buyer must carry for ten months an average $5,000 inventory instead of a $500 inventory. The buyer can readily determine if this is worthwhile by applying the principles discussed in the chapters on inventory management. If the savings exceed the additional carrying cost (less the saving in procurement cost by processing a single shipment instead of ten separate ones) and possible obsolescence, then the offer to purchase the larger quantity is attractive. The buyer should then go back to the other suppliers who quoted and ask them to requote on the same basis.

Purchase terms. The buyer should study each supplier's quotation to make certain that all offer comparable terms and conditions. For example, one supplier may quote a firm price, another may insist on some provision for escalation for labor and material costs, and a third may insist on "price in effect at time of delivery." Obviously these quotations are not comparable, even if all three suppliers quote identical prices.

The buyer should try to persuade suppliers to revise their bids and accept the terms and conditions he wants. On pricing terms, for example, most buyers prefer fixed-price contracts for short lead-time items, although they will accept escalation on long lead-time contracts in order to prevent suppliers from inflating their bids to allow for possible higher costs.

If the bidder flatly refuses to quote within the terms and conditions desired, the buyer has two choices. He may disqualify the bid, or he may accept it while making allowance for the disadvantageous terms. In the latter case, the buyer may put a price tag on the supplier's terms. Suppose, for example, that a supplier's current price is $1 and his terms are "price in effect at time of delivery." The buyer may have to inflate this bid to $1.02 or $1.03 when comparing it to the quotations of suppliers who are willing to guarantee fixed prices.

Errors. The buyer should review each quotation carefully to make certain the supplier has made no mistakes in preparing it. He should make sure that the supplier's quotation covers the exact requirements described in his quotation request. If it does not, he should return it to the supplier and ask him to requote. The buyer should be particularly wary of bids that are unusually high or low. If a dependable low-cost supplier submits a bid that is substantially higher than those of his competitors, the buyer should return it and have the supplier check it for errors. The buyer should be equally cautious about exceptionally low bids. Only the most inexperienced and naive buyers will quietly accept a bid of 10 cents for an item that is worth at least $1. This is not only unethical—it is uneconomic. The supplier eventually will detect the error and will either request a price increase or, if he feels he has been treated unfairly, refuse to do business with the buyer's company.

If a supplier rechecks a bid and insists that no errors have been made, the buyer should still be cautious if he is convinced that the bid is unrealistic. If the bidder is not too familiar with the buyer's requirements, the buyer may simply disqualify the bid. But if the bidder is an experienced, reliable supplier, the buyer may wish to review the bid in detail with him to make certain there are no errors. He also may arrange to have the specifications explained to the supplier by product or quality control engineers.

Analysis of quotations

After exceptions and errors have been taken care of, the buyer is ready to tabulate the quotations on a work sheet for purposes of comparison (see Figure 13–2). If there are no special proposals by suppliers, this comparison is not difficult to make. For each supplier, the buyer would list:

1. Net unit prices proposed for various purchase quantities.
2. Terms of payment.
3. Setup costs and minimum charges, if any.
4. Cost of any special tools to be purchased by buyer for supplier's use.
5. Unit shipping cost if the item is sold on a basis other than f.o.b. buyer's plant.
6. Other charges, if any.

In some cases, the buyer can select the lowest cost supplier with no more than a glance at his recap sheet. If the low bidder is satisfactory in all other respects, he gets the order. However, many buying decisions, particularly important ones, cannot be made so easily. Quotations must be recalculated to make them comparable, quotations may not be for identical items, or all bids may be too high.

Bids comparable economically. Quotations from suppliers frequently cannot be compared until the buyer adjusts them to make them comparable. For example, suppose a buyer gets two bids[6] for a part weighing one pound, having a usage of 10,000 units per year, and requiring an investment in special tools. Shipment is to be made in lots of 1,000 pieces.

Supplier A quotes a unit price of $1 f.o.b. buyer's plant with a $2,500 charge for special tools and a special setup charge of $10 for each

---

[6] Note that only rarely would a buyer limit himself to two bids if the purchase were at all important. Usually he would get at least three bids, and he might get half a dozen or more if he had as many qualified suppliers willing to quote.

FIGURE 13–2

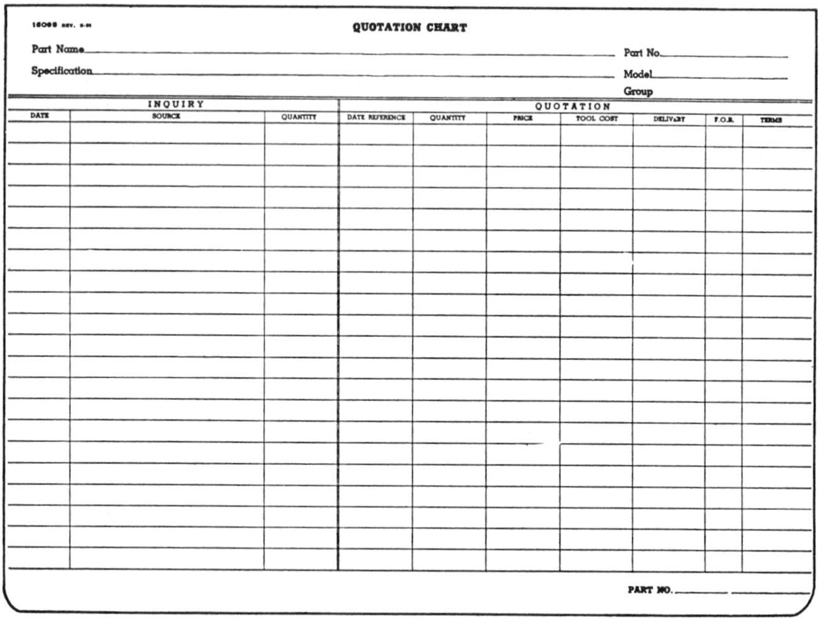

QUOTATION CHART

Part Name ______ Part No. ______

Specification ______ Model ______

Group

INQUIRY			QUOTATION						
DATE	SOURCE	QUANTITY	DATE REFERENCE	QUANTITY	PRICE	TOOL COST	DELIVERY	F.O.B.	TERMS

PART NO. ______

Courtesy Chrysler Corporation

Chrysler Corporation uses this form to compare quotations from competing suppliers of production parts. Chrysler buyers keep separate quotation records for each part.

1,000-piece lot. His payment terms are 2/10, net 30. Supplier B quotes a unit price of 95 cents f.o.b. shipping point with a $3,500 tool charge and no setup charges. His payment terms are net 30 days, and the LTL freight rate from his plant to the buyer's plant for 1,000-pound shipments is 70 cents per cwt.

It is not immediately obvious which of the two bids is the lower. The buyer must tabulate them for comparison. He would immediately make the following adjustments in the quotations:

	Supplier A	*Supplier B*
Unit price quoted	$1.00	$.95
Unit freight cost paid by buyer (1 lb. × $.007/lb.)	–	.007
Unit cost of setup charge for 1,000-piece lots	.01	–
Adjusted unit price	$1.01	$.957
Tool cost	$2,500	$3,500
Payment terms	2/10, net 30	net 30

The table above shows that the adjusted unit price of supplier B is $.053 lower but his tool charge is $1,000 higher. Therefore, B must ship 18,867 pieces ($1,000/.053) before his lower unit price more than offsets his higher tool charge. This would take almost 22 months with a usage of 10,000 pieces per year.

In practice, the buyer would want to be reasonably certain that the part will stay in production for at least two years before he would give the order to supplier B. There are two reasons for the buyer to make the break-even point between A and B more than 22 months' usage:

1. The higher tooling cost for supplier B requires an immediate cash outlay. Cash in hand is always worth more than cash derived from savings made in the future. The cash itself is worth some interest during the period. In addition, if the buyer's calculations are incorrect and the part becomes obsolete immediately, there is less loss.

2. Supplier A offers a 2 percent discount if bills are paid within 10 days; supplier B does not. If the buyer's accounting department pays bills within ten days as a matter of routine, A's discount is a clear saving of $200 per year and the piece-cost saving by buying from B is reduced from $612 per year to $412 per year. The 2 percent discount is a definite "plus" for A, even if the buyer's accounting department ordinarily takes 30 days to pay bills. The 2 percent discount is earned, in effect, if the bill is paid 20 days earlier; this is equal to an annual interest rate of 36 percent. There are few solvent companies that are so strapped for cash that they can afford to overlook such a profitable short-term investment opportunity. In fact, for most purchases any difference in payment terms between suppliers can be considered a direct difference in price.

If the buyer knows precisely how many pieces he will buy over the life of the tooling, he can compare quotations with precision. If the part in the example were to have a life of precisely two years (or a total usage of 20,000 pieces), then the buyer could make the following comparison between suppliers A and B.

	Supplier A	*Supplier B*
Total piece cost (20,000 pieces at adjusted prices)	$20,200	$19,140
Tool cost.	2,500	3,500
Total cost	$22,700	$22,640
Savings buying from supplier B		$60
Discount earned on payment terms.	$454	–
Net advantage buying from supplier A (including payment terms).	$394	

The bids above are so close that it is a toss-up whether the buyer would give the order to supplier A or B. However, there is no doubt that A offers a slightly better deal when payment terms are considered. The buyer, however, would not necessarily give A the order after making the comparison. He might ask B why he did not offer better payment terms if they were normal in his industry.[7] Or he might suggest to B that he review his tooling cost to make certain he had received the lowest possible quotation from the tooling shops he contacted. Many suppliers quote on the basis of rather careless estimates of tool costs— made, in many cases, before they have even obtained quotations from tool shops. Thus, they are sometimes willing to reduce tool quotations after they have studied their needs in greater detail. While it is unethical to disclose competitors' bids, some negotiation of this sort is normal before an order is placed.

Bids for nonidentical items.   The example above is applicable primarily to production parts made to the buyer's specifications. An entirely different problem is encountered in evaluating supplier-designed items. In such cases, bidders usually are quoting on performance specifications. They may be bidding on a machine tool to do a given job or a component to perform a given function. In each case the supplier is selling both his design efforts and his manufacturing skills. Since each supplier's design is unique, bids are not comparable. Technical evaluation is necessary.

In such cases, engineers carefully review each supplier's proposal. They indicate not only which proposals they prefer but which are acceptable. Suppliers whose bids are not acceptable may be asked by the buyer to requote, especially if their proposed prices are attractive.

The final buying decision is based on both the buyer's evaluation of the economic factors of the bid and the engineer's evaluation of the technical factors (see Figure 13–3). Some companies evaluate bids on a point basis. Engineers assign preference ratings to each bid which reflect their technical evaluation of the supplier's product. They list their preferences in sequence (1, 2, 3, 4) and also indicate separately bids that are unacceptable to them. The buyer lists his preferences in sequence. If a bidder gets a top rating from both the buyer and the engineer, there obviously is no problem. But what of a bidder rated only second or third by an engineer is rated tops by the buyer? In such cases, the buyer and engineer usually try to resolve their differences. In many instances the buyer's preference will prevail if the engineer agrees that the third-best bid is still technically acceptable. In some instances, buyer and engineer may compromise and accept a bid that is second best to both but still fulfills their objectives.

Negotiation of bids.   Good buyers do not necessarily accept the low

---

[7] On price-fixed items, many buyers get around fair-trade laws by persuading suppliers to offer better than usual terms of payment. The supplier is willing to do so to get business from a competitor because the margin of profit on such items is more than ample. Payment terms of 7%–10 days are not unheard of; they are, of course, a thinly disguised trade discount, since the buyer theoretically earns a return of 126 percent on his money by paying in 10 days instead of in 30 days.

FIGURE 13–3

November 5, 19___

MEMO TO: Chief Engineer
      cc: Plant Manager
           Project Engineer
           Plant Purchasing Agent
           Asst. Director of Purchasing

FROM: Purchasing Engineer

SUBJECT: QUOTATION ANALYSIS–ELECTROLYTIC CELL–LITHIUM HYDRIDE EXPANSION

      The following are the vendors and prices quoted for a fabricated steel electrolytic cell for the Lithium Hydride expansion:

VENDOR	DELIVERY	F.O.B. POINT	TOTAL PRICE
A_____ Welding Co.	3 Weeks	Exton, Pa.	$ 835.00*
F_____ Welding Shop	1 Week	Exton, Pa.	864.00
N_____ Steel Co.	6–8 weeks	Nazareth, Pa.	1,127.00
B & M Co.	3 weeks	Phila., Pa.	1,780.00
A. J. S & Co.	3 weeks	Exton, Pa.	840.00
P–P Co.	4 weeks	Exton, Pa.	1,235.00

      When A___, the low bidder, was contacted and advised of the special requirements as to soundness of weld, they advised that this would require a different method of welding and the cost increase would be approximately $100.00. We had also asked if they could bend two of the corners, instead of welding them, thereby eliminating about 25% of possible trouble area in the wetted section and they advised that they did not have the equipment to bend that heavy plate. A. J. S, being the next lowest bidder, were asked the same question and they advised that they had anticipated the importance of these welds and had provided for it in their original quotation of $840.00 and they also advised that they could bend two of the corners, thereby reducing the welding, with no change in price.

      On the basis of price, delivery and quality workmanship, were commended that this cell be fabricated by A. J. S & Company. S has advised that they will put a code welder on this job and make every effort to produce the very best welding possible.

W. H. Snell

Quotations on capital equipment must be carefully analyzed. Not only are prices and terms different for various suppliers, but so are the products themselves, since each supplier quotes on his own design.

bid even if they are sure it is made by a first-rate supplier and is comparable to competitors' bids. They may even reject all bids if they feel the lowest acceptable quotation is too high.

Buyers do not reject bids arbitrarily, however. They rely as much as possible on objective price data to assist them in negotiation. Even if the buyer is satisfied, there usually still is some need for negotiation. Packaging, freight rates, supplier inventories, split shipments, and so on may be discussed.[8]

SELECTING THE SUPPLIER

Buyers naturally prefer to award business to the bidder quoting the lowest prices. However, they do not always do so. If a bidder quoting a higher price offers better quality, delivery, or service, he may get the order. As we will see in the next chapter, reciprocity and other factors also influence the selection of suppliers. In general, however, the buyer is on the defensive if the low bidder does not get the job. Many companies require buyers to enter detailed explanations in their records when this is the case, and some buyers prefer to make an explanation even when it is not required in order to protect themselves against charges of collusion.

Companies may have as many as four or five suppliers for a given item simultaneously. But, in most cases, buyers rely on a single supplier for all of their requirements of a particular item. If the item does not become obsolete, they will solicit bids from other suppliers from time to time to make sure that their supplier is still competitive. In addition, they make use of learning-curve analysis[9] and other techniques to make certain that their supplier is passing on the benefits of productivity improvements by reducing prices periodically.

Advantages of a single source. By buying all requirements of a particular item from a single source, buyers can gain several advantages:

1. They make maximum use of their buying power. They concentrate all requirements for a certain item on a single supplier and thereby get the largest possible quantity discount.
2. There is less administrative work for the buyer's entire organization, since purchase orders, receiving reports, inspection reports, checks, and so on are issued to only one supplier per item.
3. Suppliers often offer special price concessions if they can make 100 percent of the requirements of a given item, since they then can set up their production in the most economic manner and invest in more efficient tooling.

---

[8] Negotiating techniques are discussed in detail in Chapter 17.

[9] This is discussed in Chapter 16.

4. Less investment in special tooling is usually needed. One supplier generally needs only one set of tools; with two suppliers each needs a set.
5. Suppliers have more incentive to aid in methods improvement. If a supplier is the sole source for an item, he is more likely to regard himself as a partner in the company's product, particularly if he is manufacturing the item under a long-term contract. As a result, he will be more likely to devote part of his research and development efforts to improvements.

Advantages of multiple sources.   Despite these advantages, many companies do their utmost to avoid relying on a single source for all but the most unimportant items. They try to have at least two suppliers for each item, and sometimes they have three or four, for one or more of the following reasons:

1. With several sources, there is less risk of interruption of supply due to quality problems, strikes, fires, and so on. If one supplier fails, the other(s) can take up the slack.
2. With two or more suppliers for one item, a healthy competitive spirit can develop in which each vies to improve methods and reduce costs in order to get a greater share of the business. With a single source, the supplier may become so well versed in making the item that he gets a virtual monopoly of its manufacture and, sometimes, no competitor brought in at a later date can meet his prices.
3. Many items either require little or no tooling or are used in such large quantities that duplicate tooling is necessary anyway. In these cases, there is no cost premium for tooling a second source.
4. The unit price of the item is no higher with two or more sources than it would be if all requirements were concentrated on a single source.
5. The buyer has found a new supplier with low prices whom he would like to introduce to the item but whom he is not yet familiar enough with to trust with 100 percent of the business.

PLACEMENT AND DELIVERY

When the buyer concludes negotiations and finally settles on a supplier, he places the order. He may simply mail a purchase order with the agreed-on terms and conditions to the supplier. Or, if he wants the supplier to start on the order immediately, he may telephone or wire him that he has been awarded the contract. The purchase order then is sent in a few days.

The buyer's job ends with the placement of the order only on minor, short lead-time items for which there is no immediate need. In such cases, the supplier ships when he receives the order and the transaction is complete. No buyer, however, would dare place an important order for parts, material, or equipment and then forget about it. He always would make some sort of routine follow-up even if there were no problems.

Acknowledgment of orders. Routine follow-up may start with acknowledgment of the order. A copy of the purchase order is kept in a separate file of unacknowledged open orders until an acknowledgment is received. If the supplier does not acknowledge within a week after he should have received the order, a buyer or expediter either phones or sends him a written reminder.

Some companies persistently follow up for acknowledgments of orders until they finally get them from suppliers. They know that in most cases the supplier is legally committed to the terms and conditions of the order only after he has formally acknowledged or actually filled the order. Also, when there is no follow-up for acknowledgments, there theoretically could be serious problems if the order should have been mislaid or lost in the mail. The company might suddenly discover a few days before the material was needed for production that the supplier had no record of the order. The result would certainly be a critical shortage, and possibly even a shutdown.

Nevertheless, many companies do not bother to follow up except when they are required to do so by government regulations, as on defense contracts. They maintain that such follow-up is expensive and never is worth the trouble or the expense it causes. The rare order that goes astray need not cause any trouble, either. In most cases, the vendor would have already been notified of the order by telephone or letter of commitment, and he would inquire if he did not receive a formal purchase order. In other cases, companies would discover that an order had gone astray through routine follow-up or when a supplier sales representative called to discuss his business prospects.

A company that insists that orders not be acknowledged can occasionally avoid disputes over purchase terms and contracts. This problem arises when the seller takes exception to the terms and conditions of the buyer's purchase order. If both buyer and seller are completely inflexible about the terms and conditions they will accept, a deadlock results. Legally the order is not binding on either party. The problem is solved in most cases by ignoring it. Both buyer and seller assume they have a valid contract (each on his own terms) and eventually the buyer gets the material he ordered. This is bad practice, but sometimes it is the only way two giant corporations with inflexible procedures can successfully deal with each other.

Although such legally vague contracts rarely create problems, some buyers attempt to circumvent a deadlock over terms and conditions by simply mailing the supplier an order and refusing an acknowledgment. For example, Magnetic Research Corporation of Hawthorne, Cali-

fornia, uses this clause as a substitute for an acknowlegment copy of
the order:

Delivery is a major condition of this order. If for any reason you cannot
meet the terms of this Purchase Order you must reply within 72 hours indicating any deviations. The absence of a reply will constitute an acceptance
of this order and an agreement to meet the terms and conditions as specified
above and on the reverse side hereof.

It is a moot point whether this clause would actually be enforceable.
That is, if a supplier simply did nothing, the Magnetic Research Corporation might not be able to hold him to the terms and conditions of
its purchase order. But the clause does open the problem up, and a
supplier who was acting in good faith would not deliberately ignore
it.

Routine progress follow-up. Regardless of whether or not they worry
about acknowledgments of purchase orders, most purchasing departments do make routine checks on suppliers' progress on orders. The
frequency of follow-up depends on the importance and urgency of the
item. Minor items may get no follow-up as long as inventories are ample.
Most of the more important items get at least one progress check, which
is most often made a week or two before the promised delivery date.

The procedure for handling such a check need not be complicated.
One of the more popular procedures involves keeping copies of the
purchase orders in file folders marked with the date for which follow-up
is scheduled. Each morning (or once a week), a secretary gives the
buyer the file folder of orders to be checked that day.

Often the follow-up process is entirely automatic and the buyer does
not get into the act at all if there are no problems. A clerk sends a
postcard requesting progress information on each order a week or ten
days before shipment is promised. The buyer is consulted only if the
vendor advises that he cannot meet his original delivery promise. When
delivery is not made on the scheduled date, the buyer may request
information using a form similar to Figure 13–4. If he needed the item
badly, however, he would telephone the supplier for information.

More complex follow-up systems are used for major production parts
and equipment. The buyer estimates what progress the supplier should
have made on the order at various dates if he is to complete it on schedule. For example, he might check progress on an order for a production
part when completion of tooling is scheduled, when tools are to be tried
out, and when initial production is scheduled. If everything is going
according to plan on each of these and other critical dates, he is reasonably certain that actual production shipments will be made on schedule.

In the typical purchasing department, more than 99 percent of all
orders can be handled with little or no follow-up. Routine progress
checks are insurance against failure, but they are not necessary except

FIGURE 13–4

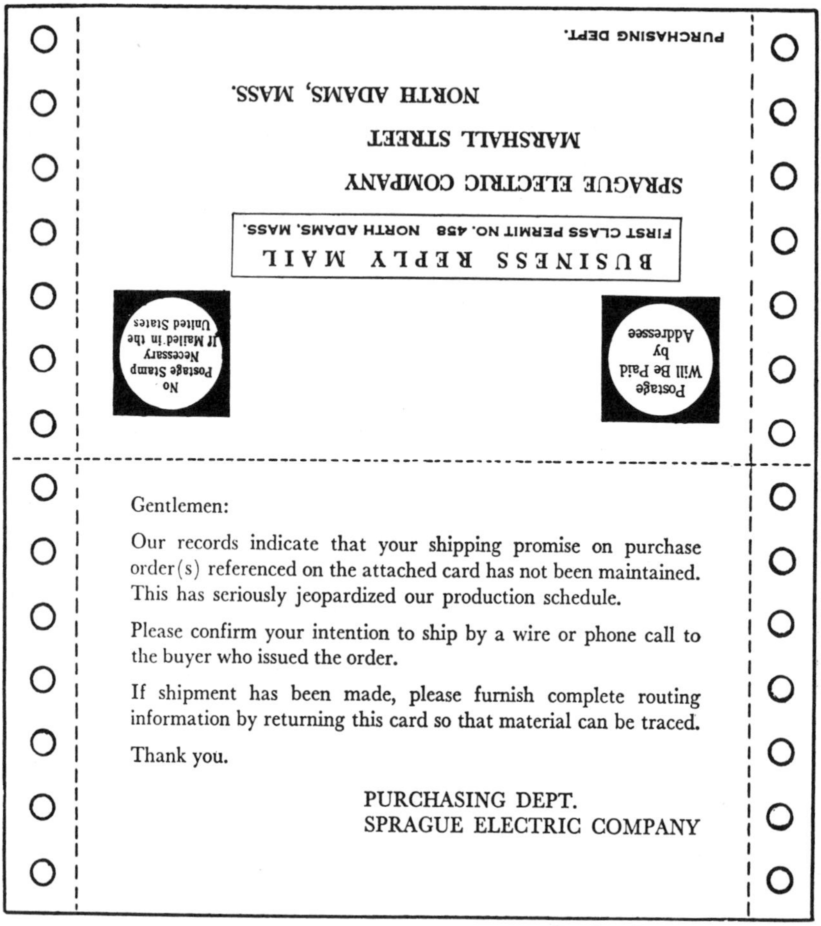

Courtesy Sprague Electric Co.

Many companies use double postcards for routine follow-up at various stages. The card above is used when the supplier has not kept his delivery promise. The supplier then returns the second card to the buyer with his shipping promise noted on it.

in a few cases. This is fortunate, since the less than 1 percent of all orders that are problems manage to take an enormous percentage of the materials executive's time. Dealing with these orders is discussed in the next chapter.

SALE OF SCRAP AND SURPLUS

The buying process does not necessarily end when satisfactory material is received on schedule. The buyer also must sell surplus and scrap materials that are inevitably generated when material is used or becomes obsolete. This is one of the incidental but by no means unimportant jobs of the materials department.

Selling scrap and surplus is a function of the materials department in most companies because the sales department concentrates its efforts on marketing end products. The materials department is much more familiar with potential buyers of scrap and salvage materials; in fact, it may sell much of its process scrap back to its raw-materials suppliers.

Even medium-sized companies may realize hundreds of thousands of dollars a year through scrap and surplus sales. Three basic types of material are sold: process scrap; miscellaneous scrap and salvage material; and surplus material and equipment.

Process scrap. There are few production processes that waste no raw material. Only rarely does all raw material wind up in the finished product; usually some becomes process scrap. For example, in the machining of metal, about half of the raw material may end up in the finished product; the rest will be process scrap, chips, and turnings. This scrap metal has a value ranging from about $30 per ton for steel chips to 25 cents or more per pound for copper and costlier metals. Since even small metalworking plants frequently use tons of metal each month, process scrap sales are an important source of revenue for them.

Miscellaneous scrap and salvage. Every plant must dispose of tons of material each year because it is usable neither in finished products nor as process scrap. Cartons, pallets, and boxes are among the most important miscellaneous items. In most areas there is a ready market for scrap paper and lumber for plants that do not find ways to reuse such materials themselves.

Surplus material and equipment. As we have seen (in Chapter 8), no company should carry inventories it does not need. Surplus materials should be sold as soon as it becomes reasonably certain that there is no immediate need for them. Obsolete equipment should also be sold as soon as no immediate use can be foreseen for it.

Scrap segregation. Scrap and surplus have value to a buyer only if they can be used. For this reason, companies are almost as careful in handling them as they are in handling newly purchased materials. It is particularly important to keep scrap segregated. In some cases, a scrap material will have no value at all if it is mixed in with other materials. In every case it will have more value if it is reasonably clean and free from impurities. Many companies use a color-code system for scrap collection and segregation. For example, red barrels at strategic locations in the plant might be used only for aluminum turnings, while yellow barrels would be used only for stainless steel.

Processing. As with any other product, top prices on scrap sales go only to those who deliver top-quality materials. Many companies invest in processing equipment both to facilitate handling of scrap and to improve its quality. For example, they may buy equipment to dry out and clean metal turnings that are soaked with oil. They may bale both metal and paper scrap to get a higher price and to make them easier to handle. They may even wind up with equipment to reprocess the scrap into usable end products. For example, several large corporations have invested in plants to convert their scrap paper into corrugated paper for new cartons.

Sale. Scrap is normally sold by asking a number of scrap brokers or dealers to bid (see Figure 13–5) on either a specific quantity or a

FIGURE 13–5
Invitation to bid for scrap materials

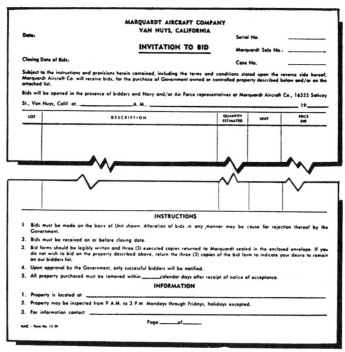

Courtesy Marquardt Aircraft Co.

The form used to solicit bids on scrap and surplus material that a company has for sale is not much different from the form used to solicit bids for material it wishes to buy.

year's needs of some commodity. Some companies sell to all comers on a cash basis; others will deal only with reputable brokers and dealers with established credit. In either case, the high bidder always gets the material. Published market prices are available for many scrap materials, and it is common practice to use these prices as the basis for long-term contracts on scrap sales. Variations in the quality of scrap sometimes forbid this, however. Regardless of the pricing technique used, the seller always can get a somewhat better price if he exercises his ingenuity.

A buyer who is selling scrap looks for buyers with the same thoroughness with which he recruits suppliers when he is buying material.

This is particularly true for specialized scrap and salvage materials for which no real market exists. In some cases, dealers will not buy such material because they do not know where they can sell it. In others, dealers may identify a market and reward their own initiative by offering the seller a price well below what they can sell it for. In such cases the buyer is much better off if he can eliminate the middleman and negotiate a deal directly with the user of the scrap material. For example, Aeroquip Corporation of Jackson, Michigan, increased its return on surplus oleum spirits 500 percent by locating a small local buyer with a specialized use for the material.

Disputes over quality are prevented by permitting each interested bidder to inspect the material physically in advance. If the material is standardized, this is not necessary; well-defined specifications are available on which buyer and seller can agree in advance. For example, the National Association of Secondary Material Industries publishes specifications on cotton rags, paper, and nonferrous scrap materials, while the Institute of Scrap Iron and Steel, publishes specifications for iron and steel scrap. In such cases it is usually fairly easy to determine whether or not the material meets desired specifications. Occasionally disputes arise over weights—often because the weight has changed in transit between buyer and seller owing to material drying out on being exposed to the hot sun, and so on. Companies prevent such disputes by insisting that the weight shown on their scales determine the buyer's payment or by using some local public scale where the weighmaster's certificate is the basis for payment.

Cases

CASE 13-1. GREAT LAKES SUPPLY COMPANY

Selecting the right supplier

Although Great Lakes Auto Supply Company does some manufacturing, it is primarily a distributor. It buys auto parts from independent manufacturers and resells them to thousands of service stations and repair shops. The parts that Great Lakes buys are almost identical with those distributed by the service departments of the auto manufacturers themselves. Great Lakes is successful because it is willing to undersell the original equipment manufacturers on service parts. For example, the manufacturer purchases mufflers at a unit price of $2.32 for one of the nation's most popular brands of car. It resells them to its dealers for $6.80, and they in turn sell them to the ultimate consumer for $10.50

plus a charge for installation labor. Great Lakes buys almost the same muffler from one of its suppliers for $2.78 (it buys in smaller quantities than the original equipment manufacturer and so must pay a higher price). It resells the muffler for $3.75 and the gas station charges the ultimate consumer $7.50 plus installation labor.

The auto manufacturers and their franchised dealers refer to Great Lakes and its suppliers as "gyp" manufacturers. They point out that the gyps do no engineering but simply copy the parts of the auto manu-facturers. They claim that the gyps produce parts of inferior quality. Consumers, attracted by the lower prices charged by the gyps, obviously do not accept the auto companies' charges. Yet the charge that the gyps copy their designs is certainly true.

For example, Walter Norris, Great Lakes' vice president in charge of purchases, recently secured quotations on replacement floor mats for 1973 Blue Motors sedans. Suppliers got no specifications; instead, they were asked to quote on the basis of "original equipment quality." Norris got the following bids for 10,000 mats:

Supplier	Price	F.O.B.	Tools	Terms
Western Rubber Products	$3.32	Shipping point	$45	2/10, net 30
Alexander Corporation.	$3.25	Great Lakes plant	$110	Net 20th prox.
Roberts Rubber Company	$3.44	Great Lakes plant	$65	1/10, net 30
Wartly Rubber, Inc.	$2.84	Shipping point	$50	Net 30 days

The mat used as original equipment on Blue Motors cars weighs 9.2 pounds, and Norris assumes that the suppliers will give him a mat of the same weight. Norris understands from one of his suppliers that Blue Motors pays an average of $2.75 for the mat. Since Blue Motors uses an average of 2,000 mats per day from each of its suppliers, Norris is not the least bit surprised that none of his bids is that low. In fact, he suspects that Blue Motors's price may be even lower than this.

Norris has made an analysis in which he compares the Blue Motors mat with mats he has purchased for various other auto models. He concludes that a fair price for the Blue Motors mat is probably between $3.10 and $3.25. He passes this on to Western and Roberts and asks them if they would be interested in requoting. Both suppliers reply that their costs have gone up since they quoted last and Norris's estimate of a fair price for the mat is out of date. Western and Roberts are currently supplying other mats to Great Lakes. Alexander and Wartly make mats for other auto part distributors but have never been Great Lakes suppliers. Norris has some doubts as to whether or not Wartly can supply the desired quality, although Wartly has had considerable ex-perience in producing mats for the "gyp" trade.

Questions

1. Which supplier should Norris choose? Support your recommendations with an anlysis, making assumptions where necessary.
2. What special studies might be called for in this case?

CASE 13–2. ST. LOUIS OFFICE FURNITURE COMPANY

A problem in user brand preference

The St. Louis Office Furniture Company is a medium-sized company that specializes in steel desks and filing cabinets. It buys steel from several mills, forms it in its press shops, welds it into desks and cabinets and then finishes and paints the completed products. The finishing operation is necessary because the metal is rough where it has been welded and worked in presses and must be sanded down to a smooth finish before painting. This is an extremely dirty and disagreeable job. Workers run abrasive wheels against the semifinished cabinets until they are smooth. Not only is this physically hard to do and requires some skill, but the job is extremely unpleasant. The wheels are noisy, the abrasive grit fills the air and settles into the workers' clothes, and the workers are invariably hot and uncomfortable. They must wear masks to prevent their lungs from being contaminated with dust, and the friction of the abrasive generates heat, which is almost unbearable in the hot summer months.

Because their job is so unpleasant, the metal finishers are extremely well paid. They average about $1 per hour more than the average worker at St. Louis Furniture. Despite the high pay, good metal finishers are scarce, and they tend to be extremely independent. Absences and tardiness are far more frequent than among other workers. The scarcity of metal finishers and their high pay gives management a double incentive to do everything it can to raise their productivity. The company's materials manager, Edward Kellogg, has been working for the past few months with Reynolds Abrasive, a major supplier, on a new abrasive that will cut at least 25 percent faster and last 10 percent longer than the abrasive currently used. Although the new product is much more expensive than the current one, if it works it will raise the productivity of the metal finishers by enough so that the cost premium will be offset many times over.

Kellogg naturally has kept the plant superintendent and others informed of his work on the abrasive. When he gets his first test shipment, he and the superintendent arrange for a test on Sunday, when the plant is shut down. The foreman of the metal finishing line and one of the company's time-study men participate in the tests. The foreman, a former metal finisher himself, uses the abrasive on a few cabinets, while the time-study man makes observations. The time studies confirm the supplier's claim: the abrasive is 25 percent faster. The foreman, however, says he doesn't like the new abrasive. He says it just doesn't feel right, although he does not dispute the time study's indication that it is faster. He says he is sure the men won't like the new abrasive. The others are reluctant to see such a big saving evaporate simply because the abrasive doesn't "feel right." They decide that the best thing to do is to change the brand of abrasive quietly and see how the men react. Then, after the workers get used to the feel of the new product, they can make new time studies and raise the standard.

The workers arrive on Monday morning and almost immediately notice the change in abrasive. They ask the foreman what is going on and are told that the company has decided to purchase a higher quality abrasive that will work faster. No mention is made of any future changes in work standards. The men grumble that the new abrasive isn't as good as the old. After giving the new product a few minutes' trial, they accuse the company of trying to slip in a cheaper new product that requires them to work harder. They flatly refuse to work until they are given the old abrasive again. The foreman gives them the old abrasive to keep production going and advises Kellogg that he had better keep on buying the old product because the men will not accept any changes.

Questions

1. Should Kellogg follow the foreman's advice?
2. What can be done to get the men to adopt the new product and accept a new time study?
3. Did Kellogg handle this problem correctly from the beginning? What mistakes did he make?

CASE 13–3. ADAMS EQUIPMENT CORPORATION

Sale of scrap iron

Adams Equipment Corporation is a manufacturer of pumps and similar equipment. Its products are made primarily from gray-iron castings, and approximately two carloads of gray-iron chips are generated in the Adams plant each day.

Eastern States Scrap Metal has been buying Adams's scrap and salvage products on a regular basis since the Adams company was founded more than 30 years ago. Joseph Adams, the founder of Adams Equipment, and Morris Levine, the founder and president of Eastern States Scrap Metal, have had a long-standing history of successful business relationships that date back to the years when both men managed rather small businesses. Now Adams Equipment employs more than 1,000 men in its factory, while Eastern States is one of the larger scrap metal brokers and dealers in the United States.

Although Joseph Adams was originally responsible for developing the relationship with Eastern States, the actual administration of the contract with Eastern States is part of the overall responsibility of Robert Hallowell, the materials manager of Adams Equipment. This has hardly been one of Hallowell's more pressing chores. The scrap contract more or less handles itself. Employees of Eastern States have complete access to the Adams plant and remove scrap iron as it is generated and load it into gondola cars in the Adams railroad siding. The cars then eventually are picked up at the Adams siding and shipped either to another scrap broker or to a foundry which deals directly with Eastern States. Eastern States forwards a check each month to Adams and a statement that indicates the total amount of scrap sold and the price per ton that Eastern States is paying.

Eastern States naturally has substantial expenses in removing the scrap from the Adams plant and, consequently, the price it pays Adams for the scrap is less than the market price. Hallowell, in studying the situation, notes that the price Eastern pays Adams is apparently about $6 per ton less than the posted price for the large metropolitan area in which the Adams plant is located. But, of course, Eastern States has several men permanently employed at the Adams plant and has also made investments in materials-handling equipment, trucks, and other items.

Hallowell is by no means convinced that Eastern States is giving Adams anything but a fair price. Relations between Eastern States executives and Adams executives have always been amicable.

Eastern States not only has been a model firm with which to deal but, in addition, has rendered services to Adams that have not necessarily been profitable for them. For example, Eastern States has been willing to purchase other types of salvage and scrap materials from Adams even when there has not been a big enough market for such material to be worth the trouble. If Adams wanted to get rid of some scrap paper products—which often have negligible scrap value—Eastern States has been willing to take it off Adams's hands and, apparently, pass on the entire proceeds of the sale to Adams (if the material has any value at all). In other cases, Eastern States has handled small amounts of miscellaneous scrap material where the value has not really been worth the trouble. For example, Adams occasionally scraps equipment that has no salvage value other than as scrap metal. Eastern States, although it really is not set up for such small-scale business, has been willing to pick up such material and to give Adams a fair price for it.

Eastern States is in a highly competitive business. From time to time other scrap firms have solicited the Adams account but, apparently, have had nothing to offer that Adams is not already getting from Eastern States. These firms were willing to pay market price but, of course, if they performed the extra services that Eastern States performs, they would charge for them. Hallowell has not personally had any contact with any of Eastern States's potential competitors as he has only been on his existing job for about two years. He has gathered, however, that there has not been too much solicitation of business by rival scrap firms in recent years because apparently they have come to recognize that Eastern States is "in" at Adams.

Hallowell wonder if it might not be a bad idea for Eastern States to get some competition, but he has no valid reason to question the quality of Eastern States service or the price it pays.

Questions

1. What are the advantages and disadvantages of a long-standing relationship such as that between Adams and Eastern States?

2. Is this relationship necessarily in the best interests of both firms? Explain.

14

Problems in supplier relations

ONE OF THE BASIC OBJECTIVES of materials management is favorable relations with outside suppliers. This is not too difficult to achieve when: suppliers perform outstandingly well on quality and delivery after they accept orders at competitive prices, and a strictly businesslike buyer-seller relationship prevails.

Unfortunately, suppliers do fail to keep delivery promises and do not always meet quality standards. Sometimes they are responsible for the failure; sometimes others are responsible. Buyer-seller relations also are subject to numerous pressures. Some of these pressures reflect the character of the buyers and sellers themselves; others are exerted by outside influences.

DELIVERY FAILURE

The most basic supplier failure is failure to deliver. There are many reasons why a supplier might not deliver on schedule. These include manufacturing difficulties, shortages of raw materials, labor trouble, transportation tie-ups, and just plain bad management.

More often than not, a supplier delivery failure creates no real problem. The material is not needed immediately, or an alternate supply is readily available. Sometimes the user of the material can work out his own solution to the problem and need not even ask the buyer for help. In other cases, the user of the material raises a lot of smoke, but the buyer later discovers that there is no fire. The buyer should not rush to head off a shortage due to a delivery failure until he investigates and is absolutely certain that a shortage will exist if action is not taken. He may also discover that the cost of eliminating the shortage is greater than the loss that results from it. It is pointless, for example, to incur substantial cost air shipping material when production control can make minor revisions in schedule that postpone the need for the material.

The shortage plan

The buyer's skill is tested only when a supplier fails to deliver material that is needed immediately. The buyer must find out the cause of the failure promptly and then develop a plan to cope with it. If he moves fast, he may be able to avoid a costly shutdown resulting from lack of material.

As soon as he learns that a supplier may fail to deliver, the buyer should get the following information:

1. When and how much the supplier can deliver.
2. Current inventories and probable requirements. (Possibly stocks are more than adequate and there is no need for the supplier to ship in the near future anyway.)
3. Cause of the delivery failure.
4. Availability of alternate sources of supply.

From this data, the buyer must develop a plan to cope with the shortage. Whenever possible, he tries to prevent production from being disrupted. But the buyer always should be realistic. If the shortage is so serious that some curtailment of output is inevitable, he should allow for this in his plan. A shutdown that is planned in advance is almost always less costly than one that comes as a complete surprise.

In some cases the buyer may be able to use his imagination and find some way to prevent a production shutdown even when the situation seems almost hopeless. Suppose, for example, that a key supplier of production parts[1] is shut down because of a strike. The buyer advises all concerned departments with a strike report. (Figure 14–1). He tries to estimate how long the strike will last; checks current stocks, both on hand and in transit; and considers ways to cope with the shortage. Perhaps it can be licked by immediately starting a second supplier on the item or by making the item in the buyer's plant. Perhaps, although not very likely, surplus stocks can be purchased from some other user. Perhaps defective or used items can be reworked to make them acceptable or a substitute can be found. Perhaps extra stock can be "discovered"

---

[1] Delivery failure is rarely a serious problem for most nonproduction supplies, since in most cases it is fairly easy to buy identical materials from another supplier on short notice. However, this is usually not true for purchases of equipment and machinery or for construction contracts, where delivery failures can seriously affect a company's sales and profits.

FIGURE 14-1

FORD DIVISION FORD MOTOR COMPANY		STRIKE REPORT			DATE	
VENDOR'S NAME		VENDOR'S ADDRESS		AFFECTED PLANT		
		NATURE OF ACTUAL OR INDICATED INTERRUPTION OF SUPPLY				
NAME OF LOCAL	NO.	UNION AFFILIATION OF LOCAL	LOCAL PRESIDENT'S NAME	NO. PERSONNEL INVOLVED	TIME & DATE OF STRIKE	
PART NO. AND DESCRIPTION		VEHICLE MODELS AFFECTED		SUPPLY CONDITION		
		STATUS OF BUYING DEPT. ACTION				
				PURCHASING AGENT OR DEPT MANAGER		

Courtesy Ford Motor Co.

When a strike stops production at a supplier plant, the buyer should immediately advise all departments concerned with a strike report and develop a plan to cope with the materials shortage that the strike probably will cause.

by shortening supply lines. For example, if a part goes into a subassembly that in turn is assembled into something else, the shortage might not be so serious as it first appears. All the in-process stock can be used before assembly of the end product is delayed.

Field expediting. Sometimes delivery failure is only partial. A supplier cannot produce desired quantities because of manufacturing problems. Or, in many cases, the supplier is not responsible for the delivery failure. Demand for material has increased, and the supplier is called on to exceed his original delivery promises.

In such cases, if the shortage is critical, a buyer or expediter may spend all his waking hours in the supplier's plant until the shortage is licked. Many suppliers privately regard their customers' expediters as a first-class nuisance. In their opinion, they accomplish nothing; if anything, they get in the way at a time when the supplier has enough problems. However, suppliers seldom dare protest openly against the use of expediters, since their customers can retort that the expediters would not be needed if the supplier had delivered the materials promptly.

Why do companies use expediters even when they are fairly certain that the supplier is doing everything he can to cope with the shortage? There are at least four reasons:

1. *The presence of the expediter may stimulate supplier personnel to greater efforts.* If a customer is interested enough in getting prompt delivery to dispatch a field expediter to the supplier's plant, supplier personnel will be more impressed with the need for delivery.

2. *The expediter can make certain that the supplier is actually doing everything possible to overcome the shortage.* If a supplier has half a dozen customers pressing him for delivery, some customers are going to be served more promptly than others. An expediter ensures that his company is getting high priority.

3. *The expediter can keep the buyer up to date with reliable, first-hand information on current delivery status.* Daily telephone reports can keep the buyer posted as to whether the shortage is going to get worse or become less critical.

4. *The expediter can sometimes assist the supplier.* If the supplier can be helped with changes in specifications or quality control procedures, the expediter can relay this information to his home office. Sometimes the supplier needs technical help or raw material. The expediter can arrange for the loan of his company's personnel and get the buyer to help in obtaining raw materials. The supplier may be willing to work his plant overtime only if the buyer is willing to pay the extra costs that will be incurred. A field expediter can evaluate the need for overtime and secure approval for the cost from his home office.

Anticipating shortages

Many delivery problems can be anticipated before an order is placed. They are the result of a supplier's having accepted more business than he is able to handle. You can understand why this would come about only if you put yourself in the other fellow's shoes. Suppose that you were a supplier and that, to the best of your knowledge, your backlog of work would prevent you from accepting any new business for deliveries prior to next July. One of your customers sends you an order demanding June delivery. Would you accept the order?

Inflated order books. If you were extremely conscientious, you might accept the order on a conditional basis, pointing out to the customer that you are now booked into July and that it might be difficult for you to deliver in June. However, most real-life suppliers are not so squeamish. They might well simply accept the order and hope for the best. There is good reason for their attitude:

1. *Their own order backlog is not firm.* It is quite possible that there will be some cancellations, making the June deadline easy to meet.

2. *They need the business.* You do not get business by turning orders down and, you want to be able to satisfy all of your customers' needs.

3. *Customers may be padding their own delivery needs.* If a buyer wants an item in June, this may mean that he actually needs the item in July and he is just giving himself a safety margin. Naturally suppliers catch on to this game and start playing it too. The buyer is padding his delivery promise, and the supplier starts to play the opposite game and pad his. On the average, everything works out all right. For all of these reasons, the supplier may be able to meet a delivery promise that is theoretically impossible to meet. However, every now and then something will go wrong, and he will fall way behind.

Cyclical effect: NAPM index. During periods of depressed business, suppliers can usually easily fill the delivery promises they make. They have enough slack capacity so that the roof must almost fall in before they fall behind. During periods when business is booming, the opposite is true. The supplier's own scheduling is so tight that a single heavy snowstorm can create a production scheduling nightmare. In addition, the supplier may be at the mercy of his own suppliers.

Thus, when the buyer places an order, he should make some mental adjustment as to possible risk of delivery failure due to business being just too good. His best overall barometer is probably the Vendor Performance Index of the National Bureau of Economic Research. This index, which is compiled monthly in cooperation with the National Association of Purchasing Management, is published on an unadjusted basis in the NAPM *Bulletin* and later in various government economic publications, including *Business Conditions Digest.* The index indicates the percent of purchasing agents reporting slower deliveries. During recessions, it is typically in the 25 percent range. That is, only 25 percent of the respondents report slower deliveries. In such cases, one can generally assume that suppliers will be able to meet their delivery promises unless there are unforeseen difficulties.

In contrast, at the peak of the business cycle, the index goes to 75 percent or more. This means that almost every purchasing agent is having trouble holding suppliers to their delivery promises. During such periods, the buyer had best accept supplier promises with some degree of reservation. It also is not a bad idea for him to pad his own requirements; that is, if he really needs the item in July, he should ask for it in June. When he does this, he is adding to the general confusion of lead times and delivery promises that prevails during boom periods. But if everyone else plays the game the same way and tacitly assumes that he does too, does he have any choice?

It is usually easy to determine when the buyer should be stretching out his own lead times if the underlying cause of tighter policy is general prosperity. It is much more difficult to determine in advance that particular suppliers may be in a bind even though general business conditions show plenty of slack. It is not always in the supplier's best interest to give his customers accurate information about his order backlog, and this is something that is not easy to estimate without access to supplier records. In some cases, conclusions must be based entirely on industry data gathered by the Department of Commerce and industry trade associations.

Overoptimism. Sometimes suppliers fall behind on deliveries simply because they are overoptimistic. The buyer can sometimes prevent this by reviewing the equipment the supplier has available to use on a particular order and then determining what safety allowance, if any, the supplier has allowed for. This is a particularly useful technique if the order involves some particularly complex piece of machinery. For example, suppose a supplier has one piece of equipment that the buyer's order will be tying up an average of 80 hours per week. This need create no problem as long as everything goes according to plan. But, of course, a minor breakdown of the equipment can immediately trigger a delivery failure.

It is, of course, almost impossible to prevent suppliers from becoming too ambitious or overoptimistic, and in many cases the buyer simply does not have enough information to know just how extended the supplier is. The problem is made more difficult by the fact that during periods when delivery failures occur, almost every supplier in an industry may be short of capacity. As a result, the buyer has little or no choice but to place orders with a supplier who is already hard pressed to keep up. In some cases, his only effective insurance is to avoid putting all his eggs in one basket and to buy the same item from several suppliers. However, one supplier's failure may still cripple the buyer. This is particularly true if a supplier suddenly starts to have quality problems. If one supplier has difficulty, chances are that the others may find themselves in the same boat. The quality problem may not shut down every supplier, but it will most likely prevent other suppliers from stepping up output enough to take up the slack of the supplier who falls behind.

QUALITY FAILURE

In many industries, the greatest single cause of delivery failure is quality failure. Quality problems begin with a complaint by either the user or the quality control department that a purchased item is of substandard quality. In the case of items purchased by brand or on the basis of performance specifications, the user may complain that the item does not perform as it should. In such cases, the buyer contacts the supplier and advises him of the problem.

The rejection process is somewhat more complex in the case of parts and materials purchased to technical specifications. In such cases quality is determined at least partly by inspection procedures. For example, suppose a company buying a part insists that one dimension be 2.000

inches with a tolerance of plus or minus 0.005 inch. This theoretically would mean that the company will reject all parts where the dimension does not measure between 1.995 and 2.005 inches. In practice, it would not reject every part not meeting this requirement. Regardless of the inspection method used, the company always tacitly agrees to accept some parts that lie outside its specifications. The reason is that no inspection is 100 percent foolproof. For example, if an inspector carefully measures each piece to make sure its dimension is between 1.995 and 2.005 inches, we still cannot be 100 percent confident that every defective piece will be culled out. In fact, so-called 100 percent inspection (where every piece is inspected) is often no more than 85 percent efficient. That is, if there are 100 defective pieces in a lot, only about 85 of them will be detected by the inspector. The others will be passed through to the final product.

Basic inspection problems

Quality control engineers are realistic about the probability of inferior quality being accepted. They design quality control procedures that will keep rejects within reasonably acceptable limits. As was discussed in Chapter 13, they recognize that a supplier's quality can never be any better than his process and devise inspection methods that will reliably indicate whether or not the process is in control.

Variables and attributes.   There are two distinct ways to inspect a product: by variables and by attributes. With inspection by variables, the characteristic is actually measured; inspection by attributes simply separates the good pieces from the bad pieces. Inspection by variables is more useful for controlling the process, while inspection by attributes may be quite adequate for the buyer who must decide whether or not to accept a shipment from a supplier.

A go, no-go gauge is commonly used to inspect hole diameters by attributes. The hole meets specifications if the go end of the gauge goes into the hole and the no-go is too large to do so. For a 2.000-inch hole with a tolerance of plus or minus 0.005 inch, the go end of the gauge might be 1.9945 inches in diameter. With an allowance of 0.0005 inch for clearance, the gauge enters any hole that is at least 1.995 inches in diameter. Therefore, when the go gauge goes, one can be certain that the hole meets the requirements for the minimum diameter of 0.995 inch. Similarly, the no-go gauge might be 2.0045 inches in diameter. Allowing for 0.0005-inch clearance, it will not enter any hole smaller than the maximum diameter of 2.005 inches.

Inspection by attributes is fast and relatively cheap. In many cases it is the only inspection technique that is available. There is no way to inspect by variables when the quality being measured involves human taste or smell. Color also is often measured by the inspector's eye rather than instruments so inspection must be by attributes. For example, inspectors of dyed cloth or printed labels make visual comparisons with standard color samples. The two colors either "match" or they do not.

One can be more precise when gauges are available to measure a specific physical quality. For example, an inside micrometer or dial indicator will measure the precise diameter of a hole. It might indicate that a particular hole is 2.004 inches in diameter. The inspector knows not only whether or not the hole meets specifications but also how close it comes to the desired mean diameter. This additional information is invaluable in controlling the process. If holes gradually start getting bigger, the process can quickly be corrected (perhaps by sharpening the drill) before it drifts out of control.

Acceptable quality level (AQL). In theory, the supplier need not concern himself with his customers inspection methods. All he need do is meet specifications and he has done his job. In practice, however, inspection methods are often all-important to both buyer and seller and must be well defined. If an item is critical enough so that quality becomes a problem, then agreement on inspection methods is essential. The standard is often more lax than would be indicated by literal interpretation of the specifications.

For example, if the specification calls for a hole to be 2.000 inches with a tolerance of plus or minus 0.005 inch, the uninitiated might assume that all holes must fall between 1.995 and 2.005 inches. This may not be true, however. In some cases, the tolerance was put on the blueprint by a draftsman who was simply following empirical rules. It appears to be fairly easy to hold this tolerance, so that is what the draftsman specifies. The engineer may not care at all what tolerance this particular dimension is held to as long as the hole is made with a standard half-inch drill. When a particular specification causes quality problems, the buyer should immediately make certain that the specification is really vital to the functioning of the product.

In most cases, the decision is almost entirely economic. In general, the tighter the quality standards, the higher the cost. Offsetting this higher unit material cost, entirely or partly, is a reduction in the cost of inspecting and using material made to tighter specifications. Material that barely meets the buyer's standard can often fall below standard. In this case, careful inspection and control in succeeding operations is essential. If the material is much, much better than minimum, this costly control is not needed.

Actual quality. The real quality may be different from the indicated standard even if the engineer actually believes the specification is essential to the product. The real quality standard is not known until the supplier also knows how the buyer will measure how this standard is being met and how much allowance he will make for deviations from it.

Most real-life quality limits fall between two extremes. At one extreme, the most quality-conscious buyer would tell the supplier he would reject an entire shipment if a single piece falls outside his desired quality limits of 2.000 inches plus or minus 0.005 inch. If the buyer were really fussy, he might inspect every piece by attributes with an inspection machine that automatically rejects any part that falls outside the desired limits. A single rejection would cause the entire shipment to be rejected. The reasoning behind this blanket rejection is logical. The buyer is requiring the supplier to select a process where all output falls within required specifications and a single defeat then becomes excellent evidence that the supplier's process is out of control.

Few buyers would want to pay for such perfection—and they probably would not get it even if they were willing. A supplier who stands to have an entire shipment refused if there is a single reject would not dare to use the process that is really suitable for the item. He would have to use the next best process—if one were available. The reason for this is that the ideal process may be only 99.9 percent perfect even if it is always in control. Thus there would be at least one defective piece in almost every shipment. If the buyer inspected every piece, he would probably find the defective piece and would then reject the entire shipment.

Random fluctuations will always produce an imperfect piece occasionally. The odds against this can be narrowed even further by selecting even better and more expensive processes. But, unfortunately, there is no foolproof method to assure that standards will always be met. In addition, the supplier will not necessarily adjust his process if a single reject is detected. He would simply reinspect the lot and then resell it to the same customer. Experience would prove that the rigid quality requirements still would not prevent an occasional reject from sneaking through—particularly if the reject did not trigger a change in the basic process.

At the other extreme, the buyer who is not worried about quality would simply make certain that the item was made by the desired process. He would be satisfied with whatever the process would produce as long as it was functioning—in control or out of control.

These two extremes represent rather wide differences in cost even if the same process is involved. In the first case, the supplier would have to exercise great care in manufacture and would also be forced to subject his production to elaborate quality control procedures. In extreme cases, he might spend a great deal more on inspection than on production. In the second case, the seller need not spend anything on quality control.

Most real-life quality problems are caused by requirements that fall between these extremes of perfection and indifference. The acceptable quality-level (AQL) measures the buyer's willingness to take material that does not meet specification. For example, an AQL of .97 indicates that the buyer will accept shipments in which he estimates that 3 percent of the items do not meet specifications. Naturally, the lower the AQL, the easier it is on the supplier.

100 percent inspection. If the supplier does not meet the requested AQL, the buyer is free to reject the entire shipment. In practice, however—if he desperately needed the material—the buyer would probably return only the defective items.

For example, suppose the AQL on a particular item is .97 but the supplier is unable to keep his process in control. The supplier's own rejection rate is 50 percent. But sufficient defectives pass through his inspection procedures so that shipments actually sent to the buyer have an AQL of only .85. The buyer can reject the entire shipment if he likes, since the supplier clearly is not living up to his part of the bargain. In practice, however, when the supplier has this much trouble, the buyer is almost always desperately in need of the item. He cannot afford to be highhanded. As a result he would probably inspect every piece, returning only the defectives to the supplier.

This practice would not be desirable, however, even if the buyer did not worry about the costs of 100 percent inspection. When the process itself is out of control, sufficient defectives would pass through both the supplier's and the buyer's inspection to affect the quality of the end product. In fact, quality would probably deteriorate simply because the item was in short supply. The buyer's inspectors cannot afford to be as tough in such cases. If there is any chance that the item will function they will let it pass through. The supplier also senses that the buyer's inspectors will be more lax so the emphasis shifts from quality to quantity—usually with adverse effects on the former.

Statistical inference

When supply conditions are normal, not only is quality higher but inspection costs are lower. Usually, 100 percent inspection is not standard practice. Instead, the buyer's inspectors select a sample from the shipment at random, inspect it carefully, and use statistical inference to draw meaningful conclusions about the entire shipment. Many different sampling plans are used.[2] Each plan requires that a sample of predetermined size be selected at random from the shipment. The entire shipment is always accepted if every item in the sample is acceptable. In some

---

[2] For examples of various sampling plans, see *Sampling Procedures and Tables for Inspection by Attributes,* MIL-STD-105D, and *Sampling Procedures and Tables for Inspection by Variables for Percent Defective,* MIL-STD-414. Both are available at modest cost from Superintendent of Documents, U.S. Government Printing Office, Washington, D.C. 20402.

cases, the shipment may be returned if there is a single reject in the sample, or the plan may permit a certain limited number of rejects. Some plans may call for a second or even a third sample to be drawn under certain conditions.

Each plan is designed to achieve some predetermined level of reliability at the lowest possible cost. The plan's effectiveness is measured by its operating characteristic curve. For example, Figure 14–2 shows the

FIGURE 14–2

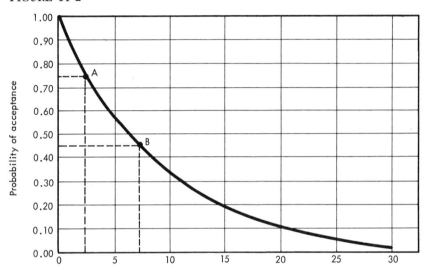

Percentage of defectives in lot

Operating characteristic curve: Lot 200; sample 10; no defectives allowed.
Source: Theodore H. Brown, "Quality Control," *Harvard Business Review*, November 1951, p. 75.

operating characteristic curve of a relatively simple plan that calls for inspection of a sample of 10 pieces in each lot of 200, with no defectives allowed. The curve shows the probability of acceptance (or, conversely, the probability of rejection) of lots with various percentages of defects. If the lot is perfect, there is 100 percent probability that every piece in the sample of ten will also be perfect and the lot will be accepted. However, if the lot is 5 percent defective (10 rejects in a lot of 200), there is only a 60 percent probability that none of the defects will show up in the sample. Conversely, there is a 40 percent probability that one or more of the ten defects will be in the sample of ten and the lot will be rejected.

Type I and Type II errors. Note that it is possible to make two types of error with this and any other sampling plan. In statistics jargon, these are appropriately known as Type I and Type II errors. You make a Type I error when you reject a lot that should be accepted, and you make a Type II error when you accept a lot that should be rejected.

Suppose, for example, that the sampling plan shown in Fig. 14–2 is applied to an item with an AQL (acceptable quality level) of 95 percent. This means that you would like to reject shipments with more than 5 percent defectives and accept those with 5 percent or less.

The operating characteristic curve indicates the probability of your making an error when the lot actually contains various percentages of defects. First, suppose that the lot of 200 actually contains about 5 defective pieces and is therefore 2.5 percent defective. This shipment should be accepted, since it exceeds your AQL of .95. The operating characteristic curve (see point A in Fig. 14–2) shows that there is about a 75 percent probability that you will draw 10 perfect pieces from your lot of 200 and, therefore, accept the shipment. Conversely, there is a 25 percent probability (100 percent minus 75 percent) that you will make a Type I error. That is, one of the five defectives in the lot will show up in your sample, and you will incorrectly reject the shipment.

Similarly, suppose that the shipment contains 7.5 percent rejects. It doesn't meet your AQL and should be rejected. But the operating characteristic curve shows (see point B) that there is a 45 percent probability that the shipment will be accepted. This would be a Type II error. Conversely, there is a 55 percent probability (100 minus 45) that one defective will appear in the sample of ten and the shipment will quite rightly be rejected.

The inspection plan outlined in Figure 14–2 would not be useful for most items. The probability of Type I and Type II errors is too high. These probabilities can be reduced either by increasing the size of the sample or by plans calling for additional samples to be drawn under various circumstances. The probability of Type II errors can be reduced most conveniently by simply increasing the size of the sample. Type I errors can be prevented more economically with sequential sampling plans which call for an additional sample to be drawn if one or two pieces are defective in the first sample.

Supplier quality problems

The quality control manager, not the materials manager, is responsible for selecting appropriate sampling plans to control the quality of incoming material. The plans represent his evaluation of engineers' specifications. The engineers who write the specifications would like to have 100 percent of the vendor's shipments fall within tolerances even though they know that this will never be the case. In fact, some companies refuse to disclose to suppliers precisely what their acceptable quality level is because they are afraid that by doing so they will encourage them to reduce standards to the minimum needed to pass inspection.

As a result, many inexperienced vendors may find shipments rejected simply because they underestimated the buyer's quality standards.

In such cases both buyer and seller lose. When there is no mutual trust on quality standards, the buyer does not get something for nothing. On the contrary, the experienced seller will soon learn how to beat his system. There are enough quality problems even if buyer and seller have an excellent relationship. Otherwise, there will be constant problems even if specifications are seemingly consistent.

Conflicting standards. For example, if a supplier manufactured and inspected his product so that 95 percent of the pieces were within tolerances and the buyer's inspectors worked to a sampling plan that required 99 percent reliability, practically all of the supplier's shipments would be rejected. A supplier might get occasional rejections even if his quality standards were identical to those of the buyer. For example, while the supplier might check a small sample and find it within tolerances, the buyer might check an entirely different sample from the same shipment and find it exceeded acceptable tolerances. In practice, many suppliers find they must manufacture to quality standards slightly higher than those required by their customers in order to eliminate occasional rejections of this sort and also to provide themselves with a little leeway on quality before it becomes a problem.

This can also cause conflict to develop between the materials department and quality control. In many cases, quality control's interpretations of specifications are not consistent with what materials managers regard as good purchasing practice. The buyer likes to pay for precisely the quality he needs—no more, no less. It is obviously wasteful for suppliers to manufacture a higher quality standard than is really indicated by the specification. Theoretically, there should never be a conflict where specifications are clearly spelled out. However, in most real-life cases, specifications are simply not all that well defined. In the aerospace and electronics industries in particular they are almost never as tight as would normally be dictated by good purchasing practice. Suppliers are often working with newly developed technology, and the problems have not been ironed out.

This may be true even of items that suppliers have been making for years. For example, it is quite difficult for automotive engineers to specify precisely how smooth a "chrome-plated" part such as a bumper guard should be. The process of making the bumper guard automatically generates a number of scratches which must be buffed out at considerable cost. The buyer naturally wants to pay for the minimum amount of buffing that will do the job. Inevitably, cases arise where after the supplier gets the order, he complains that his quotation was based on less buffing than is presently being required by quality control. As a result, the supplier's shipments are not accepted. The buyer is in a quandary. He cannot help but ask himself whether or not the supplier is just using this as an alibi to get a higher price for the item after he gets the order. Or, for all the buyer knows, quality control has quietly restructured its own ground rules. Inspection of "appearance" items on automobiles involves a great deal of latitude. Each inspector is supposed to look at the item and determine whether or not it is suitable in appearance to go on a finished automobile. Unfortunately, it is the last scratches that are the most difficult and most costly to get rid of. Whenever a new supplier is introduced, there is almost always a lot of disagreement that must be resolved before the supplier knows what is really required on the item.

Quality certification

When buyer and seller agree on quality levels, it is sometimes possible to eliminate a great deal of extra inspection with quality certification. A supplier whose quality control procedures meet the buyer's standards then simply ships the material, which gets little or no incoming inspection by the buyer.

With this approach, the buyer specifies in considerable detail precisely what tolerances must be maintained, the AQL for each dimension, and the inspection and sampling procedures to be used. The supplier then certifies that he meets these requirements on each shipment. The buyer need only make occasional spot checks of shipments to make certain that the supplier is not getting lax.

With quality certification, much duplicate inspection is avoided, since for most shipments the buyer's receiving inspection can be quite superficial. This can reduce costs substantially, especially for precision parts with many dimensions that must be held within close tolerances. Certification also has boosted quality for most companies that have tried it. Supplier responsibility is clearly specified, and most suppliers take pride in having their quality level certified by their customers.

Companies with quality certification programs are careful, however, to limit their use to suppliers of proved reliability. They rarely have so much faith in a new supplier that they will accept shipments without a thorough inspection. If the volume of business with the supplier is substantial, the buying company may station one of its inspectors at the supplier's plant to monitor the process. This is more likely to assure high quality than inspecting after material is received, since it helps assure that the supplier's process is in control. The obvious disadvantage is the cost of maintaining an inspector in the field. This tends to limit the practice to military and aerospace products where quality problems are particularly acute. Most other organizations settle either for a quality certification program or conventional receiving inspection.

Buyer's quality role. When a shipment is found defective, the buyer first investigates to make sure that the supplier is really responsible for the defects. He may discover that the rejection was due to changes in specifications, inspection procedures, and so on, that were not incorporated into the purchase agreement. If this is the case, the supplier is not responsible for the rejection.

In most cases, however, the rejection is either wholly or partly the supplier's responsibility. The usual procedure is for the buyer to review the inspection report and pass it on to the supplier. If the supplier agrees that the shipment should be rejected and accepts responsibility for the defects, he will indicate how he wishes to dispose of the shipment. (This is often covered by a standing agreement.) The supplier may want to have the shipment returned to him, scrapped, or salvaged by the buyer. If it is scrapped or salvaged, there must, of course, be agreement concerning scrap credits to the supplier (if the buyer sells it to a scrap dealer) or on charges to the supplier for the buyer's salvage work. Should the supplier deny responsibility for the rejection, the buyer must thoroughly investigate and try to reach an amicable agreement with the supplier that still protects his own company's interests.

Regardless of who is responsible for the quality problem, the buyer should do everything he can to prevent recurrence. He should make certain that the supplier is taking all possible measures to boost quality. If the supplier persists in shipping merchandise that does not pass inspection, the buyer may have to switch suppliers.

Poor quality creates the worst possible type of delivery failure. Unlike other supply failures, there is no advance warning before the material is actually received. Nor is the problem necessarily solved if the supplier succeeds in making a shipment to replace the rejected one, for that shipment may also be rejected. Fortunately for many a buyer of precision parts, quality control departments often relax standards and accept shipments with minor defects when there will be a critical shortage if they are rejected. But this does not by any means take the pressure off the buyer to get suppliers who can consistently meet quality standards.

Zero defects. Quality has a natural tendency to get sloppy. In fact, experience shows that it automatically deteriorates if buyer and seller become the least bit complacent. The zero defects program is designed to fight complacency. Its theme is that nothing less than zero defects is good enough. Zero defects programs were originally developed to boost quality of components used on missiles and spacecraft, but the idea has spread to other industries. The concept of zero defects is simply that quality depends on the motivation of the people who make the product. If you tell these people that you are willing to accept 4 or 5 percent defects, you will probably get just that and maybe a lot more. Instead, you set your goal at zero defects and try to motivate everyone in the organization to work toward this target.

The materials manager and his buyers are catalysts in zero defects programs. They are administered by the quality control department (which is usually part of the manufacturing organization) and applied to both purchased and manufactured items. The materials department is responsible for getting the message through to the company's suppliers, and it works with quality control in arranging seminars and other programs designed to make supplier personnel conscious of the need for zero defects. The end result may not literally be zero defects but at least a higher quality level than prevailed before the zero defects program was begun.

PROBLEMS IN SOURCE SELECTION

Even if a buyer succeeds in getting suppliers who offer outstanding quality, delivery, and service at rock-bottom prices, his selection of sources will not satisfy everyone in his company. In fact, in many cases there are strong forces pushing business toward suppliers who do not necessarily measure up to these basic but tough economic criteria. The environment in which a buyer and his company operate also influences selection of suppliers. Relations with customers, top executives within a company, and the community in which the company operates may dictate selection of suppliers on other than strictly economic terms.

Reciprocity

When a company makes a point of buying from its customers, it is practicing reciprocity. For example, an oil company may buy its pipe only from those steel companies that use its industrial lubricants. Or a chemical company may sell one raw material to another chemical company and buy a second material from that company.

Such reciprocity (or "trade relations," as it is often called) is more widespread in American industry than many business executives care to admit. Purchasing executives often consciously favor their company's customers when selecting suppliers. One purchasing executive for a chemical company (who prefers to remain anonymous) was able to increase his company's sales by $3,516,000 in a single year by calling on his 50 largest suppliers and asking them to become better customers of his company if they wished to continue as important suppliers. On his travels, the purchasing agent was armed with statistics indicating precisely how much his company sold to each supplier and how much it purchased from him.

Many company salesmen travel from customer to customer equipped with similar statistics. Usually it is considered fair and ethical to deal reciprocally on a proportionate basis—as long as quantities purchased are reasonably great. For example, if a chemical company bought 10 percent of its bags from a paper company, it might reasonably expect to get 10 percent of the paper company's chemical purchases (provided, of course, that the chemical company made the chemicals needed for making paper).

Economics of reciprocity. Proponents of reciprocity maintain that it is simply an application of the Golden Rule: "Do unto your customers as you would have them do unto you." Actually, reciprocity is a vicious practice that saps the efficiency of the economy. When firms can sell on some basis other than the price, quality, and delivery of their product, their efforts are unavoidably misdirected. There is bound to be some waste.

In some cases, the waste is obvious. For example, if all firms could secure business only on the basis of the price and quality of their products, the efficient, low-cost firms would get the business and the marginal producers would disappear. When reciprocity permits an inefficient firm to stay in business and prevents the efficient producer from getting the business he deserves, the real costs to the overall economy are slightly higher and aggregate productivity is reduced. This happens every time a purchasing agent accepts slightly higher prices or slightly inferior quality from a supplier because of reciprocity considerations.

It also happens—although much less obviously—when reciprocity is the basis for selecting among suppliers who offer identical prices and almost identical quality, service, and delivery. Even in the tightest oligopoly there is usually a faint flicker of competition. Reciprocity reduces constructive competition even further. The result inevitably is slightly higher costs and less efficiency, which cannot be detected because low-cost producers make little or no effort to undercut their less efficient collaborators in the oligopoly.

Effect on firm. Few economists would deny that reciprocity reduces the efficiency and productivity of the economy as a whole. But economists do not necessarily make good businessmen. The businessman's job is to manage his firm, not the economy as a whole. And the plain fact is that reciprocity need not hurt an individual company. On the contrary, reciprocity is so widespread that many firms' sales and profits would be reduced substantially if they did not practice it.

Suppose a company has a choice of buying materials from two competing suppliers who charge identical prices. One supplier is a customer; the other is not. Should the company offend a good customer by buying from his competitor? The only excuse for doing so would be if it could make the competing supplier a customer, too. So the only "right" decision from the viewpoint of the business executive is one that is based on reciprocity.

The situation is only a little different when the customer and would-be supplier offers to sell goods that are either slightly more expensive or inferior in quality to those of other suppliers. In such cases, the company is paying a definite price for reciprocity. Whether or not it accepts the deal depends on whether or not the premium is worth the benefit that is gained. Most companies refuse to pay higher prices to suppliers who are also customers. They usually find it more profitable to buy from the more efficient suppliers and bluntly demand that these suppliers reciprocate by becoming customers. Sometimes, of course, this is not possible. For various reasons the more efficient supplier may not be able to use the company's products. In that case the price premium paid to hold a customer by making him a supplier should be regarded as an indirect price reduction on the products sold to that supplier.

Reciprocity is a significant problem only in industries selling goods to other industries. Few consumer-goods manufacturers can push reciprocity on their suppliers, nor would it be worth the trouble to do so. For example, not only would the R. J. Reynolds Tobacco Company have a hard time trying to force all employees of its suppliers to smoke Camels or Winstons, but the effect on sales would be negligible if it did succeed in doing so. Not so with a company that both makes and buys products of industrial consumers. For example, a typical chemical company's major purchases are chemical raw materials, and as much as 50 percent of its sales go to other chemical companies. Every major chemical company is both customer and supplier to a number of other major chemical companies. Under the circumstances, reciprocity is inevitable.

Organization for reciprocity.   Many companies have a rather casual approach to reciprocity. The company's own salesmen work informally with purchasing in attempting to solicit business from suppliers. Conversely, the purchasing department will give a courteous reception to all company customers who desire reciprocal business.

Big corporations formerly had a more structured approach to reciprocity. There was often a "trade relations department," sometimes headed by a vice president, responsible for coordinating reciprocal purchasing and marketing efforts. In recent years, however, the Justice Department has forced several big corporations to disband their reciprocity organizations under threat of prosecution for violation of the antitrust laws. Other big companies have taken the hint and quietly disbanded their own trade relations departments. Reciprocity still exists, but its presence is more muted than before.

The role of the purchasing agent or materials manager in reciprocity is essentially defensive. He is always courteous to company customers who want reciprocal business, but he often tries to give them less business than they request. For example, an oil company would almost certainly buy steel pipe on a reciprocal basis. If reciprocity were strictly a numbers game, the oil company's purchases of steel pipe would be made from steel companies in exact proportion to their relative importance as company customers. If the oil company sold $10 million worth of petroleum products to the steel industry, a steel firm that took 10 percent of this, or $1 million worth of oil, might feel it had a "right" to 10 percent of the company's pipe purchases.

The oil company's purchasing agent probably wouldn't give the steel company quite that much business, however. He might attempt to keep some flexibility by giving the steel company only perhaps 6 or 7 percent of the available business. If he shortchanged every steel supplier-customer proportionately, he would have a fair "kitty" that could be awarded either to exceptionally good suppliers—exclusive of reciprocal considerations—or to assist company salesmen in landing new accounts among steel firms.[3]

Reciprocity is perfectly legal as long as it does not serve an "unreasonable" restraint of trade. If a very large corporation uses reciprocity in a coercive manner—forcing its suppliers to purchase its products or risk being dropped as vendors—it may well be violating the antitrust laws. For example, the government held that General Motors Corporation violated the antitrust laws when, as the single largest purchaser of railroad transportation, it used reciprocity to persuade railroads to purchase GM locomotives.

Tarnished image. Although reciprocity is usually legal—especially when practiced by smaller firms—its image is basically unfavorable. Both buyers and sellers often have pangs of conscience when they engage in it. Our "free enterprise ethic" dictates that products should be bought and sold on their own merits. It somehow seems dishonorable to favor a supplier simply because he is an existing or potential customer. Yet, as we have already pointed out, reciprocity may be a useful policy for an individual firm.

When a useful practice has a bad name, it makes sense to change the name. This explains why reciprocity is almost universally described as "trade relations" in the business community. Trade relations is reciprocity with good manners. Both involve the use of a company's buying power as a marketing device. Those who engage in trade relations merely point out that an interdependent relation exists between customers and suppliers. The end result is the same as with reciprocity, but the trade relations people are gentlemen about it.

Back-door selling

When a salesman deliberately bypasses the purchasing department and makes a sales call on personnel in the department using his product, he is engaging in "back-door" selling. Most companies frown on back door selling. Many companies go so far as to require supplier salesmen

---

[3] More detailed information about reciprocity and purchasing is included in Dean S. Ammer, *Trade Relations—Guide to Purchasing* (New York: National Association of Purchasing Management, 1965) and "Realistic Reciprocity," *Harvard Business Review,* January 1962, pp. 116–24.

to get written permission from the purchasing department before they may call on engineering or manufacturing personnel. (A salesman's interview permit is shown in Figure 14–3.)

FIGURE 14–3

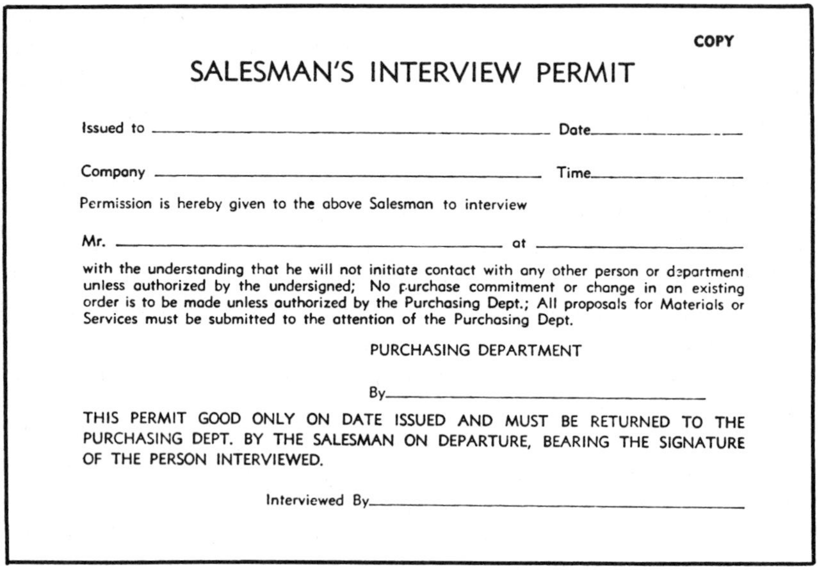

```
                                                              COPY
              SALESMAN'S INTERVIEW PERMIT

      Issued to _____ Date_____

      Company _____ Time_____
      Permission is hereby given to the above Salesman to interview

      Mr. _____ at _____
      with the understanding that he will not initiate contact with any other person or department
      unless authorized by the undersigned;  No purchase commitment or change in an existing
      order is to be made unless authorized by the Purchasing Dept.; All proposals for Materials or
      Services must be submitted to the attention of the Purchasing Dept.

                        PURCHASING DEPARTMENT

                  By_____

      THIS PERMIT GOOD ONLY ON DATE ISSUED AND MUST BE RETURNED TO THE
      PURCHASING DEPT. BY THE SALESMAN ON DEPARTURE, BEARING THE SIGNATURE
      OF THE PERSON INTERVIEWED.

                  Interviewed By_____
```

This interview permit is designed to regulate back-door selling. The purchasing department uses it to control supplier sales calls on operating personnel.

Discouraging back-door selling.. Companies try to prevent suppliers from making sale calls on operating personnel for at least four reasons:

1. *To increase efficiency.* They simply do not want salesmen to waste the time of operating personnel. The company's purchasing personnel get paid to interview supplier salesmen; operating personnel are supposed to concern themselves with their own operations.

2. *To control purchase commitments.* If personnel outside of purchasing have dealings with suppliers, they may innocently commit the company to purchases that have not been properly authorized. Expenditures can be closely controlled only if the authority to commit the company is limited.

3. *To maintain competition.* If a supplier persuades the user of a material that his product is the only one that will do the job, the purchasing department may be handicapped in its efforts to reduce costs. If it is forced to buy one brand exclusively, it cannot get bids from competing suppliers. Sometimes a supplier can gain a tremendous advantage by working with the user of the material even if he does not succeed in getting preclusive specifications tailored to his products. He

can become more familiar with the operating problems in the buyer's plant and can more easily locate applications for his products. This, of course, is to the buyer's advantage, but not if it is done at the cost of freezing out all of the supplier's competitors.

4. *To maintain security.* Many companies, even those not engaged in defense work with security regulations, do not like to have outsiders strolling around almost at will in their plants and offices. They do not want their new product plans and other advance efforts to become widely known. Since supplier salesmen usually call on the company's competitors as well and often are not averse to gossip, better security is maintained by restricting them to the purchasing department except under special circumstances.

Need for calls. Despite the efforts to discourage them, most salesmen make as many calls on operating personnel as they do on purchasing personnel. Many salesmen get more business by calling on the engineers who specify material and the factory superintendents who use it than they do from the purchasing personnel who theoretically buy it. If engineers or superintendents can be sold on a supplier's brand, sometimes the salesman's job is done. The brand is specified on the requisition, and the buyer buys it. Most companies permit their buyers to ignore a brand name on a requisition so they can get quotations from manufacturers of competing brands. But some buyers will go to great lengths to avoid offending the requisitioner, and most buyers will try to give some consideration to the requisitioner's preferences.

Thus back-door selling is effective. In fact, from the marketer's point of view, it is absolutely essential for any product that is not sold on the basis of detailed specifications. For most specialized equipment purchases as well as countless other items, the user of the item is the real buyer. In many organizations, top management interferes with the buying process for totally nonrational reasons. For example, a marketing vice president may be personally very interested in cars, so he interferes with the purchasing department in the purchase of company-owned salesmen's automobiles. Friendships between top managers and suppliers also influence the procurement process.

While no form of back-door selling is good practice, few would deny that there is a real need for contact between suppliers and operating personnel. Materials managers and buyers cannot be experts on every product. In most cases, they cannot hope to know as much about the details of the product as the engineer who specifies it or the manufacturing supervisor who uses it. This is particularly true when the product is designed partly or wholly by the supplier. In such cases some exchange of information between supplier and user is essential and should be encouraged.

The question is—when does an innocent exchange of information become back-door selling? This varies with the product and the personnel involved. Well-managed materials departments are careful to devise procedures that prevent unauthorized purchases from being made and brand preferences from creeping into specifications. However, rules and regulations will do only half the job. The other half can be done only when there is goodwill between the materials department and the departments it serves. Good purchasing executives do their best to cultivate good interdepartmental relations. Some even go so far as to hold seminars for operating personnel in which they explain their objectives and why it is to the company's best interest to have purchases made by professional buyers rather than by persons who use or specify the material purchased.

Personal purchases

Many purchasing departments use one hand trying to avoid being bypassed through back-door selling while with the other they try to be bypassed on personal purchases. It is safe to say that personal purchases are a problem in every company. Should the company use its buying power to purchase things for employees at a discount, or shouldn't it? In general, companies have one of three policies on personal purchases:

1. *They explicitly forbid them.* In this case, a buyer may ignore the rules for his personal friends by informally lining them up with suppliers who, he knows, are willing to sell at a discount. But this would have to be a clandestine procedure and would occur only occasionally.

2. *They permit suggesting sources of supply.* Most companies permit buyers to suggest sources of supply to company personnel if they have the time and desire to do so. In such cases, the buyer will often make a deal with a supplier whereby any employee of the company can get a discount if he is sent by the buyer.

3. *They encourage personal purchases.* Some companies will cooperate on personal purchases to the extent of issuing company purchase orders for the material and then reinvoicing the employee. With this approach, the employee can buy at the same price as the company. Most companies restrict issuing of purchase orders for personal purchases to top executives. Some are less strict, and a few firms even operate company stores. For example, oil companies operating in remote areas of the Middle East are almost forced to assist employees with personal purchases through operating company stores that sell at relatively low prices.

Policies on personal purchases vary not only from company to company but with rank within a company. Generally, top executives and purchasing personnel themselves make far more extensive use of the company's buying power on personal purchases than others in the organization.

A lenient policy on personal purchases helps boost employee morale. It also can increase employees' effective purchasing power, particularly in areas where there are no "discount houses" and there is little price competition among retailers. On the other hand, personal purchases are expensive for a company.[4] Valuable purchasing department time is wasted on trivial purchases. Vendor goodwill can be endangered by nuisance purchases for employees. If the company uses its purchase orders to make them, personal purchases can take accounting department time, and there also is the problem of collecting an invoice rendered to an employee. Community relations also can become a problem. Local merchants resent a company that uses its buying power to help employees purchase at a discount from out-of-town suppliers.

Local purchases

If all other factors are equal, it is to the buyer's advantage to buy from a local supplier. He usually can get prompter service, and his lead time will be shorter. In addition, it makes for good community relations when a company spends its money locally whenever possible. This is particularly true of a franchised monopoly like a public utility, which must maintain the goodwill of the community and is also trying to stimulate business in its service area.

Municipal and state purchasing agents usually encounter strong pressure to buy within the boundaries they serve. The money they spend comes from taxes collected within the state or city, so it is reasonable that they should make some effort to spend it on businesses in the same area. However, public purchasing agents should not subsidize local industry with tax money if they can buy more cheaply elsewhere—unless they are forced to do so by statute. Federal government agencies, for example, at one time could lawfully buy from a foreign supplier only if his delivered price was more than 25 percent below that of the lowest cost domestic supplier. This "buy American" act resulted in millions of dollars of hidden subsidies to higher cost domestic producers.

ETHICS

Ethics is perhaps the only problem in purchasing and materials management that receives widespread publicity. A big-city newspaper can count on at least three or four big stories a year concerning purchasing ethics. A top federal government official accepts entertainment from

---

[4] Sometimes the cost can be staggering when compared with the results achieved. A number of years ago, I was asked to get some bolts for the general manager of the firm in which I was employed. I spent about one hour of time plus $2 for a long-distance phone call to get bolts directly from the manufacturer that could have been bought retail for 30 or 40 cents at any hardware store.

a major defense contractor; a city purchasing official favors a supplier who is a close personal friend; the president of a large corporation is part owner of a firm that is a major supplier. These are typical stories that make the front page periodically.

On the average, professional buyers and materials managers probably have higher moral standards than most of their fellow citizens. But they also are subjected to more temptations. Buyers spend millions of dollars of their company's money each years. As a result, they wield tremendous economic power and are the objects of considerable attention from suppliers. They are in an excellent position to be dishonest if they want to be. Buyers can bluntly demand kickbacks and other favors from suppliers. Sometimes they can almost make themselves millionaires before they are caught. For this reason, materials managers are careful to select buyers with strong character and high moral standards, as well as to devise procedures and controls to prevent them from giving in to temptation. Partly because of this practice, many of the scandals that have been exposed did not involve materials personnel but improper relations between operating executives and suppliers. One case that received widespread publicity involved William C. Newberg, president of the Chrysler Corporation, and Chrysler suppliers in which Newberg was a silent partner.

Gifts and entertainment

Even though they may be completely honest, buyers and top management executives will often receive many wholly unsolicited favors from suppliers. These range from an occasional lunch or entertainment at a convention to Christmas gifts, theater or football tickets, and other favors.

Recipients include not only buyers and materials managers but everyone else who is someone's customer. In many cases, marketing managers regard the practice as a waste of money, but they often continue out of force of habit, if for no other reason. Even if a company spends substantial sums on gifts and entertainment of customers, the cost in relation to sales is trivial. For example, a supplier may give an $8 bottle of whiskey to a customer from whom it received $100,000 worth of business during the year.

Tax deduction. Business gifts are normally deductible as business expense by the supplier. This is defended on the basis that the purpose of the gift is to influence the customer, and it is, therefore, part of the customer's marketing effort. A gift given purely for the sake of giving would not be a legitimate business expense. Thus, "friendship" in the purest sense has nothing to do with the average business gift.

Considering this simple fact, what then should the buyer's attitude be if a supplier or potential supplier offers him a gift or other favor?

Under no circumstances should he accept anything from a supplier if it will tend to obligate him directly or indirectly to favor that supplier. There is no general agreement on what a buyer can ethically accept from a supplier. Some believe the buyer should refuse anything except gifts of nominal value used for advertising and sales promotion purposes. Most managements have a somewhat more lenient attitude.

No gifts. A few companies and most government agencies have written policies forbidding any employee to accept any favors from suppliers. When a buyer receives an unsolicited gift, he is expected to return it with a letter advising the supplier of the no-gift policy. The top procurement official often goes even further and warns the supplier that he will lose business if he continues to send unsolicited gifts. When a company receives gifts that are perishable and cannot be returned (food, flowers, and so on), it may donate them to some charitable institution. The only gifts that are acceptable are advertising novelties such as ballpoint pens with the supplier's name on them, calendars, and the like, which are often passed out at conventions and trade shows by the exhibitors.

Gifts of nominal value only. In the course of normal business relations, certain amenities are both accepted and customary. Buyers and sellers often conduct business over cocktails and lunch or on the golf course at the local country club. In such cases, either may pick up the check. Many completely honorable buyers and sellers remember each other with a gift at Christmas. In many cases, their frequent business dealings have led to friendships that endure even after they are no longer active in business. They naturally would resent any implication that such gifts were unethical. However, there is no doubt that there have been some misguided applications of the Christmas spirit in the business world.

Ethical behavior

A buyer can be completely honest, resolutely refusing all favors from suppliers, and still be guilty of unethical behavior. In fact, it is extremely difficult for a buyer with the best of intentions to be wholly ethical at all times. To do so he must always be completely equitable and honest in his dealings with all suppliers. This is not easy in an atmosphere in which each supplier is vying for the buyer's favor. The buyer is bound to be attracted to the personalities of some supplier salesmen and repelled by others. Theoretically, this should not influence his buying decisions. But since buyers are human beings, they are bound to be influenced by the personalities of the people with whom they deal. The best buyers can subordinate their personal feelings with respect to suppliers and make fairly objective buying decisions that bring maximum benefit to their company, even if this involves awarding business to suppliers whom they personally dislike and not awarding it to individuals they like.

Although a buyer is expected to work hard to negotiate the best possible purchase for his company, he should never stoop to unethical techniques for achieving this goal. If he does, he will eventually develop a reputation for underhanded dealing, and suppliers will no longer trust him. Among the practices in which no ethical buyer indulges are:

1. *Permitting a favored supplier to examine the quotations of his competitors.* All quotations submitted to a buyer are confidential and should not be shown to any outsider. Nor should a buyer disclose to competitors any information he might have about a supplier's costs, processes, new products, or the like, unless he has the supplier's explicit permission to do so.

2. *Giving the supplier misleading information to get him to reduce his prices.* The buyer with scruples never asks a supplier to meet a lower bid that exists only in the buyer's imagination. Nor does he give the supplier fictitious information regarding planned production schedules, and so forth, so that the supplier will be encouraged to grant bigger discounts or other benefits.

3. *Using his company's buying power to force suppliers to sell at prices well below cost.* This is not only unethical but uneconomic, since only a reasonably prosperous supplier can be useful for future contracts. The buyer need not be carried away with compassion for the supplier, however. Every supplier has a right to go broke if he wants to. The buyer can prevent cases of undue supplier dependence by avoiding excessive commitment to a supplier who could be badly hurt if the buyer withheld his business.

4. *Asking suppliers for quotations when they have no chance of getting the business.* It often is convenient for a buyer to use quotations from an outside supplier to check up on an established supplier or to compare with shop costs. The quote is used only to negotiate a price reduction from the established supplier or stimulate a cost-reduction drive in the buyer's manufacturing plant. The supplier who quotes has absolutely no chance of getting the business regardless of his quotation. Since quotations are expensive to prepare, the buyer who requests them under false pretenses is, in effect, guilty of stealing from the supplier.

5. *Having a financial interest in any company that is a supplier.* In such cases there is an obvious conflict of interest. Most companies do permit buyers to own stock in suppliers that are so large or diversified that the buyer's actions would have no significant effect on sales or profits. For example, few would object if a buyer of utility services owned a few shares of American Telephone & Telegraph. AT&T is so big that no buyer could significantly affect its profits; it also is a monopoly in its service areas, so the buyer would not have an alterate source of supply, anyway.

Few business executives would deny that industrial purchasing ethics today are higher than they have ever been. Scandals make news because they are relatively rare. One reason for this is the work of the National Association of Purchasing Management in boosting the stature and recognition of purchasing. The NAPM's code of good practice, to which its members subscribe, is illustrated in Figure 14–4.

FIGURE 14–4

Principles and Standards of Purchasing Practice

1. To consider, first, the interest of his company in all transactions and to carry out and believe in its established policies.
2. To be receptive to competent counsel from his colleagues and to be guided by such counsel without impairing the dignity and responsibility of his office.
3. To buy without prejudice, seeking to obtain the maximum ultimate value for each dollar of expenditure.
4. To strive consistently for knowledge of the materials and processes of manufacture and to establish practical methods for the conduct of his office.
5. To subscribe and work for honesty and truth in buying and selling and to denounce all forms and manifestations of commercial bribery.
6. To accord a prompt and courteous reception, so far as conditions will permit, to all who call upon a legitimate business mission.
7. To respect his obligations and to require that obligations to him and to his concern be respected, consistent with good buisness practice.
8. To avoid sharp practice.
9. To counsel and assist fellow purchasing agents in the performance of their duties, whenever occasion permits.
10. To cooperate with all organizations and individuals engaged in activities designed to enhance the development and standing of purchasing.

This code of ethics was developed by the National Association of Purchasing Management to guide the conduct of its 18,000 members.

PROMOTING SUPPLIER GOODWILL

Supplier relations are a problem even when both buyer and seller have the highest possible ethical standards. A supplier who does not get business may sometimes wonder if the buyer isn't unjustly favoring some "pet" supplier.

Buyers try to promote supplier goodwill as much as possible. Salesmen never are left waiting in the lobby for more than a few minutes without some explanation. If a buyer is busy, he will usually try to arrange for the salesman to see another buyer, if he wishes to do so. If the salesman is from out of town, buyers often will make a prearranged appointment to make certain they are not busy when he calls.

Buyers always will listen sympathetically to the salesman's presentation, even though they may not have any foreseeable need for the product. Seasoned buyers also have mastered the art of ending an interview. If they are busy and the salesman has nothing new to say, they know

FIGURE 14–5

CONTENTS

Courtesy General Electric Co.

Many companies have "welcome" booklets in which they describe their purchasing policies, organization, and products to suppliers. Shown here is the table of contents of *Selling to General Electric*.

how to rise, thank the salesman for calling, and conclude the interview in a tactful way. They want the salesman to like them and to like the company, and they do their best to make his visit a pleasant experience.

Large companies even publish purchasing directories to help their suppliers. In them they list the major commodities they buy and a breakdown of their purchasing organization, so that the visiting salesman can readily locate the buyer specializing in his product line. They also try to explain company purchasing policies and procedures so that there will be no misunderstandings. Figure 14–5 illustrates the contents page of the booklet, *Selling to General Electric,* which was prepared to help the 45,000 firms that sell to that company.

Many companies go still further to bolster supplier relations. They arrange hotel and transportation reservations for visitng salesmen. Most firms permit purchasing personnel to buy lunches for suppliers and extend other courtesies. A few firms even remember suppliers with a Christmas gift of nominal value.

Why do they go to the trouble? Suppliers not only can use a company's products but they also may become some of the company's biggest boosters if they are sold on the company as a customer. More important, suppliers can be an important source of cost-reduction ideas. This aspect will be discussed in detail in the chapters on price negotiation and cost reduction.

Cases

CASE 14–1. COLONIAL LAUNDRY EQUIPMENT COMPANY

Coping with supplier labor trouble

Production will shut down at the Colonial Laundry Equipment Company's main plant in Louisville, Kentucky, unless the company's purchasing director, Kenneth Caldwell, can achieve "the impossible." Colonial makes coin-operated washing machines for use in apartment buildings and stores. The transmission housing in its product is made from a gray-iron casting that the company buys from the Allied Foundry Company.

Allied has now been shut down by a strike. Its union, the United Foundry Workers, is demanding a wage increase of 50 cents per hour for its members. Allied insists that it cannot afford any increase at all and cites its shrinking profit margins and the price cutting currently prevalent in the industry as evidence. Caldwell believes that the strike may be a long one, not only because the company and union are so far apart on a wage settlement but also because Allied's labor relations have never been too placid. The UFW local at Allied is unusually belligerent, according to Allied's management. In addition, Caldwell suspects that the company's labor relations policies have been a little heavy-handed.

Allied has suffered from a series of one-day walkouts over the past year. In addition, its quality has suffered; apparently some of its workmen no longer take any pride in their work. For these reasons, Colonial's inventories of castings are somewhat lower than they would be otherwise. Although Caldwell was aware of the fact that the company's union contract expired on June 30 and that a strike was likely on July 1, he was unable to accumulate more than one week's inventory of castings. He had hoped to get at least three weeks ahead, which would take up all available storage space at the Colonial plant.

Because Allied had definitely been slipping on both quality and delivery, Colonial had already solicited bids from other foundries, as follows:

Supplier	Price	Cost of patterns	Delivery promise after receipt of order (weeks)
Consolidated Gray Iron	$2.65	$1,950	8
Archer Foundry.	3.10	1,800	6
Young Industries	2.40	2,200	6

Colonial is currently paying Allied $2.20 per casting. Allied's price and its competitors' bids all are based on shipment of approximately 4,000 castings per month in lots of 1,000, and each supplier would be willing to quote the same price for a volume as low as 2,000 castings per month. Caldwell has hesitated to switch sources previously because he was unable to find a supplier who could meet Allied's price. He hoped that Allied would straighten out its problems without a price increase. Now he doubts that Allied will be able to hold to the $2.20 price, since the settlement of its strike will be too costly to permit it to do so. Caldwell expects a price increase of at least 10 cents after Allied settles with the union.

Of course, Caldwell has no idea when the settlement will be made, but he doubts that Allied's workers will still be on strike in six weeks, when he can get his first castings from Archer or Young if he places an order with them now. This is not Caldwell's only alternative, however. The patterns that Allied uses were paid for by Colonial. If Caldwell can get them from the Allied plant, he can cut the lead time needed to start up a new source by at least several weeks.

None of the other foundries can give Caldwell a firm promise as to when it can start production with Allied's patterns, since none of them has ever seen the patterns. It might be possible to use them without any rework at all, or it might be necessary to make substantial changes. Nor can the other vendors be held to the prices they have quoted if they use Allied's patterns. Their quotations are based on patterns of their own design. But Caldwell doubts that there would be more than a small price increase were Archer, Young, or Consolidated to use Allied's patterns.

However, Caldwell does have another problem, even if he can get the patterns out and they can be used. If Archer, Young, or Consolidated work hard to deliver castings as promptly as possible during Allied's strike, they naturally expect some reward in the form of future business. They believe it would be unfair to extend themselves to help Colonial in an emergency and then promptly lose the business once Allied settled its strike. On the other hand, Allied has been supplying Colonial for several years, and except for occasional difficulties resulting from its poor labor relations, it has been a dependable, low-cost supplier. Also, it is possible that Allied's competitors may likewise be faced with labor problems and higher costs in the next six months when their union contracts expire.

Questions

1. What course of action do you recommend that Caldwell follow to cope with the shortage of castings?
2. What should he do after Allied's strike has been settled?
3. What, if anything, could he have done to prevent these difficulties from arising?

CASE 14–2. JOHNSON INSTRUMENT COMPANY

Gifts and entertainment from suppliers

Johnson Instrument Company manufactures a line of precision instruments that have both civilian and military applications. Because of its defense business, the company is especially careful to keep its relations with suppliers "as clean as a hound's tooth." It takes great pains to get competitive bids on every order. When a contract is not placed with the low bidder, an explanation is written into the purchase record so that government contract auditors will know there has been no collusion.

Naturally, the company has a firm policy prohibiting any of its employees to accept gifts or gratuities from suppliers. The only exceptions to this rule are business lunches and advertising novelties of nominal value. Johnson Instrument does not even like to have its suppliers pay for all lunches. Its materials executives have expense accounts and are expected to pick up their fair share of the checks.

George Browning is one of the company's buyers. He handles a wide variety of maintenance, repair, and operating supplies, including all of the lumber used by the plant. One of his major suppliers is the Warren Lumber Company, a well-known local firm with a deserved reputation for integrity and dependability. Browning is a dedicated baseball fan, and Ned Warren, the young sales manager of Warren Lumber, knows it. Warren is also familiar with Johnson's policy on gifts and has never offered Browning any gift of more than nominal value at Christmas.

Two days before the World Series, Browning receives two box seat tickets for a week-end game, with this note:

> DEAR GEORGE:
>
> I intended to use these myself. Unfortunately, I had forgotten that my brother and sister-in-law are coming to stay with us for the weekend. They're not interested in baseball, and at this late date I don't think I could get tickets for them anyway. So it looks as if I'm going to miss the game. I know how crazy you are about baseball. Why don't you use them?
>
> Cordially,
> NED

Needless to say, Browning would very much like to go to the game. But there is no doubt that the tickets are of more than nominal value. The list price is $10 each, and they're actually worth more, since scalpers are selling them for as much as $20. Not only would it be against the company's policy for him to accept the tickets, but Browning is honest enough to admit to himself that while Warren may have sent him the tickets as a gesture of friendship, he will undoubtedly regard them as a legitimate deduction for "sales expense" and not as a personal gift.

On the other hand, Browning is equally certain that the gift is not going to influence his buying decisions in any way. Warren is his lowest cost lumber supplier (in fact, he is the only major lumber supplier in the area), and Browning will not buy any more lumber than what the plant requires, regardless of how much he likes Warren. In addition, Browning can say with complete objectivity that he wouldn't think of jeopardizing his reputation or integrity for the sake of $20 worth of baseball tickets. If he returns the tickets to Warren, he is saying in effect, "This $20 gift will corrupt me." Also he is, by implication, insulting Warren, since he is then tacitly accusing Warren of trying to bribe him when, in fact, Warren might have no such intention. So, in returning the tickets, Browning might well jeopardize what has been an excellent business relationship between Warren and himself.

Questions

1. What should Browning do?
2. If Warren should offer to let Browning and/or other employees of Johnson's purchasing department make personal purchases of lumber and other supplies at the same wholesale prices paid by the company, would

it be ethical for Browning to accept this offer? Should Browning attempt to solicit such a discount for personal purchases?

CASE 14–3. NORTHEAST ELECTRONIC PRODUCTS, INC. (A) & (B)°

Quality problems on purchased materials

On February 1, 1960, Albert Whitmore, Manager of Manufacturing, received the following memorandum from Mr. James Barker, design engineer for the Airguide Project:

> To: A. Whitmore
> FROM: J. Barker
> cc to: Willet, Jorgensen, Johnson
> On Friday we received an assembly request for investigation of an interference problem on the ring and spacer of Airguide Module #57. After investigation it is clear that the design is correct and that any problem must lie within the production operation. See Exhibit 1 for analysis.

Mr. Barker's investigation of the ring and spacer assembly had been prompted by a memorandum which he had received earlier from Mr. George Willet, an assembly foreman. That memorandum read as follows:

> DEAR JIM:
> This week we began pilot assembly operations for module #57 in the Airguide system. So far we have been having a great deal of trouble with dimensional interference on the ring and spacer components. Our pilot quantity is 30 units and they are scheduled for shipment in just a week. So far we have been able to get only 19 good modules out of the 30 sets of parts delivered to the assembly department. The other 11 have been held up because the ring and spacer pairs fitted improperly. The design specification calls for a nominal thickness of .062 plus or minus .006 on the spacer and .057 plus or minus .005 for the ring. The specification also requires that each spacer be thicker than the mating ring. As simple arithmetic will show, the smallest acceptable spacer is .001 smaller than our nominal specification for the ring. Will you please see that these dimensional specifications are changed and that satisfactory parts are supplied to this department.
>   /s/ GEORGE

Background of the contract

The Airguide system was a military airborne radar navigation system developed by the Western Aircraft Corporation. Western Aircraft was

---

acting as the prime contractor to the Department of Defense in supplying these systems and had agreed to deliver the first three pilot systems on March 15, 1960, and to commence production of a lot of 1,000 systems upon government approval of the pilot model. Each system contained 3,000 prime parts assembled into 72 basic modular subassemblies which were to be interchangeable from one system to another. The production contract was negotiated on a fixed-price basis specifying a total price of $20,000 per system. Northeast Electronic Products, Incorporated, acted as a subcontractor supplying 12 of the modular subassemblies to the Western Aircraft Corporation. Under the contract, Northeast Electronic would receive $2 million for the components it would produce as part of the initial production lot of 1,000 systems.

The #57 module

One of the 12 Airguide modules being produced at Northeast was the #57 module, a critical component in the system and one that was used ten times in each finished system. To supply the requirements for the first three pilot systems, Northeast had to produce 30 of the #57 modules. The contract price for each #57 module was $25.

The heart of the #57 module was a 2-inch diameter steel spacer and a 5-inch diameter nylon plastic ring. Copper strips which served for electrical contact were fitted in recesses on the upper surface of the nylon ring in such a way that the surface of each strip was flush with the surface of the ring. The spacer fitted through the hole in the center of the ring and separated two parallel metal plates above and below the ring. The device would not function if the upper surface of the ring and the lower surface of the upper plate were in contact, but high performance depended upon those two surfaces being as close together as possible without actual contact. The thickness of the space determined the distance between the upper and lower plates. Thus, it was essential that the space thickness be slightly greater than the ring thickness.

The ring

The ring was injection molded of nylon 66 which was shrunk under controlled conditions after molding to achieve the nominal thickness dimension of .057. Because of random variations in material content and other factors in the process, the actual thickness of each ring might vary from the nominal dimension. A study of the first batch of rings molded as well as their experience with similar molded products led the process engineers to the conclusion that the population of parts produced in this manner formed a characteristic random normal distribution around the nominal dimension. The engineers believed that "it would have been fundamentally uneconomical to try to refine the process beyond the sixth standard deviation band of normal chance variation." For the process which produced the molded ring, one standard deviation was found to be .001667.

The spacer

The metal spacer was a simple stamping made from $2\frac{1}{4}$-inch-wide high-carbon steel strip specified as SAE1080 for long-wearing characteristics. The nominal thickness of the steel strip was .062 and the tolerance guaranteed by the supplier was plus or minus .006. A set of go, no-go snap gauges was used to inspect the thickness of all the steel strips used for these purposes, and a similar set was used in inspecting the thickness of the finished stamping.

The steel strip from which the spacer was stamped was purchased from a nearby steel warehouse in 4,000-pound lots, each of which included about 100 ten-foot strips. Each lot cost $350 delivered to the Northeast plant. High-carbon cold-rolled strip of SAE1080 specification was commercially available also in nominal thicknesses of .068 and .056 inches in the $2\frac{1}{4}$-inch width.

Assembly operations

Prior to assembly of the modules, the component parts were sorted into part bins so that all of the parts used at a given assembly station were moved to that station together. The bins for assembly station Number 2, at which the spacer and ring assembly took place, contained 30 spacers and 30 rings when prepared for the pilot assembly operation. These parts were drawn in the stockroom from bins containing a much larger number of parts. During the full-scale production run it was expected that each assembly station would be furnished daily with enough parts to complete the expected average daily production of fifty #57 modules. Assembly station Number 2 was not equipped with any measuring equipment and the operator was not expected to do selective fitting of components. In other words, he would draw one ring and one spacer from their respective bins and assemble them.

The assembly operators were paid $1.95 per hour and inspectors were paid $2.50 per hour at Northeast Electronic Products, Inc. For cost accounting purposes, the company allocated its overhead at a rate equal to 100 percent of direct labor. The cost accounting department valued the ring at $1.50 and the spacer at 30 cents prior to assembly.

At the final station on the assembly line the #57 modules were encapsulated by immersion in a bath of epoxy plastic resin. When hardened, the plastic formed a tough protective coating which adhered to the exposed surfaces of the module. Because it would be impossible to rework rejected modules after encapsulation, each module was first visually inspected by the operator to ensure that all components were assembled and in the proper location.

According to the planned procedures, the completed modules would remain at the end of the line on special racks until the next morning when the day's production would be moved in one lot to the testing department. There each module would be tested for performance under normal and extreme environmental conditions and one of every 50 would be subjected to a destructive test to determine operating life. After test the modules would be shipped to the Western Aircraft Company to be inspected and tested again as components of an operating Airguide system.

Airguide design requirements

In investigating the problem, Mr. Barker restudied the design specifications furnished by the Western Aircraft Corporation. The specifications made it clear that the performance of the #57 modules was directly related to the gap between the ring and the plates. If the ring and plate were in contact, the module would certainly fail to perform. If the two components were separated by a very small gap the module was almost certain to perform satisfactorily. As the gap increased, however, the level of performance would fall off and the probability that the module would fail the qualification test would raise. Because of the advanced technology of the product, however, Mr. Barker could not develop any direct quantitative relationships between the size of the gap and the probability of failure without testing a large number of modules. He did believe, however, that for modules with a gap larger than .008 inches the probability of failure might be as high as .1 and that for a gap larger than .012 inches the probability of failure would be approximately .3.

Mr. Barker's report

On the afternoon of February 1, Mr. Whitmore had to decide what to do about the ring and spacer assembly. As Manager of Manufacturing,

Mr. Whitmore was responsible for all fabrication and assembly operations and for some related activities, including purchasing and industrial engineering, but not quality control or product design. Mr. Whitmore, as well as the Quality Control Manager (Mr. Frank Jorgensen) and the Chief Design Engineer (Mr. Johnson) reported to the company's executive vice president. As Quality Control Manager, Mr. Jorgensen was responsible for the quality assurance lab, incoming parts inspection, the in-process production inspectors, and the final test department. Copies of Mr. Barker's memorandum were sent to Willet, the assembly foreman, and to Jorgensen and Johnson.

After reading Jim Barker's memorandum (see Exhibit 1) about the ring and spacer problem in the #57 module, Mr. Albert Whitmore, Manufacturing Manager, called in an industrial engineer to investigate the production process. The engineer's report was as follows:

REPORT OF INDUSTRIAL ENGINEERING INVESTIGATION OF MODULE #57 SPACER AND RING

The thickness of molded plastic rings and purchased steel strip for spacers was investigated as a first step in evaluating the control of these processes.

Our entire supply of rings—118 units—was examined and the thickness of each ring measured with a micrometer. A tabulation of these readings is as follows:

Ring thickness	Number of rings	Ring thickness	Number of rings
.052	1	.058	23
.053	5	.059	12
.054	4	.060	7
.055	14	.061	1
.056	21	.062	2
.057	28		

One load of SAE1080 cold-rolled strip, $2\frac{1}{4} \times \frac{5}{8}$, was measured to determine the distribution of thickness dimensions. One measurement was made at the approximate midpoint of each of 100 strips. The measurements are tabulated as follows:

Strip for spacers		Strip for spacers	
Thickness	Frequency	Thickness	Frequency
.0600	2	.0575	21
.0595	2	.0570	10
.0590	12	.0565	3
.0585	22	.0560	—
.0580	28		

The steel supplier's only thickness specification is given as .062 ± .006. It is clear that the strip meets that specification but not our need. Our purchasing agent believes that this situation is a consequence of the great improvements made in recent years in steel mill control of the rolling process. This much tighter control of thickness variation has permitted them to concentrate the product on the low end of the specification, at least in this instance.

EXHIBIT 1
Mr. Barker's analysis

1. Call the ring thickness "R" and the spacer thickness "S".
2. Accept Assembly if $S > R$
   Reject Assembly if $S \leq R$
3. *For the moment*, assume that the processes for S and R are mutually independent and under statistical control.

   If this is so, let $\bar{S}$ = mean of S
   $\bar{R}$ = mean of R
   σ_S = standard deviation of S
   σ_R = standard deviation of R

Assume that the occurrence of S and R forms a random normal distribution about $\bar{S}$ and $\bar{R}$. Thus:

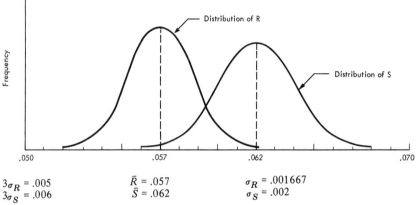

$3\sigma_R = .005$	$\bar{R} = .057$	$\sigma_R = .001667$
$3\sigma_S = .006$	$\bar{S} = .062$	$\sigma_S = .002$

For any ring and spacer pair selected at random, call (S-R) the "*clearance*," C. For a large number of pairs, thus selected, the distribution C would be:

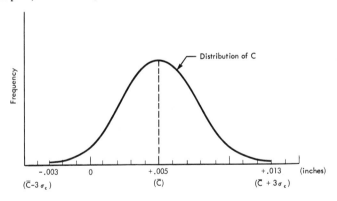

$$\bar{C} = \bar{S} - \bar{R} = .062 - .057 = .005$$
$$\sigma_C = \sqrt{(\sigma_S)^2 + (\sigma_R)^2} = \sqrt{(.001667)^2 + (.002)^2} = .00268$$

The smallest "C" in the distribution is $\bar{C} - 3\sigma = .005 - 3(.00268) = -.00304$. The smallest acceptable C is $+.00001$. The difference of $(.005 - .00001) = .00499$ is 1.87 standard deviations. From a table of the area under a normal curve, we find that 46.93% of occurrences lie between $\bar{C}$ and .0001. Thus 3.1% of occurrences are $<.00001$.

4. If the assumptions of (3) were correct—mutual independence and statistical control of processes—the reject rate would be 3.1%. Since actual rejects are 11 of 30 = 36.5%, the assumptions of statistical control must not be correct in this case. Thus we conclude that, at the moment, the process is not being controlled to give the proper distribution of dimensions.

15

Traffic and physical distribution

PHYSICAL DISTRIBUTION is concerned with getting goods from the manufacturer to the customer. While physical distribution usually involves substantial expenditures for warehousing and internal materials handling, the biggest element in the process is usually transportation. In the aggregate, American industry spends at least $50 billion per year to ship materials and finished products from mines and quarries to factories and, finally, to end-product consumers. Many manufacturing and marketing organizations operate their own fleets of trucks not only to deliver goods to market but also to pick up purchased materials from suppliers. Occasionally, organizations that are not primarily in the transportation business also operate their own ships, pipelines, barges, aircraft, and railroads.

Most organizations, however, rely on common carriers for most or all of their transportation needs. In the economic sense the common carrier is like any other supplier the company might have. The carrier performs a service and gets paid for it. The main difference is that common carriers whose vehicles cross state lines are very tightly regulated by a federal government agency, the Interstate Commerce Commission, as well as by various state agencies.

Were it not for the unique character of its regulation, transportation services would probably be just another purchasing function in most organizations. However, complex regulations make transportation purchasing sufficiently different from conventional purchasing activities so that in larger companies it is usually not carried on in the purchasing department but in a separate traffic department.

THE TRAFFIC FUNCTION

Traffic management is a big job in most industries. In the typical manufacturing company, transportation services are the third greatest expenditure; only purchased materials and labor are more important. Producers of bulky, low-cost materials may spend as much as one-fourth of their sales dollar on transportation, and even those who produce items of very high value may directly or indirectly pay out 5 or 10 percent of their sales dollar for transportation services.

Most larger companies have a separate traffic or physical distribution department. The traffic manager is a major executive; in some cases he reports directly to the president of the company. Even when he does not, he may be only one echelon lower in the organization, reporting to the materials manager, purchasing manager, or marketing manager. Growing recognition of the importance of the physical distribution function (see Chapter 1) is not only upgrading traffic but bringing it closer to related materials activities.

Basic responsibilities

The traffic department is responsible for problems related to the purchase of transportation services, including the selection of mode of transport and of carrier, negotiation of rates, tracing and expediting of shipments, filing and negotiation of claims for lost or damaged shipments, and audit of freight bills. In addition, as the company's experts on transportation, traffic personnel are involved in many special studies designed to minimize transportation costs or to advise management about the effect that various decisions (such as plant location or product distribution) would have on transportation cost.

Traffic is intimately involved in materials management and physical distribution even in companies where there are no organizational ties linking traffic with other materials management activities. The choice of a carrier automatically influences inventory levels. Fast, highly reliable modes of transportation permit less inventory than is required for slower, more erratic modes. The traffic function is also intimately related to problems of warehouse and plant location. In simple cases, the location must be easily accessible to low-cost transportation; in more complex cases, inventory investment, transportation cost, and other variables combine to determine optimum location.

The typical traffic department also has a number of miscellaneous functions, including the handling of all passenger reservations for employees traveling on company business and the moving of household effects of employees transferred from one company plant to another. Sometimes the traffic manager also is responsible for the operation of all company-owned vehicles; even if he is not, he should always be consulted prior to their purchase.

Traffic also is concerned with packaging material. The heavier the package, the higher the freight costs to ship the product. On the other hand, lightweight packaging is more liable to damage in shipment. For this reason, many tariffs are based on shipments being made in certain types of packaging.

Traffic usually is concerned with both inbound and outbound shipments of materials and finished products. Many traffic departments become intimately involved with charter carriers or company-owned trucks. Normally, however, most of their dealings are with various common carriers, including railroads, trucks, pipelines, and water carriers.

Picking the carrier

Railroads are by far the most important common carriers in terms of tonnage handled (about half the total). Trucks are second in tonnage but lead in dollar volume. Pipelines handle almost as much tonnage as trucks but get only a small fraction of their revenue. The reason for the discrepancies between shares of tonnage and revenue of the various carriers is obvious: the rate per ton-mile for all commodities is not the same. A trucker who hauls a ton of household goods for one mile may get 100 times as much as a pipeline gets for moving a ton of crude oil the same distance.

A company should buy transportation services just as it buys any other commodity—on the bases of quality, price, and service. It should try to direct its business to carriers that provide prompt delivery with a minimum of lost or damaged shipments, cooperate readily in tracing and rerouting shipments, make a minimum of errors in invoicing, and so on. These are sound criteria for selecting among like types of carrier, which charge identical rates when they are subject to regulation.

The transportation buyer must also select among various types of transportation service. His two basic criteria should be price and service. Carriers that give fast service charge relatively higher tariffs and those charging the lowest rate usually provide the slowest service. Shipment over water is the cheapest and usually the slowest way to ship any commodity—particularly in specialized bulk carriers that transport oil, coal, grain, and like commodities. Pipeline is the lowest-cost overland mode of shipment—so cheap that even coal is pulverized and mixed into slurry so it can be pumped through special pipelines. Most materials cannot be transported in ships or pipelines, however, and shippers must choose among a variety of higher cost, but usually faster, carriers. Figure 15–1 illustrates a chart used by North American Rockwell as a general guide to the services and relative costs of various types of carriers.

Rail freight. Although the relative importance of railroads has declined substantially since World War II, they still are the most important carriers. Rail freight rates in carload lots are always lower than air freight, parcel post, or rates charged by freight forwarders. For many commodities they are cheaper than truck rates, and sometimes they are competitive with barge and ship rates. They rarely are cheaper than pipeline rates.

With the exception of materials that can be pumped through a pipeline, for most commodities rail shipment—particularly in trainload quantities with oversized box cars—is the cheapest possible mode of overland shipment. Shippers of manufactured goods rarely are able to generate enough traffic to move their goods in trainload quantities; their lowest-cost mode of shipment is often in full carload lots for shipments between points equipped with railroad sidings. When a company does not have a siding, it must transfer its shipment from the railroad boxcar to a truck. This creates extra transport and handling expenses which usually make it more economic to ship 100 percent by truck or may even force a company to relocate near a siding if its costs are to remain competitive.

Truck freight. Almost every factory is equipped with a dock to receive truck shipments; in fact, truck lines are the most important common carrier for many types of manufactured goods. Truck rates often are as low as those charged by railroads for finished manufactured products, and service usually is faster. Trucks are especially competitive on shorter hauls. They may offer overnight service between cities that are only a few hundred miles apart. Both interstate truck and rail rates are regulated by the Interstate Commerce Commission, which tries to set rates that permit fair competition between the two carriers. Trucks have substantially increased their share of traffic at the expense of the railroads since the 1950s, but recently the railroads have been holding their own despite fierce competition from competing carriers.

Shipment by air. Air cargo shipments have increased at a fantastic rate as technology has worked to reduce real costs. Since the end of World War II physical volume of air freight has increased at least 50 times, although total tonnage is still a small fraction of that carried by rail and truck. The only factor that has tempered growth is the fact that air tariffs are still two to ten times higher than those charged by railroads and truck lines.

If rates are so high, how have air shipments managed to gross so fast? Obviously because for some shipments, speed is the only important factor and the shipment must be made in the fastest possible manner, almost regardless of the cost. There are at least two other reasons for the rapid growth of air shipments. First, air tariffs are not as high as they appear. In most cases, it is possible to use much lighter containers when shipping by air, and sometimes no packaging at all is needed.

FIGURE 15–1
Transportation method on comparison chart

Transporta-tion media	Description	Application	Can be traced
Carload and truckload	Full rail car or trailer	Where quantity is sufficient to warrant (differs with product)	Yes
Truck	Motor truck	For all shipments over 50 lbs. not requiring emergency air service	Yes
Freight forwarder	Truck pickup for assembly into carloads, includes truck delivery at destination	For all shipments over 50 lbs. not requiring emergency air service. Forwarder usually on long haul	Yes
Railway express	Freight handled by express company on passenger trains. Includes pickup and delivery	To or from out-of-way points. Also between large cities when expedited service is required	Very difficult
Air freight	*No. 1.* Regular passenger airlines which also handle air freight up to a limited size and weight	Rush shipments over 20 lbs. Usually as fast as Air Express	Yes
	No. 2. Cargo air carriers handling freight only	Rush shipments over 20 lbs. Usually as fast as Air Express	Yes
Air express	Complete pickup and delivery service using all commercial airlines on shipments of limited size and weight	Extreme emergency only! Of little value to and from points not on a scheduled airline	Very difficult
Air freight forwarder	Brokerage service using all commercial airlines and surface transportation when necessary	Extreme emergency only!	Yes
Parcel post	4th class regular mail	Up to 20 lbs. when transit time is not important. 40 lbs. up to 150 miles.	No
	4th class airmail	Very small rush shipments!	No

Buyers at North American Rockwell's Columbus, Ohio, plant use this chart as a guide to the relative merits of various types of transportation service. In recent years, the United Parcel Service has become a low-cost, reliable substitute for parcel post and Railway Express.

Thus the total weight paid for when shipping by air is often less than it would be if shipment were made by surface transportation. This reduces the premium paid for air shipment. For certain extremely fragile shipments that would require especially heavy packaging if shipped by surface freight, it may actually be cheaper to ship by air. Air shipments also permit buyers to carry lower inventories. If they can get overnight shipment, they need not carry an item in inventory. For this reason, air shipment is quite commonly used for repair parts for machinery.

The cheapest type of air shipment is air freight. The shipper delivers the goods to his local airport and they are handled by a regularly scheduled passenger airline or air cargo carrier. For a substantial premium (usually about 200 to 300 percent), the shipper can get faster, more complete service with air express or by using an air freight for-

FIGURE 15-1 (Continued)

Can be expedited	Cost comparison	Remarks
Yes (in advance)	Cheapest method	Total charges depend upon minimum weight required, routing used, and many other factors. *Contact Traffic Department* for best method.
Yes (in advance)	Most economical method of shipping over 50 lbs.	Recommend truck routings when single-line service is available
Yes (in advance)	Most economical method of shipping over 50 lbs.	Superior to motor truck service in many specific cases. Should never be used on shipments over 10,000 lbs. without consulting Traffic Department
Difficult	Generally cheapest under 50 lbs.	Inferior to truck service in many cases. *(Contact Traffic Department)*
Yes (in advance)	2½ to 3 times more costly than truck or freight forwarder. Cheaper than Railway Express in many cases. (Check with Traffic Department)	In rare cases may be delayed to give priority to mail or Air Express
Yes (in advance)	2½ to 3 times more costly than truck or freight forwarder. Cheaper than Railway Express in many cases. (Check with Traffic Department)	Good service between major cities; only one flight daily into Columbus.
Difficult	3 to 4 times more costly than Air freight generally	We have no choice of airlines used or routings chosen by express company. Air freight service is comparable in most cases. *(Contact Traffic Department)*
Yes (in advance)	Usually more costly than Air Express (except over 100 lbs.) *Always more costly than air freight.*	Cost is prohibitive except in cases when a few hours' transit time differential is vital. *(Contact Traffic Department)*
No	Cheaper than Railway Express	Generally not advisable except on very small packages on which delivery is not urgent.
No	Approximate to Air Express up to 5 lbs.	Generally not advisable except on very small packages on which delivery is not urgent.

Courtesy North American Rockwell

warder. The tariff for such shipments includes pickup and delivery by truck and routing over the best available commercial air routes.

The U.S. Postal Service provides the forwarding service if the shipper uses air parcel post. This is economic on very light shipments but, for larger shipments, the shipper should (and sometimes must) use private forwarders or the airlines themselves.

Barge and pipeline. Shippers of bulky, relatively inexpensive raw materials try to ship by water or pipeline whenever possible in order to keep transportation costs at a minimum. In fact, chemical, aluminum, steel, and power plants often are intentionally located at deep-water ports or on inland waterways in order to reduce the cost of inbound raw materials. Water shipment is slow, but the rates always are low.

Also, when railroads or trucks are faced with competition from water carriers, they are more prone to offer rate reductions.

Only fluids can be shipped through pipelines, and pipeline shipment often is more expensive than water shipment. However, the pipeline is the most economic vehicle for shipping natural gas, oil products, and anything else that can be made into a fluid to inland points.

Piggyback and fishyback. Sometimes the most efficient way to ship is by using two carriers—truck trailer and either railroad or ship. "Piggyback" shipments are made by loading truck trailers aboard railroad flatcars for shipments between cities. The trailer is delivered from the shipper's plant to the flatcar by truck, which also moves it to the customer's plant. "Fishyback" shipments are made by loading the truck trailers on a barge or ship. After the water shipment, the trailers can be towed by truck to their final destination.

Piggyback and fishyback shipments combine many of the advantages of shipping by rail, barge, or ship with those of shipping by truck, including the following:

1. *Reduced handling expense.* Material need be handled only when it is loaded into the truck trailer and when it is unloaded at the final destination.

2. *Lower rates.* Shipment between points not on rail sidings often is cheaper by piggyback than by motor freight, since the long intercity haul can be made by rail. With fishyback, it is possible to eliminate extra handling and packaging for export by loading the truck trailer directly onto the ship.

3. *Faster service.* Since they minimize handling and enable shipments to be routed by the best service available, piggyback and fishyback usually permit quicker deliveries than the conventional approaches to surface transportation.

Piggyback and fishyback are by far the fastest growing modes of shipment and, in recent years, their expansion has been limited largely by carriers' ability to buy and finance additional equipment.

Small shipments

Every common carrier has minimum rates that are charged regardless of how small a shipment is. Railroads and trucks always charge for 100 pounds even when a shipment weighs much less. In addition, they charge premiums for LCL (less than carload) and LTL (less than truckload) shipments. Table 15–1 shows rates for various shipments of iron and steel articles between Cleveland and Akron. Note that rates are much higher for small shipments. For example, it costs 91 cents per cwt. to ship 2,000 pounds but only 12 cents per cwt. when the shipment weighs more than 26,290 pounds.

If the shipment is small enough, it does not pay to ship by truck

TABLE 15–1
Routings and rates—Cleveland to Akron (iron and steel articles)

Weight (lbs.)	Rate (per cwt.)	Carrier
0–2,160	$0.91	Allmen Transfer Co.
2,160–5,450	.51	Allmen Transfer Co.
5,451–11,200	.26½	Allmen Transfer Co.
		Lake Erie Cartage Co.
		Kaplan Trucking
11,201–26,290	.17½	Allmen Transfer Co.
		Modern Motor Express
		Kaplan Trucking
26,291 and over	.12	Lake Erie Cartage Co.
		Kaplan Trucking
		Glenn Cartage
40,000 and over	.13	Erie R.R.
80,000 and over	.12	B & O R.R.
		Penn Central R.R.

Source: Purchasing manual, B. F. Goodrich Co.

or rail. Shipments of 100 pounds or less can usually be shipped at much lower cost either by parcel post or United Parcel Service. When the package is small and fast service is desired, intercity bus service is a somewhat higher cost alternative. Commercial freight forwarders are a possibility for somewhat heavier shipments. They consolidate small shipments from a number of customers into carload and truckload quantities. Their rates often are lower than those of Railway Express, but their service sometimes is not as fast. Forwarders also handle shipments from overseas points; in routing a shipment, they may make use of almost every means of transportation.

Nonprofit shippers' associations also help cut costs of small shipments. Shippers—usually smaller businessmen and manufacturers in a particular area—band together for the purpose of consolidating shipments and negotiating with common carriers. They usually hire a traffic expert as director of their association. As long as the group is nonprofit, it is exempt from ICC regulation. Otherwise, its basic function is not much unlike that of the freight forwarder, except that the shippers get all of the benefits when they have their own association.

Routing, delays, and damage

Once the carrier is selected, the traffic manager's job would seem to be complete—but it rarely is. The carrier does not necessarily carry out its part of the bargain. Trucking companies do not always have trucks immediately available and, if they are busy, do not maintain their promised schedules. With railroads, the problem may start when boxcars are requested. Plenty of them are usually available in periods of depressed business, but during boom periods there is often a shortage. The shipper frequently has no recourse but to wait his turn, although he can ask the Interstate Commerce Commission for help. The ICC has the power to allocate cars to various railroads (and even can, for example, order a railroad to supply some of its cars to a competing road that is hard pressed). But, of course, the ICC cannot create cars out of thin air—so shipments are delayed during periods of car shortage.

Routing.   The traffic manager's problems do not end when his shipment is loaded on the railroad boxcar or truck. If he is on the job, he will direct the originating carrier to use a particular routing. Railroad and truck lines crisscross the United States in a huge grid. There are almost always two possibilities on an interstate shipment, and there may be dozens. For example, one of several possible routings between Portland, Maine, and Greensboro, North Carolina, would be the Boston and Maine Railroad to Hartford, Connecticut; the New York, New Haven and Hartford Railroad to New York City; the Penn Central Railroad to Washington, D.C.; and the Southern Railroad to Greensboro.

If you are a shipper in Portland, Maine, all you need do in theory is to tell your friendly Boston & Maine freight agent that you want a car to go to Greensboro, North Carolina, and he will pick the routing for you. But the best routing from the point of view of the originating carrier is not necessarily the best one for you as the shipper. Left to his own devices, the originating carrier may carry you as far as possible on his own lines. This may not be the fastest routing, but it gives the originating carrier maximum revenue. Then the originating carrier may turn the car over to another railroad with whom it has friendly relations—either common financial control or reciprocal agreements on freight. This again is not always the quickest route. Occasionally, it is not even the cheapest way although, in general, tariffs between two points are identical regardless of the routing.

Thus, companies with professional traffic managers always give their carriers precise routing for each shipment. In most cases, responsibility rests with the firm that is purchasing the material rather than the supplier. The routing becomes a standard part of the purchase order, and the supplier's traffic department follows its customer's instructions.

Tracing.   The supplier's traffic department may trace shipments for its customers. Typically, the buyer follows up with the supplier's sales department to determine why a particular shipment has not yet been received. The sales department may then discover that the item has been shipped. It might give the appropriate bill of lading or waybill number to the buyer so his own traffic department could trace the shipment, or it might do the tracing for the customer.

In big companies, dozens of traffic clerks spend almost all of their working lives on the telephone tracing shipments. The procedure is fairly simple. Given the waybill or bill of lading number (i.e., the shipper's receipt for the shipment), the carrier's clerk can determine precisely what boxcar or truck the shipment is on. The clerk then traces the car or truck and reports back to the shipper when it is due at its destination.

Big shippers often find it convenient to reroute full truck or carloads. For example, at any given time an auto producer might have hundreds of boxcars en route from its major manufacturing plants in Michigan to assembly plants scattered throughout the country. If shortages develop at a particular assembly plant, a boxcar can be rerouted in transit to that plant. This practice cuts lead time substantially and permits the firm to get along with a lower inventory investment.

Damage claims. Even if cars are not rerouted, goods are shuffled back and forth a great deal while they are in transit. Not surprisingly, there is a good deal of damage. Common carriers are forced to pay out more than $200 million per year in damage claims to shippers. Even if the shipper is reimbursed in full, damaged shipments cause production delays, and the processing of claims is a huge burden on the typical firm's traffic department.

Not all claims are the carrier's fault. In fact, the carriers maintain that most claims occur as a result of inadequate packaging. One problem is that frugal shippers keep using the same cartons over and over again. Carriers maintain that most corrugated cartons are designed for one-shot use and should then be discarded.

The exact cause of damage is not clear-cut in many cases. The shipment would certainly not have been damaged if it had been handled with sufficient care. But it might also be true that there need not have been any damage had the merchandise been packed more carefully in costlier containers. Traffic departments spend a great deal of time investigating damaged shipments and making claims against carriers. They also work with their own company's packaging engineers and others on ways to reduce damages. Shippers are becoming increasingly conscious of the simple truth that they are losers on damaged shipments even if they are reimbursed in full by carriers.

The procedure for claiming damages is fairly straightforward. The shipper presents the carrier with a claim similar to that shown in Figure 15–2. He also gives him his bill of lading, the paid freight bill, and a copy of the supplier's invoice or other evidence that establishes the value of the damaged merchandise. The claimant may include photographs of the damage both to help verify his claim and to serve as a basis for the development of ways to prevent future damage. Naturally, carriers must include an allowance for damage claims in their tariffs, and it is to everyone's interest to help minimize such claims.

FIGURE 15–2

The Mason & Dixon Lines, Inc.

STANDARD FORM FOR PRESENTATION OF LOSS AND DAMAGE CLAIM

Brown Toy Company   115 King Street, Kingsport, Tennessee
(Name of firm by whom claim is presented)   (Address of claimant)

The Mason & Dixon Lines, Inc.   November 17, 1958
(Name of Carrier)   (Date)

Knoxville, Tennessee
(Address)

(Claimant's Number)

(Carrier's Number)

This claim for $ **$3.00** is made against the carrier named above by **Brown Toy Company**
(Amount of claim)   (Name of claimant)

for **Damage** in connection with the following described shipments:
(Loss or damage)

Description of shipment **Toys, iron and rubber**

Name and address of consignor (shipper) **John Jones Manufacturing Company**

Shipped from **Knoxville, Tennessee** . To
(City, town or station)   (City, town or station)

Final Destination **Kingsport, Tennessee** Routed via
(City, town or station)

Bill of Lading issued by **shipper** Co.; Date of Bill of Lading **November 17, 1958**

Paid Freight Bill (Pro) Number **3-1875** ; Expense Bill Serial No.

Name and address of consignee (Whom shipped to) **Brown Toy Company, 115 King Street, Kingsport,**

If Shipment reconsigned enroute, state particulars: **Tenn.**

DETAILED STATEMENT SHOWING HOW AMOUNT CLAIMED IS DETERMINED
(Number and description of articles, nature and extent of loss or damage, invoice price of articles, amount of claim, etc.)

2 - Sleepy -time Dogs (Rubber) - Damaged   @ 1.50 each   3.00

Total Amount Claimed   **$3.00**

THE FOLLOWING DOCUMENTS ARE SUBMITTED IN SUPPORT OF CLAIM.
(X) 1. Original bill of lading, if not previously surrendered to carrier.
(X) 2. Original paid freight ("expense") bill.
(X) 3. Original invoice or certified copy.
     4. Other particulars obtainable in proof of loss or damage claimed.

Remarks

The foregoing statement of facts is hereby certified to as correct. **Brown Toy Company**
                                                                  Per:
Write any further remarks on back hereof: (Signature of claimant)

Courtesy The Mason & Dixon Lines, Inc.

To speed claim processing, motor carriers request that claimants use standard forms like that above. Railroads have a similar form. Claims should be backed by a copy of the bill of lading, the original paid freight bill, and a copy of the invoice for the material to prove that the claim does not exceed the value of the loss.

TARIFFS OF COMMON CARRIERS

Like other prices, the tariffs charged by common carriers are influenced by supply, demand, and cost of production. They also are influenced by peculiar variables of their own. Unlike most other sellers of goods and services, common carriers are not free to set their own rates, nor can they operate wherever and whenever they please. Each carrier must have a franchise to operate at all, and, as a condition of the franchise, almost every phase of the carrier's business is subject to regulation. In fact, carriers are not even free to cease operations without getting approval from one or more regulatory agencies.

The Interstate Commerce Commission is the most important regulatory agency for interstate railroads, motor carriers, and barge line operators. The Federal Power Commission regulates pipelines. Intrastate shipments are regulated by various states agencies.

Economics of rate structures

Regulatory agencies try to set rates that are fair to shippers and at the same time permit carriers to earn an adequate return on their investment. This is not an easy job. It is almost impossible to determine the cost of handling a particular type of shipment. In addition, regulatory agencies are subject to considerable noneconomic pressures.

Cost determination. Each carrier ships thousands of different items between thousands of different terminals. A big railroad, for example, is available to carry any type of shipment from any terminal on its own or another railroad's line to any other station. It would be a difficult enough job to determine the cost of an individual shipment if all costs were direct. Unfortunately, most costs do not vary directly either with the type of shipment or with the distance it is carried. They are fixed, or nonvariable.

For example, railroads must spend prodigious sums on maintenance of their roadbed. Most such expenditures are necessary regardless of whether the road handles one train a minute or one train a year. How then does one calculate the wear and tear on the road from an LCL shipment of shirts from the factory in Troy, New York, to a department store in Memphis, Tennessee? The shipment may move over several railroads, and chances are that several alternate routes are available. The expenses of each road involved will be almost exactly the same whether or not the shirts are shipped.

It is impossible for a carrier to determine the real cost of any single shipment or even any group of shipments. About the best it can do is determine the average cost per ton-mile for all shipments by dividing total costs shipped by total ton-miles. It also can calculate the average cost per shipment by dividing total costs by total number of shipments. Special studies also can yield valuable information concerning the relative costs of handling various types of shipment. But when it comes to determining what the costs and rates should be for transporting a particular commodity such as shirts from one point to another, arbitrary assumptions must be made.

Almost any rate can be justified, depending on the assumptions that are made. Competition can sometimes be used as a basis for rate setting, but competing modes of transport often find themselves in the same boat. None of them can assign costs so well that rates make much sense. Competition does work in some respects, however. Carriers "discover" that costs are lower when competing modes of transport are available. Costs often are high and service is poor on routes where a carrier enjoys a monopoly.

Pressures or rates.   Tariffs are influenced by both political and economic forces. Since a company in a given community can compete more effectively if it has favorable freight rates, regulatory bodies often are pressed by local communities and industries to set low rates. In fact, much of the original pressure for regulation of carriers came from farmers and small businessmen who believed that the railroads were getting too big a share of their output by charging high tariffs to ship their goods to market.

Even today, rates are almost always lower when carriers have competition. For example, on coast-to-coast shipments, railroads are conscious of competition from ships using the Panama Canal. This sometimes makes the coast-to-coast rate lower than rates charged for shipping identical commodities to inland points. Competition from barge traffic on the Mississippi and Ohio rivers keeps rail rates low in those areas. Railroads in the Great Lakes area have been forced to reduce some rates because of competition from ships using the St. Lawrence Seaway.

Even if a carrier has little effective competition, it cannot afford to charge too high a tariff. If it does, the traffic may simply disappear. A rock quarry, for example, will go out of business if it cannot negotiate a competitive freight rate. The major cost of the rock delivered to the user is freight. The lower the freight rate, the greater the distance from the quarry that the rock can be shipped and still remain competitive with rock from other quarries.

In some cases, the traffic is created only if the rate is sufficiently attractive to make it possible for the shipper to earn a profit. For example, the Kaiser Steel Corporation began shipping sheet-steel coils across the country from its plant in Fontana, California, to Hennepin, Illinois, in 1972 only because it was able to negotiate a special 50-car-unit trainload rate of $19 per ton. This rate, which is divided among the carriers—the Southern Pacific, Rock Island, and Milwaukee railroads—is less than half that of the single-car rate. Without it Kaiser Steel could not possibly hope to compete with steel firms in the Midwest for business in that part of the country.

What traffic will bear.   In general, most tariffs are based on "whatever the traffic will bear." If the product has an extremely high value per pound, freight cost is relatively unimportant to the shipper. For example, a freight cost of $5 would have an almost insignificant effect on the cost of a very fine chair designed to sell for $400, but it would be quite significant for a chair intended to sell for $40. Whenever possible, carriers try to distinguish between inexpensive and expensive products in order to charge what the traffic will bear. Usually only part of the premium paid to ship the higher cost commodity is justified by the greater cost of damage claims and other costs that characterize the more expensive item.

To add to the confusion, the rate is not necessarily identical in both directions. For example, the lowest rate at which one could ship a truckload of "printed matter" from Boston to Philadelphia is 87 cents per cwt. But one could ship a truckload of the same printed matter from Philadelphia to Boston for only 72 cents per cwt. The rates should be identical. Why do they differ by more than 20 percent? The most likely explanation is that shippers of printed matter from Philadelphia to Boston were more successful in negotiating with carriers and arguing the validity of a lower rate before the Interstate Commerce Commission than shippers in the opposite direction were. Or possibly there is more southbound traffic, so that trucks sometimes must travel partly loaded or empty northward from Philadelphia to Boston. The northbound traffic will not take as high a tariff as the southbound traffic, so the carriers established a differential designed to encourage more northbound shipments.

Similarly, it has traditionally been cheaper to ship something from Europe or Japan to the United States than vice versa. For example, iron or steel pipe costs $38.25 per ton to ship from New York to Germany but only $20.75 to ship from Germany to New York. Similarly, it costs $0.00664 per ton-mile to ship automobiles from New York to Rio de Janeiro but only $0.00222 to ship from London to Rio. American manufacturers have complained bitterly that this discrimination in ocean freight rates puts them at a competitive disadvantage with foreign manufacturers. The conference of shipping lines that sets the rates justifies them on the basis that cargo space that is outbound from the United States is relatively more scarce than inbound space. This, of course, is a roundabout way of saying that rates are set for what the traffic will bear.

The density of the product also is important in determining tariffs. A carload of lightweight, bulky material costs almost as much to transport as a carload of very heavy materials. The carrier naturally must charge a higher rate per hundredweight for the low-density material in order to recoup his costs. For example, the *National Motor Freight Classification*[1] indicates the following rates per hundredweight on LTL

---

[1] The *National Motor Freight Classification*, published by the American Trucking Association, 1424 16th Street, N.W., Washington, D.C., provides up-to-date information on truck rates. Its counterpart for rail rates is the *Uniform Freight Classification*, available from the Tariff Publishing Office, 202 Union Station, Chicago, Illinois. Since tariffs change quite frequently due to economic and competitive conditions, the real-life traffic manager must subscribe to these services to keep up to date. Because of these frequent changes, the examples of freight rates quoted in this text are for comparative purposes only. The odds favor their being out of date before the printer's ink is dry on this page.

(less than truckload) shipments from Washington, D.C., to Atlanta, Georgia:

Density (per cu. ft.)	Rate (per cwt.)
Less than 6 pounds	$7.31
6–12 pounds	3.79
More than 12 pounds	3.26

Class and commodity rates

So complex are rate structures that it is even possible to pay two different rates for identical shipments with identical origins and destinations. For example, the tariff for shipping a carload of steel from Baltimore to San Francisco can be either $3.98 per cwt. or $2.43 per cwt. The higher is the "class" rate, the lower is the "commodity" rate.

Carriers have class rates for almost everything. As the term implies, the rates are created by dividing goods into classes (or classifications) and setting rates for each class. An occasional shipper of a commodity will check first to see if there is a commodity rate for the shipment he wishes to make. If there is not, he will always find a class rate.

A frequent shipper of a commodity between two points is foolish to pay a class rate. When no commodity rate is available, he negotiates one with the carrier. The proposed rate is reviewed by the ICC and hearings are held. At these hearings, the shipper's competitors may object if they feel the proposed rate is too low and gives him an "unfair" competitive advantage. Competing carriers also may protest if they feel the rate is too low and will cause them to lose traffic. The final commodity rate[2] usually represents a compromise among the conflicting interests of the shipper, his carrier (or carriers), competitors of the shipper, and competing carriers. However, in every case the commodity rate is lower than the class rate, so it is well worth a big shipper's trouble to obtain commodity rates for all key commodities he handles.

COST-REDUCTION OPPORTUNITIES

Because rate structures are so complex, there are many opportunities for traffic experts to make tremendous savings in buying transportation. They often can save their companies millions of dollars by finding "loopholes" that permit shipments to be made at lower tariffs and also by spotting errors that carriers make in computing charges. For example, North American Aviation Division of North American Rockwell Corp. was able to reduce its $2,929,400 annual freight bill by $597,344 in

---

[2] Note that there is a separate rate for each commodity and each point of origin and destination. Thus, a traffic department in large corporation may be working with hundreds of thousands of rates, each of which must be approved by the ICC.

a traffic cost-reduction program. More than $180,000 of the savings came from overpayments detected in audits of freight bills that had already been paid. The balance came from more economical shipping methods. More than $143,000 was saved by making increased use of pool car shipments. Savings of more than $230,000 came from consolidation of service from air cargo carriers, use of company-owned trucks returning empty from deliveries, special fixtures in freight cars, and so on.

Auditing freight bills

Of the savings made by the North American Aviation traffic department, the most surprising may well be the huge sum recouped by auditing freight bills to detect overcharges. It might appear that North Amercian had been extremely inefficient to accept such overcharges in the first place or that its carriers were either inefficient or dishonest. Neither is true.

Every well-managed company audits its freight bills and makes enormous savings as a result. The rate structure is so complex that errors are inevitable. Moreover, when two different rates apply to the same commodity (and there is always the problem of classifying the shipment), who is to blame the carrier if it charges the higher of the two rates? Many such mistakes are the shipper's fault. The carrier's rate clerk never sees the shipment and must rely on the shipper's description of the material. If the description is incomplete, he naturally applies the higher rate. The lower the class number, the lower the rate. In other words, a Class 77½ rating carries a lower tariff than a Class 100 rating. Class ratings vary substantially with the completeness of the shipping order description. For example:

If you ship:	And describe them as:	They will be rated:	They should be rated:
Cotton work shirts	Cotton shirts	Class 100	Class 77½
Crude sulfate of soda	Chemicals	Class 100	Class 50
Wooden forks or spoons	Woodenware	Class 100	Class 50
Portable phonographs	Phonographs	Class 125	Class 110
Solid toy blocks	Toy blocks	Class 85	Class 70
Cotter pins, iron or steel	Hardware	Class 70	Class 50

Even after freight bills have been audited once, it is still possible for a skilled auditor to detect errors. For this reason, almost every big corporation sends bills that its own auditors have checked to an independent auditing firm for a second review. Such firms find it profitable to check clients' bills for a commission of 30 to 60 percent on the errors they detect. They will also provide complete traffic management service for smaller companies.

Not every freight bill is incorrect, of course. In fact, more than 99 percent usually are not challenged. Monsanto Chemical's experience is not untypical. It limits its audit to invoices that exceed $100; at that it must check about 600 of them a day. About 20 of these are "pickups," that is, bills picked up for further investigation because of some discrepancy. On about half of the pickups there is a discrepancy between the rate charged by the carrier and the rate Monsanto feels should be paid. The balance of the pickups result from errors in computation. Monsanto's experience in auditing freight invoices is typical of most large companies with first-rate traffic departments.

Charter truck

Switching from common carriers to private chartered truck has been a surefire cost-reduction technique for many traffic departments. For example, Montgomery Ward cut its transportation costs by $2,500,000 a year with a company-operated fleet of 280 trucks. Big savings result mainly because charter rates are not regulated. A company can carry the "cream" of its traffic in its own trucks and ship the balance by common carrier. It saves enormous amounts in this way because common carriers charge rates much higher than their true cost for some shipments in order to offset losses on other shipments. For example, almost all common carriers lose money on LTL and LCL shipments, whereas carload and truckload rates for most finished manufactured goods are extremely profitable, especially when shipment is between two points on the carrier's main line.

Interstate Commerce Commission regulations may prohibit common carriers from cutting rates in order to hang on to business they might lose to captive carriers. Only common carriers of agricultural products are exempt from ICC regulation. In some cases, manufacturers make use of farm trucks to haul merchandise one way—and the trucks presumably haul produce the rest of the time. Care must be taken to avoid violation of ICC regulations, however. And, in recent years, the ICC has tried to crack down on what are really unlicensed common carriers.

It is perfectly legal for a company to use a chartered truck to deliver goods and then return empty to the plant, and many companies believe that this seemingly uneconomical mode of transport is much cheaper than common carrier. Naturally, traffic managers try to route their trucks so that they expend a maximum amount of time traveling with payloads. One way to do this is to use the trucks to pick up materials from suppliers after they have made deliveries to customers in the same area. One New York–based manufacturer of steel laboratory furniture uses a charter truck to make weekly deliveries to customers in the Milwaukee and Chicago area. The truck returns with steel purchased from Chicago mills. In this particular case, the company's choice of steel suppliers is influenced by the fact that many of its customers are in the Chicago area. Were the company to buy its steel from mills nearer New York—in Bethlehem, Pennsylvania, or Sparrows Point, Maryland, for example—it would have to ship by common carrier, since it does not have many customers in these areas.[3]

Individual firms can also cooperate with one another in order to make more efficient use of charter trucks. For example, a manufacturer in New York might have heavy outbound traffic to Chicago, while a Chicago manufacturer might have heavy shipping to New York. If the two can cooperate in some fashion, they can get more efficient utilization of their charter trucks. They have to be careful to avoid acting as a common carrier, but in many cases such cooperation is possible and does not violate ICC regulations.

Many companies claim they would prefer charter trucks even if they made no direct cost saving with them. With their own trucks they are able to work on tighter schedules and enjoy lower cost packaging and materials handling. The trucks may even be used as a promotion device with the firm's brand name prominently displayed on them.

Tighter scheduling. When a shipper controls his own fleet, he can more easily regulate relative priorities of various shipments. Sometimes he also can offer prompter service to customers or reduce his in-transit inventories. For example, the Admiral Corporation reduced its average time to ship TV sets from several plants near Chicago to its New York distributor from 50 to 30 hours when it started using chartered trucks.

Packaging and materials handling. It often is practical to equip chartered or company trucks with special racks or other materials-handling devices to cut packaging and materials-handling costs. Comparable savings often can be made by leasing specially equipped railroad cars from common carriers. Even when special racks will not eliminate packaging, it still is possible to cut packaging costs by using company trucks. Since carriers are responsible for damage to goods in transit, they naturally insist that shipments be securely packaged. In some cases, it is possible to ship in lighter, cheaper containers with little increase in damage. For example, the Douglas Furniture Company cut packaging costs $25,000 per year because it was able to use 150-pound test cartons in its own trucks instead of the 200-pound test cartons required by common carriers. In addition, it cut its damage losses 80 percent because merchandise was handled more gently in company-operated trucks.

Good will and convenience. A company-owned truck with the company name and trademark emblazoned on its side is a rolling advertisement. In addition, customers are more likely to be impressed when delivery is made by company truck instead of by common carrier. There

---

[3] Close cooperation between purchasing and traffic is essential to take advantage of deals like these. This is obviously much easier to effect when the two functions are grouped together in a unified materials organization similar too those discussed in Chapter 4.

is good reason for this. A company often can give better service with its own trucks, and it is almost always more convenient to dispatch a company-owned vehicle than to call on a common carrier.

Despite their advantages, however, there is no doubt that charter trucks would not be used so widely today were it not for the rate structure and antiquated regulations governing common carriers. Few manufacturers or distributors can operate truck lines as efficiently as common carriers, and most would not want to do so were it not so advantageous.

Other cost-reduction techniques

Sometimes a company can get common carriers to reduce rates simply by threatening to charter its own trucks. The process is an involved one, because the carrier cannot cut rates unless it has approval to do so from the ICC or some other regulatory body. The carrier's competitors will often resist its request for rate reduction. Competitors of the shipper benefiting from the reduction also may protest.

Classification change. An easier route to rate reduction sometimes lies in creating a brand-new rate classification for the item. The shipper must convince the carrier and the regulatory body that his product is unique and should get a lower rate because it either costs less to ship or is worth less than other products in the same rate class. For example, the *National Motor Freight Classification* shows the following classifications for a simple item like a garment hanger:

> Hangers, garment, aluminum, aluminum alloy, magnesium
>   metal, or magnesium metal alloy, NOI, in boxes . . . . Class 100
> Hangers, garment, plastic, or plastic and metal combined,
>   in boxes . . . . Class 100
> Hangers, garment, NOI, in barrels, boxes, or crates. . . . . Class 100
> Hangers, skirt or trouser, cast aluminum, in boxes . . . . Class 85
> Hangers, garment, wire, or wire and paper combined, in barrels,
>   boxes, or crates. . . . . Class 70
> Hangers, garment, wood, or wood and wire combined, in barrels,
>   boxes, or crates. . . . . Class 70
> Hangers, garment, pulpboard, printed or not printed, in barrels,
>   boxes, or crates. . . . . Class 55

The lower the class number, the lower the tariff that will apply. Thus the cheapest hanger to ship is one that is "garment, pulpboard, printed or not printed, in barrels, boxes, or crates." The most expensive is the first one listed. If a company should develop a new type of garment hanger—one of molded Fiberglas, for example—how does it determine what rate class should apply? Of course, it always can ship the product as "hangers," but then the carrier would apply the highest tariff. Or it could describe the item in terms of the rate class that best fitted it. Fiberglas hangers presumably would be considered "hangers, garment, plastic, or plastic and metal combined in boxes." In this case they would be shipped as Class 100.

If there were any legitimate basis for doing so, the traffic manager would try to get the Fiberglas hangers assigned to a lower class than the plastic hangers. He might claim, for example, that Fiberglas hangers had a higher density, were of lower value, or less subject to damage than ordinary plastic hangers, and therefore they were entitled to a lower rate class. In this particular case, he probably would not be successful since Fiberglas would probably be considered a superior form of plastic.

Needless to say, shipper should be extremely careful in describing shipments. To earn a lower rate, the shipment not only must fit the specifications of that rate but must be described as such.

Reducing demurrage charges. Railroads allow 24 to 48 hours to unload a boxcar. If the car is held beyond this free time, they make a penalty charge called "demurrage." This charge has been increased several times in recent years because railroads complained that approved demurrage rates did not permit an adequate return on their investment in boxcars. However, the charge has apparently not increased enough to make it profitable for railroads to invest in boxcars, and idle cars remain a problem for the railroads. From the shipper's point of view, the boxcar is a reasonably cheap storage area even if demurrage charges must be paid. However, shippers naturally try to keep demurrage charges low, and the traffic department makes periodic studies to analyze charges and recommend changes in procedure that will reduce them.

In many cases, materials managers can reduce demurrage charges substantially by carefully scheduling shipments so that unloading facilities are never overtaxed. Periodic studies show whether or not cars are being handled in the most economical fashion. They must take account not only of demurrage charges but also of unloading and storage costs. Sometimes it pays to incur extra demurrage charges; for example, it may be cheaper to pay demurrage than to have an unloading crew work overtime at premium rates. Also, many companies prefer to pay demurrage during peak production periods rather than to invest in the additional storage space that would be required to eliminate it. Partly as a result of this practice, the average boxcar moves loaded in trains only about 23 days per year and moves empty for 14 days. The rest of time the car sits idle on various sidings.

Specific projects

Every traffic department always has at least one or two special cost-reduction studies underway. Particularly promising for cost reduction are changes in packaging specifications, various pool car arrangements, and various facilities studies.

Packaging. Although it may not be directly responsible for package design, the traffic department should be concerned with packaging specifications. It can analyze damage claims, and, if there is almost no damage because of poor packaging, perhaps a less expensive package can be used. If damage claims are high, more costly packaging might be worthwhile. Needless to say, traffic men prefer to select the lightest possible package. A shipper must pay freight not only for the product but also for the package that holds it. In some cases, costs can be reduced by selecting a container that weighs less even though it may cost slightly more.

Pool cars. Shippers try to avoid paying high LCL and LTL rates whenever possible. One way to do this is to pool a number of small shipments headed in the same direction. For example, many Eastern manufacturers load orders for a number of West Coast customers in a single car. Thus a manufacturer may load orders for distributors located in a number of California cities in a boxcar with a San Francisco destination. When the car arrives, the orders are separated and carried by company-owned truck or by some other conveyance to their separate destinations.

Pool cars also can be used for purchased materials. In this case the company pools all shipments from suppliers in a given area. For example, an auto company with a Los Angeles assembly plant might arrange for pool cars to leave at regular intervals from all cities in which it has a number of parts suppliers. Suppliers then deliver to the loading point, where a carloading firm pools their shipments. Such arrangements may save hundreds of thousands of dollars. Needless to say, purchasing and traffic must work together closely when there are pool car arrangements. In many cases, choice of a supplier will be influenced by his proximity to a pool car loading point.

Facilities studies. Traffic considerations also are important in determining the location of any new facilities. Using linear programming and other operations research techniques, the physical distribution or traffic manager can determine the relative transportation costs to and from various proposed locations. Frequently there are substantial differences. Linear programming and other cost-reduction techniques are discussed in Chapter 18.

Cases

CASE 15-1. EACKER TELEVISION AND RADIO CORPORATION

Creating a traffic department

Eacker Television and Radio Corporation of Chicago, Illinois, has always specialized in high-quality, semi-custom-made electronic equipment. The company was founded in 1946, and its first major product consisted of a radio-phonograph combination designed to retail for $900. In 1949 the company produced its first television set. It did not attempt to compete with the big mass producers of TV sets; its design emphasized quality and retailed for about $475. Practically all sales went to six distributors in New York, Atlanta, St. Louis, Chicago, Dallas, and San Francisco. In 1964 the company broadened its line and introduced color television. Again the emphasis was on quality, not price.

The color TV line was an immediate success, and the company began to grow. By 1966 there were 500 employees, compared to fewer than 100 just ten years earlier. Don Eacker, the company's founder and president, felt that the company had now grown to the point where it could profit from an integrated materials activity. He promoted his purchasing agent, Robert Strong, to materials manager and made him responsible for inventory control, shipping and receiving, and traffic, as well as purchasing.

Strong in turn hired Robert Alexander as a traffic expert. He explained to Alexander when he hired him that he himself knew very little about traffic management but was certain that substantial savings could be made, since the company was currently spending nearly $550,000 per year on transportation services.

Prior to the creation of the independent materials department, traffic had been something of a stepchild in the Eacker organization. The sales department was responsible for all outbound shipments. Practically all shipments were made by the Great Lakes Trucking Company, a leading Midwestern trucking firm. If the shipment was directed to a destination outside of Great Lakes's territory, the Great Lakes traffic manager routed it through other trucking firms.

Inbound shipments were the responsiblity of the purchasing department. As Strong puts it: "I buy from suppliers within a 300-mile radius of Chicago and require all vendors to quote f.o.b. our plant. This makes it easier to compare bids of competing suppliers and makes the vendor responsible for delivery to our plant on the date we request it. It also gives the vendor an incentive to combine shipments in one geographical area and thus keep his costs down."

While Strong is convinced that this approach may have been the most economic one while the Eacker Company was small, he is open to any suggestions that Alexander may have for improvement.

Questions

1. Prepare a program of traffic management for Eacker Televison and Radio Corporation.
2. What should Alexander's duties and responsibilities as traffic manager be?

3. Suggest specific areas of investigation reduce the company's transportation costs.

CASE 15–2. MOHAWK ALUMINUM AND CHEMICAL CORPORATION

Freight rate negotiation

Mohawk Aluminum and Chemical Corporation ships bauxite from its mines in the Carribean to a tidewater plant in Louisiana, where it converts the bauxite into alumina. Currently, it is shipping 400,000 tions of alumina per year to a reduction plant on the Ohio River, where the alumina is converted into aluminum. The Ohio River facility is strategically located for several reasons. First, it is reasonably close to most of the major aluminum fabricators in the East and Midwest. Second, it can get favorable rates from huge steam power plants located close to the West Virginia coal fields. Third, it can get alumina by both barge and rail.

Currently, Mohawk gets all of its alumina by rail. The current rate is $6.10 per ton. Mohawk's traffic manager, Herbert Reynolds, has been working hard to get the railroads to reduce this rate. He warns the carriers that they must be competitive with barges if they are going to continue to haul Mohawk's alumina. He says that he believes he could get water carriers to transport alumina for as little as $5 per ton and suggests that the railroads try to meet this rate.

The railroads point out that it is not fair to compare their rates with those charged by barge companies. Their service is faster. In addition, Mohawk cannot handle barge transportation until it invests in terminal facilities. Reynolds is fully aware of this, of course, and has already gotten an estimate on the cost of constructing such facilities. Mohawk's investment would have to be at least $4 million.

Reynolds believes that his position would be strengthened for negotiation with the railroads if he actually had river terminal facilities to handle barge shipments. But, on the other hand, $4 million is a lot of money to spend for bargaining power. His guess is that the railroads have an out-of-pocket cost of $4.00 to $4.50 per ton for hauling alumina. If they had to, he is quite certain that they would be willing to cut rates to as little as $4.75 per ton in order to hold the traffic. He believes that the best barge rate he could negotiate would be between $5.00 and $5.25 per ton—after having invested $4 million in terminal facilities.

Recently, Reynolds called in top railroad officials and bluntly informed them that Mohawk would go ahead with construction of barge terminal facilities if it were not possible to get a more favorable rate on alumina. He pointed out that the traffic currently was worth more than $2,400,000 to the railroads, and in the future it would be worth a lot more, since demand for aluminum was steadily increasing. He said he preferred the faster rail service to barge, but in most cases Mohawk is in no hurry to get material, since it carries large inventories of alumina at its Ohio River plant.

Questions

1. What is the highest rate Reyonlds can afford to accept from the railroads before he seriously proposes construction of terminal facilities to his company's finance committee?

2. Has Reynolds exhausted every possibility for rate negotiation other than actually going ahead with building terminal facilities?

CASE 15–3. CONTINENTAL COPPER & STEEL INDUSTRIES

Negotiation of a reduction in freight rates

Donald S. Helm, director of traffic, Continental Copper & Steel Industries, Inc., keeps a detailed record of distribution costs as percentages of gross sales by area. Early in 1964 he analyzed shipments of insulated copper and wire cable moving from his company's Hatfield Wire & Cable Division plants in the New York area to Kansas City, Missouri, Omaha, Nebraska, and Minneapolis. He determined that the transportation costs involved were excessive when compared to those on similar shipments to other areas.

The rates were as follows:

To Kansas City: $2.15 per cwt with a 24,000-lb minimum; $1.90 per cwt with a 30,000-lb minimum; $1.82 per cwt with a 34,000-lb minimum.

To Omaha: $1.96 per cwt with a 30,000-lb minimum.

To Minneapolis: $1.83 per cwt with a 30,000-lb minimum; $1.75 per cwt with a 34,000-lb minimum.

Helm realized that the motor carrier industry had worked with truck manufacturers to develop bigger semitrailers and more powerful tractors capable of pulling heavier loads. He also knew many states had gradually liberalized highway restrictions of motor vehicle sizes and weights. He reasoned that motor carriers could transport 40,000-pound payloads from New York to the destination points of the shipments involved.

Helm concluded that if he could offer the motor carriers larger shipments, which would increase their revenue per truckmile, they might be willing to reciprocate with lower rates.

To determine whether or not Hatfield Wire and Cable could take advantage of bigger shipping quantities, Helm checked with his sales manager, who assured him that customers in the area he was studying would purchase in 40,000-pound truckload volumes. He also checked warehouse inventory costs to determine if an increase in inventory was worthwhile.

Helm's next job was to find a carrier who would work with him to develop and propose lower freight rates based on a higher minimum weight. The proposal would have to be made before the Standing Rate Committee of the Eastern Central Motor Carriers Association, the tariff publishing agency for the motor carriers serving the area in which the shipments moved.

Helm knew that technically he could appear before the ECMCA and propose the rates himself. But as a practical matter he also knew that a rate sponsored by a carrier member has a better chance of being approved. The carrier has to meet several requirements. First, he must be sympathetic to the proposal. Then he must be authorized to serve the points involved. The carrier's equipment must be able to handle the heavier shipments contemplated. Service in general has to be good. Finally, the carrier must have a low claims ratio (the ratio of the number of lost or damaged shipments to the number of claim-free shipments). Helm considered a low claims ratio important because cable can be damaged easily if it is not handled carefully.

All Helm's qualifications were met by Interstate System, operating out of Grand Rapids, Michigan. Helm and his assistant traffic manager, Floyd Machette, worked closely with John P. Ryan, director of sales for Interstate, and on May 20, 1964, Helm submitted his proposal to Interstate's traffic department.

The proposal for the New York to Minneapolis rates included the following data (similar information was submitted for the other two destinations):

Full description of the commodity as it was described in the existing tariffs: Cable, electric, brass, bronze or copper, NOI. Wire, brass, bronze or copper, covered, insulated or plain.

Origin and destination point: New York to Minneapolis.

Mileage between the two points: 1,232.

Number of tariff containing the class rates: 25-E.

Existing first-class rate: $5.45.

Proposed rate: $1.65.

Percentage relationship between the proposed rate and the first-class rate: 30.3%.

Proposed minimum weight: 40,000 lbs.

Carrier truck-mile earnings the proposed rate would produce: 53.6¢.

Present rates, their percentage relationships to the first-class rate, minimum weights, and current truck-mile earnings: $1.83; 33.6%; 30,000 lbs.; 44.6¢. $1.75; 32.1%; 34,000 lbs; 48.3¢.

Present rates and minimum weights via rail piggyback service ($1.83, 30,000 lbs.; $1.75, 34,000 lbs.).

Present rates and minimum weights via regular rail service ($1.55, 30,000 lbs., with $1.24 per cwt. applying on any excess over 30,000 lbs.).

FIGURE 15–3

STANDARD
DOCKET PROPOSAL FORM
(Submit in duplicate)

Do not use this space

Dkt. No. ________

Proponent's File No. ________
Date ________

NAME OF TARIFF PUBLISHING AGENCY WITH WHICH PROPOSAL IS FILED: ________

PROPOSAL ORIGINATED BY: (Company) ________

Check one: ☐ Motor Carrier ☐ Consignor ☐ Consignee

(Official) ________
(Address) ________ (Street) ________ (City) ________ (Zone) ________ (State)

1. PROPOSED COMMODITY DESCRIPTION AND PACKING, or RULE OR REGULATION: (Show the exact commodity description to be employed using classification description where possible. If a change in rule or regulation is involved, quote the entire rule or regulation as it is desired, or state the desired change and clearly identify it in connection with the present rule or regulation with item and tariff where published.) ________

REMINDER - DOES INVOLVED COMMODITY DESCRIPTION CONFORM TO N.M.F.C. DESCRIPTION IN FURTHERANCE OF E.C.M.C.A CONTINUING TARIFF IMPROVEMENT PROGRAM?

2. N. M. F. CLASSIFICATION REFERENCE OF ARTICLES SHOWN IN PARAGRAPH 1: Item ________ N.M.F.C. No. ____ Supp. ________, Ratings: LTL ________, TL or Vol. ________, Min. Wt. ________ lbs.

3. BASIC DETAIL: (GIVE FULL TARIFF AUTHORITY FOR ALL PRESENT AND COMPETITIVE RATES SHOWN BELOW.)

TERRITORY				PROPOSED BASIS				PRESENT BASIS			
								MOTOR		RAIL or OTHER	
FROM (Unless otherwise indicated)	TO	MILES	First Class Rate	* Rate or Rating	% of First Class	Min. Weight	Truck Mile Earnings	Rate or Rating	Min. Weight	Rate or Rating	Min. Weight

* Is proposed rate subject to increase under Conversion Table, Master Tariff, etc? Yes ☐ No ☐

TARIFF AUTHORITY	Item No.	Tariff No.	MF. I.C.C. No.†	Issued By
MOTOR Rate				
MOTOR Rating				
RAIL or OTHER Rate				
RAIL or OTHER Rating				

† If tariff is filed under I.C.C. No. or I.C.C.F.F. No., so state.

Docket proposal form calls for information on movement, including present and proposed rates, and detailed statement of justification for rate change. ECMCA officials say inadequate information is a primary reason why proposals are rejected. Forms are available from ECMCA and other carrier tariff bureaus.

In each case, the truck-mile earnings via Helm's proposed rates were higher than earnings via the rates then in effect: 53.6 cents on 40,000-pound minimum shipments, compared with 44.6 cents on 30,000-pound minimum shipments and 48.3 cents on 34,000-pound minimum shipments.

In effect, Helm was proposing a rate of \$1.65 per cwt. with a 40,000-pound minimum, compared with \$1.75 per cwt. for the lowest existing rate, which was based on a volume minimum weight of 34,000 pounds.

Meanwhile, Interstate's sales director, Ryan, was asked by his traffic department to fill out a detailed questionnaire on the proposed change.

This gave the traffic department additional data it needed to determine whether or not to support the rate proposal.

In reviewing the proposal, Interstate considered such factors as the amount of tonnage moving annually from the account, whether the new rates would discriminate against any shippers or geographic areas, the annual tonnage involved in the particular movement, whether the volume warranted a deviation in the established rate structure, the existence of a precedent for the new rates, and the competitive necessity for the new rates.

On June 23, 1964, Interstate submitted the proposal to the Standing Rate Committee of the Eastern Central Motor Carriers Association. The proposal was assigned Docket No. SR-18192 and the hearing date was set for July 13, 1964.

To notify all members and interested shippers of the hearing, ECMCA published the proposal, along with 35 other new rate proposals, in its weekly docket bulletin (No. 287, dated July 4, 1964), which was mailed to all subscribers. This publication alerts interested shippers and carriers to pending rate proposals. They can support or object to the proposals by appearing in person, by mail, or, in the case of ECMCA, by telephone. Speakerphone facilities permit full discussion between any interested party and the entire Standing Rate Committee at one time via one phone call.[4]

Here is the proposal as it was published in the Docket Bulletin:

> SR-18192 Amend ECMCA Tariffs 22-K and 27-C as follows:
>
> (TARIFF 22-K)—Add rates from New York, N.Y., to Kansas City, Mo., 171¢ and Omaha, Neb., 179¢, min. wt, 40,000 lbs to apply on Cable, electric, copper steel armored lead covered or armored lead covered, NOI; Wire, brass, bronze or copper, insulated or plain or copper clad steel, covered, insulated or plain.
>
> (TARIFF 27-C)—Add a rate of 165¢ @ 40M from New York, N.Y., to Minneapolis, Minn., to apply on Cable, electric, brass, bronze or copper, NOI; Wire, brass, bronze or copper, covered, insulated or plain.

The Standing Rate Committee, composed of three members of the ECMCA staff, heard testimony in support of the proposal from Interstate System and from Continental Copper & Steel Industries, Inc. It also heard testimony from other motor carriers and shippers opposing the new rates.

On July 18, 1964, the Standing Rate Committee issued its report rejecting the proposed rates. The committee stated that there appeared to be no competitive necessity for the setting of new rates.

At this point, the carrier had three choices: appeal the Standing Rate Committee's decision to the General Rate Committee, composed of ap-

---

[4] The docket bulletin is indispensable for anyone who hopes to keep informed of pending rate changes. Other carrier tariff publishing agencies issue bulletins. Subscription fees are nominal.

proximately 30 members; accept the decision; or take "independent action" and have the rate published to apply via its line, with other carriers free to have the rate published for their account also.[5]

In this case, Interstate decided to take independent action and had the rates published for its account. They became effective on October 16, 1964 (New York to Minneapolis) and November 13, 1964 (New York to Kansas City and Omaha). Other carriers became party to the rates, meaning that they too agreed to charge the new rates.

Helm estimates that the publication of the three rates is saving his company between $6,000 and $7,000 annually.

In 1964 Helm was able to negotiate 20 freight-rate adjustments which now trim the company's transportation bill by an estimated $50,000–$60,000 annually.

"Good traffic management," says Helm, "is good business. We hear a lot of talk to the effect that nothing can be done about the trend toward higher freight rates. That's just not true.

"Freight rates can be negotiated just as the price of any other service or product can be negotiated. If you can show carriers how they can increase their earnings through greater revenue per trip, as we did in this case, or through reduced operating expense, or that the present rates are discriminatory or unjust or unreasonable, the carriers will listen to you.

"But be reasonable," continues Helm. "Remember, they're in business to make money, just as you are. Be frank with the carriers. Give them all the facts they need to help you, and when they do succeed in lowering your freight rates, be appreciative."

Questions

1. How does negotiation of a freight rate differ from negotiation of price paid for a conventional purchase?

2. Why would Interstate be willing to cut its tariff in order to please Hatfield, since Hatfield would have to ship its products in any case, even if it were forced to continue to pay a higher tariff?

3. Is the new tariff fair to smaller producers of insulated copper wire who do not have enough volume to ship in 40,000-pound lots?

4. What would you guess the Rate Committee meant when it said there was no competitive necessity for the lower rate? Why did Interstate go ahead and cut the rate anyway?

---

[5] Carriers are always free to publish any rate they wish, regardless of the action of the Standing Rate Committee or General Rate Committee. This freedom is guaranteed by the Interstate Commerce Act. However, if a carrier publishes a rate independently and the rate is investigated by the Interstate Commerce Commission, the carrier must defend the rate without the assistance of a rate bureau such as the ECMCA. On th other hand, if the bureau approves a rate and it is investigated by the Commission, the bureau will assume responsibility for defending the rate.

16

Purchase price analysis

THE MOST BASIC materials management objective is low prices, which have a more direct effect on profits than any other factor. It was noted in Chapter 1 that if the average manufacturing company can reduce materials costs by just 2 percent it can boost its profits by 10 percent.

The cost structure of a typical 500 ton/day superphosphate fertilizer plant provides an extreme example of the effect of changes in materials costs on profits. The principal raw materials for the plant—phosphate rock and sulfuric acid—together cost $12.15 per ton of fertilizer or slightly more than 82 percent of the $14.79 per ton total manufacturing cost. The cost of sulfuric acid alone is $8.46 per ton of fertilizer, or slightly more than 82 percent of the $14.79 per ton total manufacturing cost. The cost of sulfuric acid alone is $8.46 per ton of fertilizer, or 57 percent of the total production cost. Figure 16–1 shows the effect of changes in sulfuric acid prices on net profits. When sulfuric acid costs $1.17 per pound, the plant makes a profit of 50 cents per ton of superphosphate (based on a price of $16 per ton). When the price of sulfuric acid goes up to $1.25 per pound, the break-even point is crossed and the plant is unprofitable. A difference of only 8 cents per pound in the price of sulfuric acid therefore signifies the difference between satisfactory profits and loss.

THE PRICING PROCESS

It is no wonder, therefore, that materials managers devote a great deal of their time to price negotiation and cost reduction. Their actions

FIGURE 16-1
Effect of purchase price on profit

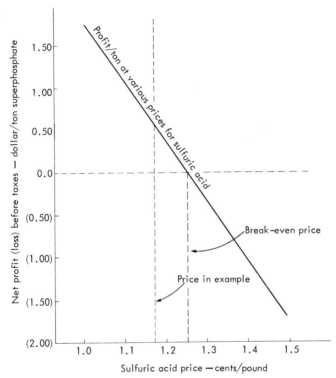

Superphosphate fertilizer provides a classic example of the effect of relatively minor changes in purchased material prices on product profits. When its key ingredient, sulfuric acid, costs $1.25 a pound, the fertilizer plant breaks even. When it costs $1.40 a pound, the plant loses more than $1 a pound, on each ton of fertilizer it produces.

can have considerable effect on the prices they pay for purchased materials. For, contrary to what some students learn in elementary economics courses, the prices of most commodities are *not* determined by the impersonal interaction of supply and demand forces in "pure" competition. Instead, they are what economists call "administered" prices, determined by a process of "imperfect" competition. When there is relatively little competition among producers, the administered price usually is high enough to yield handsome profits. When there are many producers and competition is keen, profits shrink even though an individual producer theoretically is free to charge any price he pleases.

Administered prices are quite different from prices determined by pure competition (see Chapter 6). Pure competition prevails only when there are a large number of buyers and sellers and the product is homogeneous. One seller's product is as good as that of any other seller, and no single buyer or seller can influence prices. Everyone must do business at the prevailing market price, which is determined by the collective action of all buyers and sellers.

Imperfect competition

When reasonably pure competition prevails, as it does for most materials traded on commodity exchanges, materials management is primarily concerned with price forecasting and timing of purchases. When imperfect competition prevails, as it does for 99 percent of the items that a typical company buys, the scope of the materials management job is far broader. It is intimately concerned with the pricing process and product quality.

Product differentiation. The outstanding feature of imperfect competition is product differentiation. The products of the producers are not homogeneous; each is unique. For example, Ford and Chevrolet are competing brands, but they are completely different; only a few of the components they use are interchangeable. Unlike commodities, whose prices are determined by pure competition, Ford and Chevrolet prices are not identical. The higher price presumably is justified by higher cost of production or higher quality.

Product differentiation creates tremendous opportunities for sellers. If a company can successfully convince its customers that its product is substantially different from those of its competitors, it can charge slightly higher prices and earn much greater profits. For example, the Polaroid camera is a unique product that is protected from imitation by patents. The prices and profits of Polaroid reflect this position. At the other extreme, prices of textiles also are determined by imperfect competition, but there is little product differentiation among producers. Quality standards are almost identical, there are a large number of competing producers, and it is relatively easy to go into the textile business should it look profitable to any would-be producer. As a result, price competition in the textile industry is extremely keen and profits of producers are very low.

Manufacturers know that profits are almost always higher when they can convince buyers that their product is unique. They attempt to do this through advertising and sales efforts. In some cases they are successful in establishing product differentiation for products that are almost identical with those sold by competitors. This is true of both consumer and industrial products. Consumers may pay 79 cents for a bottle of 100 brand-name aspirin tablets that are identical with and may even have been made by the same chemical company as those sold for 12 cents a bottle. An industrial buyer may pay a premium for a brand-name cleaning fluid when the identical material is available at a lower price directly from the manufacturer of the basic chemical ingredient.

Industrial buyers are not nearly so naive, and, in most cases, they can use their skill to negotiate lower prices. Only relatively few items have rigid, inflexible prices. On these, there often is genuine product differentiation, or there are a limited number of producers who control the market and can arbitrarily set prices and make them stick regardless of the buyer's skill or the state of the market.

The buyer's economic role. In most cases the supplier does not have the last word on prices. Able buyers can exert tremendous leverage if they understand how prices are set and do not hesitate to use their skills. In doing so, they are doing a service not only to their own company but also to the supplier and to the economy as a whole.

When competition is imperfect and prices are not regulated impersonally by market forces, some other regulatory force is needed. In a totalitarian economy, the force is exerted arbitrarily by government officials. In a free economy, it is exerted by negotiation between buyer and seller. Every time a buyer challenges a vendor's bid, he forces the vendor to recheck his costs and review ways in which productivity can be increased. He becomes a substitute for the impersonal competitive market forces that determine the prices of materials traded on commodity markets. In this role, buyers are collectively a tremendous force in the overall economy. When they award business to the efficient, low-cost producers and force the high-cost producers either to mend their ways or to go out of business, they help make the overall economy wealthier and more productive.

Suppliers also benefit when buyers challenge their prices, although few suppliers are aware of the benefit and even fewer would admit it. Pressure from buyers stimulates improvements and prevents complacency. Although sloppy purchasing will certainly permit a supplier to boost profits temporarily, the day of reckoning comes eventually. Only the supplier who is efficient can hope to earn high profits indefinitely.

Administered prices

Pricing can be a real problem with imperfect competition. The supplier cannot simply sell at some market price, because there is no market. Nor, in most cases, can he set a price that will yield the highest possible return. Instead, he must grope for a price that is high enough to be profitable but not so high that a buyer will turn to a competitor's product.

In many cases, the supplier's estimate of what the "right" price should be is not much better than the buyer's estimate. Few suppliers will admit this, of course. But the reasons are obvious in the light of the supplier's pricing process on items where imperfect competition prevails and prices must be administered. In such cases, prices are determined by each producer on the basis of:

1. Probable demand at various prices.
2. Selling prices of similar products by competitors.
3. Profit objectives.
4. Cost of production at various levels of output.

Establishing an administered price is as much an art as it is a science. Each of the four factors above must be considered in making the final pricing decision. The desired profits often are not achieved because of changes in demand, lower prices of competitors, or the cost of production.

Effect of demand. When a supplier gets an inquiry from a buyer, he knows what the immediate demand is. He may not know what the ultimate demand from that buyer will be. In most cases, the buyer does not know either; he can only guess what his company's future prospects are. But he should pass on to the supplier any information on future demand that is not confidential in order to help negotiate the most realistic price.

The buyer also should try to determine what demand, if any, buyers in other companies will have for the supplier's products. He will not necessarily get accurate information from the supplier; he may have to base his estimate on his own general knowledge of the market. In general, the stronger the demand for the supplier's products and services, the higher the price the supplier can seek. It is the buyer's job to undermine this demand by finding numerous alternate supply sources that are eager, able, and available.

Competitors' selling prices. Every company's sales department tries to keep up to date on the selling prices of competitors. With some products this is easy. Published prices are readily available, and producers actually sell at the published prices. For other products the job is more difficult. In fact, in many cases neither buyer nor seller is fully informed about the selling prices of all possible competitors. The buyer often is better informed than the seller, since he can always solicit bids from a number of suppliers. But many suppliers are better informed than some buyers give them credit for. Only a foolish (and unethical) buyer will deliberately mislead suppliers as to their competitors' selling prices. But a buyer need not go out of his way to tip off a supplier when his competitors are raising their prices.

However, it may not do any harm to "leak" news of price cutting. The supplier who cuts prices on a selective basis would prefer that competitors not know what he is doing, since they will usually match or even try to beat his prices. From the buyer's point of view, competition is increased if each seller is well informed on the pricing strategy of competitors—provided there is no collusion among suppliers. If such price competition is concealed, it is possible that a company competing with the buyer's firm may be gaining a price advantage in purchasing. In most cases, sellers are extremely well informed on competitors' strategies, and the buyer can tell them nothing they do not already know. In fact, it is usually the buyer who can learn from the seller, rather than vice versa.

Profit objectives. Well-managed companies almost always set specific targets for profits in relation to both sales and net worth. For example, a company might seek to earn 15 percent before taxes on sales and 25 percent on net worth or invested capital. One of the easiest ways to achieve this objective is to set selling prices high enough so that they virtually guarantee success. Almost every supplier will do this if demand, competitors' selling prices, and customer acceptance of his prices permit it. No smart buyer objects if a supplier achieves his profit objectives, but he prefers to have it done through lower costs and increased efficiency rather than through high prices.

Cost of production. No supplier is eager to sell below his total costs, and any supplier would be extremely foolish to sell for less than his cash out-of-pocket cost. Cost of production is the single most important factor in price determination, since it sets the minimum level below which prices drop only on rare occasions. The supplier's pricing theoretically rests firmly on his estimates of cost of production. To this cost estimate he adds a profit that reflects his profit objectives, moderated by his estimate of competitors' selling prices and demand.

For example, if a supplier calculates that unit costs will total $1.00 for an item and his profit objective is a 20 percent return on sales, his bid would be $1.25. Up to this point, the estimate may well be made by a junior employee in the cost-estimating department or even by a computer. But before the bid is submitted to the customer, a top executive—the sales manager, general manager, or president—will usually study it. The price may then be modified to reflect overall demand and competitors' selling prices. Usually the senior executive will reduce the bid. Strong competition or a weak market prevent the desired profit markup from being added in full to the estimated cost. When business is booming, the senior executive may raise the bid and shoot for a higher than standard profit. No executive ever was fired for making too much profit for his company.

SUPPLIERS' COST ESTIMATES

The vendor pricing process is much less exact than we have implied so far. The supplier does not work with a rigid estimate of costs to which he adds a profit that is flexible and determined by market conditions. Instead, his whole cost estimate is quite flexible. The reason for this is that costs can never be calculated exactly until after they have actually been incurred. And sometimes they can never really be determined. One major problem is that of joint costs chargeable to several products. For example, if a mining company recovers several minerals from the same ore, how does it allocate the cost of digging the ore to the finished minerals? Or how does a company allocate the salary of its chief executive to its various products? By the amount of time he spends on each product, by sales volume, by gross profit on each product, or by some other means? Regardless of the method used, the allocation is arbitrary, as any student of cost accounting knows.

A supplier's price quotation is, of necessity, based on estimated future costs that he thinks will be incurred if he gets the business. Such estimates are no more than educated guesses, regardless of the proficiency of the estimators. This is true regardless of the cost-estimating system used. Most systems break cost into four major components: direct-material cost, direct-labor cost, manufacturing overhead, and administrative expenses. Each component is estimated separately.

Direct material cost

The easiest component to estimate is usually direct material cost. Direct material includes any purchased part or material that is used directly in the product. Some cost accountants even consider paint, packaging, and plating materials direct material, although there is no universal agreement on this. Cost accountants do not regard materials consumed in the production process (such as cutting oils) as direct material. All maintenance, repair, and operating supplies are considered indirect material and are part of the manufacturing overhead, since they are not incorporated directly into the product.

Usually the cost estimator determines the cost of direct material simply by asking the purchasing department for the price. He then calculates usage and multiplies by the unit price. It is not necessarily an easy job to estimate materials usage. The estimate of the stainless steel molding shown in Table 16–1 is a case in point. The estimator must be able to calculate the initial blank size of stainless steel needed from the blueprint of the finished molding. Once he knows the blank size, the job is not too difficult. He calculates the weight and then multiplies by the price per pound to get the cost. Sometimes estimates of material cost are wrong because the unit price changes. The most common error, however, is a bad estimate of usage. Either the estimator's calculations are incorrect, or he fails to make the proper allowance for process scrap and shrinkage.

Direct-labor cost

Errors are made even more frequently in estimating labor costs. Direct labor includes all work performed directly on the product—assembly,

TABLE 16–1
Cost estimate, automobile door molding

Material cost:

SAE 51430 stainless steel
.018" × 1.6125" × 42.32" = .3470 lbs.
  .3470 lbs. × $.4456/lb. $0.1546
  Packaging material 0080

Labor cost:

Equipment	Operation	Minutes	Labor rate per minute	Cost
Roll form	Load coil, form, sweep & cut-off	0.063	$0.035	$0.0022
Light press (2 stage die)	Open flange, notch, trim end to shape	.165	.033	.0054
Light press.	Form end, close flange	.165	.033	.0054
Light press (2 stage die)	Open flange, notch	.132	.033	.0044
Light press (2 stage die)	Form end, turn down flange	.132	.033	.0044
Automatic polish	Load & unload – 3 at a time, 2 men	.088	.038	.0033
Hand polish	Polish formed ends	.165	.038	.0063
Packaging	Package	.110	.032	.0035

      Total labor cost 0349
Manufacturing overhead 0698
      Total manufacturing cost. $0.2673
Commercial and administrative expense 0133
      Total cost. $0.2810
Profit. 0420
      Price. $0.3230

machine operations, and so on. It does not include work that is indirectly performed on it—inspection, materials handling, maintenance, supervision, and so on. The estimator first decides what operations are needed and estimates the time required to perform each of them. He then calculates the cost by multiplying the time by the wages that must be paid. For example, suppose a worker who is paid $4.20 per hour can consistently produce at the rate of 120 units per hour. The worker's time costs $0.07 per minute ($4.20 per hour divided by 60 minutes per hour), and each operation takes 0.5 minutes (60 divided by 120). Therefore the direct-labor cost per operation is $0.035 (0.5 times $0.07). Similar calculations are illustrated in Table 16–1 above.

Errors rarely are made in estimating wages, since the estimator knows what the average wages are for each job skill. Actual labor costs differ from estimates mostly because of variations in the time required to perform various operations. In calculating the time, the estimator must be able to visualize an operation and, in effect, make a mental time study. To the actual standard, the estimator then adds an allowance (usually about 10 percent) for delays, rest periods, and other inefficiencies. Even if the estimator makes no errors, his estimate will be unrealistic if the workers fail to perform up to his standard.

Overhead

Manufacturing overhead and sales and administrative expenses both are overhead. One is overhead associated with the factory—MRO supplies, indirect labor, depreciation, and so on. The other is overhead associated with the office—clerical and executive salaries, office supplies and rent, and the like. A cost estimator has little difficulty in estimating overhead. For example, note how easy it is to calculate the overhead in the estimate in Table 16–1. The estimator assumes that manufacturing overhead is 200 percent of direct labor and that administrative overhead is 5 percent of total manufacturing cost.

These calculations are deceptively simple. Allocation of overhead is essentially arbitrary and usually has little relation to the direct cost of making the product. The reason for this is the nature of overhead, which includes all costs other than direct-labor and direct-material costs. Overhead must be charged in some way to the product in order to be recouped. In calculating overhead, accountants try to include all miscellaneous costs directly associated with the product or its manufacturing operations, but in many cases this is not feasible. Important expenses—building depreciation and maintenance, part of the payroll, and expenditures for various supplies—cannot be traced directly to any one product or operation. Allocation must be made on some arbitrary basis, usually as a percentage of the direct-labor cost or total cost.

Types of overhead.   There are three types of manufacturing overhead: fixed, nonvariable, and variable.

Fixed overhead means exactly what the term implies. It includes costs that are incurred regardless of how much the plant produces. Real estate taxes, certain insurance premiums, depreciation on buildings and some equipment, salaries of certain personnel (like watchmen), and so on, all cost the same regardless of whether the plant is operating at 100 percent capacity or at only 10 percent.

Nonvariable overhead is not quite so rigid as fixed overhead. It will vary slightly with changes in production volume but will not vary in direct proportion to such changes. For example, when a plant is producing near capacity, there might be a need for two receiving department foremen, one on the first shift and one on the second. When the plant is operating at 75 percent capacity, these foremen are still needed, and nonvariable overhead remains unchanged. But when operations are cut back to 40 percent capacity, it is possible to get along with a single receiving department foreman, and the "nonvariable" overhead varies.

Sales and administrative expense (i.e., the cost of operating the "front office") usually behaves very much as nonvariable manufacturing overhead. It is relatively unresponsive to small changes in sales or production volume, but when there are major changes in sales it will increase or decrease.

Variable overhead is similar to direct-labor and direct-material costs in that it varies in direct proportion to production volume. If production volume doubles, variable overhead also doubles. Examples of variable overhead include the cost of most public utility services, perishable tools, various operating supplies, and depreciation that is calculated on the basis of machine hours.

Changes in fixed costs. Variable overhead can usually be related to product cost reasonably accurately. It is fixed and nonvariable overhead that create problems in pricing. Product and equipment mix can affect overhead and product costs even though a particular product continues to be made in exactly the same way as before. For example, suppose that products X and Y are made in the same department. Total fixed and nonvariable overhead costs are $100,000 per year and, since direct labor in the department amounts to about $50,000 per year, the overhead is recovered by a 200 percent charge to direct labor.

The company then buys a new machine that will be used only on product Y. Depreciation and other nonvariable costs associated with this machine amount to $10,000 per year. This automatically raises the overhead rate by 20 percent to a new level of 220 percent of direct labor. This change causes the reported costs of *both* products to increase even though the new machine is used exclusively on just one product! If the company were producing both products on a cost-plus basis, it might be able to collect higher prices for both—provided the customer's auditor did not complain.

Cost-volume relationship

Misleading information. Companies often get misleading information from their accounting systems even when they are not trying hoodwink customers. No company can predict precisely what its future production volume will be, yet volume is a major factor in determining overhead absorption and product cost. Table 16–2 shows why this is true. One column shows costs for a hypothetical manufacturer whose production volume is 100,000 units of an item that he sells for $1.00. At this volume, his unit profit is 10 cents. A total profit of $10,000 or 10 percent on sales permits him to achieve his desired return on investment.

Now suppose that this manufacturer is able to boost his sales by 10 percent, to 110,000 units. Note that his costs do not go up proportionately. They increase by only $5,750—from $90,000 to $95,750. In other words, the additional 10,000 units produced cost only 57½ cents each ($5,750/10,000). If the manufacturer can maintain his selling price of $1 each for the extra volume, he can boost his profits 42½ percent

TABLE 16–2
Costs, profits, and prices at two production levels

	100,000 units production		110,000 units production	
	Total cost	Unit cost	Total cost	Unit cost
Direct material	$ 15,000	$0.15	$ 16,500	$0.15
Direct labor	20,000	.20	22,000	.20
Fixed overhead	25,000	.25	25,000	.225
Nonvariable overhead.	10,000	.10	10,500	.096
Variable overhead.	15,000	.15	16,500	.15
Sales and administrative expense	5,000	.05	5,250	.048
Total operating cost	$ 90,000	$0.90	$ 95,750	$0.869
Profit.	10,000	.10	14,250	.131
Sales (selling price)	$100,000	$1.00	$110,000	$1.00
Profit (as percent of sales).	10.0%		13.0%	

Note: This table shows the effect of an increase in production volume on unit cost. When volume goes up, fixed overhead is overabsorbed and unit costs decline, opening opportunities for buyers to negotiate price reductions.

(from $10,000 to $14,250) with only a 10 percent increase in sales. The reason for this, of course, is that fixed and nonvariable costs do not increase proportionately as output expands. These costs are what accountants call "overabsorbed"—i.e., already paid for by being allocated over a lower level of output.

Of course, if the company could plan on a production of 110,000 units it could cut prices and still achieve its profit objective. If we assume that a $10,000 profit provides an adequate return on investment, then a unit profit of just over 9 cents would be required if production were 110,000 units. With costs of $0.869 at this level of output (see Table 16–2) the price could be cut from $1.00 to about $0.96.

The break-even chart. If a series of cost-volume relationships is calculated and plotted, the result is a break-even chart. Figure 16–2 illustrates such a chart for the data in Table 16–2. The break-even chart is invaluable for pricing decisions. With it, the supplier can determine the precise effect of any change in volume on costs and profits. He also can use the break-even chart to predict costs and profits from his sales forecast.

The break-even chart graphically illustrates the effect of relatively small changes in volume on costs and profits. It proves that there is nothing sacred about a supplier's cost estimate regardless of how ably it is made. Unit costs of a given product are affected not only by the proficiency with which the product is made but also by the supplier's overall efficiency and by the amount of business he succeeds in getting from other customers. Thus no buyer need feel restrained from asking a supplier to reduce a bid.

FIGURE 16–2

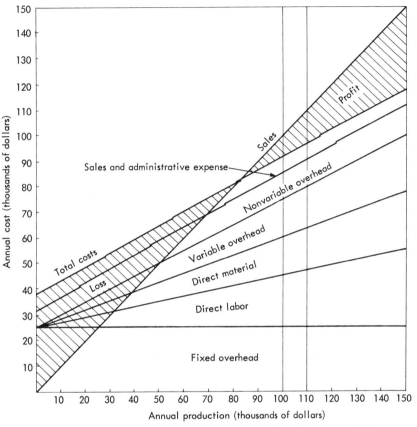

The break-even chart is an excellent guide for profit planning and forecasting of costs. It shows what costs will be at any level of production.

Despite the buyer's best efforts, suppliers usually succeed in avoiding price cuts when costs decline because of an overall increase in sales. During these periods, demand is strong and markets are tight. The result is sharply higher profits. On the other hand, when sales drop off during business downturn, suppliers will study their break-even charts. They may decide that it pays to sell below full cost if necessary in order to keep plants operating at levels sufficient to absorb overhead costs.

Using the chart. Suppose a supplier with a break-even chart like that in Figure 16–2 is operating at 50 percent capacity. He is producing 50,000 units and his price is $1 per unit. A mail-order house offers him a contract to produce 20,000 units for 70 cents. Can the supplier afford to take the order? He looks at his break-even chart. With present volume, he is losing $13,000. With the additional order, his revenues rise by

$14,000, but the break-even chart shows that his costs only rise by $11,000, from $63,000 to $74,000. Obviously it pays the supplier to take the order (provided that his other customers do not insist on price cuts) even though the business is not theoretically "profitable."

USING COST DATA

The cost-volume principle is particularly applicable when a supplier enters a foreign market. He maintains a high price in the home market and then sells his surplus production for whatever the traffic will bear in a foreign market. Naturally, this type of competition is not welcomed in the market that is being invaded, and it is not permitted under the rules of the General Agreement on Trade and Tariffs (GATT). Nevertheless, it is clear that American purchasing managers have sometimes saved substantial amounts of money for their company by buying from foreign producers at prices lower than those charged either by American producers or by foreign producers in their own home markets.

A buyer need not understand supplier pricing to buy from a foreign producer who quotes a lower price. This knowledge has other applications, however. Fortunately, in some cases the supplier may be quite willing to give the buyer access to his cost estimates and records. The buyer definitely has the right to examine the supplier's costs if there is provision for him to do so in the purchase contract. For example, price redetermination and cost plus fixed-fee contracts always include some provision for an audit of costs. If there is no provision, however, the supplier has every right to keep his costs to himself. In many cases, this is no handicap to the skilled purchase analyst or buyer. He can accurately estimate the costs anyway. When it is difficult to estimate the absolute level of the supplier's costs, the buyer can still apply the cost-volume principle and accurately estimate the effect of a change in volume on the supplier's cost.

Applying the cost-volume principle

Every supplier's cost curve resembles that in Figure 16–2. Costs are always lowest and profit margins greatest when the plant is operating near maximum capacity. Suppliers always have extra incentive to build sales volume when their plants are operating below their optimum. As we have noted, they not only stand to make their standard profit on this business but will also gain increased overhead absorption. The cost-volume relationship can be profitably applied to make-or-buy decisions. It should also be taken into account when volume rises either because business is good or because a buyer groups orders of like items to make them more attractive to a supplier.

Make or buy. It sometimes pays to make an item even though it can be bought more cheaply from an outside supplier. When it makes an item a plant is able to absorb part of its fixed overhead. This is true only when the plant is operating at a fraction of its normal capacity. When it is operating at capacity, on the other hand, it sometimes is economical to buy items from an outside supplier even though they theoretically can be made at lower cost in the buyer's plant. The reason for this is that costs can soar over standard when a plant is operated beyond its normal capacity. Expansion may not always be a solution, since additional capacity increases the fixed and nonvariable costs that must be absorbed.

Grouping orders. Many buyers get spectacular cost reductions by offering suppliers a "package" of business for all requirements of a group of similar items. Both buyer and seller benefit, since it is possible to process like items in large quantities at lower costs. Production is greater and unit overhead is lower. As is obvious from the figures in Table 16–2, a supplier making 100,000 units of an item often is willing to offer price concessions if he can get a customer to take an extra 10,000 units. His costs justify a price reduction and his profits will be greater if he offers a price cut less than his actual reduction in costs.

Exploiting sales gains. When business is good, companies buy more from their suppliers. Since the extra volume helps reduce costs, smart buyers do not hesitate to ask their suppliers to pass on the benefits by cutting prices. If suppliers know that no one else will sell the item at lower prices, they usually will refuse to cut prices. (Needless to say, they are usually less than candid about the real reason they decline to reduce prices; generally they insist that costs have gone up.) Even when costs have gone up, the buyer's efforts may not have been in vain. In some cases he can persuade the supplier to absorb increases in wages and materials costs that are almost inevitable when business is good.

Basis for negotiation. Suppose, for example, that a purchase agreement is negotiated for a particular item at a time when volume is 1,000 units per month. The buyer estimates cost of manufacture as follows:

Material	$0.50
Direct labor	.15
Overhead	.30
Sales and administrative expense	.05
Profit	.10
Price	$1.10

Business conditions improve and volume gradually increases to 1,200 pieces per month. Meanwhile material prices advance by 3 percent and wages go up 5 percent. The supplier would like to boost his price.

The buyer counters by requesting a price reduction. He agrees that a 5 percent increase in material costs should boost the price by about $0.025. He also admits that a 3 percent wage boost would boost the supplier's direct labor costs by almost $0.005 and that when this boost is applied to indirect labor and salaries, the total applicable increase in the wage bill could be the equivalent of as much as $0.01 per unit.

Thus, if the supplier seeks an increase of about $0.015, it is justified by higher costs. However, the buyer points out that this is more than offset by reductions in cost. Perhaps half of the supplier's overhead may be fixed or nonvariable. Once this overhead is absorbed, the supplier need only allow a 15-cent overhead charge in his price, instead of 30 cents. Thus if the supplier could afford to sell the first 1,000 units per month for $1.10, he should be able to sell 200 additional units for 15 cents less, or 95 cents. His average price should therefore be $1.075 per unit $\left(\dfrac{1,000 \times \$1.10 + 200 \times \$.95}{1,200}\right)$ when volume is 1,200 units per unit. This price gives the supplier the same unit profit of 10 cents that he enjoyed before. And it gives him a higher total profit—$120 per month when volume is 1,200 units, compared with $100 when volume was only 1,000 units. Thus, the supplier is ahead when he cuts prices, as long as volume increases.

The supplier and the buyer might finally agree on a price of $1.09— deducting $0.025 for increased volume and allowing $0.015 for higher basic costs.

Amortization. Supplier costs may also be reduced when special set-ups, tooling, start-up costs, or equipment associated with a new order are amortized. Suppose, for example, a supplier must spend $1,000 to rearrange his plant when he accepts a particular order. He does not dare propose that the customer pay for this as a separate charge, since his quotation, almost by definition, indicates he is fully able and ready to handle this order. But the rearrangement cost is real. If the supplier simply lumps it in with overhead, the cost will be spread over a number of jobs, implying, incorrectly, that costs on these other jobs have increased. Instead the supplier amortizes the special cost over the life of the initial contract. If this is for 10,000 pieces, the amortization of $1,000 would then amount to 10 cents a unit. If the supplier gets a second order, his profit will increase by 10 cents a unit, since the $1,000 extraordinary will have been fully recouped.

Smart buyers study the supplier's operation and try to identify such nonrecurring costs so they can get the benefit of lower prices after all special costs have been fully organized. Suppliers do not necessarily cut prices without a struggle. But the buyer still has a few more aces up his sleeve, if he needs them. He may want to make a fresh study of the overall cost of making the item or he may wish to apply the learning curve.

Buyer cost estimates

A buyer should be able to estimate the direct material cost of a purchased part as accurately as the supplier's estimator can. He can readily calculate the amount of material that will be used, and he usually knows the price of the raw material. The buyer should also be able to estimate the approximate labor cost. He is familiar with his supplier's equipment and processes, and he should be able to estimate how fast they will operate. He easily can find out what wage rates are in the supplier's area from employers' associations or from his own industrial relations department. The buyer normally can get burden rates for various types of manufacturing operation from his own company's cost department.

Thus, the buyer has all the raw material to make a reasonably good cost estimate. And, in fact, many skilled buyers can estimate costs with at least 95 percent accuracy. Some of them follow the same procedure as the accountant, estimating labor, material, and overhead separately. Others do just as well by comparing the new item with similar items and by drawing on their past experience.

The buyer's estimate becomes a useful target price. If the buyer calculates that the price of an item should be $1.00, then he will certainly think twice before he accepts a bid of either $0.50 or $2.00. In both cases he should ask the supplier to double-check his quotation for errors. He may, provided the supplier is willing, compare his cost estimate with that of the supplier.

While many buyers can prepare reasonably accurate cost estimates, they are not professionals. Some large companies have expert cost estimators working on purchased parts. Their estimates are used to budget costs, negotiate purchase prices, and measure the performance of purchasing personnel. Table 16–3 illustrates an estimate of an automobile-engine air cleaner that was used for this purpose. The estimator believes that a price of $2.54 would provide the supplier with an adequate 10 percent profit on the air cleaner. The actual price is $2.65.

Th 11-cent difference between the estimator's target price and the actual price is a target for the buyer in negotiation. The buyer can ask the supplier why he cannot produce the cleaner for $2.54. This may result in a detailed comparison of the buyer's estimate with the supplier's estimate. If the buyer's estimator is competent, the supplier may be hard put to justify the 11-cent price difference.

Detailed buyer cost estimates normally are used only for major items that are made by highly specialized suppliers. Since they are expensive to prepare, it is pointless to do so unless expenditures for the item are substantial. It also is pointless to make them if the normal process of soliciting competitive bids brings prices down to the level of the estimates. However, for many components there is not that much com-

TABLE 16–3
Purchased part price objective (14″ air cleaner and silencer assembly, dry type, 8 cyl.)

Objective price	$2.5400
Current price . . . . , ...	2.6500
Current price (over) under objective	$(.11)

Comments:

Material cost of make parts–steel	$ .6343
Purchase cost of element assembly, including freight	.4850
Purchase parts cost, including paint and carton.	.2415
Labor cost @ $.0346/min	.2488
Burden cost	.5476
Total manufacturing cost–painted and packaged	$2.1572
Product development engineering @ 3% of manufacturing cost. . .	.0647
Adjusted manufacturing cost	$2.2219
Administrative and commercial @ 5%	.1111
Total cost with administrative and commercial.	$2.3330
Profit on element assembly @ 5% of total cost	.0262
Profit on remainder of assembly @ 10% of total cost.	.1808
Estimated selling price–painted and packaged	$2.5400

Source: Ford Motor Co.

petition. Some are so complicated that only a few suppliers can produce them. Others, like the automotive air cleaner in Table 16–3, are not complicated, but one or two suppliers have become so adept at making them that their costs are much lower than those of any other potential producer. Their know-how gives these suppliers an advantage that effectively eliminates most potential competitors. In this case, the buyer's cost estimate is a substitute for a more competitive market.

The learning curve

Every supplier selling a custom-made product is to some extent a monopolist. Competition is restricted because: (1) The supplier has unique experience with the item that makes his production costs inherently lower than those of an inexperienced producer. (2) It is both costly and troublesome for the buyer to change suppliers. Often new tooling must be made. Quality and delivery problems develop. Sheer inertia makes it easier to continue doing business with the existing supplier.

If the purchased part or assembly is extremely complicated and order quantities are small, it will not do the buyer much good to negotiate strictly on the basis of cost of production. The supplier's skills will increase so much with experience that past costs are not a good guide to future costs unless the supplier's experience is taken into account. The solution in such cases is the "learning curve" approach, which is widely used in the aircraft and missile industries where order quantities are quite small, parts are extremely complex, and labor input per unit is very high.

Basic calculations. The principle behind the learning curve is quite simple: each job is performed more efficiently as it is repeated. While this relationship between efficiency and experience has always been obvious, it was not until World War II that any attempt was made to quantify it. At that time, studies showed that labor hours per unit of product in the airframe industry declined by about 20 percent whenever the production count was doubled. This is an 80 percent learning curve. It means that if the first unit of a product takes 100 hours of labor, the second unit will take 80 hours, the fourth unit 64 hours, the eighth unit 51.2 hours, and so on.

The cost of any lot with any learning curve can be calculated with the formula:

$$\log Y_i = \log Y_1 - b \log i$$

where:

i = Production count beginning with first unit or lot.

Y_1 = Direct labor hours (or dollars of direct labor cost) required to produce the first lot.

Y_i = Direct labor hours (or dollars) required to produce i^{th} lot.

b = Slope of the learning curve calculated from the formula:
2^b = Learning curve rate

For example, for an 80 percent curve, 2^b = .80, and therefore b = .322.

Now apply the formula to a case where the curve is 80 percent and the ith unit in which you are interested is the eighth unit or lot. Y_1 = 100 hours. You want to calculate the hours required to produce the eighth unit or lot. Therefore, i = 8. Substituting into the formula:

$$\log Y_8 = \log (100) - (0.322)(\log 8)$$
$$\log Y_8 = 2.000 - (.322) \times (.903) = 1.709$$

therefore,

$$Y_8 = 51.2 \text{ hours}$$

To get this answer, you must be proficient in the use of log tables. But it is easy to verify the formula when the production count is 8. The correct answer is equal to 80 percent of 80 percent of 80 percent, or 51.2 percent of the original cost, because production is doubled three times.

Plotting the results. Calculations with the formula are slow and tedious. It is much easier to use a chart. Learning curves can be calculated for various levels of operating efficiency on log-log paper. For example, Figure 16–3 shows an 80 percent learning curve used by North

FIGURE 16–3
Learning curve

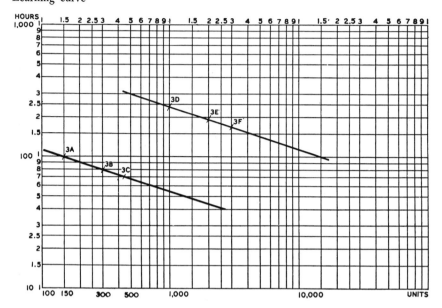

The learning curve is based on the principle that the number of man-hours needed to produce an item declines as the supplier gains experience. This 80 percent learning curve is used by North American Rockwell Corp.

American Rockwell Corp. The vertical scale indicates the vendor's direct labor costs and the horizontal scale shows units of output. The curve slopes downward because as the vendor gains experience he is able to make the product with fewer labor hours.

Applications. The learning curve is an excellent negotiating tool. Two typical applications are given below.

Problem No. 1. 150 pieces of a special machined forging were purchased from company A for $100 each. You now want 300 more pieces to be made and shipped in two lots of 150 pieces each. How much should you pay?

Plot point *3A* (see Figure 16–3) at $100 (or 100 hours if you were measuring your learning curve in hours rather than dollars) and 150 units. Plot point *3B* for double this total quantity, 300 units, and 80 percent of the price of $80. These two points establish the 80 percent slope.

The principle behind the learning curve is that costs decline in an arithmetic progression as quantity increases in a geometric progression. In this case, the cost of the second lot is 80 percent that of the first lot and the cost of the *fourth* (and not the third) lot is 80 percent of the cost of the second lot. The cost of the third lot cannot be calculated so readily. It is an easy matter to pick it off the chart, however, at point *3C* where the curve intersects the cumulative production count of 450 which would be reached when the third lot is completed. The chart indicates that the cost is $71.

You may wish to price the second and third lots separately at $80 and $71, respectively. Or you may wish to negotiate a combined price, equal to the average of the $80 price and the $71 price, or $75.50. Note, however, that if the supplier is going to make and ship the second order in one lot of 300, this learning curve does not apply; instead, you use a different rule which will be covered later.

Problem No. 2. This example shows the most typical use of the learning curve. Suppose you made an initial purchase of 1,000 pieces of a welded forging assembly at a price of $300 each. Now 2,000 additional pieces are needed, to be shipped in two lots of 1,000. What should the price be?

Analysis of supplier's costs shows the following: $10,000 was spent for tooling that was amortized over the first order and will not contribute to the costs of the additional order. Raw-materials costs were $65 per piece on the first order, but, due to the general price increase, they will go up to $70 on the subsequent order. Plating and heat treating costs totaled $5 per unit and are not subject to the learning curve. X-ray cost $2 per piece on the first order. They are believed to be subject to the curve, and the supplier intends to negotiate a lower price.

The supplier has just granted a 10 percent wage increase to his production workers and is going to be forced to go on a 48-hour week because of the increased work load. Direct labor amounted to $100 per part on the first lot. The supplier made no profit on the original order and feels he is entitled to a 10 percent price increase in order to earn a fair profit.

The computation is as follows:

Original price		$300.00 ea.
Less tooling, $10,000, for 1,000 pieces equals $10 ea.		10.00
Less items not subject to curve:		$290.00
Material	$65.00 ea.	
Plating and heat treating.	5.00	
	$70.00	70.00
Balance of costs subject to learning curve		$220.00
Plus:		
10% wage increase	$10.00	
Overtime cost	8.80	
	$18.80	18.80
Adjusted costs (including X-ray) subject		
to learning curve		$238.80

In Figure 16–3, plot point *3D* at 1,000 units and $238.80. Then plot point *3E* at double the quantity and 80 percent of the price ($191) to establish the 80 percent curve. Point *3F* then shows that the cost of the third lot of 1,000 pieces is $167.

If you wish to get a single price on a lot of 2,000 pieces, to be shipped in lots of 1,000, you would average these two costs of $167 and $191, giving you an average cost of $179 subject to the learning curve. Total costs would then break down as follows:

```
Costs subject to learning. . . . . . . . . . . . . . . . . . . . . . . . . . . . . . . $179.00
Raw material ($65 previously subcontracted and $5 increased cost) . .    70.00
Plating and heat treating (previously subcontracted) . . . . . . . . . .     5.00
        Net price before profit . . . . . . . . . . . . . . . . . . . . . . . . . $254.00
        10 percent profit on sales . . . . . . . . . . . . . . . . . . . . . .    28.22
        Adjusted price for new order . . . . . . . . . . . . . . . . . . . . $282.22
```

Limitations. The example above probably is not realistic, however. The supplier might well make and ship a lot of 2,000 rather than ship in lots of 1,000. In fact, one major problem in using the learning curve is change in purchase quantity. Only rarely is the second order for the same quantity as the first order. In some cases, the change in quantity is more significant to pricing than the supplier's experience. A company can determine the effect of change in quantity and experience on various types of item only by studying cost changes on a number of items. North American Rockwell's materials department made such a study. It believes that an 80 percent learning curve with various changes in purchase quantity results in the following relationships:

Percent increase in quantity (new order divided by old orders)	*Percent of old price that should be paid for new order*
10	67
50	63
100	60
150	57
200	55
500	47
1000	41
1500	37

The learning curve has other limitations. The most obvious one is that buyer and supplier often will not agree on which learning curve should be applied. The differences in price that result from using various learning curves can be enormous. With a 90 percent curve, prices on succeeding orders would run 100, 90, 81, 72 and so forth. With a 70 percent curve, the decline would be much steeper: 100, 70, 49, 35, and so forth. Such disagreements can best be resolved by comparison of the cost experiences of a number of companies making similar products.

But, obviously, the learning curve serves as a basis of negotiation; it is not so precise that the buyer can present the supplier with his learning curve analysis on a basis of take it or lose the business.

The learning curve should be used carefully. It cannot be applied to standard items on which a supplier has already reached optimum efficiency. Nor can it be applied to a cost estimate. If there are errors in the estimated price for the first order, the errors will not be magically eliminated by applying the learning curve to determine the price for the second order. Nor can one curve be applied universally to all items. The 80 percent curve works for certain types of aircraft parts; it will not work for everything. Each company must devise its own learning curves after making a study of the effect of production experience on the costs of various items.

Application to production control. A study of the effect of the learning curve on a company's own operations has applications that are by no means limited to purchasing problems. The learning curve is also useful for production control—particularly when the product is a new one and subject to rapid improvement. In such cases, productivity of both manpower and equipment may increase rapidly with the learning curve.

Suppose, for example, that eight workers are employed to assemble some new product and it takes them exactly one week (or 320 hours of labor) to complete the first job. If an 80 percent learning curve applies, the second unit should require 80 percent of 320 hours, or 256 hours. Required labor hours can then be calculated for every succeeding job using the learning curve formula previously described and a schedule can then be prepared. This schedule is different from the conventional one in that it shows steadily increasing production as the crew gains experience. When the schedule is made up in this fashion, production control will automatically make certain that a sufficient amount of material is always on hand. Otherwise, the company will not be in a position to take advantage of rising productivity because it simply will not have enough material on hand.

Cases

CASE 16–1. BLUE MOTORS CORPORATION (B)

Submission of identical bids

Blue Motors Corporation (whose periodic ordering system was discussed in Case 9–3) makes both passenger cars and light trucks. It has a central purchasing department headed by John Stone, vice president in charge of purchasing. Stone puts constant pressure on his staff to reduce costs. Blue Motors is not nearly so integrated as its major competitors and spends 64 percent of its sales dollar on purchased parts and materials. As a result, its competitive position depends heavily on how successfully it can control prices charged by suppliers.

Stone sets cost-reduction quotas for each of his buying supervisors, and their year-end bonuses are based partly on their success in meeting these quotas. Stone's electrical buying section is headed by Walter Karney, who was recently transferred to the purchasing department from the electrical components section of the company's engineering department. Karney is especially eager to meet his cost-reduction quota, since he wants to make good on his new job.

One of the items that attracts Karney's attention is the parking and tail-light light bulb that the company will be using on its new model cars, coming out the following autumn. Usage of this light bulb is quite heavy (more than one million units annually), and even a modest reduction in unit price will bring a substantial yearly saving. Traditionally, Blue Motors has divided its business equally among all four producers of the bulb, since there was no incentive to concentrate business with any of them. On the new bulb, Karney got the following quotations from the company's suppliers:

Alpha Electric.	$4.8117/C
Consolidated Electronics.	4.8117
California Lamp Corporation	4.8117
Donaldson Lighting Company.	4.8117

Karney cannot understand how four competing suppliers can quote independently and come up with prices that are identical to four decimal places. Naturally, he suspects collusion, and he decides to talk to each of the suppliers' sales representatives separately.

Roger Alpert of Alpha Electric says, "Our prices are carefully calculated in our estimating department and reflect not only our cost of production but also the extensive research program we have for developing new types of electrical items." Alpert denies having prior knowledge that his competitors would charge the identical price but agrees that "competitive forces" often result in identical prices from competing producers on identical products.

George Watson of Consolidated Electronics also emphatically denies having had any advance knowledge of what his competitors would charge. He points out that, although its price may be the same, Consolidated offers better quality and service than its competitors because it is the largest producer in the industry.

Charles Sincere of California Lamp observes that prices of competing producers must be identical, although he denies that there has been collusion. The reason for this is the Robinson-Patman Act, which requires that identical prices be charged to like customers. Blue Motors's competitors will also be using the new type of lamp in their new models, so California had to quote the same price to Blue Motors that it quoted to its competitors.

Joseph Allison of Donaldson Lighting, the smallest producer in the industry, points out that his firm is a licensee of patents vital to the process, which are owned by Alpha Electric and Consolidated Electronics. While Alpha and Consolidated make no attempt to dictate the prices to be charged, they have exercised a traditional role of price leadership in the industry.

Karney is reasonably certain that his suppliers have not violated any of the antitrust laws in their pricing. But he is equally convinced that competition among them is not as vigorous as it might be. He also suspects that the companies' prices on the bulbs will yield them substantial profits.

Question

How can Karney stimulate price competition among his light-bulb suppliers?

CASE 16–2. NUCLEONICS CORPORATION

Use of the learning curve in negotiation

Nucleonics Corporation of America is the prime contractor for the U.S. Air Force's Greyhound missile. The company has relied heavily on subcontractors in the development and manufacture of the missile, and about 65 percent of the sales dollar is for purchased components. In the early stages of the missile's development, when Nucleonics had an Air Force research and development contract, the company did a great deal of contracting on a cost- plus-fixed-fee basis. These contracts were converted to price redetermination as soon as suppliers knew enough about specifications to quote reasonably realistic prices.

Now many suppliers have had sufficient experience to be willing to quote on a fixed-price basis, and the materials manager, Mr. Swinbourne, buys a number of small components at fixed prices. However, he prefers to continue to buy the more complex items on a basis that permits prices to be redetermined periodically by either party. He believes these items are so specialized and his suppliers now have so much experience with them that no competitor could successfully produce them at lower cost. As a result, if suppliers were awarded fixed-price contracts after competitive bidding, they could easily charge prices high enough to earn rather exorbitant profits.

This is true even of some relatively simple parts. For example, Boston Electronics makes a special resistor used in the missile's guidance system.

Tolerances on this resistor are extremely tight, and at first the company had a fantastically high scrap rate. At least 100 resistors were rejected for every one accepted. The company accepted its first order for 2,000 resistors at $6 each, with price redetermination. After it completed half of this order, the company submitted the following cost breakdown and requested a new price:

Material	$ .92
Labor	1.22
Manufacturing overhead	9.24
Total manufacturing cost	$11.38
Sales and administrative expenses	.56
Total cost	$11.94

Nucleonics' materials manager was particularly shocked by Boston's enormous overhead charge. Boston's sales manager explained that these charges included the cost of scrap that had been run. After substantial negotiation, Nucleonics finally agreed to pay Boston $11.94 for the second batch of 1,000 resistors provided that Boston would stick to a price of $6.00 for the first batch. Boston agreed, since it believed it had found a way to reduce its scrap substantially.

While Boston was completing this order, Nucleonics got an extension of its prime contract from the Air Force. It placed an order with Boston for an additional 4,000 resistors. The order was priced at $6 with a redetermination clause. Calculating that Boston should be gaining additional experience and should be reducing costs, Nucleonics' materials manager decided to invoke the redetermination clause and reopen price negotiations on the second order.

In accordance with the provisions of the clause, Boston submits the following unit cost breakdown for the final lot of 1,000 pieces made on the initial production order:

Material	$ .87
Labor	1.05
Manufacturing overhead	2.25
Total manufacturing cost	$4.17
Sales and administrative expenses	.21
Total cost	$4.38

Boston suggests that since the second order will be manufactured in lots of 2,000, it can afford to reduce its price to $4.85 and still make a 10 percent profit on sales. It regrets that it cannot make any further price reduction because its suppliers are increasing prices and so materials costs will rise by 2 cents per resistor. In addition, Boston recently negotiated a new two-year contract with its union that called for wage increases of 15 cents per hour. Boston's current average wage is $2.65 per hour.

Questions

1. Should Nucleonics accept Boston's offer of a $4.85 price?

2. What price would be reasonable based on Boston's current costs, its projected increases in cost, and the experience it has gained, based on an 80 percent learning curve?

17

Negotiation with suppliers

NEGOTIATION is one of the most interesting phases of buying.[1] It may be limited to a three-minute telephone conversation about the details of a purchase or it may consist of several all-day sessions involving top executives in both the buyer's and the supplier's organizations. If the purchase is a minor one, the buyer may not negotiate at all; he may simply get a bid and place the order. It is pointless to make any effort to negotiate the purchase of a low-value nonrecurrent item. Negotiation may be unnecessary even for fairly high-value purchases. If the supplier's proposal is entirely satisfactory, the buyer may simply place the order.

The buyer should concentrate his efforts on negotiating the high-dollar-volume items for which some phase of the supplier's bid is not entirely satisfactory. Particularly suitable for negotiation are purchases with one or both of the following characteristics:

1. Competition is so limited that the buyer feels all bidders are quoting excessive prices or offering unsatisfactory delivery terms.
2. Prices are fixed (because of patents, collusion, fair trade, or trade custom) but it is possible to wangle "fringe" concessions from the supplier.

---

[1] This chapter is primarily concerned with negotiation of parts and materials prices, but the principles developed can also be adapted to negotiation of freight rates. Regulated interstate rates can be treated not unlike price-fixed purchased materials, while nonregulated rates can be negotiated just as any other commodities whose prices are determined by imperfect competition.

NEGOTIATION WITH LOW BIDDER

Experienced buyers do not automatically award business to the lowest qualified bidder. The low bidder may be disqualified if the buyer feels his bid is too low and reflects lack of familiarity with the specifications. Nor will he necessarily get the job if the buyer feels that the item is worth less than the low bid. In the latter case, the buyer may bluntly inform all bidders that he considers their bids too high and ask them to requote, or he may deal only with the low bidder or the bidder to whom he would like to award the contract. Such favoritism need not indicate collusion. A buyer may feel it is advantageous to give preference to a certain supplier for a number of legitimate reasons, including reciprocity, proximity of the supplier's plant, a history of favorable relations with a particular supplier, or the belief that a particular supplier will, in the long run, be the lowest cost producer and the greatest contributor to the buyer's cost-reduction program, new product efforts, and so on.

Possibly minor changes in specifications can be made that will reduce costs. Sometimes the supplier will permit the buyer to compare the details of his cost estimate with the buyer's own estimate. When this is done, differences often can be resolved. For example, a supplier may have included a certain manufacturing or inspection operation not considered necessary by the buyer. The buyer's quality control or product engineers can be called on to clarify specifications and ascertain if the operation is really needed.

Persistence needed. The buyer doesn't necessarily give up even if the lower bidder flatly refuses to reduce his quotation. If he still is convinced that the supplier's price is too high after he has unsuccessfully attempted to negotiate a price reduction, the buyer may take one of several courses of action:

1. *He may solicit bids from new, untried suppliers.* When he does not have time to do this because of delivery pressures, the buyer may be forced to accept the existing supplier's bid, but he should then go to work to locate new suppliers. He may wish to warn his existing supplier that he is looking for a new source. This will put some pressure on the supplier to reduce his costs.

2. *He may suggest that the item be made in the plant rather than bought from an outside supplier.* The threat of an adverse make-or-buy decision may put pressure on the supplier to reduce his costs and prices. For example, in Chapter 11, it was brought out that automobile companies invested in glass-making facilities primarily because they were not satisfied with prices charged by their suppliers for windshield glass. The case of the Mohawk Aluminum & Chemical Corporation in Chapter 15 is a good example of how this technique can be applied to transportation charges. Mohawk uses a threat to build dock facilities to handle

barge shipments as a lever to negotiate a substantial reduction in rail freight rates for alumina.

3. *He may propose that a high-priced component be "designed out" of the product.* For example, high and wildly fluctuating prices of copper have encouraged users of that metal to search for substitutes. Similarly, aluminum and plastics have been widely substituted for steel. The price of steel advanced more than twice as fast as other industrial prices during the 1950s and early 1960s. While aluminum and other substitutes are most costly per pound of material, they are lower in density·and often are low-cost substitutes. In construction, architects have made greater use of concrete and less of structural steel.

Buyer's concessions.   The measures above are fairly drastic. The buyer need not go to such trouble until he is certain that he really has negotiated the best possible price with his supplier. He should continue negotiations until all possibilities for reducing prices have been exhausted. In many cases, the supplier will be willing to cut prices if the buyer in turn makes certain concessions. The buyer can offer:

1. *A long-term contract for the item.*   With such a contract, the supplier may feel secure enough to invest in additional specialized equipment that will reduce his costs. He may also be persuaded to regard the contract as "bread and butter" business that will pay his overhead and permit him to make profits on his standard line. The mail-order houses buy in this way. They offer long-term contracts provided that the supplier will quote rock-bottom prices. A review of the break-even chart illustrated in Chapter 16 shows why this approach is attractive to both buyer and seller.

2. *Changes in specifications or design that permit the item to be adapted to the supplier's manufacturing processes.*   In many cases minor changes bring substantial savings. Both buyers and engineers should be alert to such changes; in many cases the value analysis techniques discussed in the following chapter help stimulate suggestions for change.

3. *Additional business on similar items to permit grouping of shipments and production runs in order to cut costs.*   This technique can be applied to any material or service. For example, a buyer may be able to get price concessions if he offers to buy all his office supplies from a single vendor. The same approach may work with production parts and materials (although here the buyer may not want to become too dependent on a single supplier). Even if the buyer gets no price concession, order grouping will almost always reduce both administrative and freight costs. Fewer shipments weigh more, and lower rates are charged per pound; they also cut administrative costs for both buyer and seller. This idea has become so popular in recent years that it is sometimes considered a basic buying concept. It is described as *systems contracting.* The idea is that the buyer looks upon the vendor as a supplier of a "system" of related items and gets the best possible terms of purchase

by relying on a single supplier for each "system" or "subsystem." In some cases the supplier operates almost as a direct adjunct of the buyer, and he, rather than the buyer, provides inventory protection and synchronizes his operations with those of the buyer.

4. *Contracyclical buying.* Some industries are seasonal or cyclical. Suppliers in these industries will make major price concessions during their slack season. A good example of this is the electrical equipment industry. Although the demand for electric power increases each year and is relatively unaffected by the business cycle, equipment demand is quite unstable. Utilities tend to be either in a rush for equipment or not the least bit interested in it. As a result, the equipment manufacturers either are operating at full capacity with an enormous order backlog or their plants are almost idle because of lack of business. In return for price concessions, the purchasing department of the Tennessee Valley Authority tries to do much of its buying during the slack season. Other utilities have not been so farsighted—or they have hesitated to tie up their money in equipment until there is a definite need for it.

Some purchasing departments deliberately negotiate long-term contracts during the industry's slack season. Suppliers in such industries know that depressed business during this period is normal. Theoretically, they should have no more reason to offer a price concession on a long-term contract when business is temporarily slow than at any other time of the year. But suppliers are human. An almost empty factory has a psychological effect on a businessman even though he knows the condition is temporary. He is more likely to be inclined to cut prices than he would be during the busy season—even though delivery dates on the orders are identical.

One purchasing agent in a small Midwestern city claims that he cut costs by nearly 5 percent by negotiating all of his contracts for mill supplies during the month of August. His suppliers are in a one-industry area, and during August the industry is almost completely idle. The purchasing agent solicits quotations for the following year during August. Although suppliers are fully aware that they will be delivering against the purchase order throughout the year, the purchasing agent claims that psychologically they feel less secure during this slack month and will quote slightly lower prices.

FIXED-PRICE ITEMS

If the purchased material is industry priced, the buyer usually is wasting his time if he tries to negotiate a price reduction, particularly if his company is not a significant user of the item. In such cases the supplier often is selling the identical item to many customers, and in some cases other sellers also are selling the identical item. It is both illegal (according to the Robinson-Patman Act) and unethical for a supplier to discriminate among customers. If a supplier cuts the price for one customer, he must cut it for all customers. This makes price cuts extremely expensive and very difficult to negotiate. In some cases, if the item is legally price fixed by fair-trade laws, it even may be illegal for the seller to reduce the price under any conditions.

Even such rigid pricing leaves the buyer plenty of room to negotiate lower prices. He often has the opportunity to:

1. *Become a "unique" user.* Sometimes it is possible to become a "unique" user of a material with changes in specifications. When this is the case, buyer and seller can negotiate any price they please. Then, if the supplier reduces his price, he need not reduce prices of similar items sold to other customers. This is one of the reasons large mail-order houses use private brands. For example, the Whirlpool Corporation makes refrigerators and home-laundry equipment both under its own brand name and under Sears, Roebuck's Kenmore brand. Whirlpool presumably charges Sears less for equipment carrying the Kenmore brand name than it charges its own wholesalers for almost identical merchandise carrying the Whirlpool name. Were Sears to attempt to get similar prices on the Whirlpool brand, it would almost certainly run afoul of the Robinson-Patman Act (see Chapter 5).

When a company succeeds in becoming a unique user of an item that would otherwise be price fixed, the resulting price structure is sometimes weird. Auto companies, for example, pay less for exhaust tail pipes than they would have to pay for the steel tubing from which the tail pipes are made. The tail pipes are designed to fit each model of car, and their prices are negotiated by the auto company and its suppliers. The tubing from which the pipe is made is a standard commodity, sold at identical fixed prices by all producers. Tubing prices cannot be reduced through negotiation but tail pipe prices can. As a result, auto companies use their buying power to get low prices from tail pipe fabricators, whose costs are low because they have their own tubing mills to convert steel strip into the tubing that is made into finished tail pipes.

2. *Negotiate payment terms.* Although the price of a material may be fixed, individual sellers of the material often have different payment terms. For example, mill supply houses have been known to offer thinly disguised reductions on price-fixed items by offering unusually generous payment terms. The standard discount for paying an invoice within ten days is either 1 or 2 percent, but some buyers get trade discounts as high as 7 percent from distributors. Obviously this is a concealed price cut, not just a concession to get the buyer to pay his bill promptly. A price reduction of 7 percent for paying a bill in 10 days instead of 30 is the equivalent of paying interest at the rate of approximately 150 percent per annum. Needless to say, few distributors are so hard

pressed for cash that they will pay such an interest rate; most can borrow from a bank at 8 percent per annum or less.

3. *Use concealed discounts.* When a company buys both price-fixed and non-price-fixed items from the same supplier (as is often the case in buying from mill supply distributors), it is not difficult to negotiate discounts on the price-fixed items. The buyer simply lists both price-fixed and nonprice-fixed items on the purchase order. By previous agreement he deducts his negotiated discount on the price-fixed items from the prices of the nonprice-fixed items.

4. *Use vendor inventory.* As we saw in Chapters 9 and 10, inventories are expensive to maintain. If a buyer can get a supplier to carry part of his inventories for him, he is getting the equivalent of a reduction in purchase price. For example, a buyer may negotiate an agreement whereby the vendor guarantees that a 60- to 90-day stock will be maintained exclusively for the buyer's requirements. The buyer then can operate on a hand-to-mouth basis with no fear of stockouts. He buys small quantities from the vendor, who periodically replenishes his stock when it drops to some predetermined level. As noted previously, so-called "stockless" purchasing is often part of an overall "systems contract" in which a buyer makes an agreement to purchase all items of a particular type from a single supplier.

5. *Obtain quantity discounts.* Sometimes a buyer can persuade a supplier to give him a quantity discount even though he is not actually buying the quantities required for such a concession. For example, suppose a supplier's price schedule provides for an extra 10 percent discount on purchases of more than 1,000 units. If the buyer uses only 100 units per month, he certainly would not want to buy a ten-month supply to earn the discount. But he might be able to persuade the supplier to give him the discount anyway. His gimmick: a purchase order for 1,000 units that does not call for immediate delivery but permits the buyer to draw on material as he needs it. Then the buyer can get 100 units each month as he requires and still get the discount for buying the larger quantity.

Companies with several plants often can persuade suppliers to consider companywide volume when calculating quantity discounts, even though each plant may order its needs separately. For example, products such as light bulbs are often sold on a "national accounts" basis. If a company with several plants bought light bulbs on a hit-or-miss basis, it might get hardly any discount from the list price. But if it combines the buying power of all its plants and buys directly from the manufacturer on a national accounts basis, it may get a discount of 30 percent or more. Centralized purchasing of this sort also permits a company to exercise more effectively its reciprocal power to persuade suppliers to become customers.

6. *Adjust packaging and shipping.* There is almost no limit to the number of ways an imaginative buyer can find to reduce costs—even when the prices of the items he buys are theoretically fixed. Various packaging and shipping arrangements offer numerous possibilities. The simple act of buying "f.o.b. our plant" instead of "f.o.b. shipping point" can in itself bring substantial savings. Packaging and palletizing arrangements also can cut costs. For example, one company has persuaded its vendors to ship in cartons that it can reuse for shipments to its own customers.

7. *Get extra services.* Sometimes a supplier can be persuaded to render extra services. If these have economic value to the buyer, they are obviously worth negotiating. If scrap generated by the buyer's process has no market value, the supplier is doing the buyer a service by hauling it away. (But the buyer had better be absolutely certain he cannot make a profit on the scrap by selling it himself.) Similarly, suppliers may train buyer's personnel in the use of his equipment or material.

Among smaller hospitals, suppliers sometimes take over much of the materials management function. They periodically check buyer's stocks and automatically replenish them if they feel they are too low. In most cases, the supplier is overly generous in keeping the hospital well stocked with his product but chances are that inventories would be no lower if the hospital tried to manage them, especially in hospitals that are too small to be able to justify employment of a full-time, well-trained materials manager.

NEGOTIATING PRICE INCREASES

Since about 1941, the prices of finished and semifinished materials have advanced steadily, despite the best efforts of buyers. The reason is that rising wages have increased both manufacturing costs and materials costs.[2] When demand for their products is weak, suppliers usually are forced to absorb wage increases from profits, and occasionally they are even forced to cut prices in the face of rising costs. When demand is strong, however, the shoe is on the other foot: suppliers not only can pass on the full costs of wage hikes to their customers but sometimes can also boost prices to more than offset the cost of future wage and materials increases. The result has been that prices have gone up when business is booming but have not declined substantially when business has dropped off. This has meant an average rise in prices of at least 2 to 3 percent a year.

When demand is strong, no materials manager can expect consistently

---

[2] Wage increases naturally drive a supplier's materials costs up because the supplier's suppliers also are confronted with higher costs that they pass on through price increases.

to avoid compensating suppliers for increases in cost. But often he can prevent suppliers from getting price increases in excess of cost increases. Suppose a materials manager gets a letter from a supplier saying that "effective immediately, the prices of our products are hereby increased 5 percent." What does he do? His course of action depends on the nature of the commodity. If it is one that is standard and sold to a number of users, he has much less flexibility and bargaining power than if the commodity is made to order for the materials manager's company.

For example, if there is an industrywide price adjustment on a standard commodity like copper, it would be a waste of time for an individual buyer to try to persuade Kennecott Copper Corporation that this increase should not be applied to him. The best he can do is to look for a lower cost supplier or for a substitute material. The buyer is not so restricted on items made to his company's specifications, where the price is determined by negotiation between buyer and seller. When a supplier increases the price of these items, he must give the buyer a good reason for doing so. The usual reason is "higher costs," and few would deny that both labor and raw-materials costs progressively creep higher and higher year after year.

Justifying the increase

No buyer worth his salt will accept a price increase on a purchased component with the simple explanation of "higher costs." He will insist on substantiation from the supplier that costs really have risen. Sometimes the supplier will furnish a breakdown of his costs (and, in fact, such a breakdown may be provided for in the purchase order terms and conditions). In any case he should be willing to furnish some quantitative evidence.

If the price increase is caused by higher labor costs, the supplier normally will tell the buyer what his average increase is in cents per hour. He also should be willing to indicate either the number of standard hours of direct and indirect labor used in making each part or the total old and new labor cost in dollars per unit. If the price increase is caused by higher materials costs, the supplier should be willing to disclose his materials costs, materials specifications, and the precise materials usage per unit.

Needless to say, the documentation offered by a supplier will always "prove" that his price increase is completely valid. This does not mean that the buyer should accept the "proof," however. The fact is that many suppliers have never attempted to calculate closely the unit costs of the items they produce. When overall costs rise, they simply add enough to the price of each item to achieve their profit objective. Often the individual price increases represent the sales manager's best estimate of "what the traffic will bear." Some parts are increased by less than the amount of the cost increase because the supplier feels his competitive position on these items is weak; others are increased by much more. Thus the buyer should never be reluctant to ask for substantiation (or feel that he is challenging the supplier's integrity by doing so).

Cost analysis

Since the "evidence" submitted will always "prove" the increase justified, how does the buyer determine whether or not he should accept it? The skilled buyer can determine with amazing accuracy precisely how much a supplier's costs have increased if he is given a little data to work with. Suppose, for example, that a supplier wishes to increase the unit price of a part by 5 percent, from $1.00 to $1.05, on account of higher labor and materials costs. The supplier submits the following cost breakdown to prove that his increase is justified by higher cost of production:

	Old cost	New cost
Materials cost: 0.5 lbs. brass bar stock		
@ 62¢/lb.	$ .31	@ 66¢/lb. = $ .33
Labor cost	.20	.21
Overhead (@ 200%)	.40	.42
Total cost	$ .91	$ .96
Profit	.09	.09
Price	$1.00	$1.05

Before the buyer even bothers analyzing the supplier's cost breakdown, he should ask himself these questions:

1. Is the supplier's proposed new price still competitive with that of other qualified producers?
2. Do purchase order terms and conditions permit price escalation?
3. Are other producers in the supplier's industry also confronted with these higher costs, and are they succeeding in passing them on to their customers?
4. Has the supplier passed on, in the form of price reductions, the benefits of increased productivity or other changes that have cut his costs?

If the answer to any of these questions is no, then the buyer has a basis for negotiation with the supplier other than cost of production. In such a case, he might possibly be able to convince the supplier that he should forego his price increase without making any analysis of cost.

But assume that the buyer must analyze costs. He does this most easily by analyzing each basic component: material, labor, overhead, and profit.

Material. This is the easiest component to analyze. Most raw-material costs are readily available, and it does not take too much study to verify the weight of material used by the supplier. In the example cited, which is a part made of brass bar stock, the buyer would check the supplier's old and new costs per pound against price lists available from the major brass mills. These price lists would include also the weight of each diameter bar per linear foot. Thus it would be simple to verify the supplier's estimate of unit weight.

When the buyer is reviewing a price increase charged to higher materials costs, he should be sure to check also for a change in the value of scrap material. Usually when the price of the finished raw material goes up, so does the price of scrap. If the material has a relatively high value, the value of process scrap can become significant. This is true particularly if the design of the part generates a great deal of scrap. For example, some finished brass screw machine parts weigh only about half as much as the bar stock from which they are machined. Since brass is a relatively expensive metal, this scrap is valuable. If its price goes up, the price the buyer pays for the finished part should be reduced.

In some cases, the buyer may wish to determine the market in which the supplier is buying his raw material. In the United States, there is sometimes a significant difference between the price quoted by domestic producers and that charged for material of foreign origin. There is almost always a major price difference between different modes of distribution—e.g., purchasing direct from a mill rather than from a distributor. The buyer should insist that his purchase be based on using the lowest cost material available—even though this may not be identical with that used by the supplier. The supplier may bitterly resist the buyer's attempt to "interfere," but this is nevertheless a reasonable subject for negotiation.

Labor. In the example given, the supplier indicated that his direct labor cost per unit had increased by 5 percent, from $.20 to $.21. The buyer should ask the supplier what the wage increase is in cents per hour and also what the new average wage is. Naturally, these figures should indicate a 5 percent increase. The buyer should then compare the supplier's wage figures with overall wage averages issued by the Bureau of Labor Statistics for the supplier's industry and his area. In addition, the buyer can often get excellent wage statistics from his local Chamber of Commerce or manufacturers' association. In most cases, the buyer will not have to get such data at first hand; his own industrial relations department often has excellent statistics on average wages and is also familiar with the pattern of wage increases. Needless to say, the supplier's indicated wages and wage increases should not be too far out of line with industry and area averages. If they are, the buyer has a point for negotiation.

Overhead.   As all students of cost accounting soon learn, all labor is not "direct" labor. Wages paid to employees who are not directly concerned with making the product are an "indirect" labor expense and are charged to various overhead (or burden) accounts. Indirect labor in most manufacturing companies is by no means an insignificant expense. Typically it amounts to between 60 and 75 percent of direct-labor costs. In highly automated plants, of course, the ratio is much higher. In fact, in a completely automated plant (i.e., with no production workers), the ratio of indirect-labor to direct-labor costs would be infinite. In such a case, the cost accounting convention of separating direct-labor cost from overhead would be meaningless, since there would be no direct-labor costs and buyers would concern themselves only with changes in direct materials and overhead costs.

In any event, overhead consists of many costs in addition to indirect labor. Therefore, in no case does a 5 percent increase in wages automatically increase a supplier's overhead costs by exactly 5 percent (from $.40 to $.42) as it does in the example given above. The buyer thus has a negotiating point even if the 5 percent wage increase is completely justified.

Frequently buyers and suppliers will disagree about the total labor cost content of a given part. The supplier's estimate of the cost of direct and indirect labor as a percentage of selling price usually will be higher than the buyer's. Smart buyers try to accumulate as much comparative data as possible. They try to get estimates from their own cost department of what relative costs should be on the type of work the supplier is performing. They also build up files of comparative data from competing suppliers. Buyers should always remember, however, that cost data they get from suppliers are nearly always confidential. They should never show such data to a competing supplier without the express permission of the supplier from whom they obtained the information. Nor should they attempt to play off one supplier against another by implying they have data that they actually do not have. Experienced buyers can follow these rules of the game and still be able to estimate a supplier's cost structure with considerable accuracy.

Profit.   The example given shows that the supplier theoretically is not increasing his unit profit of 9 cents with the price increase. This may mean that the supplier feels his competitive position is such that he cannot hope to boost profits when he raises prices. Or—and far more likely—it means that the supplier has made up a cost breakdown especially designed to please the buyer and convince him that higher prices do not mean higher profits.

One of the major objectives in setting administered prices is an adequate return on investment. Many companies try to achieve this objective by setting as a target a given percentage of profit on sales. Naturally, when costs and prices go up, profits go up proportionately. Most suppliers follow this accounting convention. Therefore a buyer can assume, regardless of what the supplier's cost breakdown shows, that a request for a price increase includes a request for added profit. If competitive conditions warrant it, the buyer should not be outraged at such a request. And in fact he should hesitate to use his buying power (if he has enough) to push down the price of an item so far that there is no profit in it for the supplier. However, the buyer who feels his suppliers are "entitled to a profit" is naive. It is not the buyer's job to help his suppliers make profits. On the contrary, the buyer's role is to serve as a countervailing force that limits supplier profits. If the buyer is really effective, he may occasionally eliminate the inefficient and un-profitable supplier from his ranks. He will be looked upon as a villain by that supplier but to the overall economy and to his company, he will just be doing his job. No buyer can prevent the most efficient pro-ducer from being very profitable indeed. And, of course, in a free society, neither buyer nor seller is forced to accept the other's terms. The agree-ment is voluntary and must therefore be mutually advantageous.

Need for pressure. In the example given, cost analysis has opened up several areas for negotiation of the supplier's price increase. The buyer could ask for a credit against the increase in materials cost because the scrap being generated also had a higher value, or claim that the supplier's wage increase was being applied to his entire overhead even though indirect labor was probably less than half of total overhead.

The supplier, of course, can always flatly refuse to reduce the amount of the price increase. Or, as is far more likely, he can attempt to work up new figures to "prove" that the increase is really justified and that only the original "justification" was in error. Sometimes the supplier will cheerfully reduce the amount of the increase. In this case, it is quite possible that he has anticipated the buyers attempts at price reduction and has deliberately padded his estimates so that he will end up with what he actually wants after he has made substantial concessions in negotiation with the buyer.

Error in supplier pricing

So far we have discussed only price increases that result from higher wages or raw-material costs. These are the most common price increases. But buyers sometimes encounter suppliers who accept an order at a certain price and then find they cannot meet this price. There has been no change in basic wages and materials costs. The supplier's problem is that he finds he is using either more material or more direct labor hours than he had anticipated.

Unless the purchase order terms permit price redetermination (see Chapter 5), the buyer should normally treat such requests unsympatheti-cally. No supplier can be right all the time, and the best supplier will sometimes be too optimistic when he is making the cost estimate on which he bases his quotation. But this will be offset by the jobs on which the supplier's profits are higher than expected. If a buyer permits suppliers to charge higher prices every time they bid too low on a job, his competitive bidding process will become a farce. Suppose, for example, that a supplier bid $100 on a job and the next lowest bid was $105. If the supplier later requests a higher price, the buyer might well have been better off if he had given the order to the competitor who bid $105.

"Buying" the business. Suppliers themselves are familiar with the buyer's dilemma. It is a time-honored strategy to "buy" business by deliberately quoting low prices. Suppose that XYZ Company has been doing business with ABC Company for years. ABC's prices are reasonable and its quality and delivery are excellent. As ABC's competitor, you would like to get a slice of XYZ's business. You are as good as ABC but no better. How do you go about getting your foot in the XYZ door? One common strategy is to undercut ABC's price, selling below cost if necessary. Then, after you are in, you will try to recoup your losses over time from more profitable XYZ business.

This strategy occasionally backfires badly. A new supplier underestimates the difficulty of a particular job and costs begin to run away from him. While the buyer's reaction may be unsympathetic in such cases, his bargaining position may also be weak when a supplier exerts strong pressure for a price increase. Suppose, for example, that the buyer places an order with a supplier in June for delivery in December. If manufacturing lead time is six months, what does the buyer do if in November the supplier refuses to ship unless he is awarded a general price increase? In practice, the buyer probably would settle with the supplier. If he wanted to, he could refuse to adjust the contract and attempt to enforce it with legal action. However, this is rarely done by industrial buyers, whose supplier relations seldom deteriorate to the point where even a threat of legal action is necessary.

Honest error. A far more common problem in industrial purchasing is the supplier who comes to the buyer and says: "We bid too low on this job. We just didn't anticipate the difficulties we've had. Costs have been so high that we cannot continue to produce on the job unless we get some sort of price relief." The buyer investigates and discovers that costs have indeed been so high and the job has actually been more difficult than either he or any of the suppliers who quoted on the job probably could anticipate.

Even then the buyer may insist that the supplier deliver at the purchase order price. Buyers for government agencies have no other choice. If their purchase order does not specifically call for price redetermination or escalation, they can do nothing. Industrial buyers usually can be more flexible. If they feel that specifications were misleading or that the supplier might be useful for future contracts, they may wish to renegotiate the contract even though they are under no obligation to do so. In such a case they normally would insist on a detailed substantiation of costs. They might even call on their own company's internal auditors for help in checking the supplier's cost records. Then they would try to negotiate a price that was somewhere between the original price and the supplier's actual cost.

PRINCIPLES OF NEGOTIATION

The word "negotiation" carries many connotations that are not consistent with modern industrial buying practices. To some, negotiation means the haggling that might take place in a public market in the Eastern Hemisphere. Buyer and seller carry on an animated conversation, exchanging either insults or compliments. The buyer starts negotiation by offering a price well below that which he knows he ultimately must pay. The seller's demands are equally outrageous; his first offer may be two or three times what the merchandise is actually worth. After some time spent in haggling, buyer and seller finally agree on a price that is close to what each could have predicted before negotiation was begun.

Some buyers use a rather crude version of this basic approach to negotiation. They are never satisfied with any quotation, regardless of how low it is. Some of the more obnoxious buyers try to browbeat suppliers into submitting lower quotations. Their negotiating techniques are pretty much limited to pounding on the table and demanding concessions. Such buyers are quite rightly called chiselers by their suppliers. In most cases, the price reductions they negotiate are illusory. Suppliers who know them for what they are simply quote higher than normal and then make "concessions" when the buyer figuratively—and, occasionally, literally—pounds on the table and demands them.

Basic rules

Successful buyers have a more sophisticated approach to negotiation. They know that they can negotiate nothing but what suppliers are willing to concede. So they concentrate on creating an environment conducive to voluntary concessions by suppliers. Some of the principles applied by successful negotiators include:

1. *Put yourself in the supplier's shoes.* One of the most basic principles of successful selling is to think in terms of the customer's requirements. When a buyer is trying to wangle concessions from a supplier, the shoe is on the other foot: he is trying to sell the supplier. So he should think in terms of the supplier's objectives, not his own. For example, he might say to the supplier: "If you offer me a price concession,

I will try to work you in as a supplier of some new products that we currently have in the development stages." He would *not* say: "If you cut prices, you will help me meet my quota on cost reduction." If you were the seller, which approach would appeal to you—the one where the buyer in effect says, "Let me help you," or where he says, "Help me"?

2. *Let the supplier do most of the talking.* The vice president in charge of purchases of a large electrical equipment manufacturer once said: "Supplier salesmen can't stand silence. They'll talk just to fill the vacuum, and in the process they often talk themselves into making just the concessions you want." This is the exact opposite of the approach used by "old-school" buyers who try to browbeat suppliers into making concessions, and it is infinitely more effective. After all, salesmen are professional persuaders. They consider overcoming customer resistance to be the greatest test of their skill. If a buyer challenges the price or quality of their product, they're ready with arguments to sell him. But what if the buyer says almost nothing? In this atmosphere, the salesman is at a disadvantage and may well end up making concessions that he never intended to make at the outset.

The deadpan approach has another basic advantage. The supplier may begin to believe that the buyer's position is much stronger than it actually is. The ethical buyer never lies. But he doesn't spill everything he knows. It would be unethical, for example, to tell the supplier that you can buy the item at a lower price if this just isn't true. But if the supplier begins to believe this himself because of the buyer's silence, that is the supplier's problem.

3. *Let the supplier save face.* The buyer should at all costs avoid a showdown. He never wants to force the supplier into a position where he says, "Here are my terms—take them or leave them." Once the supplier does this, he must lose face if he makes further concessions. Similarly, a buyer should never imply, directly or indirectly, that cost breakdowns or similar data submitted by a supplier are false or misleading. Such breakdowns always justify the supplier's position. When the buyer analyzes them and finds they are incorrect, he should point out the "errors" or "misinterpretations" in them. But under no circumstances should he imply that the data were created solely for use as a sales tool by the supplier.

4. *Satisfy the supplier's needs.* Most suppliers have two outstanding characteristics. They genuinely like selling, and they feel somewhat insecure. Smart buyers cater to these characteristics. They give the supplier a chance to sell them. Thus a good buyer provides a test for the supplier's skills that is both stimulating and satisfying. The buyer should also remember that many of his suppliers are in businesses that are subject to violent ups and downs. Suppliers inevitably are attracted to buyers who make them feel secure and who do not unnecessarily increase their

insecurity so long as their terms are competitive. They often will offer better terms to such buyers simply because their emotional needs are partly fulfilled.

5. *Talk to the proper person.* Some buyers make the mistake of trying to negotiate with the wrong person in the supplier's organization. When they do, they are simply wasting their time. For example, most supplier sales representatives have limited powers to negotiate purchase terms and conditions. Sometimes they have no authority at all. Most suppliers give their salesmen a little leeway. For example, they may be instructed to quote a price of $100 for an item, which they can cut to $95 without consulting the home office if they are forced to do so in negotiation. In such a case, the buyer should try to estimate in advance approximately what concessions the supplier is willing to make. If he is satisfied with these concessions, he can conclude negotiations shortly with the salesman. If he is not satisfied, he should negotiate with higher level officials in the supplier organization. If the purchase is an extremely important one for both buyer and seller, the top management of both companies may become involved before negotiations are concluded. Minor purchases, on the other hand, rarely involve much negotiation. If the desired agreement cannot be reached with the supplier sales representative, the buyer will either accept the supplier's terms or start looking for another supplier.

6. *Sell the supplier.* Intelligent suppliers try to get business from companies that are going places. They very wisely recognize that their own growth is linked to that of their customers. The buyer should try to convince the supplier that the buyer's firm is worth doing business with over the longer term, even if this involves temporary sacrifices on the part of the supplier. This approach obviously has its limitations. It can be used with considerable success for a buyer who works for IBM or Polaroid but it is a moot point how effective it would be were it applied by a purchasing agent of a bankrupt railroad.

7. *Take up one point at a time.* A series of little concessions will add up to a big concession. Each little concession is relatively painless, but taken together they may be more than the supplier can swallow. It can safely be assumed that the supplier can figure out what is going on in this process. But it is just possible that he will wind up conceding slightly more than he originally intended if the process represents a series of little nibbles instead of one big bite.

8. *Don't rush the process.* Of course, only major purchases are worth the trouble of prolonged negotiation. But if it is worth the effort, give yourself sufficient time to be effective. The seller should never get the idea that you are eager to wrap up negotiations so that you can proceed to more important business. On the contrary, you should try to make him eager to conclude negotiations by giving you at least part of what you request.

The negotiating session

Major purchases of equipment or parts almost always require formal negotiating sessions. Usually they are held in the purchasing agent's office. The vendor generally will send a top sales official to assist the local sales representative. He may also send his controller, chief engineer, or manufacturing superintendent if the discussion involves their specialties. The purchasing executives also may draw on other departments for technical assistance, especially on quality control and engineering.

Advance planning. The participants in a negotiating session accomplish more if the session is planned in advance, with an agenda indicating what is to be discussed. Purchasing should be prepared to discuss price and delivery terms. Engineering and quality control experts may be called upon to discuss the proposed purchase in terms of their specialties. Shrewd purchasing executives never go into a negotiating session unprepared. They try to anticipate what the supplier will propose so they can be ready with a counterproposal. Some go so far as to conduct prenegotiating sessions in which all the participants except the supplier's representatives meet to plan the real session. Good planning pays off. In some cases, the supplier can be caught off guard, and the result is a greater concession than he had originally intended to grant. In every case, good planning reduces the probability that some important area for negotiation will be neglected.

Negotiating sessions take varying amounts of time. Two hours may be adequate for many rather important purchases. Sometimes a full day or longer must be allowed, particularly if there are a great many engineering details to review. In any event, the atmosphere should be calm and unhurried. Some purchasing executives even believe in spending the first few minutes of the session in discussing completely irrelevant subjects—such as who won yesterday's ball game—in order to create the proper atmosphere.

Every effort should be made to prevent the participants from becoming the least bit emotional. When there is sharp disagreement, the chairman should make note of it and pass on to the next topic on the agenda. Perhaps the disagreement can be resolved at another session, or one party may concede to the other rather than see negotiations broken off. When every point has been covered, the chairman should summarize all points of agreement—and disagreement—and conclude the meeting. Many materials executives follow up such meetings with a written summary of the minutes in order to prevent any possible misunderstanding. A letter would then be sent to the supplier which outlined the areas where agreement was reached and also made counterproposals to resolve questions on which agreement has not as yet been reached.

Prenegotiation. The formal negotiation session is a simple straightforward approach to the problem of reaching agreement with the supplier on prices and other contract terms. Many Americans and almost all foreigners prefer a less direct approach in which business and social activity are intermixed.

For example, buyer and seller may enjoy 18 holes of golf together without discussing business problems at all. Then in the locker room each may gently sound the other out on the basic problem. Neither party presents anything that could be construed as a formal offer or counteroffer at this time. Each simply listens sympathetically as the other discusses his problems and objectives. No attempt is made to conclude an agreement.

The basic purpose of the locker-room session is for buyer and seller to understand each other's attitudes and problems. Each can then tailor his formal proposal to fit more closely the needs of the other. The buyer-seller golf game (or hunting and fishing expeditions, or similar jaunts) may be regarded as fun by the casual observer. And it is. But when he gets closer to the process, he realizes that its major purpose is still business—and the salesman on the golf course may be working just as hard as the man who is beating the bushes for customers in more obvious ways. While it may be inefficient and wasteful, the pre-negotiation session that is conducted on the golf course is often the most effective way that buyer and seller can reconcile differences and concentrate on common objectives.

Cases

CASE 17–1. BLUE MOTORS CORPORATION (C)

Negotiating a supplier price increase

Blue Motors (see Cases 9–3 and 16–1) spends about $10 million a year on "chrome" moldings used to decorate the sides of its various automobile models. The moldings are made from a relatively low-cost type of stainless steel. There are three basic steps in the process. First the stainless steel is run through a series of rollers to form the desired cross section. Then the rolled molding is cut to length, and notches and holes are pierced in a press operation. Finally, the completed moldings are inspected for scratches, polished if necessary, and packaged for shipment. Most suppliers perform the two basic operations—rolling and forming—on a single machine. Occasionally, supplementary press operations are required. Inspection and buffing out of scratches are always necessary.

All together, Blue Motors buys about 40 different moldings, but it uses only two different cross sections. Most of the differences between parts come at the press stage rather than at the rolling stage. For example, a four-door car might have four different moldings running along each side—on the front fender, the front door, the rear door, and the rear quarter panel. The moldings are almost identical (in fact, to the casual observer they would blend together to look like a single molding running the length of the car); the only differences are in length, holes, and the forming of the ends.

Blue Motors buys its moldings from three suppliers: Detroit Molding Corporation, Galway Corporation, and Stainless Forming Company. In addition, there are two other suppliers of moldings to the auto industry, Great Lakes Molding Company and Albertson Corporation. Blue Motors has done business with Great Lakes and Albertson in the past. But it prefers to limit itself to three suppliers, and these two firms were not competitive when the last buy was made.

The technology of the stainless steel molding industry is far from complex. Almost anyone who has a quarter of a million dollars to invest could go into the business. The equipment is standard throughout the industry, and relatively little know-how is required to operate it. There is just one big problem: making a profit at the prices the auto companies are willing to pay. Although there are only five producers, competition among them is so keen that four of them have been forced to move their plants from the Detroit and Cleveland areas to the South, where wages are much lower.

The lowest cost producer in the industry is the Galway Corporation, which has always been located in South Carolina. Until 1955, the company was exclusively a manufacturer of eaves troughs and similar rolled products used in construction. At that time, Blue Motors's assistant purchasing agent, Edwin Barnes, felt that there was not enough competition in stainless steel moldings, and he decided that he would try to persuade new producers to enter the field. The ideal new producer, Barnes reasoned, would already be familiar with the techniques of forming metal by rolling and would have the necessary equipment. He also would be in an industry that was price-conscious and in an area where labor costs were relatively low.

Barnes was looking for a supplier with a completely fresh approach, one who had never done any business with the auto industry. He particularly wanted a supplier located in the South. Not only did the lower labor cost in that area appeal to him, but there also might be some savings in transportation costs with a southern supplier for 15 to 20 percent of the total requirements. In 1955 Blue Motors was shipping moldings from Detroit and Cleveland suppliers to all 18 of its automobile assembly plants. A southern supplier would have a definite freight advantage on shipments to Blue Motors's Memphis, Houston, Norfolk, and Savannah plants.

After several trips to the South visiting supplier plants and discussing the possibilities of their doing business with Blue Motors, Barnes finally met Joseph Galway of the Galway Corporation. Galway was eager to diversify. His company looked efficient and well managed to Barnes. The workers were capable, conscientious, and well trained. Since Galway was the sole stockholder and had no need for dividends, finances were remarkably strong for a company of Galway's size (sales about $10 million in 1955). Galway was an excellent manager. There was only one problem. As in so many companies with a strong owner-manager, Galway Corporation was a one-man show. No one but Galway himself made any but minor decisions.

Barnes broke the market for stainless steel moldings when he brought Galway in as a supplier. Galway's original prices were nearly 20 percent lower than those charged by the northern companies. Galway had no difficulty in increasing its share of Blue Motors's business to 33 percent of total requirements, and it later got substantial contracts from Blue Motors's competitors. The northern companies could not compete. They tried to get their employees to either take wage cuts or boost their productivity. They were unsuccessful on both counts. To stay in business, they moved their plants South to get a more placid and lower cost labor supply. By 1961, they had managed to get their new plants operating efficiently and were making modest profits at prices that averaged about 5 percent above those charged by Galway.

Although materials and wage costs have climbed more than 20 percent since 1955, Blue Motors in 1961 calculates that its prices for moldings are slightly lower than they were six years before. This is only an estimate, of course. A direct comparison is not possible, since new moldings appear on almost every new model of car.

Blue Motors recently negotiated prices for the moldings for its 1962 models. Despite slightly higher labor costs, it was successful in persuading suppliers to forego price increases. But it met strong resistance when it tried to negotiate price reductions, and it wound up with no change in price. In 1962, as in 1961, Galway would again be Barnes's lowest cost molding supplier, with prices averaging 5 percent below those of its competitors.

On June 10, 1961, Barnes received a letter from Galway requesting a 10 percent general price increase for the 1962 moldings. The letter said that the reason for the increase was higher costs of labor and materials. Barnes wrote Joseph Galway and asked him to substantiate the increase, since he knew of no increase in wage and materials costs since the contracts for the 1962 moldings had been negotiated three months earlier.

The following week Galway arrived at Barnes's office in Detroit accompanied by his Detroit sales representative, controller, and general sales manager. Galway had work sheets on which he had broken down what he claimed were the actual manufacturing costs of each molding, based on the most recent production run. Typical is the breakdown

of part CF-101172, the right rear quarter panel molding for Blue Motors'
Stardust sedan:

.32 lb. of stainless steel @ 46¢/ lb.	$0.1472
Labor.	.1600
Overhead.	.4900
Total manufacturing cost	$0.7972
Sales and administrative expense	.0797
Total cost.	$0.8769
Loss	(.0269)
Price.	$0.8500

Barnes was ready to talk to Galway. His purchase analyst, Roger
Spade, had prepared detailed cost estimates of the moldings. His breakdown of part CF-101172 was as follows:

.30 lb. of stainless steel @ 46¢/lb.	$0.1380
Labor–2.1 minutes @ 6.5¢/minute	.1365
Burden @ 250%	.3413
Total manufacturing cost	$0.6158
Sales and administrative expense	.0300
Total cost.	$0.6458
Profit.	.0720
	$0.7178
Estimated price	$0.7180

After exchanging pleasantries, Barnes said to Galway, "I'm glad you're
up in Detroit to discuss molding prices again. We have made a detailed
cost analysis, and frankly we think there's still plenty of room for price
reduction."

Galway replied, "That isn't what my records show. I know we're
the lowest-cost producer in the business—and you know it, too—and
we just can't make out at these prices. Here are my records to prove
it."

Galway's controller then produced detailed records of actual direct
labor and overhead costs for Spade and Barnes to examine. Spade immediately asked if he might study the records for a few days. Galway
refused. He said that his costs were actually nobody's business but his
own, and he didn't intend to let these detailed records out of his sight.
Spade then made a superficial examination of the records in the presence
of the others. He concluded that the records supported Galway's statement that he was losing money on Blue Motors's molding orders.

Spade and Barnes now pointed out that their orders were not issued
on a cost-plus basis. They said their estimates showed that an efficient
producer should be able to cut prices and still make money on Blue
Motors's orders. Galway asked them if they could support their claim.
Spade then showed Galway his own detailed estimates.

"That estimate looks mighty fine on paper," Galway declared, "but you've never had any experience running a molding factory."

Spade replied that he had spent some time in almost every molding plant in the country, including Galway's own, and that these figures were based on efficient operation of modern equipment not unlike that he had seen in the Galway plant.

The group then proceeded to compare estimates. The difference of .02 lb. in stainless steel usage was readily resolved. It turned out that Galway's costs were based on a size he had purchased some months before to protect himself against a steel strike. He agreed that his materials cost would drop to the $.1380 shown in Spade's estimate as soon as he started using stainless strip of exactly the right size.

The difference in labor cost between Galway's and Spade's estimates was all but resolved. Spade agreed that he had neglected to include all of the hand-polishing operations that Galway insisted were necessary to meet Blue Motors's inspection standards. But he claimed that total labor cost, including the polishing costs, should not exceed $.15. Galway finally agreed that $0.15 was a good target, provided that Barnes would get Blue Motors's quality control manager to visit the Galway plant and agree to accept parts with the polishing labor possible with a $0.15 direct-labor allowance.

Galway and Spade found it impossible to reconcile their differences on overhead and administrative expense. Spade claimed that these costs depended heavily on volume of production and that Blue Motors could not be held responsible for Galway's underabsorbence of overhead. Spade suggested that the reason that Galway's overhead was high was because his sales volume was off from the previous year. Galway had lost part of the business it had previously enjoyed from one of Blue Motors's competitors. Overall auto sales were off from the year before and auto manufacturers were using less molding on each car because of the increased popularity of compact cars, which had less "chrome" decoration.

Galway declared that the breakdown showed his actual costs, and that he knew full well he was the most efficient producer in the industry. He told Barnes that no "young punk" (meaning Spade) was going to tell him what his costs should be and how his business should be run. He said he expected an answer from Barnes when he returned to Detroit the following week.

Barnes knew that if he awarded any increase to Galway his other molding suppliers would undoubtedly hear of it and also ask for price adjustments. Negotiation with the others would be particularly difficult if Barnes were forced to give Galway a price increase that eliminated the differential between Galway and his competitors. Since Blue Motors had already announced that it planned no increase in auto prices on the 1962 models, any increase in costs would be a direct charge to profit.

Question

How should Barnes and Spade plan negotiations with Galway and the other molding suppliers?

CASE 17–2. HARRISON MACHINERY CORPORATION*

Conflict between reciprocity and "fair trade"

Harrison Machinery Corporation is a leading producer of equipment used in the construction industry. Much of the company's output is sold to contractors in the United States and abroad, but a substantial share is also sold to various manufacturers in the United States who use the equipment in their own maintenance and construction departments. Harrison has an integrated materials department. It is headed by a corporate materials manager, Ralph Hyde. Hyde directs a small staff at corporate headquarters and is also functionally responsible for materials management at the company's 13 decentralized plants. Each plant has its own purchasing agent or materials manager who reports to the plant or division manager.

Most purchases are made at the plant level, and Hyde is responsible only for broad policies and procedures. However, a substantial part of the corporation's purchasing is done at the corporate office. In general, most items that are sold on a "national account" basis are at least negotiated at corporate headquarters; on other items, Hyde's staff may actually issue purchase orders. To be handled by the corporate materials staff, an item must meet one of the following criteria:

1. More than one Harrison plant uses the item, and central purchasing can get a lower price by combining the requirements of several plants. For this reason and no other, the central staff at Harrison corporate headquarters buys various production parts that are common to a number of Harrison products.

2. The item is "customer sensitive." Corporate purchasing buys all products used in significant amounts which are manufactured by Harrison customers. The corporate purchasing staff works closely with the corporate marketing staff on reciprocal arrangements. For example, Harrison's steel purchases are awarded on the basis of reciprocal purchases of Harrison's products by the various steel companies. From time to time, Hyde has deviated from this policy. As he says, "I won't buy from a company just because it buys Harrison products. Every supplier, including suppliers who are already customers, has to earn our business and give us the quality, price, and delivery we want and need." But Hyde admits that since steel prices are identical and that all of the

---

major firms offer comparable quality and delivery, he winds up buying steel pretty much on a reciprocal basis.

On occasion, he has purchased foreign steel at prices 5 to 10 percent below those offered by American firms and so far has had no complaints from his American suppliers. One reason for this, Hyde is the first to admit, is that they just haven't known about it. None of his American suppliers is so well informed as to Harrison's precise needs that Hyde does not have some flexibility. The foreign steel purchases were made during a period when both the steel industry and its customers were girding themselves for an industrywide steel strike. So Hyde would have had a good excuse for buying the foreign steel had one of his steel suppliers heard about it.

Some of the commodities that Hyde's staff buys meet both criteria for central office purchase: it is not only the cheapest way to buy them but also a practical way for the company to earn "reciprocal credit" among its customers. Fluorescent light bulbs are a good example. Harrison spends about $90,000 per year on fluorescent light bulbs used in its various factories and offices. This business is split among three major light bulb producers, all of whom are Harrison customers. Traditionally, the division of business has been in direct proportion to the importance of the light bulb manufacturer as a Harrison customer. The division is based on the previous year's reciprocal sales. For example, Harrison is now buying about half of its bulbs from one of the three firms and the balance of the business is shared almost equally by the other two firms.

Harrison's sales records show that the three light bulb manufacturers purchase about $800,000 worth of Harrison products each year. Consolidated Electric accounts for 50 percent of this, while the other two manufacturers each purchase about $200,000 worth of Harrison products. Consequently, Harrison has traditionally divided its bulb purchases on a 50–25–25 basis, with Consolidated getting the lion's share. Harrison need not have divided its purchases so precisely. None of the three bulb manufacturers knew exactly what his relative importance was as a Harrison customer. As long as each got a reasonable share of the Harrison business, there probably would not have been any complaints. But Harrison had no incentive to do anything other than give its customer its fair share of reciprocal business. All three manufacturers offer excellent quality and service and charge identical prices.

By buying directly from the "national sales office" of each of the three firms, Harrison is able to get the maximum discount. This discount brings Harrison's prices down to a level that is only about 10 percent higher than that which the light bulb manufacturers charge their own distributors.

Harrison formerly bought bulbs from local distributors. However, several years ago, the bulb manufacturers set up national accounts sales offices that catered especially to the needs of large corporations like Harrison that operated plants all over the country. These industrial users were often more important as customers than many distributors and they had long been pressing the bulb manufacturers for more favorable prices. Moreover, the large users do not need many of the services offered by the distributor, and the bulb manufacturers can enjoy bigger profits if they bypass their distributors on such sales. Sales to national accounts also give the bulb manufacturers valuable statistics so that they may know if they are getting their share of reciprocal sales from their suppliers.

The distributor in Harrison's area felt the loss of business keenly when Harrison switched over to buying directly from the light bulb manufacturers. Six months ago, this distributor presented one of Harrison's buyers with an attractive proposition which Hyde finally approved. The distributor agreed to sell light bulbs to Harrison at a price that was only 5 percent above the distributor's cost and 5 percent below the price charged Harrison by the bulb manufacturers. The distributor pledged Harrison to confidence, however. His agreement with the manufacturer requires him to sell light bulbs according to a price schedule that is set by the manufacturer. The schedule allows the distributor approximately 25 percent over cost for most accounts. The distributor can do business with Harrison for much less because of Harrison's enormous volume. Also, this represents marginal business to him and any profit he makes is "gravy." Both Harrison and the light bulb distributor benefit from the new arrangement and, of course, Harrison is continuing to use its customers' products even though it is not buying them directly.

However, Consolidated Electric, the biggest light bulb manufacturer, recently asked Hyde why he was no longer buying its light bulbs. The national accounts sales manager of Consolidated politely pointed out that Consolidated was continuing to buy Harrison's products and he could see no reason why Harrison should not reciprocate. He asked Hyde if he had any reason to consider Consolidated's service or quality to be inferior to that of its competitors. As he put it, "I don't think you should buy our products just because we buy your products. However, as long as our price, quality and service are as good as our competitors, I think you should definitely consider us when you are buying fluorescent light bulbs. Yet, our records show that you have not bought a single bulb from us for six months now. What is wrong? If our service or quality has fallen down we want to hear about it. On the other hand, if it hasn't, I think you owe us some explanation."

Question

What are the issues in this case? How can Hyde best resolve them?

18

Cost-reduction techniques

THE BEST-MANAGED materials departments have continuing cost-reduction programs. They would have them even if it were possible to negotiate the lowest possible prices for every purchased item. Price negotiation is only one of many contributions the materials department can make to reduce costs. Others include:

1. Design or specification changes that permit suppliers to manufacture at lower cost.
2. Materials substitution, either to reduce the cost of material or to secure a superior material with no change in cost.
3. Reduction of the number of items carried in inventory through standardization or through weeding out obsolescent material.
4. Application of analytical operations research techniques that permit costs to be reduced with no change whatever in prices paid for materials or transportation services.
5. Purchase of materials and equipment that reduce labor costs or boost efficiency of materials management operations in other ways.

VALUE ANALYSIS

One of the most widely accepted cost-reduction techniques is value analysis. The term was coined by L. D. Miles, manager of value analysis services at General Electric Company in 1946. Others use the terms "purchase analysis" or "purchasing research" to describe cost-reduction activities that are substantially the same as Miles's value analysis.

There are almost as many specific definitions of value analysis as

555

there are value analysts. But few would quarrel with this general definition:

Value analysis is the study of the relationship of design, function, and cost of any product, material or service with the object of reducing its cost through modification of design or material specification, manufacture by a more efficient process, change in source of supply (external or internal), or possible elimination or incorporation into a related item.[1]

The objective of value analysis is to get more value from an item in terms of function. As the examples in Figure 18–1 graphically show,

FIGURE 18–1
Examples of value analysis

This push button was made as a screw machine part. Research among suppliers turned up one that could cold head the part from aluminum wire. Cost of the item dropped from 19 to 2 cents.

Readily available zinc die-cast nuts were successfully substituted for acorn brass nuts turned out on screw machines. Use of a standard reduced cost from $12.24/M to $5.76/M.

 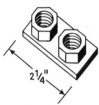

This machined clamp bar cost 32 cents. The design was changed so that the item could be made from a stamping with two nuts resistance welded on. New cost: 8 cents, plus $350 for tools.

A rolled thread specialist studied this steel J-bolt and suggested the words "cut thread" be removed from the drawing. The part is bought now for 1.5 cents as against 11.7 cents—an $80,000 saving.

Courtesy General Electric Co.

the value analyst seeks to perform a function at lower cost. The function of the J-bolt in Figure 18–1, for example, is performed equally well whether the threads are rolled or cut. But there is an enormous difference in cost between the two processes; switching from cut threads to rolled threads reduces cost by nearly 90 percent.

---

[1] Dean Ammer, "What Value Analysis Is All About," *Purchasing*, May 1957, p. 38.

Organizing for value analysis

While every firm can benefit from value analysis, only the bigger companies can afford full-time value analysts. At present, no more than a few hundred companies have them; some of these, however, are fairly small companies. For example, the A. C. Gilbert Company of New Haven, Connecticut, has a value analyst in its purchasing department even though it spends only $6 million a year for purchased parts and materials. In some cases, it may be economic to hire a value analyst in a company with a volume of purchases as small as $2 million to $3 million, provided that the company buys many parts and has frequent design changes.

According to experienced practitioners, a full-time analyst should be able to save more than eight times his salary even in a small company. Even so, only very large companies in the process industries tend to have full-time analysts. One reason is that opportunities for savings are limited to nonproduction materials. There are no production parts in the process industries, and it is difficult to save through value analysis on basic raw materials.

The staff function. Anyone can apply value analysis principles: buyers, manufacturing engineers, design engineers, and others. However, some special training is necessary before an individual becomes proficient at value analysis, and it is best carried on by someone who is free from the distractions of other duties. For these reasons, value analysis is normally organized as a separate staff activity,[2] except in small firms that cannot afford to hire a full-time analyst. Typically, the chief analyst reports directly to the director of purchases or the materials manager. The value analysts usually work on value analysis projects of their own and also coordinate value analysis activities of other materials personnel.

The typical value analyst has several projects of his own to work on at all times. He periodically reports his progress on existing projects and also suggests new projects. In addition, he might instruct other materials personnel in value analysis techniques and assist in getting their ideas approved by all the departments involved.

When a value analysis project is completed, a written report usually is submitted to all interested parties. Figure 18–2 shows a typical value analysis report. The Celanese Corporation saved $1,490.25 by changing its specification for cresylic acid. Before the change was approved, it was analyzed by the Celanese laboratory, and the accounting department audited the savings estimate to make certain it was realistic.

Value analysis committees. The committee approach to value analysis is particularly well suited to the small company that cannot

---
[2] For example, the research specialists shown in the organization chart in Figure 4–5 in Chapter 4 could be responsible for value analysis.

FIGURE 18–2

Value analysis report

COMPLETED COST REDUCTION PROJECT
PURCHASING DEPT.   GEH-1479 (4-58)

COMMODITY

Cresylic Acid (meta para feed)

TYPE OF REDUCTION	PROJECT STARTED	PROJECT COMPLETED	LOCATION	PROJECT NUMBER
☒ A ☐ B	Nov., 19—	March, 19—	Point Pleasant Plant	12

DESCRIPTION OF COST REDUCTION

By special arrangement with Productol Company samples of certain mixtures were obtained and evaluated in the plant laboratory. It was found that certain blends would result in a feed equal to that which normally would be priced to us at $1.15 per gal. and that components would be priced so that a savings would be realized. Therefore, 26,000 gals. was purchased for blending and it is hoped this can be repeated once each quarter in the future.

20,392 gals.   Grade 25A (MP) @ $1.15/gal less freight equalization $20,163.73
5,961 gals.   Grade 2876 (special xyl) @ $0.90/gal less freight
                                                      equalization   4,413.28
26,353 gals.   Blend equal to Grade 25 (MP) delivered for $24,577.01
Normal cost @ $1.15/gal. less $4,238.69 (freight equalization)
                                        would have been   26,067.26

                                    One time saving $ 1,490.25

No extra handling occurred since materials could be mixed either in feed or product tanks.

ONE TIME SAVINGS	AMOUNT OF SAVINGS		
	RECURRING SAVINGS		
$1,490.25	ANNUAL VOLUME	UNIT SAVING	ESTIMATED ANNUAL SAVINGS
			$6,000.00

	OFFSETTING COSTS		
CAPITAL	EXPENSE	INVENTORY LOSS	TOTAL OFFSETTING COSTS
$	$	$	$ None

DEPARTMENT AFFECTED	OTHER PARTICIPATING DEPARTMENTS		
Production	Plant Manager. Laboratory, Central Purchasing, Operations Control (NYO),		

AUDITED BY: *Accounting* DEPARTMENT   *JBL* *QEA.* INDIVIDUAL

SUBMITTED BY: *H. O. Vrombio,* Mgr. Operations Service Dept.   4/22/—
                INDIVIDUAL   TITLE   DATE

Courtesy Celanese Corp. of America

Many companies have standard forms for reporting value analysis projects. This report of the Celanese Corporation of America is typical.

afford a full-time analyst. The typical value analysis committee includes members from the purchasing, production, product engineering, manufacturing engineering, and cost departments. It might meet once or twice a month. Specific projects—for example, a commodity group such as steel stampings or specific products—are selected for analysis at each meeting. Each member of the group studies the project in advance of the meeting. The combined and varied skills of the group frequently lead to ideas that cut costs.

The committee form of organization works well in value analysis. It helps generate ideas that no individual member of the group could probably come up with on his own. However, after the committee meets, someone must see that these ideas are thoroughly investigated and, if possible, applied. If a company has full-time value analysts, they can handle the necessary follow-through. Otherwise, the chairman of the committee must administer the program to make certain that the committee's recommendations are acted on.

Value analysis projects often take months to bring to a successful conclusion. In some cases, almost every major department in the company must approve suggestions before they are incorporated. As a result, committee members cannot simply meet, dream up new ideas, and then go back to their regular jobs and forget all about value analysis until the next meeting. Someone must follow through ideas if anything is to be accomplished.

Value analysis techniques

Tests for value. One of the simplest—and sometimes one of the most effective—value analysis techniques was developed by General Electric Company. Each part being analyzed is subjected to "Ten Tests for Value." The value analyst asks himself these questions as he studies the part:

1. Does its use contribute value?
2. Is its cost proportionate to its usefulness?
3. Does it need all of its features?
4. Is there anything better for the intended use?
5. Can a usable part be made by a lower cost method?
6. Can a standard product be found that will be usable?
7. Is it made on proper tooling, considering the quantities used?
8. Do material, reasonable labor, overhead, and profit total its cost?
9. Will another dependable supplier provide it for less?
10. Is anyone buying it for less?

If a part "flunks" any of these tests, the analyst makes a more detailed investigation. For example, the high-cost design of each part in Figure 18–1 would flunk one or more value tests. The push button fails tests 2, 4, 5, and 9, and the acorn nut fails tests 2, 5, and 6. What tests would the clamp bar and J-bolt fail?

As the tests for value imply, the value analyst believes in creative skepticism. He is never satisfied that any item has the ideal design and is being produced at the ideal cost. An item that may pass all the tests for value today may fail one of them tomorrow as lower cost processes and designs are discovered. The value analyst must keep abreast of all new developments. He must also be versed in cost estimating in order to evaluate the effect of new developments on the cost of the items he analyzes.

Comparative analysis. Sometimes the analyst can get more leads on potential savings by making comparative analyses of similar items rather than by applying tests of value individually to each item. For example, the analyst might review all of the die castings his company buys. Simple comparison might give him some clues. Castings should get progressively more expensive as their weight increases, special features such as inserts are added, usage decreases, and so on. Whenever there is an inconsistency, the analyst investigates.

Some analysts plot the weight of like parts against their cost per pound. As indicated in Figure 18–3, the price per pound should progres-

FIGURE 18–3

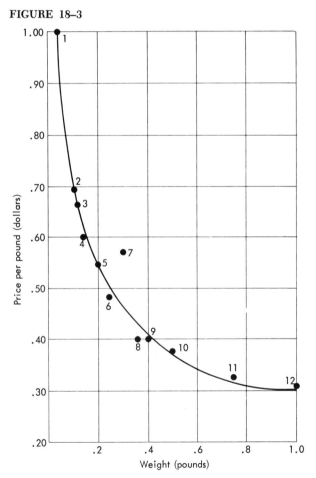

Weight analysis is a widely used value analysis technique for comparing like items. As weight increases, cost per pound should decrease. Parts that do not follow the pattern (such as No. 7 above) are analyzed in more detail.

sively decrease as weight increases. Parts that do not follow the curve (for example, part 7 in Figure 18–3) are not necessarily poor values, since they may have special features that justify a cost premium. But they should be investigated, and in many cases they are good prospects for a detailed individual analysis.

Even if the cost curve fails to locate any good prospects for value analysis, it still may be useful. The curve can be used to make quick cost estimates of new items. Suppose that a new part weighs 0.8 pound and is similar to the parts in Figure 18–3. A glance at the chart shows that this part should cost about 31 cents per pound, so the unit price must be about 25 cents (0.8 lb. × 31¢/lb.).

Cost of each property. Another basic technique of value analysis is to determine the cost of each property of the item. For example, if the purpose of the item is to cover something, its cost per square foot might be calculated and compared with the cost per square foot of other materials. If the item does some other job, it might be analyzed in terms of the properties needed. For example, light bulbs can be analyzed on the basis of their cost per watt-hour of life, electrical capacitors on the basis of their capacitance, and so on.

A variation of this approach is to evaluate an item on the basis of its cost per function. This approach would work well with the machined clamp bar in Figure 18–1. This bar performs the function of holding two bolts or studs. The cost of this function with the old design is 32 cents. This cost is high, since ordinarily nuts will hold studs or bolts for a cost of only a penny or two each. This approach would naturally lead the analyst to look for a way in which nuts could perform the function at lower cost. The result is the 8-cent design that uses two standard nuts fastened to a small plate.

Brainstorming. The advertising industry originated brainstorming as a technique to stimulate creative thinking of advertising copy. Its applications broadened after Alex Osborne of the advertising firm of Batten, Barton, Durstine & Osborne popularized the technique.[3]

Brainstorming is a group activity in which four to ten persons participate. Each participant applies his imagination to a single problem and is encouraged to propose any idea that occurs to him, no matter how ridiculous it may seem. Every idea is duly noted by the chairman; none is criticized during the meeting lest this inhibit the creative power of the participants. The hope is that one idea, even though it may be ridiculous, will touch off other suggestions, which ultimately will lead to a genuinely original and workable solution to the problem.

Brainstorming is as useful in value analysis as it is in creating advertising copy. Value analysis ideas often are inhibited by preconceived notions and prejudices. The value analyst gets used to being told, "Why change, we've been doing it this way for twenty years," "It just won't

---

[3] Alex Osborne, *Your Creative Power* (New York: Charles Scribner's Sons, 1948).

work," and the like. He often gets results only if he can remove all preconceived ideas about how a product should be made and concentrates on the function of the item. Brainstorming can provide an ideal environment to shake out old prejudices and look at a problem in a new light. If some of the ideas proposed are a little wild, they can readily be discarded in the evaluation stage following the brainstorming session. Most sessions last no more than a couple of hours (the participants generally are exhausted by then). Usually dozens of ideas are generated, and only one good one is needed to solve the problem in question.

Buyer-supplier seminars. Even small companies often have thousands of suppliers, and each supplier usually knows far more about his specialty than any of his customers do. One of the most profitable value analysis techniques is to draw on this pool of supplier know-how for cost-reduction ideas. Buyers try to do this in their day-to-day contacts with suppliers. Some companies go further: They organize supplier seminars to which they invite top executives from all the companies with which they deal.

The seminars are usually held at the buyer's plant or at a nearby hotel. They almost always feature a luncheon or dinner at which company executives introduce new products, outline corporate objectives, and discuss future plans and their effect on suppliers. But the real purpose of the meeting is to permit suppliers to tour the company's facilities and study its products in detail.

Some companies make up special product displays in which they have every detail part of their product spread out on a table or attached to a display board. Suggestions for improvement are solicited from suppliers, even for items that the supplier does not manufacture. The results can be amazing. For example, a few years ago the Whirlpool Corporation held a supplier seminar at its home laundry plant in St. Joseph, Michigan. Suppliers made more than 300 suggestions for improvements. About a dozen of these were acceptable, and they resulted in unit savings of more than 90 cents on every combination washer-dryer made by the company.

Some companies that have held successful supplier seminars try to stimulate supplier suggestions on a continuing basis. They do this with permanent product displays in which they show all of the major components of their product. One of the "Big Three" auto companies goes even further: Its product display room has components of not only its own cars but competitors' products as well.

Selling value analysis

Value analysis is a staff activity. The value analyst can accomplish nothing without the help and cooperation of those with whom he must work—buyers, engineers, suppliers, and others. A considerable part of his time must be spent in arousing enthusiasm for cost reduction and value analysis in everyone he contacts.

To suppliers. Seminars do a lot to stimulate supplier interest in value analysis, but some companies do even more. For example, many have published booklets in which they explain their problems to suppliers. Others go in for gimmicks like that used by Aerosol Techniques, Inc., shown in Figure 18–4. International Minerals & Chemicals Corpora-

FIGURE 18–4

Aerosol Techniques, Inc., uses this simulated theater ticket to stimulate supplier cost-reduction ideas. "Tickets" were mailed to all suppliers and also were available in the reception room of the company offices. They have space on the back for the supplier to note his ideas.

tion puts to good use a blackboard in the room where suppliers wait to see the company's buyers. On the board is lettered a "Dear Mr. Supplier" message. One such message read: "What have you contributed to IMC's Purchasing for Profit Program this year? Be prepared to give a definite written answer by July 1."

Many companies have had considerable success with vendor value awards (see Figure 18–5). If a supplier has been consistently helpful with cost reduction, he gets a certificate in recognition of his achievement. Suppliers receive the certificates gladly both because they like to know that their efforts are appreciated and because they can use the certificates as a selling tool. What better advertising is there than the written testimony of satisfied customers?

Suppliers are catching on to the fact that value analysis can be a tool they can use to boost sales and profits. Their sales message in effect becomes, "Buy from me because I can help you save with value analysis." Suppliers whose products are suitable offer value analysis service to their customers. Figure 18–6 shows typical promotional material used by a supplier to promote his value-oriented approach to customer problems.

A few firms go even further. One foundry in the South invited its

FIGURE 18-5

An Award of

VENDOR VALUE

conferred upon

_____ABC Supply Company_____

In recognition of consistently helpful service and cooperation
in the field of cost reduction.

The Purchasing Department of

_____John Manufacturing Company_____

makes this award in conformance with the principles appearing below.

"The Vendor's Know-How is the Buyer's Greatest Asset".

___Jan. 2, 19—___   ___Richard Roe___
Date   Purchasing Agent

_____

The tests of a

VENDOR'S VALUE

1. He knows precisely how the customer uses his product.
2. He makes every effort to help the customer with standardization.
3. He tries to help customers cut costs by eliminating unnecessary features in his products.
4. He knows all his own capabilities and how they can help the customer.
5. He stays informed on—and tries to top—features of competitive products.
6. He tries to simplify his products before he's forced into it by the customer.
7. He stays informed on new processes and materials, and discusses them with the customer.
8. He tries to package his products in the cheapest and most efficient way.
9. He promotes the idea of blanket orders and other devices to help the customer cut costs.
10. He tries to give each customer the best possible price on his product.

Copyright 1957, Purchasing Magazine

Some companies present vendor value awards to suppliers who have made outstanding contributions to their value analysis programs. Suppliers like the awards because they can use them as a selling tool with new prospects.

FIGURE 18–6

TI MATERIALS SYSTEM **APPLICATION REPORT**

M4-2

TEMPERED TOP-LAY

APPLICATION:

Contact blade assembly with contacts over and under.

ORIGINAL DESIGN:

Fabricate spring blade and then stake rivet and washer to it.

Disadvantages: Mass of rivet head is limited by shank diameter, thus restricting current capacity of assembly; staking operation often breaks web; difficulty of achieving symmetry by double heading, especially with less ductile materials like silver cadmium oxide.

TI DESIGN:

Bond contact segments to top and bottom of blade material and then fabricate by conventional tooling.

Advantages: Greater design freedom since contact mass is not restricted; reduced costs inherent in "over and under" design; higher quality because the bonding process continuously monitors bond strength.

DESIGN NOTES:

1. Tri-layer contacts (copper core as heat sink, for example) reduce need of precious metal to fill contact gap.

2. When design requires segment thickness less than ⅓ the width, consider use of clad profile-shaped wire rather than strip.

3. The TI bonding process yields a composite with segment stock parallel to grain of base material. Where this is objectionable, 45 degree blanking or use of base metal without grain orientation is recommended.

TEMPERED TOP-LAY

... featuring continuous bonding of two contact segments to thin–gauge material without compromise in temper.

OLD METHOD

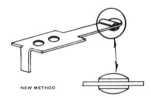

NEW METHOD

ORIGINAL DESIGN
Rivet and washer staked to pre-fabricated blade.

TI DESIGN
"Over and under" contact segments bonded to base material prior to fabrication.

METALS & CONTROLS INC.
34 FOREST ST. • ATTLEBORO, MASS.
A CORPORATE DIVISION OF
TEXAS INSTRUMENTS
INCORPORATED

HCG B5460-2 8-64
Printed in U.S.A.

Typical example of value analysis promotional material developed by suppliers who offer a marketing approach oriented to value analysis to their customers.

customers to a three-day value analysis seminar at which they had one of the top analysts as a guest lecturer. The foundry made no attempt to sell customers on its products. In fact, they even charged tuition to the customers to attend the seminar. "We benefit even though there was no sales pitch," the foundry's president explained "because if our customers learn about value when they're visiting us, they will associate us with the concept and we're bound to benefit eventually."

The Defense Department now includes value analysis clauses in many of its contracts. These give contractors tangible incentive to cut costs. Expenses of the value analysis program are allowable as costs, and the supplier is permitted to add to his profit part of the savings made with successful value analysis programs.

Within the company. The value analyst must not only sell value analysis to others in his company; he must also sell himself. Almost all of the value analyst's proposals will mean stepping on someone's toes. His forte is change, and this means, in effect, proving that what is being done now is not too good. If the value analyst does not tread carefully, his ideas will inevitably be taken as implied criticism of those responsible for the older, higher cost approach.

Value analysts sell themselves and their ideas with talks and presentations in which they explain value analysis concepts to others in the organization. Value news bulletins are another means of doing this (see Figure 18–7). Their objective is to stimulate enthusiasm for value analy-

FIGURE 18–7

Purchasing Cost Reduction
⸺ News Letter

CENTRAL PURCHASING DEPARTMENT • CHARLOTTE, N. C.

July 1, 1959   No. 59-3

At the halfway mark in 1959, our "buying for value" policy has resulted in a savings of almost $200,000 in purchased materials. This indicates the responsibility each of us feels to contribute to Corporate profits. For the second half of the year, it is the considered opinion of most economists that we are facing a period when prices will be firmer and higher and an increased demand will be evident in some lines. This may make cost reductions more difficult to accomplish and will call for greater effort on our part to do the best buying job possible.

COST REDUCTION

Cost Reductions for the first six (6) months of this year are running at a rate well ahead of our target level with a notable increase in savings during the second quarter. Number of projects completed together with total savings compare with target as shown below:

	1st Qtr. 1959	2nd Qtr. 1959	Total 1st 6 Mos. 1959	1st 6 Mos. Target-1959
Projects Completed	66	63	129	---
Savings	$74,933	$123,797	$198,730	$157,000

As shown on the Detail Sheet (attached) the increase in activity, as measured by the number of projects completed, during the months of May and June is particularly creditable in view of the heavy buying load currently being experienced at all locations.

Courtesy Celanese Corp. of America

A few companies keep interest in value analysis at high pitch by publishing cost-reduction newsletters in which they report progress and discuss value analysis techniques.

sis. They review the cost-reduction progress that has been made to date and also single out individuals who have made outstanding contributions to value analysis. Full-time analysts usually try to give all the credit for successful projects to others. That way they get better cooperation on future projects.

STANDARDIZATION

Value analysis programs are usually designed to reduce the cost of an item. Standardization programs may eliminate the item entirely. For example, Figure 18–8 illustrates what happened as a result of a standardization program at Bryant Electric Company, Bridgeport, Connecticut. The company reviewed 1,447 items carried in stock and found it could eliminate 794 of them. Unit costs were reduced because fewer items were bought in larger quantities; carrying costs were reduced because of a net reduction in inventories. Total savings are estimated at $102,000 in the two years since the program was started.

Bryant's experience with standardization is not unique. For example, before it set standards, one large Cleveland auto parts manufacturer stocked several hundred different types of oil and other lubricants in its plants. Each production supervisor requisitioned the precise type of oil he thought would best serve his needs. A standardization study showed that less than 50 different types of oil were needed to do every possible lubrication job in the company's factories. As a result, the company uses 80 percent fewer types of lubricant than before. Inventories are lower, and prices have also been reduced because the company can buy each type of lubricant in larger quantities.

The standardization program

The examples cited above are dramatic, but they illustrate why standardization is important in industry. Standardization is essential to a modern mass production economy. Almost every major industry has standards to classify its products. The American Standards Association coordinates and promotes standardization of thousands of products for the 122 technical societies and trade associations and the 2,000 companies that are its members.

A standard is defined as "that which has been established as a model to which an object or an action may be compared."[4] The purpose of a standard is to provide a criterion for judgment. Companies are concerned with standards both for the products they design and for the materials designed by their suppliers. In the former case, the company's

---

[4] *Industrial Standardization—Company Programs and Practices,* Studies in Business Policy No. 85 (New York: National Industrial Conference Board, 1957), p. 7.

FIGURE 18-8

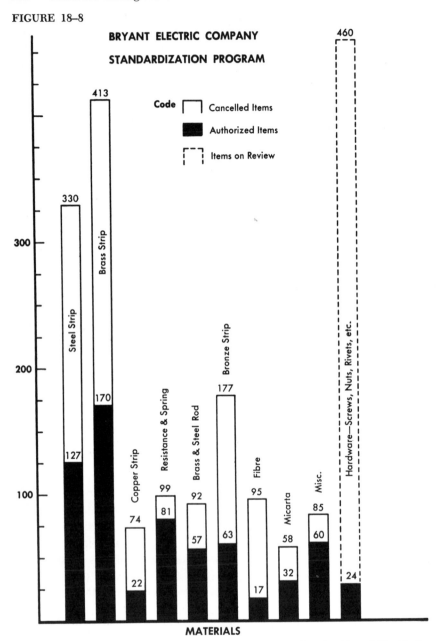

BRYANT ELECTRIC COMPANY
STANDARDIZATION PROGRAM

Code

☐ Cancelled Items

■ Authorized Items

⌐ ⌐ Items on Review

MATERIALS

Courtesy Bryant Electric Co.

The standardization program of Bryant Electric Company was an outstanding success. In two years the number of items stocked was reduced by more than 50 percent, and savings totalled $102,000.

engineer may create his own standards or work to the standards of an industry. For example, when an engineer in an office-furniture factory designs a drawer pull, he may work within industry standards for strength, shape, durability, and so on. But his final design is unique—although it may become one of the company's own standards for drawer pulls. The materials the company buys usually are in accord with the supplier's industry standards. For example, the engineer may specify that the drawer pull be made of steel specified in an American Iron & Steel Institute standard.

Companywide standards. Although industry standards help prevent unnecessary variation in specifications, the needs of our economy are so great that each industry usually offers many more standard products than any single consumer can possibly use. In addition, many industries try to sell by brand name rather than by industry standards. For this reason, many companies establish their own standards, not only for products they design for themselves but also for products designed by their suppliers. For example, Chrysler Corporation has set its own standards for the carbide tool inserts it buys (see Figure 18–9) by specifying the exact dimensions and grades it requires. If Chrysler did not go to the trouble of doing this, it would soon find itself using far more different types of carbide insert than it does at present.

When there are no written standards, each user of material has carte blanche to specify what he needs. For example, note that Chrysler has five different types of square carbide insert. No. SQ–122 has a $\frac{3}{8}$-inch square cross section with .2156-inch clearance and $\frac{1}{32}$-inch corner radius. The comparable dimensions for the next size, SQ–163, are $\frac{1}{2}$ inch, .386 inch, and $\frac{3}{64}$ inch, respectively. If one size is too small, the next size is used. But what would happen if there were no standards? Each user would calculate the dimensions that most closely suited his needs. Eventually Chrysler would wind up buying and stocking several dozen different sizes of insert with dimensions intermediate between those of SQ–122 and SQ–163.

The experiences of Bryant Electric, the auto parts company, and numerous other companies prove that there is a natural tendency for companies to stock more and more different items to do the same job. Each user likes to get the item that is *exactly* what he wants and will not settle for the nearest standard item if he can help it. As a result, standardization is a continuing process. Periodic reviews of every item are essential to root out the items that are no longer needed.

How to standardize

Bryant Electric's standardization program is fairly typical. Decisions were made by a committee that included representatives from every major department. The chairman was the company's standards engineer.

FIGURE 18–9

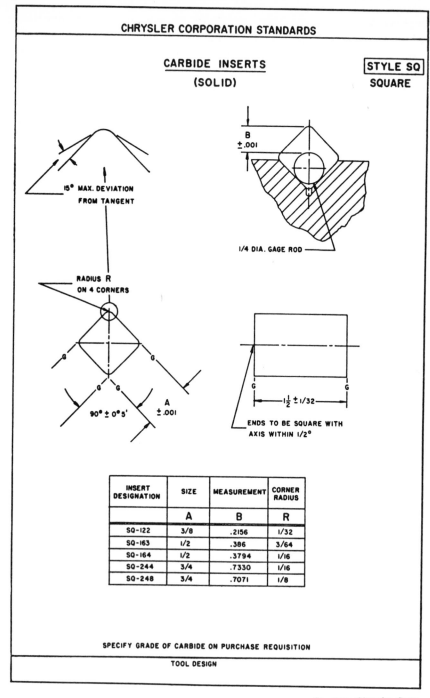

CHRYSLER CORPORATION STANDARDS

CARBIDE INSERTS
(SOLID)

STYLE SQ
SQUARE

15° MAX. DEVIATION
FROM TANGENT

B
±.001

1/4 DIA. GAGE ROD

RADIUS R
ON 4 CORNERS

90° ± 0° 5'

A
±.001

G G
G G

G   G

$1\frac{1}{2} \pm 1/32$

ENDS TO BE SQUARE WITH
AXIS WITHIN 1/2°

INSERT DESIGNATION	SIZE	MEASUREMENT	CORNER RADIUS
	A	B	R
SQ-122	3/8	.2156	1/32
SQ-163	1/2	.386	3/64
SQ-164	1/2	.3794	1/16
SQ-244	3/4	.7330	1/16
SQ-248	3/4	.7071	1/8

SPECIFY GRADE OF CARBIDE ON PURCHASE REQUISITION

TOOL DESIGN

Courtesy Chrysler Corp.

A company can limit the number of items it stocks by developing its own specifications. For example, this standard indicates that Chrysler Corporation uses only five sizes of square carbide insert.

The first step in the program was to list all inventory items in detail on large $(14'' \times 24'')$ accounting sheets. (Figure 18–10 shows a part of Bryant's listing of various types of brass strip.) Listed initially for each item was a description of the material, its usage, and how it was

FIGURE 18–10

							Material Substitution				
Material Description	Ann.	Part	Dwg.	Part	Cat.	Dwg.					
Thk Width Length PDS	Act.	No.	No.	Desc.	No.	No.	Thk Width Length PDS				Remarks
016x5/32xC Brass 2676-6	570	E27214	14514C	Bracket	FS40	14526A	016x5/32 Brass 2676-6 Bracket width				
		E27844	15207C	Bracket	FS40	14540C					5/32 required
016x255xC Brass 2676-6	100	E21236	9922C	Contact	20	9920L	016x1/4 Brass 2676-6 1/4 width o.k.				
		E21237	9921B	Contact	20	9920L					
016x255xC Brass 2676-10	360	E29438	15914D	Brush	207	8051L	016x1/4 Brass 2676-10 Ex. Hd. Tem-				
		E29439	15913D	Brush	204	8014L					per required
		E29440	8030C	Contact	200	15455L					
		E20654	8979C	Contact	4013	B01076					
		E21287	10015B	Brush	5128	10012A					
		E21679	10213C	Contact	310	14141A					
		E24024	8979C	Contact	15	Cat.card					
016x255xC Brass 2676-4	48	E28254	15600C	Strap	5269	15599A	016x1/4 Brass 2676-6 1/2 hd. o.k.				
016x255xC Brass 2676-11	924	E20126	8943C	Brush	706	6294B	016x1/4 Brass 2676-10 -10 o.k. per				
											6/10 lab rpt.
016x7/16xC Brass 2676-8	10	E2737	3125A	Washer	392	4957B	Slit from 1" wide 2676-5 1/4 hd.o.k.				
016x13/32xC Brass 2676-10	2376	E2757	7671C	Contact	70	1800A	016x13/32 Brass 2676-10 Ex.hd.				
		E4238	6340C	Contact	4229	4299A					Temper
		E13064	7671C	Contact	4190	Cat.card					Required
		E16123	6180C	Contact	421	10783B					
		E18213	6180C	Contact	421	10783B					
		E22163	10459C	Contact	337660	4299A					
016x15/16xC Brass 2676-3	500	E17718	7152C	Housing	746	SK521	016x15/16 Steel 7300-5 Steel o.k.				

BRYANT MATERIAL STANDARDIZATION PROGRAM

Courtesy Bryant Electric Co.

The first step in a standardization program is to list all items stocked. Bryant Electric Company did this for the brass strip listed above and changed much of the 0.255-inch-wide material to a standard 0.25-inch width.

used. (Potential substitutes for the material were listed later.) The committee then reviewed the list to make certain that there were detailed buying specifications for each item, and possible substitutions were proposed.

Economic substitution. Even if a substitute is technically feasible, it is not necessarily economic to use it. The economics of standardization are not complex. All one need do is compare cost of acquisition and carrying cost before the substitution was made with costs after it was made.[5] For example, suppose an item costs $0.10 and 500 units per year are used. Its substitute, which is also stocked, costs $0.105. Assume that ordering cost is $10 and carrying cost is 24 percent. If the higher

---

[5] These terms and this type of analytical approach were discussed in some detail in Chapter 10.

cost item is substituted, purchase cost is increased by $5 per year (500 units × $.005). But, assuming that the item formerly was purchased once a year, ordering cost by $10 and carrying cost by $6 (24 percent of $25).

Items not needed. A similar approach can be used for obsolescent items. An item is worth eliminating entirely if the carrying cost which probably will be incurred before it is used exceeds the purchase cost less the scrap or salvage value. Many well-managed companies consider an item obsolescent if it has not been used for the past 12 months and there is no immediate need for it. If they can sell the item back to the supplier or to another company that needs it, they do so, even if they must take a 50 percent loss to make the sale.

Standardization programs are designed primarily to root out unneeded inventories, but they also can bring direct savings on material. Most companies must stock thousands of repair parts for their equipment. Standardization programs can locate duplicate inventories—cases, for example, where a spare fan belt or ball bearing stocked for one manufacturer's machine is identical with a spare part for a different manufacturer's machine. Stocks of such components can be combined by tracing each component back to the standards of the original manufacturer. Once the buyer knows who made the component, he is foolish to pay a premium price for it to the equipment manufacturer. He can buy at much lower cost directly from the original manufacturer's distributor.

The Tennessee Valley Authority made substantial savings in buying spare parts by doing just this. For example, it used to buy replacement V-belts for certain pulverizing equipment from the equipment manufacturer (who, in turn, had purchased them from a V-belt supplier). The price of the special steel-cable V-belts was $12.08 each from the equipment manufacturer. It was reduced to $5.67 by buying directly from the V-belt manufacturer. The TVA and numerous private companies have made comparable savings on other items. Most manufacturers can make enormous profits (markups of 400 to 500 percent are not uncommon) on their service-parts business. Smart buyers often can circumvent the equipment manufacturer and buy at lower prices directly from his supplier.

Specials sometimes cheaper. Another by-product of a standardization program is that it sometimes leads a company back to "specials." Standardization is not always economical. It pays to consider a special when:

1. *The standardized item is price fixed.* Sometimes the manufacturers of a standard item set an extremely high price on a semiproprietary product. Steel tubing is a good example. Hardly any major user of parts made from steel tubing can afford to pay the official posted steel-mill price. Instead, larger users either make their own tubing or they buy tubing fabricated to their specifications—and thereby avoid paying the standard price for the standard item. In other cases, the semistandard

item is sold under a brand name and priced like a proprietary product. Costs may be reduced 50 percent or more by developing unique specifications so that suppliers can quote a special price without upsetting the market for their branded products.

2. *Volume is large.* A standard item is relatively cheapest when the user's needs are limited. When volume increases, it often pays to use a special that is designed exclusively for one product. Specials may also offer a marketing advantage. If a company's product is made from standard items, the customer can buy his repair parts anywhere. If they are specials, the user may be forced to buy the parts from the original equipment manufacturer at high prices that yield substantial profits. Users may not be happy about this, of course, but there is no denying that the practice is prevalent and presumably profitable.

LINEAR PROGRAMMING

Sometimes costs can be reduced without making any changes whatever in design, price, or number of items carried in inventory. A few materials managers are giving their companies a competitive edge with operations research techniques. Two techniques are especially applicable to materials management: linear programming and simulation.

As the term implies, linear programming can be applied to any problem in which the mathematical relationships are linear (i.e., in algebraic terminology, $a + bx = c$.) Typical are problems with these characteristics:

1. One plan of action must be selected from many possible plans. For example, which of 200 parts used in the product should be manufactured, and which should be subcontracted?
2. The objective is to maximize or minimize a critical factor, such as to minimize the cost of buying silicon.
3. Relationships in the problem are linear. This means, for example, that it costs ten times as much to buy ten gallons of paint as it does to buy one gallon.
4. The resources you can use in achieving your objective are limited. Perhaps the amount of steel you can buy in any one month is limited by your storage capacity.

In materials management, linear programming can be applied to make-or-buy, inventory management, scheduling, and physical distribution problems. To date its most popular materials management application has been in transportation and physical distribution. For example, Western Electric has applied linear programming techniques to 39 different items that have a total annual purchase volume of $84,500,000. Its savings with the technique have totaled almost $2,500,000, or 3 percent, on the items for which it has been used.

The transportation problem

Many large companies buy material from several suppliers that is shipped to several plants. In considering how business is to be divided, they must take into account not only the price charged by each supplier but also the cost of shipping the material to each plant.

Take the case of the hypothetical Rocket Chemical Corporation, which has three plants, A, B, and C. Each plant uses a certain chemical that it buys in 100-pound bags. Requirements for the next three months are:

Plant A.	1,200 bags
Plant B	4,800 bags
Plant C	3,000 bags

Four vendors, W, X, Y, and Z, have agreed to supply this material. Each has a capacity restriction limiting the total amount he can supply during the next three months. The capacities and selling prices are as follows:

Vendor	Capacity (in bags)	Price
W	5,000	$30
X	2,500	25
Y	1,200	20
Z	1,000	15
Total capacity	9,700	

The costs of shipping from each vendor to each plant are:

Vendor	Plant A	Plant B	Plant C
W	$10	$5	$6
X	4	3	5
Y	1	7	6
Z	4	9	3

By adding the shipping costs to the selling prices, we can determine the cost per bag of material delivered from each vendor to each plant:

Vendor	Plant A	Plant B	Plant C
W	$40	$35	$36
X	29	28	30
Y	21	27	26
Z	19	24	18

The problem is to decide on the quantities to be purchased from each vendor and where they are to be shipped so that the plant's requirements will be met at overall minimum cost. If there were no restrictions on the amounts that could be purchased from each vendor, the problem would be simple. We can see that the lowest delivered cost for each plant is obtained by buying from vendor Z. The solution would call for buying the total requirements from vendor Z and nothing from the other vendors. Vendor Z, however, cannot supply the total requirement for any one plant, let alone for all plants. Therefore, this plan is not feasible, and we must analyze the problem further.

The first solution. The first step in solving the problem is to construct a grid like that in Figure 18–11, listing the unit delivered costs from

FIGURE 18–11

Plant / Vendor	A	B	C	D	Available
W	40	35	36	0	5,000
X	29	28	30	0	2,500
Y	21	27	26	0	1,200
Z	19	24	18	0	1,000
Required	1,200	4,800	3,000	700	9,700

each vendor to each plant and the total requirements of each plant. Note that in addition to plants A, B, and C we have also listed plant D. This is a dummy plant that is needed to balance out the problem. Also note that while we need only 9,000 bags of material, our vendors have the combined capacity to produce 9,700 bags. The extra 700 bags are assigned to the dummy plant D; the delivered cost to plant D is 0 since we won't actually be making any shipments to this plant.

To solve the problem, it is essential that each vendor ship his quota and that each plant (including dummy plant D) get its requirements. The first solution does not give the lowest cost plan, but it can lead to it. Figure 18–12 illustrates a typical first solution. Each vendor's capacity is allocated to each plant in sequence. Vendor W satisfies all of

FIGURE 18–12

Vendor \ Plant	A	B	C	D	Available
W	40 (1,200)	35 (3,800)	36	0	5,000
X	29	28 (1,000)	30 (1,500)	0	2,500
Y	21	27	26 (1,200)	0	1,200
Z	19	24	18 (300)	0 (700)	1,000
Required	1,200	4,800	3,000	700	9,700

plant A's and part of plant B's requirements; vendor X satisfies the balance of plant B's and part of plant C's needs; and so on. The final 700 units of capacity are assigned by vendor Z to the dummy plant D, so the sum of the shipments from each vendor equals the sum of the shipments received by the plants.

Cost of this solution is as follows:

```
Vendor W to plant A: 1,200 bags @ $40 . . . . . . .   $ 48,000
Vendor W to plant B: 3,800 bags @ $35 . . . . . . .    133,000
Vendor X to plant B: 1,000 bags @ $28 . . . . . . .     28,000
Vendor X to plant C: 1,500 bags @ $30 . . . . . . .     45,000
Vendor Y to plant C: 1,200 bags @ $26 . . . . . . .     31,200
Vendor Z to plant C: 300 bags @ $18 . . . . . . . .      5,400
Vendor Z to plant D: 700 bags @ $0 . . . . . . . . .         0
    Total cost . . . . . . . . . . . . . . . . . . . .  $290,600
```

Evaluation. Now we must make an evaluation to see if we have the lowest cost solution to the problem. This can be done by determining the net effect on cost of buying one bag through a vendor-plant combination different from those in our solution. For example, what happens to cost if we have vendor X ship one bag to plant A at a cost of $29? To do this, we must deduct from X's shipment to some other plant. If we deduct from B, we cancel one bag worth $28. If we replace the bag for B with a shipment from vendor W, the cost is $35. To stay within W's capacity, we must cancel a shipment to A costing $40.

Since we are considering adding one shipment from X to A, we retain our balance with these changes. The net effect on cost of these changes is equal to the sum of the costs of the shipments that were added less the sum of shipments that were eliminated. This gives $29 − $28 + $35 − $40 = −$4. In other words, by reallocating our shipments we have reduced net costs by $4.

The values for all the unused routes have been entered in Figure 18–13, and several of them are negative. Therefore, we can improve the plan.

FIGURE 18–13

Plant Vendor	A	B	C	D	Available
W	40 (1,200)	35 (3,800)	36 -1	0 -19	5,000
X	29 -4	28 (1,000)	30 (1,500)	0 -12	2,500
Y	21 -8	27 +3	26 (1,200)	0 -8	1,200
Z	19 -2	24 +8	18 (300)	0 (700)	1,000
Required	1,200	4,800	3,000	700	9,700

Total cost = $290,600

In general, to evaluate an unused route, add the unit cost shown for that route, move horizontally to a circled value in the same row, and deduct the unit cost. From there move vertically to a circled value in the same column and add the unit cost. Move along that row to a circled value and deduct the unit cost. Proceed in this way, alternately moving horizontally and vertically, adding and subtracting, until you are back in the same column as the unused route to be evaluated. Enter the sum of the additions and subtractions in the unused route column.

All the unused routes should be evaluated in this way. If it turns out that all the unused routes have positive values, this means that you already have the lowest cost plan and using any other routes would only add to the total cost. If, on the other hand, one or more unused routes have negative values, this means that the plan can be improved.

Solving the problem

Figure 18–13 shows that the largest negative value for an unused route is −19 for shipments from vendor W to plant D. We would like to change our plan to ship as much as possible by this route, as every bag shipped will save us $19.

To determine how much we can ship by this route without violating the restrictions on requirements and capacities, we proceed as follows. First, trace a path from WD horizontally to a circled value in the same row, then vertically to a circled value in the same column, continuing, as we did in evaluating unused routes, until we are back in the same column in which we started. This path will be:

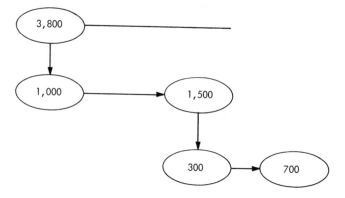

Let the quantity to be shipped by route WD be Q. Then, in order to keep within the restrictions of the problem, the amounts shipped by other routes in the path we have traced must be adjusted in the following way:

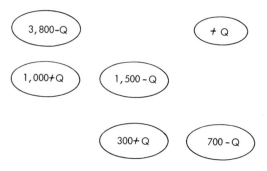

Q will be that amount that will just reduce one or more of the quantities being shipped under the first plan to zero without making any of the quantities negative. In this case Q will be 700, eliminating shipment from vendor Z to plant D.

Making the adjustments above, the new solution is shown in Figure 18–14. The total cost associated with this solution is $277,300, obtained

FIGURE 18–14

Plant \\ Vendor	A	B	C	D	Available
W	40 / (1,200)	35 / (3,100)	36 / -1	0 / (700)	5,000
X	29 / -4	28 / (1,700)	30 / (800)	0 / +7	2,500
Y	21 / -8	27 / +3	26 / (1,200)	0 / +11	1,200
Z	19 / -2	24 / +8	18 / (1,000)	0 / +19	1,000
Required	1,200	4,800	3,000	700	9,700

Total cost = $277,300

in the same way as the total in the first solution. This is $13,300 less than the first plan, which would have cost $290,600.

We determined before that we would obtain a saving of $19 per bag shipped over route *WD*. As our second plan calls for shipping 700 bags over this route, the saving is 700 × $19, or $13,300, which checks with our calculations above.

Evaluating the unused routes in the second solution, we find that some still have negative values, indicating that we can reduce the total cost further. The largest negative value for an unused route in Figure 18–14 is —8 for shipment from vendor Y to plant A. Proceeding as we did in changing the first to the second solution, we find that we can ship 1,200 bags from vendor Y to plant A. In adjusting the amounts shipped by other routes, shipments will be eliminated from Y to C and from W to A. The total number of routes used will be reduced from seven to six. In order for us to be able to evaluate the unused routes, however, we need to have a solution that uses a number of routes equal to the number of vendors plus the number of plants less one, or 4 + 4 —1 = 7.

To meet this requirement, enter ϵ (epsilon), meaning a very small quantity, in one of the routes that was eliminated. In Figure 18–15 we have entered it in route WA. In arriving at the final solution, ϵ is treated

FIGURE 18–15

Plant Vendor	A	B	C	D	Available
W	40 ϵ	35 4,300	36 -1	0 700	5,000
X	29 -4	28 500	30 2,000	0 +7	2,500
Y	21 1,200	27 +11	26 +8	0 +19	1,200
Z	19 -2	24 +8	18 1,000	0 +19	1,000
Required	1,200	4,800	3,000	700	9,700

Total cost = $267,700

just like any other quantity being shipped. Once the final solution is achieved, however, ϵ will be ignored.

The largest negative value for an unused route in Figure 18–15 is −4 for shipments from supplier X to plant A. Changing the plan according to our previous methods involves adding ϵ bags to route XA and WB and deducting ϵ bags from routes WA and XB (see Figure 18–16). As ϵ is very small, this does not change the cost of the plan, and the total costs associated with the third and fourth solutions are both $267,700. However, this does help us in finding the final solution, as we see that of the unused routes in Figure 18–16, only one, WC, has a negative value.

The final solution. To obtain the fifth solution from the fourth, we add 2,000 bags to routes WC and XB and deduct 2,000 bags from routes WB and XC. This plan has a total cost of $265,700, a saving of $24,900 over the first plan developed. We now find that all unused routes have positive values. No further improvements are possible; we now have the minimum total-cost plan. If any of the unused routes had zero values, it would mean that though no better plans were available there was another plan just as good.

FIGURE 18–16

Plant \ Vendor	A	B	C	D	Available
W	40 +4	35 (4,300 +ϵ)	36 −1	0 (700)	5,000
X	29 (ϵ)	28 (500 −ϵ)	30 (2,000)	0 +7	2,500
Y	21 (1,200)	27 +7	26 +4	0 +15	1,200
Z	19 +2	24 +8	18 (1,000)	0 +19	1,000
Required	1,200	4,800	3,000	700	9,700

Total cost = $267,700

The final plan can be transcribed directly from Figure 18–17 by simply ignoring the shipments to dummy plant D. The plan is:

1. Buy 4,300 bags from vendor W and ship 2,300 to plant B and 2,000 to C.

FIGURE 18–17

Plant \ Vendor	A	B	C	D	Available
W	40 +4	35 (2,300 +ϵ)	36 (2,000)	0 (700)	5,000
X	29 (ϵ)	28 (2,500 −ϵ)	30 +1	0 +7	2,500
Y	21 (1,200)	27 +7	26 +5	0 +15	1,200
Z	19 +1	24 +7	18 (1,000)	0 +18	1,000
Required	1,200	4,800	3,000	700	9,700

Total cost = $265,700

2. Buy 2,500 bags from vendor X and ship to plant B.
3. Buy 1,200 bags from vendor Y and ship to plant A.
4. Buy 1,000 bags from vendor Z and ship to plant C.

Other applications

While the above example is a reasonably typical application of linear programming to materials management, it is only one of many possibilities. Linear programming is applicable to any problem where a fixed amount of resources must be allocated to several users. It can be used in scheduling allocated machine time to various products and in make-or-buy decisions. However, as is now obvious to the reader of the foregoing section, the calculations are complex and tedious and it is easy to make errors. In practice, a computer is now commonly used to solve real-life linear programming problems. "Canned" programs are available to reduce costs; even so, as much as $5,000 to $10,000 worth of staff and computer time may be needed to solve a single problem. Thus, linear programming is too complex a technique to be used except by large organizations for major problems. When applied to them, however, savings can be considerable.

MONTE CARLO SIMULATION

Basic principles

Simulation, in contrast, can probably be applied occasionally even by smaller materials management organizations. Simulation is a device that permits the materials manager to predict what will happen to a system when demand changes. At any given time, the materials management is concerned with efficient use of a fixed bundle of resources subject to fluctuating and often unpredictable demands, or "input." While the input may follow some pattern, any particular unit of input occurs at random. For example, while a materials manager may be able to estimate fairly accurately the total annual work load of his receiving department, he may not have the vaguest idea how much work the department will have next week at 11:30 A.M. Each input of work (in this case, a truck making delivery of purchased materials) arrives more or less at random. For short periods of time, for no reason that can be explained, the receiving department may be confronted with far more deliveries than it can handle. Other periods may be extremely quiet.

Queue forms. Similar patterns may occur in other activities where there is a tendency for a queue to form. For example, sometimes there may be a line of workers waiting for service from a single nonproduction stores clerk. Other times, the clerk may be able to work uninterruptedly on records for an hour or more without any interruption from any employee who wishes to requisition material.

This same queuing pattern occurs with machines as well as men. In a job shop, a machine may be idle for a day or two. Although no one planned it that way, dozens of different parts in process that may have required work on this machine simply do not reach this stage of the process at that particular time. In contrast, on another day the same machine may be flooded with more work than it can possibly handle, and a queue forms. The ebb and flow of demand for particular machines can occur, despite the most careful planning, because of random variations in the factors (machine time on previous operations, changes in priorities, and so forth) that determine when the demand for service will actually occur.

These unpredictable changes in input pose a real dilemma for the manager. Delays can be prevented only by having available manpower and/or machines that will be idle except during periods when a queue tends to form. For example, a company may have only 1,000 hours of work per year for a particular machine. If demand for the machine is reasonably regular, it can obviously get along easily with just one machine. But if demand fluctuates unpredictably, the company may find that occasionally so much work piles up in front of this particular machine that it becomes a bottleneck that holds up other operations. In this case it may pay to purchase at least one additional machine, even though it may be idle 11 months out of 12. Conversely, the company may have two partially utilized machines and discover that the saving made from eliminating one machine more than offsets and loss that results from the long queues that occasionally form in front of the single machine that remains.

Study model. Simulation is the device that permits a company to measure what will happen when a particular group of resources is subject to input that varies at random. The materials manager first creates a "model" that represents numerically what he thinks happens in his system. Then he simulates operation of the system by subjecting it to random variations of input, using the Monte Carlo technique (so called because the probability of any particular event is no more predictable than a particular outcome on an honest roulette wheel).

Application to dispatching

For example, suppose that you operate a job shop using a dispatching procedure similar to that described in Chapter 8. There is one major difference, however. Because your job shop has hundreds of machines it is impossible for you to visualize exactly what happens as work flows through it. You can fairly easily do this if your shop has just a few machines, as in the oversimplified models in Chapters 7 and 8 did.

You run a wide variety of work through you shop, and the routing of almost every item is different. Your overall utilization of machinery is no more than about 50 percent. That is, your average machine is actually making money for you only about 20 hours of the single 40-hour shift which you presently find adequate to handle all of your orders. You would like to increase your utilization of equipment, but you know from past experience that it is very difficult to get a much higher rate of utilization. If business increases substantially, you will probably have to do the extra work on either overtime or a second shift. Bottlenecks will inevitably develop that will prevent you from increasing you equipment utilization much beyond its present 50 percent on each shift worked.

Bottleneck identified. In fact, you already seem to be plagued by bottlenecks at several stages of your process; a centerless grinder operation seems to be a particular problem. This operation is one of the last performed on a number of jobs that pass through your shop. It is impossible to predict precisely when any particular job will reach the grinder. A study of your job dispatching system shows that orders requiring centerless grinding are released to the first work station (which is not centerless grinding, of course) at fairly regular intervals. But since each job requires widely varying amounts of work at various work stations, it is impossible to predict when a job will arrive at the centerless grinder. As a result, your four centerless grinders are sometimes out of work. At other times, there are substantial backlogs, and your foreman claims that delays in completing centerless grinding have caused serious scheduling problems in subsequent assembly operations.

You can find nothing in your dispatching procedure that causes these occasional pileups of work. In fact, they seem to occur at random and to be completely beyond your control. One possible solution to the problem is to buy another centerless grinder, but you wonder if this will be profitable since, obviously, there will be periods when this costly equipment is idle. In addition, when a pileup of work does occur, it is sometimes so big that a single grinder would not make much headway in working off the backlog rapidly.

Basic steps. You decide to try a simulation to determine (1) exactly how work does flow to your centerless grinders, and (2) whether or not a fifth grinder would solve your problem. You would then follow the steps outlined below.

First, you go through your records and study past demand for centerless grinder time. As long as your product mix does not change, the past is a reasonable guide to the pattern you can expect in the future.

Your records reveal that you have required a total of 27,000 hours of centerless grinder time in the past 1,000 working days, or an average of 27 hours per day. Since your four grinders have a capacity of 32 hours per day, they are obviously adequate as long as you are willing to let backlogs of work build up during periods when demand is temporarily greater than 32 hours per day. But, of course, it is these backlogs that are apparently your problem. So you proceed to analyze the distribution of demand. You discover that new demand on any single day varied between zero hours and a maximum of 45 hours. For convenience in analysis, you divide daily demand into eight groups, with each group embracing a five-hour interval, as shown in Column 1 of Figure 18–18.

FIGURE 18–18
Probable demand for a specialized machine

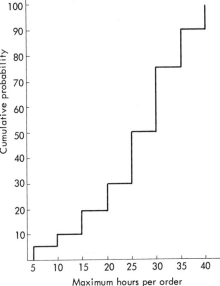

(1) Demand hours machine time)	(2) Number of occurrences	(3) Prob- ability	(4) Cumulative probability
0–5	50	0.05	0.05
5–10	50	.05	.10
10–15	100	.10	.20
15–20	100	.10	.30
25–30	200	.20	.50
30–35	250	.25	.75
35–40	150	.15	.90
40–45	100	.10	1.00
	1,000	1.00	

Average 27.0 hours demand per day

You then count the number of days during the 1,000-day period that demand fell within each of these clusters. Thus Column 2 of Figure 18–18 shows that during 50 of the past 1,000 days, total new work arriving in the centerless grinder department amounted to less than five hours for each day. These 50 days represent 5 percent of the 1,000 days that you study (Column 3). Similarly, on another 50 days the daily input of new work to the department ranged between 5 and 10 hours; on 100 days, it ranged between 10 and 15 hours; and so on.

Second, you then calculate the cumulative probability of the various inputs, as indicated in Column 4. Thus there is a 5 percent probability of demand ranging between 5 and 10 hours and a cumulative probability of 10 percent that demand will be between 0 and 10 hours. Similarly, there is a 10 percent probability of a daily demand for 10 to 15 hours of grinder time and a cumulative probability of 20 percent that demand will range between 0 and 20 hours.

Third, you then plot the cumulative probabilities that you have calculated in a chart like that in Figure 18–18. This chart indicates that your four machines, whose daily capacity is 32 hours of work, should be able to get out work the same day it is received at least half of the time. The other half of the time, work arriving at the grinders on a particular day will exceed capacity. There will be some carryover to a succeeding day when new work is less than 32 hours and the backlog can be reduced.

Monte Carlo in action. You are now ready for the simulation. In real life, you would probably use a computer, although with a little patience calculations for this simple example can be carried out manually, as illustrated in Table 18–1. Two-digit random numbers, which

TABLE 18–1
Simulation of demand for centerless grinder time

(1)	(2)	(3) Backlog with four grinders		(4) Backlog with five grinders	
Random number	Mean hours of demand	Hours	Days	Hours	Days
98	42.5	10.5	0.3	2.5	0.1
93	42.5	21.0	.7	5.0	.3
79	37.5	26.5	.8	2.5	.1
54	32.5	27.0	.8	–	–
15	12.5	14.5	.5	–	–
57	32.5	15.0	.5	–	–
80	37.5	20.5	.6	–	–
81	37.5	26.0	.8	–	–
59	32.5	26.5	.8	–	–
13	12.5	7.0	.2	–	–
43	27.5	2.5	.1	–	–
6	2.5	–	–	–	–
90	42.5	10.5	.3	2.5	.1

can be copied from any statistics text if you do not generate your own in a computer, are shown in Column 1 of Table 18–1. Each random number determines how much work will reach the centerless grinders on a particular day. For example, 98 is the first random number drawn. It means that on that day, the amount of work reaching the centerless grinders is in the 98th percentile.

Figure 18–18 indicates the number of hours of machine time that a demand in the 98th percentile would require. For convenience, various possible demands have been assigned together to eight clustered groups in Figure 18–18. Note that the greatest possible values—those lying between 40 and 45 hours—occur 10 percent of the time and that these fall between the 90th and 100th percentiles, as indicated in Column 4 of Figure 18–18. Thus, the first random "arrival" of 98 has a value between 40 and 45 hours. You arbitrarily assume the mean value of this range, 42.5 hours, for ease of calculation. (Any error we make will be automatically canceled out.) You enter 42.5 hours in Column 2 of Table 18–1. You then calculate the effect of this initial input on operations. If you have four grinders, your capacity is 32 hours per day. Therefore, this initial order exceeds capacity by 10.5 hours. As shown in Column 3, you end the day with a backlog of 10.5 hours, which is equal to about 0.3 days' production.

If you use five grinders, your capacity is 40 hours of grinder time. The initial demand of 42.5 hours leaves a backlog of 2.5 hours or about 0.1 days production, as shown in Column 4.

The second random number you draw is 93. This also falls between the 90th and 100th percentiles of the table illustrated in Figure 18–18, so the second day's demand also has a mean of 42.5 hours. With four grinders, the backlog increases to 21.0 hours and with a five-grinder setup it becomes 5.0 hours.

In Table 18–1, a series of random numbers under 90 follows. This causes the backlog of five grinders to be eliminated by the end of the third day. For the next nine days, there is insufficient work to keep five grinders busy until, finally, another job comes along that is in the 90th percentile, so that the five grinders are fully employed and the day ends with a 2.5-hour backlog. In contrast, the simulation shows that with four grinders, there is almost always some carryover of work to the following day. With the four-grinder setup, the backlog is wiped out on only one day.

Conclusions. The simulation shown in Table 18-1 has not been carried out for a sufficient number of transactions to be useful for a real-life problem. However, if the pattern shown in the 13 transactions in the table essentially repeats itself, we could reach these conclusions:

1. With five grinders, work would normally be completed the same day it was received and there would never by more than a very small carryover of work until the following day. On a typical day, however, at least one of the five grinders would be idle for the entire day.

2. With four grinders, work would sometimes be finished on the same day it was received. Just as often, however, it would carry over until the following day. Under ordinary circumstances, production control could assume that work that arrives in the grinder department on the morning of one day will have left the department at least by the afternoon of the following day.

3. In view of the above, it is highly unlikely that the company would buy a fifth grinder. The cost of owning it would almost certainly be greater than the possible saving from a modest reduction in in-process inventory. The simulation would also prove that if there is a problem with pileups of work in the grinder department, the cause is nonrandom and, therefore, the problem can be solved with a change in dispatching or some other procedure over which management has control.

A real-life simulation in production would be far more complex than the example shown above. In most cases the materials manager would want to simulate the operation of a plant's complete production control system under various conditions. A computer would be essential and, in fact, "canned" programs are available to perform such simulations. The underlying principle, however, would be no different from the over-simplified example shown in Figure 18–18 and Table 18–1.

Other applications

Simulation can be used for any materials management problem that involves waiting. For example, a materials manager may want to simulate operation of a receiving or a purchasing department. In both cases, the flow of work is irregular and, during peak periods, a queue of either purchase requisitions or stores requisitions would form if capacity were temporarily exceeded. The same technique can be applied to any type of materials-handling equipment. For example, the best way to determine whether a materials manager needs five fork trucks or four of them is to simulate what would happen in each case, following a procedure like that illustrated above. Simulation can prevent costs from rising as a result of adding equipment or manpower that really is not needed, or it can be used to weed out redundant manpower and equipment.

CAPITAL EQUIPMENT ANALYSIS

The materials manager is both a user and buyer of equipment like fork trucks. Most of the time, however, he is a buyer of capital goods that are used by others in the organization. Regardless of who uses it, equipment should meet two basic purchase criteria: engineering and financial. The materials manager relies almost entirely on the judgment of users of the equipment for engineering evaluation. The financial evaluation of equipment is primarily a responsibility of the organization's controller. However, materials management should also play a major role in the economic evaluation of proposed equipment purchases. In addition to being a user of certain types of equipment, the materials manager should also serve as catalyst to acquaint others in the organization with equipment that might help reduce costs.

The materials department normally buys capital equipment to specifications developed by the company's manufacturing engineering department. The engineers play a more active role in buying equipment than they do in the purchase of parts and materials. But otherwise the process is essentially the same; the principles discussed in Chapters 12 through 14 apply equally to equipment and other items.

The materials department has a special interest in capital goods purchases, however, because of the opportunities they offer for cost reduction. It is particularly interested in the economics of equipment that is acquired to permit the company to make something it formerly purchased, but it also should participate less directly in all cost-reduction programs that involve capital investment.

MAPI formulas

Buying decisions for capital equipment are usually based on an analysis prepared by the company's finance staff which, in turn, is based on data submitted by manufacturing engineering and purchasing. Usually, the decision is based on a comparison of the reduction in operating cost resulting from use of the new equipment with the investment required. The Machinery & Allied Products Institute (MAPI) has developed numerous formulas to evaluate the profitable purchase of equipment. The application of one such formula by the Norton Company, a leading manufacturer of abrasives, is illustrated in Figure 18–19.

Norton is considering the purchase of a new handling system for abrasive grain. Norton estimates that the new equipment will reduce labor and other costs by $96,000 a year. On the other hand, the older equipment has operating advantages amounting to $14,500 a year because of lower taxes, less power consumption, and less maintenance. Net operating advantage of the new equipment thus is $81,500 ($96,000 — $14,500). To this must be added the capital cost (prorated over 15 years) and interest of $2,500 to cover needed improvements on the old equipment. These capital charges plus the $81,500 adverse operating cost of the old machine total $85,670, compared with an annual charge of $93,000 for interest and depreciation on the new equipment. Thus costs are theoretically $7,300 higher if Norton buys the new equipment. Norton decides to buy it anyway because it feels the intangible benefit of improved product quality with the new equipment is worth $7,300.

Note that Norton's profits will actually increase when it buys the new machine. Included in the "cost" is an allowance of 10 percent for interest. If we assume that Norton buys the equipment with idle cash, its profits increase because the 10 percent interest charge was included in the cost calculation.

Note also that if Norton were willing to accept a 5 percent return on capital, the interest cost of the new equipment would drop to $34,460. The "adverse minimum" on the new equipment would be $58,540 per year, and on the old equipment (giving effect to an interest rate reduction on the $25,000 investment in improvements) it would be $84,420. Thus the company would theoretically save $25,880 per year by investing in the new equipment instead of incurring a $7,300 cost increase to improve quality.

The MAPI formulas are very useful in comparing the relative desirability of investing in various types of equipment. The interest rate

FIGURE 18–19

```
                                                           Sheet 1 of 3 Sheets
  1926
                        NORTON COMPANY                Est. No.  7831
                   EQUIPMENT REPLACEMENT ANALYSIS     Date  4/20/54
  Line
  No.                          PRESENT                                 PROPOSED
   1  Description  Present Grain Handling System    Description Pl. #2 Portable Grain
        in Plant #2                                 Tanks, Bldg. Add.; TBS & Magnorite
   2  Salvage value                  $   0          System
                                                    Cost installed            $ 689,200
   3  Age                          40    yrs.       Service life              *   31    yrs.
   4  Equipment Number                              Est'd. salvage value      $   0
   5  Department           Pr. Whl.-Abr.#2          Salvage ratio                 0     %


      ADVERSE MINIMUMS


   6  Operating inferiority (line 29)   $ 81,500    Total cost installed       $ 689,200
   7  Loss salvage value - next year        0       Chart %                       31    %
   8  Interest - salvage value              0       Interest %                    10    %
   9  Proration - capital addition 25,000  * 1,670  Total %                             %
  10  Interest - capital addition @ 10%   2,500

                                                        *
  11           ADVERSE MINIMUM $ 85,670   (A)       ADVERSE MINIMUM $ 93,000   (B)
  12  GAIN FROM REPLACEMENT (next year) (A - B)      $ - 7,300
```

OPERATING ADVANTAGE (next year)		
	PRESENT	PROPOSED
Income Advantages		
13 **X** Superiority of product	$	$
14 Increased output		
15 **X** Other		
Cost Advantages		
16 Direct labor)		* 75,000
17 Indirect labor)		
18 Fringe benefit cost (20 %)		15,000
19 Maintenance	* 6,000	
20 Supplies Cap Replacement		1,000
21 Tools		
22 Spoilage Reduction in Rejections due to streaks		5,000
23 Down time		
24 **X** Floor space		
25 Power	500	
26 Property taxes and insurance	* 8,100	
27 **X** Other		
(8½ year payback period DCF return on investment 11½%)*		
28	$ 14,500 (C)	$ 96,000 (D)
29 Net Operating Advantage (D - C)		$ 81,500 (to line 6)

```
  Remarks: This analysis has been computed without appraisal of intangible benefits
  checked above, and discussed in detail on attached sheet. Acceptance of this
  proposal is tantamount to evaluating all these benefits at a minimum of $7,300
  Recommendation: per year. This is considered satisfactory.
               Approval recommended.
  Signed  _____           Approved _____

  Date  4/20/54                                     Date _____
```

Norton Company uses an analysis technique developed by the Machinery & Allied Products Institute to determine whether or not it pays to replace capital equipment.

can be varied to reflect the company's availability of capital and willingness to invest in a not too certain future.

Other approaches

The MAPI method is probably the most widely used approach to capital equipment analysis. It is easy to use and leads its users to the correct investment decision most of the time. However, the method has its weaknesses. All versions of the MAPI method involve comparison of a first-year return with the amount of the investment. But, of course, a company does not buy new plant and equipment just for the first-year return; the return is spread out over a number of years. In effect, a company gives up cash today for new equipment in order to get a series of cash returns that are spread out over the life of the equipment. The problem is to relate the value of future payments to present costs.

Proponents of the MAPI method claim that its alleged weakness in considering only first-year results is unimportant. The future is so uncertain, they argue, that it is hard enough to estimate what will happen in the first year, let alone in succeeding years. Also, they point out that highly subjective factors such as higher quality are major determinants of investment decisions, and there is no point in being more precise numerically if the heart of the decision is really qualitative. Nevertheless, the MAPI method has lost popularity gradually as the controllers' offices of more companies have become staffed with business school graduates trained in the application of more complex methods.

Payback period. One simple calculation is almost always made, regardless of what other methods are used. Payback period is calculated by relating the cost of the equipment to the profit it earns and then estimating the number of years it takes for the equipment to pay for itself. The basic objective is to purchase the equipment with the fastest payback period. Suppose, for example, that a company can eliminate an employee whom it pays $5,000 per year by buying a machine that costs $10,000. If there were no income tax, the machine would pay for itself in two years. The corporate income tax and various tax credits make calculations more complicated.

To keep things from getting too complicated, assume that the machine has a ten-year life and is depreciated on a straight-line basis with a depreciation charge of $1,000 per year. In addition, assume that there is a corporate income tax rate of exactly 50 percent.

To figure the payback period, first deduct $1,000 for depreciation from the $5,000 return. This leaves a $4,000 gross profit from the machine. Half of this profit is taxable, so after corporate income tax there is a net profit of $2,000. The cash flow is equal to the $2,000 net profit plus the $1,000 depreciation, or $3,000. Therefore, the machine should pay for itself in about three and one-third years.

Discounting future payments. Many companies use a more sophisticated approach: discounted cash flow. They assume that a minimum return must be made on their capital, and an investment is not made if this standard is not met. For example, a lot of companies assume that they must earn a 20 percent return after tax on new investment in plant and equipment. They then discount the value of future cash flows to the present at this rate. Table 18–2 shows a discounted cash flow analysis at 20 percent per year for the $10,000 machine described

TABLE 18-2
Present value of future payment of $1,000 discounted at various rates°

Year	6%	9%	12%	15%	18%	20%	22%
1	$0.971	$0.956	$0.942	$0.929	$0.915	$0.909	$0.901
2	.914	.874	.836	.799	.764	.751	.731
3	.861	.799	.741	.688	.639	.621	.593
4	.811	.730	.657	.592	.533	.513	.482
5	.764	.667	.583	.510	.446	.424	.391
6	.719	.610	.517	.439	.372	.350	.317
7	.677	.557	.459	.378	.311	.290	.258
8	.638	.509	.407	.325	.260	.239	.209
9	.601	.466	.361	.280	.217	.198	.170
10	.566	.425	.320	.241	.181	.164	.138

*Calculations assume that return from the investment is continuous throughout the year. For example, a payment of $1 for an entire year would be continuous if you receive roughly 0.3 cent per day starting January 1 and continuing until December 31. This is, of course, a closer approximation to actual operating conditions than discounts based on the return being received at the end of a period (as would be true of deposits in a savings bank, for example).

above. The machine yields a net cash flow of $3,000 per year. This return is then discounted to present value at 20 percent.

The discounting factor assumes that the return is spaced out evenly during the year. For example, the payment of $1 spread out at regular intervals over the course of the next year (for example, at the rate of about 0.4 cent for each of the 250 working days in the standard year) has a present value of 90.9 cents discounted at a rate of 20 percent per year.

Similarly, a payment of $1 spread out over the second year would have a value of 75.1 cents. Thus, a $3,000 cash flow spread out over the next year has a present value discounted at 20 percent equal to .909 times $3,000, or $2,727. Applying this approach over the ten-year life of the machine gives a $13,377 discounted present value. Since this compares favorably with the $10,000 that must be laid out to buy the machine, the purchase would be approved.

Management can vary the discount rate to reflect its relative availability of capital. If it is very hard pressed for funds, it can raise the discount rate and, automatically, the most attractive projects will be picked. The materials manager, like all other executives in the company, should always be alert to new opportunities for profitable investment and for cost reduction.

PREPRODUCTION PURCHASE ANALYSIS

The newest and least direct cost-reduction technique is preproduction purchase analysis (PPA). All the cost-reduction techniques discussed so far are designed to reduce the cost of existing parts and materials. Preproduction purchase analysis aims to reduce the cost of an item before it is produced, while it is still being designed. It encompasses all value analysis techniques and makes considerable use of the cost-estimating techniques discussed in Chapter 16.

Preproduction purchase analysis was first developed in industries where rapid product obsolescence made value analysis impractical. If a product is never going to be made again, it is pointless to make a detailed value analysis of it. With PPA, materials personnel work closely with product designers and follow every stage in the evolution of a new product, from the point at which ideas áre first developed to the point where production drawings are made and purchase orders issued.

The objective of PPA is to steer the designer into concepts that result in maximum value. This may mean suggesting that a product be made of a lower cost material. More likely, it means that the designer will be guided into components that cost less because they are standard for some other product.[6] This approach works especially well for companies making extremely complex and expensive products in small volume—computers, missiles, ships, and so on.

The technique also works well in the mass production industries. For example, Ford Motor Company's Ford Division has 180 purchase analysts working on PPA. They begin to deal with new car models about three years before actual production commences, and their cost estimates guide stylists in preparing preliminary designs. More detailed estimates are made from clay models of the new cars. By the time production blueprints are prepared, which may be a year or two after the design was first proposed, purchase analysts have highly refined estimates that often are accurate within a fraction of a penny. These estimates permit engineers to select the lowest cost designs and materials long before funds must be committed to tooling. PPA is essentially cost prevention rather than cost reduction, since the higher cost design that would be approved in the absence of PPA never becomes a reality.

Cases

CASE 18–1. CONSOLIDATED ELECTRIC COMPANY*

A problem in value analysis

Consolidated Electric Company has designed a system to measure impurities of gases. It anticipates that this system will have wide application among natural gas pipeline and distribution plants, chemical producers, and others. The system picks up a sample of gas (see Figure

---

[6] In many cases, this approach results in the designer's specifying a component that theoretically costs more but actually costs less because it is standard with a number of manufacturers. To cite a simple case, suppose the ideal design indicated that a screw should be $^{127}/_{128}$ inch long. This screw theoretically would be cheaper than one that is $1''$ long, but naturally the 1-inch screw is standard and is available in large volume at prices that may be a fraction of the cost of a $^{127}/_{128}$-inch screw.

* This case study is based on an actual value analysis problem encountered by the General Electric Company.

FIGURE 18-20

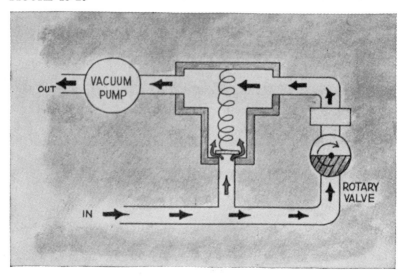

18-20) that is sucked into a chamber where its composition is measured. The sample is then discarded and the process is repeated. During the moment when one sample is being measured, the rotary valve is closed. This causes the gas to force the relief flipper valve up (see Figure 18-20), providing an alternate and continuous path of flow. As the rotary valve opens for a new sample, the spring closes the flapper and shuts off the alternate path.

FIGURE 18-21

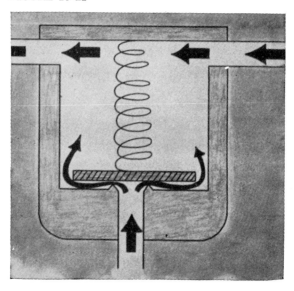

FIGURE 18-22

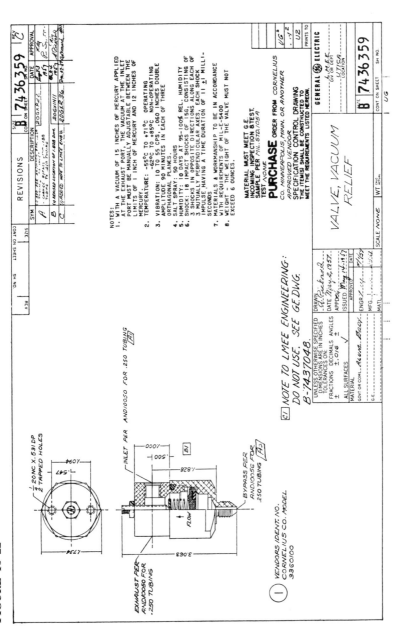

Roberts Company, one of Consolidated's regular suppliers of special valves, has designed a relief valve, model No. 3360100, for the system. Stated simply, the function of the relief valve is to provide a continuous flow. Its function is illustrated schematically in Figure 18–21, and engineering details are shown in Consolidated's drawing No. 7436359 (see Figure 18–22).

The valve has an aluminum body (see illustrations in Figures 18–23 and 18–24) and male and female half sections. It is assembled with mating threads that are made airtight by means of a Neoprene rubber "O" ring. The female body has a male AN (i.e., made to Army-Navy standards) air-line fitting, while the male body has two threaded holes for accepting AN fittings and two for stud mounting. The female body has two decals, one indicating the direction of flow and the other identifying the supplier. The flapper has a molded Teflon surface that seats on a knife-edge diameter to provide a closed-valve position. It is held in place and can be adjusted with a spring, stud, and locking nut. The assembly contains ten individual parts.

FIGURE 18–23   **FIGURE 18–24**

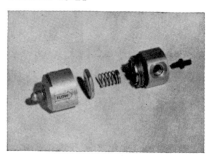

Roberts Company has quoted a unit price of $73.20 for an order of 546 pieces.

Questions

1. Does Roberts's quote represent good value?
2. How might costs be reduced through value analysis?

CASE 18–2. MID-STATES TELEPHONE COMPANY

Use of linear programming

Mid-States Telephone Company uses large amounts of "K" rural wire to support telephone lines. The wire is stored in five warehouses scattered throughout the company's service area. The company buys the wire from four sources, and because of price, quality, capacity, and other factors, business has been divided among them as follows:

Supplier	No. of reels of wire purchased per year	% of purchases
Allen	1,795	40%
Bruce	1,120	25
Carter	1,120	25
Doner	450	10
Total	4,485	100%

The requirements of each warehouse and delivered costs of a reel of wire from each supplier to each destination are as follows:

Destination	No. of reels required	Delivered prices per reel			
		Allen	Bruce	Carter	Doner
Johnston City	950	$299.50	$304.85	$311.25	$303.70
Kankakee	1,105	307.10	305.90	308.40	312.10
Laramay	770	310.80	310.40	311.60	314.20
Montook	1,080	310.40	311.10	314.80	316.50
Norrisfield	580	321.15	321.85	325.25	326.10
Total	4,485				

Mid-States is presently trying to have the lowest cost supplier ship to each destination—within the limits of its allocation of business. The current shipping pattern is as follows:

Destination	Supplier				Total no. of reels
	Allen	Bruce	Carter	Doner	
Johnston City	950				950
Kankakee		1,105			1,105
Laramay		15	755		770
Montook	845		235		1,080
Norrisfield			130	450	580
Total	1,795	1,120	1,120	450	4,485

Question

Using linear programming, determine the lowest cost shipping pattern from Mid-States's four suppliers to its five warehouses.

CASE 18–3. STANFORD SHIRT COMPANY

Purchase of capital equipment

Stanford Shirt Company has a national reputation as a manufacturer of high-quality shirts. For 40 years the company has catered to the executive who likes the very finest ready-made shirts. Until recently, Stanford's cheapest shirt retailed for $7.50. While the company has earned an enviable reputation for quality, its growth has been limited by its pricing policies. Very few men are willing to pay premium prices for shirts. Finally, the company decided to enter the medium-priced shirt field and created its Stanfast line. The brand name chosen was designed to be similar to the Stanford brand name in the hope of trading on the company's reputation but sufficiently different to prevent the two lines from being confused.

The Stanfast line is designed to retail for $4.50. Part of the savings comes from narrowing the dealer's profit margin from nearly 50 percent to the 30 percent that is more common on lower priced shirts. The Stanfast shirts also are made of cheaper cloth and buttons. In the manufacturing operations, the company is able to make only minor savings through the elimination of a few sewing operations. It is difficult to make greater savings because both shirts must be sewed together in approximately the same way.

As a result, the company's profits on the new line have been disappointing. The company's profit plan calls for a 20 percent return after taxes on investment in all new projects. The new line of shirts definitely is not earning its fair share of the desired return on investment and, in fact, unit profits are currently less than 5 cents per shirt, and everyone in the organization is searching for ways to widen the profit margin without hurting quality.

The purchasing director, Frank Adams, believes he may have the answer. Currently, all of the company's shirts are ironed by hand. Finished shirts are conveyed in hampers to women workers, who pick them out of the hamper, iron them, and then fold and pack them in boxes. The women work on piece rate, and the company's total labor cost per shirt for these operations is 11 cents. The company controller estimates that the variable overhead applicable to this operation is about 6 cents.

Laundries have been using semiautomatic shirt ironing machines for years. The freshly laundered shirts are folded over a series of forms, and it is possible to iron and pack a shirt with about 1.2 minutes of direct labor. Ironing machines have never been used much by shirt manufacturers, however. Newly manufactured shirts are much harder to iron, and the laundry equipment will not remove all of the wrinkles. In addition, shirt manufacturers are convinced that their products will sell better if they are ironed perfectly. So far, laundry equipment manufacturers have failed to devise a machine that can approach the quality achieved by a skilled woman equipped with a hand iron and ironing board.

Alma Laundry Machine Corporation thinks it has made a breakthrough. Its M–9 shirt-ironing machine will turn out 60 shirts per hour that are almost wrinkle-free. Adams arranges to ship a gross of newly manufactured Stanfast shirts to the Alma plant and himself watches the machine iron them. Accompanying him on the trip is Stanford's quality control manager, John Connally. The two men agree that while the M–9 doesn't do a good enough job for the Stanford line, it should be adequate for the Stanfast line.

On checking with the personnel department, Adams discovers that an operator for the machine would probably have to be paid $2.40 per hour. In addition, fringe benefits (which would become part of variable overhead) amount to $.60 per hour.

Alma insists that its estimated production rate of 60 shirts per hour includes more than adequate allowances for downtime, delays, rest periods, and so on. The supplier also claims that maintenance expenses on the machine will average less than $500 per year, and that it probably has a useful life of at least ten years on three-shift operation. All other variable overhead expenses in connection with the machine total about $0.001 per shirt ironed. The machine costs $20,000 installed, and Stanford can easily make use of at least one machine working two shifts, five days per week. Adam doubts that the scrap value of the hand equipment that the machine would replace is more than $100.

Question

Should Stanford buy the machine? Support your conclusions with (1) a MAPI investment analysis, (2) a calculation of cash payback period, and (3) a discounted cash flow analysis. Assume corporate income tax rate of exactly 50 percent and straight-line depreciation.

19

Control of administrative costs

A COMPANY with 2,000 employees may have 100 persons working in its various materials activities: purchasing, production control, traffic, and so on. More than 85 percent of these jobs are predominantly clerical. A fantastic number of man-hours are devoted to filling out thousands of different forms, keeping records, and the like. One company with about 5,000 employees found that its materials personnel filled out more than one million pieces of paper a year. The computer is taking over much of the processing of this paper work, but everything that goes into the computer is usually written on a piece of paper and is then keypunched. So while the computer speeds analysis of business data, it may in effect mean more paper work.

PAPER WORK IS COSTLY

All surveys show that paper work in materials management is increasing much faster than general business activities. The costs of this paper work are obviously substantial. It probably costs at least 10 cents to fill out each purchase requisition, request for quotation, purchase order, receiving report, inspection report, and accounts payable voucher, and 5 cents for posting each inventory record and keypunching each tabulating card. Even a small company will issue thousands of purchase requisitions per year. Since each requisition may generate a need for one or more quotation requests, purchase orders, and so on, clerical costs can easily mushroom.

Accountants sometimes divide a materials department's total operating costs by the output of some key document, such as a purchase order.

Such comparisons have limited usefulness as barometers of operating efficiency, but they can dramatically illustrate the high cost of paper work. For example, the writer once estimated that it cost the purchasing department of Ford Division of Ford Motor Company $58 to issue each of its purchase orders. The full cost of carrying an inventory of medical-surgical supplies in a large hospital for one year may be equal to as much as the value of the inventory itself. Most of the carrying cost is represented by salaries paid to clerks and other stores personnel whose job is mostly record keeping.

Need for paper work. Is all this paper work necessary? Much of it is. The materials management process inherently involves a lot of detail. A company with only a few hundred employees will have thousands of different items that must be controlled in some fashion, while a big corporation may have hundreds of thousands of items to control. Records must be kept for each item. If a company is to do a first-rate job of materials management, it must have systems designed to bring any deviation from routine to the attention of the materials manager immediately.

It behooves each materials manager to get the information he needs for making decisions with a minimum of paper work and clerical manpower. In so doing, he helps achieve one of his primary objectives: to manage materials with minimum operating cost. This in itself is adequate motivation for a program to eliminate clerical effort through improved forms and procedures and mechanization. But managers should be interested in reducing the enormous amount of clerical effort required in materials management even if they were able to persuade clerks to work without pay.

Effect on materials. The bigger the clerical work force, the more complex the materials organization structure inevitably becomes. As was explained in Chapter 4, each supervisor has a limited span of control. As the work force grows, more supervisors are required; inevitably more levels of organization are needed. The organization becomes progressively more complex. Top materials managers are forced to devote an increasing amount of their time to managing people rather than managing materials. This reduces their efficiency.

In a large, complex organization, procedures for transmitting information to make decisions become cumbersome and time-consuming. All other factors being equal, a small organization can always move faster than a big one. In materials management, speedy transmission of information permits faster materials cycles with lower inventories and less obsolescence.

When clerks are eliminated through improvements in procedures or through mechanization, it is not just the simpler organization structure that permits faster flow of information. The new methods can speed data transmission directly, since they are inherently faster. For example, if a company computes its investory balance by manually totaling and extending the balances on thousands of record cards, the job will probably take a week or two, regardless of how many clerks are assigned to it. On the other hand, if inventory records are kept on the memory drum of an electronic computer, it is easy to get daily inventory reports.

Reduction of errors. Not only do people require far more management effort than machines do, but they also are more prone to make mistakes. If a clerk is posting hundreds of inventory records each day, it is inevitable that he will occasionally make an error. Most such errors can be detected by having the work double checked by another person. But management can be certain that on rare occasions an error will go through undetected, regardless of how many different persons try to spot it. A clerk will enter "100" as an inventory balance when he should enter "10," or a form will be mislaid and he will simply overlook an item entirely. If the error is not detected, the item will not be available when it should be, and a costly shutdown may result.

Companies will have problems of this sort as long as they have employees, but they can reduce the chances for error by reducing the number of times basic data must be transcribed by human beings and by giving as much of the job as possible to machines. No machine can actually think, but it can perform repetitive operations without fatigue and with built-in controls that detect any errors that might occur.

CLERICAL QUALITY CONTROL

Clerical errors are a perpetual source of nightmares for materials managers. There are thousands of opportunities for such errors to be made every day. And many of them can be serious—a purchase order is directed to the wrong vendor, a shipment is routed to a destination where it is not needed, and incorrect amount of material is ordered, and so on. Procedures in materials departments are very carefully designed to minimize errors, but a few inevitably sneak through the best designed system. All that the materials manager can do is devise the best system he can afford and then be certain that it operates the way it should.

Design of the system. Materials managers do not always like to admit it, but every paper-work system represents a compromise among conflicting objectives. The simple fact is that the manager can spend only so much to prevent errors, and it is never economic to have a system that is so foolproof that all probability of error is eliminated. In the ideal system, the marginal cost of preventing errors is roughly equal to the losses suffered from errors.

Suppose, for example, that a company presently suffers from one serious clerical error in the materials department each month. It guesses that it suffers from perhaps a hundred or more other minor errors. Many of these are never detected, since they create no problems. The materials manager is convinced that he has the best possible procedures for error prevention that he can afford with his present budget. His employees are conscientious and motivated and, in general, are doing a satisfactory job.

The materials manager believes that the only way he could reduce errors is by hiring an extra clerk to proofread key forms. He estimates that if he does this the number of important errors will decline by about 50 percent. Instead of 12 serious errors per year, there will be just 6. Should the materials manager add the extra error checker to his payroll? To decide, he should balance the cost of the extra employee against the benefit. If the checker's salary and fringe benefits add up to $6,000 per year, then errors must be worth $1,000 each to the materials manager if he is to hire the extra employee to eliminate them. They may not be worth this much; if so, in theory, the materials manager should not hire the extra checker. In practice, he might do it anyway. Errors are visible and very embarassing. There are noneconomic reasons why the materials manager would try to eliminate them. In any event, an extra clerk soon gets built into the budget structure and is readily accepted.

Monitoring the process. When the materials manager is convinced that he has the best system he can afford, he should still look for better ways to do the job. But his day-to-day job is largely control—making certain that the system operates the way it should. Quality control principles can be applied to such systems just as if they were tangible products. In both cases, the concept is based on the principle that a process will fluctuate at random within some predetermined case when it is "in control." When it moves out of this range, it is "out of control" and should be corrected.

The process is monitored with a control chart on which sample data are periodically plotted. In industrial quality control, an inspector periodically checks a group of parts and plots the results. In paper work quality control, the procedure is essentially the same: a sample of paper work is inspected periodically, and the results are tabulated and plotted.

As in statistical quality control, the process will fluctuate at random in a range that is three standard deviations around the mean. The mean is found experimentally. Suppose that, over a long period of time, as a materials manager you make random checks of your paper flow, comparing actual error with possible errors. You discover that three and one-half errors are made in every 100 occurrences and are satisfied that this is normal behavior of the process. You recognize, however, that the error percentage will fluctuate at random around this mean.

You know from your study of statistics that 99.72 percent of all occurrences will fall within three standard deviations of a normal distribution. You expect to control your process by periodically inspecting a sample of paper work where there are 100 opportunities to make an error. You expect on the average to find three and one-half errors in the sample. You calculate your expected standard deviation with the formula

$$s = \sqrt{\frac{P(1 - P)}{n}},$$

where P = the percent defective and n = number of observations.

$$s = \sqrt{\frac{.035(1 - .035)}{100}} = .0184$$

If one standard deviation is .0184, then three standard deviations is equal to about 0.55. Therefore, the upper control limit of the process becomes .09—the mean defective of .035 plus three standard deviations, or .055. Thus, 100 samples drawn from your process can contain as many as nine defectives. However, the probability that the process is going out of control increases as you drift away from the expected mean. This shows up clearly on the control chart shown in Figure 19–1.

FIGURE 19–1

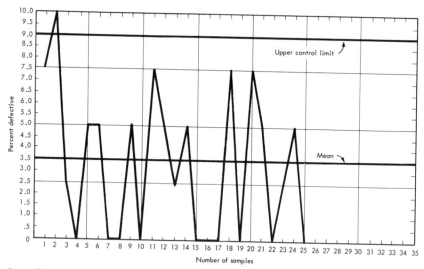

Control limits can be established for statistical quality control of paper work just as they can be used to monitor manufacturing processes. In this example, an average of three and one-half errors is expected in each sample. When the paper-work process is "in control," errors will fluctuate at random between a maximum of nine errors per sample and a minimum of no errors. If more than nine errors are made in a sample, something has gone wrong, and management should investigate.

The first sample drawn from the process has 7.5 percent defectives. This warns management that while the process may not yet be out of control, it could be headed in that direction. Observation 2 confirms this suspicion; the defective rate is 10 percent and beyond the upper control limit. Something is obviously wrong; management would investigate and take corrective measures. Observation 3 indicates that the process is back in control again. Observation 4 indicates no defectives whatever. This is the effective lower control limit. When the process goes down to this limit, management might also investigate—not to find out what went wrong but to find out what has changed. Sometimes improvements sneak into the process undetected. They may disappear spontaneously unless management discovers them and incorporates them into operating procedures. Statistical quality control not only is a device to detect processing faults but also can detect changes that help improve the process. When the process breaks through the lower control limit, the odds heavily favor some favorable change having occurred that should be investigated. The behavior of the process as plotted in Figure 19–1 implies that the true mean of the process is now lower than the original estimate of 3.5 percent. Note that a majority of observations fall below 3.5 percent.

SHORT CUTS WITH FORMS

In bigger companies, the materials manager may have an administrative assistant (sometimes even an entire staff department) who devotes a major share of his efforts to improving forms and procedures. Periodically, each form and report used should "stand trial for its life." If its existence cannot be justified, it should be eliminated. Even in the best managed departments, such "trials" occasionally uncover paper work that can be eliminated. Conditions change but if there is no control the obsolete forms and procedures will continue anyway unless someone does something about them. Periodic reviews are valuable even if they do not reveal any paper work that can be eliminated. They can alert management to savings in clerical time, which can result from such improvements as special ordering procedures, combining of forms, and changes in forms design.

Special ordering procedures

Transactions in materials departments vary widely. Consecutively numbered purchase orders may be issued for a $20,000 machine tool, a $2 charge to fix a flat tire on a company truck, and a contract to purchase $100,000 worth of production parts. Different types of orders warrant different treatment if they are to get the control they deserve without excessive paper work. This can be done with blanket orders, cash pickup orders, and similar procedures.

Blanket orders. Items that are used regularly often require a dozen or more purchases a year. Each time inventory drops to the reorder point, the stores department issues a requisition that touches off a complete purchase transaction. A company can cut paper work, of course, by ordering less often and in larger quantities, but this is an expensive solution to the problem. Increased inventory carrying cost may more than offset the savings in paper work. Blanket orders offer a better solution. The buyer issues an order good for a year's requirements to be shipped "as released." Then, whenever stock of material runs low, the buyer simply telephones the supplier and asks him to ship against the outstanding blanket order.

Blanket orders help save on repeat items in four ways:

1. *They usually reduce paper work.* A single blanket order is substituted for many individual orders. There is some saving in paper work even when the buyer sends written release forms (as is customary on important purchases) to the supplier each time he wants a shipment. In this case the buyer still is relieved of the need to get quotations for each transaction. And, in most cases, the releasing procedure is less complex than the ordering procedure.

2. *They save the time of skilled buyers.* Once a blanket order is placed, the job of ordering can be transferred from a skilled (and highly paid) buyer to a clerk (or even to a machine, if the company has electronic data processing equipment). The clerk simply writes out a release against the blanket order and mails it to the supplier.

In some cases, it is convenient for the user of the material to do his own ordering—especially in cases where the user is in charge of the inventory. For example, a hospital materials manager may establish a blanket order for drugs, but the inventory is under the direct control of the hospital pharmacist who then has authority to issue releases against the blanket order.

3. *They facilitate price negotiation.* Suppliers often will quote lower prices when they are bidding for a year's requirements rather than for a single order. Multiplant companies can go even further; they can combine requirements for all plants on a single blanket order in order to maximize their buying power.

4. *They permit closer inventory control.* Blanket orders help companies operate with shorter lead times and lower inventories. If they can get an order for a year's requirements, suppliers often can be persuaded to stock the material so it is available for immediate delivery. This permits the buyer to operate hand to mouth, with almost no safety stock.

Cash pickup orders. Few companies can process the paper work necessary for a complete purchase transaction for less than $10,[1] and

---

[1] Surveys made of the cost of issuing a purchase order have been inconsistent because there is no agreement on what costs should be charged. However, big

the supplier who "cannot enter the smallest order at less than $10 cost"² also is typical. Small orders are money-losers for both buyer and seller. Yet, of necessity, a substantial percentage of the orders issued (50 percent in many smaller companies and 25 percent in big corporations) are for $50 or less. Even though such orders may comprise less than 5 percent of total expenditures, they can consume a disproportionate share of the total administrative and clerical expenses.

With conventional purchasing procedures, an order for a $5 item will get the same administrative treatment as a major order. Special procedures help bypass costly administrative controls on small orders. One of the simplest is merely to authorize a supplier to ship and bill on the basis of a telephone order. The only records of the transaction are the requisition and the receiving report. No purchase order is issued; the purchase is cleared by matching the requisition, the receiving report, and the supplier's invoice.

Another short cut eliminates the invoicing process; the buyer pays cash for the order. Typical is the small-order procedure used by Argus Cameras, Inc., Ann Arbor, Michigan, for local purchases (see Figure 19–2). The purchase requisition doubles as a purchase order. When the buyer gets it, he telephones the order to the supplier, fills in the supplier's name and price on the requisition, and makes out a check to pay for the order. When the supplier delivers, the check and one copy of the purchase order–requisition are ready for him at Argus's receiving dock.

"Blank check" orders.   Other companies go one step further. In effect, they give the supplier a blank check for purchases that may amount to as much as $1,000. Typically, the buyer's data processing system automatically generates a purchase order when inventory of a particular item reaches the reorder point. A purchase order form is automatically printed out. Into it is incorporated a bank draft made out in the supplier's favor. When the supplier delivers the item, he fills in the bank draft for the amount due him. He then deposits the draft in his own bank on the date called for on the payment instructions that are enclosed with the purchase order. The bank draft is usually limited to $500–$1,000 in order to limit the buyer's potential liability. Technically, it is a "draft" rather than a "check." If the seller does not deliver material satisfactory to the buyer, the draft may be rejected by the buyer. Otherwise, the draft works just like a blank check. Neither buyer nor supplier need

---

companies that have made detailed studies usually have found their costs to be much greater than $10 when they consider the cost of the complete materials cycle, from initiation of the requisition to the point where the material is received, stored, and used. However, the *marginal* cost (i.e., the cost of one extra order) is in most cases probably less than $10.

² *The Small Order—Asset or Liability?* Studies in Business Policy No. 21 (New York: National Industrial Conference Board, 1956).

FIGURE 19–2
Small-order purchase requisition form

This Argus Cameras purchase requisition doubles as purchase order on small orders. The buyer phones the order, and the supplier gets a copy and payment upon delivery.

bother processing an invoice for the material. Some companies have succeeded in reducing the number of purchase invoices they process by as much as 75 to 80 percent using this "blank check" system.

Many managers view special small-order procedures with mixed enthusiasm. They like to eliminate paper work, but they are afraid that small orders will encourage unnecessary expenditures, discourage grouping of orders that might reduce costs even more, or stimulate a lax environment where there will be repeated last-minute "emergencies" calling for small orders. Companies that do have small-order procedures maintain extremely close control over them for these and other reasons.

Combining forms

Certain data are repeated again and again in materials transactions. Part numbers and names appear on almost every form used in every department in a company. Supplier names appear on buy records and quotation requests and are repeated on numerous other forms, including purchase orders, receiving reports, inspection reports, inventory records, and so on. Order quantities and prices similarly are repeated again and again.

Each time information is transcribed, not only is clerical cost incurred but a costly error is risked. Thus it pays to combine forms to make use of common information whenever possible. This can be done both by making one form do several jobs and by preparing different forms with a single, simultaneous operation. The traveling requisition is a good example of the former; combination purchase-order, receiving-report forms and various duplicating techniques are good examples of the latter.

The traveling requisition. With conventional procedures, a separate requisition is filled out to authorize each purchase of an item. This means that common data, such as item number, description of the item, and so on, will be copied over and over again in requisitioning frequently used items. The traveling requisition is larger than the conventional requisition form and also is made of heavier paper. A permanent traveling requisition is kept for each item in stock (see Figure 19–3). On it is space for common data and also for data specifically describing a particular purchase.

When stock drops to the reorder point the stores clerk pulls out the traveling requisition from the file and sends it to the buyer. After the purchase is made, the buyer or his clerk posts the order data to the requisition, which travels back to the stores clerk. He notes that the purchase has been made and then refiles it until it is needed for the next purchase. Since the traveling requisition form provides a complete purchase history, some buyers also use it as a purchase record. Other buyers, particularly of commodities with high dollar volume,

FIGURE 19-3
Traveling requisition form

54612 Impeller Assembly, part no. 625 Type 316 Elc Stainless Steel 22" diameter, 3 vane, right hand								ORDER POINT 1
								E.O.Q. 2
								PURCHASE UNIT ea
								ISSUE UNIT ea

BY REQUISITIONER					BY PURCHASER				
REQUIRED		CHARGE NO.	P. O. NO.	V E N	PRICE	TERMS	F.O.B.	#	VENDOR
DATE	QTY.							1	City Supply Co.
6/4/—	2	160401	9-16/20	1	320.00	2/10/30	St Louis	2	ABC Dist.
10/7/—	2	16040l	9-19960	4	318.00	2/4/30	Baltimore	3	J. Doe & Co.
9/4/—	2	16040l	0-13240	3	300.00	Net	Bartow	4	State Mfg. Co.
								5	
								6	
								7	
								8	
								LOCATION 3R4-5	
								EQUIPMENT	
								For Type 2,	
								Model B, Pump	

In a typical traveling requisition form, the requisitioner fills in data on the left of the card, and the purchaser acts on this data and returns the form to the requisitioner, who files it until stocks drop again to the reorder point.

prefer to keep separate purchase records. They wish to keep a more detailed record than is possible on the traveling requisition, and they often are afraid that stores personnel or others will reveal competitive price data to favored suppliers.

Occasionally, traveling requisitions also double as inventory records. It is not difficult to include space for stores receipts and withdrawals on the form. Most companies prefer to post to a separate stores record, however. Then, if the traveling requisition is lost, there is still a basic record of the item in the stockroom.

Other combination forms. With electric typewriters, which can make about ten reasonably clear carbon copies, it is possible to combine physically many forms that use common data. Most common is the purchase order–receiving report, which consists of an 8″ × 10″ copy "snap-out" type of form with one-time carbon paper inserted. The first four or five copies of the form are a conventional purchase-order set. The last copies become the receiving report. Since most of the basic purchase-order data is also needed for the receiving report, this combination of forms can save a considerable amount of typing. It does not completely eliminate the need for separate receiving reports, however. Many orders are not completed in a single shipment, and, of course, a separate receiving report is needed for each shipment.

In similar fashion, many companies have a combined receiving report and inspection report or inspection report-move ticket. The combination can also be achieved with duplicating equipment. For example, a purchase order set might include a duplicate master, which in turn is used with a second master to run off copies of receiving reports and other documents.

Forms design

The materials department usually does not design its own forms. Larger companies have separate "office services" or "procedures" departments (usually as a staff activity reporting to the controller) staffed with forms and procedures experts who serve the entire company. Smaller companies usually rely on their forms suppliers to assist them in design.

The materials department should naturally make use of any help it can get in designing forms. However, the materials manager should never forget that he—not the manager of the procedures group—is ultimately responsible for every phase of administering his department, including its forms and procedures. Therefore the materials manager should be familiar with the general principles of forms design, since he is responsible for and should approve every form his department uses.

Principles. A good form transmits needed information at minimum cost. The forms designer should observe six principles:

1. *Keep design as simple as possible.* The more complex the form, the more difficult (and costly) will be its use. Procedures and forms should be as foolproof as possible.

2. *Allow adequate space.* Forms that are tight on space are inefficient. If data is filled in by typewriter, there should be space between lines equal to typewriter double spacing. If the form is filled in with pencil (and this may be preferable because it eliminates the need to type a "finished" copy from a rough, handwritten copy), there should be enough space for rather large handwriting and rather lengthy descriptions.

3. *Keep copies to a minimum.* Naturally everyone vitally concerned with a transaction should get a copy of the form, but copies never should go to persons or departments with only occasional interest in the transactions. Instead, if anything, such persons should have forms directed through them—that is, they receive the executed form, look at it, and then pass it on to someone who actually uses the information it contains.

4. *"Try each form for its life" at least once a year.* Forms and procedures frequently become obsolete, but sometimes they live on simply because no one periodically reviews their application to make certain that there still is good reason for their existence.

5. *Reduce handwritten data to an absolute minimum.* Use multiple-choice answers on a form when there are a limited number of alternatives; then all the clerk need do is check the appropriate one. If the information required should change, do not be afraid to scrap existing forms and change the design to accommodate the new data. The cost of the paper and printing is negligible compared to the cost of the time of those who fill out the forms.

6. *Keep data in sequence.* Information on a form should be listed in the sequence in which it naturally comes to the person filling in the form. If a form moves from department to department, the first department using the form should fill in the top part of the form, with succeeding departments filling in information in sequence.

Design criteria. Typewritten forms should be laid out to minimize carriage returns, positioning, and spacing required to type in the data. Each of these has a price in keystrokes:

Carriage return.	5 keystrokes
Horizontal space	1 keystroke
Tabular stop	5 keystrokes
Hand positioning	12½ keystrokes
Vertical space	2½ keystrokes

The materials manager can evaluate the forms designs he approves simply by adding the number of keystrokes. The fewer the keystrokes, the lower the clerical cost. If one form requires 1,200 keystrokes and another form doing a similar job requires only 600, the materials manager may well consider requesting that the first form be redesigned, since it costs about twice as much to fill out as the second one does.

INTEGRATED DATA PROCESSING

The techniques discussed so far help reduce paper work. But, to be realistic, their impact on the overall materials job is minor. Even if they are applied intensively, 80 to 90 percent of the work of materials management will continue to be clerical. Mechanization is more promising: It permits machines to be substituted for people.

Every materials department is mechanized to some extent. It has duplicating equipment, copying machines, dictating machines, electric desk calculators, electric typewriters, and so on. At this stage of mechanization, machines do various jobs, but data continues to flow in conventional fashion on conventional forms and records.

Integrated data processing is more advanced. Data moves from operation to operation in a form that permits each machine to operate automatically from the instructions it receives in some "common language." The vehicle of the common language is either punched cards or punched tape. Numbers and letters of the alphabet are coded by changing the position and frequency of holes in cards or tape.

Punched-tape systems. One of the simplest systems on integrated data processing involves the use of a patented Flexowriter machine made by the Friden Division of Singer Corporation. A typical application of the system starts with a traveling requisition form printed on an envelope. Stored inside the envelope is a punched tape generated the last time the item was bought. On this tape is punched all the data that was typed on the last purchase order. If the buyer wishes to issue another order to the same supplier at the same price as before, the tape can be fed into the Flexowriter, and a new order will be generated almost entirely automatically. The machine types at the rate of 600 characters per minute with no errors. Carriage return and line spacing are also regulated by the punched tape.

Usually the old order tape cannot be used to type out a new order so directly. For example, the buyer may wish to send quotation requests to a number of suppliers. In this case, the old order tape (or the previous quotation request tape) will permit a large part of the job to be done automatically. Information not on the tape is added manually. The machine can be set to stop at predetermined points to permit the typist to enter such variable information as the date of the order, the date delivery is required, price, and so on.

The purchase order tape is saved. It can be used to issue purchase order amendments and also for receiving reports. In either case, most of the needed information is already on the tape. The balance can be typed in manually. Sometimes Flexowriters are used from remote points. For example, the purchasing and receiving departments can have their punched-tape systems linked by wire. When a shipment is received, the receiving clerk pulls the appropriate order tape, inserts it in the Flexowriter, and prepares a receiving report, typing in variable receiving information. Two receiving reports are typed simultaneously. One is typed in receiving on a conventional machine. The other is typed in purchasing on a slave machine connected by wire to the conventional machine. Connection can even be made by leased telephone wire to connect plants that are hundreds of miles apart. This eliminates the day or two lost mailing receiving reports and thereby shortens purchase lead time and reduces inventory needs.

Punched-card systems. Data on punched tapes can be run through tape-to-card converters and automatically transferred to punched cards. Systems involving punched cards are now used in the materials departments of all but the very smallest companies because they are compatible with company computers. As a result, the same basic data can be used over and over again to generate many different documents and reports. With a punched-card system, every transaction that has any effect on inventory is keypunched on the cards. In some cases, this is done auto-

FIGURE 19-4

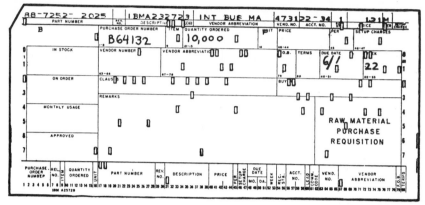

Courtesy Sprague Electric Co.

Sprague Electric Company uses punched cards as purchase requisitions. Buyers fill in purchasing data, which is then punched on another "buy" card.

FIGURE 19-5

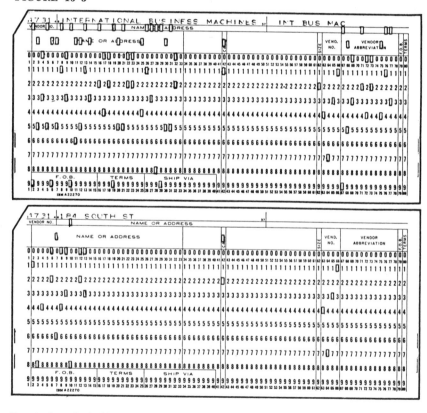

Punched cards hold a limited amount of data. Four cards (above and on facing page) are needed to print a typical supplier's name and address.

FIGURE 19–5 (Continued)

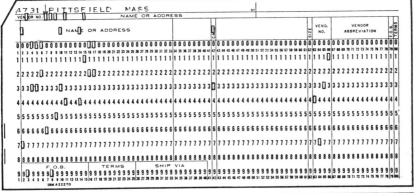

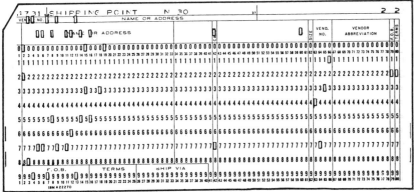

Courtesy Sprague Electric Co.

matically when a form is typed; special typewriters are available that can be set to keypunch certain data after it has been typed. In most cases, a keypunch operator must record the data onto the cards in a separate operation.

Punched cards also can be used to automate purchasing operations. Typical is a system used by the Sprague Electric Company, in which the purchase requisition is a punched card (see Figure 19–4). The buyer fills in the variable data—purchase order number, purchase quantity, vendor's promised delivery date, and so on—in pencil, and a keypunch operator punches this information on a new "buy" card. This buy card, along with a deck of cards for the vendor's name and address (see Figure 19–5) is fed into a machine that automatically prints a purchase order (see Figure 19–6).

The cards used to print the purchase order are saved until the supplier delivers. They then can be combined with another punched card and used to print a receiving report. They also can be used to print reports on open orders. For example, Sprague Electric makes run-offs of all

FIGURE 19–6

FORM 481 REV.

SPRAGUE ELECTRIC COMPANY
NORTH ADAMS, MASSACHUSETTS
Telephone: MOhawk 3-5311

PURCHASE ORDER

VENDOR

INTERNATIONAL BUSINESS MACHINES
184 SOUTH ST
PITTSFIELD MASS

DATE: 05 12

• RECEIVING STATIONS •
1. Bldg. 15, Marshall St., North Adams, Mass.
2. Bldg. 17, Marshall St., North Adams, Mass.
3. Bldg. 21, Marshall St., North Adams, Mass.
4. R & E Library, North Adams, Mass.
5. Brown Street, North Adams, Mass.
6. Beaver Street, North Adams, Mass.
7. Union Street, North Adams, Mass.
8. Factory Street, Nashua, New Hampshire
9. Pembroke Road, Concord, New Hampshire
10. Ashe County Div., Lansing, N. C.
11. Benmont Ave., Bennington, Vermont
12. Rock of Ages Capacitor Div., Barre, Vt.
13. S. Mooney Blvd., Visalia, Calif.
14. Sprague Caribe Company, Ponce, Porto Rico
15. Bldg. 19, Marshall St., North Adams, Mass.

PLEASE FURNISH THE FOLLOWING, SUBJECT TO ALL CONDITIONS ON BOTH SIDES HEREOF:

F. O. B.	TERMS	SHIP VIA (UNLESS SPECIFIED SEE SHIPPING INST. REVERSE SIDE)
SHIPPING POINT	N/30	

INCLUDE ON ALL PACKAGES AND DOCUMENTS — INCLUDE ON ALL PACKAGES AND DOCUMENTS

PURCHASE ORDER NUMBER	RELEASE NO.	TYPE	QUANTITY	U/M	PART NUMBER	DESCRIPTION	UNIT PRICE	PER	SETUP	DUE DATE MONTH	DUE DATE DAY	SHIP TO
864132		A	10000	P	88–7252– 2025	IBMA23272	1 21	M		6	01	1

A Barrels, B Boxes, C Cases, D Drums, E Pair, F Feet, G Gallons, H Board Ft., I Square Ft., J Grams, K Kilograms, L Pounds, M Gross, N Pints, O Ounces, P Pieces, Q Quarts, R Rolls, S Sheets, T Tons, U Sets, V Pads, W Troy Oz., X Bottles, Y Yards, Z Tubes

▼ NOTE ▼

PRICE PER: C — Hundred, D — Dozen, E — Each, L — Lot, M — Thousand

1. INVOICE IN DUPLICATE AND MAIL TO: SPRAGUE ELECTRIC COMPANY NORTH ADAMS, MASS.

DO NOT ACKNOWLEDGE

2. THIS ORDER IS PLACED ACCORDING TO YOUR LEAD TIME AND PRICE QUOTATION. OBJECTIONS SHOULD BE DIRECTED TO THE BUYER FORMALLY.
3. NOTE: A REQUISITE OF YOUR SERVICE IS TO ADVISE IN ADVANCE IF DELIVERY WILL BE LATE.

VENDOR'S COPY

R A FAIRBANKS
PURCHASING DEPARTMENT

Courtesy Sprague Electric Co.

When the punched buy card and the vendor deck are fed into the proper tabulating equipment, a purchase order like the one shown here is printed automatically.

FIGURE 19–7

JUNE 10, 19—

Vendor	Po#		Item		Part No		Unit	Quantity	Week Due
ELECT IND	A29517	20	A		44	162K	P	40000	24
BARBER LTHR	A32481	35	A		4062	119U	P	5000	24
ALCOA	A33181	6	A		75	65	P	75450	24
NATL LEAD	A39525	42	A		1223	17E	L	2000	24
NATL LEAD	A39525	45	A		45	63	L	400	24
AM EXTRUSIN	A39636	9	A		31	106A	P	25000	24
ELECT IND	A40965	18	A		44	162B	P	20000	24
INSULAT FAB	A41834	9	A		27	1020	P	25000	24
N BERKSHIRE	A41877	75	A		407	382C	P	2500	24
N BERKSHIRE	A41877	77	A		407	381G	P	2500	24
N BERKSHIRE	A41877	79	A	4	407	51Z	P	1000	24
OAKITE	A44912	6	A		4506	436	L	800	24
MIN MINING	A45012	71	A		23	16	R	1440	24
MIN MINING	A45012	79	A		23	51B	R	72	24
MIN MINING	A45012	80	A		23	16M	R	288	24
MIN MINING	A45012	81	A	4	23	1D	R	12	24
SPEC INSUL	A50019		C		400	47D	P	3500	24
[illegible]	A50045		A		118	1	L	74	24

Punched buy cards can be used also to print various reports. Sprague Electric Company, for example, prints a weekly report of all open orders due the following week.

open orders the week before they are due (see Figure 19–7). It also makes separate run-offs of orders where delivery is behind schedule, and uses the same punched cards to print out expediting notices that are mailed to suppliers.

Punched cards have many other uses in materials management. If a card is punched for each materials transaction, it is possible to use the cards to print almost any form used in materials management. In addition, the cards can be combined and recombined to produce a wide variety of reports. Cards for each withdrawal, receival, rejection, and purchase can be combined to run off a complete inventory report. The report can be made according to supplier, product, part number, or in almost any other way desired.

ELECTRONIC DATA PROCESSING

Punched-card data processing systems predate the electronic data processing computer. Now the two are almost synonymous. Companies that use punched-card equipment almost always analyze this data in a computer. EDP systems still use punched cards for much of their input data, but cards play a minor role in the overall EDP system. The bulk of the data processing job is done by the "memory" cells, transistors, and other components of complex computers. The computers will not think, but they can carry out complicated instructions and perform calculations at fantastic speed, as well as store enormous amounts of information in their magnetic memory cells.

Advantages of electronic data processing

Electronic data processing has revolutionized materials management within the last decade. It is taking over control of the entire clerical phase of materials management and is giving managers tools to manage materials as they've never been managed before. The computer can analyze, in minutes, data that would take a small army of clerks weeks to process. As a result, the materials manager can get data for making decisions much faster than before; he also can get more data than would be possible with manual or mechanical techniques. Even a rather small computer can store about ten million characters of information (enough to fill about 25 ordinary-size books). In addition, the computer has access in minutes (or even fractions of seconds with some designs) to a number of reels of magnetic tape, each of which will hold about ten million characters of information.

Materials management by computer normally starts with a magnetic tape that is, in effect, a list of the items to be controlled, and a program that tells the computer what to do with this basic list and the variable data fed into it. The program is an attempt to simulate a clerk's reaction to data; it permits the computer to regulate itself and make basic operating decisions. This ability to "think," plus its fantastic operating speed, are what make a computer and electronic data processing different from punched-card mechanical processing.

The basic magnetic tape consists of more than a simple parts list. Included are not only such basic data as each part number, part name, and product usage, but also such materials management information as safety stock, unit weight, lead time, inventory balance, and inspection requirements.

When a program is devised and desired basic information is on tape, variable information is fed into the system. Every transaction affecting the status of the items controlled is fed into the computer for compilation and analysis. Included would be all receivals and withdrawals of stock, placement of purchase orders, and usage schedules. The usual procedure is to describe each transaction on punched cards, usually punched by a keypunch operator. This is virtually the only manual operation required with EDP and sometimes even it can be eliminated. The data can be entered with a "mark-sense" pencil that permits the cards to be punched automatically. Or, in some cases, information can be transmitted directly to the computer as it is generated.

The information on the cards may be read directly into the computer. Usually, however, it is transferred to magnetic tape which, in turn, is fed into the computer. This additional operation is needed to keep the costly computer working at peak efficiency. It is physically impossible to feed data from punched cards into the computer at a rate much faster than 2,000 characters per second. This is wasteful, since computers are capable of handling an input of 1,000,000 characters per second or more, and magnetic tape feeds in data at the rate of about 50,000 characters per second.

Periodically, usually once or twice a week, the magnetic tape listing transactions is fed into the computer and compared with the permanent data already in the program. The computer compares the two sets of data and makes necessary calculations. Its conclusions appear on reports made on a high-speed printer to which it is linked.

A well-designed EDP system will handle all routine materials management transactions. It will:

1. *Provide up-to-date reports.* Current inventories of each item can be calculated and printed in detail. In addition, almost any type of inventory summary can readily be compiled for analysis. The computer can also be programmed to compile estimates of future inventories based on projected schedules of purchase and usage.

2. *Complete materials transaction records.* Not only the inventory balances but a complete record of each transaction for each item can be compiled and printed automatically.

3. *Compute economic order quantities and usages.* The computer can automatically analyze previous usage of an item and revise anticipated usages in accordance with some formula. It then can recompute

economic order quantity. If there is a need for them, the computer can be programmed to use mathematically complex ordering formulas for which a clerk would have neither understanding nor the time to make the necessary calculations.

4. *Make routine materials decisions.* The computer can review the lead time and planned usage of each item. When inventory drops to the reorder point, it can be programmed to print automatically a purchase requisition calling for a new buy. If there is no need to get competitive bids, the computer can be programmed to print a purchase order instead of a requisition.

The computer would not necessarily take action whenever it receives a requisition or when inventory drops to a reorder point. It might be programmed to wait until there was further demand for an item. For example, suppose the computer received a requisition for an item on June 1 that was required on September 1 and lead time was 4 weeks. The computer would hold off ordering that item until late in July and, in the meanwhile, would go ahead and accumulate other orders for that item, grouping them together into a single big order. Thus, the computer can automatically be programmed to search for the biggest possible quantity discount.

Computers can also be made delivery-conscious. For example, when a predetermined lead time has elapsed or when inventories drop to some dangerously low level, the computer can be programmed to print automatically a notice calling for expediting. The supplier's promised delivery date also can be fed into the computer, and another expediting notice is generated if the material is not received before this time. If an item needs expediting for several consecutive buys—or if delivery is consistently early—the computer can analyze the purchase history and calculate a new time.

5. *Provide up-to-date cost data.* The computer can easily be programmed to multiply purchase quantities and inventory balances by unit prices. This gives the controller current reports on inventory investment and also an accurate estimate of future cash needs to pay for deliveries against open purchase orders.

The computer can also be programmed to make a special report on all items where there is a price change; this naturally would facilitate the materials manager's control over purchase prices. It would also be easy to print from data already in the computer special reports showing expenditures by supplier. This information would be useful both for reciprocity and for various reports that prime contractors must make for the armed services on relations with small business, and so on.

Problems with electronic data processing

Although they are revolutionizing business procedures, computers are not a completely unmixed blessing. They are extremely expensive. Big firms often have several million dollars invested in a single computer center, in addition to paying substantial sums in monthly rental for the computer itself. The smaller firm can get along with a smaller computer or may even simply rent time on someone else's machine.

The cost of developing a program and transferring data from manual records to the computer can also be enormous. Between 20,000 and 50,000 man-hours of labor may be needed to translate the basic data for an inventory of 6,000 items into "machine language." Many companies that have adopted EDP systems control 20,000 or more items with them. Needless to say, their investment in EDP start-up cost is even greater.

Because of these high costs, only a few giant corporations could conceivably afford to use a computer exclusively for materials management. The normal practice is to share the computer among all the major departments of the business. Usually the biggest user is finance—for payroll, general accounting, and cost accounting. The marketing and engineering departments also can be big users of computers.

When a computer is used reasonably close to its effective capacity, it will normally effect savings in clerical costs that will more than offset its high operating costs. In some companies, materials management employment has been reduced by 50 percent or more after the introduction of the computer. In most cases, however, reduction in employment has been more modest. In fact, it is a moot point whether or not the computer has actually reduced materials management operating costs. Instead, its real benefits are represented by tighter control. If the personnel relations problems that are inevitable when the computer requires large-scale reclassification and transfers of employees is taken into account, its impact on materials management operations (as distinct from overall performance) may be negative on balance.

There are also problems in programming the computer. Even the most routine clerical job has dozens of minor problems that require decisions. Each problem must be anticipated in programming the computer. A few of them are bound to be overlooked. For example, suppose a company has programmed a computer to generate a buy notice if safety stock drops to a given level. Regardless of the reason the stock drops, the computer faithfully follows instructions and generates the buy notices. This can create problems if other controls are not programmed into the computer as well.

Suppose, for example, there are engineering or quality control problems with a given product. Management wants to let stocks run down until the problem is solved. With manual inventory control, the clerks would simply ignore the declining stock balances on the items affected and would write no requisitions until they were told the problem was solved. With automatic control, the computer would flood the buying department with dozens or even hundreds of useless buy notices. If they are not properly regulated, automatic systems can generate so much unnecessary paper work that their usefulness is substantially reduced.

Every company that has attempted to set up an EDP system for materials management has encountered expensive and troublesome "bugs" that must be ironed out before the system works well. However, practically all of them agree that the results are worth the effort and cost.

A typical application

Fairchild Industries Corporation uses an IBM computer and related equipment for materials management. Basic scheduling data and parts lists are stored on magnetic drums in the memory part of the computer. Every materials transaction—schedule changes, purchase orders, receivals, and so on—is recorded on punched cards (see Figure 19–8).

FIGURE 19–8

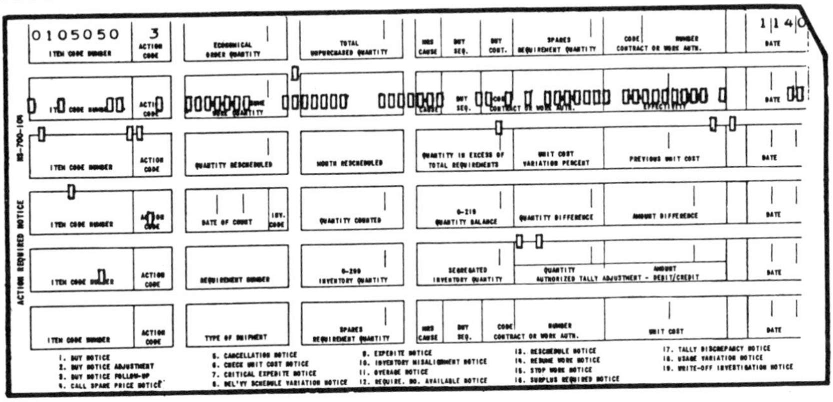

Fairchild Industries Corporation keypunches every materials transaction on 21,000 components onto cards like this one. The data are then transferred to magnetic tape.

Information is then transferred to magnetic tape so it can be fed to the computer at a faster rate.

Nine times per month the tape is fed into the computer, along with a predetermined program (i.e., set of instructions that tell the computer what to do). The computer automatically performs the calculations that the program directs. Results of these calculations are printed on individual material inventory status reports for each item controlled. Figure 19–9 shows transactions for a typical active item.

Reports for action. In addition to status reports for each of 21,000 active items it controls, the computer simultaneously prints orders calling for specific action on items that need it. When stocks of an item drop

FIGURE 19–9

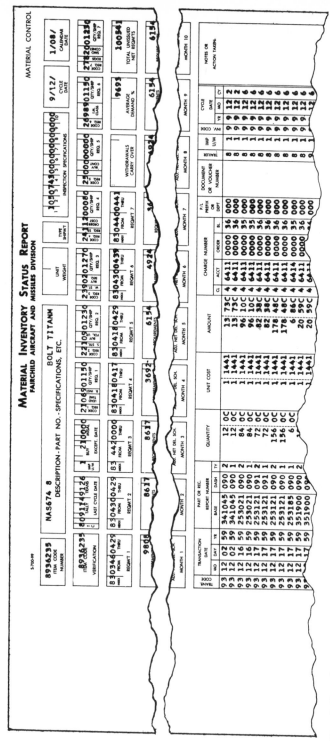

Fairchild Industries Corporation runs a magnetic tape of all materials transactions through its computer nine times per month. Every transaction for each item is automatically printed on a Material Inventory Status Report.

to the point where they equal probable usage during the lead time plus the safety stock, the computer calculates the economic order quantity and prints a buy notice. Similarly, if stock on hand or on order exceeds foreseeable demand, it prints a cancellation notice. The computer also prints three different types of expediting notice:

1. When there is a variance between the planned delivery schedule and the supplier's actual schedule.
2. When inventory drops to one half the safety stock.
3. When there is not enough stock for current operations.

If some purchasing action is not taken, the computer is programmed to find out why. If an order is not placed after the computer issues a buy notice, the computer asks why when the follow-up time programmed into it has expired. For example, the computer might print a buy notice on March 1 requesting that a purchase order for material be placed by March 15. If the order is not placed and recorded on the magnetic tape, the computer may print a notice asking why the order was not placed when the tape is run through it on March 15. If engineering has issued a "hold" on the item requesting that all new commitments for an item be delayed because of possible design changes, the computer is programmed to take this into account and refrain from printing new buy notices until the part is taken off the "hold" list.

Quantities calculated by the computer include predetermined contingency factors. Lead times are always up to date, since the buyer must indicate a new lead time when he places the order and this information is passed on to the computer. Order points also are regularly brought up to date. The computer is programmed to forecast demand and calculate order points, using the exponential smoothing techniques discussed in Chapter 9.

Fairchild's gains. Electronic data processing has helped Fairchild do a better materials management job at lower cost. Before EDP, the company had 26 persons in its material control department and 41 persons in its procurement department. After the introduction of EDP, there were only 38 persons in a new combined purchasing and material control department. The heavy personnel cut came in material control activities, where the computer took over about 90 percent of the clerical work. In addition to cutting administrative overhead (most of which is offset by the share of the computer's rental that is chargeable to materials management), Fairchild has enjoyed these benefits through EDP:

1. *Fewer delays in manufacturing due to late deliveries, and less expediting expense.* With the computer there are fewer cases where material is ordered late and delivery must be rushed to meet schedules.

2. *Lower average inventories.* The computer issues a buy notice only when needed. Long lead-time items are bought before short lead-

time items; material is scheduled for delivery only when it is actually required. This reduces average inventories. Stockouts from excessively low inventories are prevented because the computer maintains a much closer surveillance of inventory position than was possible before. The computer makes a complete review of all inventory items nine times a month and recomputes safety stocks and order points to take account of changes in usage.

3. *Lower average costs of material.* Economic order quantities are programmed into the computer. Buy notices are accumulated until they are absolutely needed because of lead time. As a result, there are fewer buys in larger quantities, and purchasing can get lower prices.

4. *Better planning of cash flow.* Reports of open purchase commitments (the computer is informed whenever a purchase order is issued) permit the controller to project cash needs with precision. Funds not needed can either be invested in short-term securities or used to reduce loans.

5. *Improved cost control.* Product costs can be tabulated from data on the computer. Changes in costs can be picked up accurately and rapidly. Formerly the controller got monthly product cost tabulations two weeks late; now he gets weekly reports with only five days' delay. Major cost changes get special attention. Any price change greater than 10 percent for an order of more than $25 is picked up by the computer and reported separately for review and analysis.

6. *Faster purchasing.* Formerly, contract extensions had to be added manually to each material control card before new requirements could be figured. This was a slow, tedious job. Now the change in end-product requirements is put into the computer and all of the detail work is done automatically. Purchasing knows the effect of a contract change almost in a matter of hours. Similarly, when a contract is cut back, purchasing can move faster on cancellations.

Fairchild's price. All these benefits were not gained without sacrifice. Besides the recurring expense of operating the computer, Fairchild had to make a one-time investment of roughly 5,000 hours of labor, including 1,800 hours at overtime rates, to translate its materials records into a form that could be handled by the computer. Even with the best programming that can be devised, the computer cannot do what the lowliest clerk can: think. If some data must be handled in a slightly different fashion, a clerk will automatically make allowances. With a computer the problem must be anticipated, or there will be trouble.

For example, with conventional programming the computer will not issue a buy notice until the lead time requires it. This is desirable in most cases, of course—but not always. If a certain item is in short supply, a buyer may wish to order as soon as there is a requirement, even if this is months before he would be required to do so by the lead time. A clerk could work from a special list of all such items.

A computer can only follow the instructions in its program. Fairchild overcame this particular problem by programming the computer to handle certain items as "buy instant." The computer is programmed so that it generates a buy notice for such items as soon as there are requirements.

Other problems have not been solved that easily. One that took a great deal of time to overcome was minimum buys. Suppose the computer calculates that 12 cotter pins are needed and generates a buy notice to that effect. If the buyer's vendor requires a minimum order of $5, the actual purchase quantity might be 1,000 cotter pins.

When the purchase order data are fed into the computer, the trouble begins. The computer compares a requirement of 12 pieces with a potential inventory of 1,000 pieces and proceeds to take steps to prevent excessive inventories from accumulating by printing a purchase order cancellation notice for 988 pieces. This wasted paper work can be corrected by another special addition to the program that tells the computer to handle minimum order parts in a special way.

The computer will not solve the problem of usage variation, either. It can compute procurement lead times and safety stock by almost any mathematical technique. But if usage varies erratically, eventually the computer will make a mistake: either safety stock will be inadequate and there will actually be a stockout before a new shipment arrives, or the safety stock will be so big that inventories will be excessive. Clerks also have trouble with erratic demand fluctuations, but sometimes they manage to do a better job of controlling them than a computer can.

For these and other reasons, Fairchild still has about 1,400 items under manual control. For these items, clerks keep records and relate past usage to future sales. Customer-choice items are also controlled manually; it is not worthwhile to put them into the system because the item is being bought only for one customer's special order.

The future. Despite the cost and the problems, Fairchild has no intention of ever going back to manual methods of materials management. It believes EDP is here to stay. In fact, it anticipates further improvements that will result in even wider applications. The role of EDP in the materials organization of the future will be discussed in Chapter 21.

Cases

CASE 19–1. CAROLINA PAPER COMPANY

Improving records and administrative controls

The Catawassa mill of the Carolina Paper Company was built in 1910 to take advantage of the ample supplies of timber in the area as well as the almost unlimited water supply available from the Catawassa River. Since 1945, the mill has more than trebled its capacity. Now it has reached a period of consolidation. The entire paper industry is currently suffering from overcapacity. Every producer is hard pressed to preserve profit margins. Carolina is no exception, and it has called in a management consulting firm, David–John–Karen, for advice. One of the changes the consultants recommend is that Carolina adopt a materials management type of organization. The following year this recommendation is followed, and George Jenkins, from a leading New England paper company, is hired as Carolina's materials manager.

One of Jenkins's first jobs as materials manager is to analyze the procedures and records in his department. He discovers that the company's single most important material, logs for the pulp mill, is controlled almost entirely by the log buyer, Alan White. Logs are purchased from dozens of small lumber mills and are also supplied by the company's own forestry department, which White treats as an outside supplier. White's procedure is to get a copy of the company's pulp-mill schedule and to determine from it what the demand for logs will be. He then places order with his suppliers. The traffic department arranges with the railroad to have cars available to pick up logs from White's suppliers.

White keeps a separate record for each supplier. Whenever he places an order, he posts it to the appropriate supplier's record. When a shipment is received, White gets a copy of the receiving report and credits it against the open order. White also keeps a separate inventory record for hardwood and softwood logs. As cars come in from the suppliers, he debits this record; as they are unloaded for the logs to be cut into pulp, he credits the record. His inventory is represented by the full cars waiting in the company's switching yard.

Somewhat different systems are used by the company to control other raw materials (mostly chemicals used in papermaking and for maintenance supplies. Raw materials are stored either in the mill's yard or in a storage shed. Manufacturing makes withdrawals whenever necessary. The buyer knows from experience approximately what usage will be, and he schedules his purchases so that they will approximately equal usage. Occasionally he also makes physical checks of the stock to make certain there are no drastic fluctuations. When usage is extremely heavy, the mill's general foreman will sometimes warn him that his stock of a particular chemical is getting low. The buyer then gets on the telephone immediately and places a rush order. This is rare, however, since the buyer normally protects himself with a more than adequate safety stock. He readjusts this stock once a year, when the annual inventory is taken. Last year, the inventory indicated that he was carrying $500,000 in chemical inventories, which was an average three months' usage.

Carolina's maintenance storeroom is organized somewhat like a grocery supermarket. Whenever they need material, individual maintenance men walk into the storeroom and help themselves to whatever they need. They record their withdrawals on a stores requisition form. The maintenance men on the day shift simply give the form to the stores clerk, who then posts it to perpetual inventory record cards. The men on the afternoon and evening shifts leave the forms in a box to be posted later by the clerk.

The clerk reorders whenever there is a stockout or when his records show that the stock has dropped to the reorder point. He calculates the reorder point by studying usage history and comparing it with the lead-time estimate he gets from the purchasing department. His reorder point is normally equal to his estimate of usage during the lead time plus a 50 percent safety allowance. Whenever there is a stockout, however, the clerk increases his safety allowance a little to try to prevent a recurrence. Stockouts do not occur too often, even though the annual physical inventory always indicates that there have been more withdrawals from stock than were ever recorded in stores requisitions; the safety stocks are more than adequate to take care of shrinkage.

When stock does drop to the reorder point, the clerk prepares a purchase requisition for the desired purchase quantity. The purchasing department then issues a conventional purchase order for the required material. The stores department gets a copy of this order, which it posts to the perpetual inventory card. In most cases, it then can forget about the order until the material is received and it posts the receiving report and move ticket to the inventory card. If there is a stockout before the material is received, the stores clerk calls purchasing and requests that the purchase be expedited. He also increases the lead time shown on his inventory card to prevent a recurrence of the stockout.

Questions

1. What improvements, if any, can be made in Carolina's materials management procedures?

2. How can control be improved or cost of paper work reduced?

CASE 19–2. VERTOL DIVISION, BOEING COMPANY

Data-Phone system speeds order processing

John Brane, materiel director of the Vertol Division of the Boeing Company, Morton, Pennsylvania, decided to make a 30-day tour of other companies' procurement installations with his top aides in order to search for ways in which to improve his own company's techniques and procedures. He then established an "improvement board" staffed on a rotating basis with members from purchasing, outside production (subcontracting), warehousing, and various other materiel groups. The improvement board meets regularly to search for improvement procurement techniques. Its first recommendation was installation of a Data-Phone system to purchase office supplies. It was believed that this would lead to similar installations to purchase other items. The Data-Phone installation permits information to be transmitted from Vertol's EDP system over telephone lines to that of the supplier.

Brane declared, "If you have good blanket orders to begin with, you're probably ready for Data-Phone. There is nothing mysterious about the system. It's simply an ultra-efficient technique for making blanket order releases."

Al Martorell, manager of materiel, programming, and planning (one of the materiel groups reporting to Brane), points out that "all of the advantages of Data-Phone stem from its ability to transmit releases faster and more accurately. As a result of these benefits, we've reduced inventory, cut paper work, freed the buyer from petty details, and lowered administrative expenses.

"These are impressive savings, but they're tough ones on which to hang a definite price tag. So, at least for now, we don't attempt to do so. Instead, if price, quality, service are the same among competing bids, we give the nod to the supplier equipped to plug into our Data-Phone system."

Philadelphia Stationers was Vertol's first Data-Phone connection, since it was fully equipped with a receiving set, a transmitting unit (to feed conventional orders into its automated system) and auxiliary data processing equipment. Under Vertol's setup, when an item in the stationery storeroom hits the reorder point, a stores clerk calls purchasing. One of the purchasing department clerks accumulates reorder requests and transmits once or twice a week to Philadelphia Stationers. To do this, he:

1. Dials Philadelphia Stationers' number on the Data-Phone and waits for the dial tone that indicates all is clear for transmitting.
2. Inserts Vertol's identifying master card into the IBM 1001 card reader, an adjunct to the Data-Phone.
3. Inserts each item card into the 1001, and keys in quantity required.
4. Hits the "end" button when all cards have been processed.

Whenever necessary, the clerk can establish voice communication with the supplier. An example is if he wishes to segregate certain items against a specific release number. Ordinarily, release numbers and release dates are programmed in at Philadelphia Stationers. For purchasing's records, the clerk handwrites date and quantity ordered on each item's card.

Receiving equipment at Philadelphia Stationers triggers an 026 keypunch unit to bang out duplicate IBM cards. When these cards are run through a 402 accounting machine, they produce a four-part continuous-form packing list. This list is used for stock picking and accompanies the shipment (usually within 48 hours) to Vertol.

Vertol, in turn, uses the packing list for receiving purposes. The receiving clerk signs two copies for the supplier's deliveryman, sends the third copy to the finance department, and forwards the fourth copy, with the goods, to the stationery storeroom.

A key feature of this operation is that Philadelphia Stationers lists items on the packing slip in the same order as on the original blanket order. It sorts the IBM cards manually on small releases and uses automatic equipment on large ones. Vertol's finance department, consequently, need not skip from page to page of the master order to check invoice prices.

With the supplier's shelf stocks backing up the stationery storeroom so effectively, Vertol has trimmed its on-hand investment in office supplies by one third. While part of this reduction is due to conventional blanket orders (about 80 percent of office items are covered by some type of annual agreement), purchasing stresses Data-Phone's key role in shrinking the buyer-supplier communications loop.

On virtually all other Data-Phone links established by Vertol following its success with office supplies, purchasing has dealt itself out of the paper-shuffling game completely. "After six months' experience with office supplies," explains Carroll Parrish, manager of purchasing, "we started converting other blanket orders to Data-Phone. We soon had eight more. Since seven of these involve standard floor supplies like nuts, bolts, and rivets, we put the Data-Phone equipment right in the warehouse stocking the items."

"We've got about 1,500 of these supply items on Data-Phone now," Parrish continues, "and one of the orders is with a West Coast firm. We use a WATS line to make transmissions there. Or, I should say, the warehouse inventory supervisor does. We don't touch the cards in purchasing. Instead, we negotiate blanket orders annually."

When traffic from the stationery storeroom warrants, Vertol plans to install another Data-Phone there. Having the equipment in purchasing provides some decided advantages. "We use it for demonstrations to other suppliers," says Parrish, "to help sell them on the simplicity and efficiency of Data-Phone."

A significant difference between the original Data-Phone agreement covering office supplies and subsequent ones is that release cards for floor supply items are prepunched with "order quantities." On stationery orders, the clerk in purchasing keys in this information.

To make sure all stationery releases are in standard packaging units, Philadelphia Stationers ran a data processing report on all of Vertol's releases after three months on the system. Then it provided Vertol with a run-off sheet, showing item description, unit of measure, lead time

FIGURE 19–10

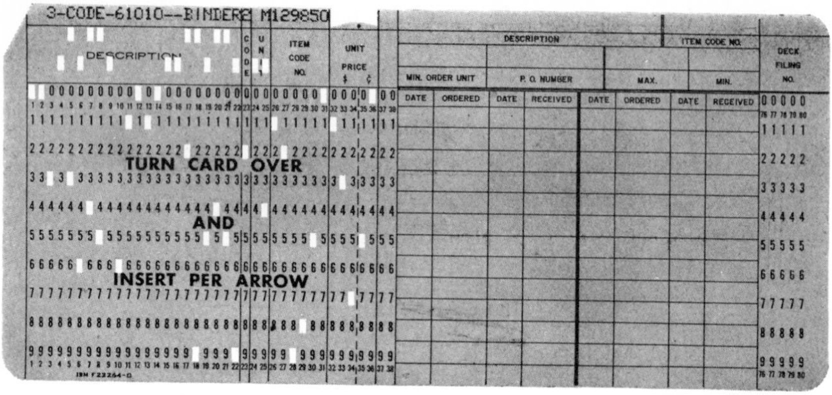

Vendor-supplied tab cards cover every item on the blanket order for office supplies. A purchasing clerk uses these cards to transmit fast, completely accurate releases. (Unit price has been deleted from this sample.)

FIGURE 19–11

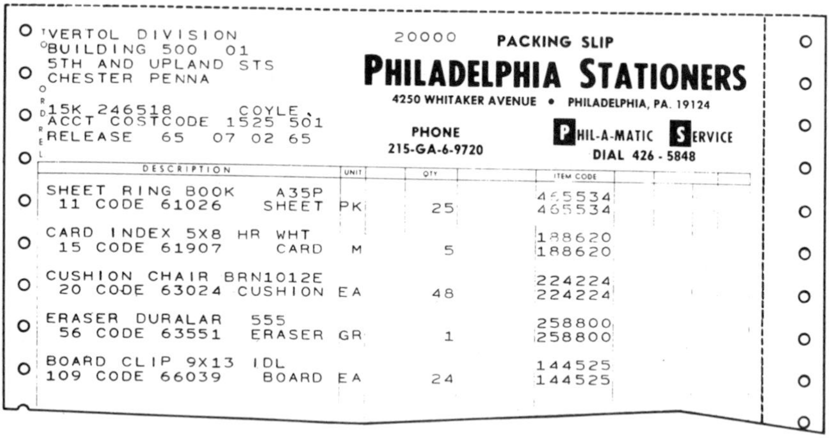
VERTOL DIVISION
BUILDING 500 01
5TH AND UPLAND STS
CHESTER PENNA

15K 246518 COYLE
ACCT COSTCODE 1525 501
RELEASE 65 07 02 65

20000 PACKING SLIP
PHILADELPHIA STATIONERS
4250 WHITAKER AVENUE • PHILADELPHIA, PA. 19124
PHONE 215-GA-6-9720
PHIL-A-MATIC SERVICE
DIAL 426 - 5848

DESCRIPTION		UNIT	QTY	ITEM CODE
SHEET RING BOOK 11 CODE 61026	A35P SHEET	PK	25	465534 465534
CARD INDEX 5X8 HR WHT 15 CODE 61907	CARD	M	5	188620 188620
CUSHION CHAIR BRN1012E 20 CODE 63024	CUSHION	EA	48	224224 224224
ERASER DURALAR 56 CODE 63551	555 ERASER	GR	1	258800 258800
BOARD CLIP 9X13 109 CODE 66039	IDL BOARD	EA	24	144525 144525

Packing list, developed by the supplier's data processing equipment, serves as a receiving report on incoming shipments. The fact that this form always lists items in the same order as they appear on the original blanket order is a big help for accounting.

for the few nonshelf items on the blanket order, unit price, package quantity, standard carton quantity, and suggested order quantity.

This sheet guides the clerk so he can amend quantities requested to the nearest standard container quantity. In addition, every month Philadelphia Stationers submits three copies of a complete analysis of all items shipped. The office supplies buyer keeps one copy for his own use, sends one to the stationery storeroom, and routes the third to procurement and material management.

Philadelphia Stationers also submits a consolidated report of usage at the end of each annual contract, or whenever Vertol requests one. The Data-Phone setup is now in its second year with the office supply house, and Vertol is very pleased with it.

Purchasing is convinced that its approach to Data-Phone—paced by the office supplies agreement—really works. No problems have arisen in the warehouse from having several vendors handle similar items by Data-Phone. Recently, for example, the inventory supervisor there sent releases on 16 items to six vendors in just eight minutes.

Currently, Vertol is considering perishable tools and maintenance supplies as likely Data-Phone candidates. Backstopped by its acquired know-how and experience with office supplies and other items, the division figures to make the switch quickly, easily, and without violating its competitive buying policies.

Questions

1. Is Data-Phone likely to limit competition among suppliers or increase it? Explain.

2. What should Vertol guard against in expanding its Data-Phone system?

3. Suppose a supplier not equipped with Data-Phone offers Vertol lower prices than a supplier equipped with Data-Phone. How would Vertol go about deciding which supplier's bid to accept?

20

Measuring materials management performance

THERE ARE four basic steps in measuring the performance of any manager or department. They are:

1. Define the limits of the job.
2. Determine the objectives to be achieved within these limits.
3. Develop a program to meet these objectives.
4. Compare progress on the program with the objectives.

The limits of the job are defined by the organization structure and policies and procedures. In previous chapters, it was noted that the ideal materials organization embraces all related materials activities: purchasing, traffic, material control, and so on. The typical objectives of the materials organization were defined as:

1. Low operating costs (i.e., low costs of acquisition and possession and low payroll costs).
2. Low prices of purchased material.
3. Minimum investment in inventory (i.e., high inventory turnover).
4. Superior supplier performance (i.e., adequate quality of purchased materials, prompt delivery, and generally favorable vendor relations).
5. Development of materials personnel.
6. Good records.

DEVELOPING THE PROGRAM

The third basic step in measuring performance—developing a program to meet objectives—was discussed in Chapter 7. The program normally would include both qualitative and quantitative goals. Among the latter would be a detailed budget to control operating costs and specific cost-reduction and inventory management performance. Other goals are inherently qualitative, however, including those of better supplier relations, development of personnel, and good records.

The materials manager should have a program for the department to achieve these goals. In addition, he should require each of his key subordinates to develop programs to achieve similar goals. Authority to develop a program should be delegated to the lowest possible. level in the organization. In doing this, the materials manager ensures that the efforts of everyone in the organization will be directed toward goals that are consistent with those of the whole department and of the company.

In the larger corporation, each divisional materials manager should develop his own program. Typically, he might submit a plan to the corporate materials manager once a year in which he describes his goals for the coming year. The corporate materials manager would then review and compare the plans submitted by his subordinates. Some of them he might accept without any questions. Others would have to be reviewed in some detail in order to make them consistent with department-wide goals.

Each divisional materials manager is encouraged to exercise his initiative and set standards against which his performance could be measured. He naturally would set goals for cost reduction and inventory turnover. In addition, he would encourage his subordinates to control their own operating costs, budgeting themselves on travel, telephone calls, and personnel. In this plan, the materials manager would not only include how he intended to develop his subordinates but also indicate—after a frank discussion of his own strengths and weaknesses with his boss—how he proposed to correct his own shortcomings.

With this approach, not only is responsibility for performance delegated to the lowest possible level, but the practice in planning is itself a management development tool. Men and women become experienced in planning and administration while they are still in junior jobs. This permits management to test their managerial ability long before they advance to levels where their mistakes can seriously hurt the organization.

The materials manager's plan is a composite of the plans of his subordinates and would also be submitted annually. If accepted by top management, it would become a standard against which the department's performance would be measured. Performance measurements of individual parts of the plan might be made annually, quarterly, monthly, weekly, or even daily. In general, performance in achieving the qualitative goals would be measured less frequently than that in achieving the quantitative goals. For example, an annual or quarterly report would usually be adequate to measure progress in personnel development. On the other hand, deviations from operating budgets might be reported monthly, while price changes often are reported weekly or daily.

The quantitative phases of performance measurement get more attention for several reasons. Among them are the following:

1. *Quantitative data are more objective.* They are based on operating statistics, whereas qualitative data reflect, in large part, the opinion of the observer. It would be hard for a materials manager to distort performance on cost reduction, where progress is measured in dollars and cents. But it would be very easy for him to exaggerate the progress he is making on such intangible goals as personnel development or improved supplier relations.

2. *Quantitative data usually change faster.* Most of the materials management goals that can only be measured qualitatively are long range in nature. Progress on them is usually so slow that it is pointless to attempt to measure it weekly or daily. On the other hand, progress on quantitative goals should be measured frequently, so that remedies can be applied immediately should performance fall short of expectations.

3. *Quantitative data are more directly related to company profits.* Top management has an immediate interest in materials management goals such as cost reduction and inventory turnover which can be measured quantitatively. Performance is directly related to day-to-day operating decisions. On the other hand, management is usually interested in qualitative goals only when it is planning for the future.

CONTROL OF OPERATING COSTS

Managements have been measuring how effectively purchasing agents and materials managers control operating costs for years. In fact, in the less progressive companies this is the only performance measurement that is applied to the materials department. The assumption is that the materials department is a service activity and should be interested primarily in providing its service at the lowest possible cost. Implicit in this assumption is the concept that the materials department is a clerical activity, and its performance should be measured in terms of how much it costs to process each purchase order, requisition, or production release. Accountants then carefully calculate the department's costs and divide them by the number of forms it processes. By this criterion, a purchasing department whose operating costs are equal to $10 for each purchase order it issues is considered more efficient than one that spends $12 per order.

This is a false concept, of course. Control of operating costs is just one objective of the materials department, and not the most important one, by any means. For example, the typical materials department can save $50 by buying materials at lower prices for every $1 that it can shave from its operating costs. And the best materials departments usually have rather high operating costs because they are willing to pay higher salaries to attract highly skilled personnel who are capable of doing an outstanding job of materials management.

Nevertheless, control of operating costs is still a fairly important objective. Were there no control, costs would soon get out of hand. Operating costs should be budgeted as part of the overall materials plan. Performance can be measured in two ways: (1) measurement of the productivity of the persons employed in the materials department with either absolute or relative standards; (2) measurement of success in controlling direct materials department expenses by comparing actual costs with budgeted costs.

Control of personnel

The materials department plan should include an estimate of personnel needed to achieve objectives. This estimate, if approved, becomes the department's personnel budget. Whenver possible, it should be based on objective criteria. For purchasing and material control jobs, the criterion may be the number of parts of a given type that a person can handle. For example, one company calculates that each buyer should be able to handle 250 complex parts and about 500 simple items; this company also needs one materials planner and two clerks for each 1,000 items that are controlled. Similar criteria can be applied to other materials activities. For example, personnel requirements in traffic, shipping, and receiving can be measured in terms of the number of shipments handled.

All the standards mentioned so far are relative. They are useful in determining personnel needs when work loads change. For example, if one buyer is needed for each 250 parts, we know that we must hire two buyers if 500 parts are added because of a new product. Absolute standards are more difficult to justify. How do we know that a buyer cannot handle 400 parts, for example, instead of only 200? For some jobs, particularly the highly skilled ones, the answer is mostly a matter of judgment. The materials manager draws on his own experience and that of his supervisors, and he may also make comparisons with companies with similar materials management problems.

Time studies. More exact methods can be used to measure the less skilled jobs. Any job that involves doing something—as distinct from thinking about something—can be measured with conventional time-study techniques. The time-study man breaks the job into its basic components and calculates how much time it takes to perform each element at some standard of efficiency. Work standards can easily be set for such repetitive materials operations as typing purchase orders, filing various documents, processing various types of shipments and receivals, and so on. Many large corporations have made time studies of their highly repetitive materials jobs. A few even have introduced incentive pay on certain jobs. For example, one company boosted the productivity of its purchase order typists by more than 20 percent with incentive pay. Current output averages about 125 orders per typist per day.

Work sampling. It is difficult to make time studies of the less repetitive jobs, but they can be analyzed with ratio-delay, or work-sampling, studies. The first step in making such a study is to break the job into a series of simple elements that can readily be observed—walking away from the desk, talking to visitors, typing, talking on the telephone, doing nothing, and so on. Then an observer, unknown to the subject, notes the subject's activity at random intervals. Usually several thousand observations are made over a period of several months.

Accuracy of the data increases in proportion to the square of the number of observations. It is measured with the formula

$$s = \sqrt{\frac{p(1-p)}{n}}$$

where s is the standard deviation for an event that occurred p percent (expressed as a decimal) of n observations. For example, suppose that a buyer was attending meetings 1,000 times in the course of 10,000 observations. Thus, p obviously equals 10 percent, or 0.10.

Therefore,

$$s = \sqrt{\frac{.10(1-.10)}{10,000}} = .003$$

Converting to a percentage, the standard deviation is therefore 0.3 percent. Since we know that three standard deviations embrace 99.72 percent of a normal curve, we can then be more than 99 percent confident that the buyer spends at least 9.1 percent of his time attending meetings (10 percent *minus* three times 0.3 percent) and not more than 10.9 percent (10 percent *plus* three times 0.3 percent). If we made 100,000 observations, we could reduce our standard deviation to 0.03 percent, while it would be but 3.0 percent if we made just 100 observations.

Ratio-delay studies are not foolproof, but they can give clues to improvements, both in the average performance of everyone performing the job being studied and in individual performance. A large appliance firm made such a study of secretaries and buyers in its materials department. Figures 20–1 and 20–2 show the results. Note in Figure 20–1 that the average buyer's secretary spent 10 percent of her time on the telephone. Investigation might show either that the company was too lenient about personal calls or—as was actually the case at this appliance company—that secretaries were wasting too much time placing long-distance calls for buyers, which could be handled more efficiently by the operator on the company's switchboard.

The studies also are useful for individual comparison of performance.

FIGURE 20–1
Ratio-delay study of secretaries' performance

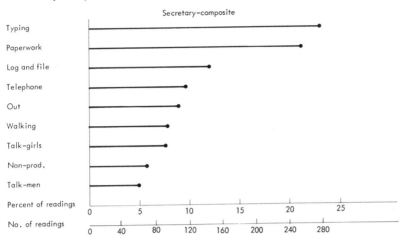

This chart shows the results of ratio-delay studies made of ten buyers' secretaries. Managers get clues to performance when they compare studies of individual secretaries to this average.

FIGURE 20–2
Ratio-delay study of buyers' performance

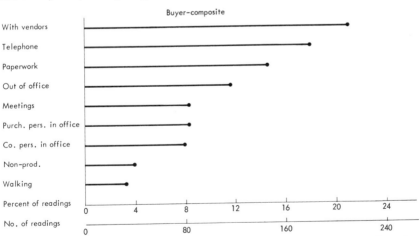

This chart shows how the average buyer in a midwestern appliance manufacturing company spends his time. It is based on ratio-delay studies of ten buyers in the purchasing department.

Figure 20–1 shows, for example, that the average secretary spent 5 percent of her time doing nothing, 10 percent away from her desk, and 7 percent talking to other girls in the office. One would have little doubt as to the efficiency of the secretary who spent 10, 15, and 10 percent of her time on these activities respectively and correspondingly less on her more productive (and less pleasant) jobs: typing, paper work, and filing.

Usually there is an excellent correlation between ratio-delay studies of clerical workers and other evaluations of their efficiency. The least efficient secretary will have the highest average of nonproductive time. With the more highly skilled jobs, however, this may not be true. The best buyer may spend a greater percentage of his time doing nothing than the average buyer (see Figure 20–2), who spends only 4 percent of his time engaged in no apparent activity. The reason for this, of course, is that the best buyer may be able to perform routine tasks with dispatch and devote a greater part of his time to planning and generating ideas for cost reduction and product improvement.

Control of direct costs

The materials manager rarely has any problem controlling his biggest operating expense: wages and salaries. He gets his personnel budget approved and allows for salary adjustments. His performance will inevitably be satisfactory so long as he does not grant salary increases or increase his staff in excess of the budget.

Nonsalary costs. Other expenses are harder to control. Travel and telephone expenses can easily get out of hand in a materials department, particularly if there are many unexpected quality and delivery problems with suppliers. Such expenses are heavy enough even when everything goes according to plan. Contact must be maintained with thousands of suppliers. A materials department responsible for annual purchases of $30 million may have telephone and telegraph bills that exceed $2,000 per month, and it may spend as much as $20,000 per year on travel.

Telephone and travel expenses are controlled much as personnel expenses are. A budget for each is included in the overall purchase plan. Standards are based on past experience. For example, both telephone calls and travel expenses would tend to vary with the dollar volume of purchases, the number of suppliers, and the number of employees in the department. Suppose that telephone expenses totaled $30,000 in a year when there were 100 persons in the materials department, 6,000 suppliers, and a $30 million purchase volume. Then a budget of $32,000 would not be unreasonable for a year when volume of purchases rises to $35 million, there are 110 persons in the department, and it is planned to introduce a number of new suppliers.

Most other expenses can be controlled in similar fashion. Expenses for office supplies, for example, should vary almost directly with either the number of persons employed in the materials department or the number of purchase orders and other forms being processed.

Comparison with results

Salaries and other direct costs are not ends in themselves; they are incurred to achieve results. The materials manager is concerned with both quantity and quality of the output of his staff. Quantity is easier to measure. It involves comparison of actual operating costs with tangible output: number of purchase orders issued, the rate at which requisitions are processed, stock withdrawals, receivals, and so on.

Many materials managers keep their finger on their departments' performance with charts that graphically measure output. For example, Figure 20–3 shows one of the operating charts used by I. T. T. Kellogg

FIGURE 20–3
Performance chart

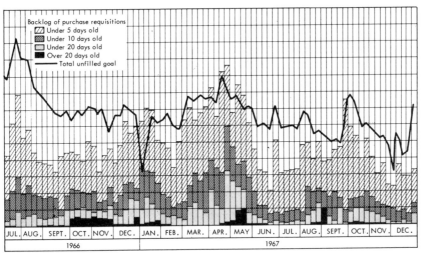

Chart measures performance in processing requisitions. Solid line shows permissible backlog (determined by comparison of requisitions on hand with department capacity). Bars show number of requisitions in various age categories. By December 1967, the department's productivity had improved markedly. The backlog is only about half what would be expected (solid line compared with top of bar chart), and most of the requisitions in the backlog are less than 5 days old.

Communications Systems to show how rapidly the purchasing department is processing requisitions. Each week, a clerk checks all open requisitions for material that has not yet been ordered. He classifies them into four groups: those that have been in the department less than 5 days, less than 10 days, under 20 days, and over 20 days.

Of course, the object of the game is to fill all requisitions as rapidly as possible. Unfortunately the requisition load fluctuates erratically, while purchasing's ability to fill requisitions is fixed by the size of its staff. The permissible backlog is represented by the difference between purchasing's capacity to issue orders and the actual backlog. During dull periods, the permissible backlog declines and almost all requisitions can be filled within five days of their receipt in the department.

During exceptionally busy periods, the permissible backlog grows, and the age composition of open requisitions also shifts. An increasing percentage is more than five days old simply because the department has more work than it can handle. The purchasing manager can study this chart and measure how well his department is doing and, also, determine whether or not he is falling behind.

Similar charts can be constructed to measure the percentage of purchase orders on which suppliers have fallen behind in meeting delivery dates, and in processing orders. They can also be used to control operating costs.

CONTROL OF PRICES

The charts above are good measures of the *quantity* of work that is being done. But the materials manager is also interested in the *quality* of this work. He wants to know how effectively his staff is contributing to the company's profit objectives. The biggest contribution comes when costs of purchased material are reduced. Department operating costs are usually almost trivial compared with what is spent for purchased parts and materials. For example, if a typical materials department cut its telephone bill or its office-supply expenses by 2 percent, it might save a few hundred dollars per year. There would be no perceptible change in the company's profit margin. But if it could reduce the prices of all purchased materials by 2 percent, profits would rise noticeably. In an average manufacturing company that spends 50 percent of its sales dollar on purchased materials and earns a pretax profit of 10 percent on sales, a 2 percent reduction in purchased materials cost would boost profits by 10 percent. This leveraged effect of purchased materials cost on profits explains why price is perhaps the single most important objective in the typical materials department.

Performance in meeting the price objective can be measured in three ways: by comparing actual costs with the materials budget, by cost-reduction reports and bogies, and by price indexes.

The materials budget

Price performance is most directly related to overall company objectives when actual costs are compared with a materials budget. Most well-managed companies try to budget sales and costs at least a year ahead. Such projections help management evaluate overall performance in reaching profit and sales goals. Usually the cost department calculates standard unit material costs for each product. The materials budget is then calculated by multiplying these standard costs by proposed production volume for each product.

Performance is measured by means of variance accounts that show the difference between actual costs and budgeted costs.[1] Variances can arise both because the unit cost of the material was different from the plan or because usage (or scrap) varied. The former is the materials manager's responsibility; the latter is the manufacturing manager's (unless extra scrap resulted from defective purchased material).

Top management often likes to use the materials budget to measure the materials department's performance because it is so directly related to the objectives of the business and neatly ties in the department with other company activities. However, the materials budget has serious shortcomings for performance measurement. These include:

1. *The materials budget includes only direct materials.* Yet most companies spend substantial sums for indirect materials, which should not be overlooked in cost-reduction programs.

2. *Actual costs show up in variance accounts weeks after they are incurred.* This is because of the lag between the time material is ordered and the time it is finally used after having been in inventory. Because different items have different lead times, it is extremely difficult to reconcile the usual cost department records with purchase records.

3. *Variance figures rarely, if ever, show why a price changed.* Usually price increases and decreases are balanced against one another and are not segregated. In addition, cost department records often are not set up for item-by-item analysis, yet this procedure is essential for good materials management.

Cost-reduction reports

For the reasons above, most materials departments maintain their own controls over cost-reduction efforts. They cannot use cost department records.

The simplest, and one of the most effective, controls over purchase cost is a daily or weekly report of price changes on purchased materials (see the sample form in Figure 20–4). The report lists each item on which there is any price change, the reason for the price change, the amount of the price change, the percentage change, and the cost per month.

---

[1] The reader not familiar with this terminology should consult any accepted text in cost accounting or Robert Dickey (ed.), *Cost Accountants' Handbook*, 2d ed. (New York: Ronald Press Co., 1960).

FIGURE 20-4

WEEKLY REPORT OF PRICE CHANGES   X _____ DIVISION
PURCHASED PARTS AND MATERIALS
PRODUCTION ITEMS ONLY   DATE _10-19-_

PART NO OR MAT'L SPEC	PART NAME OR DESCRIPTION	SUPPLIER	% BUY	OLD PRICE	LOT BUY	EFF DATE	NEW PRICE	LOT BUY	EFF DATE	% OF CHANGE	REASON FOR CHANGE	PRESENT AVG. MO. REQ'MTS.	EFFECT OF PRICE CHANGE Month
345675	Housing	A	100	.275	1000	1-56	.205	1000	10-56	+3.5	LM	300	3.00
356305	Body	B	100	.960	300	1-56	1.017	300	10-56	+3.8	M	100	3.70
367557	Bracket	C	25	3.10	15000	3-56	3.01	15000	9-56	-2.9	M	15000	-1350.00
370752	Cap Screw	D	100	.43	2000	1-56	.45	2000	10-56	+5.7	LM	735	14.70
370941	Bolt	E	100	.77	2000	1-56	.79	2000	10-56	+2.8	M	1045	20.90
383610	Brace	F	70	3.63	2000	3-56	3.46	5000	10-56	-4.9	N	1000	-170.00
381226	Valve	G	100	.57	BLKT	1-56	.59	BLKT	10-56	+3.6	M	41108	622.16
361754	Dowel	H	100	.205	BLKT	1-56	.216	BLKT	9-56	+5.2	LM	1466	16.13
534516	Cover	I	100	.050	300	1-56	.052	300	6-56	+3.2	LM	25	.05
740330	Valve	J	100	.2902	1000	8-56	.3250	1000	8-56	+12.0	LM	525	18.27
737337	Fitting	K	100	.900	10000	5-56	.869	20000	10-56	-1.2	Q	6070	-66.77
739746	Gear	L	100	.0095	10000	7-56	.0092	10000	10-56	-3.2	N	4125	-1.24
35630	Plug	M	100	3.42	100/499	3-56	3.37	500	3-56	-1.4	M	300	-15.00

CODE FOR PRICE CHANGE
M - CHANGE IN MATERIAL COST   N - NEGOTIATED CHANGE   S - SUBSTITUTE MATERIAL
L - CHANGE IN LABOR COST   B - PRODUCT DESIGN CHANGE   Q - QUANTITY ONLY
                                                                                       O - OTHER, EXPLAIN

Courtesy Eaton Corporation

Weekly reports of changes in purchase prices help keep purchasing managers appraised of department performance on cost reduction and also expose any price increases that should be investigated.

Each buying group normally makes its own report. Materials managers can use the reports both as a control and as a measure of performance. When the price for an item rises sharply, they can ask for an explanation. Similarly, when there is a sharp decrease, they may wish to know why the price was so much higher on the previous buy—or they may congratulate the buyer on a skillful job if he exercised considerable ingenuity in finding ways to reduce costs.

Cost-reduction reports can also be used to measure performance of individual buying groups. Data can be accumulated by buying group and by reason for change and compared with budgeted price changes. The reports can be used to generate a healthy spirit of competition among the various buying groups. If each group has a cost-reduction target, then each will not only carefully study the report to see what progress it is making in meeting its own bogey but also be keenly interested in the progress of other groups.

Usually the cost-reduction target is orginally determined as a percentage of purchase cost for each group. Percentages are helpful because they present fewer forecasting problems. For example, a 2 percent quota would hold regardless of whether purchase volume were $10 million or $11 million, whereas an absolute quota would be easier to meet if business were slightly better than expected.

Cost-reduction quotas of 2 to 3 percent are fairly common. The targets then are translated into estimated absolute quotas, which are subject to change should actual dollar volume of purchases be different from forecasted volume. Different buying groups normally would get different quotas, both as a percentage of cost and in dollars. Ideally, the quota should reflect the cost-reduction opportunities of each group. For example, a group buying steel or other commodities where there is little price competition may have a quota of only 1 percent. If its dollar volume were $10 million, the quota would be $100,000. Another buying group might have a 4 percent quota, but its absolute quota would also be $100,000 if its dollar volume were only $2,500,000.

How is the quota determined? First, an overall quota should be set for the entire materials department. It should be based on:

1. *An economic forecast.* If the outlook is for booming business, the quota will have to be quite low, since suppliers will be operating at near-capacity levels and will not be too responsive to cost-reduction efforts. On the other hand, if business is not too good, competition among suppliers will be keen.

2. *Price forecasts for key commodities.* In many companies, a few commodities account for a large share of the volume of purchases. Predicted prices for these commodities should be taken into account when computing overall cost-reduction quotas.[2]

3. *Past performance.* This is one of the most widely used criteria. Managers naturally like to see some improvements each year. On the other hand, buyers sometimes complain that if they succeed in reducing costs for a number of years it becomes progressively harder to meet quotas because the opportunities for cost reduction keep diminishing.

4. *Relation to company profit objectives.* Sometimes cost reduction is necessary if the company is to achieve desired profits. In some cases, top management may exert rather arbitrary pressure on its materials department to reduce costs in order to achieve these overall profit objectives.

5. *Opinions of materials personnel.* The materials manager and each of his commodities specialists know from past experience and from "feel" of the market the cost-reduction quota that can reasonably be achieved.

After an overall quota is agreed upon, individual quotas are set for each group, following the same basic criteria. Individual supervisors should have as much latitude as possible in setting their quotas. This boosts morale and stimulates effort to meet quotas, since they become

---

[2] The principles of price forecasting were discussed in Chapters 6 and 7.

bogies that the supervisor agreed were reasonable rather than targets imposed on him from above. Higher management sometimes finds, however, that it must stimulate supervisors to raise their sights in setting quotas. In some cases, supervisors try to make their jobs too easy; occasionally they are so eager to make a showing that they become overoptimistic.

Obviously, all price reductions are not the result of the buyer's efforts. Market prices drop through no effort on the buyer's part, products are redesigned to reduce cost, and so on. And price increases may reflect superior performance on the part of the buyer when they are held below the amount justified by increases in wages and raw material cost. Therefore, some evaluation of price changes is essential if they are to be good guides of purchasing performance. In a big company, this would be done by someone on the materials manager's staff, usually a purchase analyst or value analyst. In a small company, the materials manager himself may have to do it.

Actual performance on price reductions attributable to buyer action can be charted against the savings objective for each buying group. Figure 20–5 illustrates how one company charts price-reduction progress for each of its buying groups.

FIGURE 20–5
Cost reduction comparison chart

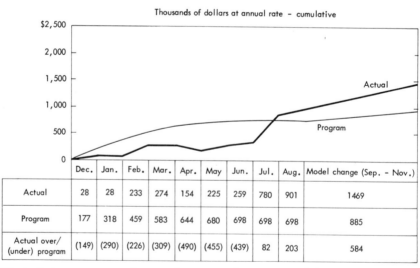

	Dec.	Jan.	Feb.	Mar.	Apr.	May	Jun.	Jul.	Aug.	Model change (Sep. – Nov.)
Actual	28	28	233	274	154	225	259	780	901	1469
Program	177	318	459	583	644	680	698	698	698	885
Actual over/ (under) program	(149)	(290)	(226)	(309)	(490)	(455)	(439)	82	203	584

Charts that compare actual cost reductions with quotas can help stimulate interest in reducing prices, in addition to serving as measures of performance.

Price indexes

Although weekly or daily price change reports are useful to keep materials management informed of price actions by subordinates, they are not ideal for performance measurement. There often are hundreds of price changes each month, even in small companies. Tabulating and evaluating each of them from a price-change report is costly. In addition, errors are almost inevitable. Either buyers will incorrectly estimate usage in computing the monthly cost effect of the price change, or usage will change and their estimate will be inapplicable.

With a price index, on the other hand, estimates can be made with precision. In addition, they can be related directly to the cost of the company's products. There will be fewer errors and less clerical work, since a good index need contain only about 15 percent of total items.[3]

Once the overall index is established and a price-reporting system is operating, it requires relatively little effort to break up index items by buying group so that each group has its own index. This permits comparison both for performance evaluation and to generate a spirit of competition. Purchase-price indexes can also be compared with the indexes of the U.S. Bureau of Labor Statistics and other organizations.[4] For instance, an index made up primarily of metal parts can be compared with the Bureau's wholesale price index of metals and metal products.

INVENTORY PERFORMANCE

Every materials manager strives to operate with minimum inventories, provided that in so doing he does not jeopardize achievement of other objectives (especially low prices and prompt delivery of materials to manufacturing when they are required). In some companies, inventory performance is measured simply by comparing present inventories with those of some base period.

Figure 20–6 shows how a southern textile firm measures performance in inventory management. Index numbers permit easy comparison of present inventory levels in each of its plants with inventory levels that prevailed during the base period. The lower the index number, the greater the progress that has been made in reducing stocks.

Though this measuring technique is simple, it can also be misleading, for it implicitly assumes that the need for inventories is constant from year to year in each plant. In most companies this would not be the case; the need for inventories would vary with the level of output. A more sophisticated approach is to set inventory standards for various levels of output and then compare actual inventories with these standards.

In general, the need for inventories does not rise in direct proportion to output. If $1 million in inventories is needed to maintain a production volume of $1 million per month, substantially less than $2 million in inventories will be needed for an output of $2 million per month. The

---

[3] How to make and use purchase-price indexes is described in detail in Chapter 7.

[4] Many price indexes appear monthly in the *Survey of Current Business,* published by the U.S. Department of Commerce.

FIGURE 20–6
Inventory management performance chart

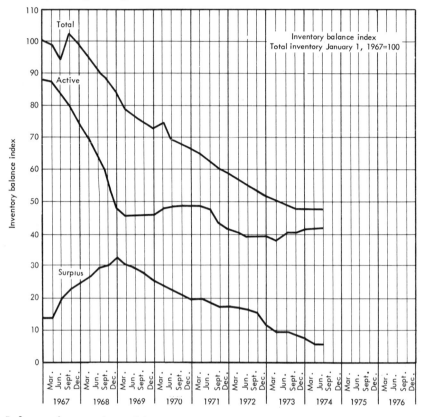

Index numbers can be useful in comparing inventory performance of various buying groups or various plants within the same company. The index number indicates the relative progress each unit has made in relation to some base period.

inventory standard either can be for a specific investment or it can be measured as a rate of turnover (annual dollar volume of purchases divided by average purchased materials inventories). Whenever possible, inventory standards should be established for every subclass of inventory. Then the materials manager can compare actual performance with the standard and locate imbalances. It is possible, of course, to have too little of one class of inventory and too much of another class. Then overall turnover figures would be in line with standards, but individual turnover statistics would highlight imbalances.

Obsolescence should also be budgeted. The budget should be based primarily on past performance, but it should also reflect special conditions. For example, if obsolescence losses the previous year were unusually low because of special circumstances and higher losses will be inevitable during the current year, this should be allowed for in the budget. Otherwise materials personnel will be tempted to continue to carry inventories that should be declared obsolete. Special reports on inventory items for which there is little or no recent demand help the materials—manager eliminate obsolescence.

SUPPLIER PERFORMANCE

Three major materials management objectives directly involve outside suppliers. They are adequate quality, prompt delivery, and favorable vendor relations. It is doubly important that performance in achieving these objectives be measured. It is essential not only to measurement of the materials department's performance but also to measurement of supplier performance by the materials department itself. Good buyers should regularly evaluate the performance of their existing suppliers. Not only should they visit supplier plants regularly, keep up to date on supplier finances and products, and so on, but they should try to keep objective records of supplier quality and delivery performance.

The quality objective

The materials department achieves its quality objective only when all supplier shipments meet standards and the cost of inspecting these shipments can be eliminated. Few materials departments can reach this ideal, but they can work toward it by selecting suppliers with good quality records and educating delinquent suppliers in quality procedures.

Every salesman will maintain that his company's quality is unsurpassed. How can the materials manager evaluate such claims objectively? He does so by analyzing records of his own company's receiving inspection reports. He may simply keep a record of rejects in the form of percentage of total shipments received from each supplier for each basic type of material. Naturally rejects will be higher for some items than for others. What is important is the trend of rejections for a given commodity and the performance of competing suppliers on like commodities. If a supplier starts slipping on quality, the buyer first should warn him that he is falling behind his competitors. If there is no improvement, the buyer may be forced to give his next order to a different supplier.

Figure 20–7 shows the quality records of three competing suppliers. The percentage of rejections by each supplier was plotted each month. The supplier with the highest rejection rate will first be warned—and he may even be shown the chart that compares his quality record with those of his two major competitors. If he fails to improve, the materials manager may try to locate a fourth supplier who can deliver higher quality merchandise at the same or a lower price.

Tabulating the results. Reports such as this can rarely be made

FIGURE 20–7
Suppliers' performance chart

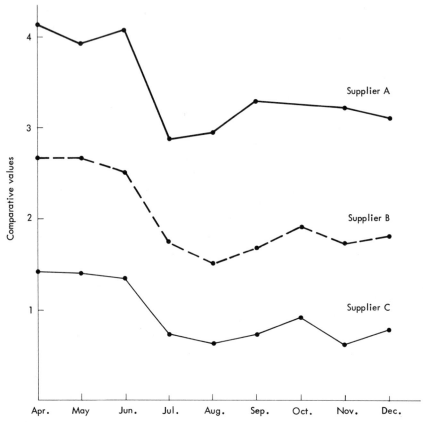

Quality performance of competing suppliers can be measured by plotting rejects as a percentage of monthly shipments. This not only permits comparison of suppliers but also indicates whether or not a poor-quality supplier is showing any signs of improvement.

unless the company tabulates quality statistics with electronic data processing equipment. With this equipment, data from inspection reports for every shipment is keypunched on cards (see Figure 20–8). The actual quality level, determined from the inspection reports, is then compared with the acceptable quality level (AQL).

Various formulas are used to make comparisons; typical is the following quality-scoring formula used by an electronics company:

$$\text{Quality conformance} = 100 - \frac{30 \text{ (percent defective)}}{\text{Acceptable quality level}}.$$

This formula is designed to give a "passing grade" of 70 when the supplier's quality meets the standard exactly. For example, if the AQL

FIGURE 20-8
EDP data on supplier performance

VENDOR NO	PT NO	TL	DATE	RPR	PO #	CC	QTY REC	DEPT	QTY AC	NAME	DEF	#	CRIT	INSPECT MAJ	MIN 1	MIN 2	CRIT	DEFECT MAJ	MIN 1	MIN 2
A NA NA			002 001 003																	
6468233	10-1-9			34716	61		36	335	36					7						
6672455	10-13-9	23621		34798	61		24	335	24		160	1		7					7	
6678114	10-28-9			34721	61		17	335	17					7						
							77*		77*					•	•	21*	•	•	•	7*	•
A																				
							•		•					•	•	•	•	•	•	•	•
NA A	087		007 001 008																	
6010117	10-19-9			75568	61		36	345	36					25	7	3				
6010120	10-19-9			74400	61		12	345	12					12	7	3				
6015276	10-19-9			75568	61		36	345	36					25	7	3				
6015277	10-19-9	23663		75568	61		36	345	34		64	2		25	7	3	1	1		
6015280	10-20-9			75568	61		36	345	36					25	7	3				
6015281	10-20-9			75568	61		57	345	57					25	15	3				
6015282	10-20-9			75568	61		36	345	36					25	15	3				
6015283	10-20-9			75568	61		36	345	36					25	15	3				
							285*		283*					•	187*	80*	24*	•	1*	1*	•
NA NA A	075		003 001 004																	
6010769	10-20-9			35309	74		6	345	6					6	6	3				
6010771	10-20-9			35309	74		526	345	526					50	50	50				
6011087	10-14-9	23679		73869	74		150	345	144		33	1		25	15	3	2			
6013217	11-04-9			35309	74		50	345	50					25	7	3				
							732*		726*					•	106*	78*	59*	•	2*	•	•
A A A	100		001 000 001																	
6015841	10-12-9			77629	74		475	345	475					50	35	35				
							475*		475*					•	50*	35*	35*	•	•	•	•
NA			000 001 001																	
6010844	10-16-9	23658		35367	74		225	3												
							225*														

Courtesy International Business Machines Corp.

Tabulating equipment facilitates measurement of vendor quality performance. Data from inspection reports is punched on cards, and the equipment then calculates quality performance and prints the necessary reports.

permits a 2 percent rejection rate (i.e., two pieces out of a hundred do not meet the quality standard) and 2 percent of a supplier's shipment is actually found defective, then quality conformance = $100 - 30(.02)/.02 = 70$. Superior quality would earn the supplier a score higher than 70. Most companies would regard any score below 70 as the point where the supplier's shipments become completely unacceptable.

When a company has punched-card tabulating equipment, it can prepare quality conformance reports similar to that shown in Figure 20-9. These reports are mailed to the supplier and indicate whether or not he has earned a passing grade on quality during the preceding month. Most companies prefer not to reveal their AQL to vendors, however; they are afraid the vendor will begin to cut corners on quality and

FIGURE 20-9

IBM   INTERNATIONAL BUSINESS MACHINES CORPORATION

FORM 920 7847 2

OWEGO, N. Y.
PLANT LOCATION

PURCHASED PRODUCT QUALITY CONFORMANCE REPORT

TO:

ABC Company
J. Doe QC Manager
Hometown
New York

	PERIOD ENDING	VENDOR NO
	Nov 15 19—	00000

THE QUALITY CONFORMANCE INFORMATION BELOW REPRESENTS IBM'S EVALUATION OF YOUR PRODUCTS UPON RECEIPT

QUALITY CONFORMANCE			SHIPMENTS		
THIS PERIOD	LAST PERIOD	TWO PERIODS AGO	RECEIVED THIS PERIOD	ACCEPTABLE AS RECEIVED	UNACCEPTABLE AS RECEIVED
Acceptable	Acceptable	Unacceptable	18	17	1

SHIPMENTS LISTED BELOW WERE FOUND TO BE UNACCEPTABLE AS RECEIVED. YOU WERE ADVISED OF THE RESULTS BY THE REJECTED PURCHASE REPORT INDICATED. SHIPMENTS ACCEPTED AS RECEIVED ARE EXCLUDED FROM THIS LISTING.

*INDICATES SHIPMENT RETURNED

PART NUMBER	PURCHASE ORDER NUMBER	QUANTITY RECEIVED	SAMPLE QUANTITY INSPECTED	SAMPLE QUANTITY DEFECTIVE	REJECTED PURCHASE REPORT NO	
6000000	12345	50	25	3	54321	*

Courtesy International Business Machines Corp.

International Business Machines Corporation and other companies periodically mail reports to suppliers that indicate their quality performance. These reports can be generated easily if the company has data processing equipment and is already calculating quality performance for internal use.

try to beat the system. Instead, they simply translate their quality tabulations into "acceptable" and "unacceptable" ratings. Vendors who get unacceptable ratings usually are invited to attend a meeting with quality control personnel to discuss ways to boost their quality.

Buyer quality performance. If quality ratings for each shipment from each supplier are accumulated, a computer can easily be programmed to calculate a combined vendor quality performance report for the entire materials department. This is an excellent barometer of the progress being made by the department in meeting its quality objective. The records can also be made up for individual buyers and used to measure their performance. It is not the only useful performance barometer, however.

Achievement of the quality objective affects other departments, too. When quality is poor, the operating costs of the quality control department are high, since each shipment must be carefully inspected. On the other hand, when vendor quality standards are extremely high, it may even be possible to use purchased material on receipt with no inspection whatever.

Many companies "certify" suppliers with good quality control performance. These suppliers certify that each shipment meets the AQL, and the customer's inspectors content themselves with occasional spot-checks to make sure that the supplier's quality has not slipped below the certified standard.

When the materials department selects suppliers who meet quality standards with little inspection, it is making a considerable contribution to profits. Some companies—most notably General Electric Company—use the cost of operating the receiving inspection department as a barometer of materials management performance. The cost of shutdowns in manufacturing because of poor-quality purchased materials often can also be used legitimately as a barometer of materials management efficiency.

The delivery objective

Most shutdowns, however, result from the supplier's failure to deliver on schedule. Getting material, the most basic job in materials management, is one of the most difficult to measure objectively without data processing equipment. Records of each shipment from each supplier must be tabulated. Figure 20–10 shows how one company plots delivery performance of its suppliers. Another company uses barometers—a time rating and a quantity rating—to rate its suppliers.

Time and quantity ratings. The time rating is calculated by comparing the date when a shipment is actually received to the date for which it was promised. Early shipments are penalized less than late shipments, because it usually is more desirable to carry excess inventory than to risk a stockout. However, for many companies it is probably more important to detect early deliveries than late ones. The latter will be noticed anyway if they are important, but it is possible for a seller to deliver ahead of schedule wtihout the buyer ever knowing about it. As long as everything is in order, the shipment will be processed routinely, and the company will wind up with inventory it does not really need until some weeks or months in the future. In some cases, the supplier may even wind up getting paid well ahead of schedule, resulting in cash being invested in unneeded inventory.

FIGURE 20-10
Delivery performance chart

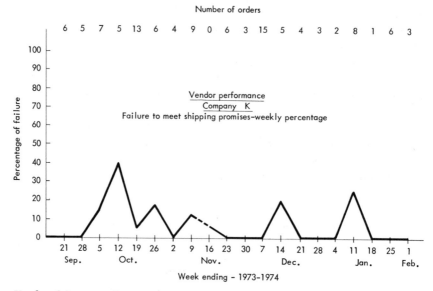

Vendor delivery performance can be measured simply by dividing the number of times a vendor fails to keep a shipping promise by the number of shipments he makes. Listing the number of orders per week on the chart shows the significance of the failure. A high percentage of failures on a large number of orders is more serious than the same percentage of failues on a smaller number of orders.

Scoring which takes both late and early shipments into account could be as follows:

100 . . . . .   Shipment received the week it was due or one week early.
80 . . . . .   One week late or two weeks early.
60 . . . . .   Two weeks late or three weeks early.
40 . . . . .   Three weeks late or four weeks early.
20 . . . . .   Four weeks late.
0 . . . . .   Five or more weeks late.

Partial receipts also serve as a barometer of delivery performance. A supplier who must make a lot of unscheduled extra shipments in small quantities is not doing as good a job as one who can accumulate the desired quantity and ship it according to schedule. Performance in avoiding partial shipments is measured by a quantity rating, which is calculated by dividing the number of scheduled receipts by the number of shipments actually made by the supplier.

The combined delivery performance rating is calculated by averaging the time delivery rating, weighted 70 percent, with the quantity delivered rating, weighted 30 percent.[5] For example, suppose a supplier is scheduled to make three shipments. His first shipment is two weeks early, his second scheduled shipment is received in two parts and the first part is two weeks late, and his fourth and final shipment arrives on schedule. The supplier's time delivery rating is equal to the average of his individual ratings—80, 60, and 100—or 80. Since he made four shipments when three were scheduled, his quantity delivered rating is 75. The combined rating equals 70 percent of 80 and 30 percent of 75, or 78.5.

This would not be good performance on most rating scales. The following scale is used by the New England company that devised this formula:

> 95–100. . . . . . . Excellent performance
> 90–94 . . . . Good
> 80–89 . . . . Fair
> Under 80. . . . . . Unsatisfactory

Once a company is set up to tabulate delivery statistics, it can use them not only to measure supplier performance but also to measure how well the overall materials department and the groups within it are doing in achieving the delivery objective. Performance of the department, of course, is equal to the combined performance of all suppliers on all shipments. Performance of individual groups within the department is calculated from statistics on the shipments for which they are responsible. With tabulating equipment, it is easy to keypunch receival cards not only with the vendor's code but also with the buyer's or expediter's code. Then it becomes a routine matter to run off not only delivery performance reports on suppliers but also on buyers, expediters, or some other organizational unit within the materials department.

Other barometers. Delivery performance statistics may be fairly difficult to compile even when a company has data processing equipment. Punched cards must be made up for each shipment, and equipment must be programmed to run off the necessary reports. This is usually practical only if delivery performance reports are a part of an overall data-processing system.

Other barometers of delivery performance may be easier to use. They involve studying the effect of delivery on operations rather than analyzing the delivery statistics. When delivery performance is poor, the internal operating costs of the materials department are high.[6] Travel

---

[5] Note that this weighting is quite arbitrary. Different companies would apply different weights, depending on what they believe to be the relative importance of the two factors.

[6] This also illustrates how various materials objectives are interrelated. If a materials manager successfully achieves the objective of getting suppliers to deliver promptly, he also achieves his objective of low department operating costs. But he may have to make some sacrifices to get prompt delivery.

and telephone costs go up, and payroll costs rise because more expediters are needed. Each is a barometer of delivery performance.

Costs also rise in manufacturing, because scheduling of production is less efficient when materials are in short supply. Shutdowns also are more frequent. Many slowdowns in manufacturing are charged to variance accounts (in companies with standard-cost systems), which are designed to show why costs are higher than anticipated. If a company has a variance account for premium costs incurred on account of lack of material, this account in itself is a measure of the materials department's delivery performance. Of course, a barometer like this is not as useful as delivery statistics because its use is limited to measurement of department performance. It cannot easily be adapted to measure delivery performance of individual suppliers or buyers.

Vendor rating

The best suppliers do more than meet quality standards and ship according to schedule. They offer shorter lead times than their competitors; their prices are lower; and they offer more new products, ideas and miscellaneous services.

The combined rating. Various materials managers have attempted to weigh all these factors and develop numerical ratings for each of their suppliers. A supplier's price performance can be calculated by comparing his price with that of the lowest bidder on the order. A similar comparison can be made for lead time. In each case, the supplier's rating is calculated by averaging performance on a series of orders. The formulas are:

$$\text{Percentage of price performance} = \frac{\text{Lowest price or bid (any vendor)}}{\text{Actual price}}$$

$$\text{Percentage of lead-time performance} = \frac{\text{Shortest lead time (any vendor on comparable item)}}{\text{Actual lead time}}$$

Some companies consider only quality and delivery in developing composite delivery ratings. Others also take price and lead time into account. Such weighting is arbitrary and depends entirely on the materials manager's judgment of the relative importance of the various factors. One company uses the following weighting to rate its suppliers:

Quality 40%
Delivery 20%
Price 35%
Lead time 5%

Favorable relations. Such composite ratings may be useful as buying tools, and they also provide clues to how good a job the materials department is doing in terms of its objective of maintaining favorable supplier relations. But they do not tell the full story about performance on the latter objective. It shows up directly in cost-reduction reports and less directly in supplier assistance in product development. Presumably good relations help stimulate suppliers to generate helpful ideas for their customers. These result in new products or basic improvements that, while they are never reflected in cost-reduction reports, do have tremendous impact on customer profits.

Stimulating supplier R & D. Some materials managers operate on the theory that since their orders help support supplier research and development (R & D), they should see some of its tangible benefits. A few go so far as to ask each supplier quite bluntly what they have done for them in the past year. For example, one purchasing agent sends a letter every year to each supplier which reads as follows:

> During the year —— ——, our purchases from you totalled $—— ——. We assume that you spend roughly five percent of your sales dollar on research and development. And certainly we at the —— —— —— —— Company welcome your R & D efforts and believe that we have greatly benefited from them. Last year, your sales to us should have supported $—— —— worth of research and development. In addition, we believe that your excellent sales engineers undoubtedly made a number of tangible contributions to our success in the course of their work with our people. We would like evidence of such assistance. It is our intention to favor those suppliers who have done the most for us. Would you please give me a comprehensive report of the help you have given so that we may use it to evaluate your success as a supplier.

This purchasing agent's requests for substantiating evidence of supplier R & D have not been particularly successful. Most suppliers are unable or unwilling to provide him with evidence of how their R & D have helped him. But his principle is sound: Research and development is being paid for by every supplier's customers, and buyers should be interested in how successful it is in solving their own companies' problems.

Unfortunately, supplier research cannot always be related to customer objectives year by year, even if it is very useful over a longer term. This is just one of the reasons why evaluation of supplier relations performance is difficult. There is usually considerable lag before a successful vendor relations program shows measurable results. This year's performance in developing supplier relations may show up in cost-reduction reports or quality statistics in succeeding years. It is not possible to rely entirely on objective measures to determine whether or not the objective of favorable supplier relations is currently being achieved.

The best the materials manager can do is to have a program and then report progress as best he can. For example, he may occasionally try to summarize the contributions that each supplier has made in suggesting new products or ideas or in helping operating personnel with their problems. This would be a barometer of past performance and might provide clues to current performance.

Carrier performance. The vendor performance measurements described above can readily be adapted to a specialized type of supplier: the common carrier. There is some difference in objectives, of course. In most cases, the particular carrier cannot be measured on price performance, since under ICC regulations his tariffs most likely are identical with those of his competitors. Quality and delivery objectives for the common carrier are essentially merged into a single service dependability objective.

There are two measures of a carrier's service dependability: time required to pick up a shipment (or to make a box car available) and time required to deliver the shipment to its destination. With electronic data processing, it is relatively easy to calculate the time required both for order processing and actual shipment of each order. Performance ratings can then be developed for each common carrier, using essentially the same techniques that have been described for purchased-materials suppliers.

In addition, the traffic department may wish to monitor the quality of the carrier's service either by keeping track of damage claims or by having the consignee of the shipment fill out a short report indicating the condition in which the shipment was received. A composite rating can then be developed for each carrier. Changes in the carriers' ratings are more important in such a system than the absolute ratings themselves. For example, it would be significant if a particular carrier demonstrated either improved or deteriorating performance. But it might not be fair to compare an absolute rating of one carrier with another, just as it is not fair to compare ratings of two conventional suppliers who are in different businesses.

DEVELOPMENT OF PERSONNEL

Supplier performance is a valid measure of the performance of materials management personnel. For example, the best buyers are able to get better performance from their suppliers, and it is common practice to tabulate vendor performance by buyer. The materials manager must be cautious in comparing buyers on this basis, of course. The very best buyer may be assigned to a commodity group where there are inherent problems in achieving superior vendor performance. On the other hand, relative comparisons by buyer of vendor performance are perfectly valid. If the aggregate performance of a particular buyer's suppliers declines from 90 to 80, then the buyer is not doing as good a job for his company as he was before.

The concern of the materials manager should go beyond whether or not his staff is carrying out its present assignments in an efficient manner. He should also be contributing to the future strength of his company. Survival is one of the most basic objectives of any organization. To perpetuate itself and the company of which it is a part, every department should strive to develop and train future managers. Historically, the materials department has done a rather poor job on this objective. Proof of this is the minute number of chief executives who are former materials managers. For example, the author of one study of the backgrounds of chief executives in big business did not even bother to list purchasing or materials management as a department through which one could advance to become a chief executive.[7] Presumably the category "operations and production" in this study embraced materials management as well as manufacturing. Only 40 percent of the chief executives had this background (the balance came from finance, sales, legal departments, receivers in bankruptcy, personnel, and other departments), and undoubtedly practically all of them were from manufacturing or its equivalent in service companies.

One of the major reasons that materials departments have done such a poor job in developing chief executives is historical. As we saw in Chapter 1, it is only quite recently that materials departments have developed enough stature and attracted enough high-caliber personnel to become logical training grounds for future top executives.

The materials department has done a better job in perpetuating itself by developing future purchasing agents and materials managers. Many, if not most, top materials managers have worked their way up through the ranks of the materials department. The materials manager should always be grooming potential replacements for each of his key subordinates. Personnel development is one of his most important objectives.

Unfortunately, it is not easy to measure year-to-year performance in achieving this objective. The results will be reflected in the performance of future managers, and it will be difficult, if not impossible, to trace them back to any particular period or program. The only practicable measure of year-to-year performance is to compare the materials manager's plans for achievement with those of previous years and to measure his actual progress in carrying out his plans.

The materials manager is interested not only in developing future managers but also in getting the best possible performance from every person in his department. His own performance should be measured by his success in reaching these goals. It is measured both by the

---

[7] Mabel Newcomer, "The Big Business Executive," in W. Lloyd Warner and Norman H. Martin (eds.), *Industrial Man* (New York: Harper & Bros., 1959), p. 142.

programs he proposes for personnel development and by his ability to execute those progams.

High-potential employees

The materials manager's program should include regular appraisals of the performance and potential of every member of the materials organization. Particular attention should be given to development of the high-potential employees who are the company's future managers. Figure 20–11 shows appraisal forms used by Ford Motor Company to

FIGURE 20–11

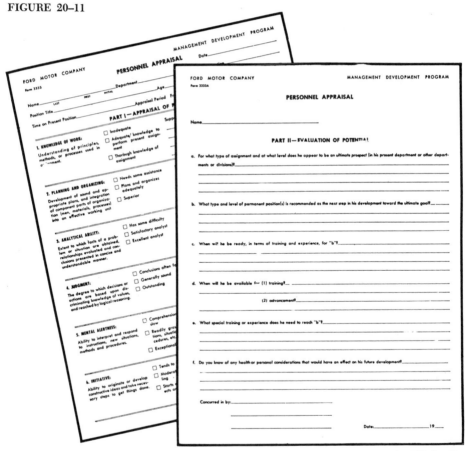

Courtesy Ford Motor Co.

High-potential employees capable of assuming greater responsibility are essential to a company's growth and survival. Ford Motor Company uses this form to appraise the performance of the executives in its management development program who are being groomed for future top-level jobs.

evaluate high-potential employees in its management development program.

To become "high potential," an employee must not only perform well in his present job; he must also show promise of being able to perform well in jobs with substantially more responsibility. He must have the personality, intellect, and education of a manager.

There should be high-potential persons at almost every level of organization. This insures the orderly progression of competent executives that is essential to perpetuate the organization. In his annual report to top management, the materials manager should describe in some detail the progress being made by each of his high-potential employees. When there are insufficient high-potential employees, at any level in his organization, he should indicate how he proposes to fill the gap— through hiring new people, transfers, and so on.

Ideally, he should have replacements who are capable of filling any vacancies that might occur because of death, retirement, or resignation. Some managers use color-coded, phantom organization charts to help them plan. For each position, they list not only the incumbent but also his or her potential successors. Color codes indicate whether the potential successors are presently ready to handle increased responsibilities or require additional training. For example, the top candidate for promotion might carry a green color code, which indicates he or she is ready to move or without any additional training or experience. Other candidates might carry yellow color codes, indicating that they are not quite ready. The materials manager should then make certain that these candidates get the training and experience needed to qualify them for future promotion.

Developing managers

The materials manager should not assume that managers can be developed automatically, with no effort on his part. He should have a positive program designed to permit each employee to make a greater future contribution to company objectives. Included in this program would be such time-tested techniques as job rotation, special training programs, and special assignments.

Job rotation. Some materials managers deliberately rotate jobs in their department. Others prefer to make changes only when required; they dislike going to the trouble of retraining men and women for new jobs when it is not absolutely necessary.

The former approach is the better one both for management development and for overall efficiency. People inevitably get stale on their jobs; occasional job rotation brings a fresh approach to the job and boosts morale. With a planned rotation program, the materials manager can eventually train several persons in all phases of every job in his department.

With a planned approach to job rotation, individuals are transferred from job to job not only when there is a basic need for the shift, on account of promotions, retirements, and the like, but also for the mere sake of rotation. For example, suppose there are ten buyers in a purchasing department, each specializing in some group of commodities. Buyer A might buy gray-iron and malleable castings; buyer B, permanent mold and die castings; and so on. One plan of rotation would be simply to have the buyers switch jobs; thus B might switch duties with A. With such a program, eventually every buyer would become familiar with every commodity.

Some materials managers might hesitate to follow this plan because it involves forcing a person to become immediately familiar with commodities entirely different from those he has handled. They prefer a more gradual approach, in which, for example, buyer A might continue to handle gray-iron castings but would swap his malleable castings for buyer B's die castings. With this type of change, neither B nor A would have to learn a brand-new job all at once and, after enough of these changes each still would have learned how to buy every commodity in the department.

Special training programs.   Each supervisor in the materials department should evaluate his subordinates. If there are gaps in their knowledge, he should try to fill them by means of training programs. High-potential employees should be encouraged to take special courses in night schools and take similar steps to broaden themselves. Many companies encourage such study by paying all or part of the tuition. Materials personnel should also be encouraged to participate in activities of such organizations as the National Association of Purchasing Management, the American Production and Inventory Control Society, the National Institute for Governmental Purchasing, the National Association of Educational Buyers, and various traffic clubs.

Many companies have training programs designed to give a broad overall understanding of company operations to young men fresh out of college. Figure 20–12 shows an outline of the training program of the Stromberg-Carlson Division of General Dynamics Corp. The materials department should play an active role in such company wide programs. In this way it can keep itself supplied with young high-potential employees by regularly providing jobs for a few trainees who have completed the course. Also, trainees destined for other departments will be able to work better with the materials department if they know how it operates.

The materials department can make a valuable contribution to the company's sales training program. Fledgling salesmen can learn how

FIGURE 20–12
Personnel training program

Typical Program Schedule					
DEPARTMENT	**ASSIGNMENT**	**WEEKS**	**DEPARTMENT**	**ASSIGNMENT**	**WEEKS**
ENGINEERING	General Orientation (Projects, Design, Value, Systems Engineering, Project Control, Components and Materials, Services, Mechanical Design)	2	PRODUCTION ENGINEERING	General Orientation	½
				Industrial Engineering	½
				Tool Engineering	½
				Test Equipment Engineering	½
				Value Engineering	½
	Work Assignment (In one or more of above areas)	5		Project Engineering or Assignment to one of the above areas	4½
		TOTAL 7			TOTAL 7
INSPECTION AND QUALITY CONTROL	Purchased Materials Inspection	1	PRODUCTION CONTROL	General Orientation	½
				Material Inventory Control	1½
	Project Inspection	1		Requisitioning and Scheduling	2
	Quality Control	1		Planning and Expediting	3
	Work Assignment (One of the above areas)	4			TOTAL 7
		TOTAL 7	MARKETING	General Orientation	½
PRODUCTION	General Orientation (Organization, Labor Relations, etc.)	1		Military Marketing	3
				Industrial Marketing	1
				Contracts Administration	2
	Work Assignment (Capacity of Assistant Foreman)	6		Advertising	½
		TOTAL 7			TOTAL 7
PURCHASING	General Orientation	½			GRAND TOTAL 49*
	Value Analysis and Standardization	1			
	Buying (Production)	1			
	Buying (Engineering)	1			
	Order Control	½			
	Work Assignment (One of the above areas)	3			
		TOTAL 7			

*The total of 49 weeks does not in all cases terminate the training of the individual. Depending upon the trainee's desires and qualifications and the needs of the company, the opportunity is afforded to spend two to four weeks in one or more of the following areas:

Plant Engineering
Value Engineering
Accounting
Research
General Services
Other-Operating Divisions

Courtesy Stromberg-Carlson Division, General Dynamics Corp.

The materials department should participate actively in companywide training, both to recruit high-potential employees and to indoctrinate future executives in other departments in the importance of materials management. As this chart shows, two sevenths of the Stromberg-Carlson Division's training program is devoted to the materials management functions of purchasing and production control.

customers react to various sales approaches either by trying them out on purchasing personnel in their own company or by actually watching supplier salesmen in action. Several companies make their sales trainees serve a short stint in the purchasing department as a buyer's assistant. They can see other salesmen at work and objectively appraise the impact of each on his customers.

Special assignments. The materials manager often can use special assignments to test his subordinates. One assignment that can help develop future managers in two ways is that of organizing a training program. The subordinate who runs the training program is being developed, and the program itself helps develop others. High-potential subordinates should be tested regularly with special assignments. These may include special reports, development of new procedures, participation in various companywide activities (Community Chest drives, and so on), and various commodity studies.

GOOD RECORDS

The materials manager can achieve two objectives simultaneously when he assigns a high-potential subordinate to audit the department's records. He is developing personnel and he also is making certain that the department's records and procedures are satisfactory.

Many materials managers prefer to have their records checked by someone outside the department, however. They have the company's internal auditors make detailed examinations; a few even use outside auditing firms. Auditors are experts in checking records and in detecting deviations from standard procedures. They can be used as an independent check on the materials department, much in the same manner as they are used in the accounting department.

The internal auditor will first make a detailed review of the materials department's procedures in order to make certain that they provide adequate control. He will occasionally suggest changes that will either tighten control or cut costs. After he is satisfied with procedures, the auditor spot-checks a number of materials transactions to see if procedures have been complied with in practice. He then notes each case in which there is some deviation or in which records are incomplete. In a materials department, he would make a special effort to be absolutely certain that business was awarded to suppliers in the best interests of the company. For example, the auditor would expect to find clear records of each supplier's bid. If the contract were not awarded to the lowest bidder, he would expect to find evidence justifying the decision.

After he checked a satisfactory number of transactions, the auditor would make a report summarizing his findings. This report would provide an impartial measure of the departments' performance in meeting its objective of having good records.

We have now covered measurement of performance of all of the basic objectives of a typical materials department. One question that may arise in the reader's mind must remain partly unanswered: How does one arrive at a combined rating that shows overall performance in meeting all objectives? It would not be too difficult to calculate a combined rating. All one need do is determine the relative importance of each objective, give it a percentage weight, and then calculate some cumulative performance rating for the overall performance.

The writer believes, however, that such a combined rating would be almost meaningless. Not only is weighting of individual objectives arbitrary, but it would be necessary to combine objectives that can be measured quantitatively with those that can only be measured qualitatively. The writer believes that the only practical approach to performance measurement in materials management is to measure progress on each objective as accurately and impartially as possible. Then whoever is responsible for performance can be the judge whether or not the department's efforts were directed toward the right objectives.

Cases

CASE 20–1. CONSOLIDATED BUSINESS MACHINES CORPORATION

Measuring supplier performance

George Matheson, president of Consolidate Business Machines Corporation, is concerned about the company's choice of suppliers for sensor brushes, which are used in the company's data processing equipment. Matheson occasionally plays golf with Harold Adams, president of Adams Machine Company, one of the company's suppliers of brushes. Recently, Adams complained to Matheson that his firm has been having difficulty in getting its traditional share of Consolidated's brush business. On the last buy, Adams's firm failed to get any business, even though Adams believed he was the low bidder. Matheson tells Adams that normally he does not get into the details of procurement, but he promises to ask his purchasing manager, Sloan Howard, to investigate.

The following morning Matheson calls Howard and tells him of Adams's complaint. He says he does not want to influence the company's procurement policies, but he does feel that Howard should investigate to make sure that Adams was treated fairly.

Howard discovers that Adams was indeed the low bidder on the last buy. Quotations for an order of 10,000 units were as follows:

Adams Machine Co.	$2.22
Burlington Electronics Co.	2.23
Zenith Tool & Machine Co.	2.25

Zenith and Burlington each got orders for 5,000 pieces. Zenith has done considerable development work on brushes, while Adams and Burlington have done very little. The quality and delivery records of the three suppliers on the last ten orders for the brush are as follows:

Supplier	Quantity ordered	Quantity defective	Delivery
Zenith	4,000	122	One week early
Burlington	4,000	92	One week late
Adams	3,000	120	On time
Adams	6,000	162	Two weeks late
Zenith	4,000	38	On time
Burlington	5,000	29	One week early
Adams	2,000	88	1,000 pieces on time; 1,000 pieces four weeks late.
Burlington	6,000	98	Two weeks late
Zenith	4,000	45	One week early
Adams	5,000	162	One week late

Consolidated's quality control department has set an acceptable quality level of 3 percent on the brush.

Questions

1. Is Howard justified in eliminating Adams as a supplier of brushes?
2. In what respect is the complaint from Adams justified?
3. Prepare a report for Matheson explaining the decision to eliminate Adams as a supplier; use quantitative data as much as possible to support your position.

CASE 20–2.   BORG INSTRUMENTS DIVISION*

Use of bid handicaps to stimulate supplier performance

By putting a dollar sign on how well vendors do on quality, reliability, and service, Borg Instruments, a division of Amphenol Borg Electronics Corp., has taken vendor rating to its logical conclusion.

Using a special formula, buyers convert vendors' monthly performance ratings into cash values. They add these amounts to suppliers' bids as handicaps or "fines." The poorer a supplier's performance rating, the higher the bid handicap he gets.

By using this system, the purchasing department of the Delavan, Wisconsin, maker of auto clocks and synchronous motors is able to buy on the basis of the total cost of doing business with a vendor—the sum of his quotaton plus the money Borg must expect to spend to offset his lapses in quality, reliability, and service.

---

* The performance measurement system described is actually used by Borg Instruments, a division of Amphenol Borg Electronics Corp., but names of suppliers used in the case are fictitious.

Because they are based on past performance, the penalties against suppliers are realistic and fair. According to Deane Grether, purchasing agent, weighting the bids of vendors is "a harsh stimulus, but it's effective because it's applied where it will do the most good."

Each month, Borg buyers rate suppliers' quality, reliability, and service. A buyer can give a vendor up to 40 points each in quality and reliability—or 10 points for each standard. The vendor can get up to 20 points for service—or 5 points per standard. A perfect score would be 100 points, which is rarely attained.

The buyer bases his ratings on facts rather than opinion. To score a vendor on quality, for instance, he goes to the supplier's inspection report form, which contains a running record on all questionable and rejected shipments. This form has previously been filled out on the basis of reports from the inspection department.

After a buyer has finished scoring a vendor, he totals the points and enters them in the summary box of a supplier evaluation report. At the bottom of the report is a table showing the penalty factors for various scores. A score of 97 points, for example, draws a penalty of 3 percent—which means that the supplier bid is to be handicapped (increased) by 3 percent.

On the reverse of the supplier evaluation report are complete explanations of Borg's rating criteria (see Figure 20–13) to ensure that all buyers use the same yardsticks in rating vendors.

The evaluation reports go to Grether for his review and signature. Afterwards, they are mailed to vendors—usually to the presidents of small companies and sales managers of large ones. They are thus sure of reaching interested and influential executives.

When a buyer has finished an evaluation report, he pulls the supplier's evaluation rating card from a file and enters the latest monthly score (See Figure 20–14). Every six months, he computes the average score and notes it on the card. The latest semiannual score determines the vendor's bid penalty.

In the Borg rating system, vendors have the right of appeal. They can express dissatisfaction with their scores and give Borg the chance to correct the infrequent scoring error. Recently, for example, a supplier protested a low quality score. When investigation proved his claim correct, the score was changed.

When a job is put on quote, the buyer enters all bids on a quotation record card. Then he picks up the latest ratings and penalty factors for the bidders from their evaluation rating cards. On the back of the quotation card, the buyer lists the bids and applies the proper penalty factor to each one.

To illustrate, a supplier with a semiannual average score of 94 points has a penalty factor of 6 percent. His bid is inflated by 6 percent. If this bid was $1000, it is raised to $1060. The supplier with the lowest

FIGURE 20–13

BORG INSTRUMENTS
A DIVISION OF AMPHENOL BORG ELECTRONICS CORPORATION
DELAVAN, WISCONSIN

SUPPLIER EVALUATION REPORT

SUPPLIER _A·B·C Co._   ATTN: _M SELLER_   MONTH _MAY 19—_

QUALITY	1	2	3	4	5	6	7	8	9	10	Mo. Grade	REMARKS
APPEARANCE/DIMENSIONAL							X				8	
SPOILAGE									X		10	
MATERIAL/PACKAGING									X		10	
DEFECT COSTS									X		10	
QUALITY RATING											38	

RELIABILITY	1	2	3	4	5	6	7	8	9	10	Mo. Grade	REMARKS
DELIVERY PERFORMANCE								X			9	
ACQUISITION COSTS								X			9	
REPORTS, INFORMATION & RECORDS									X		10	
PRICE RELIABILITY									X		10	
RELIABILITY RATING											38	

SERVICE	1	2	3	4	5	Mo. Grade	REMARKS
SALES PERFORMANCE					X	5	
TECHNICAL PERFORMANCE					X	5	
FINANCIAL PERFORMANCE					X	5	
MANAGEMENT PERFORMANCE					X	5	
SERVICE RATING						20	

NOTES: _____

RATING SUMMARY CHART

Item	Possible Rating	Your Rating
QUALITY	40	38
RELIABILITY	40	38
SERVICE	20	20
TOTAL	100	96

COST RATIO FACTOR	PENALTY FACTOR	COST RATIO FACTOR	PENALTY FACTOR
100	0	94	6%
99	1/2%	93	8%
98	1%	92	12%
97	2%	91	15%
96	3%	90	20%
95	5%	89	3% Ea. Pt. Below 100

COST RATIO FACTOR	Last 6 Mos.	This 6 Mos.
	97	

SIGNED _D·T· Shutler_
Purchasing Agent

(See Reverse Side for Rating Explanations)

EXPLANATION OF RATING TERMS

QUALITY RATING

1. **Appearance/Dimensional:** This refers to the over all appearance of your product, such defects as dirt, scratches, pits, bad paint, faulty plating, etc., and any defect caused by not being to print dimension.

2. **Spoilage:** This refers to costs incurred due to spoilage of materials over and above our regular inspection procedure.

3. **Material/Packaging:** This refers to any defect in the materials used in your product and poorly designed packaging or faulty packaging material.

4. **Defect Costs:** This refers to the cost incurred to Borg Instruments for premium inspection, rejections, waivers to use, specification revisions, and manufacturing losses.

RELIABILITY RATING

1. **Delivery Performance:** This refers to your ability, flexibility and performance in meeting our required delivery schedule.

2. **Acquisition Costs:** This refers to the costs incurred to Borg Instruments for expediting, telephone, telegraph, premium transportation charges, manufacturing losses, due to delinquencies and shortages.

3. **Reports, Information & Records:** This refers to your adherence in submitting all requested reports and information, and maintaining good records such as purchase order balances, engineering changes, invoices, request for quotations, cost estimates, etc.

4. **Price Reliability:** This refers to your ability to hold firm prices for at least one model year, and your completeness and reliability of your quotations.

SERVICE RATING

1. **Sales Performance:** This refers to the performance of the sales representative in calls (too little, too much), purchase order follow up, cost reduction ideas, availability and emergency help.

2. **Technical Performance:** This refers to the excellence and extensiveness of your design and development engineering, production engineering and tool engineering, as well as ability to assure quality before, during and after production.

3. **Financial Performance:** This refers to your adequacy of credit standing, cash flow, equity and working capital.

4. **Management Performance:** This refers to the scope and quality of your system, procedure and administration controls over facilities, materials, manpower, time and costs, and your ability to plan, organize, integrate and measure them effectively.

Borg instruments vendors receive a monthly supplier evaluation report which shows them how they fared in three rating categories and gives them their total score. Rating terms are fully defined on reverse side of the monthly form.

FIGURE 20–14

SUPPLIER INFORMATION & EVALUATION RECORD

ADDRESS _1001 MAIN ST._	**CONTACT PERSONNEL**
CITY & STATE _HOMETOWN ILL._	
TELEPHONE _HU 3 - 2100_	PRESIDENT
TERMS _2% 10 NET 30_	_JOHN POWERS_
F. O. B. _OUR PLANT_	SALES MGR.
ROUTING _TRUCK_	_MIKE SELLER_
DELIVERY _4 WKS_	ENGINEERING
D & B or NCO RATING _AAA #1_	_HENRY MARKUM_
PRODUCTS MFGR. _STAMPINGS_	QUALITY
	HARRY CHECKER
	PLANT MGR.
SALES REP. _JOE BROOKS_	_ROBERT OVERSEER_
ADDRESS _2121 ELM ST. SUBURBIA ILL._	ORDER DELIVERY
TELEPHONE _CL 4 - 9981_	_RICHARD TELLER_
SUPPLIER	EVALUATION REPORT TO: _M. SELLER_
_A. B. C Co_	

EVALUATION RATINGS

YEAR	JAN.	FEB.	MAR.	APRIL	MAY	JUNE	6 MOS. COST FACTOR	JULY	AUG.	SEPT.	OCT.	NOV.	DEC.	6 MOS. COST FACTOR
1962	95	97	95	92	100	99	96	94	96	98	98	97	100	97
1963	96	94	100	98										

COST RATIO FACTOR	PENALTY FACTOR		COST RATIO FACTOR	PENALTY FACTOR
100	0		94	6%
99	1/2%		93	8%
98	1%		92	12%
97	2%		91	15%
96	3%		90	20%
95	5%		89 and under	3% Ea. Grade Below 100

A supplier's monthly performance scores are recorded on an evaluation rating card and are averaged for six months.

bid will often lose the business if his penalty factor is significantly higher than those of his competitors.

Besides rewarding virtue, Borg's vendor-rating system helps eliminate marginal suppliers and is a defense against the occasional vendor who bids low to "buy" business, intending to recoup later by relaxing on quality. Monthly ratings are frequent enough to permit buyers to detect waning quality almost as soon as it develops. They can take prompt, effective action.

New vendors bidding for Borg business naturally do not have ratings and penalty factors, and it would be unfair to permit them to compete without any handicaps. Grether solved this problem by giving each new bidder the same handicap as the best established supplier against whom he is competing. New vendors thus receive a generous benefit of the doubt.

Most suppliers—especially the better ones—have praised the vendor-rating program. By introducing dollar values for quality, reliability, and service into the bidding process, the Borg system favors the good vendor and penalizes the poor one. In the meantime, scoring vendors on the major areas of their performance pinpoints their weaknesses and permits buyers to help them improve.

Has vendor rating been successful? Rod Burghoff, Borg's vice president of manufacturing, figures that the system is saving about $50,000 per year. And Grether reports that the number of suppliers with grades of 98 and better has more than doubled since the program started two years ago.

Questions

1. Suppose a Borg buyer receives three quotations on a part. The ABC Company quotes $95.00 per thousand in lots of 25,000; J. Brown Co. quotes $93.00; and R. James & Co. quotes $96.50. The part requires a four-cavity mold for which quotations from the three suppliers are $2,100, $2,050, and $1,995, respectively. It is expected that the part will continue in production at the rate of about 25,000 units per month for at least one year. Borg would like to have two suppliers and is willing to reward the best one with 75 percent of the order. Based on previous performance, ABC has earned a cost ratio factor of 94, J. Brown & Co. has 95 and R. James Co. has earned 98. Prepare an analysis of the three bids using Borg's rating system, and recommend suppliers.

2. A new supplier offers the same item at $97 per thousand. As the buyer, you investigate and discover that the supplier's reputation is excellent, but, nevertheless, you have never actually had any experience with it. Should the new supplier be given any business? Back up your recommendation with an analysis based on Borg's evaluation system.

3. Suppose the new supplier is given the lion's share of the business and one of the established suppliers complaints. He tells you, "I agree with your rating system when you are comparing established suppliers. But I heard via the grapevine that you gave business to this fellow without having ever had any experience with him. And his price was higher than mine! The implication is that he will do a better job on quality and delivery than I do. But this just isn't true. This fellow is a competitor of mine on three other accounts and I get the biggest share of the business because my price

is lower and I do at least as well on quality and delivery. You are making a decision without evidence when you favor him over me. This isn't fair."

Is the supplier's argument reasonable? How would you counter it?

CASE 20–3. CONTINENTAL AIRCRAFT CORPORATION

Choosing a new materials manager

Charles Harrington, vice president in charge of materials of Continental Aircraft Corporation, is looking for an assistant who can succeed him when he retires in two years. Harrington has three possible candidates for his job: Robert Clement, 37 years old, materials manager of the company's California Division; Alex Dawson, 48 years old, materials manager of the Texas Missile Division; and Glenn Wilcox, 58, manager of materials research and administration on the corporate staff. Clement and Dawson report directly to the managers of their respective divisions and functionally to Harrington. Both men are highly regarded by their division managers. Wilcox reports directly to Harrington and has earned the respect of everyone on the corporate staff.

Clement is a relative newcomer to Continental. He has degrees in aeronautical engineering and business administration, and he joined the company just five years ago as an executive in the customer relations department. He was appointed assistant materials manager of the California Division two years later and was made materials manager a year later. A young, aggressive executive, Clement has already racked up an enviable record at the California Division, which is the company's largest. Last year he exceeded his cost-reduction quota by nearly 20 percent and managed to keep inventories from rising, despite a 25 percent increase in division sales volume. Clement is a good leader and morale in his department is high, although he sometimes is a little impatient with others when they fail to match his fast pace.

Dawson was Clement's predecessor as materials manager of the California Division. He joined the company as an engineering trainee shortly after he received his B.S. degree. His advancement in the organization was rapid, and he became materials manager of the California Division ten years ago. Harrington chose Dawson to take charge of materials activities at the rapidly expanding Texas Missile Division because of problems that were being encountered in producing satisfactory missiles. Before Dawson arrived, the division was plagued with both quality and delivery problems on purchased materials. Now, although costs are still much higher than Harrington believes they should be, suppliers are delivering on schedule material that meets the fantastically close tolerances required in missile manufacture.

Dawson has an excellent record for developing personnel. Clement was one of his protégés at the California Division, and other "alumni" who formerly worked for him now hold key posts both in other departments of Continental and in several outside companies. Compared with Clement, Dawson is much better at working with people, but he also has faults. Clement, in Harrington's opinion, has more imagination than Dawson, he drives both himself and his subordinates harder, and he may well have potential that will carry him beyond the position of top materials executive in some company.

Wilcox, the third candidate, is a real veteran of the company. He joined Continental 37 years ago as a draftsman, shortly after his graduation from college. His advancement has been steady if not spectacular. He has informally acted as Harrington's No. 2 man for more than ten years, and it is generally assumed that he will succeed Harrington. Wilcox has been employed strictly on staff work for the past ten years. He has spark-plugged a companywide materials training program and has done an excellent job working out ticklish policy and procedures problems. Before that, he acted as assistant materials manager under Harrington. This was a line job, since at that time all of the company's products were made by what is now called the California Division, and Harrington was its materials manager.

Questions

1. What qualities should Harrington look for in a successor?
2. Which, if any, of the three candidates should he choose?
3. When should he make his final decision?

21

The future of materials management

EVEN IF there were no sound economic reasons for adopting materials management forms of organization, companies would probably continue to do so. One reason is simply imitation. When the time comes to make a change in organization, the chief executive is primarily concerned with what seems to work in practice, he is rarely eager to be organizationally innovative. This pragmatic approach was an inhibitive factor in the development of materials management as recently as the 1960's. At that time, accepted practice called for divided materials responsibility. The integrated materials organization was sufficiently esoteric so that hardly any chief executive wanted to take the risk of experimenting with one.

Now the situation is reversed. Materials management has become almost fashionable. At least one leading company in every industry has an integrated materials management set up, and chief executives have a convenient model they can copy. When they observe that XYZ Company is very successful and has materials management, their resistance to proposals that they adopt comparable organizations is overcome.

ORGANIZATION BEHAVIOR

In most cases, the chief executive would probably be too preoccupied with other problems to worry about materials management were there not pressures that encourage him to consider a change in organization. Sometimes the pressures are the product of specific materials management problems. In many cases, they are at least partly contrived. Every real-life organization is a political entity in which change is far more likely to occur when some person or group has a vested interest in that change.

Sources of support

This is certainly true when a company creates an integrated materials management organization. Support for the change inevitably comes from would-be candidates for the material management position. Such support is almost automatic; the author's studies show that more than three fourths of all newly appointed materials managers are promoted from within their own organizations.[1] The director of purchases is the strongest single candidate for promotion to materials manager, followed by the production control manager in manufacturing companies. However, at least half of all newly appointed materials managers are promoted from a variety of nonmaterials management positions.[2]

While the executive who is trying to promote himself as materials manager is obviously a strong advocate of change, there is entrenched opposition to change in every organization. For every "winner" in an organizational change there may be one or more "losers"—those who will enjoy less prestige and power as a result of the change. The purchasing manager is not only the most likely "winner" in materials management if he should be chosen materials manager, he is also the most probable "loser." When a company adopts a materials management organization, it is all but inevitable that the purchasing manager will wind up one or more organizational levels lower than he was before. If purchasing reported to the general manager before the change, the very best it can expect afterward is that it will drop one level, reporting to materials management which, in turn, reports to the general manager.

But even less favorable developments are possible. A purchasing agent who reported directly to a general manager may find himself reporting to a materials manager who reports to a manufacturing manager who, in turn, reports to a general manager. In this case, not only the purchasing manager but also the production and inventory control manager and the traffic manager may find themselves effectively demoted when a materials manager is appointed.

Timing of change

Most top managements are sensitive to the feelings of their subordinates—particularly if no overriding emergency forces them to get tough.

---

[1] Based on a survey I made of 4,000 U.S. manufacturing companies under a grant from the American Production and Inventory Control Society. Part of the results were published in Article 3.6, "Materials Management," in the *Guide to Purchasing* of the National Association of Purchasing Management, as well as in various commercial publications.

[2] Ibid.

The concept of "don't rock the boat" is tacitly accepted in almost every real-life organization. Major changes often are postponed until they can be made smoothly. Sometimes retirements or resignations provide the opportunity, as illustrated in the Gamelin case in Chapter 1. In other cases, organization changes can be grouped together so that almost everyone winds up with at least as good a job as he had before. For example, a purchasing manager who is downgraded by the creation of a materials manager may be promoted to purchasing manager of a larger division. In other cases, a severe recession may provide an opportunity to make changes gracefully. Reductions in staff can automatically create a need for organization changes, and materials management can be slipped in as a by-product. In some cases, the rationalization for the change may rest on even flimsier grounds.[3]

Eventually, however, every chief executive does make changes that he believes will strengthen his organization. Since the materials management organization has been widely accepted, it can be safely assumed that there is now a "backlog" of companies waiting to make the change when a strategic opportunity arises. There are also far more rational reasons for the materials management form of organization to gain wider acceptance. They are both technological and politico-economic.

POLITICO-ECONOMIC CHANGE

Current-politico-economic change is working to make materials management and the supply function increasingly important. Ironically, it is probably also working to reduce the number of top-ranking positions in the field. In 1950, there may have been more positions in materials management paying over $100,000 per year than there are today—even though the purchasing power of the dollar has declined by more than 50 percent during that period, while the economy is twice as big. The big jobs of that time almost always carried the title of vice president—purchases. Almost every huge corporation had one. Many big companies still do, but each year the number seems to shrink.

Decentralization

The underlying cause of the dearth of lush jobs in materials management is decentralization. In the beginning, at least, the motive for decentralization was economic: to increase efficiency. For example, until the 1950s General Electric Company had a huge, centralized purchasing operation in Schenectady, New York, headed by a vice president. Later

---

[3] In one company I know, the general manager simply announced he was filling a long-standing "vacancy" for the position of materials manager after having made an "exhaustive search" for the right man. Until this announcement, no one knew that the position existed! But presumably, since it had "always" existed, obviously no one was being reduced in status when the position was finally filled.

purchasing responsibility was dispersed to individual operating departments. The purchasing manager typically reported to a materials manager who, in turn, was responsible to manufacturing. The materials management concept was also adopted at the corporate level, but so much authority had been delegated to individual operating departments that the highest ranking materials manager in the company did not have nearly as much authority or prestige as the former purchasing vice president.

Reciprocity. Other companies have followed the GE example—for reasons not always related to operating efficiency. It has been deemed politic for purchasing at the corporate level to assume a low profile simply because centralized purchasing records are essential to efficient reciprocity.[4] Reciprocity can be illegal if the Justice Department or the Federal Trade Commission can prove that it substantially lessens competition. Conglomerate corporations—which might otherwise provide a number of high-level purchasing jobs—can most easily prevent possible antitrust problems by simply not having a purchasing activity at corporate level. All buying is done by decentralized divisions and, in the absence of centralized purchase records, it becomes all but impossible to practice reciprocity on a wide scale. Other companies that still have centralized purchasing departments have been specifically enjoined by the Justice Department from maintaining corporate records of sales and purchases. Although no one likes to admit it, this action by the Justice Department eliminates a high-level purchasing function. In the process industries in particular, the chief purchasing executive was as concerned with reciprocity or "trade relations" as he was with more conventional purchasing activities.

While the Justice Department's antireciprocity drive has undoubtedly worked to reduce the number of top-level purchasing positions, it has probably helped accelerate the movement toward materials management. When the rules on reciprocity were free and easy, purchasing departments were sales-oriented. In the paper, chemical and petroleum industries in particular, sales and purchasing were sometimes combined organizationally. When they were not, the purchasing director was often an ex-sales manager, and he usually played a critical role in reciprocity that informally linked purchasing and sales, even if the combination was not part of the formal organization.

Production orientation. Former marketing-oriented purchasing departments are gradually becoming part of production-oriented materials management departments. In larger corporations, these departments occur primarily at divisional level, and there may be no corporate purchasing or materials management staff whatever. Worse yet, from the

---

[4] This is discussed in Dean S. Ammer, "Realistic Reciprocity," *Harvard Business Review*, January–February 1962.

point of view of concerned materials managers, at least half of all materials managers do not report directly even to a division manager but to a second-level divisional executive—usually the manufacturing manager.

There are two basic reasons for this state of affairs, from top management's point of vew:

1. A company whose purchasing department is "buried" in a materials management department which, in turn, is part of manufacturing, is less likely to be regarded as a potential antitrust offender—particularly if the organization is at divisional level.

2. The manufacturing manager may oppose creation of an independent materials management organization if this requires him to give up jurisdiction over production and material control activities. But he may welcome materials management if it is placed under his jurisdiction.

Government regulations.   The Justice Department's antireciprocity stand is by no means the only government-inspired force working indirectly to spur wide adoption of the materials management form of organization. Other governmental actions are also favorable. Increasing governmental regulation of business forces top management to consult with its materials manager or purchasing manager before making major decisions. By measures both legal and unlegislated but with the force of law, the government is guiding seemingly private corporate purchasing decisions. Materials managers must work actively to develop minority suppliers and to encourage smaller vendors to attempt to compete successfully with larger ones.

In many cases, there are pressures to "buy American" even if a foreign firm offers better quality at lower prices. In addition, almost every larger corporation must keep abreast of the twists and turns of American foreign policy. At one time, for example, it was perfectly acceptable for American firms to purchase nickel from the Soviet Union, while Cuba was off limits. It mattered not that the Cubans undoubtedly sold their nickel to the U.S.S.R. in order to permit the U.S.S.R. to sell its nickel to the United States. While government guidance in purchasing is seldom welcomed by American business, it undoubtedly works to strengthen the purchasing organizations involved.

Full-employment economy

The by-products of the Full Employment Act of 1946 are not welcomed by most American managements either, but they, too, work to make the role of materials management more critical. This act requires the federal government to intervene in the economy to maintain full employment. The side effects of these policies are now well known. They include steady inflation, historically high interest rates, and turbulent labor relations.

Inflation. One need have no forecasting ability to predict that the general price level will be higher next year than it is this year—and even higher the year after. Inflation is part of our way of life. If all prices and costs were to rise predictably at the same rate, inflation would pose no real problem for the materials manager. His increases in purchased materials costs would be more than offset by increases in his company's selling prices. Unfortunately, the rate of inflation is uneven. While selling prices of most finished goods and services eventually go up to reflect higher basic costs of material and labor, there often is a rather painful lag. This puts special pressure on the purchasing agent and materials manager who may be responsible for at least half of product costs. Increasingly, company managements are discovering that they must have a first-rate purchasing department if they are not to be caught in squeezes where company costs are rising faster than selling prices.

Interest rates. When prices are expected to go up, the logical response is to boost inventory, to stock up at a lower price. This is inhibited, however, by the high interest rates that are another by-product of successful full-employment policies. The combination of soaring prices and rising inventory carrying costs makes it imperative that a company work for optimum purchase prices and inventory levels. This is easiest to accomplish with an integrated materials management organization.

Strikes. Every employee would like to get a bigger slice of the total economic pie. Everyone also occasionally has the urge to tell off his boss. In the past, fear of unemployment worked to inhibit workers from expressing these fundamental human urges. Full employment and generous unemployment benefits take away almost all of the penalties of work stoppages. In addition, as explained below, technology gives the protesting worker a great deal more economic leverage than he had before. The net result is that from the worker's point of view it often pays to strike—and disruptions in supply from labor unrest seem to be increasing in frequency, especially in the English-speaking countries. This inevitably makes it more desirable for managements to have integrated materials management departments to minimize the effect of supplier strikes.

AUTOMATION AND THE SUPPLY PROCESS

It is no accident that employees in capital-intensive highly automated industries are both higher paid and far more likely to strike than their less fortunate brethren in labor-intensive, unautomated industries. The barber continues to cut hair with essentially the same tools he used in 1920, but production of most other goods and services has been greatly changed by technology. Jobs that used to be done by many workers with relatively simple tools are now done by relatively few workers using very costly tools. In the factory, this process of using fewer workers and more complex machinery is called automation. But the same process of technological change has also affected most major service industries. In the hospital clinical laboratory, a $60,000 machine can perform in minutes tests that formerly required hours of a skilled medical technologists' time. Similarly, a Boeing 747 airliner is able to transport almost 20 times the number of passengers carried in the piston-engine airliners common until 1960.

Automation in manufacturing and services has greatly reduced costs. And, of course, with their relative absence of workers, automated plants look as if they should be low-cost producers, and they are. But they are not *no-cost* producers. Even though direct labor costs may have been virtually eliminated, all other costs still exist—purchased materials, administrative costs, maintenance and depreciation, interest and return on invested capital, and so on. In fact, some of these costs will be much higher in the automated plant. Its more complex equipment costs more to maintain. It also requires a greater initial investment, which means higher interest and depreciation charges.

As yet no one has built a workerless plant. But some of the highly automated plants in the electrical equipment, electronics, and auto industries provide clues as to what happens to costs when processes are automated. The following example is representative:

	Before automation	After automation
Material	$1.00	$1.02
Labor	.38	.04
Overhead	.57	.55
Manufacturing cost	$1.95	$1.61
Sales and administrative cost	.08	.08
Profit (to yield 20% return on investment)	.17	.34
Selling price	$2.20	$2.03

As expected, automation drastically reduces labor costs and also reduced total costs. Not so obvious, however are other by-products.

1. *Overhead is practically unchanged.* Although there is less indirect labor in the automated plant, what labor there is will be more highly skilled and higher priced. The greater capital investment in automated equipment raises depreciation charges and probably also general maintenance and operating costs. As a result, the composition of the overhead changes. Fixed charged (depreciation and so on) increase, while variable charges (mostly indirect labor) decrease. This makes costs more rigid.

2. *Profit Requirements are greater.* Automation requires a bigger investment in facilities. Naturally this means that profits on each unit produced must be higher to yield the same return on investment. In the example above, a 17-cent unit profit might be adequate, at standard

volume, to provide a 20 percent return on a $1 million investment in facilities. Suppose the investment in facilities increases to $2 million when production is automated. Then a 34-cent unit profit would be needed to provide a 20 percent return on investment—assuming there is no change in volume of output.

In addition, many managers believe that automated facilities should earn a greater return on investment than nonautomated facilities (although competition usually prevents this). The reason: the risks are greater with automation. In a completely unautomated plant, if a product fails to sell management can simply lay off workers and thus minimize losses. With automation, it cannot get off so easily. It is likely to be stuck with an enormous investment in equipment that is not good for much of anything except making a product that no one will buy.

3. *Tighter specifications may be needed.* When there are slight deviations in quality of parts and materials in a nonautomated plant, workers often are able to use the materials anyway by making minor adjustments. In a fully automated plant this might not be true. The automated equipment may not be able to compensate for off-standard materials; machines can never be as flexible as skilled human hands.[5] Inevitably, increasing automation will bring demands on suppliers to adhere more rigidly to specifications. This may raise costs of purchased materials slightly. It may also increase the probability of supply failure due to poor quality.

4. *Costs of supply failure increase.* In a nonautomated plant, if a supplier fails to deliver materials of satisfactory quality the plant is shut down and the workers are sent home. This is costly enough. But in a fully automated plant, the costs of shutting down are many times greater. Since there are fewer workers, less can be saved by sending them home without pay. Substituted for the workers is a tremendous investment in equipment that goes right on depreciating, whether it is being used or not.

What happens to the costs in the example when there is a shutdown?

---

[5] I observed an excellent example of this several years ago when touring the factory of a leading manufacturer of electronic data processing equipment. Electronic control panel boards were being assembled and soldered on an automated line. The new process required just two workers to load and unload parts from the line. The old process had required more than a dozen workers, who assembled and soldered various components—capacitators, resistors, transistors, and so on—to the printed circuit panel boards. Now the job was done by machine, only the machine wasn't working when I saw it. A shipment of capacitators had arrived, and some of them had wires that had been bent slightly in packing. Were the capacitators being soldered to the board by hand, this defect probably would not even have been noticed. The workers would simply have bent the ·vires to make them fit when they soldered them to the panel board. With the automated setup, each capacitator with a bent wire shut down the line for 10 or 15 minutes. It jammed the magazine feed at one station in the line, and no sooner would it be unjammed by a worker when another bent capacitator would jam up another station. The problem was finally licked by packing and unpacking with special care to prevent the wires from being bent. Naturally this raised costs slightly.

In both the automated and the nonautomated plant, the material and direct-labor costs can be largely eliminated; material is not used and workers are laid off.[6] Nevertheless, a supply failure even in the nonautomated plant can be costly. Note that the product in the example has a unit overhead cost of 57 cents when made in a nonautomated plant. Perhaps 30 cents of this is fixed or nonvariable overhead, which is incurred regardless of whether or not the product is made. In addition, the company naturally loses its 17-cent unit profit when there is a shutdown so its total loss on each unit not produced is 47 cents. If the plant has a standard volume of 1,000 units per hour, then the supply failure costs $470 per hour.

The costs of a shutdown almost double in the automated plant. The 55-cent unit overhead cost in the automated plant is a little lower than the overhead in the nonautomated plant. But much more of it—at least 45 cents—is fixed and nonvariable, incurred regardless of whether or not the plant operates. In the automated plant, the variable indirect-labor cost that was incurred for inspectors, material handlers, and so on, is replaced with nonvariable maintenance and depreciation expense needed because of the added investment in plant and equipment. As a result, the automated plant has 15 cents (45 cents minus 30 cents) more fixed and nonvariable overhead per unit than the nonautomated plant. In addition, the profit loss is greater when the automated plant shuts down. It is 34 cents instead of 17 cents, or 17 cents greater. Thus a shutdown in the automated plant results in a total additional loss of 32 cents (the 17-cent profit loss plus the 15 cents in extra fixed overhead) per unit. At standard volume of 1,000 units per hour, the supply failure in the automated plant is $320 per hour more costly than the same failure in the nonautomated plant. The total cost of the failure is $790 per hour.[7]

5. *Probability of supply failure increases.* The extremely high cost of shutting down automated equipment is not lost on the employees who operate it. The costlier the shutdown, the greater their bargaining power. It is no accident, for example, that airline pilots are far more likely to strike than taxicab drivers. The airline pilot who strikes causes a $25,000,000 aircraft to sit idle, and the loss to airline management for each idle plane can be several hundred thousand dollars per day. From the pilots' point of view, strikes are profitable because managements cannot afford to let their aircraft sit idle for prolonged periods, thus each strike brings new gains in wages and fringe benefits. In contrast,

---

[6] This is an oversimplification. Employers incur substantial labor costs even when they lay off workers, because union contracts call for supplementary unemployment compensation. In addition, state workmen's unemployment compensation benefits are paid from taxes levied on employers in proportion to their workers' needs for such benefits.

[7] Based on 45 cents for unit fixed and nonvariable overhead in the automated plant, plus 34 cents in unit profit, multiplied by 1,000 units per hour.

the owner of a taxicab loses relatively little if his driver refuses to work, and the driver has far less incentive to strike.

Thus automation in the factory and in service industries not only greatly increases the cost of supply failure but also tends to increase its probability. This unfavorable aspect of automation makes managements more conscious of the need for capable materials management personnel to minimize the effect of supply failures.

AUTOMATION IN THE OFFICE

Automation in the factory will put tremendous pressure on materials managers by increasing the costs of supply failure. The use of computers and other automated equipment in the office will relieve some of this pressure, because it allows for radically different materials management techniques.

It will also bring substantial changes in the organization structure for materials management. Chapter 1 noted that in many companies materials activities are not unified organizationally. The typical manufacturing company has separate purchasing, traffic, and production control departments. The only person responsible for all three activities in most cases is the company's president or general manager, and often he is much too busy with other problems to worry much about materials management. In the typical company materials get managed if the managers of the various materials activities have learned how to work together and responsibility is divided among them quite precisely by policies, procedures, tradition, and habit.

There are at least four reasons why this approach does not work well when the computer takes over the routine tasks of materials management:

1. *Computer programs stimulate unification of materials activities.* Computer programming is extremely costly. Even fairly simple business systems require a programming investment of several thousand dollars; major systems require several man-years of work because of the many exceptions that must be allowed for in creating the program. Programming is a problem even when cost is no object. Demand for programmers has been increasing much more rapidly than the supply and this imbalance will probably continue.

For all of these reasons, it is obvious that interrelated activities like purchasing, production control, and traffic cannot develop programs independently of one another. Materials management must be considered an integrated activity in developing a single program. This, in turn, will help break down the functional lines between departments and help unify them organizationally.

2. *Reports from computers encourage a unified, integrated approach to materials management.* Companies rarely invest in computers simply

because they want to cut clerical overhead. They are every bit as interested in another objective: to speed the flow of information needed for making decisions. Computers permit daily inventory status reports in companies that formerly were forced to use monthly reports (issued up to a month late) as a basis for materials management decisions. Such rapid reporting is useful only if management is able to use it promptly in making decisions.

This is more likely to be the case in an integrated materials department. In such an organization, one person can be delegated all the authority he needs to take action on most materials problems. This is not the case in the conventional materials organization with separate purchasing, production control, and traffic departments, particularly if these departments are not even unified under a common materials manager. In such an organization, basic materials decisions can be made only after there is some consultation among individuals in the interested departments. Inevitably, this is more time-consuming than if responsibility rested with one person who is responsible for all phases of materials management for a particular item. It is also more wasteful, since it causes several persons to check similar materials problems for identical products.

3. *Manpower needs will be substantially reduced.* It was noted in Chapter 19 that about 90 percent of the materials jobs in a typical pre-EDP company are clerical. In the future, fewer than 50 percent will be clerical. A materials department that requires 200 persons without automation will ultimately require no more than 100 persons, with computers and other equipment taking over much of the routine work. This reduction will be felt more heavily in some functions than in others. It may, for example, virtually eliminate what is currently the biggest materials activity in terms of manpower, the production control department.

Computer programs already have been developed (e.g., at Fairchild Industries Corporation, as described in Chapter 19) to take over all routine production control activities. Once the problem of data transmission is solved so that operators no longer are needed to record materials transactions on punched cards or punched tape, clerical manpower needed to manage materials will be reduced further. As a result, the production control department will shrink so that its supervision ceases to be much of a problem.

The purchasing and traffic departments will also shrink, although not as much as production control. Suppliers of materials and transportation services must still be dealt with by people, but machines can take over much of the clerical drudgery in purchasing and traffic, including invoice checking, posting of records, and the like.

These reductions in manpower will make it more convenient to group these heretofore independent functions under a single manager.

4. *Computers may reduce flexibility.* Computers are not as versatile as human clerks. Their programs must be carefully designed to allow for every exception. This makes programming costly and expensive to change. Materials management by computer will be practicable only if the authority for basic changes in policy centers on a single materials manager. If materials management authority is dispersed, as it is in the conventional organization, there will inevitably be problems. This need not mean that the materials manager should be directly responsible for operating the computer; that can be done by a highly specialized service department. But a single materials manager should be the basic authority on what programs are devised for managing materials with the computer. The service department can then translate his instructions into an actual program for the computer.

MATERIALS MANAGEMENT AND EDP

The computer is now so widely applied in materials management that its effects can be observed. The application of electronic data processing to materials management follows a predictable pattern[8] in terms of industry, size of company, and type of application.

Applications of EDP

Big companies lead. Inventory control is often the first application of EDP to materials management. The big companies began to use computers for inventory management in the 1950s, but smaller firms often did not undertake their first applications until the late 1960s and early 1970s. In both large and small companies, EDP is typically used for scheduling and material control concurrent with its adoption for inventory control, or soon thereafter. Other applications soon follow.

The bigger companies were not only the first to apply EDP but, because of economics of scale, they also make more extensive use of it. Table 21–1 shows materials management applications of EDP broken down by size of company. While most smaller companies are using it for major materials management applications, they often find manual methods quite satisfactory for minor applications. For example, 43 percent of the companies with sales of $1 billion or more use EDP in their traffic operations, while no respondent in the $5 to $10 million sales group uses it in traffic (and, of course, most companies this size do not even have a full-time traffic manager).

Most applications of EDP to materials management are fairly recent. More than 80 percent of all EDP users had not made their *first* applica-

---

[8] All data on materials management applications of EDP discussed in this chapter are based on a survey of 4,000 manufacturing companies I conducted under a grant from the American Production and Inventory Control Society.

TABLE 21-1
Percent of companies making various materials management applications of EDP

Type of activity	Total all respondents (%)	Over $1 billion sales (%)	$250 million to $1 billion sales (%)	$100-250 million sales (%)	$50-100 million sales (%)	$25-50 million sales (%)	$10-25 million sales (%)	$5-10 million sales (%)	$5 million or less (%)
Scheduling. .	55	75	70	60	58	54	50	48	24
Material control. . .	63	67	76	74	59	62	66	43	52
Inventory control. . .	76	78	87	78	84	75	77	63	58
Purchasing . .	52	65	67	69	56	50	45	29	38
Expediting. .	36	51	47	45	41	33	32	21	22
Receiving and shipping . .	33	48	47	39	37	36	30	12	18
Traffic	12	43	20	19	16	9	6	0	4
Stores	39	72	45	44	42	41	39	17	14
Other.	16	14	14	13	17	21	16	16	24

tion as recently as 1960, and almost every company has made at least one or two new applications in the past year or two. Thus a majority of companies are still learning new ways to apply EDP to materials management.

Industry pattern. The application of EDP to materials management varies from industry to industry. It is most likely to be found in highly concentrated industries dominated by large companies, especially when that industry's materials management process generates a great deal of paperwork. There is also, as indicated in Figures 21-1 and 21-2, a relationship between the application of EDP to materials management and the existence of a materials management type of organization.

Figure 21-1 compares companies in various industries that use EDP in materials management with those that have materials managers. In general, industries that use EDP in the materials management process are likely to have materials organizations headed by materials managers. For example, about 68 percent of the respondents in the aerospace industry indicated that they used EDP in materials management, and 62 percent reported that they had unified materials organizations headed by materials managers. The relationship is not quite so perfect in other industries, however. In the chemical industry, EDP is widely used in materials management, but the materials management form of organization is less prevalent than in other industries. This is also true of the food industry. Both industries typically have strong centralized purchasing departments, while other materials management activities often appear only at plant level. In the chemical industry, purchasing departments have often been more marketing-oriented than production-

FIGURE 21–1

Comparison of application of EDP for materials management in various industries with incidence of materials manager title*

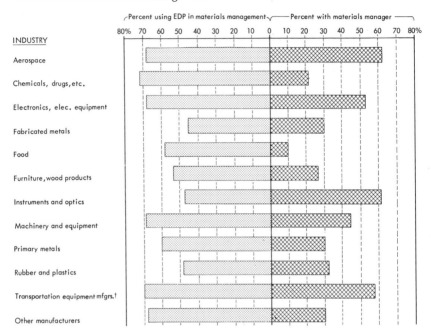

*Includes titles comparable to materials manager, such as director of material, vice president purchasing & production control, etc.
†Includes auto, truck, railroad equipment, shipbuilding, etc., but not aircraft, which is included in aerospace.

oriented. The other materials activities, in contrast, have tended to be production-oriented. These organizational relationships create an additional obstacle that must be overcome before an integrated materials management organization can become a reality.

EDP use and materials management adoption. In the cases described above, EDP is less effective as a stimulus for adoption of the materials management organization. Yet in most industries, EDP users are more likely to have materials managers than companies that do not use it. This is shown in Figure 21–2, which compares by industry the prevalence of materials managers among EDP users and nonusers.

For example, more than 70 percent of the EDP users in the aerospace industry are likely to have a materials manager, while only 50 percent of the nonusers have one. This relationship is valid even in industries like food and chemicals where the materials management form of organization is still relatively rare. Note that in the food industry, for example, only about 8 percent of the companies that do not use EDP in materials management have materials managers, while about 11 per-

FIGURE 21–2
Comparison by industry group of adoption of materials management organization among firms using EDP and those not using it

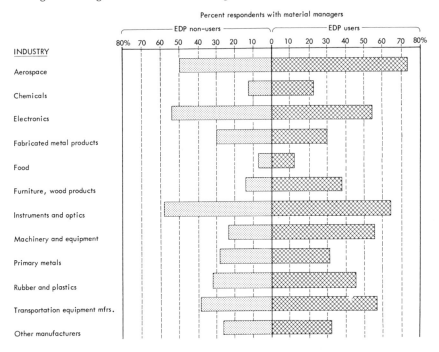

Percent respondents with material managers

cent of the EDP users employ them. In chemicals, the relationship between EDP and materials management is even more apparent. About 22 percent of the EDP users have materials managers, while only 12 percent of the nonusers have them. In electronics, fabricated metals, and primary metals, the EDP users are apparently just as likely to have materials managers as are nonusers. Nevertheless, there appears to be a correlation between adoption of the materials management organization and application of EDP to materials management.

Future effect. The relationship between EDP and materials management will almost certainly become more pronounced when managements learn how to use their computers to manage materials in new ways. At present, the computer is still a glorified clerk as far as materials management is concerned. Its speed permits much tighter control of inventory and other materials management activities, so materials managers can make better decisions sooner. As yet, however, there has been little change in the basic techniques of materials management. In fact, EDP is still in a shakedown stage in many materials departments. This is evidenced by the fact that the computer has not apparently caused any great reduction in materials management employment. Companies reporting sharp reductions in employment are almost exactly offset by companies reporting increases. Eventually, however, the computer is destined to increase sharply the productivity of materials management personnel. Clerical employment is certain to decline universally among materials departments. While employment of professional-level staff will undoubtedly increase sharply, the net change in employment will be negative.

Many new positions will be developed in materials management as companies begin to use their computers to manage materials in totally new ways. For example, few if any of today's materials departments are staffed with mathematicians. There is no need for them. Present-day materials management problems can be solved with arithmetic and high-school alegbra. This will not be true in the future; computers will permit the use of highly sophisticated inventory control formulas devised by trained mathematicians.

Similarly, the demand for economists in materials management will grow enormously. The inflexibility and high fixed costs that characterize the automated factory and office make it more important to forecast demand accurately. Computers will help economists in forecasting by digesting and analyzing complex statistics. Automation will also increase the demand for men and women with engineering backgrounds in materials departments. The tighter quality standards, closer scheduling, and more complex manufacturing processes that automation permits will require materials personnel with a real understanding of manufacturing and engineering.

No longer will it be possible—as it still often is today, particularly in smaller companies—to promote a man to the job of buyer or purchasing agent simply because he is a competent clerk in the stockroom and knows how to get along with people. Other qualifications will be required. A college degree will be almost mandatory and advanced degrees will be commonplace, particularly in large companies. The opportunities should be challenging enough to test the mettle of even the most talented.

The systems approach

To an increasing degree, materials management will be looked at as a subsystem operating within an overall management system. The setup will be quite different from the traditional approach to organization in which management was looked at as group of specialized functions—purchasing, manufacturing, engineering, marketing, finance, and so forth. This traditional approach is essentially static organizationally. Each department has a role that is quite rigidly defined. The new computer-age systems approach to management completely changes this. This systems approach is essentially dynamic; that is, functions are not static and well defined, but fluid. Each activity interacts with every other activity. The specialist who is used to minding his own business discovers that he must become involved in the activities of others. All management is seen as a system—a closed loop.

The materials management type of organization—in which all materials activities are grouped together under a common manager—is uniquely suited to a computer-oriented systems approach to management. The materials group is a subsystem interacting with other subsystems. Its main source of input is the engineering subsystem, which also feeds data to the manufacturing subsystem.

PERT network.[9]   The first step in applying the systems concept to materials management might be to construct a complex program evaluation and review technique (PERT) network detailing all the thousands of steps needed to translate a top-management decision into a tangible reality. The product must be engineered; special tools and equipment must be designed and built; suppliers of purchased parts and materials must be located; sample parts must be tested and approved; and materials and components must be ordered and received—all before production can begin.

Expected times would be calculated for each path of the PERT network, and the entire network would be coded on cards or tape and put into a computer. The project itself would form a new subsystem which would coexist, of course, with various other subsystems, including materials management. All systems would interact with each other.

Suppose, for example, that a major supplier is hit by a long strike which causes delayed delivery of a component. The materials department would have to feed this information into the materials subsystem and analyze it, along with thousands of other bits of information. The computer would then recalculate the paths in the PERT network, taking all the new facts into account.

The supplier's delay might not create a critical path. In this case, management would know that there was no real problem. On the other hand, the delayed delivery might lengthen a path that was already critical for the entire project. Everyone in the project group involved in this specific path would then know where to apply maximum effort. The materials manager would, of course, have to expedite all critical path activities in the materials subsystem.

The same subsystem would continue to operate when the new product went into production. A new production system would then evolve. Inputs into the production materials subsystem would come from the marketing subsystem (basic demand), engineering (design changes), quality control (reliability standards), and suppliers (delivery information). Output would consist of a flow of purchase orders, change notices, and receiving reports.

The materials group would make many decisions almost indepen-

---

[9] The PERT technique is discussed in Chapter 7.

dently of other subsystems. It would decide how much and how often to order. It would also regulate the flow of various materials and adjust it to accommodate minor changes in demand and supply. And, of course, it would have to adjust to the changing needs of other subsystems. For example, if the marketing subsystem indicated a major increase in demand, the materials subsystem would report back on how rapidly it could respond and would automatically make the necessary schedule adjustments.

Use of Computer. This rundown of how a computerized materials subsystem would work might cause a precomputer purchasing agent to ask:

1. Isn't the systems approach just a lot of gobbledygook for what we have been doing for years?
2. Why can't there be a "purchasing subsystem" rather than a "materials subsystem"?

The answers to these questions are interrelated. It is true that a lot of specialized jargon is used in the computerized systems approach (such as "software" to describe computer programs and "hardware" to describe the computer equipment itself). But the systems approach is distinctly different from what has been done in the past. In fact, it is not insignificant that the approach is applied mostly in new industries. When it catches on in an established firm, it is usually because of a merger with an avant-garde company.

A computer is all but essential to a systems approach, since the concept is based on management's being able to react rapidly to changes in operating conditions. The systems approach is impractical without a computer. Noncomputerized information is too dated to be more than a historical guide.

With the systems approach each manager can figuratively (and sometimes literally) do his job by quizzing the computer on what is happening inside his subsystem. For example, the manager of a materials subsystem can ask, "What should I worry about today?" and get back a typed list of jobs by order of urgency.

The systems-type organization tends to follow patterns set up by the computer program. Materials management can be programmed into a group of routines that carries material through its entire cycle—from specification of materials to delivery of end products. This automatically draws together the traditional purchasing, production control, and traffic departments, along with their usual subfunctions of receiving, stores, shipping, transporation, and materials handling as well.

Purchasing itself, however, is not a subsystem. It is not able to regulate its input. Therefore, there is no real need for the feedback that is the vital element of the systems approach. The traditional purchasing department buys what it is told to buy (although it controls its output by selecting supply sources). In addition, purchasing is usually not linked to any real product system.

The project-oriented organization is closely related to the systems approach. Each project group becomes a separate small system linked to the bigger system of the overall company. Materials forms a subsystem within each project system. This arrangement is logically consistent with the dynamics of computer programs, but not with the rigid structures of conventional organization.

Application of management science. There are other reasons why a materials group is a more logical subsystem than a regular purchasing department. The computer makes it practical to use scientific management techniques such as economic order quantities, queuing theory, line of balance, PERT, and linear programming. Most of these techniques were devised years ago but never became widely accepted because the calculations were too cumbersome.

It was the computer—not the techniques themselves—that actually made seat-of-the-pants materials management obsolete. The inevitable result is that purchasing and production control—natural rivals in the usual organization—have been drawn closer together. Either a hybrid department develops, or the stronger of the two takes over.

DEVELOPMENT OF THE PROFIT CENTER

The department that emerges may well become a separate profit center. In the past, materials management activities have been regarded as "services" that help other profit centers within the company do a better job. In this respect, materials management resembles a department like maintenance which makes an indirect contribution by preventing breakdowns. Neither maintenance nor the various materials management activities have traditionally been regarded as direct profit markers. Their contribution has usually been too indirect and too difficult to measure.

Criteria for profit center

Every materials manager can improve his own performance by applying profit-center techniques to the management of his department. And, in the future, the materials department may well turn out to *be* a profit center. The purpose of profit centers is to focus management's attention on the most basic objective of the business: profits. For this reason, manufacturing is almost always broken up into profit centers in big companies. Sales and engineering may also be legitimate profit centers.

Organization. A profit center is created by drawing an imaginary line around some part of the organization and arbitrarily treating it as a separate business whose manager is responsible for profits. For example, an automobile assembly plant may be a separate profit center.

It may "buy" engines, bodies, and other major components from the company's own manufacturing plants or from outside suppliers. It assembles these components into complete automobiles which it "sells" to the company's sales organization which, in turn, sells to dealers. The plant "profit" represents the difference between cost and selling price.

A company's sales organization may ·also be considered as a profit center. It "buys" finished products at some predetermined price from the company's manufacturing organization and then resells them to company customers. Thus the marketing organization of a large manufacturer may be treated somewhat as a department store. It buys material from the factory; adds value to it with its own advertising, sales promotion, and distribution; and finally resells at a profit to the ultimate user.

Materials management can be treated the same way. It buys material from others, adds value to it in the form of distribution, and then "sells" it to the company's own manufacturing organization. The difference between the price at which material is transferred to manufacturing and the total cost of procurement represents the "profit" from materials management. This profit can be related to the capital that is employed in the materials management process.

Essential factors.   Every profit center has these basic criteria: (1) value is added, (2) capital is employed productively, and (3) costs are incurred. The materials management organization in any profit or nonprofit company or institution can meet these criteria as well as a "captive" manufacturing profit center such as the Fisher Body Division of General Motors. Nevertheless, few captive materials management profit centers actually exist. One major reason is that most top managers either are not familiar with the concept or do not believe it is advantageous. Also, the application of the profit-center concept implies the existence of an independent materials management organization, and this idea is not always welcome in companies where materials management ·is subordinate to manufacturing, finance, or some other function. The materials manager who is recognized as a "value adder" in his own right is the organizational equal of the manufacturing, marketing, and other second-level managers of the business. While few real-life materials managers head genuine profit centers, the concept is not entirely theoretical. The procurement activities of several department-store chains are almost independent profit centers. They buy for a group of stores and charge them an amount that at least equals the cost of the service. The General Services Administration also buys and stores materials and supplies which it then resells at cost plus markup to other government agencies.

Profit center accounting

While top managements may not have any interest in putting the materials manager in charge of a profit center for the sake of his prestige, they are sympathetic to any program designed to boost profit. The materials department can set up its own system of profit control without any formal organization changes. The end result is a profit-and-loss statement and a balance sheet for the materials department that resemble those of other profit centers.

Assets. If you were a materials manager setting up a profit center system, you would first list the value of all assets under your jurisdiction. (You can get part of the data from accounting; some you may have to estimate yourself.) A medium-sized firm might have the following materials management assets:

ASSETS

Raw-materials inventory	$1,000,000
Office equipment and floor space.	200,000
Factory floor space and equipment.	300,000
	$1,500,000

If yours is a manufacturing company, the purchased-materials inventory would include not only direct but also indirect material. In nonmanufacturing organizations it would, of course, include only inventories of supplies and other materials not incorporated into any product. Office equipment and floor space would include the allocated share of those assets that are employed in the complete materials management process. For example, if purchasing, production control, and other materials management activities occupy 10 percent of an office building with a value of $1,000,000, then the value of the space these activities occupy is 10 × $1,000,000, or $100,000. A similar approach is used when materials management shares factory floor space with manufacturing.

You would have no liabilities (as long as you assumed that all material in stores had been paid for), so the company's net investment in its materials management operation would be $1,500,000. Like the company's other investments, this is expected to earn a return. If it provides no economic return, then the company should liquidate it. Companies usually set target returns on capital employed. For example, the General Motors Corp. allegedly will not invest money in a project unless it promises a 25 percent return on investment after taxes.

Suppose your company has profit objectives more modest than General Motors's and is willing to settle for a 20 percent return. Then the materials management profit objective becomes 20 percent of the $1,500,000 investment in materials management assets, or $300,000 per year. If you can reduce your investment, however, you can get along with less profit. Suppose, for example, that you succeed in reducing inventory investment by $200,000. This reduces total assets from $1,500,000 to $1,300,000. With assets of only $1,300,000, you need earn but $260,000 per year in order to achieve management's 20 percent profit objective.

Focus on profit. So far, all you have done is draw up a theoretical balance sheet to guide you in managing materials. Nevertheless, note how this automatically helps focus your efforts on management's profit objectives and works to boost efficiency. If you occupy more floor space, buy equipment for your own use, or boost inventory, you automatically boost your department's total capital. This, in turn, boosts your profit bogey—forcing you to make 20 cents extra profit for every $1 extra investment. Conversely, you can make yourself look good by whittling down your investment, as long as this does not impair operating efficiency. You will not invest in additional facilities or inventory to provide better "service" but to make more money. This is as it should be in a competitive, profit-lean economy.

There is no way in which you can separate the return earned by assets employed in materials management from assets employed in other basic activities of the business. This is true of any "captive" profit center which does not sell its output on the open market. The reason for this, of course, is that your profit or that of any other captive profit center is heavily dependent on the price charged for goods and services. If these are sold on the open market, you can charge whatever the traffic will bear, and there is no doubt that a profit has been earned. If they are sold within the organization, there is no "free market," and the earnings of every captive profit center are at least partly suspect.

To start a captive profit center, however, it is probably reasonable to assume that it earns the same return on its capital as other profit-centers in the same company earn on the capital they employ. If the company earned, for example, a 15 percent pretax return on all of the capital employed in every phase of its business, it is reasonable to assume that, in the beginning at least, materials management and every other activity in the company made this same contribution. So you arbitrarily assume that as materials manager you are neither better nor worse than any of the company's other managers, and, like them, earned a 15 percent return on the capital.

Income statement.   This preliminary estimate of a target return on capital gives you a basis for pricing and creating an income statement. You incur two types of cost in the operation of your materials management profit center: cost of goods and services purchased for resale, and operating expenses. Suppose, for example, that you purchased $10,000,000 worth of goods and services from outside suppliers last year. Total expenses associated with all materials management activities— salaries, fringe benefits, depreciation on buildings and equipment, and so forth—amounted to $300,000. Thus the total materials management effort had total costs of $10,300,000 last year, exclusive of any return earned on capital. But, of course, $1,500,000 of the company's capital is needed for the assets employed in materials management. If this capital has been used productively it must have earned some return, and we arbitrarily assume that this return is identical with that earned by the company's combined activities. If this overall return is 15 percent, the "profit" earned in materials management must be equal to 15 percent of the capital employed: 15 percent of $1,500,000, or $225,000. Total value added by distribution in the materials management process then becomes $225,000 plus the $300,000 of operating expenses, or $525,000. Therefore, the $10,000,000 worth of value added by suppliers has a value of $10,525,000 by the time it is used by "customers" of the materials management department in manufacturing or other company activities.

You now have all the figures you need to construct the following income statement:

"Sales"	$10,525,000
Cost of goods sold (annual purchase volume)	10,000,000
Gross margin	$ 525,000
Expenses incurred in the materials management process	300,000
Profit earned in materials management	$ 225,000

$$\frac{\text{Materials management profit} = \$225,000}{\text{Capital employed} = \$1,500,000} = 15 \text{ percent return on capital}$$

Purpose of the profit center

So far, we have gone through what could be a meaningless exercise in bookkeeping. It has significance, however, even if we go no further. It proves rather conclusively that $1 worth of purchased material is worth more than $1 by the time it reaches the using department. Conventional accounting systems assume that there are no costs associated with each purchase and that, therefore, the using department incurs a cost that is no greater than the cash purchase price plus inbound freight. This simply is not true. Value is always added by distribution in the materials management process, and the costs of using activities are understated if they do not reflect full cost of purchased materials to the user.

This can be particularly misleading in cases where the materials management process is extremely costly. For example, the true cost of $1 worth of medical-surgical supplies delivered to a hospital nursing station may be $1.50 or even $2 by the time all materials management costs, including return on capital, are taken into account. Profit-center calculations that take into account value added by materials management help shift costs to the parts of the organization where they are actually incurred. This makes for more precise financial reporting and should lead to greater overall efficiency.

Even more important, however, is the impact that a materials management profit center may have on the ways in which materials are managed. For the first time, the performance of the materials manager is directly related to the primary economic mission of the organization: to achieve maximum results with minimum resources. The efforts of the materials manager are automatically focused on economic performance. The materials manager behaves like a businessman and works to maximize his return on capital. He can do this by reducing purchase costs or operating expenses. He may also succeed in employing less capital in the materials management process, as suggested in the three simple examples given below.

1. *Inventory reduction.* The materials manager decides to cut inventories by 10 percent. He purchases smaller quantities than before and also reduces order points, thereby cutting back on safety stocks. As a result, he is able to operate with an inventory investment of only $900,000, and capital employed in materials management is reduced by $100,000 to a net total investment of $1,400,000. If we assume competent inventory management in the past, this reduction cannot be made "for free." Materials management operating expenses should go up, since shortages will occur more frequently and increased expediting will be needed.

In addition, there may be an increase in supply failures. Buck-passing is not allowed in the materials management profit center. The materials manager earns his profit by guaranteeing delivery of material to users in accordance with some prearranged schedule. If material is not available because inventories are too low, then materials management must absorb any losses incurred by the using department that result from material not being on hand when needed.

Assume arbitrarily that these extra expenses and losses resulting from the cut in inventory amount to $10,000 per year. If there are no other changes in costs or revenues, this means that the "profit" earned in the materials management process declines by $10,000 to $215,000. However, this $215,000 profit is earned by an investment of only $1,400,000 because inventories are $100,000 lower than before. Consequently, the return on capital is $215,000 ÷ $1,400,000, or 15.4 percent. Thus tighter inventory control has increased return on capital by 0.4 percent.

2. *Lower purchase costs.* The materials manager embarks on a campaign to reduce costs of purchased parts and materials. He believes that if he hires a specialist in cost reduction, the savings made from value analysis (see Chapter 18) will more than offset the salary and other costs incidental to the program. So he hires a value analyst, and operating costs increase by $20,000 per year. However, the value analyst succeeds in reducing purchase costs by 1 percent, so the saving is $100,000 per year (.01 × $10,000,000). As a result, profit from materials management increases by a net of $80,000 per year. Provided there are no other changes, total profit will then be $305,000 per year, and return on capital increases to about 20 percent per year.

3. *Methods are improved.* The materials manager discovers that he can reduce payroll and other operating costs in his department by $20,000 per year if he spends $100,000 on new materials-handling equipment. The reduction in operating costs increases profit by $20,000, to $245,000, but capital employed in materials management increases by

$100,000, to $1,600,000. As a result, return on investment is 15.3 percent, a modest increase over the 15 percent overall return that was earned prior to the investment in new equipment.

Ground rules

If the materials manager is able to continue to make improvements in his operations like those described above, his return on capital will begin to increase gradually. Initially we assume that materials management earns exactly the same return as the rest of the company. At this starting point, the calculated return on capital employed in the materials management process has no real meaning. However, successive calculations of return on capital are significant. Suppose, for example, that the materials manager begins in year 1 with the same 15 percent as the rest of the company, but by year 5 he has managed to increase return on capital to 20 percent. Meanwhile, the company has made no progress in boosting overall profitability, and total return on capital continues to be exactly 15 percent. This means that over this five-year period materials management has become relatively more profitable, while other company activities have become relatively less profitable. If the ground rules for measuring profitability are correctly constructed, then this relative improvement in materials management profitability is a fair measure of the materials manager's performance.

However, tough ground rules are needed if change in return on investment is to be a valid measure of materials management performance. The exact rules would have to be tailored to fit the unique needs of each organization, but the following rules illustrate the principle.

1. *Materials management pays for all supply failures.* Losses resulting from supply failure are absorbed by materials management rather than the department that uses the purchased material. For example, suppose that late delivery of purchased materials from a supplier forces manufacturing to schedule overtime for operations that fall behind schedule due to lack of purchased material. This cost would be chargeable to materials management, not to manufacturing, even if the supply failure was more or less an act of God. For example, if an outside supplier is held up because of a fire or flood, the materials manager cannot disclaim responsibility simply because he could not anticipate the disaster. He is automatically held responsible for the performance of all outside suppliers, regardless of cause. The using departments, in effect, pay materials management to assume this responsibility so that they, in turn, can concentrate their efforts exclusively on the activities in which they specialize.

2. *Transfer prices are relatively rigid.* Materials management is a "cost plus" operation only in year 1, when a markup is added to purchased materials costs sufficient to cover both materials management

operating expenses and a return on capital equal to that which is earned companywide. From then on, materials management is on its own. If a supplier increases his price, the added cost is absorbed by materials management, not by the department that actually uses the purchased material. This tough rule applies even to purchased materials whose prices cannot possibly be influenced by the materials manager. However, the rule does work both ways. If the materials manager succeeds in reducing the price paid for purchased material, the saving is *not* passed on to the user.[10] Reductions in cost automatically work to increase materials management profit and return on capital.

Similarly, changes in operating costs would not immediately be passed on to users in the form of higher transfer prices. In practice, this means that the materials manager would probably find himself in an almost continuous profit squeeze. Like every other department in the company, materials management is confronted with steady wage and salary inflation. Employees are typically given raises of 5 percent or more per year, even though there may have been no improvement whatever in their productivity. Thus it would hardly be surprising if a materials management department that has operating expenses of about $300,000 per year would suffer a creeping inflation of about $15,000 per year in its operating expenses. Profits decline by a like amount unless the materials manager figures out a way to offset this inflation. The easiest way to do this is simply by increasing transfer prices and, in effect, making the using departments pay for higher costs of materials management. But the whole purpose of the profit center is to make the materials manager, not the using departments, responsible for all aspects of materials management. Inevitably, this means steady pressure on the materials manager to prevent his profit from being eroded by higher costs.

3. *Price changes are market determined.* The materials management profit center must be prevented from increasing transfer prices whenever it pleases simply because it is a monopoly supplier to the using departments. Ideally, the ground rules should simulate the existence of competition even when the environment does not actually permit it.

Yet it is unrealistic to assume that transfer prices must be maintained at the same level for all time. Adjustments are needed periodically to compensate for higher costs. These become related to a real-life free market if they can be tied to the company's selling price for end prod-

---

[10] The only exception to this rule would be a case where the using department is at least partly responsible for the reduction in purchase price. Then it would naturally share in the benefit. For example, if the using department agrees to relax purchase specifications, then it should naturally benefit from the lower costs that result. On the other hand, if the cost reduction comes about simply because the purchasing department is able to buy identical material from another supplier at a lower price, then the saving need not be shared with the using department, and the transfer price to the user would not be reduced even though costs are lower.

ucts. Every time the company's end-product prices can be increased, materials management and other captive profit centers can share the benefit in proportion to the value they add to the product by manufacture or by distribution. In a small, single-product company, a 5 percent increase in the price of that single product would automatically permit a 5 percent increase in the transfer price of all purchased materials "sold" by the materials management profit center. On the other hand, a 5 percent decrease in end-product prices would automatically trigger a 5 percent decrease in materials management transfer prices, even if materials management costs and purchase prices were rising.

With this system of periodic price, adjustment, the return on capital earned by the materials management department would parallel the company's overall rate of return except to the extent that materials management succeeded or failed in its attempts to increase its return on capital. And, of course, the basic purpose of the profit center approach is to identify and encourage actions by materials management that result in lower costs and/or less capital employed.

Advantages of the profit center

The materials management profit center is primarily a device by which materials management performance can be measured objectively. It encourages decisions which tend to increase the return on capital employed in the materials management department (and, indirectly that of the entire organization) and to discourage decisions which reduce return on capital. But there are also some major ancillary benefits.

1. *Unified materials management is encouraged.* Purchasing, production control, traffic, and other materials management activities have a natural tendency to operate independently of one another, even after they are brought together organizationally. In addition, some materials management decisions may continue to be made by the using departments rather than by materials management. The profit center approach tends to define materials management responsibility more sharply and to force materials functions to work together toward common objectives.

2. *Emphasis is on profit, not cost.* When materials management is not a profit center, it is looked upon as a service activity that, in effect, is a helper to the profit makers. As a result, considerable materials management effort may be directed toward pleasing the using departments that are served, even though this may not necessarily be in the best overall interests of the organization. For example, a materials manager whose performance is measured on the basis of "service" would try to avoid situations where inventories became uncomfortably low, and he would also be quite willing to cater to the brand-name preferences of using departments, even if it caused costs to be somewhat higher. In contrast, the manager of a materials profit center would tend to

be more concerned with the economic performance of his department than with its popularity.

3. *Responsibility is defined more clearly.* Real-life materials managers and their subordinates are all too quick to blame someone else when there is a supply failure. They are usually able to "prove" that they were misinformed by the using department. Or, with a straight face, they may say that a supply failure is the supplier's fault, implying that somehow this relieves them of any responsibility. The plain fact is, of course, that using departments cannot be held responsible for supply failures unless they do their own materials management. The risk and the responsibility for failure must be assumed by the materials manager. If his failures cause losses in the using departments, then it is only fair to consider them as part of the costs of materials management, even with failures that no reasonable person could foresee or prevent.

4. *Rational risk taking is encouraged.* There is some element of risk in every phase of a business. However, managements have traditionally taken substantial risks in marketing and design and avoided them in materials management. For example, a company might, in effect, take a risk at 50–50 odds when it launches some new product with a costly advertising campaign. In the same company, a purchasing manager may decline to take a chance on a new supplier, even though the odds may be 5 to 1 in favor of that supplier being as successful as the higher cost supplier that would be replaced.

In the traditional organization, the penalty for failure that is suffered by the staff executive is much greater than the reward for success. In materials management, this may mean that the saving from successful buying simply is not noticed but the failures (e.g., when the plant is shut down because of supply failure) are extremely conspicuous. It is a wonder, then, that a materials manager is willing to take any risk whatever, even when it is to his company's advantage. In the materials management profit center, in contrast, risk taking that is profitable on balance is encouraged. As long as the "winners" outnumber the "losers," the return on investment earned by materials management should increase. And, of course, this gain is not at the expense of any other activity, since materials management assumes full responsibility for supply failures.

5. *Materials management can spend money to make money.* In the conventional organization, materials management is treated as a cost center, not a profit center. The budget is the major tool for control and for performance measurement. When times are tough, the materials manager is expected to reduce his budget. When the outlook is rosy, top management will listen sympathetically to a materials manager's pleas for a bigger budget. Cost-center control may lead the materials manager to overstaff during boom periods so that he is not badly crippled when management forces him to make cuts during periods

of austerity. (The basic work load in most materials management activities is largely independent of the business cycle.)

In many cases, top management may be so preoccupied with budgetary control that it refuses to authorize materials management projects that increase profitability. For example, one manager of a materials management cost center (i.e., a conventional materials management department) requested an increase of $50,000 per year in his budget to initiate a value analysis program that promised to reduce costs by at least $200,000 per year. The materials manager's boss was sympathetic to the idea but suggested that it be tabled for a few years until the company "got back on its feet again" and could afford to take on new programs!

In the materials management profit center, the materials manager would probably still be forced to get top-management approval if he wanted to boost his operating budget. But the focus is quite different. The materials manager could point to an expected increase in profit rather than an increase in cost, and approval would be far more likely. For example, even in the toughest of times, a marketing manager may be able to hire extra salesmen provided he can convince his boss that they will earn their keep. And, of course, the manufacturing manager hires extra workers as long as customer demand provides work to do. There is no reason why the same reasoning cannot be applied to a decision to boost the materials management payroll, provided this results in a higher return on capital.

6. *Managers will develop in materials management.* At present, very few top managers begin their careers in materials management activities. For example, only two of the presidents of the 500 largest manufacturing companies have backgrounds in purchasing and, apparently, none is a specialist in production control or traffic. In contrast, marketing and manufacturing supply hundreds of top management executives. The basic reason these functions breed top managers is because their executives learn how to make basic profit-and-loss decisions at relatively early stages in their careers. Their counterparts in materials management, in contrast, tend to be more concerned with pleasing the real decision makers rather than making any decisions themselves. In effect, marketing and manufacturing provide an environment that makes their practitioners think like businessmen; materials management activities often seem to create merely timid bureaucrats. The harsher, less sheltered environment of the materials management profit center should develop more businessmen who can go on to assume top-management responsibilities.

Profit-center problems

While its advantages outweigh its disadvantages, the materials management profit center is not an unmixed blessing. All types of captive profit centers—materials management or any other variety—encourage interdepartmental bickering. There is strong incentive for the profit-center manager to try to look good at the expense of his fellow manager. He can do this by padding his transfer prices and also by taking actions that reduce his costs at the expense of increasing costs in some other department. In the case of the materials management profit center, there might be temptation to try to cut costs by purchasing merchandise of inferior quality while maintaining the same transfer price. There would also almost certainly be difference of opinion on responsibility for stockouts. For example, if a plant suddenly ran out of material, the stockout might be blamed on the supplier, while the materials manager would claim that the plant did not have sufficient foresight to advise him of a basic change in its requirements. Well-defined ground rules could eliminate most such disputes—but not all of them.

In addition, breaking up an organization into a group of captive profit centers may create additional administrative costs. There is more bookkeeping. More time is spent negotiating transfer prices and ground rules, as well as attending to the other details of profit-center administration.

Use of index numbers

Most of these intrinsic disadvantages can be avoided by using index numbers as a basis for a profit center. When this is done, a materials management department can set itself up as a profit center simply as a means of monitoring and improving its own performance. There would be no complicated bookkeeping and it would not be necessary to negotiate profit-center terms and conditions with using departments.

Two indexes needed.   In the simplest case, just two sets of index numbers would be needed: purchase costs and end-product selling price as illustrated in Figure 21–3.

Suppose, as in the earlier example, you work for a company that has annual purchases of $10,000,000, materials management expenses of $300,000 per year, and employs $1,500,000 worth of company capital in the materials management process. If the company earns a 15 percent return on capital, it would then be assumed that during this base year materials management will also have earned a 15 percent or $225,000 return on its capital. To recoup the $300,000 materials management expenses and earn the $225,000 profit, it is necessary to mark up purchase costs of $10,000,000 by $525,000 or 5.25 percent, so that "sales" to using departments become $10,525,000. The $10,000,000 spent for purchases is determined by two basic variables: physical quantities and price. Price changes can be measured with an index following the procedure outlined in Chapter 7. During this base period, the index of purchase prices is 100.0.

Second-year results.   The materials management profit center does

FIGURE 21-3

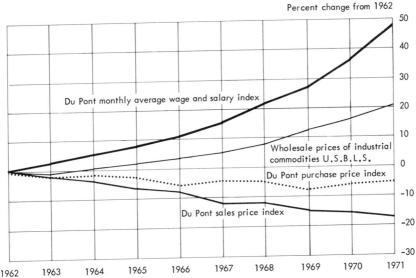

Percent change from 1962

DuPont's purchasing department accomplished something that is seemingly impossible during a period of inflation: It reduced its purchase prices about 5 percent between 1962 and 1971. But if DuPont had a materials management profit center, the purchasing manager would be reminded that this performance was not good enough. During the same period, DuPont selling prices declined about 18 percent. As a result, the purchasing or materials management profit center would almost certainly be operating in the red, indicating that purchasing and materials management were making a smaller contribution to return on investment than they were at the beginning of the 1962-71 period.

Source: Annual report to stockholders, E. I. duPont de Nemours & Company

not really begin to operate until the second year. During that year, suppose that:

1. Actual withdrawals of purchased materials inventories at cost plus direct purchases are $10,800,000. (This figure is easily obtainable from conventional accounting systems.)
2. Year-end inventory is up $50,000 over the previous year. No other changes are made in materials management assets, so capital employed in materials management increases by exactly $50,000, to $1,550,000.
3. The purchase price index increases by exactly 2 percent to 102.00. The company boosts its end-product prices by exactly 1 percent.
4. Operating expenses incurred in materials management increase by exactly 5 percent, to $315,000.

From this data, you can construct a hypothetical income statement for the materials management profit center, but you first must make these adjustments:

1. Actual purchase volume must be adjusted to reflect base period

purchase prices, since the materials management profit center must base its "sales" on base period rather than actual purchase prices. To do this, simply divide actual purchase volume of $10,800,000 by the price index of 1.02. This indicates that volume of purchases would have been $10,588,235 had supplier prices not increased by 2 percent.

2. Applying a 5.25 percent markup to adjusted purchase volume of $10,588,235 indicates that "sales" would have been $11,144,117 had there been no change in hypothetical transfer prices charged to using departments by materials management. However, the company was able to increase its overall selling prices by 1 percent. Therefore, materials management is entitled to a 1 percent price increase. This boosts "sales" to $11,255,558.

It is now possible to calculate an income statement, as follows:

"Sales"	$11,255,558
Cost of goods sold	10,800,000
Gross margin	$ 455,558
Operating expenses	315,000
Profit	$ 140,558

Return on capital employed in materials management $= \dfrac{\$140,558}{1,550,000} = 9.03$ percent

Thus, in this example, the materials management department has permitted its costs and expenses to increase more rapidly than its revenues, and return on capital has declined to 9.03 percent. If the decline in the company's overall return has been even greater, then materials management can be assured that it is providing its fair share of support of the company. Otherwise, the materials management department should not be satisfied with its performance.

When indexes are used, the entire profit-center system may take up no more space than a file folder and, since there are no genuine transactions, there is no need to involve departments other than materials management. After he has acquired experience with this dummy system, the materials manager may suggest to top management that it be used as a basis for measurement of materials management performance and, eventually, a formal profit center may evolve.

Production versus nonproduction

In most real-life companies, the materials management profit center should be divided into two or more parts. Even in the smallest manufacturing companies, there is a substantial difference between the value added by materials management on purchases of nonproduction items and that added on production material. The 5.25 percent markup used in the example is more typical of production material. On nonproduction items it must be higher.

Inventory turnover is usually much lower on nonproduction supplies. In extreme cases, each $1 of "sales" of nonproduction supplies requires as much as 50 cents of assets. If the return on capital is 10 percent, this 5-cent profit alone creates a markup of 5 percent. In addition, the costs of operating nonproduction storerooms may be greater relative to the volume of material handled than is the case with production stores. In fact, value added by materials management for nonproduction materials may be as much as 20 percent in manufacturing companies. This is roughly equal to the markup of many industrial distributors that handle approximately the same kinds of materials. Among nonmanufacturers, storage costs may be even higher and true value added by materials management may, in extreme cases, exceed value added by the supplier.

If a materials department handles classes of material that are as widely different as production parts and nonproduction materials are in most manufacturing companies, it can measure performance on each class of material far more precisely if it sets up at least two different profit centers with markups over cost that more accurately reflect the nature of the service performed.

In some cases, of course, the materials department may perform only a buying service for the using department. It gets a requisition for the item, buys it, and the using department takes possession of it on delivery. There is no inventory carrying cost for this type of transaction, so the markup need cover only the allocated costs of making the purchase. In at least one real-life materials management profit center, the London County Council (Case 21–1), this type of transaction is performed gratis for clients and its cost is, in effect, buried in the markup applied to items that are carried in inventory.

Other materials management profit centers will no doubt find it convenient to make similar compromises between convenience and accounting precision. While each profit center must be tailored to the unique needs of the organization, the case studies that follow provide a guide to successful implementation of the profit-center concept.

Cases

CASE 21–1. GREATER LONDON COUNCIL SUPPLIES DEPARTMENT*

A materials management profit center in the public sector

The City of London began to expand beyond its original boundaries hundreds of years ago. By 1960, the built-up area that was then known as Greater London had an area of about 840 square miles and a popula-

---

* This case was prepared by Dean S. Ammer of the Bureau of Business and Economic Research, Northeastern University, Boston, as a basis for classroom discus-

tion of almost 9,000,000 persons. While Greater London is a single economic entity, it was governed in 1960 by more than 90 separate local authorities including country councils, country borough councils, and urban and rural district councils with overlapping jurisdictions.

The London Government Act of 1963 greatly simplified this structure. It created the Greater London Council, the first regional elected authority in the United Kingdom. The Council is presently responsible for providing a long list of municipal services to a local government area of 610 square miles of Greater London with a population of about 7,500,000 persons. The Act also created the Inner London Educational Authority which consolidates the educational facilities of the 13 boroughs that comprise London's core.

The Greater London Council Supplies Department was created in 1965. It is one of the 15 specialized departments that serve the Council. Of the Council's 120,000 employees, approximately 2,000 work for the Supplies Department. The Department provides a supply service for the Council, the Inner London Educational Authority, as well as London area boroughs that wish to make use of its services. In addition, other public agencies in the London area may purchase from the Department on a voluntary basis.

The Department is fully self-supporting and normally makes a small profit even after making an allowance for interest on the funds it employs in the business. In 1972, its total volume of business had reached ₤46,278,932, divided among four classes of customers:

Greater London Council	₤13,337,257
Inner London Educational Authority	15,303,452
London boroughs	16,348,873
Others	1,289,350
	₤46,278,932

The Supplies Department's business is classified into four basic categories: direct supply; issues from depot stocks; repair work, sales, services; and local order contracts and joint contracts. On direct supply transactions, the Supplies Department acts as a purchasing service for the agency that needs the material. In general, direct supply is used for items where the requirements of a particular agency are unique and not shared with other agencies. The Supplies Department is responsible for buying the item and delivering it to the agency that uses it. To cover its costs, the Department adds a 5 percent service charge

to each purchase. However, the maximum charge for any purchase is
£30, and there is a minimum fee of 25 pence. Direct supply sales were
£19,552,738 in 1972.

Direct supply may not be practical for items that are used regularly
by a number of agencies. In such cases, it is often more economical
to purchase in large quantities and have each user draw upon the Supplies Department's inventories. In 1972, the Department's sales from
its depot stocks amounted to £10,617,350. In general, the Department
tries to carry sufficient stock of each item to guarantee a 95 percent
service level. According to Mr. Sam Swallow, Director of the Supplies
Department, "the mark-up over purchase cost varies by type of item
but in general is designed to recoup the department's total operating
costs. These costs include annual repayments of the capital cost of depot
real estate and interest on the capital amounts outstanding, together
with interest on stocks. Interest rates are related to the current rates
at which the Council borrows."

The Department normally carries an inventory equal to about a three
months' supply of materials that are issued from stock. Inventory naturally varies from item to item. In general, higher stocks are probably
required in the United Kingdom than are needed in the United States
because of the U.K.'s great dependence on imports of food and industrial
raw materials. In some cases, the Supplies Department, in effect, buys
food and other material by the shipload that it then issues from stores
in smaller quantities.

Substantial safety stocks are sometimes needed to protect against substantial variations in usage that result from long and often erratic fluctuations in procurement lead time. As a result, a substantial increase in
inventory would be essential if the Department were to increase its
stock-out protection from its present level of 95 percent to 99 percent.
The extra cost would have to be passed on to the using agencies and
ultimately to the overall British economy.

The using agency normally has no contact whatever with vendors
who supply material that the Supplies Department carries in stock. However, this policy simply is not practical for all purchases. For example,
perishable foods are delivered directly from the vendor to the user and
day-to-day contact is necessary to keep demand and supply in balance.
Similarly, using agencies find it convenient to deal directly with vendors
when specialized equipment breaks down and a repairman is needed
immediately. The solution to problems of this sort is joint or local order
contracts whose terms are negotiated by the Supplies Department on
behalf of the agencies, who then deal directly with the appropriate
vendors.

Joint and local order contracts amounted to £13,375,000 in 1972.
Major commodities included fuel and marine oil, meat, milk, gasoline,
rent of Rank-Xerox copying machines, and a variety of services such

as window cleaning, laundry, etc. While negotiation of these contracts requires a substantial effort on the part of the senior staff of the Supplies Department, it is not practical to pass on the Supplies Department's costs directly to the users because they are invoiced directly by the outside vendors and not by the Supplies Department. However, the cost of negotiating local contracts is passed on indirectly to users since the Supplies Department is self-supporting and its overall administrative costs are eventually passed through to users by a surcharge on materials on which it can take a mark-up.

In its fourth major activity, repair work, sales and services, the scope of the Supplies Department extends well beyond that of a conventional supply agency. The Department operates a printing and bookbinding service for its client agencies that had gross sales of £1,225,357 and profit of £53,488 in 1972. Advertising printing grossed an additional £349,724 with surplus of £1,824. The Department also grossed £234,695 and lost £21,572 on six restaurants it operates primarily to serve employees of the Greater London Council and related agencies.

The Supplies Department also operates a motor pool and garage. In 1972, it had gross income of £1,183,808 and profit of £24,594 on automotive repairs and income of £1,289,000 and profit of £14,275 from vehicle rentals. In addition, the Department provides various general services such as maintenance, a central reprographic service, office services, etc., whose costs are mostly shared on an allocated basis.

The Supplies Department operates two major supply depots. The larger and more modern of the two is the Tottenham Hale Depot which has 288,000 square feet of space. This depot handles five major groups of materials: building materials and supplies; scientific and electrical equipment and supplies; cleaning materials, uniforms, and textiles; furniture, furnishings, and floor coverings; and food. The depot's basic function is to buy merchandise in large quantities, store it, and then deliver it to client agencies. The depot is also a processor of materials. It operates both a sawmill and a butcher shop. Basic reason for these operations is that the United Kingdom is not self-sufficient in either lumber or meat. The Supplies Department buys both of these commodities abroad in partially finished form (the lumber as timber and the meat as frozen carcasses) and then must carry on further processing before delivery to using agencies.

The Supplies Department is also responsible for disposing of surplus materials on behalf of its agency customers. Centralized surplus disposal often permits material and equipment that is surplus with one agency to be transferred to another agency which has a need for it. An important by-product of this responsibility is the school furniture repair shop at the Tottenham Hale Depot. When furniture becomes unusable, schools send it to the Tottenham Hale Depot. In some cases, the Supplies Department is not able to repair the furniture or can find no use for it.

It is then sold for the best price that can be obtained. Such sales totalled £4,982 in 1972. In most cases, furniture can be repaired either at the depot or by outside suppliers. Issues of repaired furniture amounted to £515,728, and the repair operation earned a profit of £6,293 after incurring internal costs £142,367 and paying outside contractors £372,050.

The Southfields Depot is older and smaller than the Tottenham Hale Depot. It has 142,000 square feet of space and is used primarily for office supplies, stationery and similar materials, as well as fuel. Like the Tottenham Hale Depot and the Supplies Department's other facilities, it maintains separate accounts for each category of business.

Exhibit I, which shows the general stores and textile accounts at

EXHIBIT 1
London County Council Supplies Department, Tottenham Hale general stores and textile accounts, fiscal year 1972 (in British pounds sterling)

Stock account (in British Pounds Sterling)				
Issues to other Supplies Department Depots.			118	
Issues to GLC and ILEA			1,583,515	
Issues to Boroughs and others.			1,818,354	
Total gross value of issues			3,401,987	*(3,188,610)*
Opening stock.	155,861			
Purchases	2,887,513			
		3,043,374		
Less closing stock.		189,117		
Total net value of issues		2,854,257	2,854,257	*(2,673,268)*
Gross trading surplus			547,730	*(515,342)*
Clerical salaries and wages	61,000			
Operative salaries and wages.	106,170			
Superannuation deficiency	5,932			
Premises	85,456			
Supplies and Services.	9,527			
Office expenses	15,386			
Carriage	146,410			
Computer	44,517			
Interest.	8,999			
Central expenses	18,591			
Balance transferred to Stores Surplus Account	45,742			*(+27,338)*
	547,730		547,730	

Tottenham Hale, is representative of the Department's accounting system. Note that this particular account shows a surplus for the year of £45,742, after allowing for interest expense of £8,999. Also note that the accounts are limited to operating expenses and inventories. While fixed assets obviously exist, they are not accounted for in the Department's annual report but are presumably treated simply as government-owned buildings.

While the Department strives to make a modest profit on every account, deficits are sometimes incurred. Using agencies have fixed budgets for each fiscal year, and to permit them to stay within their budgets, the Supplies Department guarantees fixed prices for all stock items for the British April–March fiscal year. Unfortunately, the Department's suppliers do not necessarily keep their prices at fixed levels. Thus, the Department is often squeezed between relatively fixed prices and rising costs. This is aggravated by a rate of domestic inflation in the United Kingdom that since World War II has been consistently greater than that of the United States and some of the U.K.'s major trading partners in Western Europe.

As a result, Mr. Swallow explains that "the trading objective is to break even overall taking one year with another but to accumulate and carry forward a small surplus to safeguard the fixed prices against unexpected inflation of purchase prices or falls in demand. Part of the accumulated surplus has recently been used for repayment of some of the capital cost of the Tottenham Hale Depot and certain other items of non-recurrent expenditure."

Consequently, cost reduction and value analysis are major objectives of the Supplies Department. The Department maintains a laboratory at its Tottenham Hale Depot for testing materials to assure maximum value and also makes use of outside laboratories, as required. The Department has been successful, in many cases, in getting greater value by purchasing on a competitive basis materials for which it has developed its own specifications. For example, in 1972 the Department was testing a new type of work uniform it had developed for the London Fire Brigade and was also in the process of developing new designs for school and office furniture.

Unlike some American government agencies, the Supplies Department is not required to accept the lowest bid that it gets. Contracts are awarded on the basis of overall value, not exclusively on price. The Department maintains its own quality control activity to monitor supplier quality and to make certain that its specifications are being met. Competitive proprietary products are also evaluated on the basis of performance and other quality characteristics. Many of the Department's suppliers are in the Greater London area, since this is, of course, the economic, as well as the political, capital of the United Kingdom. However, there is no requirement that the Department buy locally, although the Director and other senior executives are conscious of the public relations impact of their decisions.

Questions

1. Is the GLC Supplies Department a profit center? How does it differ from a materials management profit center one might find in a private company?

2. How does the British taxpayer benefit from the GLC Supplies Department's operations? Why might a similar setup be resisted in the United States or (perhaps elsewhere in the United Kingdom)?

CASE 21–2.   QUEENSTOWN CHEMICAL CORPORATION (B)*

Evolution of the purchasing profit center

In 1968, the management of the Queenstown Chemical Corporation (see Case 8–1) called upon a major consulting firm to make a "top management" survey of the company. For the past decade, Queenstown had enjoyed a better-than-average rate of growth in sales of roughly 10 percent per year. Management fully expected this growth to continue and anticipated that the 1970 sales volume of approximately $100 million would double by 1978 or 1979. To date, profits have not kept pace with growth of sales. Return on capital after taxes has declined from about 12 percent in 1959 to slightly less than 10 percent in 1968. It was easy to blame this modest decline on price cutting in certain of the company's product lines and also on heavy starting and development costs in a few of the company's newer products. But management was not convinced that the company was realizing its full potential and therefore called upon the consultants to make a broad survey.

Of the consultants' many recommendations, one was of particular interest to George Mead, the company's director of purchases. The consultants proposed that the company distinguish more clearly in its organization structure between manufacturing and materials management activities. In the past, Mead had been responsible not only for the company's purchases but also for all inventories. Mead's responsibility in the purchasing area was very well defined. The company's buyers reported directly to him, and they were responsible for purchasing all the company's raw materials, operating supplies, purchased services, and equipment.

The inventory responsibility was not so well defined. It dated back about ten years to the time that Mead had joined the company. Mead had insisted on inventory responsibility as a condition of his employment by the company as director of purchases. As Mead put it at the time, "Every purchase decision is also an inventory decision, and when you try to separate purchasing from inventory control, you inevitably wind up with less-than-adequate performance from both."

There was no opposition to Mead's request for authority over inventories. In effect, Mead moved into what had been an organizational void. Various supervisors of stores areas in manufacturing had always had jurisdiction over inventory, of course. But their control was routine and of little interest to the manufacturing manager himself, who devoted

---

practically all of his time to production and quality problems. When he did become involved in inventory management, it was almost always a matter of the company having run out of some particular material and this was, of course, regarded as a purchasing problem. Thus the manufacturing manager regarded Mead's request for authority over inventory simply as a formal confirmation of what had been normal practice for years.

While Mead had authority to set reorder points and purchase quantities in what he believed to be the company's best interest, blue-collar hourly personnel directly responsible for inventory and stores control remained in the manufacturing organization. Mead was directly responsible only for the white-collar salaried personnel employed in the purchasing department.

Although they continued to be part of the manufacturing organization, the foreman and workers in the various stores departments cooperated willingly with Mead's staff. The consultants nevertheless recommended that they be transferred directly to Mead. In their opinion, there was no reason not to make such a transfer and plenty of reasons for favoring it. The workers in the storerooms were members of the same bargaining unit as production employees but this posed no problem, since all union contract negotiations were handled by the labor relations department anyway. So it made no difference whether these workers reported to materials management or continued as part of the manufacturing operation.

But there were distinct advantages, the consultants felt, in making this group part of purchasing. One major advantage, according to the consultants, was morale. The men were "lost" in the manufacturing organization. They could not really relate their objectives to those of manufacturing. The consultants felt that their problems—real or imagined—would get a much more sympathetic ear if these workers were part of a department which was concerned only with materials management. In addition, the new atmosphere would be more likely to stimulate suggestions for improvement and strengthen the rapport among all company employees concerned with materials management. In subtle ways, the consultants also felt that the stores personnel would be overly concerned with manufacturing objectives to the extent that they might not carry out their own jobs effectively if they continued to be part of the manufacturing orgainzation.

This argument was also used by the consultants in proposing that shipping and materials handling personnel be transferred to materials management. There seemed to be direct conflict of objectives in the materials-handling area, in particular. In order to achieve maximum production it was sometimes necessary to handle materials two or three times simply to get them out of the way. While this may have made production's job easier, it was often debatable whether or not this was in the company's best interest because of the extra handling expense. In addition, the consultants sensed that the materials-handling personnel, in particular, felt like a tail being wagged by a large production dog. Their morale would be higher, the consultants believed, if they could identify even indirectly with a major company official who was not subordinate to production.

The company's top management accepted the consultants' recommendations and transferred all personnel identified with materials management to Mead's department. This included all employees in stores, receiving, shipping, and materials handling. Manufacturing continued to schedule its own production in accordance with plans acceptable to Mead and to the company's marketing executives.

Mead's new responsibilities were formally acknowledged when his title was changed to materials manager. Mead continued to function as chief purchasing officer and, as before, purchasing agents responsible for direct and indirect materials continued to report to him. In addition, Mead created the position of manager—materials handling and control and appointed one of the former supervisors of materials handling to this position. The manager—materials handling and control was made responsible for all nonpurchasing materials management activities of the company and reported directly to Mead.

It was understood by everyone, however, that a future traffic manager might report directly to Mead rather than to one of Mead's immediate subordinates. To date, the company had operated without a formal traffic department, with traffic reponsibility dispersed among Mead's buyers and the shipping supervisor. Mead had suggested some months before the consultants made their study that the company's growth seemed to have created a need for a genuine traffic specialist. The consultants concurred, so top management gave Mead authority to plan a traffic department.

Mead was naturally delighted with his new responsibilities. For the first time he looked upon himself as a director of a complete function. At the first staff meeting with his three department heads (the two purchasing agents and the manager of nonpurchasing materials activities), he said, "In a way, the four of us are partners in what is really a little business in itself. We coordinate the efforts of thousands of suppliers so that we get a smooth flow of materials into the plant, and then we get rid of the materials in finished product form after manufacturing does its job. To do our best, we should think like businessmen and try to get a maximum return on investment."

In the past, Mead had always tried to measure his accomplishments in terms of company objectives. Since the company strived for a 25 percent return on capital before taxes, Mead had initiated routine use of economic order quantity formulas which assumed that the company's cost of capital was 25 percent. He also tried to report department accomplishments in terms that related them directly to the corporation's financial objectives.

For example, in one year, Mead not only reported that the purchasing department had saved $225,000 through negotiation, materials substitution, and changes in suppliers but also related this to earnings per share on the company's stock. In that year, the company had managed to boost pretax earnings per share from $4.50 to $4.84 on the 2,000,000 shares that were outstanding. According to Mead's calculations, about 11½ cents of this gain ($225,000 ÷ 2,000,000 shares) came about because of the purchasing department's cost-reduction efforts. Therefore, he could report that purchasing was responsible for about one third of the company's 34 cents per share increase in earnings that year.

This figure was challenged by the company's controller, who pointed out that purchasing's savings not only did not come without cost but were probably largely the result of good luck, since chemical prices had declined sharply that year. Mead agreed that it helped if one were lucky in purchasing, as in marketing when a salesman might land a fat order simply because he happened to be available to receive it. But he found it difficult to counter the controller's argument that while cost reduction was certainly useful, it could not properly be related to earnings per share, since this represented a return from the company's total resources and had to be related both to costs and to capital employed to be really useful.

It occurred to Mead that in his new role as materials manager he could effectively counter the controller's claim that materials management was not really a profit-making activity. He explained:

Look, the industrial distributor doesn't do anything we don't do for our manufacturing activities and various other user departments. The distributor doesn't make anything. He is entitled to a profit only because he carries items in stock that his customers want. His profit is a reward for the capital he has tied up in inventories and facilities and the risk of obsolescence and loss that is incurred. The controller is right in one thing, however. The distributor can't be measured by how much total profit he earns. For example, if a distributor carries a $1,000,000 stock and only earns a $50,000 profit, he is not especially successful. But if he can make the same $50,000 profit with a $200,000 inventory he's got an operation he can be proud of.

Similarly, we can be proud of ourselves only if we carry our weight and earn as high a return as other units of the company. Right now, we're responsible for nearly 15 percent of the company's total assets. This includes about $1,000,000 of nonproduction inventories and $6,000,000 in production materials. Our production inventory turns over about seven times per year, while the turnover in nonproduction stock is about four. We have maybe $300,000 invested in facilities and equipment, about two thirds of which is associated with production and the balance with nonproduction stocks. Our total operating expenses—payroll and other costs of operation—are divided in probably the same ratio and currently amount to about $900,000 per year.

We usually manage to save at least $100,000 in purchasing, and we are also working to improve our inventory turnover. But, frankly, I don't know whether this is good performance or not; after all, we are really only doing what we get paid to do. The fact of the matter is that purchase costs have tended to increase year after year, irrespective of the savings we've made. This hasn't hurt the company since it has also usually been able to boost its prices on finished products and ride with the inflation.

I wonder how good our performance would really be in a year in which the company was not able to boost its prices but all other costs and prices kept going up. Let's suppose that next year, the company's sales go up 5 percent to $105 million. Prices stay the same, so this gain is real in terms of physical volume. Unfortunately, costs rise even faster than sales, so net profit before tax declines by $1,000,000 to $9,000,000. Salary inflation pushes up the budgets of the materials department along with every other department, and our operating expenses increase by $100,000. We manage to hold the line on nonproduction inventories, which remain at $1,000,000. Prices sneak up 1 percent, however, and this is the sole reason that disbursements of nonproduction inventories increase from this year's $4,000,000 to $4,040,000. We also manage to hold production inventories in line with sales growth and they increase by 5 percent, to $6,300,000. Disbursements from inventory increase slightly less than sales. With no change in price, they would tend to increase from $42,000,000 to $44,100,000. But at cost, we wind up spending only $44,000,000 and our production materials price index verifies this by declining by 0.2 percent.

The company's total investment in net plant, equipment, inventory, and so on increases by $4,000,000, to $54,000,000, mostly as a result of the addition of new production facilities. However, there is no change in the 300,000 investment in equipment and facilities of the materials department; depreciation charges are exactly offset by additional purchases of equipment.

I would guess that we would have done a pretty good job under such conditions. But I would be hard pressed to prove it, especially since manufacturing would probably still be on my back about occasional supply failures of material for the flotation process. We had two such failures this year because of defective purchased material, and there's no arguing with their claim that these must cost the company at least $10,000 each time. To be realistic, I think we can expect two such failures next year. Hopefully, by the following year, we will be out of the woods on this problem—but something is sure to turn up. It always does.

Happily, reciprocity should be less of a millstone next year than it currently is. This year we are pretty much locked in with the Dorset Company as one of our key suppliers. Dorset is a good outfit, and, in theory, their prices are competitive. But everyone knows we're tied to Dorset because of all the material they buy from us, so I doubt if I've even got a good feel for the market when I check prices. No one bothers to be competitive. Now that Dorset is being absorbed by Consolidated, I can buy wherever I please next year, since our marketing people expect that Dorset will almost certainly then favor Consolidated's Prager subsidiary over us, so there will be no latent threat of reciprocal action if I get tough with Dorset. I would guess that I will wind up sticking with Dorset—they're a good outfit—but I should be able to get their prices down by about $50,000 next year. This means that we only have to pick up a net of $50,000 from everything else to realize our projected drop of 0.2 percent of $100,000 in our purchased-materials price index.

Question

1.   Construct a tentative balance sheet and operating statement for a materials management profit center at Queenstown Chemical.

Selected bibliography

Organization and management

Ammer, Dean S. "Materials Management." *Guide to Purchasing*, Sect. 3.6. New York: National Association of Purchasing Management, 1971.

——. "Materials Management as a Profit Center." *Harvard Business Review*, January–February 1969, pp. 72–82.

Dale, Ernest. *Planning and Developing the Company Organization Structure*. Research Report No. 20. New York: American Management Association, 1952.

Drucker, Peter F. *Managing for Results*. New York: Harper & Row, Publishers, Inc., 1964.

——. *The Practice of Management*. New York: Harper & Bros., 1954.

Haas, George; Krech, E. M.; and March, Benjamin. *Purchasing Department Organization and Authority*. Research Study No. 45. New York: American Management Association, 1960.

Koontz, H., and O'Donnell, C. *Principles of Management*. 5th ed. New York: McGraw-Hill Book Co., 1972.

Newman, William H.; Summer, Charles E.; and Warren, E. Kirby. *The Process of Management: Concepts, Behavior and Practice*. 3d ed. Englewood Cliffs, N.J.: Prentice-Hall, Inc., 1972.

Forecasting and planning

American Management Association. *Evaluating and Using Business Indicators*. Management Report No. 25. New York, 1959.

715

Ammer, Dean S. "The Effectiveness of Opinion Surveys." *Guide to Purchasing,* Sect. 2.10. New York: National Association of Purchasing Management, 1970.

———. "The Side Effects of Planning." *Harvard Business Review,* May–June 1970.

———. "What Businessmen Expect from the 1970's." *Harvard Business Review,* January–February 1971, pp. 41–52.

Arthur, Henry B. *Commodity Futures as a Business Management Tool.* Boston: Division of Research, Harvard Business School, 1971.

Bach, George Leland. *Economics—An Introduction to Analysis and Policy.* 7th ed. Englewood Cliffs, N.J.: Prentice-Hall, Inc., 1971.

Baer, S. B., and Saxon, O. G. *Commodity Exchanges and Futures Trading.* New York: Harper & Bros., 1949.

Dauten, Carl A., and Valentine, Lloyd M. *Business Cycles and Forecasting.* 3rd ed. Cincinnati: South-Western Publishing Co., 1968.

Ewing, David W. *The Practice of Planning.* New York: Harper & Row, 1968.

Fearon, Harold E. "Purchasing Economics." *Guide to Purchasing,* Sect. 2.10. New York: National Association of Purchasing Management, 1965.

Gardner, Robert L. *How to Make Money in the Commodity Market.* New York: Prentice-Hall, Inc., 1961.

Samuelson, Paul A. *Economics—An Introductory Analysis.* 9th ed. New York: McGraw-Hill Book Co., 1973.

Schmeckebier, Lawrence F., and Eastin, Roy B. *Government Publications and Their Use.* Rev. ed. Washington, D.C.: Brookings Institution, 1961.

Silk, Leonard S., and Curley, M. Louise. *A Primer on Business Forecasting.* New York: Random House, Inc., 1970.

Steiner, George A. *Top Management Planning.* New York: Macmillan Co., 1969.

Stigler, George J., and Kindahl, James K. *The Behavior of Industrial Prices.* New York: National Bureau of Economic Research and Columbia University Press, 1970.

Wasserman, Paul. *Sources of Commodity Prices.* New York: Special Libraries Association, 1960.

Purchasing practices

Aljian, George W. (ed.). *Purchasing Handbook.* 2d ed. New York: McGraw-Hill Book Co., 1966.

Bean, C. C. *Procurement Handbook.* Washington, D.C.: U.S. Government Printing Office, 1959.

Berry, H. A. *Purchasing Management.* Englewood Cliffs, N.J.: Prentice-Hall Inc., 1964.

Dowst, Somerby R. *Basics for Buyers.* Boston: Cahners Books, 1971.

England, Wilbur B. *Modern Procurement Management: Principles and Cases.* 5th ed. Homewood, Ill.: Richard D. Irwin, Inc., 1970.

————. *The Purchasing System.* Homewood, Ill.: Richard D. Irwin, Inc., 1967.

Farrell, P. V. *The First Fifty Years of the N.A.P.M.* New York: National Association of Purchasing Management, 1965.

Fearon, Harold E., and Hoagland, John H. *Purchasing Research in American History.* Research Study No. 58. New York: American Management Association, 1963.

Gross, H. *Make or Buy.* Englewood Cliffs, N.J.: Prentice-Hall, Inc., 1966.

Heinritz, Stuart F., and Farrell, Paul V. *Purchasing Principles and Application.* 5th ed. Englewood cliffs, N.J.: Prentice-Hall, Inc., 1971.

Jennings, George W. *State Purchasing: The Essentials of a Modern Service for Modern Government.* Lexington, Ky.: Council of State Governments, 1969.

Lee, L., Jr., and Dobler, D. W. *Purchasing and Materials Management.* 2d ed. New York: McGraw-Hill Book Co., 1971.

Leenders, Michiel R. *Improving Purchasing Effectiveness through Supplier Development.* Boston: Graduate School of Business Administration, Harvard University, 1965.

National Association of Purchasing Management. *Guide to Purchasing.* New York, 1965. Loose-leaf, plus quarterly supplements.

Nicholson, J. W.; Nammacher, T. J.; and Smith, K. L. *Guide to Governmental Purchasing.* Minneapolis, Minn.: Lakeside Publications, Inc., 1965.

Nierenberg, Gerard I. *The Art of Negotiating.* New York: Hawthorn Books, Inc., 1968.

Pooler, Victor H., Jr. *The Purchasing Man and His Job.* New York: American Management Association, 1964.

Ritterskamp, J. J., Jr.; Abbott, F. L.; and Ahrens, B. C. *Purchasing for Educational Institutions.* New York: Teachers College, Columbia University, 1961.

Westing, J. H.; Fine, I. V.; and Zenz, Gary J. *Purchasing Management: Materials in Motion.* 3d ed. New York: John Wiley & Sons, Inc., 1969.

Willetts, Walter E. *Fundamentals of Purchasing.* New York: Appleton-Century-Crofts, 1969.

Production and inventory management

Brown, Robert G. *Decision Rules for Inventory Management.* New York: Holt, Rinehart & Winston, 1967.

————. *Statistical Forecasting for Inventory Control.* New York: McGraw-Hill Book Co., 1959.

Conway, Richard W.; Maxwell, William L.; and Miller, Louis W. *Theory of Scheduling.* Reading, Mass.: Addison-Wesley Publishing Co., Inc., 1967.

Greene, James H. (ed.). *Production and Inventory Control Handbook.* New York: McGraw-Hill Book Co., 1970.

Magee, John F., and Boodman, David M. *Production Planning and Inventory Control.* 2d ed. New York: McGraw-Hill Book Co., 1967.

Moore, Franklin G., and Jablonski, Ronald E. *Production Control.* 3d ed. New York: McGraw-Hill Book Co., 1969.

Physical distribution and traffic

Constantin, James A. *Principles of Logistics Management.* New York: Appleton-Century-Crofts, 1966.

Fogg, Charles J.; Weller, Walter W.; and Strunk, Arthur B. (eds.). *The Freight Traffic Redbook.* New York: Traffic Publishing Co., Inc., 1955.

Knorst, William J. *Transportation and Traffic Management.* Vols. I–IV. Chicago: College of Advanced Traffic, 1947–49.

Lochlin, D. Phillip. *Economics of Transportation.* 7th ed. Homewood, Ill.: Richard D. Irwin, Inc., 1972.

Magee, John F. *Physical Distribution Systems.* New York: McGraw-Hill Book Co., 1967.

National Motor Freight Classification. American Trucking Association, Washington, D.C. (published periodically).

Taff, Charles A. *Commercial Motor Transportation.* 4th ed. Homewood, Ill.: Richard D. Irwin, Inc., 1969.

————. *Management of Physical Distribution and Transportation.* 5th ed. Homewood, Ill.: Richard D. Irwin, Inc., 1972.

Uniform Freight Classification. Tariff Publishing Office, Chicago (published periodically).

Wilson, G. Lloyd. *Freight Service and Rates.* Washington, D.C.: Traffic Service Corp., 1952.

————. *Freight Shipping Documents & Claims.* Washington, D.C.: Traffic Service Corp., 1952.

————. *Railroad Freight Rate Structure.* Washington, D.C.: Traffic Service Corp., 1951.

Miscellaneous

Ammer, Dean S. *Manufacturing Management and Control.* New York: Appleton-Century-Crofts, 1968.

Buzzell, Robert D. *Value Added by Industrial Distribution and Their Productivity.* Columbus: Ohio State University, 1959.

Clark, Charles. *Brainstorming.* New York: Doubleday & Co., Inc., 1958.

Croxton, Frederick E.; Cowden, Dudley J.; and Klein, Sidney. *Applied General Statistics.* 3d ed. Englewood Cliffs, N.J.: Prentice-Hall, Inc., 1967.

Fetter, Robert B. *The Quality Control System.* Homewood, Ill.: Richard D. Irwin, Inc., 1967.

Grant, Eugene L., and Leavenworth, Richard S. *Statistical Quality Control.* 4th ed. New York: McGraw-Hill Book Co., 1972.

Gray, A. W. *Purchase Law Manual.* New York: Conover-Mast Publications, 1954.

Heiland, Robert E., and Richardson, Wallace J. *Work Sampling.* New York: McGraw-Hill Book Co., 1957.

Kaplan, A. D. H.; Dirlan, Joel B.; and Lanzillotti, Robert F. *Pricing in Big Business.* Washington, D.C.: Brookings Institution, 1958.

Kollios, A. E., and Stempel, Joseph. *Purchasing and EDP*. New York: American Management Association, 1966.

Magee, John F. *Industrial Logistics: Analysis and Management of Physical Supply and Distribution Systems*. New York: McGraw-Hill Book Co., 1968.

Miles, L. D. *Techniques of Value Analysis and Engineering*. New York: McGraw-Hill Book Co., 1961.

Oxenfeldt, Alfred G. *Make or Buy: Factors Affecting Executive Decisions*. New York: McGraw-Hill Book Co., 1956.

Terborgh, George. *An Introduction to Business Investment Analysis*. Washington, D.C.: Machinery & Allied Products Institute, 1958.

Wyatt, John W., and Wyatt, Madie B. *Business Law—Principles and Cases*. 4th ed. New York: McGraw-Hill Book Co., 1971.

Index